DATE DUE

AUG 0 2 2000		
NOV 0 5 2002		
FEB 2 4 2003		
MAR 2 5 2003		
APR 1 5 2003		

GAYLORD   PRINTED IN U.S.A.

The Terror
of the Machine

CMAS BORDER & MIGRATION STUDIES SERIES
Series Editor: Gilberto Cárdenas

The Terror
of the Machine

*Technology, Work, Gender, and
Ecology on the U.S.–Mexico Border*

DEVON G. PEÑA

CMAS Books
The Center for Mexican American Studies
The University of Texas at Austin

A CMAS BOOK

Editor: Víctor J. Guerra
Assistant Editor: Jess Jackson
Production Editor: John Bodinger de Uriarte

The publication of this book was assisted by a grant from the Inter-University Program for Latino Research.

The author's royalties from sales of this book go toward the funding of college scholarships for maquiladora workers. The fund is administered by the Centro de Orientación de la Mujer Obrera, A.C., in Ciudad Juárez, Mexico.

HD
8119
.M49
P46
1997

Library of Congress Cataloging-in-Publication Data

Peña, Devon Gerardo.
    The terror of the machine : technology, work, gender, and ecology on the U.S.–Mexico border / Devon G. Peña. — 1st ed.
        p. cm. — (CMAS border & migration studies series)
    Includes bibliographical references and index.
    ISBN 0–292–76561–4 (alk. paper). — ISBN 0–292–76562–2 (pbk. : alk. paper)
    1. Women offshore assembly industry workers—Mexican-American Border Region—Interviews. 2. Labor—Mexican-American Border Region. 3. Quality of work life—Mexican-American Border Region. 4. Industrial hygiene—Mexican-American Border Region. 5. International business enterprises—Mexican-American Border Region. 6. Mexican-American Border Region—Economic conditions. 7. Mexican-American Border Region—Social conditions. 8. Canada. Treaties, etc. 1992 Oct. 7. I. Title. II. Series.
HD8119.M49P46   1996
331.4′87042′09721—dc20   96-2352

♻ ∞ This book is printed on recycled, acid-free paper that conforms to the American National Standard of permanence for printed library materials, as approved by the American National Standards Institute.

Printed and bound in the United States of America.

First edition (April 1997).
Second paperback impression, May 1998.

To the memory of
Guillermina Valdés de Villalva
1939–1991

Contents

Figures and Tables

Acknowledgments

The creation of a book, like all forms of knowledge production, is always a collective endeavor. I must acknowledge the lasting influence and guidance of the late Dr. Guillermina Valdés de Villalva. Guillermina was my mentor, colleague, and friend. I learned two ethical principles from Guille that forever changed the manner in which I conduct myself as an activist-scholar. She taught me that researchers have a moral and political responsibility not only to "take sides" (and stand with the underdog) but to let the "subjects" define the research agenda. When I first arrived at COMO in the summer of 1980, Guillermina and her staff were adamant about not letting any more academic researchers come in, clean up, and leave—with scarce another word to be heard from them again. They were justifiably tired of being exploited by intellectuals. It was bad enough that capitalists were only too eager to exploit maquila workers. It was appalling that presumably progressive intellectuals would do the same for the sake of publication, recognition, or career.

Another lesson Guille taught me was that workers have the most vital and important knowledge to contribute in the struggle for a safe, humane, and democratic workplace. It was Guille and the COMO staff who led me on a journey through the unfamiliar territory of *tortuguismo* and worker inventions, innovations, and modifications of the labor process. It was the workers at COMO who taught me about the existence of hidden workplace struggles inside the maquilas—the subaltern life of the ghosts in the machine. In this fashion, Guille encouraged me to develop the research process so that it evolved out of constant discourse among the workers.

I will never be able to adequately express what a terrible, profoundly unequivocal loss her untimely death will turn out to be. Guille was a pioneer of maquiladora research and a tireless champion of workplace democracy and sustainable development. She also mentored an entire generation of borderlands research scholars. The most I can do at this point, however feeble a gesture it may appear to be, is to dedicate this book in her honor.

Gil Cárdenas, my academic mentor, provided advice, guidance, and tough standards during my years as a graduate student at the University of Texas. He got me through a challenging and difficult time in my life. I owe many thanks to the other faculty who assisted me in graduate school: Rose Brewer, Harry Cleaver, Joe Feagin, Doug Kellner, Bill Kelly, Gideon Sjoberg, and the late Lou Zurcher. Special gratitude is owed Rose Brewer for insisting that women are not just a "proletariat in drag" and Harry Cleaver for introducing me to the perspective of *la autonomía obrera*.

Countless other friends, relatives, and colleagues supported me over the past thirteen years of work leading to this publication: José Eduardo Peña, Cristina Peña, Jorian Clair, Víctor Nelson Cisneros, Julia Curry, César Caballero, Jorge Carrillo, Estevan Flores, Teresa Córdova, Cindi Delgado Noel, Dawn Gettman, Suzi Aiko Nishida, Margi Duncombe, Jeff Livesay, Robert Dunne, Beatriz Vera, Luz María Villalva, Ron Takaki, Reyes García, Kathleen Staudt, Susan Tiano, Vicki Ruiz, Leslie Sklair, Ellwyn Stoddard, and Vandana Shiva. All of you are warmly and gratefully acknowledged. Víctor and Estevan are due special thanks for burning so much midnight oil with me over the years.

A great debt is owed the activists, educators, organizers, and workers who generously shared their time and knowledge with me: Jesús "Chuy" Montenegro, Gustavo de la Rosa Hickerson, Graciela Delgado, Olga Calderón, Luis Herrera, and the entire staff and student body at the Centro de Orientación de la Mujer Obrera.

I would like to acknowledge the support of the Danforth Foundation, the Center for Mexican American Studies at the University of Texas at Austin, and the Colorado College Benezet Grant Program and Research and Development Board for financial support. I am especially grateful to Rodolfo de la Garza, Joe Gordon, Glenn Brooks, and Tim Fuller. Without this institutional support I could not have completed the second-phase field-research seasons for this study. Thanks go to Kathy Kaylan of the Hulbert Center at Colorado College for assisting with research on NAFTA; Jane Stark of the Political Science Department for correcting the bibliography; and Sariya Jarasviroj, my former research assistant at Colorado College, for her untiring support and good cheer during the long and difficult editorial process. I owe a great deal to my editor at the University of Texas, Víctor Javier Guerra, whose dedication to quality was a real inspiration to me.

Finally, I would like to thank the people of the San Luis Valley in Colorado for their generous support while I was preparing the final version of this manuscript. I am especially indebted to Corpus, Yvette, and

Joe Gallegos of San Luis. As I sit here looking out the window toward the snowy peaks of Mount Blanca, I am reminded of a story Corpus told me a few years ago: "Yes," he said, "that stuff about struggling with the machines, that's pretty old stuff. It's been going on a long time. When I was a boy, my dad and I would work with these *gringos* who had huge grain threshers. They came to help us with our crop. Well, that driver, he was always going way too fast. But we figured how to plug the machine up by feeding the grain stalks sideways. That way, the machine broke down and it took about an hour to fix it. We could take a nice break." *Tortuguismo* in the bottomlands of the Río Culebra in Colorado's San Luis Valley. Should make a good topic for the next book.

— DGP
El Rito, San Luis Valley, Colorado
November 16, 1996

The Terror
of the Machine

The U.S.–Mexico Border Region

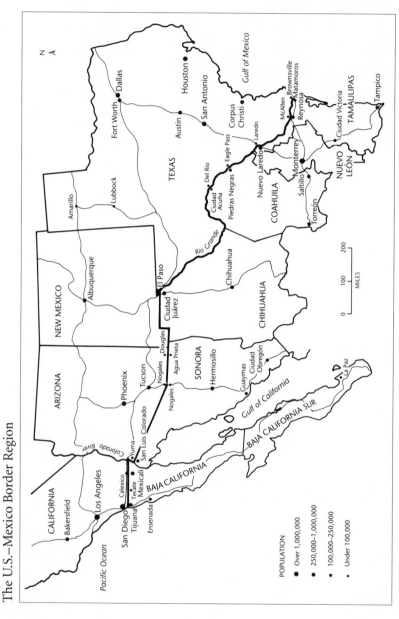

Adapted from Lawrence A. Herzog, *Where North Meets South: Cities, Space, and Politics on the U.S.–Mexico Border* (Austin: CMAS Books, University of Texas at Austin, 1990), 34.

Part One

THE TERROR OF THE MACHINE

1

"No Terrors, to a Certain Kind of Mind"

Repetitive labor . . . is a terrifying prospect to a certain kind of mind. . . . but to other minds, perhaps I might say the majority of minds, repetitive operations hold no terrors.
— Henry Ford (*My Life and Work*, 1922)

This job is a terror. The noise. The monotony. The constant danger of the machine. . . . Sometimes I have a nightmare . . . in which the machine swallows me whole. In the factory, the [assembly] line is the worst, it crushes your fingers and in the end your mind as well.
— Juana Ortega, maquiladora worker (Ciudad Juárez, 1982)

If Henry Ford Had Gone to Mexico . . .

. . . he probably would have built a maquiladora. In 1922, Ford published his autobiography, *My Life and Work.* "The Terror of the Machine" is the most intriguing chapter in a book unjustly relegated to obscurity within the annals of industrial history and industrial sociology. It is also one of the more deliberately honest autobiographical moments in the memoirs bequeathed by the generals of the U.S. Industrial Revolution—Carnegie, Rockefeller, and Ford. "The Terror of the Machine" is Ford's cynical account of industrial workers at the dawn of the age of mass production. Describing workers on the assembly-line system, Ford said:

> And then there is the pressing to take away the necessity for skill in any job done by one. . . . Repetitive labor—the doing of one thing over and over again and always in the same way—is a terrifying prospect to a certain kind of mind. It is terrifying to me, . . . but to other minds, perhaps I might say the majority of minds, repetitive operations hold no terrors. In fact, to some types of mind thought is absolutely appalling. To them, the ideal job is one where the creative instinct need not be expressed. . . . The average worker . . . wants a job in which he does not have to put forth much physical exertion . . . above all, he wants a job in which he does not have to think.[1]

3

Ford battled workers for power by reducing them to appendages of the assembly line. He then blamed them for an alleged deficiency in creative instinct. As a book, *My Life and Work* remains obscure. But the technological and social system spawned by the terror of Ford's machine remains a central problem for late-twentieth-century industrial sociology.[2] Fordism is perhaps the most perplexing and complex institution in the history of workplace organizations. The development of Fordism has posed a constant, formidable challenge to social scientists and workers alike.

Ford presents a paradoxical view of labor in "The Terror of the Machine." His worker is essentially a mindless automaton. In Ford's view of work, human beings fulfill their roles as unthinking industrial workers only by withstanding the terrors of repetitive labor. This gives us the figure of the sturdy yet hopeless factory idiot—the stereotype captured brilliantly by Charlie Chaplin in *Modern Times*. Ford's worker is a quiescent being, sequestered in the shadows of history without much of a script to read. Paradoxically, Ford expressed concern for the potentially disruptive power of the proletarian masses, and felt compelled to strip workers of their skills and knowledge: "the pressing to take away the necessity for skill in any job done by one." Perhaps the mindless automatons were mindful after all? Indeed, the traditions of skill and knowledge that workers brought to the factory with them were real sources of power over production. The reality of workers' knowledge forced Ford into accepting a dual philosophy of labor: Workers were ideally mindless automatons but were in reality persistent foes of capitalist command and control. So, Fordism also gave us the oppositional figure of the sit-down striker—a figure at center stage of history, fully capable of writing an original script.

Recognizing the strength workers had in preserving their skill-and-knowledge traditions, Ford presumably found a key to management's complete conquest inside the factory. Even Ford's script endows the mindless automatons with enough creativity to become saboteurs, agitators, and organizers—as long as they possess the knowledge necessary to control their own work. Building on an awareness of the connection between knowledge, power, and the control of work, Ford masterminded a series of technical and organizational revolutions that forever changed the nature of the human experience of work.

Ford, like Frederick Winslow Taylor before him,[3] understood that knowledge is power. He further understood that in capitalist production, power means control over work. So, to wrest control of production from the workers, Ford implemented an ingenious strategy that combined technological domination with bureaucracy and ideological control. We thus have the three mainsprings of Fordism: the assembly line, the five-dollar day, and the "social department."[4] Ford presumed absolute moral authority when it came to establishing the rules of workers' conduct both on the line and outside the factory. He established the rules (did the thinking), and the workers were expected to follow orders (without thinking). Managerial authority was to reign supreme, and workers were expected to submit and acculturate to the new demands of an industrial work ethic.

But Henry Ford and industrial sociology do not have a monopoly on truth claims about the nature of workplace politics. Workers have always had their own visions of the workplace. It hardly matters if you call them "oppositional workplace cultures" or "informal shop-floor networks of resistance." What matters is that workers have alternative understandings of the underlying politics of production, and they have long struggled to organize the workplace in a manner consistent with their views. In the case of the Ford Motor Company, the sit-down strikers at the River Rouge Complex and at the Highland Park and Dearborn factories decided once and for all to rewrite their role. They went on strike during the Great Depression until Ford recognized their union. These struggles led to the dismantling of the repressive surveillance machine in the so-called social department, notorious for its midnight raids on workers' homes to see to it that they were abiding by Ford's notions of cleanliness and citizenship.[5] Listening to workers' stories of lived experience in assembly-line factories, a startling contrast to Ford's fearless yet passive automaton emerges. If one goes to the U.S.–Mexico border, which is the focus of this book, one will find an even more startling contrast to Ford's mutant proletariat.

From River Rouge to Juárez, Mexico

Mexico's maquiladoras are third-world versions of assembly-line mass production. And in the maquilas, the battle between Ford's repressive system and the workers' efforts to assert their autonomy and creativity continues as a fact of daily life on the shop floor. The story of labor repression and resistance in the Fordist assembly-line factories that we call maquiladoras has not been written. This book is the story of struggles against domination. Henry Ford never went to Mexico as an industrialist, but his technological and organizational systems eventually did. The maquilas are third-world heirs to Ford's assembly-line terror.

These factories are based on the same repressive technological and management systems pioneered by Ford and his engineers at the River Rouge Complex outside Detroit during the early to mid 1900s.[6] Ford's terror of the machine has come to the third world, where it manifests itself in a vastly unregulated and uncontrolled border industry that is rapidly transforming the ecological, economic, and political landscapes of Mexico's northern border.

But Mexico's maquila workers, like workers the world over, are not the unthinking automatons envisioned by that most inventive of all American automakers. From the worker's perspective, the problem of workplace politics resides not in labor's lack of creativity but rather in the capitalist organization of work itself. To hear workers tell the story, the hierarchical and technological organization of production under capitalism is the primary source of struggle. "You ask if my life is a struggle. You would do better to ask why the struggle is my life," Juana Ortega once told me over a rushed cup of coffee during her lunch break at RCA. Ortega is a veteran of the RCA plant, a sprawling, semiautomated electronics assembly-line factory that has been producing color television sets in Juárez since 1967. RCA–Juárez was one of the very first consumer-electronics assembly plants established under the auspices of the Border Industrialization Program (BIP), a bilateral agreement between the United States and Mexico negotiated in 1965.[7] The exterior and landscape architecture of RCA–Juárez looks more like that of a college campus than like that of a postmodern version of William Blake's dark, satanic mills.[8] As Juana Ortega says, "It has a friendly exterior to mask the ugly brutality inside."

Ortega describes her job in terms that are a mirror reflection of Ford's own twisted lament over the loss of labor's creativity: "This job is a terror. The noise. The monotony. The constant danger of the machine. . . . In the factory, the [assembly] line is the worst. It crushes your fingers and in the end your mind as well." In the workaday world inhabited by Ortega, the assembly line is a nightmarish machine come alive in the form of a hand-mangling, spirit-crushing monstrosity. Unlike Ford's unflinching automaton, Ortega is not always fearless before the terror of the machine.

> In the morning about five I get up to fix breakfast for my son and two daughters, my sister Clara, and my uncle Roberto. They will eat it when they wake up at six to go to work and school. But I am gone before they wake up. I go to the bus stop to meet my friends and co-workers. I hate the bus, but it is better than the vans. You might think that I am just nagging about this but the fact is that when they cram us into those vans and buses

like sardines in a can, well it just symbolizes everything that is wrong with our country. They stuff us into vans. They stuff us into factories. They stuff it to you at work. It's stuff! Stuff! Stuff! The work I do is nothing to be proud of. Any donkey can do it, and faster to boot! It's not that I am incapable. It's more like the job is not a challenge. In fact, it's an insult to my intelligence. . . . You work till your bones hurt. You work till your eyes hurt. The engineers make you work till you think you will drop. They really are . . . always watching and hovering, stopwatch and clipboard in hand. What I regret the most is not the pain of working at something so degrading, so meaningless. It is instead the pain of knowing that we, the laborers, are capable of doing so much more. Of living and working in a more meaningful way. Of controlling our own lives, our own resources, our own destinies. This is what I struggle for then. For a job to make full use of my imagination. And to change the world. To make it more just. Happier, full of love and cooperation. I dream of a world that lives within its own means. Within limits, free of excesses. The maquilas? Well, you know, it's crazy to work so fast all year round to make so many useless things. But I guess as long as the *americanos* want cheap TVs then there will always be maquilas. But you know at the same time we are exhausting Mexico's resources, especially its workers. We are wasting human lives. I say: this is too high a price to pay for a job, food, and shelter. (Interview, Ciudad Juárez, May 1982)

My first impression of Ortega's life was that she was trapped in a grinding struggle to survive. But from her point of view she is involved in a struggle to create a new way of life. Her commitment to an ideal of social change is the result of many years of thoughtful reflection regarding the present and future struggles of women in building a more just Mexican society. It was only later, after conversing with Ortega for over seven years, that I came to understand that her terror was also the source of a great inspiration to resist and invent. Perhaps the old Wobbly lawyer Austin Lewis had it right after all? Workers learn struggle from the capitalist organization of the factory itself.[9]

More Akin to Ludd

Juana Ortega is the antithesis of Ford's mindless automaton. She is a thinking, creative, feeling human being who also happens to be an industrial worker in a foreign-owned, assembly-line factory. She is proud of her skills and, although frustrated by her oppression, determined to change the lot of workers like herself. Her story is not one of despair, although it is full of adversity. Her life is not one of poverty, at least not of the spirit, although her family must scrimp just to put food on the table. Her work is alienating not because she lacks skill but because the job degrades her integrity as a feeling and thinking human being. Despite such frustration, Ortega struggles to empower workers on the shop floor. She has a bit of the terrorized victim that is Ford's automaton and a lot of the rebel that is more akin to Ludd, the original machine-smasher.[10]

And like that renowned nemesis of English textile machines, Juana Ortega demonstrates unbounded creativity in her daily combat against the terror of the machine. She discusses her participation in acts of sabotage in the maquila:

> When I see that they are about to increase my standard [of output], . . . that motivates me. I accumulate units without testing them. . . . I always have some pretext on hand. Sometimes I'll break the chassis for the circuit board or I'll take the fuses off the visual [sic]. . . . That is what counts because that is what you can get away with, little bits of sabotage . . . just enough to slow the work down. (Interview, Ciudad Juárez, May 1982)

Another worker—from a maquila that assembles electronic surgical tools—expresses similar knowledge of sabotage:

> The conveyor belt [*banda*] is really made up of several pieces held together by metal and rubber clamps. One of the tools we use is a screwdriver which is the right size for working on the clamps. When they speed up the line, we agree to unclasp the belt. I'll do a little at a time, and everyone does their own little part. After an hour or so, the belt comes undone and we take a rest while the engineers fix the damage. (Interview, Ciudad Juárez, April 1982)

Indeed. Mexico's maquila workers provide a striking contrast to Ford's automaton. Through thirteen years of field research and library study for this book, I have documented hundreds of cases of worker informal resistance and sabotage in the maquilas.[11] This book traces various workplace stories of struggle—the intrigue and stress, mishaps and successes of workers' direct confrontations with technology and management on the shop floor. These struggles are the outcomes of a subaltern organization created by workers inside the factory.[12] Working at the pace of turtles, or what the workers call *tortuguismo,* is perhaps the most widespread tactic of resistance. Sabotage of machinery, tools, components, and other work materials is common. Playing "sick" or "stupid" are also common forms of resistance used by maquila workers. But this resistance sometimes erupts into unofficial and illegal "wildcat" strikes and other work stoppages.

On occasion, maquila workers have escalated informal shop floor struggles to higher levels of organization and to wider arenas of confrontation. This was the case during the Nuevo Laredo strike wave of 1974–75 when more than ten thousand workers, out of a total maquila workforce of fifteen thousand, staged a protracted and violently suppressed general strike protesting against poor working conditions and low wages and for democratic unions.[13] Other groups of workers in Juárez, Mexicali, Tijuana, and Matamoros have struggled to establish independent unions and worker coalitions, solidarity networks, and even self-help and producer cooperatives. It would appear from this that the working women of Mexico's maquilas are not quite the quiescent victims of managerial fantasies and scholarly theories.

I do not see a quiescent victim in Juana Ortega. She is both an oppressed worker and a tireless agitator for workers' rights. Her oppression does not reduce her to the status of a helpless victim. She is too dignified for that. Instead, she remains unquestionably clear and eloquent in explaining the conditions that ensnare our lives in a web of suffocating and contradictory interdependencies. She does not fit the stereotype of the happy Juárez factory worker impatiently yearning for the next paycheck to hurry on across the border in search of a Big Mac and fries at the gleaming, golden-arched temple of North American capitalism. While she readily accepts the wages she needs to help a family survive, she remains critical of the excessive *gringo* appetites that fuel the growth of the maquila industry and keep people like herself trapped in underpaid, meaningless, and dangerous work producing electronic gadgets for consumers north of the border. But her insightful criticisms strike at the heart of the dilemma. The maquiladora industry continues to grow because consumers in U.S. markets demand cheaper TVs and other assembled products. Yet, a job in an assembly-line factory remains an alienating, dehumanizing, and hazardous experience for many workers like Juana Ortega. The organization and technology of maquiladoras can crush the workers' spirits, deny them opportunities to develop and express working knowledge, and endanger their health.

Ortega understands this, and so she questions the rationality of the entire system that gives rise to the terror of the machine. She sees the maquiladora strategy as an invention of unbridled transnational corporate power, which she thinks also menaces the environment. She says: "These plants are everywhere, aren't they? I bet wherever they go it's the same thing: The workers, all the people, and the land just the same. In the end, we are the ones that get hurt" (interview, Ciudad Juárez,

May 1982). Maquilas send Mexico down the dangerous road to ecological and cultural degradation.[14] To Ortega, the signs of environmental degradation are plainly visible in every drop of water she is afraid to drink because of pollution from chemical wastes and untreated sewage. She is wondering: Should Mexico, or any other third-world country, accept the maquiladora strategy as an appropriate model of development? Should not Mexico find alternatives to the current wave of rapid "development" through mass-production industries? Does not such "development" carry too high a price in the destruction of human life and ecological balance?

Modernization at Too High a Price

Maquiladoras are part and parcel of the "modernization" of Mexico. During the recent postwar phase in the global expansion of capital the distinctions between first and third worlds were increasingly blurred. The third world is no longer an exotic, faraway place. The rise of multinational corporations has brought the third world home to the first and the first to the third.[15] The process of multinational capitalist development has dramatically transformed the ecology, political economy, and local cultures of the third world. If the multinational corporations are the flagships of the new modernization, then assembly lines are their most common weapon. For capital, the most critical transformation brought about by the global diffusion of the assembly line is the imposition of new social and technological forms of domination on a newly emerging third-world industrial working class. Internationalization of production also provides a strategic escape valve from the pressures caused by the struggles of organized workers in the first world.[16]

Modernization theory holds that industrial development is a necessary step toward progress, civility, and modernity.[17] Backward peoples are brought out of the dark malaise of preindustrial traditions and into the shining light of the modern industrial city and factory.[18] Rapid industrial development of the third world is said to be a necessary step in meeting the demands of a growing global population. Only modern mass-production techniques can meet the challenge of feeding, housing, and caring for the growing third-world masses. "Developing" countries must therefore open their borders to foreign investment and technology. This is the same ideology that drove the Bush-Salinas negotiations for a North American Free Trade Agreement (NAFTA).[19] A growing population means more jobs are needed, and transnational corporations from the United States, Europe, and Japan are supposedly best able to provide the jobs and technological resources to meet this challenge. Third-world people must accept progress, even if that progress is accompanied by the terror of the machine and the destruction of nature and local cultures. The story is an old one, but it is being repeated today along the U.S.– Mexico border.

What is wrong with modernization? For Juana Ortega and other maquila workers, modernization means they must now confront work that is full of danger and degradation. As Ortega puts it,

> There should be other ways to make a living. Work should never be drudgery. It should be something you look forward to. It should be a time of joy and not just a burden. If the best we can do is come up with a machine that does the job fast while it smashes your fingers, then we are really in trouble. These factories are bad. They are bad for your health and, look around, this is really bad for the land and water and air. Everything in Juárez has changed. But it is all part of a bigger scheme. The entire world is dying from pollution and waste, and our children are like the first warning sign. When they get sick from the food and water they consume, you know something is terribly wrong. (Interview, Ciudad Juárez, October 1983)

In this narrative, modernization is a process riddled with inequities. Ortega understands that "modernization" undermines the right livelihood of third-world men and women. It imposes limits on Mexico's options for development. If given a choice, workers like her would opt to not follow the path of big industry and environmental degradation: Why trade a child's health for a dirty, low-paying job? It does not seem worth the cost. For Ortega, maquilas are also bad because they sever the workers from democratic participation in the solution of workplace problems; management resists the workers' struggles for safe and healthy workplaces. Workers are also denied the opportunity for conviviality, since their communities are threatened by environmental degradation and poverty. Industry is a menacing threat to a vulnerable planet. Alternatives to such destruction are possible and must be fought for.

Third-world women and men have more often experienced development as "maldevelopment."[20] Maldevelopment forces colonized peoples to conform with Western industrial capitalist values, purposes, and methods of production (and destruction). The Western model is offered as the only true path to progress. This has the effect of locking the planet's entire array of local cultures into an expanding international system of rampant industrialism. Global capitalist industrialization destroys the diverse and endangered original livelihoods of third-world peoples. Present and future options for new, more just, and ecologically sound economic arrangements and institutions are being destroyed. The most profound destruction unleashed by capitalist industrial development is easily the one most often overlooked: people's original livelihoods. People of color are also endangered species. This is the point that Vandana Shiva makes when she describes modernization as being associated with the introduction of new forms of dominance.[21] Shiva recognizes that maldevelopment is an inevitable outcome of the imposition of "western technological man as a uniform measure of the worth of classes, cultures, and genders." This is a form of domination that is destructive of both ecological and cultural diversity. In capitalist maldevelopment, ethnocide is the brother-in-arms of ecocide and patriarchy.[22]

But there is another side to this process of supposed modernization. And this is that third-world women are emerging in struggle against the ecologically destructive and spirit-crushing nature of capitalist industrialization. Not all classes and cultures subscribe to the technological myths of Western progress. Not everyone worships at the altar of technical rationality. And reason and wisdom are not the exclusive possessions of Western capitalist societies; in fact, much of what passes for Western rationality seems quite irrational.[23] Maquila workers, despite the terror of the machine, are capable of thinking for themselves, of inventing alternatives to capitalist production/destruction, of creating cooperative forms of organization that link workplace democracy with ecological sustainability.[24]

Juana Ortega understands that the destruction of workers and the environment in the third world are both consequences of the excessive levels of consumerism generated and satisfied by mass-production systems. Workers such as Ortega question the absence of democracy in the workplace. They question the legitimacy of a system of production that endangers the mental and physical health of workers. They challenge the production system's degradation of skill and craft. And they question the rationality of a mass consumer society that is based on the destruction of nature. The sit-down strikers at River Rouge, Highland Park, and Dearborn forced Ford to recognize their union and abandon his repressive social department. The maquila workers of Mexico's northern border are also challenging the assumptions of the dominant Western paradigm of progress and industrial development by taking a stand for an alternative to mass production and assembly-line work.

"My Girls Respect Authority"

Unfortunately, Ortega and her co-workers are not, at this point, in a position to implement an alternative model of workplace organization or economic development. They are confronted by a type of management that is as ruthless in pursuit of profit as Ford was in the days of the Model A. Courageous and creative, Ortega and her co-workers remain a study in the nuances and limits of self-empowerment. And maquila management is ultimately a study in the refinement of Ford's terror. I will never forget what the manager of a U.S. electronics assembly plant in Juárez told me, when asked about the level of skill in the maquilas: "You know, we are doing real good for Mexico. My girls, well, they have no skills at all coming into these factories. What they have is a respect for authority and an ability to work long and hard at the same thing, over and over again" (interview, Ciudad Juárez, June 1981).

At the time of the interview with the plant manager these words did not strike me as familiar. On further reflection, I can now see the connection between the maquila manager's views and those expressed in Ford's "Terror."

> The work here is difficult. A good operator will excel at her output within six weeks. It really is all about output levels when it comes to skill [in the maquiladora], the higher skill required to reach higher levels of output with minimum quality-control problems. That is not as easy as it seems when you consider the amount of concentration necessary to perform the same job at the same quality for long hours. (Interview, Ciudad Juárez, August 1981)

Part of the problem with industrial work relations in the maquilas is that plant managers and production engineers really do seem to believe that what they are doing is good for Mexico. I do not question their sincerity, but their delusions regarding the tyrannical nature of work and the horrific working conditions in the maquilas are unforgivable. The manager is correct on at least one point, even if he overlooks its significance. One does not have to look too hard at the statement to get at the underlying kernel of truth. Maquila work is certainly "not as easy as it seems." But what the manager does not say is that the "concentration necessary to perform the same job at the same quality for long hours" is exactly what Ford had in mind when he described "repetitive operations [that] hold no terrors." Ford has indeed come to Mexico, not only in the form of the assembly line but also in the echoing thoughts of the maquiladora plant manager.

This [repetitive labor] also reinforces discipline and self-worth. We are helping Mexico become more modern. The technology we use here is high-tech. We are upgrading Mexico's technological infrastructure, and this is a big part of the progress we are bringing to our good neighbors south of the border. And so this opens up new possibilities for the girls who work for me. I mean, these girls don't have a lot of other options: stay at home, sell trinkets or candies on the street, work at a sewing factory, or, worst of all, prostitution. People accuse us of exploitation, but we are bringing a superior technology, good jobs at decent wages, and a better business climate to Mexico. The way I figure, these plants are good for Mexico because they . . . offer the young women a chance to be something better. At Electro-Fixtures we have a slogan: "Working hard for EF is working hard for self-improvement." Our goals are the same: developing a good personality and good civil conduct in our employees is as important to us as producing a good product. We are proud of our technology. It provides solutions to a lot of problems and brings superior skills to Mexico's labor force. This is what progress is all about; the key is technology. It has nothing to do with exploitation. (Interview, Ciudad Juárez, August 1981)

Nearly all the elements of Fordism are present in the manager's sentiments: An emphasis on "output levels," and the equating of skill with the ability to "reach higher levels of output with minimum quality-control problems." An obsessive concern with "respect for authority" and with discipline. For the manager in the maquilas, discipline is the same as "developing a good personality and good civil conduct." This is frighteningly reminiscent of Ford's social department. And the machine. It seems the machine is always there, a presence that simply cannot be undermined or erased. And so the manager's statement closes with expressions of reverence for technology as a measure of progress, as the key to solving Mexico's problems.

The statement also reflects the prejudices of a manager born and raised in the United States. The idea that maquilas are "helping Mexico become more modern" by "bring[ing] superior skills to [its] labor force" conveys the same attitude that describes Mexico as a backward nation. This statement reminds me of a declaration once made by Eduard Bernstein, the German Social Democrat: "We shall condemn certain methods by which the savages are subjected, but we shall not condemn that savages are subjected and that we claim the right of the superior civilization with regard to them."[25] Would our maquila manager, I wonder, condemn the terror of the machine? Would he question the hazards and degradation of the assembly line and repetitive labor? Not likely. The manager believes that his factory system is superior to anything Mexico offers. He truly believes that the maquilas are a major contribution to the salvation of Mexico from the grinding poverty of "underdevelopment." So, he resents the allegation that maquilas exploit workers. He believes that the "superior technology" and "good jobs at decent wages" are proof enough that the intentions of foreign multinational corporations are noble. Our manager truly believes that the presence of the maquilas in Mexico is not part of a strategy to maximize profit rates for multinational corporations through the exploitation of third-world workers. He fails to understand that workers such as Juana Ortega may not share his ideals of progress or his reverence for technology.

And how does the manager view maquila workers? They might as well be the "savages" in Bernstein's declaration. The image of the Mexican women as street peddlers or prostitutes in the absence of multinational assembly lines is too far-fetched and degrading to accept. The manager speaks in the voice of the white male, industrial capitalist worldview, a voice that gives us a distorted view of the reality of third-world women's labor. The manager's degrading view of Mexican women is suffused with sexism and racism. "These girls," he calls them. These are working women who somehow "have no skills at all" before hiring as assembly-line workers. Women who nevertheless have the ability to "respect authority" and to "work long and hard at the same thing, over and over again." Our presumed street urchins and whores should be thankful that the maquilas are there to save them from the Mexican border's immoral excesses and abject poverty. And I suppose maquila management should be equally grateful that Mexico's patriarchal culture has fortuitously produced a surplus of obedient female fodder for Ford's assembly line!

What the manager views as a quest for higher output, the maquila workers recognize as the long-hated speedup of the assembly line. The manager does not recognize that workers experience the assembly line as a steady confrontation with occupational hazards and as a source of incredible psychological pressures. He only sees the efficiency graphs and output tables used to assess workers' productivity. Our maquila manager is concerned with the workers' good personalities and civil conduct. But he fails to acknowledge the intrusive and often violent nature of managerial efforts to mold and shape workers into a compliant and productive labor force.

Our manager never seems to question whose principles of "civility" are at stake here. And he remains silent about the fact that the working women of Mexico's maquila industry are not as respectful of authority as he would have us believe. Nor are Mexican women new to work, even industrial work. Women directly participated in the first industrial strikes in Mexican history at two textile mills outside Mexico City in 1861. Women have been active in Mexican labor struggles since the famous strikes at the San Ildefonso and Colmena textile works. For well over a century—from the company towns of the Porfiriato in the late 1800s to the border maquilas of today—Mexican women have worked and struggled against their factory bosses.[26]

Does our maquila manager remain ignorant of this history because he is the product of an expansionist culture that has long regarded itself a superior industrial and political civilization? He fails to see the reality of workers' struggles against the terror of the machine. He must rationalize not just his blind faith in technology but his patronizing and myopic view of Mexican women and their place in Mexico's labor and cultural history.

Three Voices, One Truth?

Three voices then: Henry Ford, Juana Ortega, and our anonymous maquila plant manager. Which one are we to believe? Truth is problematic in the social sciences. Some argue that truth is absolute, that certain truths are universal and can be shown to operate as natural laws governing society—truth is the one true story. Others argue for relative truth—reality is in the eye of the beholder. Yet others argue that truth is contextual and subjective—truth is situated knowledge.[27] This is not the place for what would necessarily become a long-winded exegesis on the nature of the politics of knowledge and truth claims in the social sciences, what the philosophers like to call epistemology.[28]

In writing this book, I do not claim to discover or establish any universal truths about the nature of technology, work, and gender in assembly-line factories. I do not pretend to have discovered empirical laws that can describe work organizations or labor-management relations for all time and in all places. Neither do I pretend to offer an objective perspective. The social science myth of objectivity has been created largely to defend scholarly positions that are uncritical or supportive of the status quo.[29] My research may be rigorous and methodologically sound, but this I feel does not give me license to preach "truth." I am not interested in creating yet another "master narrative"—a single, true story.

What I have done in this book is to openly take the workers' perspectives. I have tried to view reality through their eyes not because I believe in "going native" or because I prefer to use "emic" research methods.[30] Rather, I have emphasized the workers' own voices simply because the workers have direct and, in my opinion, more accurate knowledge of the factory. They are, after all, closer to the work. Workers have direct access to information that not even the best field researchers or managers can tap. But the knowledge that workers hold about work is not presented here as eternal, immutable truth. I have taken from workers' narratives a body of cumulative tacit knowledge and lived experience that becomes the basis of my own analysis of the maquilas. What I share with these workers are perspectives that are critical and oppositional in character. I must honestly state at the outset my opposition to the terror of the machine. I also share the maquila workers' commitment to social change, workplace democracy, and economic justice. I share their concern for the earth and the rampant ecological destruction that capitalism produces in part because it is a brash globetrotter with little respect for local cultures and traditions.

I am in agreement with Renato Rosaldo that in remaking social analysis, research scholars must bring an awareness of their own values and normative expectations as human beings to the forefront of academic discourse.[31] Only then might we have an opportunity to candidly examine the relationship between our values and our research methods, theoretical interpretations, and efforts to shape and inform public policy. Only then will we be guided toward the formation of a social policy that is informed by our own culturally constructed values, and not just by the rules of objectivity established by the dominant canon.

My commitment to critical scholarship and to the development of an alternative epistemology are not the fundamental reasons I have championed the workers' perspectives in this book. Scholarly research on the maquila industry has thus far been limited in both its scope and methods, so that serious gaps in knowledge are apparent in the literature. I do not intend to follow the established norms of the canon and present here a step-by-step review of the literature.[32] Instead, I will identify the gaps in our knowledge and the role that workers' knowledge plays in correcting the biases and inaccuracies that have been unwittingly—or, in some cases, purposefully—perpetrated by management, unionists, and scholars.

Technology, Work, and Gender in the Maquilas: The Limits of Sociological Discourse

From a critical perspective, Mexico's maquiladoras are a new form of capitalist domination that combines first-world technology with third-world labor. But many defenders of the maquilas argue that foreign investment is integrating women into the process of third-world development—women are now becoming fuller partners in development. Pro-maquila scholars also argue that gender exploitation cannot be empirically substantiated; feminist perspectives emphasizing the role of gender in the maquilas are therefore dismissed as "ideological."[33] Social scientists have studied the maquilas for more than two decades and are in sharp disagreement over the nature of working conditions and labor relations in the industry.[34] In subsequent chapters I hope to shed some light on these disputes.

The maquila debate has covered a lot of ground and cannot be comprehensively dealt with here. There are literally thousands of research articles on the subject in numerous professional journals in the United States, Mexico, and Europe. There is a steady stream of government statistics, reports, and monographs on both sides of the border. Several major books and anthologies focusing on the working women of the maquilas have been published.[35] The subject is now familiar to academics, policymakers, unionists, and business interests. Congress has several times debated the tariff regulations that promote assembly-line factories on the Mexican border and other third-world locations, while unions in the United States have long pushed for their repeal.[36] The national news media in the United States has also recently focused attention on the maquilas, as witnessed by coverage on toxic wastes in the border region by Bill Moyers and the Center for Investigative Reporting.[37] Several documentary films have also been produced dealing with the "global assembly line."[38] With increasing media coverage we can expect higher levels of general public awareness of maquilas. Despite voluminous research by social scientists, government agencies, corporate consultants, and others, there are still large gaps in our knowledge of the maquilas. The most obvious and unsettling of these is the gap in knowledge of the relations of production in the workplace. The study of factory production as a sociological phenomenon is an area that conventional scholars typically call industrial relations or "plant sociology."[39] Marxist scholars prefer to call it labor process theory; Michael Burawoy calls it the study of the "politics of production."[40] In any case, our knowledge of the technological and social organization of work in the maquilas is severely limited.

Some very specialized research on the maquilas has focused on the organization of work and labor-management relations and on the intricacies of gender.[41] But these studies are few and far between. Prior research has generally also failed to contextualize analysis and interpretation. Researchers have failed to locate the maquilas within the context of the history and sociology of work organizations. Such a task is indispensable if we are to attain the balance of a comparative, historically grounded perspective and avoid the pitfalls of overgeneralization, ethnocentrism, or even proletarian messianism.

Research on maquila work organization has tended to emphasize capitalist control strategies. Study has focused on wage structures, seniority practices, recruitment of workers, the technical division of labor, managerial hierarchies, ideological manipulation, labor law and arbitration, the introduction of new technologies and automation systems, and other dimensions of capitalist control.[42] But such studies offer a limited perspective. There is a marked failure here to consider workers' own struggles and the impact of these on the changing organization of work. Much of this research, therefore, presents a rather one-sided view of maquila work organization. The analysis of capitalist control strategies is associated with the study of formal organizations such as unions and arbitration boards. As a consequence, most of this research has failed to consider the informal, subaltern world of workers' shop-floor struggles. Since official labor organizations in Mexico tend to be male dominated, research on formal labor-management relations is limited in what it can add to our understanding of women workers' experiences and struggles.

The failure to address what I call the subaltern dimension of work organization leads to an incomplete view of the politics of production in the maquilas. It leads to a lack of vision regarding alternatives to mass production. By silencing workers' own narratives, we contribute to this myopic view of the maquiladoras. Ironically, even managerial theory recognizes the existence of informal shop-floor networks as a major aspect of "organizational life," to be factored into planning for the social control of production.[43] The study of workers' struggles is therefore necessarily also the study of capitalist control strategies. This is a more dialectical view of the process, less one-sided than that provided by the various schools in the maquila research tradition.

Social scientists have not sufficiently grounded their research on the perspectives and working knowledge of factory workers. We have not fully tapped the knowledge that workers have of the organization of the factory. This failure is reflected in, or reflects, our inability or reluctance to integrate workers' concerns into our own research methods and agendas. It is intriguing, in the sociology of work, how a great deal of the research social scientists perform is done consulting with management. Scholars are routinely associated with management in designing and conducting research on the organization of work.[44] This has also been the case with regard to research on maquila work organization, where a large body of data has been generated to assist management in the performance of tasks such as the psychological testing and screening of potential employees.[45] If objectivity is in question, industrial sociologists and psychologists are probably more often guilty of conducting research with managerial biases. Less developed is a sociology that addresses workers' concerns. My study is therefore a contribution to the development of workers' perspectives in the sociology and history of comparative work organization. It is a study that draws directly from workers' knowledge of the politics of production in the global assembly line.

Because of my commitment to the workers' perspectives, the narrative form I have utilized in this book involves a synthesis of ethnography with survey data and field notes. Extensive and relatively unstructured oral interviews are the basis of this narrative, but I provide further interpretive context by drawing from survey interviews and records from my participant observation. If this approach seems somewhat distanced from the scholarly discussion, such is my intent—in order to highlight the voices that have hitherto remained unheard in the maquiladora discourse. Like their written textual cousins, oral narratives "can be thought to dramatize the ability of knowledge, ideology, subjectivity, and cultural productions in general to create the forces that constrain the course of narrative."[46] My contribution consists of articulating the workers' perspectives, precisely in order to change the course of the narrative surrounding the maquiladora phenomenon. For workers like Juana Ortega, the time has come to move beyond debating the merits or evils of maquilas; the time is now to search for meaningful alternatives.

Inspired by the struggles of third-world women against the terror of the machine, this book offers a first-time look at the dialectics of domination and resistance in the assembly lines of Mexico's maquiladora industry. But to fully understand the politics of production in the maquilas we must first trace the development of factory technology and workplace organization. This will take us on a long trek, from the original "manufactories" of eighteenth-century England's Industrial Revolution to the present phase of microelectronics, robotics, artificial intelligence, and global mass production.

Chapter 2 outlines the history of work organization in Western societies. It is a necessarily condensed version of a long, complex history.

I outline a historical progression in capitalist organizational forms to provide a context for my analysis of technology and workplace politics in the maquiladoras. My approach to the history of capitalist workplace organization involves a critique of the dominant discourses in the sociology of science and technology and industrial sociology. I focus on the tradition known as instrumentalism, a legacy of empirical research, philosophizing, and expert consulting that has assisted capital in evolving new forms of workplace domination. I close the chapter with a broad overview of the maquiladoras as a transnational capitalist organizational form whose ancestry traces back to the dark, satanic mills of Marx's time. Chapter 3 is a comprehensive description and analysis of the maquila labor process from the vantage point of capitalist control strategies and organizational forms. While the maquilas are located in Mexico, they are technological and organizational equivalents of the Fordist assembly-line factory. As such, maquilas have a unique place within the history of Western work organization. Fordism has come to Mexico, but it has had to adapt to the cultural and political peculiarities of the setting.

In chapter 4, I focus on maquila workers' shop-floor struggles. I describe multiple terrains of struggle and forms of resistance. Two major forms of struggle are discussed at length. The first is the so-called restriction of output (*tortuguismo*), which involves resistance against assembly-line speedup. The second involves work stoppages such as wildcat strikes and other types of collective action. The focus here is on class, gender, and cultural factors that intersect with technological arrangements and underlie the formation of the subaltern organization that workers create to resist management. But in organizing to struggle, the women workers of Mexico's maquiladoras also develop a variety of ideological and political perspectives to contest the legitimacy of managerial authority. In chapter 5, I deal with the circulation of struggle from the factory to the community. The establishment of self-managed cooperatives and other grassroots organizations in Juárez during the 1970s and 1980s is a remarkable event in the history of workers' struggles in the third world. At the heart of these struggles is the story of the Centro de Orientación de la Mujer Obrera (COMO, Center for Orientation of the Working Woman). COMO is an experiment in worker education and self-management that has attracted considerable interest among scholars in Europe, Canada, Mexico, and the United States. I document the emergence of a new social movement that involves the struggles of third-world women for workplace democracy and ecologically sustainable development. I argue that the emergence of new forms of political consciousness, ideology, and organizational forms among Mexican maquila working women has far-reaching implications for feminist and workplace democracy struggles in the third world.

In chapter 6, I return to the maquila workplace for a discussion of workers' creativity in the labor process. I examine the inventions and innovations developed by workers in their efforts to make use of their working knowledge of production. I describe the workers' struggle over unpaid technical work and the political definition of their labor as "deskilled." I challenge the perspectives of both conventional and Marxist scholars who tend to view assembly-line workers as thoroughly deskilled, haplessly exploited victims.[47] I describe an enormous reservoir of creativity and invention in the daily shop-floor activities of maquila workers. This inventiveness can contribute to self-exploitation or resistance. The role of workers' discursive practices in shaping and reshaping oppositional identities is also examined. Finally, I review the history of COMO's struggle to transfer the inventiveness and skill of maquila workers to self-managed cooperatives and experiments in community organizing.

In chapter 7, I argue that maquila workers are new social subjects with oppositional identities. They are redefining development by pointing the way to ecologically sustainable and socially responsible forms of production. I examine the case of SOCOSEMA, a dump workers' cooperative organized with the assistance of COMO. Within conventional development theory and sociology, the third-world poor and disenfranchised are viewed as hopelessly marginalized, as being peripheral to the history and politics of work. In this chapter, I argue that maquila workers, through COMO, linked with the struggles of other so-called marginals to champion the cause of workplace democracy, political self-determination, and community renewal. The struggle of the *pepenadores* (dump workers) is ultimately a lesson in sustainable development.

In chapter 8, I focus on changes in the maquila industry between 1982 and 1992, which was a decade of tremendous growth and change in the BIP. I discuss changes in technology and managerial systems; shifts in the demographic composition of the workforce, involving an increasing number of male workers; and the appearance of "maquila temps" (temporary personnel services). I also focus on the increasing presence of Japanese transnational corporations, *nihon no kaisha,* and offer a comparative analysis of work organization and shop-floor struggles in U.S.- and Japanese-owned maquilas.

Finally, in chapter 9, I closely examine the environmental impacts of the maquila industry. I develop an ecosystems approach in analyzing the maquilas as "disturbance regimes." I focus on various aspects of environmental degradation: threatened and endangered species, the contamination of surface and groundwater supplies, the diverse impacts of expanding infrastructure, the catastrophic threat of cybernetic technologies, occupational health hazards, and environmental health problems in the border region. I conclude with some reflections on the future of the maquila industry: I look at the changing role of maquilas in Mexico's development and the implications and problems posed by the North American Free Trade Agreement (NAFTA) that promises to unify Canada, the United States, and Mexico in a common market. The late Dr. Guillermina Valdés de Villalva, my mentor and colleague, was to be a coauthor of these last two chapters. Before her tragic and untimely death, she played a major role in conceptualizing my approach to the study of the changing maquila industry. Indeed, she was an important inspiration in the writing of this entire book.

With this book, I hope to bring about a clearer, and more critical, understanding of the problems that occur with the imposition of mass-production industries across the world. I do not believe we can afford to allow global Fordism to stand as the uncontested dominant model for third-world development. I believe this book demonstrates that the struggles of women industrial workers in the third world not only withstand the terror of the machine but, perhaps more important, point the way toward an alternative future—more humane, more just, and ecologically sustainable.

2

From Dark, Satanic Mills to Maquilas

And did those feet in ancient time
Walk upon England's mountains green?
And was the holy Lamb of God
On England's pleasant pastures seen?
And did the countenance divine
Shine forth upon our clouded hills
And was Jerusalem builded here
Among those dark Satanic mills?
　　　　—William Blake (*Milton*, 1808)

Discourses within Domination

The central concern of industrial sociology is the "study of the process of control over work relations."[1] The dominant discourses in the sociology of work, including the Marxist, are focused on the problematic of control. Could it be otherwise? The discourses of industrial sociology are associated with Western philosophical traditions long engaged with debating the value of controlling nature through science and technology.[2] The idea of the domination of nature by people has a basis in Plato, Descartes, and Bacon.[3] The Greeks, of course, gave us the separation of spirit and substance. Plato distinguished himself by declaring that civilization was the outcome of humankind's mastery over nature. Descartes further developed the dichotomy between mind and nature by proposing that the separation of subject and object was a precondition for the discovery of all scientific knowledge and truth. Bacon widened the chasm between "self" and "other" still further by developing the aggressive experimental methods of scientific inquiry in order to engage in the empirical "penetration" of nature.[4]

But Bacon was not just a philosopher-scientist; he fancied himself a worthy technologist as well. It is often overlooked that Bacon established an intriguing precedent by explicitly rejecting knowledge for the sake of knowledge (not that such a thing is possible or desirable) because he

25

wanted to deliver the goods to the emerging class of industrial and commercial capitalists. Bacon and his colleagues at the Royal Society were
both apologists for and beneficiaries of those who came to thrive from
the witch hunts, the slave trade, genocide, colonial conquest, enclosure,
and incipient industrialization.[5]

Karl Marx, of course, has a different place in this Western philosophical tradition. He developed an incisive and brilliant critique of the technological domination of labor under capitalism.[6] The critique was im-
passioned and poetic. We should not forget: Marx invoked William Blake's
unsettling image of dark, satanic mills in *Capital,* when he attacks the
degradation of labor in the Lancashire textile factories. But like others
before him, Marx ultimately viewed technology as essential to the human
control of nature. Science and technology were to be the tools of the
working class on the road toward a communist future free of forced and
menial labor. This is particularly clear in the now familiar passages in the
Grundrisse in which Marx outlines the emergence of science and technology as productive forces.[7]

Across the Atlantic, seemingly far removed from the domain of the satanic mills, the Western philosophy of domination gave us the scientific
management of work and the terror of Ford's machine. Engineers such as
Frederick Winslow Taylor and industrialists such as Henry Ford went beyond philosophy and social criticism by single-mindedly pursuing novel
ways to adapt and apply science and technology in the service of managerial tyranny in the workplace. Their ingenious use of science and technology was governed by the same basic Western philosophical values that gave
us Greek misogyny, the transatlantic slave trade, the "mechanical arts" of
Francis Bacon, the destruction of the "deer forests" of Scotland, and the
public spectacle of the Lancashire witch trials.[8] Like Bacon, Taylor and
Ford speak the language of technological, or instrumental, domination.

But it is often overlooked that this philosophical trajectory also gave
us the sociology of "human relations." George Homans and Elton Mayo,
the American educators who cofounded the school of "managerial sociology," have an important place in the intellectual trajectory of domination that distinguishes the history and sociology of work. Homans and
Mayo were mentors to a whole generation of American managerial sociologists, young Ph.D.s and consultants, who went on to provide capital
and management with the weapons of research on the control of work
relations in the twentieth-century industrial factory.

The "rediscovery" of informal groups by the disciples of Homans and
Mayo at the Western Electric Company's Hawthorne Works outside Chi-

cago is one of the most infamous moments in the history of industrial sociology in the United States.[9] Being good positivists, and so following in the tradition of Bacon, the managerial sociologists established a pattern of cooperation between intellectuals and management that through the present continues to be a major aspect of capitalist control of work.

Industrial sociology, like its more "hard" science cousin, industrial engineering, is one of several affiliated knowledge domains linked directly to the development and maintenance of capitalist control in the workplace. The aerospace engineer Mike Cooley, a leading critic of the human-technology relationship under capitalism, expresses this linkage most clearly:

> Employers are seeking aid from a whole host of "Hawthorne Agents" such as job enrichment specialists, group technologists and industrial psychologists. The industrial reality is that these "agents" in no way change the basic power relationships that give rise to contradictions in the first place. It is, as a Lucas [Aerospace Company] shop steward put it: "Like keeping people in a cage and debating with them the color of the bars."[10]

The industrialists that built England's satanic mills gave us the iron cage of alienation and exploitation. But it was American managerial sociology that tried to paint the bars of the cage in friendly colors.

The main point here is that instrumental reason equates objective knowledge with the technical control of nature. Knowledge is domination. Instrumental reason places ultimate value on the control of nature through technological domination. Here, both labor and nature are transformed into mere "instruments" of production and objects of domination. Here, truth is reduced to the objectivist knowledge of experts. Only experts know truth, and only experts possess the scientific methods to seek truth. Instrumental knowledge tells us that there is only one true story; universal truth can only be generated by objective experts. The rest of us are emotional and unknowing objects of experts' universal truths. The discourses of instrumental reason may thus be likened to a conversation capital has with itself in order to clarify the imperatives, methods, and directives of technological domination.[11] For the instrumentalist, the history of science is the story of the conquest and control of nature, women, workers, and colonies by means of a constant revolution in the tools of technological domination designed by experts.[12]

But the history of the capitalist workplace is much more than a discourse concerned with producing blueprints for the domination of nature, women, and labor. It is not just the story of the dominance of technical rationality—of the colonization of work through the triumph of reason and knowledge expressed as the science and technology of the workplace. The history of work is also the discourse of the *refusal* of work. It is the story of the struggle by humans against the reduction of their being to mere wage labor, variable capital, input of production—in other words, against capital's categorization of labor as mere commodity. Blake's dark, satanic mills and Ford's assembly-line terror loom large on this horizon, but so too do the Arkwright machine-smashers, the workers of the Paris Commune, the factory councils of Red Emilia, the saboteurs of the IWW, the rebellious Fiat workers of Piazza Statuto, the student-workers of the worldwide street revolts of 1968, and the turtle-pace workers of Mexico's maquiladoras.[13] Rejecting forced labor, human beings resist their objectification by capital. Workers are always more than just wage labor.[14] And most humans on the planet refuse to define their lives on the basis of their labor activity. In struggling for other ways of living, human beings develop alternatives to the capitalist organization of work. Harry Cleaver argues that "when people . . . have struggled to cease being defined as workers they have sought a richer, more multilateral existence."[15]

The point is that the study of work should not reduce human beings to mere labor power, as capitalists, positivists, and not a few Marxist intellectuals tend to do. Wage workers are much more than exploited labor power, and the majority of human beings on the planet are not even members of the industrial working class.[16] It is therefore important, in writing a history of industrial capitalist work organization, to recognize the limits of such a history. It cannot be a universal story or a master narrative. Similarly, it is important to recall that many of the technological changes that have occurred over time are consequences of workers' resistance. The history of work organization is also the history of the organized resistance that grows out of workers' own knowledge, skill traditions, ideologies, and values.[17] But we must also not deify the factory or the labor process as the highest expressions of human civilization, a well-known tendency in the discourse. The point is not to make a new religion of work, Marxist or otherwise, but to understand the dynamic and intersecting contradictions in the evolution of capitalist domination and workers' struggle.[18] And so in this and subsequent chapters, I trace the history and sociology of work in Western capitalist societies as a discourse between domination and resistance. This will take us from the satanic mills of Lancashire to the assembly-line sweatshops of Mexico's maquila industry.

Satanic Mills: The Destruction of Handicrafts and the Rise of Large-Scale Industry

The history of work under capitalism can be traced through various formations and episodes. Any history of the origins of capitalist production, however condensed, must at least acknowledge the role of the primitive accumulation—that is, the forcible separation of the peasantry from the land, or what is known as the enclosure movement.[19] It is perhaps Marx's description of the "bloody expropriation of the peasantry" that best captures the processes that led to the formation of an industrial working class. I do not intend to revisit the primordial origins of capitalist production.[20] But the separation of the peasants from their land (their means of production) is the most critical precondition for the development of capitalist production and the imposition of wage-labor exchange relations. It is only the violent and forcible separation of peasants from their original means of livelihood and subsistence that persuades them to go to the city and the factory in search of waged work. The globe-trotting violence of the primitive accumulation is the precursor to the imposition of wage labor as a means of survival. This is as true today as it was during the emergence of industrial capitalism almost three hundred years ago.[21]

The origin of the factory system is linked to the Industrial Revolution in eighteenth- and nineteenth-century England. That complex and momentous event has had many chroniclers, and Karl Marx is certainly among the most insightful.[22] Marx viewed technological change as a critical factor in the history of capitalism. But his analysis of work organization ultimately emphasized the class struggle. Marx focused on the dialectic of technological domination and workers' resistance. Here, we can find the story of workers' struggles for a legal limit to the length of the working day and the story of capital's introduction of the steam engine to "tread underfoot the growing demands of the working class."[23] Throughout his analysis of the struggle for a "normal" working day, Marx gives us a two-sided view of the politics of production as a "protracted and more or less concealed civil war."[24]

Prior to the emergence of capitalist production, work in late-medieval Europe was dominated by the artisan guilds and their handicraft workshops. The artisan craftworker was as much an inventor as a producer. Mental and manual labor were unified in handicrafts. It took many years of apprenticeship before the craftworker was prepared to perform the holistic and highly skilled intellectual and physical labor of artisan work. Artisans completely owned and controlled the means of production. This ownership of the tools of production and the control of knowledge secured a powerful and esteemed place for artisan craftworkers in precapitalist societies.[25] The emergence of capitalist production initiated a gradual assault on collective artisan power and handicraft skills. The development of the first capitalist work organizations proceeded under the rubric of what Marx calls simple craft cooperation. There were no major technological revolutions under simple cooperation. According to Marx, simple cooperation basically introduced a new form of control through the use of managers and supervisors: "An industrial army of workers under the command of a capitalist requires, like a real army, officers (managers) and NCOs (foremen, overseers), who command during the labor process in the name of capital."[26]

Simple cooperation congregated multiple groupings of independent handicrafts under the same roof and command of a capitalist owner. Cooperation was between the newly coordinated handicrafts, and command was exercised by capital's newly created supervisory strata. For the first time, artisans labored for someone else as wage workers. But craftworkers maintained control of work by preserving their monopoly over the knowledge and skills required for production. Thus the technical division of labor, in which skills are broken down and individual tasks are limited to one or several simpler operations, was yet to assert its presence in the combined handicraft workshops of simple cooperation.

With an increasing division of labor, there appeared a new form of cooperation that Marx called the "manufactory." The transition to manufacture involves two major developments: the emergence of the so-called partial worker and the specialization of job tasks. Once separate and independent craft trades were now combined into the production of a single commodity. This reorganization of work was based on the decomposition of once complex and holistic handicrafts into partialized and separate operations.[27] This was the first step toward "deskilling"—the technical dequalification of the craftworker, and his or her replacement with the partial worker. Related to this process was increasing specialization. The fragmented and interdependent nature of specialized skill enhanced the continuity of production under manufacture. Specialization was the domain of the partial worker, and the increased division of labor it represented was the result of a desire on the part of capital for greater control over the continuity and pace of work. Greater continuity in production implied an intensification of work and, therefore, higher productivity.[28] Another major aspect of the changes that occurred under manufacture was the creation of a wage hierarchy.[29] The more specialized division of labor in the manufactory included a hierarchy of skills and a concomitant hierarchy of pay. For Marx, these divisions had a political aspect: the "divide and conquer" strategy pitted the skilled against the unskilled, the manager against the worker, and the high-waged against the low-waged.

The transition from manufacture to machinery and large-scale industry was for Marx the most critical moment in the history of capitalist production. Large-scale industry, with its huge investments in machinery, came in the aftermath of a very long period of working-class struggle. The rise of protective associations, Luddite attacks on labor-displacing technologies, and other forms of resistance led to substantial gains—including legal limits on the length of the working day—for certain sectors of the English working class. Marx viewed the introduction of machinery and the creation of large-scale industry as key tactics of a capitalist strategy to restrict and undermine working-class gains. Machinery destroyed the remaining vestiges of handicraft skill. The machine replaced skilled labor in an ever-expanding variety of jobs. The remaining skilled workers were replaced by machine-tenders. Capital was seen by Marx as introducing motorized power to fortify control over the speed of work.

Marx described automatic machine systems in great detail. And he spoke of what he called the "condensation of labor" in connection with the rise of machinery. He was referring to what is perhaps the most remarkable transition in the history of work. This is the renowned, and by now theoretically famous, shift from absolute to relative surplus labor time as strategies of capitalist production. What Marx called "absolute surplus labor time" was essentially a strategy of capitalist control based on the extension of the length of the working day. If you make workers labor longer hours they produce more surplus value. This is the strategy that Marx discusses in a humorous section of *Capital*, "Senior's Last Hour," where he ridicules the argument of an Oxford professor who was called on by the English manufacturers to defend capital's position during the "Ten Hours Agitation."[30] Professor Senior claimed that reducing the workday from fourteen to ten hours would destroy British industry: the capitalists needed those extra three or four hours per day to earn a profit. But the old strategy of an absolute lengthening of the working day caved in to the demands of the organized working class.

This monumental defeat forced capital to shift its strategy from absolute surplus labor time to "relative surplus labor time." The new strategy relied on machinery to intensify the pace of work and thereby increase the productivity of labor within given time limits. This is what Marx called the "condensation of labor." The introduction of machinery, of science and technology in the service of capitalist production, revolutionized the productivity of labor. The transition from manufacture to machinery and large-scale industry provides the first great leap forward in capital's ability to mass-produce. Limits to the length of the working day could be overcome as long as capital extracted unending increments in labor's productivity through the application of science and technology. This was the key to the future of capitalist production. Marx understood the significance of the industrial and scientific revolutions that were sweeping across Europe:

> The technical conditions of the labor process may be revolutionized to such an extent that where formerly ten men using ten implements . . . worked up a relatively small quantity of material, one may now, with the aid of one expensive machine, work up to one hundred times as much raw material.[31]

Marx also noted the presence of increasing numbers of women and children in the workforce. The addition of women and child laborers accompanied the imposition of new hierarchies based on age, gender, and skill distinctions. According to Marx, divisions of age and gender were intended to further weaken the resistance of the male workers.[32] The exploitation of child and female labor in the Lancashire district was an aspect of capitalist production that greatly disturbed Marx. These were, after all, the "proletarian weeds," the most exploited of all workers in the English textile factories, on whose gates William Blake forever inscribed the appropriate appellation of satanic mills.

Marx recognized that the increasing social and technical division of labor was a powerful tool of capitalist domination in the factory: the increasing demographic diversity of the workforce functioned as a barrier to the unity of the working class as a whole. The mechanics and engineers benefited from higher wages, more autonomy, and prestige, while the machine-tenders were relegated to the ranks of the lowest-waged labor and worked under more severely dehumanizing and more dangerous working conditions. It would at best be difficult under such circumstances for machine-tenders to establish solidarity with engineers who were often busy at work in behalf of capital, trying to make exploitation ever more efficient. Marx also argued that the separation of mental and physical work originated in the transition to machine systems and large-scale industry. It is at this point that science and technology became more powerfully and clearly aligned accessories to the crime of capitalist domination and control. The mental labor of scientists and engineers became a powerful tool for undermining the struggles of "manual" labor.

Yet, the transition to large-scale industry also implied a higher level of struggle between workers and capital. The very nature of workplace organization in the dark, satanic mills gave rise to workers' resistance, as human beings struggled to empower themselves against domination. This is the most profound and enduring lesson to be drawn from a critical reading of Karl Marx's industrial-factory studies.

Designs from a Straitjacketed Engineer: The Rise of Scientific Management

Most people have never heard of Frederick Winslow Taylor. Those who are familiar with Taylor probably know him as a turn-of-the-century industrial engineer and sheetmetal expert who gained fame with his time and motion research. Few likely know that he slept strapped in a straitjacket.[33] He was reputedly so hyperactive and tightly wound that, unrestrained, he would knock himself out in his sleep. This frenetic, straitjacketed engineer gave us one of the most revolutionary transformations in workplace organization. Taylor's contribution came in the form of "scientific management." If Marx is the most insightful chronicler of Blake's satanic mills, then F. W. Taylor is the most important figure after Henry Ford in the twentieth-century history of workplace technology and organization.

Scientific management (or Taylorism) is best known for its use of time and motion study. Taylor's most enduring contributions were essentially strategies for redesigning the skill content of work and for standardizing the time and motions required for each partialized job task. Taylor, and his disciples, advanced the gospel of efficiency in an effort to justify a severe attack on skills.[34] The not-so-hidden agenda of scientific management involved a concerted attack on the greatest obstacle to industrial efficiency, what Taylor described as "the slow pace which [workers] adopt, or the loafing or 'soldiering,' marking time as it is called."[35] Taylor emphasized the problem of output restriction, or soldiering, in both of his books.[36]

Taylor designed time and motion study to prevent and control soldiering. The Taylor system was based on the assumption that conflict was an inevitable aspect of labor-management relations only as long as workers had sufficient skill to exert some control over work processes.[37] Conflict could be controlled if management appropriated workers' skills through time and motion study. This strategy promoted the constant redefinition and reduction of job skills. Time-study engineers decomposed skilled operations and then recombined them into smaller sets of fragmented and interdependent job tasks. This may be likened to a type of "methods engineering" that allows management to take over the design of labor activity in factory production.

Taylorism is not so much a system of technological innovations as it is a series of engineering methods critical in establishing managerial monopoly over the knowledge base. Workers are effectively stripped of responsibility for mental tasks. The intent is that workers follow the pace and content of unskilled manual labor as defined and designed a priori by management. The principle of absolute managerial control over the knowledge base corresponds with the separation of mental and manual labor that Marx criticized some sixty years before Taylor outlined his plan for the further deskilling of labor.[38] Taylorism was a potentially powerful weapon for combating the uncertainty that workers were capable of engendering as long as they controlled "brain work." It was really the conquest of intellectual labor that Taylor outlined in the methods of time and motion study.

Another innovation of Taylorism was the "piece-rate" system. Taylor intended that time and motion study could also be used to set optimum output rates of productivity. Workers were to be paid on the basis of the number of pieces produced. Beyond that rate, any surplus level of production was rewarded as bonus pay. In this manner, Taylor hoped to put pressure on workers to compete with each other for bonus pay. This, he felt, would serve a dual purpose. It would provide a built-in mechanism for increasing rates of output, and it would distract workers from their battle with management by converting conflict between workers and time-study engineers into competition between workers.[39]

Multiple Addition: Beyond the Mechanical Despotism of the Flow Line

Henry Ford did not invent the assembly line. The first assembly line was actually built at the Venice Arsenal in 1438. According to David Gartman, Cyrus McCormick also used the principle of the automated conveyance of work in the production of reapers in 1847. And in Chicago's slaughterhouses, mechanical conveyors were used in the "disassembly" of livestock carcasses as early as the 1890s. Ransom Olds was apparently the first to make use of "progressive layout" in the auto industry, as early as 1903.[40] But it was Ford Motor Company engineers who first achieved recognition as pioneers of the assembly line.[41] And so, Fordism has come to refer to the principles of mass production and assembly-line technology.

What exactly is the assembly line? Industrial sociologists define the assembly line as a technology that is based on the so-called flow-line principle.[42] This is the principle of the constant flow of parts on an automatic, linear conveyor belt. In Marx's time the flow-line principle was called machine-pacing. The sociologist Robert Blauner emphasizes the tyranny of machine-pacing in the following description:

> The essential feature of the automobile assembly line is the fact that the pace of work is determined by the machine system rather than by the worker. . . . Since the speed of the line is mechanically set, the cars move down the conveyor belt at a predetermined rhythm. Often, it is necessary to work at top speed to keep up with the line.[43]

Fordism is a system of factory control based on the mechanical despotism of the flow-line principle. The primacy of the flow-line principle led Guido Baldi to describe Fordism as a technological path to repression.[44] Machine-pacing was known to Marx at the time of the transition to large-scale industry, so the flow line cannot be considered the definitive characteristic of Fordism.

Gartman argues that Fordism is based on three principles: (1) division of labor, (2) accuracy, and (3) continuity. The division of labor involves increased specialization and deskilling. Accuracy involves standardizing both manual operations and assembly components. Continuity involves mass production on a continuous, nonstop basis.[45] Henry Ford's own descriptions of different phases of automobile assembly seem to confirm the existence of these three basic underlying principles.[46] But division of labor, accuracy, and continuity were already familiar aspects of capitalist production when Marx analyzed large-scale industry in *Capital*. So again, it cannot be argued that Fordism is unique in adopting these three basic principles of the capitalist organization of work. All forms of capitalist production are based to varying degrees on ever greater division of labor, and ever-increasing levels of accuracy and continuity. What, then, makes Fordism unique in the history of work organization?

In part, what makes Fordism unique is its order of magnitude. Mass production represents a quantum leap forward in the level of production compared even with large-scale industry. And also in part, Fordism merely extends and modifies Taylorist methods such as time and motion study, deskilling, the separation of mental and manual work, and quality-control supervision. However, Fordism goes beyond both large-scale industry and Taylorism in further developing the technological dimensions that strengthen and rationalize managerial control over the intensity and speed of work. While machine-pacing was known to Marx in large-scale industry, Fordism represents a higher level of technological control made possible by a larger scale of automation in the movement of work materials and in the actual process of assembly itself.

But even the dimension of magnitude falls short of describing the central innovations of Fordism. In the preceding chapter, I briefly noted that the three mainsprings of Fordism are the assembly line, the five-dollar day, and the so-called social department. Historically, the original function of the Ford social department was to exert control over the "moral" behavior of immigrant workers. It also served to control the hiring of women, as Ford preferred not to hire married women.[47] This was a system not just of economic incentives but of social controls. As Ford explained in *My Life and Work*:

> The man and his home had to come to certain standards of cleanliness and citizenship. . . . [T]he idea was that there should be a very definite incentive to better living and that the best incentive was a money premium on proper living. A man who is living aright will do his work aright. The thought of easy money breaks down work.[48]

Under Fordism the setting of wages and bonuses is more than a simple matter of controlling workers' productivity. Fordism opens new avenues, through the activities of the inquisitional social department, for controlling worker behavior by means of the supervision of domestic and civic life. Ford described this social control in no uncertain terms:

> We had about fifty investigators in the Social Department. . . . It was expected that in order to receive the bonus married men should live with and take care of their families. We had to break up the evil practice among many of the foreign workers of taking boarders. . . . Boys under eighteen received a bonus if they supported the next of kin. Single men who lived wholesomely shared [in the bonus scheme].[49]

The Ford Motor Company long reserved the right to fire workers if they refused to learn English in the school provided by the company.[50] The significance of Ford's failed attempt to impose control through social conformity must not be underestimated. His experiment in social control, while defeated during the early years of the Ford Motor Company, established an important precedent for the development of modern personnel administration systems. Similar "sociological departments" are commonplace in the modern corporate bureaucracy and are very much a part of the continuing problem of an alienated work culture, particularly in the global assembly-line factories of the third world. We now call these organizational structures "personnel departments" or "human resource departments," but the objective of managerial control remains the same.[51]

It is really the unique combination of several elements that makes Fordism a watershed in the history of work organization. Ford's genius does not reside in technological innovation so much as in organizational innovation. His genius derives from the way he combined existing and new technologies with new forms of managerial organization and social control. I have already described Ford's concept of the assembly line and the constant technological changes he thought were necessary to optimize the principles of division of labor, accuracy, and continuity. But there are two other dimensions that make the complete Fordist system: a new wage regime and a new form of social control.

In the area of wages, Ford introduced an innovation he called the bonus-on-conduct method. The Taylorist piece-rate system was rejected in favor of a minimum day wage tied to an incentive bonus scheme. This was the "Five-Dollar Day," and it revolutionized the linkage between wages and productivity in the automobile industry. While other automakers struggled with piece-rate systems, Ford increased wages and productivity on a scale unimaginable before the 1920s:

> We do not have piece work. Some of the men are paid by the day and some are paid by the hour, but in practically every case there is a required standard output below which a man is not expected to fall. . . . There must be a fixed day's work before a real wage can be paid.[52]

This concept of a flexible standard of output is one of Ford's most enduring innovations. He introduced the idea that productivity is dynamic, that increases in output are to be expected and rewarded on the basis of conduct. But this is more than just another post-Tayloristic wage hierarchy. Bonus levels were not determined solely on the basis of careful monitoring of individual worker productivity but also on the basis of the monitoring of behavior outside the factory.

Fordism also incorporates aspects of patriarchal domination. Gender is a dimension of work organization that has been overlooked or deemphasized by scholars interested in the history of the Ford Motor Company. In the early years, the Ford Motor Company did not hire married women.[53] Single women who married were summarily dismissed. And men who were found living with a partner outside matrimony were also fired. There was a definite patriarchal ideal of the family in Ford's vision of the good life. Ford never abandoned his desire to impose a patriarchal ideal of proper living on workers, despite the dismantling of the social department in the face of considerable worker opposition.

The patriarchal dimension of Fordism also includes a gender division of labor. In the early years of the company, up through the 1930s, women employees were restricted from the assembly line and from other areas with machinery and heavy equipment. There was a pronounced segregation of women into clerical and non–production line auxiliary jobs. The history of this gender segregation in the Ford Motor Company remains to be written, but it is already clear that the division of labor based on gender was never a static entity. Evidence from Ford himself and more recent research indicates that Fordism is a flexible system at the level of personnel management. It is a system that manipulates the demographic composition of the workforce in order to impose multiple divisions of power based on skill, wages, age, seniority, race, ethnicity or nationality, gender, and many other factors. This manipulation is necessary in order to make adjustments in response to fluctuations in the organized resistance of workers and in the supply and quality of available labor.

It is possible to conclude that the percentage of women on the assembly line at Ford Motor Company was never a fixed quantity. There were very likely periods when the percentage increased. For example, white women and ethnic workers played a major role in the strikes against Ford during the mid to late 1960s.[54] Fordism introduces a dynamic division of labor that is flexible despite its hierarchical structure. Gender is one quality, among many, that is manipulated as part of a complex and ever-changing division of labor that is a strategy for capitalist control. In this, Fordism relies on a strategy with roots in the satanic mills. Marx too, it will be recalled, described the "sexual" division of labor as an aspect of control in the Lancashire textile factories.

Ford's organization of the assembly-line factory, and in particular his innovative and cumulative approach to the use of machine technology and automation and his manipulation of the relationships between wages and productivity and between earnings and social behavior, revolutionized capitalist work organization to an extent unmatched even by the exemplary innovations of Taylorism. Ford was a pioneer in forging a unique combination of technological and social controls.

Describing Fordism as an ideal type is, therefore, extremely problematic since this system entails a virtual permanent revolution in organization. We might say that Fordism is a production system created through multiple addition. It is based on a constant and cumulative addition of interrelated elements. But an ideal model of Fordism may have several consistent elements, including:

1. the automated flow-line principle (continuous conveyance of parts with assembly-line speedup)
2. wage hierarchies based on careful monitoring of daily output standards (performance quotas)
3. bureaucratic controls over quality assurance (hierarchical quality control)
4. standardization and predesigning of job tasks (deskilling and separation of mental and manual labor)
5. standardization of assembly components and tools (accuracy)
6. greatly increased productivity through the combination of automation with intensive labor activity (automated mass production)
7. therefore, an increase in the frequency of both technical and bureaucratic restructuring (permanent revolution in production technologies and methods engineering)
8. dynamic and flexible concept of personnel management (oriented toward manipulating gender and other divisions of labor)
9. a mechanism for managerial control of worker social and civic life ("human resource" and "personnel management" departments)

The specific and unique combination of these organizational elements makes Fordism one of the most flexible and formidable production systems ever confronted by the working class, because it seeks to regulate not only "labor time" but *all* of the worker's time. The quest for conformity inside the factory and outside in the worker's community is the definitive element of Fordism.

Fordism extends the iron cage beyond the factory by attempting to establish a system of social regulation.[55] It goes beyond the mechanical despotism of the flow-line principle by means of multiple addition—that is, by means of a constant addition of new forms of technology and new forms of social control. Fordism is thus the logical culmination of the domination of nature, women, and labor initiated by the Greeks and perfected by their Baconian disciples. By relying on science, technology, and managerial innovation, Fordism perfects the use of instrumental knowledge to further the aims of domination.

Forging a Friendly Iron Cage: Managerial Sociology and the Social Control of Work Groups

That Ford ultimately failed to control the disenchantment (and resistance) of assembly-line workers is witnessed by the incredible rate of labor-force turnover and the great number of wildcat strikes and other work stoppages experienced throughout the history of the Ford Motor Company. Ford himself reported turnover rates of 200 percent and more as workers quit their jobs, many presumably because repetitive operations held terror for them. In 1914, for example, the Ford Motor Company had to hire at a rate of fifty-three thousand new workers a year in order to keep a constant workforce of fourteen thousand.[56] The "problem" of "labor's alienation" was reflected both in the extremely high turnover rates and in the protracted struggles by workers to gain union recognition and collective-bargaining rights. The assembly line, the social department, and the five-dollar day could not provide Ford with an effective means to control worker discontent and the struggle engendered by an oppressive system of industrial organization.

Inspired in part by the failures of Fordism, a group of U.S. sociologists trained by George Homans and Elton Mayo developed the "human relations" school of industrial sociology. These scholars argued that the problems of industrial work relations, of alienation, were caused by an underlying and generalized condition of anomie (normlessness) that afflicted industrial civilization as a whole. They saw modern society as comprising morally confused and isolated individuals ensnared in a web of social disorganization that accompanied the rise of urban, industrial systems.

Despite their belief in widespread anomie, the human-relations theorists also argued for the existence, within society, of an undercurrent of harmony and social equilibrium. Influenced by Durkheim, the human-relations school proposed reclaiming the individual and society through industrial organizations capable of inculcating and maintaining group consensus via spontaneous collaboration.[57] Modern society allegedly undermined traditional institutions of social control such as the family and church. The discipline and regime of the industrial factory could step into this vacuum and provide guidance and meaning for an increasingly atomistic urban populace.

But the nagging problem of "labor's alienation" was a barrier to the "renormalization" of the population through the social control of work. Human-relations theory fancied itself to be a new school of "managerial sociology."[58] This is a sociology of the control of work relations as a means of dealing with alienation in the workplace. Managerial sociologists believed that the discovery and analysis of informal group relations was the key to dealing with alienation and the industrial conflict it apparently bred.

Like Henry Ford, the managerial sociologists had a paradoxical view of labor. On the one hand, workers were autonomous subjects, fully capable of forming their own code of social control in opposition to managerial imperatives.[59] On the other hand, workers were also irrational opponents of managerial authority and industrial efficiency. To deal with the alleged irrationality of the working class, the managerial sociologists proposed that research on group life in the workplace be construed as a supplement and guide for management control of work relations.[60]

The managerial sociologists reported that individuals in a group situation often restrict their output. In other words, workers purposefully work slower than expected and often below their capacities. The ghost of "soldiering" that haunted Taylor some thirty years earlier reasserted its position as the central concern of industrial sociology. Output restriction, a fancy term for worker sabotage and resistance, became the obsession of managerial sociology.[61] Managerial sociologists thought they had discovered the key to the social control of work in the industrial factory, namely the existence of informal networks that could be traced to the close interpersonal relations between assembly-line operators and supervisors. These informal networks played a major role in the resistance to change that characterized the industrial workforce.[62] Management could remove resistance to control by using more direct and intense supervision. Workers were not to be left alone to their own devices but rather had to be under constant surveillance. Supervision would target the identification and subordination of informal networks because these had the power to influence social sentiments that could become a hindrance to rationality and efficiency in the factory.

The managerial sociologists followed the lead of Taylor by viewing workers as irrational opponents of industrial efficiency. Only instead of relying on the confrontational brutality and cold calculation of time and motion study, managerial sociology sought to instill labor quiescence through friendly and participative supervisory and counseling tactics. Instead of the stopwatch and clipboard of the time-and-motion-study engineer, managerial sociology emphasized the use of the "suggestion box" and the complaint session for work groups. This was management with a velvet glove, not an iron fist. Human-relations theory and practice was an experiment in "social engineering" to the extent that it attempted to get management and supervisory staff directly involved in the formation and control of the social sentiments and informal networks of primary work groups.

It is difficult to ascertain the effectiveness of managerial sociology in providing capital with new strategies and tactics for social control. But there is little doubt that the disciples of Homans and Mayo developed a model of control that continues to exert influence in contemporary management theory. Managerial sociologists anticipated many of the concerns and strategies of modern management, and in particular its focus on informal work relations and networks. The renowned managerial consultant Nathan Shefferman captures the continuing relevance of managerial sociology in the following discussion of informal networks:

> Management can no longer afford to deny, obscure, or plead ignorance of the "cliques" within its workforce. . . . "[I]nformal" power groups and their hidden leaders . . . can either help or hinder management. . . . [W]hispers can be more potent than management's commands. . . . [These] power groups [have a] relentless influence . . . on productivity, cost and profit. . . . That which makes . . . management more effective . . . is the knowledge, skill and adroitness with which management . . . recognize[s] and deal[s] with this concept of the influence of informal power groups.[63]

One of the enduring contributions of managerial sociology is the increasingly bureaucratic nature of control in the workplace. Since Max Weber, this is familiar terrain. Simply stated, heightened supervision requires long-winded policy statements and regimented rules if it is to function effectively as a mode of control over workers' behavior. Rules and regulations governing work behavior proliferate as long as the iron cage develops bureaucratic structure to complement technological domination.[64] However, more recent incarnations of managerial sociology have actually shifted away from an emphasis on social conformity and bureaucratic control. Specifically, personality and organization theory entails a rejection of the perspective of informal networks as nonconforming threats to the "rational plan of organization." Not all departures from managerial imperatives should be viewed as irrational obstacles to industrial efficiency and organizational control.[65]

Personality and organization theory admonishes management for contributing to conflict. Conflict is caused primarily by management efforts to increase the "degree of directive leadership" (the old Hawthorne formula). Imagine! The designers of Frankenstein's factory are now to assume blame for creating the monstrous machinery in the first place! Management is advised to become more "flexible" in its responses to worker initiatives and idiosyncrasies. This is a modification of human-relations theory because it decries direct coercion (Taylor's approach) in favor of more persuasive, participatory schemes. An attempt is made to rationalize informal relations. This new "humanistic management" model rewards the "positive" qualities and social-control behaviors of informal networks while attempting to rid the work groups of "negative" impulses.[66]

Accordingly, the very triumph of instrumental rationality in the workplace has produced a new, and problematic, social character that is "more oriented to self, than to craft, enterprise, or career."[67] In other words, workers are now all narcissists because the bureaucratic iron cage made them that way! For post-human-relations theorists, too much instrumental rationality actually signals the end of bureaucracy. Since disenchanted workers are more likely to become disloyal, self-serving, and cynical rebels, it is not in the interests of management to persist in the old ways of control that actually exacerbate conflict. The challenge for management, then, is to create a "corporate culture" that addresses the "personal growth needs" of individual members. Robert Howard elaborates the corporate-culture philosophy championed by the new "humanistic management" theorists:

> [T]he corporation [must] embrace this search for self and harness the new social character to its own ends. If modern management can be imbued with a "self-development ethic" . . . if workers can be made to see the corporation as the pathway not only to financial security but to personal growth and psychological identity, then the negatives of the new social character can be turned into positives. And the alienation and disloyalty experienced by workers in the bureaucratic corporation will be replaced by intense personal commitment to and total involvement in working life.[68]

We seem to have come a long way from the dark, satanic mills—a long way from Weber's disenchanted but rational bureaucracy, a longer way still from Taylor's torturous piece rates and stopwatches, and even farther from the terror of Ford's machine. Or have we? The managerial sociologists that would give us a happy corporate culture may be actually delivering as much of a "total institution" as the prison or mental hospital.[69] It seems clear that the more recent developments in managerial sociology continue to fully embrace the doctrine of absolute managerial power. Only now, instead of condemning labor's alleged irrationality and idiosyncrasies, the organizational experts seek to liberate workers from the iron cage of alienation and "narcissism" invented by capital and management in the first place. The instrumentalist tradition in industrial sociology has long been characterized by a managerial social-control bias. This bias is not a mere conceptual coincidence or ideological nicety. Rather, it is a fundamental expression of linkage between organizational theorists and management. As one critic has observed:

> In American universities [organization theorists] tend to be associated with business schools. An important criterion of their success [as academic professionals] is the amount of consulting they do with business organizations. Given the American context, they are less likely to question the entire system and the power relations in it.[70]

Managerial sociologists can be likened to an army of paraprofessional industrial mercenaries. One could think of them as snipers ready and waiting to pick at workers' alleged frailties and idiosyncrasies. Or perhaps the consultants function more like missionaries seeking to convert the unfaithful and irrational into the loyal and controllable—seeking to convert the alienated self into the "total worker," into a narcissist happily immersed in and placated by the banalities of the current fashionable corporate culture. Whatever their intentions, managerial sociologists have maintained a consistent pattern of intrusive research designed to help management control workers. In doing so, they have reshaped the face of the late-twentieth-century workplace.

The imposition of social control systems designed in part by social-science consultants contributed to the development of a destructive distortion of power relations in the workplace. The destructiveness of managerial sociology proceeds from its stark and tragic tolerance for the disempowering and sometimes violent consequences of technological and organizational change. By failing to consider the contradictory class, gender, and ethnic interests and culturally derived values that underlie social choice in the design of human-technology relationships, the adherents of instrumentalist reason tacitly endorse capital's imperatives and world-view as universal givens. The greatest folly of managerial sociology is its apparent inability to offer a critical analysis of the multiple divisions of labor created by capital on the basis of class, skill, gender, age, race and ethnicity, or any other politically and socially contrived differences. Managerial sociology is a "soft" branch of the science and technology of capitalist control of work. It is essentially an expression of capital's self-consciousness and must therefore be recognized as an aspect of the problematic of conflict in work organizations. Managerial sociology is part of the problem, rather than any sort of real solution to the alienation of the iron cage.

Capitalist Control and Transnational Labor Processes

In this abbreviated history of capitalist control strategies, I have sought to demonstrate a continuous evolution of technologies, production methods, and organizational forms. I have not dealt with more recent technological and organizational developments such as cybernetics, computer-aided design and manufacturing, flexible specialization, and robotics.[71] These more recent technological developments deserve attention, and I will address them in later chapters. The main point here is that we can trace the development of capitalist control strategies through a critical reading of the instrumentalist discourse. That is, throughout the history of capitalism, the workplace has been the contested site of a grand experiment designed and implemented by those who would use science, technology, and managerial chimeras to control the process of production and to dominate "irrational," "narcissistic" labor.

Has this progression resulted in the disappearance of the dark, satanic mills? Has the evolution of capitalist labor processes embraced human development and empowerment of workers? Has capitalism eliminated drudgery, uncertainty, low standards of living, bureaucracy, and norm-lessness? Have science and technology delivered us from the terror of the machine? These are not rhetorical questions but empirical (and political) problematics. Some argue that we have entered a post-Fordist period in which mass production is increasingly supplanted by new systems such as flexible specialization, cybernetics, and robotics (see chapter 8 for more discussion on this). Assembly-line mass production, we are told, is a relic from the 1920s and 1930s that is doomed to extinction in a postmodern world of robots, expert systems, and artificial intelligence.[72] We have moved "beyond mechanization."[73]

But mass-production assembly-line factories and their many related organizational accoutrements have not disappeared. Assembly-line mass production has certainly declined in certain sectors of the U.S. economy (for example, in automotive parts, consumer electronics, and apparel).[74] But this is symptomatic of the radical restructuring of the U.S. economy brought about by a shift to diffused global production regimes under the control of U.S. transnational corporations and is not to be accepted as evidence that an old, overexpended organizational form is somehow disappearing.[75] In the contemporary (post-1960s) period, what we find is the internationalization of the assembly line and not its disappearance. Mass production is securely entrenched in a variety of third-world settings like Mexico.

Every indication suggests that integrated transnational production will continue to expand, as corporations seek the most profitable and politically expedient locations to combat the unevenly developed power and struggles of the working class. This, of course, is what the economists misleadingly call "comparative advantage." Surely, the development of capitalist control strategies did not end with Fordism or managerial sociology.

In fact, the rise of the global assembly line suggests that Fordism and its various progeny continue to evolve, changing and adapting to new configurations of power in an international political and economic context.[76] The global assembly line is an extraordinary development that has not been thoroughly examined as a unique, historically and culturally specific reincarnation of Fordism. All of the problematics associated with this classic capitalist organizational form reemerge as characteristics of the global assembly-line factory. In closing this chapter, I will briefly sketch some of these problematics as they are manifested in the Mexican maquiladoras. This will set the stage for a more thorough description and analysis of maquila workplace organization and technology, which follows in chapter 3.

Maquiladoras: Paradise Regained or Postmodern Satanic Mills?

The maquiladoras are an example of an increasingly common form of capitalist production. The majority of maquilas are in-process assembly plants owned by transnational corporations; they operate primarily for the export market. Maquilas are not manufacturing plants (in the classic sense of horizontally integrated production systems), but rather are simply processors or assemblers of components usually manufactured in the home-base countries of transnational corporations. The maquilas assemble an amazing variety of consumer goods. They are well known for producing electronics (TVs, stereos, radios, walkie-talkies, computer circuit boards, etc.) and apparel (dresses, pants, shirts, suits, and sports coats, leisure wear, uniforms, gloves, socks, etc.). But maquilas also assemble toys and surgical tools and supplies, they fabricate wood and metal products (furniture), and even produce defense-spec precision instruments. Increasingly, maquilas include plants that assemble a variety of automotive components, including car seats, wire-harness systems for dashboards, and electrical auto parts.

But the diversity of products assembled in the maquilas is not nearly as interesting or significant as the fact that the maquilas operate on the basis of a combination of principles borrowed from Taylorism, Fordism, and managerial sociology. Maquiladoras are postmodern factory systems. By this I mean that they are characterized by fragmented and partialized labor processes, by multinational workforces, and by a pastiche-like organizational culture. In the contemporary context of labor-market structures under conditions of "flexible accumulation," maquilas are part of the international strategy adopted by capital to promote "outsourcing" of production from core to peripheral locations and social classes.[77]

Yet, there is no essential maquila organizational form. Not only are the assembly plants diverse in their technologies, organizational structures, and managerial styles, most plants are subject to constant change and restructuring.[78] There is no one permanent organizational form, even within the same plant. Instead, maquila management continually improvises new arrangements and combinations of technology, workforces, and shop-floor organization (see chapter 8). Maquilas are in a constant state of flux, an archetypically postmodern condition.[79] Their surface appearances—freshly mowed lawns and spiffy, campuslike buildings—belie the constancy of the hazardous and exploitative conditions hidden within.

Marx characterized capitalist manufactories as workplaces in which "partial workers" were subject to increasing specialization and deskilling. The manufactory also initiated the wage hierarchy. Critics of the maquilas have described the work process as "hyperspecialized."[80] Wage hierarchies are quite pronounced in the maquilas, not just in terms of differentials that separate workers, supervisors, engineers, mechanics, and managers but also within the various ranks of assembly-line operators (see chapter 3). In other words, maquilas retain many of the characteristic problematics of the ancestral manufactories. With the transition to machinery and large-scale industry, Marx observed, the workplace became even more fragmented, deskilled, and hierarchical. Large-scale industry, moreover, ushered in new divisions based on age and gender (children and women were added to the workforce primarily as machine-tenders). The definitive characteristic of large-scale industry was machine-pacing and the intensification of labor. Accompanying this intensification of labor was the separation of mental and manual work.

In the maquilas, the assembly-line workforce is also divided on the basis of age, gender, skill levels, and even nationality. And perhaps the most nefarious aspect of the maquila organizational form is the incessant speedup of the assembly line and the computer-based electronic surveillance of work (postmodern equivalents of machine-pacing and intensification of labor). Maquila work is also marked by the separation of planning (mental work) from execution (manual work).[81] The large-scale industrial factories of Lancashire were Marx's dark, satanic mills. Are maquilas their postmodern equivalents?

Again, there is no essential maquiladora organizational form. There is a great deal of variety in the maquila industry. One sociologist recently suggested that maquilas are "good, bad, or ugly" depending largely on the nature of their ownership structure.[82] The "good" maquilas tend to be wholly foreign-owned subsidiaries of transnational corporations. These companies have the resources to apply the latest technologies and presumably to promote excellent working conditions, wages, and benefits. "Good" maquilas also utilize "humanistic management" policies such as job rotation and semiautonomous work groups.

The "bad" maquilas tend to be Mexican-owned private firms or worker-owned, self-managed cooperatives. These companies presumably have fewer resources and so cannot afford the latest technologies, nor can they afford to implement and maintain good wages and working conditions. And the "ugly" maquilas include foreign-owned subsidiaries of transnational corporations that are involved in hazardous production processes with negative ecological effects. These are companies with considerable resources and state-of-the-art technologies, but presumably the very "nature" of their production activities implies that workers are exposed to occupational hazards and toxic wastes while the local environment is significantly degraded by uncontrolled emissions.

My own research supports aspects of this argument: Clearly not all maquilas are equally rife with hazardous working conditions, nor do all the factories produce negative environmental effects. This is in some ways a sectoral issue. The issue of worker-owned and self-managed cooperatives is more complex than is implied by the existence of lower wages and limited technological resources. Wage and benefit regimes also vary widely, despite the presumed constraints of Mexican law. However, the maquilas all share several characteristics, regardless of their ownership or sector. The most significant commonalities are those related to the pervasive integration of the principles of Taylorism, Fordism, and managerial sociology. Time and motion study, for example, appears to be a common practice in most maquiladoras, independent of their ownership types. Like the Taylorists, maquila management relies on the constant redefinition and reduction of job skills. Rotation through different workstations is also increasingly common. This is typical of the "job enrichment" strategy championed by managerial sociologists, but does not significantly alter the hierarchical nature of power relations in a workplace governed by the separation of mental and manual work. Maquila workers do not play a major formal role in planning production; management has a monopoly on such knowledge and on the right to use it. Piece rates have never been widely adopted in the maquilas; a few apparel factories have experimented with piecework, but the dominant exchange relation imposed on workers is actually a variation of Fordist day wages and bonus-on-conduct schemes. Thus, maquilas have integrated some Taylorist principles of labor control but not others.

Fordism combines elements of large-scale industry and Taylorism, but it goes beyond both, as we have seen, in attempting to develop a complex system of technological domination and bureaucratic social regulation. Obviously, maquiladoras are based on the flow-line principle. I have yet to see an assembly plant in the Mexican border that did not include some type of flow line (although some are not automated and may involve human material handlers and loaders, use of old-fashioned progressive layout, or semiautonomous work groups). Like Fordist factories, maquilas have a unique wage hierarchy based, in part, on contrived technical and political divisions of labor. Remuneration of workers in the maquilas follows a fixed daily wage which is subject to careful monitoring of daily output standards (i.e., performance quotas). Day-wage levels are also subject to bureaucratic controls for quality assurance. Failure to meet output and quality-control standards can easily jeopardize a worker's job security in the maquilas. All this, of course, is reminiscent of Ford's own wage hierarchy, which was a strategy with multiple functions; that is to say, it could be used to set wage levels, to reinforce productivity expectations, and to substitute "bad" workers (hence the typically high turnover rates).

Fordism is synonymous with automated mass production, which entails an immense leap forward in labor's productivity. To do this, it combines assembly workers on a semiautomated conveyor-belt system. But it also promotes a permanent revolution in production technologies and methods engineering, a point often overlooked by champions of "post-Fordist flexible specialization," who tend to view Fordism as oddly rigid and specialized.[83] The flexibility of Fordism consists in its acceptance of advances in both production technologies and management organization. This is why the Ford Motor Company has consistently been on the edge of technological frontiers (for example, in robotics, computer-aided design and manufacturing, and managerial information systems).[84] Again, maquiladoras, especially the subsidiaries of transnational corporations, integrate these elements of Fordism. Maquilas are not technologically backward sweatshops. They utilize all the latest microelectronic and robotic technologies, in combination with a large workforce of assembly-line workers. They are constantly reviewing and adopting new technologies and methods of production.

Fordism is also characteristically very flexible in its approach to the demographic composition of the workforce. In the early years, Fordism (like most other production systems at the time) was much more rigid, at least in terms of gender divisions of labor. However, the post-1960s version of Fordism reflects a willingness and ability to adapt to the changing demographic composition of the labor market, and to exploit differences in order to increase managerial control. Mexico's maquiladoras have demonstrated a similar flexibility with regard to the division of labor. For instance, in the early years of the Border Industrialization Program (prior to the late 1970s), approximately 80 to 90 percent of the workforce was female. Increasingly, and especially since the mid 1980s, maquiladoras have utilized larger numbers of male workers. These shifts in the gender composition of the maquila workforce are the result of complex factors, including incessantly high turnover rates among females; the effects of the *peso* devaluations on labor-market conditions; the availability of surplus male workers; and the growth of new, more male-dominated branches of production. The point is that maquila personnel management has been remarkably flexible and successful in responding to and manipulating local conditions.

Finally, one distinctive hallmark of Fordism is its ceaseless search for new methods of social regulation. Initially, social control was organized through rather intrusive and confrontational "social departments." Workers' struggles changed all that. In the post-1960s period, Fordism has increasingly relied on a variety of approaches to social regulation. These include modern personnel administration departments, which have staff specialists in recruitment, psychological screening, job enrichment, and ergonomics. Increasingly, these departments even include "group culture" advocates. Counseling and behavioral-modification units are also common and involve the services of in-plant or consulting industrial psychologists. In some cases, on-the-line group technologists are used by production-supervision departments to facilitate and coordinate worker participation in methods engineering on the shop floor. The addition of computer-based management information systems (MIS) has radically altered the labor process on the flow line (see chapter 8).

The late 1980s and early 1990s have witnessed an increasing level of regulation of workers' "off time." For example, control of drug and alcohol use, AIDS screenings, and even bans on smoking (both in the workplace and at home) are not uncommon. This indicates a willingness on the part of Fordist management to return to more traditional, intrusive strategies for social control. Advances in both medical and surveillance technologies have increased the accuracy and pervasiveness of these types of monitoring systems.

The maquiladoras, perhaps more so than their remnant counterparts in the first world, are engaged in all types of social regulation. My own research shows that maquilas utilize recruitment, psychological screening, and job-enrichment specialists (see chapter 3). In fact, some maquilas have a nearly paranoid approach to recruitment and have initiated psychological screening procedures to filter out potentially troublesome workers.[85] It is hardly surprising, then, that such plants report higher levels of "job satisfaction" compared to plants that do not use these procedures.[86] Many maquilas also provide counseling and behavioral-modification services, usually by contracting out with industrial psychologists, social workers, or psychotherapists. Ergonomic (or user-friendly) workplace designs and equipment are also now making an entry into the maquilas. And a significant number of plants are utilizing "corporate culture" advocates and group technologists.

With all this organizational hubbub, one might suspect that maquilas are entering a new phase of "de-bureaucratization." But bureaucratic rule and regulation of on-the-job and off-the-job performance and behavior were not considerably reduced during the decade of the 1980s (see chapters 3 and 8). If anything, in many cases the level of bureaucratization has increased in response to changing public attitudes, greater tolerance for intrusive management styles, and growing concern with the relationship between the health of workers and on-the-job safety and performance. Thus, the full range of Fordist and managerial-sociology modes of social control are available and used in the maquiladoras. But a focus on the use of formal procedures and bureaucratic power structures does not provide a complete picture of what is happening with social control in the maquilas. As we will see later, informal relations between workers and supervisors, engineers, and managers are perhaps the most effective form of social control. Sexual harassment, gift giving, socializing, and co-optation of lead operators are some of the informal methods of control used in the maquilas. Informal controls are a necessity due to the existence of clandestine shop-floor networks and the ability of these to undermine the formal plan of organization.

From the preceding broad sketch of capitalist control strategies in the maquilas, it seems apparent that Taylorism, Fordism, and managerial sociology have made significant inroads into local organizational cultures. Actually, these systems were probably already in place from the very beginning, and they have simply continued to evolve and adapt to changing circumstances and managerial imperatives. But does this mean that the maquilas are contemporary incarnations of the dark, satanic mills? Clearly, there is a huge world of difference between the conditions faced by workers in eighteenth- and nineteenth-century England and those faced by today's maquila workers. The primordial English working class was choking on smoke, soot, and grime, and its children were addicted to opiates, but it did not have to put up with a perplexing array of toxic chemicals, wastes, and heavy metals. Nor did they face ever-increasing productivity pressures induced by the science and technology of the assembly line.

In terms of environmental degradation, the maquilas are perhaps many times worse than the dark, satanic mills. The National Toxics Campaign (NTC) has characterized the U.S.–Mexico border as a "2,000-mile Love Canal." There is a growing threat to public health as the quantity and quality of toxic wastes and heavy metals illegally dumped in Mexican border waterways and surrounding lands increases with the growth of the maquila industry.[87] Research by the NTC found that some toxics are discharged into the environment at rates exceeding EPA standards by thousands of parts per million. Xylene, a carcinogenic solvent used to clean machinery, has an EPA standard of ten parts per million. The NTC samples from Mexican border maquilas were found to exceed the EPA safe-drinking-water standard by 6,300 times.[88]

Research demonstrates that many corporations have relocated to Mexico and other third-world countries to escape stricter environmental regulations in the United States.[89] Even so, bilateral regulations adopted at the 1983 La Paz Agreement require that maquilas return their toxic wastes to the United States for disposal. But SEDESOL (Ministry of Social Development) and SEDUE (which is somewhat like a combination of the U.S.'s HUD and EPA) have not consistently enforced these regulations. As a consequence, the U.S. EPA estimates that in 1988 only 1 percent of the maquilas complied with the regulations.[90] In 1990, Mexican inspectors verified that about half of approximately two thousand maquilas generated toxic wastes but only three hundred provided necessary documentation of their waste-management and disposal practices.[91]

Like the English workers in the time of Marx, maquila workers must confront the quotidian violence of the machine. Today, we are more aware of the sexual abuse and sexual harassment workers face for failing to meet managerial expectations or engaging in acts of resistance. In this regard, the workers of the English industrial factories probably faced more collective violence at the hands of capital, but they did not necessarily experience violence of the individual, interpersonal type that is common in the maquilas and is more difficult to condemn and control. Even by today's muted and often ignored labor standards, the maquilas may be likened to postmodern equivalents of Blake's dark, satanic mills. That this is so will become clearer as we venture into the hidden abode of the maquiladora labor process in the next chapter.

3

(Mis)Measuring the Ignorant

*We are into measurement here. We measure everything! That's
pretty much against the culture here, they want to sit in the corner
all day and let someone else do the work. Because we have promoted
the ones that accept measurement, they also discard the ones that
don't fit the same profile. . . . The ones that don't make it are the
more political ones.*
    —Plant manager, automotive seat assembly maquila
      (Ciudad Juárez, 1982)

*Ignorance. I use that term but I mean it in an affectionate way.
The ignorance of the Mexican workers I find is highly enjoyable.
Ignorant means you don't know any better. That is not the same
as stupid. . . . Our workers are ignorant of the industrial way of
life, and that is a major source of our control.*
    —Production superintendent, electronics assembly
      maquila (Ciudad Juárez, 1982)

The Politics of Workplace Organization
in the Maquilas

A typical electronics assembly maquila plant consists of one or two huge
warehouse structures, usually built of some combination of steel beams,
corrugated metal, and concrete slabs. The vast floors are usually cold,
bare concrete. The noise coming from the conveyor belts; soldering decks;
various pneumatic tools, jig bores, and lathes; and clattering components
is nonstop. Robotic devices known as Dynaperts provide an incessant
background staccato beat. You can feel the entire complex of building
and machinery pulse and vibrate through your body. Hundreds of workers, almost all of them women, are positioned along the conveyor belts in
groups of ten to a hundred. Small groups of engineers and mechanics in
lab white, mainly male, hover over the workers like so many predators

stalking prey. Overhead conveyor lifts shudder and whistle as they move components from one area of the factory to the next. The sound of workers talking is barely audible over the din. Chemical fumes and smoke from the soldering decks permeate the air with a metallic smell. Soon enough an acrid taste invades the mouth, nose, and throat. The exhaust fans fight a hopeless battle to circulate the foul air. Workers occasionally stop their busy work to rub their eyes and scratch their skin. Coughs and hacking sounds abound.

The organization and politics of the maquila workplace are subjects of intense debate. Many argue that the maquilas are an exploitative proposition at best. Critics point to inadequate wages, hazardous working conditions, high turnover, union-busting tactics, enormous productivity pressures, gender job segregation, overloaded infrastructures, and adverse environmental impacts. They see these problems as evidence that the industry is not a panacea for Mexico's unemployment and persistent poverty.[1] Some critics speak of sexual harassment and other types of violence against women. These problems are identified as occurring in the everyday life of the shop floor and in the home and community.[2] Feminist critics of the maquilas focus on gendered divisions of labor that segregate women in the lowest-waged and most hazardous jobs in the industry.[3] Others question the wisdom of relying on maquiladoras for border development because they are incompatible with long-range, ecological sustainability.[4]

Defenders of rapid industrialization argue that there is no gender exploitation or division of labor in the maquilas. On the contrary, women are being integrated throughout the process of development and so can benefit from access to new job and training opportunities and higher wages.[5] Supporters argue that wages and working conditions in maquilas owned by Mexican capital are worse than those found in foreign-owned maquilas.[6] Some studies suggest that maquila workers have a high level of job satisfaction, while others suggest turnover is not a managerial strategy but an unfortunate consequence of labor-market conditions beyond the control of management.[7]

If the issue is exploitation, then wages in transnational maquilas are competitive with wages in much of Mexican national industry. But this is largely due to regional differences in wage rates established under Mexican law, and is not determined solely by the type of ownership.[8] Wages in either case remain uncomfortably close to subsistence levels.[9] Real wages (adjusted for inflation) in the maquilas declined from $6.37 per day in 1982 to $3.72 in 1989.[10] This put real wages in the maquilas at a rate that is lower than the 1967 average of $3.80 a day. It might be said that in Mexico workers are "poor," with maquila workers perhaps being "less poor" than most. Typically, families have to put several members into the maquila labor market because one worker's earnings are simply insufficient to support an individual, let alone an entire family.

The nonexploitation argument rings hollow if one recognizes that maquila wages are not just inadequate, but immorally so—when judged against the backdrop of the terror of the machine. Juana Ortega once told me that no wage would be enough to compensate her for the repetitive nature and constant stress of maquila work. Workers such as Ortega may receive, on average, higher wages. But the productivity pressures they experience are also incomparably higher. The application of science and technology in transnational maquilas greatly intensifies the pace of work. Wage levels are an inappropriate measure of exploitation, unless differential productivity rates are also considered.

Despite the claims of maquila promoters, the industry is far from environmentally sound. There are few smokestacks belching obvious plumes of smog. But maquiladoras, particularly factories in the consumer-electronics, electrical-equipment, and chemical-processing sectors, utilize numerous carcinogenic and toxic substances in production. Maquila workers are exposed to these hazardous materials and wastes under virtually unregulated circumstances.[11] There is also mounting evidence of the degradation of soil and water quality as a result of toxic wastes generated by the maquilas and illegally dumped into the rivers, creeks, and lands surrounding the large industrial parks that house most of the factories.[12] Toxic wastes from maquiladoras are a veritable public-health menace to residents in communities surrounding the factories.[13] And there is, of course, the violence of the machine. Industrial accidents and medical problems associated with the organization and technology of the maquilas are pervasive.[14]

In this chapter, we venture inside the maquilas to closely examine the organization of the capitalist workplace in a transnational context. We will determine whether these assembly-line factories are happy, "brave new workplaces," to borrow a phrase from Robert Howard,[15] or postmodern reincarnations of Blake's "dark, Satanic mills." This chapter draws on my ten years of field-research experience in Juárez, Nuevo Laredo, Matamoros, and other locales in the U.S.–Mexico border region. Over the years, my research has focused on the consumer-electronics and automotive-parts sectors. These appear to embrace Taylorist and Fordist organizational principles to an extent unmatched by other sectors in the maquila industry. Foreign ownership is also strongest in the consumer-electronics and automotive-parts sectors, and my intent all along has been to study the operations of transnational corporations.

Interviews with managers, superintendents, engineers, supervisors, and workers form the basis of this description of workplace organization. Throughout, I have emphasized the discourses of managers and workers. It is their perceptions and understandings of the politics of production that I am interested in, and not so much the scholarly discourse. This chapter also incorporates results from a 1981–82 survey of 223 maquila workers. Additional data is drawn from visits I have made to several dozen maquilas and from observations recorded in a field journal that spans the decade I researched the politics of production on the border. Oral histories and unstructured interviews collected over the ten years complete the field-based data. What emerges is a portrait of complex, hazardous, and conflict-ridden workplaces.

The analysis of maquila workplace organization accompanying this description is guided by the contributions of labor-process theory. I emphasize the dialectic of domination and resistance, particularly as this involves a variety of struggles over the different forms of technical, bureaucratic, and social control.[16] My emphasis ultimately emerged from the data, from managers' and workers' perceptions, more than out of some preconceived theoretical design. I also draw from my understanding of the diffusion of Taylorism and Fordism to the third world. I focus on the intersecting nature of technological, bureaucratic, and sociocultural control strategies in mass-production assembly-line factories. This approach provides a dynamic and multitiered view of maquila workplace organization.

Several words of caution are in order. Workplace organization is seldom a static phenomenon. Work processes are subject to continual restructuring, largely as a consequence of the unfolding relationship between domination and resistance. The description of the organization and politics of maquila workplaces presented in chapters 3 and 4 reflects the state of the industry in one major border city during the early to mid 1980s. Many changes have occurred since then, and I address these in the final two chapters. Many of the events and processes that shape work organization develop outside the factory. Descriptions of workplace organization and shop-floor politics can only provide a partial view of the maquila industry. What happens in the households and communities, and in the grassroots organizations developed by maquila workers, is also important. We pursue these aspects in chapters 5 and 7. For now, a careful look inside the maquila assembly factories seems appropriate, if we are to discern the technologies and strategies of managerial control.

"Our Machines Are User Friendly": Technical Control and Division of Labor in the Maquilas

Let us begin our journey by examining the technological systems utilized in these assembly-line factories. A look at the technological layout will reveal much about how production is organized, and it will also be suggestive of the division of labor.

TECHNOLOGICAL LAYOUT IN THE MAQUILAS

Like similar assembly-line factories across the third world, maquilas utilize sophisticated production technologies:

> We are superautomated. This is the highest level of technology plant in our division, and I do mean worldwide, and in Juárez of course. There are two reasons for automation and high technology. One, . . . quality control, and two, it is cost-effective, even in Mexico. We replaced five hundred workers, who inserted components into circuit boards, with a Japanese-made robot. The Dynapert Inserter-Sequencer is an automated component-insertion, ACI, device. Before our transition to ACI, we had tremendous quality-control problems. While our workers kept a marvelous pace with our line flow, and let me tell you it was fast, the quality of work was poor. We were having to reject 30 to 45 percent of our output. Now with ACI we have quality-control rejection on the order of less than 3 percent! Sometimes we get zero rejections. . . . On one particular [color television] model, if we didn't have ACI there would be too many induced failures, too many hands [would be involved]. (Interview, Ciudad Juárez, January 1982)

John Buckner is a production superintendent at the oldest electronics assembly plant in Juárez, a wholly owned subsidiary of a U.S. brand-name manufacturer of color television sets. He shows tremendous pride while describing the advanced technological character of his plant. We circle around the Japanese-made robot, which is located in the circuit-board stuffing subdepartment. Buckner points out that the Dynapert ACI is computer controlled. A Mexican technician, young and male, sits at a video display terminal monitoring the performance of this "user friendly" machine.

Buckner's description of technology includes the central aspect of the Fordist organizational form. Assembly-line production systems combine technology-intensive layouts with large masses of workers. Fordism is both capital and labor intensive; so are the maquilas. This type of system is designed not just with cost-effectiveness and quality control in mind. Control of worker resistance is also important. As Buckner states, "there would be too many induced failures" without this technology. Workers undermine the system either consciously (through acts of sabotage) or inadvertently (as a consequence of inadequate experience). Induced failures are conscious acts of informal resistance by workers. Fordism represents a technological challenge to the power generated by workers' informal struggle, and this seems to be the case with the maquiladoras as well.

The technology of maquila production is state-of-the-art. The latest automated, semiautomated, and CAD/CAM systems are utilized, including quasi-robotic devices like the Dynapert ACI. This is hardly surprising given the resources at the disposal of the transnational corporations that operate maquilas in Mexico. Whenever possible, maquila management has opted for automation instead of reliance on a purely labor-intensive layout. This is an important point, because maquilas, especially those in electronics and automotive assembly, do not easily fit the old garment sweatshop model of eighteenth-century New England, in which masses of workers were crowded into small, unventilated rooms with old, rusty, and creaky machinery. Maquilas use automated and computerized technologies that require relatively "clean" environments to function accurately, but these are deployed in combination with a large assembly-line workforce.

It may be useful to describe the layout of the assembly line in the typical electronics maquila, to give us a better sense of the overall technological system on the shop floor. Figure 1 depicts the assembly-line layout for an electronics maquila involved in the assembly of color television sets. This is a composite picture and does not represent a specific factory. The layout is organized into fourteen stages of assembly, inspection, and packaging.[17] It includes two separate automatic conveyor belts. The first belt runs through the third and fourth stages (primary assembly and automated soldering). The second belt runs through the last nine stages of the layout, consisting of the various quality-control checks, repairs, cable soldering, frequency and power tests, prepackaging, and final packing. Only two of the stages in this layout are independent of the flow-line principle: the large-parts assembly workstations and follow-up soldering. This indicates that most of the workers in the layout are subject to machine-pacing and managerial control over the speed of the conveyor belts. The Fordist character of this layout should be obvious.

A closer look at the operation of the flow-line principle reveals some interesting variations. At one of the largest electronics assembly plants in Juárez, management has developed what it calls a "stop-start" mechanism. This contraption was designed to allow individual workers some control over the speed of the flow line. While the mechanism does allow workers a measure of control over the amount of time they take to complete specialized assembly tasks, there are other types of pressures present to keep the line from slowing down too much. The plant manager at this maquila did not think that the stop-start mechanism resulted in a slower pace of work:

> You see, the stop-start mechanism is itself automatically timed. An operator can hold her assembly for a given amount of time, within given time constraints. But we have found that the stop-start mechanism lessens some of the strain on the operators. And you know what? The operators themselves put pressure on one another to keep pace with the flow of components. If one operator is using the stop-start mechanism too much, she will be criticized by other operators. The operators must depend on each other to meet their quota standards. If one of them on the line is holding things up, then the others will also have a less-than-quota performance. (Interview, Ciudad Juárez, January 1982)

Technological innovations such as the stop-start mechanism do not alter the fundamental principle of speedup on the assembly line. They may increase the effectiveness of managerial efforts to manipulate workers' characteristics and interpersonal relationships. It is not accidental that line assignments at this plant pitted experienced rate-busters against novice assemblers, a ploy that increased quota performance pressures on the new workers.[18]

A departmental superintendent at the same assembly plant described the conveyor-belt system as a unique "user-friendly machine system." The addition of the stop-start mechanism is seen as a technology that humanizes the assembly line by giving the workers a sense of control over the pace of work. The superintendent explained how "it is in management's interest to create a work environment that is clean, safe, pleasant, and nonthreatening, and the best way to do that is to use a clean, light technology" (interview, Ciudad Juárez, January 1982). He continued his defense of the technology:

> We are centuries removed from the old sweatshops. These are modern production facilities with the best technology and management money

Figure 1. Production-Line Shop Floor, Typical Electronics Assembly Maquila

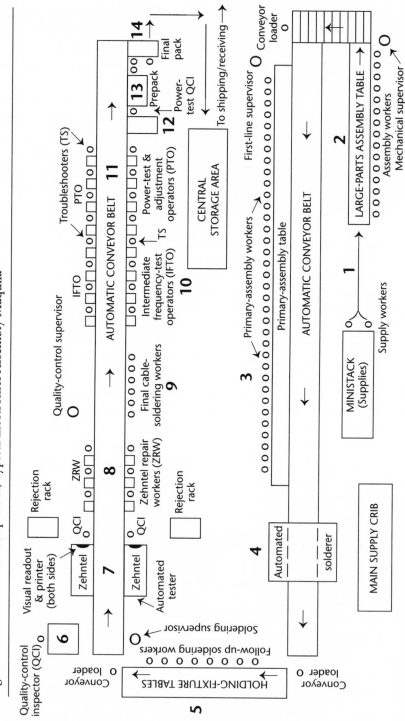

can buy. The operators know they are safe and comfortable around this sophisticated machinery, and it shows in the outstanding work they do. (Interview, Ciudad Juárez, January 1982)

Managers and production engineers at the same maquila eliminated the need for material and component carriers. Engineering staff developed an overhead conveyor system that transports materials and components automatically throughout the different areas of production and from line to line. All of the conveyor belts used in production, including the stop-start assembly-line adaptations, were designed and built at the plant by Mexican engineers and workers. All the electronics assembly plants I visited in the U.S.–Mexico border region over a ten-year period have similar assembly-line layouts.

In addition to the automated conveyor-belt systems, workers in electronics assembly maquilas are confronted by many other types of machinery, tools, and precision instruments. There are four major types: (1) various hand-operated tools such as microscopes, tweezers, and soldering irons; (2) machine tools such as lathes and jig borers; (3) numerous semiautomated or fully automated assembling and sorting machines tended by workers; and (4) a wide variety of semiautomated, interactive technical instruments such as frequency and power test equipment and other diagnostic devices.

The first group of hand-held tools are basic necessities of assembly-line work. Their use is not "technically complex" and corresponds with repetitive and partialized job tasks. More than half of the workers in electronics assembly use these tools. The second set of items are less commonly used. Lathes, jig borers, and similar machine tools are used primarily in manufacturing as opposed to assembling types of production. However, even electronics assembly plants sometimes require on-site modifications of components or production equipment that involve the use of sophisticated machine tools. Less than 1 percent of workers in electronics assembly use machine tools, and the majority of these are male technicians, mechanics, and specialized machinists. The operation of machine tools requires skilled precision labor and is the closest job in electronics assembly maquilas to craftwork.

It is the third and fourth sets of items that are fairly common sophisticated equipment used in electronics assembly. There are many semiautomated and fully automated assembling machines tended by "unskilled" operators or technicians. These include quasi-robotic devices like the ACI. Worker-tended machines used in Juárez electronics-sector maquilas include soldering decks, wiring bobbins, circuit-board printers and cutters, and component inserters. Not all of these are used directly in assembly work. Some are "prep" or setup equipment used to prepare components for assembly. Almost one third (30 percent) of the workers in electronics assembly are assigned to this type of equipment.

The semiautomated and interactive technical instrumentation in electronics maquilas includes a wide variety of frequency, power-supply, quality-control, and other testing equipment. Diagnostic and testing instruments are among the most sophisticated of the interactive technologies used in the maquilas. Some—such as the frequency, power, and quality-control testers—are basically video display terminals (VDTs) connected to computers that provide digital data to technicians. One of the most sophisticated of these is the Zehntel automated quality-control tester. The Zehntel is a computerized system that converts quality control into an information-processing task. About 20 percent of the workers in electronics maquilas use this type of equipment.

THE TECHNICAL DIVISION OF LABOR

This inventory of assembly-line technology and auxiliary tools and machinery is suggestive of the technical division of labor in the maquilas. The technical division of labor describes the division of work into different job positions in a hierarchy based on corresponding differences in skill, job tasks, and degree of control over work. Generally, it can be said that the higher positions in this hierarchy correspond to higher levels of skill (at least as defined by management), more complex job tasks, a greater span of control over the work of others, and higher wages. On the maquila shop floor, the machinery, tools, and instruments of the labor process correspond to four major groups of production workers: (1) assembly-line operators, (2) mechanics and machinists, (3) quality-control inspectors and technicians, and (4) "troubleshooting" repair technicians. However, this does not reflect the entire spectrum of job positions in the maquiladora technical division of labor. There are also a variety of other auxiliary workers, engineers, supervisors, superintendents, and managers.

The typical electronics assembly plant has thirteen basic job positions. The rank-ordered hierarchy constituting this technical division of labor is represented in table 1. The highest position in the factory managerial ranks, in terms of the degree of direct control exerted over production, is that of plant manager. Executive command, control, and communications (C3) related to plant operations are within the purview of the plant manager. Personnel and shipping and receiving managers are also part of these executive ranks. Under the authority of the plant manager is a small set of three to five departmental superintendents that have C3 authority in their respective areas of plant organization. While plant managers and departmental superintendents do not spend a lot of time on the shop floor, they have absolute decision- and policy-making powers over all aspects of production.

Production engineers are next in the hierarchy. The role of process and methods engineering in the maquilas is not well understood. This job position occupies an ambiguous location in the division of labor. This is not a managerial position, yet it involves a considerable degree of control over work. The engineer is not really a direct production worker, yet spends a lot of time on the shop floor making certain the

Table 1. Technical Division of Labor by Gender, Typical Consumer Electronics Assembly Maquiladora

Position	Number of Staff in Position	Gender Distribution (frequency)	
		Male	Female
Production			
plant manager	1	100.0	0.0
production superintendents	3–5	100.0	0.0
production engineers	6–15	100.0	0.0
quality-control supervisors	>12	100.0	0.0
mechanical supervisors	1–3	100.0	0.0
first-line supervisors	6–10	90.0	10.0
machinists/mechanics	5–10	100.0	0.0
quality-control inspectors	6–15	90.0	10.0
repair technicians	10–30	80.0	20.0
lead operators	3–10	20.0	80.0
assemblers	100–1,000	30.0	70.0
soldering operators	50–100	20.0	80.0
Nonproduction			
clerical workers	10–20	5.0	95.0

Source: Original data collected by author in Ciudad Juárez (1981–1984, 1989–1991).

Note: The positions are arranged in rank order with the higher positions in the hierarchy characterized by higher pay, greater prestige, career paths, and greater span of control.

whole process remains smooth, continuous, and free of technical log-jams. Engineers are "knowledge workers," designing, monitoring, and maintaining the continuity of production processes. You might say they do the "brain work" of production layout.[19] Working with plant management, production engineers design the flow-line principle for a given plant. It is their duty to then maintain the flow line in an operational state. A typical electronics assembly maquila will have one or two production engineers for each departmental superintendent. Production engineers usually command a team of technicians, mainly time-and-motion-study technicians and repair assistants.

Next in the ranks of the maquila division of labor are three production-level supervisory positions. These include quality-control, mechanical, and first-line supervisors. Quality-control (QC) supervisors usually number a dozen or less for each maquila. They usually work in tandem with engineering staff in making daily flow-line adjustments to establish and maintain desired quality standards. These supervisors also command teams of inspectors, who occupy a position further down in the hierarchy. Each maquila has from one to three mechanical supervisors. Their role is basically to oversee the work of repair and maintenance technicians.

The first-line supervisors are what are traditionally called "foremen." This is really the first line in production management. The job of the first-line supervisor is to exert direct control over groups of twenty to one hundred and fifty assembly-line workers. The first-line supervisory ranks are management's key to control of the informal life of the shop floor. This is the only managerial or supervisory position that involves continuous direct contact with assembly workers on the shop floor. First-line supervisors are thus a critical link in the overall technical division of labor. There are usually two first-line supervisors for each assembly line, one each for the average two daily workshifts. With an average of three assembly-line subdepartments per maquila, there are usually at least six first-line supervisors at each plant.

Below the managerial, engineering, and supervisory ranks are various types of direct production workers. At the top of this hierarchy are machinists and mechanics. These tend to be skilled male workers who work with production engineers and mechanical supervisors to maintain operations and to machine-tool other precision spec components or production devices. However, these skilled machinists and mechanics are not directly involved in component-assembly stages of production. There are relatively few of them for each assembly line.

Production workers directly involved with component assembly are in the lowest ranks in the technical division of labor. Working directly on the assembly line itself are quality-control inspectors. These workers inspect assembled components to monitor quality standards. Alongside the inspectors are quality-control technicians and repair technicians. All of these workers, inspectors and technicians alike, are invariably tied to the flow line and work with a wide variety of technical instruments and computers. Three to five inspectors and another three to five technicians are not unusual for each assembly line in an electronics maquila. At the bottom of the hierarchy are assembling and soldering operators, and most of these are women.

Assemblers constitute by far the largest group, ranging from one hundred and fifty to more than five hundred assemblers per subdepartment in each maquila. Within these ranks is an internal hierarchy that places the "novice assembler" at the bottom and the "lead operator" or group chief at the top. This is an important distinction, because management uses lead operators to help set the pace of work on the flow line and to enforce rules against acts of sabotage or output restriction. Lead operators directly assist first-line supervisors in monitoring the immediate work teams on the assembly line. They too occupy a critical position in the division of labor.

Finally, clerical workers are found under the authority of most managers, superintendents, supervisors, and even engineers. They occupy a space that is removed from the shop floor and ranks somewhat higher than assembly-line workers, at least in terms of local prestige if not in wages and better working conditions. In the maquilas, most of the secretaries and file clerks are women, while the accountants are predominantly male. Most of these workers are employed in nonproduction areas of the plant, usually in the administrative units. This study, unfortunately, did not gain access to very many clerical workers, and so discussion of their role in the labor process is limited.

Thus far, we have proceeded from the technological layout of the maquilas, to the technical division of labor, and to the role of automated systems and machine-pacing as strategies of managerial control. The approach describes the technical division of labor as a hierarchy of job positions arranged on the basis of politically defined differences in skills, wages, job tasks, and span of control. But this is a soulless description of work organization. Merely describing the technical division of labor, and the apparatus of technological control that produces it, tells us very little about what is really going on inside the factory. It illustrates how the system is based on machine-pacing and exhibits characteristics of bureaucratic hierarchy, but it ultimately tells us little about the relations of production among and between the different job positions.

To get beyond the concept that the maquilas are simply "user-friendly machine systems," one has to breach the limits of a managerial description of that technology. It is clear that technological control in the maquilas is pervasive in the form of the flow-line principle. This is the classic Fordist formula for control of work: hundreds, and even thousands, of assembly-line workers are tied to automated conveyor belts and are closely monitored by several strata of supervisors, engineers, and managers. Something else is going on underneath the apparent tyranny of machine-pacing. The manager who described robotics earlier expressed great concern for "induced failures." He described the automation of component insertion as a key tactic in management's efforts to eliminate induced failures and to restore quality standards by means of technical control. What he was referring to is, simply, sabotage. He calls it "too many hands." This is why electronics assembly maquilas rely on the Dynapert and other ACI devices to combat workers' clandestine resistance.

But technological responses to the subaltern life of the shop floor are hardly adequate. To exercise more complete control over the labor process, management must resort to other strategies as well. Beyond technical control, management in the maquilas utilizes at least four other major strategies: (1) internal labor-market policies, (2) hourly standards, (3) methods and process management, and (4) informal social regulation. The first two strategies are examples of bureaucratic control—that is, the rule of law. The third strategy is an example of an overlap between technological and social control—machine-paced processes subject to intense supervision. And the fourth strategy is a unique, cross-cultural system of informal social regulation that operates on the shop floor and beyond in the workers' personal lives. In the remainder of this chapter, I will detail the dynamics and contradictions of these four control strategies.

Managerial Control Strategies: From Bureaucratic Control to Informal Social Regulation

INTERNAL LABOR-MARKET POLICIES

Labor-process theorists have repeatedly pointed to the importance of internal labor-market policies as fundamental aspects of bureaucratic control.[20] These policies involve the use of rules and regulations governing recruitment, seniority, promotions, and job assignments, including lateral mobility. By manipulating the internal labor market, management develops the major *political* features of its division of labor. The starting point for management here are policies guiding the recruitment and screening of workers.

Recruitment in the maquilas has apparently evolved, becoming increasingly more bureaucratic in recent times. Earlier studies indicated that recruitment was highly informal, relying for the most part on word of mouth and the workers' own kin and friendship networks.[21] But this is probably due to the fact that the research was conducted in the apparel sector, which is known for its lax approach to recruitment.[22] In the electronics and automotive assembly sectors, maquila management is known to have explicit policies on recruitment that endorse the use of endurance, ability, and dexterity tests as well as sophisticated psychological screening interviews to "weed out workers with undesirable characteristics." A former plant manager at Spectronics once remarked,

> You understand that the entire issue of psychological screenings that you raise is not new. Companies worldwide have been making use of work-aptitude and emotional-disposition scales since before World War Two. I was with the Army when these tests and scales were first developed. . . . So, it's not like something new and terrible and bad. . . . The basic principle is, well, you've got the principle of private property. You know, um . . . as having a right to be protected from damage or theft. Some workers may not respect private property, and I think we have a right to protect ourselves against crime. (Interview, Ciudad Juárez, March 1982)[23]

Control of the internal labor market produces divisions based on skill, gender, wage, ethnicity, and other differences. Control over internal labor-market dynamics yields tremendous flexibility because it allows managers to manipulate these divisions politically. The political character of the technical division of labor is apparent in the manner it increases lateral, in contrast to vertical, types of conflict. That is, conflicts and power divisions between workers are manipulated through policy changes in recruitment, seniority, promotions, and job mobility. Theoretically, instead of resisting management, workers are compelled to compete with each other within and across ranks. This is the classic "divide and conquer" strategy.

Labor-market policies are common in the maquilas, and management is somewhat effective at using them to generate bureaucratic control. In a survey conducted in Juárez in 1981 and 1982 (see table 2), almost half (47 percent) of the workers reported knowledge of regulations pertaining to seniority; two thirds (67 percent) had knowledge of regulations governing promotions. But workers also reported difficulty in obtaining changes in job status. Research findings indicate that two thirds (67 per-

Table 2. Promotions and Seniority Personnel Policies

	number	frequency
Seniority Policies Exist[a]		
yes	88	47.3
no	98	52.7
Promotions Policies Exist[b]		
yes	126	66.7
no	63	33.3
Seniority Difficult[c]		
yes	93	67.4
no	45	32.6
Promotions Difficult[d]		
yes	107	75.9
no	34	24.1
Reason Seniority Difficult to Attain[e]		
regulations ignored	30	31.3
working conditions	50	52.1
other	16	16.1
Basis for Promotions[f]		
regulations	49	36.8
loyalty	84	63.2
Worker Acceptance of Promotion[g]		
yes	63	42.9
no	84	57.1
Reason for Rejecting Promotion[h]		
insufficient pay	15	17.9
endangers friendships	47	56.0
undesirable job	16	19.0
insufficient skill	6	7.1

a. Missing cases = 37.
b. Missing cases = 34.
c. Missing cases = 48.
d. Missing cases = 48.
e. Missing cases = 43.
f. Missing cases = 53.
g. Missing cases = 42.
h. Missing cases = 63.

cent) of the workers believe seniority rights are hard to obtain; and an even larger proportion (75 percent) think promotions are difficult to come by.

While maquila management has adopted formal rules to control seniority rights and promotions, most workers remain cynical and seem to doubt that management seriously and fairly follows the rules. Thirty-one percent of the workers indicated that management ignores seniority policies. Many more workers (52 percent) feel that the rules cannot be interpreted fairly because working conditions, and especially unrealistic performance expectations, make seniority difficult to obtain. Field interviews revealed that the high-productivity pressures that prevail in the workplace lead to turnover, so that workers rarely work long enough at the same plant to gain seniority rights.

A similar pattern emerges in the area of promotions. Most workers (63 percent) feel that loyalty to the company is more important than rules in determining promotions. Only one third (36 percent) feel management complies with the policies. The formal criteria used by maquila management to determine promotions are based on standard scores for skill, productivity, and good attendance. However, our survey data indicate that, in practice, loyalty comes first, quota performance second, and the other criteria a distant third. It is worth noting that poor attendance usually results in dismissal of workers.

Management's tendency to sometimes ignore the formal rules of organization may influence how workers perceive and respond to the dynamics of internal labor markets. Only 42 percent of our survey respondents indicated they would accept promotions, and more than half (57 percent) reported they would unconditionally reject promotions. This could be a reflection of workers' disillusionment with management's failure to abide by the rules. However, a closer study of worker motives for rejecting promotions reveals that this is not necessarily the case. Over half (56 percent) of the respondents cited the belief that promotions endangered friendships. Other workers cited the undesirability of the job (19 percent), insufficient pay increases (17 percent), or insufficient skill (7 percent). Thus, the overwhelming majority of workers reject promotion on interpersonal grounds. But the dynamic here certainly seems to extend beyond a desire to preserve friendships.

Interpersonal relations may also be seen as part of a class-relations problematic, particularly in the context of primary work groups in a highly stratified internal labor market. In the class politics of production, interpersonal relations are a critical aspect of informal organization.

Friendship ties may play a major role when workers create informal shop-floor networks. The networks facilitate output restriction and other types of clandestine resistance. By rejecting promotions, workers are making a conscious effort to preserve the interpersonal, small-group basis of informal shop-floor networks and not just friendships (see chapter 4).

We can see from the preceding evidence that both management and workers rely on informal strategies to obtain desired results in the struggles over internal labor-market policies. Interviews with managers revealed a variety of other issues impinging on the politics of promotions. For example, the problem of sexism was noted by the male plant manager of an automotive component assembly factory:

> We have also promoted women from the floor to supervisory positions. This first caused alarm among the males, but then was accepted. It went far in helping us eliminate the *macho* problem. Most of the women have done remarkably well in supervisory positions. But we don't see it as a sexual thing. We don't care if it is a man or a woman as long as they heed our needs and get the job done. (Interview, Ciudad Juárez, September 1982)

The manager seems oblivious to the gender division of labor described earlier: "We don't see it as a sexual thing." Most managers think the shortage of women in supervisory positions is due to their lack of experience and skill, and not to conscious or inadvertent segregation of the genders into sex-typed job positions. Yet, other managers think that you can train any worker for supervisory positions.

But it seems a majority are reluctant to promote women into supervisory roles because of what they perceive as generalized male opposition. The personnel manager at another consumer-electronics assembly plant reflected this predominant view:

> It's just too much trouble. I can move women up a notch or two—you know, from operator to group chief and maybe even quality-control inspection. But, if I was to promote women into higher supervisory levels, well, the men, the Mexican males, would be terribly upset. I'm not against the idea of women doing that type of work, but my first duty is to maintain order in the plant. The attitude of the men here, let me just say that it does not give me a lot of room to move in. (Interview, Ciudad Juárez, April 1982)

Given the Mexican context of weak laws extending equal protection to women, it is hardly surprising that maquila management does not aggressively pursue gender equality in promotions. It is perhaps even more interesting that the manager quoted above is eager and willing to attribute the problem to the *machismo* of Mexican men, a view that probably derives from a stereotypical understanding of gender roles in Mexico. Blaming the local culture and not the bureaucracy seems to be the rule of the day.[24]

Stereotypical views of gender are held also by those managers who support promoting women into supervisory positions. One manager explained that women make better supervisors than men:

> We have six unit managers. . . . The first woman we promoted is tough. When she came in, she beat the hell out of them [the line workers]. Plantwide we have ten Mexicans in managerial positions, seven male and three female. The females are much less tolerant of mistakes, poor quality, whatever. They are fantastic leaders of males. The difficult thing is making the females believe they are managers. If they want a job like a man they have to work like a man. (Interview, Ciudad Juárez, July 1983)

Here, the manager places supervisory work squarely in a male domain and categorizes women supervisors as imitation males. Only "tough" women become supervisors, and such women are presumably more authoritarian than their male colleagues. Of course, no matter how "tough" the female supervisor, she still needs to be convinced of her ability to perform as a member of the management team; typical female insecurity?[25] This context of gender role expectations may explain much about the reasons why most maquila managers do not promote women above the group-chief position, and rarely train them for or transfer them into technical jobs.

Some managers take a rather dim view of promotions, seeing them as unnecessary. From their point of view, promotions are an ineffective way of eliciting employee loyalty and high performance levels. One manager, responding to queries about rewarding workers for their creativity, stated:

> Promotion . . . we do a poor job of it. . . . The activity you refer to [worker inventions and engineering tasks] is widespread, more than perhaps what you say. It is a very definite asset. How do we recognize it? We give them gifts. Every three months, the best workers get a free vacation to Acapulco or some other such resort. Everyone out there has ideas. The workers are contributing many innovations. We try in our own poor way with little "gimmes" [gifts] to reward this activity. Our "Winning Edge" program is part of this reward system. We give them pens, blazers, and the like with company logos. . . . This is more effective than promoting people. (Interview, Ciudad Juárez, March 1982)

This indicates that some maquila managers prefer to use reward systems other than a rigorous promotions policy. The "gimmes" approach is apparently more cost-effective, and managers seem to believe that it elicits a fair amount of loyalty from the workers. The same manager explained that workers do not stay on the job long enough to be promoted, and that the gift giving was fairer in such a situation.

Other managers utilize more classical Taylorist criteria to develop and implement promotions policies. The empirical measurement of worker performance was cited by the manager of a car-seat assembly plant:

> We are into measurement here. We measure everything! Every Mexican has to make it in terms of productivity before we move them up. . . . The ones that are promoted are the ones that excel in our system. This produces integration of goals, acceptable behavior. That makes us different, even in engineering. They have to make it in production first. This has reduced the amount of conflict. We don't have that functional differentiation where staff fights with higher management because [our supervisors] have gone through production. That's where we evaluate. The production or first-line supervisor is really a long-term evaluation position. You spot your troubles there. [Many] don't make it into higher positions. The ones that don't make it are the more political ones. A lot get impatient. They see production as hard work. We expect them to stay on the floor. That's pretty much against the culture here; they want to sit in the corner and let someone else do the work. Because we have promoted the ones that accept measurement, they also discard those that don't fit the same profile. All appraisals on promotions are made by the older group. From production supervision they can get promoted to unit managers, the level at which these decisions are made. This increases integration. They choose people that are more like themselves. (Interview, Ciudad Juárez, February 1982)

This approach is distinctly Taylorist in its focus on the quantitative measurement of productivity. But productivity is not the only factor considered in this system of bureaucratic control. Equally important is identifying and reinforcing acceptable behavior. Managers tend to promote "apolitical" workers and, conversely, to fire the "political" ones. Moreover, in some maquilas these decisions are made by middle management (production superintendents and unit managers). This approach can reduce vertical conflict between middle and higher management. It presumably reduces conflict and increases integration and conformity.

Internal labor-market policies also deal with the dynamics of lateral job mobility, the reassignment of workers to different jobs with the same pay scale and social status. The survey results (see table 3) indicate that the maquila internal labor market has an unusually high level of lateral mobility. More than three fourths (75.8 percent) of the respondents reported being reassigned from one line to another.

Nearly all the workers (about 90 percent) knew the reasons for their reassignments. Thirty-six percent cited productivity; close to 20 percent were reassigned at their request; another 18 percent were reassigned due to conflicts with supervisors; and close to 16 percent reported quality-control problems. A few respondents stated that they were reassigned for having conflicts with co-workers, exhibiting patterns of absenteeism, or engaging in conversations with friends on the assembly line.

It is not surprising that so few workers are reassigned due to absenteeism. The more likely outcome for an absentee worker is getting terminated. As a personnel administrator for an apparel plant stated, "Absenteeism is not a big problem. We have very strict rules for this and emphasize to workers that failure to show up for work amounts to a forfeiture of their privilege to work for us." Another manager explained that three tardy arrivals are equal to one day of absenteeism; the result is a written reprimand and a visit to the personnel office. Four absences are grounds for an automatic suspension.

Finally, policies related to lateral mobility also involve subjecting employees to workshift reassignments. The level of workshift reassignments in the maquilas is considerably lower than that of line changes. Only 35 percent of the workers reported being reassigned to other shifts.[26] The majority of these were reassigned at their own request (42 percent). Low productivity accounted for 26 percent of the reassignments, while conflicts with supervisors were reported by 16 percent of the cases.

In the maquilas, policies governing promotions, seniority, and reassignments emphasize the measurement of productivity and the imposition of strict standards of conformity (i.e., loyalty—being "apolitical"). As is the case with most Taylorist and Fordist management systems, the maquiladoras use a highly bureaucratized system of rules and regulations to control the interpersonal dynamics of the internal labor market. This represents an elaborate technical and political division of labor. But these policies are perhaps not as significant as the widespread practice of grading job categories.

The strictly quantitative character of the criteria used in judging which job titles workers receive also indicates managerial adherence to bureaucratic forms of control. While the typical maquila has twelve basic positions in direct production categories, each position is further divided into a number of within-class grades. One manager remarked:

> Overall, we have some 280 steps that an employee could conceivably move through in going from line operator to a middle-management position. In

Table 3. Line and Workshift Reassignments
(Internal Labor-Market Mobility)

	number	frequency
Line Reassignments		
yes	169	75.8
no	54	24.2
Frequency of Line Reassignments		
very frequent	23	13.1
frequent	17	9.7
seldom	57	32.6
very seldom	78	44.6
Worker Knowledge, Reason[a]		
yes	150	89.8
no	17	10.2
Reason, Line Reassignments[b]		
productivity	28	36.4
quality-control problems	12	15.6
worker request	15	19.5
worker disliked previous job	2	2.6
absenteeism	1	1.3
conversations with co-workers	4	5.2
conflicts with co-workers	1	1.3
conflicts with supervisors	14	18.2

addition to the fifteen basic job titles in our production assembly division, each of these positions is further redivided into seventeen or eighteen different skill or performance gradings. For example, let us take the basic position of line operator. New workers start at the apprentice level. After an initial probationary period of one month, new workers are usually upgraded to the plant-worker category. Afterwards, such a worker must move through sixteen performance-level categories, each representing improvements in productivity. Their pay does not change, but they gain more positive recognition which can later pay off in a promotion or bonus. (Interview, Ciudad Juárez, May 1982)

Divisions established by an overabundance of job titles and performance grades increase managerial control over workers because vertical

Table 3 (continued)

	number	frequency
Workshift Reassignments[c]		
yes	77	34.8
no	144	65.2
Frequency of Workshift Reassignments		
very frequent	2	2.5
frequent	4	5.0
seldom	25	31.3
very seldom	49	61.2
Worker Knowledge, Reason		
yes	70	89.7
no	8	10.3
Reason, Workshift Reassignments[d]		
productivity	13	26.0
quality-control problems	4	8.0
worker request	21	42.0
worker disliked previous job	4	8.0
conflicts with supervisors	8	16.0

a. Missing cases = 2.   c. Missing cases = 2.
b. Missing cases = 73.   d. Missing cases = 28.

mobility is stifled while lateral conflict is encouraged.[27] The proliferation of job titles means workers take longer to move up through the ranks. Performance gradation means workers are so busy competing with each other that they do not have the opportunity to organize collectively against management. The introduction of hierarchical job definition is clearly a feature of bureaucratization in the maquilas. Divisions based on managerial manipulation of seniority rights and promotions appear relatively ineffective. It seems workers can overcome this particular type of bureaucratic control, in part by rejecting promotions. However, management can still disrupt shop-floor networks by resorting to line and workshift reassignments and by manipulating job titles and performance grades. Bureaucratic control of internal labor markets, at any rate, seems firmly entrenched in the maquilas.

HOURLY STANDARDS AND QUOTAS

In the realm of the capitalist labor process, the length of the working day becomes a focal point of managerial and working-class conflict.[28] Here, I will discuss how maquila management organizes the working day and the workweek. In a subsequent chapter, I will address the workers' side of the story. There are three aspects of the maquila workweek that can be examined: its length, the imposition of overtime, and the relationship between quotas and the working day. Survey data provide information for an analysis of both the length of working time and its intensity (see table 4).

The workers in the sample averaged a 46-hour workweek. Less than 7 percent of the workers reported a workweek under 45 hours; 46 percent reported the Mexican standard of 45 hours; and another 46 percent reported a workweek of 48 hours. Even by Mexican standards, many maquila workers have longer workweeks than workers in other sectors. By U.S. standards, with an average workweek of 38 to 40 hours, the maquila workweek is five to ten hours longer. Maquila workers are far from the 35-hour "European workweek."

The maquila worker's average working day is nine hours long (compared to a U.S. average of eight hours). Overtime and weekend work schedules lengthen the average maquila workweek. In addition to five days of nine-hour shifts, many maquila workers will put in another three to four hours on Saturdays. About one third (32 percent) of the workers reported regular Saturday workshifts, while another 23 percent reported intermittent Saturday overtime. Workers reporting occasional Saturday workshifts indicated such overtime was required when they lagged behind weekly production-quota standards. Saturday workshifts, however, are not usually considered overtime. On weekdays, more than one fourth (25.6 percent) of the workers reported regular overtime, 27 percent stated they never worked overtime, and close to 47 percent stated they sometimes worked overtime. For most workers, overtime is voluntary; only 39 percent stated that weekday overtime is mandatory. Overtime in the maquilas comes at the same pay rate as regular work time. In the United States most overtime work is compensated at a higher rate (usually time and a half). Maquila workers receive the same fixed day wage no matter how many hours they labor beyond the standard 45- to 48-hour workweek. Many workers appear to work overtime only in order to catch up with their production quotas.

These findings reaffirm the importance of policies governing worker productivity. If there is a consistent thread running through internal labor-

Table 4. The Maquila Workweek and Overtime

	number	frequency
Length of Workweek[a,b]		
less than 45 hours	14	6.6
45 hours	99	46.9
48 hours	98	46.5
Saturday Workshifts[c]		
yes	54	37.0
no	58	39.7
sometimes (to meet standards)	34	23.3
Overtime Work[d]		
yes	54	25.6
no	58	27.5
sometimes (to meet standards)	99	46.9
Overtime Work, Status[e]		
voluntary	96	60.0
mandatory	63	39.4
other	1	.6
Weekend Work[f]		
always	20	9.3
3 times a month	5	2.3
2 times a month	2	.9
1 time a month	6	2.8
irregular	72	33.3
sometimes (to meet standards)	57	26.4
never	4	25.0
Weekend Work, Status[g]		
voluntary	75	52.8
mandatory	67	47.2

a. Missing cases = 1.
b. Mean = 46.04, mode = 45.00, median = 45.57.
c. Missing cases = 2.
d. Missing cases = 2.
e. Missing cases = 7.
f. Missing cases = 7.
g. Missing cases = 18.

market policies in the maquilas it is the centrality of managerial efforts to sustain and control productivity standards, both on an hourly and a weekly basis. The organization of voluntary overtime and weekend work ties workers to a system in which they continuously play catch-up with quota standards. While the question of productivity in the maquilas is a complex affair, requiring analysis at various points in this text, we must clarify the nature of quotas in the context of the nine-hour working day. The data presented in table 5 show that maquila workers perform an average of 2,569 assemblies per working day. But there is considerable range in quota levels: 10 percent of the workers assemble fewer than 500 components on a daily basis, while 12 percent, at the high end, assemble more than 5,000.[29]

How high are these standards compared with similar assembly line factories in the United States? Previous research has shown that many U.S.-based transnational corporations relocate to Mexico in search of lower wages and higher productivity.[30] Several managers were quick to point this out, and noted the relative importance of wages vis-à-vis productivity. A former departmental superintendent, who was once stationed at an automotive components assembly plant in Juárez, verified this in the following statement:

> The first reason for being [in Mexico] is low-cost labor. The second reason is productivity—it is much higher here. In the U.S. . . . union negotiations often determine productivity standards. Not here. In Mexico, the firm itself solely determines the standards. Here, standards are set, firstly, by the industrial-engineering department based on time and motion studies plus U.S. estimates. I would like to point out that the U.S. estimates are usually inflated. Then, the production manager decides if the standards are attainable, and if they will fulfill production scheduling. (Interview, Ciudad Juárez, June 1982)

Another plant manager, in charge of a factory that assembles military-spec semiconductor devices, bragged about how he could get the workers to "double production every six weeks." "The absence of a union," he continued, "means that we have a virtual haven for productivity, free of bargaining fetters. This is so much easier than the U.S."[31]

Returning to the survey data, the largest proportion of cases is composed of workers who managed between 2,001 and 3,000 assemblies per working day. This constitutes an incredible rate of output. In the frame of a nine-hour working day, 3,000 assemblies translate into 333 units per hour, or 5.5 every minute. This clearly represents an example of what Marx called the condensation of labor. Given the legal limits to the length of the working day in Mexico, maquila management resorts to techno-logical means (assembly-line speedup) to drive individual and group output. Assembly-line speedup is effective only in the context of a strict supervisory regime that can continuously enforce quota standards. In the maquilas, the imposition of quota standards is strictly enforced through Taylorist methods. These include the use of time and motion study, faster-working lead operators (rate-busters), and rigid performance-improvement schedules.

All of the plant managers interviewed for this study indicated that line workers must demonstrate a consistent pattern of improvement in out-put to keep their jobs or gain promotions.[32] However, in the case of the maquilas, management also has some room for the extension of the work-week through the use of underpaid overtime and weekend shifts. In this manner, management can push productivity on the basis of increases in both the intensity of work and the length of working time. Policies gov-erning quota standards have as their primary objective the perpetual augmentation of worker output. But they are predicated on the assump-tion that the collective productivity of maquila workers will increase with higher levels of technological automation. Assembly-line speedup is more effectively managed in an automated context. Speedup increases produc-tivity because workers have less time to "waste" in nonproductive activi-ties; to waste time is to risk job security, given the policies that overlay the technological system.

Table 5. Sample of Maquila Productivity Standards
(Daily Performance or Output Quotas as Reported by Workers)

	number	frequency
Assemblies per Daily Shift[a,b]		
under 500	15	10.8
500–1,000	25	18.0
1,001–1,500	17	12.2
1,501–2,000	12	8.6
2,001–3,000	26	18.7
3,001–4,000	19	13.7
4,001–5,000	8	5.7
over 5,000	17	12.2

a. Missing cases = 84.
b. Mean = 2,569.19, mode = 1,500.00, median = 2,040.00.

In all areas of policy related to hourly standards and quotas, maquiladoras fully embrace Taylorist and Fordist organizational principles: the emphasis on time and motion study to assess and control the continuity, accuracy, and standardization of worker performance; the use of overtime and weekend work to meet unfulfilled quota expectations; the persistence of assembly-line speedup linked to policies governing quota standards. All these are indications that the maquilas combine principles of Taylorism and Fordism in order to exercise bureaucratic control over the labor process. But it is still the technological system, the tyranny of the flow line, that appears to drive the entire production apparatus.[33]

The existence of policies governing hourly standards is suggestive of a regime based on assembly-line speedup. But bureaucratic dynamics do not account for the full range of processes involved in the control of productivity. The organization of the labor process itself must be more closely examined. This takes us into the area of methods and process management.

METHODS AND PROCESS MANAGEMENT

Methods and process management deals principally with three main aspects of workplace organization: (1) the distribution of workers on the assembly line, (2) the organization and methods of productivity and quality-control supervision, and (3) the methods of control over worker resistance (tardiness, absenteeism, vertical conflict, output restriction, etc.).

The distribution of workers on the assembly line is not accidental or haphazard. Instead, it is determined through careful study and experimentation. Management, of course, utilizes time and motion study to standardize specialized job tasks for each worker (this is an important aspect of methods engineering). But there is much more to the organization of labor activity on a flow-line system. The flow of parts must be calculated both in terms of tempo and sequence; this flow must be synchronized with the distribution of workers, machines, and tools; the entire process of assembly has to be carefully supervised for bottlenecks, displacements, inaccuracies, and other breakdowns; and the flow line must be kept supplied with parts, components, chemicals, and other raw materials.

There is a high level of similarity in the types of job assignments maquila workers get (see table 6). Of 210 workers, 66.6 percent reported working on the same type of assignment with twenty or fewer other workers; 15.7 percent with twenty-one to fifty other workers; and 17.6

percent with fifty-one or more. These findings are consistent with the typical production layouts in electronics and automotive assembly maquilas. Assembly lines will usually include several groups of twenty to fifty workers; the workers in a particular primary group all work on similar job tasks.[34] Larger plants may have several primary assembly lines with between fifty and a hundred workers on similar job assignments.

There is also a high number of workers on team jobs—chores requiring several workers and centered on a particular set of components (see table 6). More than 65 percent of the respondents reported that they worked in a team assembling a component or a set of integrated components. Only 34.7 percent of the workers reported that they worked alone on their job tasks. The use of team jobs in the maquilas is consistent with Fordist flow-line layouts.

Table 6. Maquila Production Layout and Job-Assignment Characteristics

	number	frequency
Worker Assigned Machinery/Tools[a]		
yes	127	58.0
no	92	42.0
Number of Workers, Similar Equipment[b,c]		
20 or less	86	63.7
21 to 50	26	19.2
51 or more	23	17.0
Number of Workers, Same Job Assignment[d]		
20 or less	140	66.6
21 to 50	33	15.7
51 or more	37	17.6
Number of Workers on Team Jobs		
team jobs	145	65.3
individual job	77	34.7

a. Missing cases = 4.
b. Missing cases = 88.
c. Mean = 26.53, mode = 10.00, median = 67.00, range = 500.
d. Missing cases = 1.

The team approach is characterized by a high degree of functional interdependence, fragmentation of tasks, and specialization of skills. The use of quality circles and semiautonomous work groups in the maquilas probably dates back to the early 1980s. One manager remarked that putting workers together on the same job increases productivity because

> together they will motivate one another to keep pace and work harder. While we do not pay a group for its combined output, we do recognize outstanding group performance levels. A group with a record of meeting or exceeding production and quality-control standards will receive rewards and incentives. (Interview, Ciudad Juárez, July 1982)

The most important facet of methods and process management is related to the supervision of individual and group productivity. Productivity supervision in the maquilas is organized to encompass the regulation of two major aspects of worker performance and behavior: quota standards and quality of work. Who is involved in productivity supervision? There are two basic types of immediate supervisors on the maquila shop floor: group chiefs and first-line supervisors. Group chiefs are also known as lead operators. They are not formally members of the supervisory staff. In every sense, the group chief is another assembly-line worker. This is true in terms of both wage and position in the organizational hierarchy. But despite their position as line staff, group chiefs are really in the front "trenches" of maquila supervision. The plant manager of an automotive components assembly plant explains the role of group chiefs:

> We count on our lead operators to provide us with information about the daily goings-on of the shop floor. They tell us who is working hard, who is not; they tell us if there are problems with either workers or production. . . . They also provide a major incentive for other operators to keep up production, since they can admonish and reprimand. If another worker gets in bad with the lead operator, well, it will end up in the hands of management. It is not an easy position to be in, sort of in the middle. To become a lead operator you have to demonstrate extreme loyalty to the goals and philosophy of the company. (Interview, Ciudad Juárez, April 1982)

A former production superintendent at the same plant is critical of this system:

> The treatment of people is quite despotic, from the highest manager to the lead operators. This causes lack of trust and communication between the various sides. . . . So, the work is done more by force and not by desire. . . . As a subordinate one should obey orders. At [this company], orders are imposed military style. It is a very humiliating environment. . . . Here, you

forget feminine traits . . . authority is not respected. Like I said, it starts at the top because the plant manager humiliates her own supervisory staff. . . . There is constant surveillance of supervisory staff, not just operators. The group chiefs, and any other staff that can move around the plant, are a source of information for the plant manager. (Interview, Ciudad Juárez, March 1982)

The first direct contacts between workers and management in the maquilas is thus mediated through the group chiefs. This, obviously, puts them in a highly conflicted position. And yet, at some plants even supervisors are monitored. What we appear to have in the maquilas is a low-trust system, in which all participants are subject to surveillance and control, even middle managers and supervisors. Perhaps because this is a low-trust environment, management must rely on other assembly-line workers (lead operators) to initiate supervision. By enlisting select workers into supervisory roles, management hopes to lessen some of the workers' distrust, at least among the ranks of the primary work group on the assembly line.[35] The strategy is uncertain at best, but it does make the group-chief position highly conflicted and stressful.

The level of group-chief supervision reported by workers is much higher than that for first-line supervisors. The average number of daily interactions between assembly-line workers and group chiefs was eight, while the average between workers and first-line supervisors was only six. While the level of group-chief supervision is higher, survey findings indicate that there are no significant differences in quota vigilance. Sixty-six percent of the workers think their first-line supervisors were overly vigilant with regard to quota attainment, while 68 percent think group chiefs were overly vigilant (see table 7).

As we shall see later, in chapter 4, the similarities in quota vigilance may be related to the fact that group chiefs participate in the informal shop-floor networks that facilitate output restriction. While the level of group-chief supervision is higher, this does not necessarily mean group chiefs are stricter than first-line supervisors. On the contrary, research findings related to informal networks suggest that group chiefs are less likely to admonish or reprimand workers in matters related to quota attainment. The primary role of the group chief is to set the quota performance level for the immediate work team. Group chiefs tend to be rate-busters, workers who consistently meet or exceed quota standards. The label given by management to these workers, "lead operators," implies that they are the leaders in productivity.

Table 7. Productivity Supervision

	number	frequency
Frequency of Group-Chief Supervision[a,b]		
less than 4 times a day	61	40.1
4 to 9	80	52.6
10 or more	8	5.3
constant	3	2.0
Frequency of First-Line Supervision[c,d]		
less than 4 times a day	93	66.4
4 to 9	40	28.6
10 or more	4	2.8
constant	3	2.1
Supervisor Quota Vigilance[e]		
yes	146	66.1
no	75	33.9
Group-Chief Quota Vigilance[f]		
yes	134	68.7
no	61	31.3

a. Missing cases = 71.
b. Mean = 7.88, mode = 9.00, median = 7.54.
c. Missing cases = 83.
d. Mean = 6.35, mode = 1.00, median = 2.23.
e. Missing cases = 2.
f. Missing cases = 8.

First-line supervisors also play a critical role in maintaining productivity standards. They are formally members of the supervisory staff, and are considered the lowest rank in production management. Their primary responsibility is to monitor a large area of the assembly line, and they are free to roam the shop floor. While the group chief is responsible for a small primary work group of five to ten workers, the first-line supervisor normally oversees the work of an entire assembly-line unit of fifty or more. Therefore, first-line supervisors must engage the assistance of group chiefs to maintain control over a rather large area of surveillance. This has the effect of increasing informal networking through the shop-floor supervisory ranks. The relationship between first-line supervisors and group chiefs is a key strategic conjunction in the constellation of shop-floor networks (see chapter 4 for further discussion).

We have already seen that assembly-line speedup is the hallmark of Fordism, and that this system of technical control is pervasive in the maquilas. In fact, the incidence of speedup is strikingly high: close to 80 percent of the workers in our sample reported productivity drives (table 8). In the maquilas, productivity drives are organized in two basic ways: through the imposition of higher daily quota standards or through line speedups. But the imposition of higher quotas or the notorious line speedups must be coordinated with other forms of control to be effective.

My research (see table 8) indicates that there are two primary methods of control used during productivity drives: threats and admonishments, or time and motion studies and related incentives. Over 40 percent of the workers have experienced threats (layoffs and firings). An additional 38 percent have experienced reprimands or admonishments. Thus, over 78 percent of the workers reported the use of coercive methods of productivity supervision. In contrast, only 20 percent of the workers reported the use of time and motion study and incentives; these are generally considered more persuasive, but not less intrusive, forms of supervision. One former production superintendent described this process:

> Workers are given one month to reach the standard. We put together productivity reports on all workers, old and new, every hour on the hour. This is done by our time-and-motion-study people, the production supervisors, and the group chiefs. It is quite a task. If, after a series of time and motion studies, a worker still cannot meet the standards, then we admonish them. The question of intentionality is the key in determining how the worker will be dealt with. If the worker is not at fault, then we merely reassign them to another job. If they are intentionally working below their ability, we will terminate them. (Interview, Ciudad Juárez, August 1983)

Another plant manager, who oversees a plant assembling high-precision electrical instruments for defense-sector subcontractors in Juárez, voiced a very different view of effective productivity supervision:

> We have a continuous, an automatic, belt on one of our lines. We have ten, twelve workers on this line, each doing a separate and limited task. By the time you get to the end of the line you have a complete unit. If we are behind [quota standards], we meet with them. We talk directly to the workers to see what the problem is. I don't believe in industrial engineers or time and motion people. The supervisors and operators can be their own industrial engineers. They should be. But if talking to them doesn't work, we just go out there and turn up the speed of the belt. We let every worker

work harder for two, three hours. They don't even notice. Then we turn it back down. Why? I tell the workers, "You already showed me you can do it." You have to instill pride in them. You let them know they are working faster, doing it better than Texas Instruments or the Japanese. Will that slow the line down? No. Will the workers do a faster and better job? You bet! We double our production every six weeks. . . . That's one thing I like about Mexicans, they have pride; they don't want to be considered second-rate or third-rate. They want to be first so they put out for us. . . . Throughout this industry, wire stripping gives us a lot of problems. We use twenty, thirty miles of wire a day. The wire-stripping machines have a lot of downtime. I come to Mexico and some old, dumb Mexican, and I mean that affectionately, no one has told him that his machine is supposed to break down. I have this one Mexican boy. . . . He works in another building by himself on this machine that in the U.S. is always breaking down, it always has quality-control problems. There he is with his stereo headphones on listening to I guess Mexican disco or whatever. He's so ignorant, he thinks he's supposed to run the machine all day long. You'd never find someone like that in the States. He doesn't know he's supposed to have quality-control problems, so he doesn't. I don't want him to get civilized. You hit them with pride. Mexicans are very prideful people. You may drop a subtle hint. You may hint that they are doing an inferior job. They'll get mad as hell and do a better job. (Interview, Ciudad Juárez, March 1982)

It seems that some managers rely on formal supervisory schemes to control productivity; they use time and motion studies; they foster constant supervision and monitoring; and they embrace a regime of strict reprimands and admonishments. Yet, other managers seem to rely on a more informal approach to control; they eschew time and motion study and place less faith in industrial engineers; they view the automatic conveyor belt as ultimate authority in maintaining productivity standards. But they also manipulate what they think are the cultural characteristics and value orientations of the workforce: Mexicans are "prideful" and even "uncivilized" (i.e., ignorant of the industrial way of life). Apparently, pushing the right emotional buttons will get the job done every time. Apparently also, one does not have to "mismeasure the ignorant" in order to assert command over their work; keeping them "uncivilized" is enough.

How effective are these strategies for productivity supervision? If we take the level of managerial reprimands for nonquota performance as an indicator of worker compliance with productivity objectives, then it seems that the great majority of workers are complying (see table 8). Only 33 percent of the workers reported they had been reprimanded for failing to meet quota standards. The majority (66.7 percent) stated they had never been reprimanded.[36] Nevertheless, disenchantment with high quotas and speedups seems quite common among maquila workers. Over half of the workers in our sample (55.5 percent) thought quota standards in the maquilas were too high. Only 41.2 percent thought quota standards were reasonable, and 3.3 percent thought standards were low. Yet, despite the discontent, worker quota-performance reports that I have reviewed over the years suggest that there is fairly widespread compliance with managerial objectives. The survey also supports this conclusion: only 19 percent of the workers indicated they normally produced below quota; the majority normally met the quota standards (51.7 percent); and a large minority (almost 30 percent) normally exceeded quota standards (these latter presumably are the rate-busters).

High-productivity pressures, particularly when sustained over time, can create problems for management. The incidence of output restriction and other forms of resistance to speedup in the maquilas is not unusual (see chapter 4). There is also compelling evidence suggesting that productivity pressures are a major cause of employee turnover.[37] However, the capacity of the border-region labor market to absorb high turnover rates allows management to maintain a regime of both high quota standards and high turnover. The short length of training also strengthens the effectiveness of high-productivity regimes (see chapter 6). The challenge faced by maquila management is short-term: output restriction may disrupt production during brief episodes of heightened conflict. But in the long term, such resistance may not have much of an impact on management's ability to sustain productivity. And in those rare cases where worker resistance becomes protracted and effective, plant closings and relocations offer an escape.[38]

Quality control in the maquilas is organized primarily through the use of automation technologies and specialized technical staff. Often, time-and-motion-study engineers double as quality-control inspectors. Group chiefs also sometimes participate in quality-control inspections, especially at the level of the primary work group. Most quality-control work, however, is done by highly specialized diagnostic and repair technicians. But quality control is one of the areas of production in the maquilas that is becoming increasingly automated. To name a few of the plants with automated quality control (AQC): United Technologies, National Cash Register, RCA, General Instruments, Honeywell, Dale Electronics, Sangamo Electronics, TDK, Zenith, and IBM.

Table 8. Productivity Drives (Speedup)

	number	frequency
Productivity Drives (Speedup)[a]		
yes	173	78.3
no	48	21.7
Other Methods Used		
in Productivity Drives[b]		
threat of layoffs or firings	69	40.6
admonishments	66	38.8
other (*incl. multiple respon-ses, time & motion study, incentive payments*)	35	20.6
Managerial Reprimands		
for Nonquota Performance[c]		
yes	73	33.3
no	146	66.7
Type of Reprimand		
verbal criticisms	29	38.7
written report	15	20.0
visit to personnel office	8	10.7
threat of layoffs, firings, or reduced pay	7	9.3
other (*incl. multiple responses*)	16	21.3
Worker Opinion of		
Production Quotas[d]		
very high	85	55.5
normal	63	41.2
low	5	3.3
Worker Quota Performance[e]		
higher than expected	26	29.2
lower than expected	17	19.1
expected	46	51.7

a. Missing cases = 2.
b. Missing cases = 53.
c. Missing cases = 4.
d. No quotas reported by 70 cases.
e. Missing cases = 64.

Combined with automated component insertion, the use of AQC standardizes the speed, accuracy, and continuity of the process of assembly. The transition to AQC also reduces the need for inspectors, while deskilling their labor. One former inspector, angered by her demotion to what she perceived as an unskilled job, complained that the computerized quality-control system introduced at her plant had her merely sorting out the rejects, which were automatically identified. She viewed this as a degrading experience and blamed management for suspecting her and other inspectors of insubordination and then retaliating by automating their jobs. Whether or not inspectors are a significant source of resistance, AQC, like ACI (automated component insertion), reduces induced failures. There are many cases of sabotage in quality control.

However, in those situations where labor-intensive layout is the norm, quality control is exercised primarily through supervisory practices. Here, the pattern is much like that in productivity supervision. Workers are first closely monitored by group chiefs and then first-line supervisors. First-line supervisors assist quality-control technicians in compiling data for the primary work groups. The quality-control supervisors then evaluate the output for the assembly subdepartments as a whole. This way, management can control quality at several levels. Group chiefs help control the quality of individual workers. Collaborating with first-line supervisors, group chiefs also help control the quality of primary work-group output. Control at the level of the entire assembly-line subdepartments then becomes much more concise and accurate, as information filters upwards from the shop floor.

In more recent times, maquila management has instituted quality-control circles and other similar organizational innovations that presumably increase participation by line workers in the evaluation of output standards.[39] An increasing number of Japanese-owned maquilas has also reshaped the entire range of supervisory systems, especially through the use of participatory schemes, semiautonomous work groups, and quality circles (see chapter 8 for further discussion of Japanese maquilas). The predominant system of quality control in the maquilas relies on the use of specialized technicians deployed with semiautomated or fully automated diagnostic and testing instruments. Where automation is limited, more traditional Taylorist systems of supervision are in use. In either case, quality control, like productivity supervision, is still guided by the presence of bureaucratic rules and regulations that define standards and tasks for assembly workers, inspectors, and "troubleshooting" repair and maintenance technicians.

INFORMAL SOCIAL REGULATION

Technical and bureaucratic strategies are fundamental aspects of managerial control in the maquilas. Most of the time, these strategies are relatively effective in controlling the division, speed, accuracy, and continuity of the labor process. Yet the struggle over the organization of the maquila workplace often involves circumstances in which workers disrupt or challenge technical and bureaucratic forms of control. When this happens, even the tyranny of machine-pacing and the rule of law are undermined and the regime of capitalist control is weakened. In these circumstances, management often seeks to develop nontechnical and nonbureaucratic strategies to regain control. These strategies are usually twofold, involving both efforts at "ideological" manipulation, and attempts to gain control of the subaltern life of the shop floor. The first strategy involves all the classic ploys used by personnel and social departments to win the loyalty and conformity of the workforce: corporate picnics, giveaways, bonuses, vacation prizes, beauty pageants, and the like. The second, more important strategy involves micromanaging shop-floor networks with the assistance of informal contacts in the ranks of production workers in order to control resistance and inconformity.

But the fact that maquilas involve transnational labor processes, and are located in cross-cultural settings, greatly complicates managerial efforts to develop ideological and informal social control. The situation maquila managers must confront is the absence of managerial control over the organizational "work culture" of the factory. The subaltern life of the shop floor redefines the politics of production by undermining the Taylorist and Fordist designs of the would-be dominators. Management then attempts to regain control by means of a variety of ideological and informal social-control strategies. This raises interesting problems for management in their quest for effective, total control. As there is no essential maquila organizational form, so too there is no essential border working class. Maquila management must confront a variety of dynamic contradictions that emerge as a result of the unique qualities of each local workforce and community. The clandestine character of shop-floor subcultures of resistance also presents difficult challenges for managerial control. Ideological and informal social control are not that easily forged in such cross-cultural settings, despite the repugnant, prevalent stereotype of Mexican workers as uncivilized, docile pushovers.

The search for social control in the maquiladoras extends beyond the shop floor into the personal and family lives of the workers. As in the Ford shops of old, maquila management often attempts to impose on workers rigid standards and definitions of personal hygiene, citizenship, and personal values.[40] The manager of an apparel factory echoed this concern: "Of course we care what goes on in the home of the workers. We have encouraged workers to attend personal hygiene classes at the IMSS. Clean and healthy workers are more productive" (interview, Ciudad Juárez, February 1983). Efforts by maquila management to exert control over "what goes on in the homes of the workers" show mixed results. It is first of all unclear to what extent managers can intrude into workers' personal lives. In the maquilas, managerial intrusiveness seems limited, if not by choice on the part of management, then by the difficulties presented by the sheer numbers of employees. Other studies document the use of "ideological incentives" as a strategy for social control.[41] At one electronics plant, high-performing workers are rewarded with T-shirts and a chance to participate in company-sponsored raffles (for trips and other prizes). Previous research has described the use of personnel department staff to exert continuous pressure on workers to remain loyal to the company. Efforts to get workers to "feel joy and pride" in the products they assemble have been reported.[42] Other companies reportedly organize "decorate the line" contests, "beauty" pageants, and recreational sports programs. There are, in fact, "Miss Maquiladora" beauty pageants, and an annual "Race of the Lovers" is also held around St. Valentine's Day.

But these strategies of ideological control may not be very effective at all. For example, some workers report that raffle prizes are not a source of pride and joy but instead the source of a lucrative "black market" in "gimmes." Others indicate that sports programs actually provide an opportunity for workers to get together and talk about problems they share at the plant.[43] They are not that easily distracted by managerial ploys. On the other hand, there are many women workers who eagerly participate in beauty pageants. It is unclear if these contests translate into submissiveness or apolitical tendencies. One former maquila beauty-pageant prize winner summed up the contradictory forces at play in this game of ideological manipulation:

> Men have expectations and so do women. But I don't want to look beautiful according to the standards held by males. My beauty is my own definition of who I am, and it is not an ideal men have of me, of something I have to aspire to be in order to be worthy of male admiration. But, the whole thing about the pageants that troubles me the most is that the men, who usually do the judging, do think of us as bodies, sex objects. And the audience is awful, jeering and cheering like crazy. Even worse than all this

is that the plant managers think they own the workers, our beauty is theirs for the claiming. They take credit and then expect you to be the ideal, pretty worker. But beauty is not much help back inside the factory, unless you are willing to accept the sexual advances to protect your own job security. (Interview, Ciudad Juárez, November 1983)

The search for ideological control intersects with patriarchal attitudes and sexual harassment, but is not the only dimension of informal social regulation in the maquilas. Another important facet of control is centered on informal shop-floor networks. A production superintendent in a large electronics assembly plant acknowledged the importance of controlling informal "human relations" in the maquilas:

Yes, we have a human-relations, or if you like, a social-relations department. Usually the department of personnel takes care of this. But in the larger plants they have a separate division. Our basic task is to avoid conflicts between workers and managers. We try to do this by training supervisors in how to deal with people. For example, there is general resistance to unionization [among managerial staff]. There are informal contacts among workers and supervisors that are on the lookout for workers who might sympathize or who desire unionization. At MegaElectrik almost 35 percent of the workers are contacts. In return they get protection, stability of employment, and promotions. . . . To control worker organization, MegaElectrik uses these informal contacts. It's almost like you are under the eye of an invisible camera. The informal contacts are so widespread they are almost formal. (Interview, Ciudad Juárez, May 1982)

Actually, separate "divisions" dealing with the informal organization of the factory are not that common in the maquilas. Of thirty-five plants surveyed in 1981–82, only five had separate social departments charged with managerial responses to informal plant politics.[44] A more recent count (1989) yielded three departments in thirty plants. The presence of a formal social department within the organizational structure of the plant is not really necessary in order for management to deal with informal groups. As the manager above indicates, social agendas and informal networks can be pursued under the command and control of personnel managers or other strategically located officers of the plant. But even these departments and officers must ultimately rely on informal contacts within the workforce to gain entry into the subaltern life of shop floor networks.

Management's reliance on informal contacts is the key to this aspect of social control in the maquilas. The use of line workers (usually lead operators) as informants is relatively widespread.[45] These contacts provide information useful to management in exerting influence over work-ers' attitudes, and presumably their actions. The control of attitudes deal-ing with the organization of production in the plants seems particularly important. Use of informal contacts also fragments the primary work groups, creating rivalries and divisions between lead operators and other line workers. It is here that sexual harassment becomes an important as-pect of informal control strategies. Workers at several plants spoke of how first-line supervisors used sexual pressures and advances to gain control and influence over group chiefs. Oral histories with a wide variety of women workers suggest that sexual advances often lead to liaisons be-tween supervisors and the targeted victims, who tend to be rate-busters or lead operators. Lead operators who submit to sexual relations with male supervisors are rewarded with a range of "privileges," such as ex-cused absences, flexible schedules, extra wage bonuses, trips, parties, din-ners, and dances. In return for these "privileges," the lead operators are expected to function as informants (see chapter 4 for further discussion).

Two critical aspects of informal workplace politics in the maquilas are the identification and control of workers' attitudes toward unionism, and toward the organization of production. One fourth (25.6 percent) of the workers said management had expressed concern over employee attitudes toward unions. And well over half (62.8 percent) reported that management was concerned with workers' attitudes toward the or-ganization of production. This is to be expected in any industrial work-place regime informed by the principles of managerial sociology. In the maquilas, management frequently encourages workers to voice their concerns. This is one way to detect signs of discontent and to analyze complaints.

Unionism in the maquilas has always been limited in scope. Generally, few plants are organized and, in the scattered cases that involve union-ized shops, union bosses are often guilty of corruption and collaboration with management (see chapter 4). Interestingly, those maquilas that are union-free are more concerned with keeping informed about their work-ers' views of unionism.[46] One manager summed up the reasons for this concern over workers' attitudes:

> We have always been nonunion and we will always remain nonunion. The
> reason is simple. We have democracy already, and we don't need unions to
> have fair practices and good relations with our staff. Respect and being in-
> formed. Those are the two values that we use to define our whole approach
> to management-employee relations. We respect the workers' needs and
> rights. We comply with the letter of the law. In turn, the workers respect

our organization. They respect our needs, our goals and objectives. And staying informed is also important. If you are out of touch with the feelings and attitudes of your employees you are in a hell of a mess. You know how they say, "caught between the seductress and the wild blue sea"? When things are going well, smoothly and efficiently, it is very seductive. You get complacent, and then all of a sudden something blows up, the workers start a fight, or they break the machinery, or worse—they walk out on you. But if you stay informed, you know what the employees are thinking, what's the main gripe? This is good for planning, if a manager knows how to use these feelings to promote good will and trust. (Interview, Ciudad Juárez, November 1983)

Other managers are less concerned with unionism and more concerned with what workers know about the production process. Informal knowledge of work organization seems more pivotal to management in a union-free environment:

You want the workers to work at a like rhythm. . . . In the U.S., if a worker can't function with enough time in a particular assembly sequence, in the States the worker will rebel, they'll complain, make you change it. It will not go unnoticed. In Mexico, the operator is more obedient and won't complain. As a result you have more rejects. We don't want this. The operator can play an important role. If the worker speaks up, we'll listen and make changes if possible. (Interview, Ciudad Juárez, June 1982)

Tapping informal knowledge of production is the key to this strategy, but workers must be willing to exchange that information with management. Some plant managers are clearly frustrated by their apparent inability to elicit information on production processes from line workers. Here, the stereotyped expectation of worker docility ironically becomes a negative quality for management. Or, in some cases, workers may be "playing dumb" to withhold information desired by managers (chapter 4).

But why all the fuss? Many managers admit that this knowledge is important for maintaining high standards of productivity and quality. This knowledge must also be tapped if management is to exploit the wealth of technical innovations and job techniques constantly invented by workers on the shop floor. The only way to tap this "tacit" knowledge of production is by gaining access to informal shop-floor networks (see chapter 6). In the maquilas, management attempts to accomplish this by means of relations of dominance between first-line supervisors and lead operators.

Another important source of managerial concern is the fairly common occurrence of output restriction and other types of worker resistance (chapter 4). Management has an interest in understanding how workers organize responses to relations of domination and control in the labor process. This, after all, is precisely the legacy of the Hawthorne studies, which launched managerial sociology as practice, and not just theory. Maquila managers are sometimes very attentive to the existence of informal networks. They pay them due "respect." Such managers operate with group strategies in mind and rely on informal, hierarchical links that connect the plant manager's office with the shop floor. But some managers frown on all informal activities and view departures from the formal rule of organization as disruptive actions usually traceable to a few individual, disgruntled workers:

> If we didn't keep an eye out for certain types of workers, for certain views and attitudes among workers, we could get production paralyzed. You need to spot troublesome workers before they start breaking machinery, spoiling materials, or loafing time off. (Interview, Ciudad Juárez, February 1982)

Other plant managers may cling to myopic and degrading views of workers' knowledge of production. Blinded by their arrogance or ethnocentrism, such managers basically forfeit any benefit they might derive from workers' informal knowledge. A lab technician once told me that plant managers and supervisors at his plant

> don't know much about the organization of the actual work inside the plant. And this is where I criticize them. I tell them they can get such and such a thing done more efficiently. I point to mistakes and problems and suggest solutions. They get very angry and tell me, "Just do it the way we tell you to do it. Leave the thinking to us." They have a bad attitude toward the Mexican staff . . . they denigrate us. (Interview, Ciudad Juárez, September 1982)

In organizing the politics of informal control, maquila management displays a great range of strategies and tactics. Generally speaking, those managers who develop vertical links across a range of lateral supervisory ranks (i.e., who use first-line supervisors), who maintain contacts throughout the different divisions and levels of plant organization, are in a better position to exercise some control over the informal relations of production on the shop floor. The managers who are disconnected from informal networks obviously cannot exercise much of this indirect kind of control.

It is probably the case that the degree of managerial control over the informal politics of production fluctuates between periods of domination and periods of resistance. At one point, management has the upper hand; at another, workers disrupt the links and cut managers off from access to the networks that control information about the subaltern dynamics of the shop floor. This is an ongoing tug-of-war that of itself is not a serious threat to capitalist imperatives and managerial control. But this does not mean that maquila managers simply adopt some type of response or policy to control clandestine acts of resistance and sabotage. Some managers have expressed concern that informal resistance can develop a "life of its own," building in intensity and momentum. The former plant manager of an apparel factory that was closed after a protracted strike expressed this fear, in 1989, after the plant was permanently shut down:

> It started before we were aware that workers were organized. We never anticipated their unity or degree of solidarity. Their leaders were always hidden, and to tell the truth, looking back, now that I know who the leaders were, somehow I'm not surprised. It all makes sense. . . . We started having problems first with broken machines and poor-quality work on the fabric sorting. Then the problems grew, it took on a life of its own, and the sewing operators stood up and walked out of the building. There was a fire—a bundle of cloth someone had left burning on the floor. A protest was held. There were speakers. The media came. The police. It just snowballed out of proportion! We were caught off guard. And I can't tell you why. Maybe it's because we did not pay much attention to the problems, since these were always present at a manageable level. We never expected that it would explode the way it did. (Interview, El Paso, August 1989)

There are many examples of full-blown strikes and work stoppages in the maquilas that got their start as informal acts of sabotage and resistance by individual workers or small groups of workers (chapter 4). Informal resistance can evolve, under certain conditions, to reach a more generalized and open level of struggle by well-organized workers.

In their efforts to control informal resistance, some managers "pander" to what they think are the "emotional needs" of their workforce. This is the style championed by the type of manager that thinks Mexicans are "affectionately ignorant" and "uncivilized." Other managers "respect" the knowledge workers have of production, and they try to listen and to integrate suggestions. This is the style preferred by managers who think of themselves as being more enlightened because they rely on the objective, "empirical measurement" of work. Yet others exercise control through sexual harassment and informal surveillance networks; they, in effect, build a counterinsurgency network through the constant "camera eye of informal contacts."

❖

Whatever the strategies—and I will not dwell on the racist and sexist attitudes that inform them—management's objective is to win back the shop floor and to reintroduce and reinforce managerial authority and control at all levels, including that of the individual rate-buster. But a common, fatal flaw in maquila management's efforts to reconquer the subaltern life of the factory stems, ironically, from the mismeasurement of "ignorance," if I may play with the words of my managerial informants. Sometimes managers get so obsessed with measurement, with the quantitative reality of the flow line, that the social relations of production become obscured to them, rendered invisible as if behind a smoke screen of denial. For such managers, the "laws" of capitalist production appear to be unconscious, unquestioned assumptions. Conflict is viewed as an anomaly. And workers are viewed as "ignorant" or "uncivilized." Of course, the "uncivilized" worker is both an asset and a potential threat. Managers who see only the "negative" aspects of departures from bureaucratic rules risk mishandling the informal shop-floor networks. To ignore the potential for creativity and autonomy among the line workers is to make management vulnerable to informally organized resistance. In these cases, subaltern resistance may develop into an open, more general struggle. Managers may then respond with a new set of technological strategies—for example, by automating the jobs of workers who have gone out on strike. In fact, this has often been an outcome of worker resistance: plants automate or relocate in response to persistent, or protracted, work stoppages.

To the extent that managers are serious about "scientific management" and "empirical measurement" of labor processes; to the extent that managers conduct their own ongoing "research" on workers' performance, behavior, attitudes, and knowledge; to the extent that principles of Taylorism, Fordism, and managerial sociology are embraced and put into practice in the maquilas—to that extent, management establishes a complex, cross-cultural apparatus for the formal and informal social control of the sites of transnational production. But this is not the only side of the story. Workers have their own discourse on the politics of production in the maquilas. They have their own perspective on the dynamics of domination and resistance on the shop floor. The fact that management must respond to the subaltern life of the shop floor means that workers have created their own (albeit hidden) organization inside the factories. And to the extent that maquila managers mismeasure the "ignorant" by underestimating the knowledge, vitality, and creative potential of workers or by ignoring their struggles, to that extent the workers on the line can continue to build their own alternatives to managerial imperatives. It is to the development of these struggles and subaltern organizations that we now turn.

Part Two

TERRAINS OF STRUGGLE

4

Like Turtles on the Line

We put the brakes on it all the time. As the engineers like to say, we withdrew our efficiency. We did . . . what do we call it? . . . tortuguismo. We worked at a tortoise's pace.
> —Former RCA worker and staff member of Centro de Orientación de la Mujer Obrera (Ciudad Juárez, 1983)

From the start the group was clandestine. Our actions in the factory were invisible until the time we hit with the walkout and sabotage. Sometimes it was necessary to meet after work since they closely watched over us. . . . We made little groups [bolitas], had dinners and parties. We talked about the problems and made plans for the next day at work.
> —Maquila worker, active in the Acapulco Fashions strike (Ciudad Juárez, 1981)

I feel that the workers woke up to defend their rights. They were not afraid to fight the supervisors and management. Workers started to make demands, to speak up and demand their rights. We stopped allowing this open-ended exploitation.
> —Electronics maquila worker, active in Despacho Obrero (Ciudad Juárez, 1982)

Ghosts in the Machine? The Subaltern Life of the Factory

When workers rebel they challenge the open-ended exploitation capital seeks to impose in its Edenic "haven of productivity." The workplace is more than the sum of capitalist imperatives. The factory is not just a collection of "dead labor"—that is, machinery and technology.[1] The politics of the workplace is not limited to the organizational designs imposed by engineers and managers in an effort to control the production apparatus.

Many "ghosts" would appear to inhabit the machine as well: the gremlin of output restriction, the shadow of absenteeism, the poltergeist of sabotage, the spirit of resistance, and even the specter of autonomy![2] The history of workplace organization includes the subaltern struggles of the workers. But are there ghosts in the maquilas? Workers in the maquilas have often been described as quiescent by many researchers and other experts.[3] Trade unionists, on both sides of the border, do not seem to think that Mexican women can be successfully organized.[4] One AFL-CIO journalist writes that maquila workers are unorganizable "low-wage lures, south of the border."[5]

Leftist intellectuals, including dependency theorists and other neo-Marxists, have depicted maquila workers in a slightly more positive light. In this version, workers are courageous but ultimately hapless victims. They are the brave, hungry, and outgunned third-world proletarians who are systematically brutalized by imperialist exploiters. The only way for the third-world proletariat to find liberation is by fighting dependency and its resulting underdevelopment.[6] Nay, says management. Our workers have always had a high level of job satisfaction. They are grateful for their jobs; they are learning new skills; and they beat the pants off any American worker when it comes to quota performance.[7]

Quiescent labor? Low-wage lures? Exploited victims of underdevelopment? Happy rate-busters? These are disturbing labels. However, these models of the maquila worker are more ideological constructs than accurate portrayals of "real" workers. The search for an archetype is itself suspect. The abstractions of quiescent subject, low-wage lure, and happy worker are not rigid modes of existence for maquila workers, even if they were invented by expert observers. Experts want to define an *essential* subject, they want a "one-and-only true" maquila worker. Such categories convey a rigidity that simply does not exist in actual situations of inequality and struggle. Human beings are much more diverse and complex than the labels that experts impose on them for the sake of analytical convenience. Witness how many apolitical, seemingly passive workers turn into both rate-busters and clandestine leaders. Anyone may become politicized. People are complex, contradictory creatures with life histories that challenge generalization.

In a more interesting and promising vein, some scholars have correctly pointed out that unionism in the maquilas is hampered by the nature of Mexican labor law—a law that requires unions to follow a lengthy and highly bureaucratic process of review before a strike can officially take place.[8] The process of "tripartite arbitration and conciliation" favors managerial over union interests. The manner in which mediation of industrial conflicts is organized does seem to give management the advantage, the opportunity to neutralize strike threats (*emplazamientos a huelga*). This makes the historically low number of formal, officially approved strikes in the maquilas easier to understand.[9] But does this mean that there are no "ghosts" in the maquilas? Are these transnational assembly-line factories largely free of struggle?

Clearly the maquiladora industry does not have a history of generalized, sustained work stoppages. Strikes have historically been concentrated in the larger assembly plants owned by transnational corporations in the electronics, automotive, apparel, chemical, and furniture-making sectors. The larger strikes, involving more than five hundred (and as many as ten thousand) workers, have been limited to sporadic struggles in several different locales. For example, there have been large strikes in Nuevo Laredo (1973–1975), Juárez (1979–1985, 1987–1989), Mexicali and Tijuana (1973–1979), and Matamoros (1989–1991).[10] Yet, the majority of maquila workers have never participated in a formal strike, and the level of unionization remains suppressed at about 20 to 30 percent for the industry as a whole.[11]

But it is a mistake to assume that organized struggle by workers is expressed only through registered strikes and official unionism. Ghosts, and their unending pranks and hauntings, are not always easily noticed or appreciated. The most prevalent form of struggle in the maquilas is subaltern, or clandestine, resistance articulated by workers inside the factories. The subaltern struggles of maquila workers involve direct, often spontaneous actions by informally organized networks on the shop floor. These struggles are very difficult to control because, like fleeting ghosts, the protagonists move unpredictably through hidden networks. Workers have the additional advantage of using the equally concealed practices and knowledge bases invented by shop-floor subcultures of resistance. Some of these struggles are not directed against management, but against the vagaries and abuses of *charrista* (male-dominated) business unions. Often, these shop-floor struggles mature into full-scale battles: collectively organized strikes, walkouts, or political protests.

Much of the research on industrial organization and conflict in the maquilas treats the realm of production politics as the exclusive domain of trade unions, management, arbitration boards, and other formal, male-centered institutions. This institutionalist error leads many scholars to overlook the multiple forms of autonomous struggle developed by workers. The focus on formal organization ignores most of the subaltern continuum of resistance: from clandestine shop-floor struggles to wildcat strikes and other, more generalized forms of political protest. These struggles depend on creative resources that James Scott has eloquently described as the "weapons of the weak."[12] To disregard the subaltern life of the workplace is to risk misunderstanding the politics of production as a whole.

A growing body of work, which includes invaluable "factory ethnographies," documents numerous forms of working-class organization and struggle in the maquilas.[13] Worker insurgency in the maquilas has been found to include every imaginable, direct form of action: from informal, individual acts of sabotage that occur on the shop floor every day, to sporadic, collectively organized strikes with the potential to paralyze the industry for weeks and months. Maquila workers have launched a diverse movement that has led to the establishment of independent unions, interplant coalitions, solidarity networks, legal-aid centers, research groups, and other autonomous organizations. Several important strikes have been won and, in other cases, valuable concessions have been secured.[14] Independent groups such as the Centro de Orientación de la Mujer Obrera (COMO), Despacho Obrero, Solidaridad Obrera, and Coalición para Justicia en las Maquiladoras[15] have long worked on issues related to toxics and other occupational hazards, sexual and political violence in the workplace, wage equality, job desegregation, and workers' legal rights; they have also helped create and maintain strike support networks, alternatives to mass production, and worker-owned, self-managed cooperatives.

There is nothing wrong with studying exploitation and the relations of domination that sustain it. An understanding of capitalist control strategies is necessary to develop a balanced analysis of the politics of production. But a balanced analysis must also recognize that workers are by no means always quiescent dupes or powerless victims. The two-sided character of class politics in the workplace must be revealed by giving attention to the changing forms and terrains of workers' struggle. We must develop an approach that can discern and describe the class and cross-cultural dynamics that impinge on the politics of production. We must listen to the voices of the ghosts in the machine.

There is no complete conquest of power by capital in the workplace any more than there is a universal proletariat. Global Fordism must adapt its systems of control to the local cultural context in which the politics of production unfolds. And similarly, Mexican women must in this case adapt to the circumstances of their employment as assembly-line workers in transnational factories. The subaltern struggles of each community have a history and logic of their own, and are capable of influencing the development of workplace organization in antagonistic interaction with capitalist imperatives.

Why is clandestine struggle so much more prevalent than official strikes and unionism? The institutional deck is stacked against maquila workers, largely as a result of the corruption and co-optation of many of the labor unions and administrative agencies that have a direct stake in the mediation of industrial conflict. The rules of the game are rigged against the workers. Why should maquila workers risk engaging in formalized procedures to secure the right to strike, when such institutionalized processes are essentially designed to suppress struggle? Too many workers have gone through the process of trying to get a strike approved, to discover that all that awaits them in the end is a negative decision by the arbitrators and a dismissal slip from management.[16] As it stands, the Mexican system for arbitration and conciliation basically serves to delegitimize rationales for strikes and at the same time provide management with a buffer of time within which it can develop counterplans against the organizers of impending work stoppages.[17] Maquila workers have consistently demonstrated good sense by circumventing formal mediation and opting instead for underground struggle, which is organized as direct attacks on technological, bureaucratic, and social forms of control. In the realm of subaltern struggle, workers can dispense with the ever elusive strike permit.

But then, why would workers risk their jobs and lives by participating in "illegal" wildcat strikes and other work stoppages? Such forms of struggle are inevitably repressed through violent force, plant closings and relocations, or massive layoffs. Often, wildcat strikes end with attacks by "goon squads," producing numerous casualties with smashed skulls, broken limbs, and even miscarriages.[18] Tens of thousands of workers have also been laid off in the aftermath of strikes, usually with insurgents especially targeted. And there are several cases in which management closed and relocated plants that were undergoing a strike.[19] Somehow, despite the institutionalized violence and displacement invoked by capital and the state to restrain collective struggle, maquila workers continue to risk life and limb by engaging in an extraordinary level of shop-floor struggle, wildcat strikes, and other acts of organized political protest.

"We Had the Dignity to Defend Ourselves"

I never thought of myself as a political person. I have never voted, and before coming to work, I never protested. . . . I was unsatisfied with my life. That is why I got a job in the maquila. A friend worked at Automotive Wiring Assemblers. She said the pay was good, the place was nice, and the managers were young, good-looking, and kind. . . . [T]he first day . . . I walked in alone, and a little late. My troubles started right away. The personnel manager brought me into his office and gave me a long lecture about being prompt and the importance of being a reliable operator. . . . After I had worked there for about a year, a group of us decided we should get a raise. All of us were good workers. We were producing 30 to 40 percent above quota and our quality was impeccable. After our shift was over, five of us went to the engineer in our area and made our case. It wasn't even a demand, we were very polite. . . . Well, he got very upset with us, sent us home, and warned us that the head of personnel would get a report. The next day, we were all sent to the personnel office. María and Angélica were fired as the instigators. Ramona, Clara, and myself were issued reprimands that went into our personnel files. We were told that a promotion was now most unlikely, and that we were lucky to have a job at all. . . . It was after this that we decided to fight back any way we could. And so we started very cautiously and deliberately, by sabotaging components. . . . Other workers noticed. They got encouraged too, and pretty soon everybody was doing their part to slow production and bring the quality standards down. . . . It got to the point where the girls competed with each other to see who could come up with the smartest, fastest way to mess things up. . . . We taught each other, and we learned to watch out for each other. I have to admit it was a lot of fun! . . . Yes, this led to an unofficial strike. It lasted for three months. The conclusion was inevitable. We had dignity to defend ourselves. We were all terminated. Without indemnification. [*She shrugs.*] What did they call it at the arbitration council? Justifiable dismissals! I have no regrets. . . . I came alone, joined together with many, and left, fighting back against the managers. (Interview, Ciudad Juárez, July 1989)

I first met Elena Villarejo outside the COMO building in Colonia Exhipódromo in July 1989. I was in Juárez visiting with Guillermina Valdés, coordinating a new survey, and conducting interviews with managers, engineers, and workers. I had not counted on meeting Villarejo. She had heard about me from Chuy Montenegro and others on the COMO staff. In the friendly, jesting manner of a *norteña*, she mumbled something about rumors that people were always bailing me out of the Juárez municipal jail. She was very eager to tell the story of how she became a "radical," as she put it. She knew I would be a good listener.

What strikes me about Elena Villarejo and her story is the same thing that impresses me about other workers I have spoken with over the years, Juana Ortega, Chela Delgado, and Olga Calderón among them. All share a vision and a vitality, an inventiveness, that makes me a bit more hopeful for the future of the border. None of these women workers came to the maquilas as ready-made militants. Certainly none of them planned on getting fired as troublesome activists. They made friends, shared lessons of survival on the flow line, and eventually used their friendships as a basis for resistance. They came alone, joined together with many, and then eventually left fighting against management. For many border women, the maquilas offered an opportunity to develop new friendships and community with other women. But these were not ordinary friendships: in many cases the *amistad* evolved from a purely emotional bond into a crucial political alliance.

A WILL TO STRUGGLE OR A CLASSROOM FOR SUBVERSION?

Where does this will to struggle come from? I have often been asked this question. But this is probably not the correct query. The issue is more one of necessity being the mother of invention than a matter of the eternal will of a transcendental subject that has mastered its own destiny. It is my argument in this chapter that the shop floor is a "classroom" where workers first "learn" strategies of resistance and the nature of collective organization. But just because workers become students of resistance and agents of struggle does not mean that they can *will* their way to liberation or define their own destiny. Such matters are determined by collective struggle and depend on broader, more complex political processes that are often beyond the direct influence of small groups of workers.

In a fundamental way, maquila workers are learning struggle from Henry Ford's ghost. It is in the labor process that workers first learn to confront the authority and command structures of management in direct practice. It is through participation in the informal politics of workplace organization that workers learn to coordinate and communicate, and protect shop-floor networks. It is by working with machinery that workers learn to understand technology: its operation, dangers, and vulnerabilities. It is inside the factory that workers learn to become "like turtles on the line" by utilizing the power of their collective, tacit knowledge. And it is inside the factory that workers first learn to use that knowledge in an effort to gain some measure of control over working conditions and production processes.

As much as workers learn from the capitalist organization of the labor process, subaltern shop-floor networks of resistance cannot be invented nor sustained without the vast inventory of cultural, political, and social knowledge workers bring into the factory with them.[20] Workers are not blank slates. The knowledge that workers bring to the factory is knowledge shared with the communities they come from—communities that maintain strong links with those who have already interacted with the mass-production regime. In other words, workers rely on their own local community resources to strengthen the organization of subaltern struggle in the factory. And, eventually, this may increase the tendency to circulate struggle from the factory back to the community (see chapters 5, 6, and 7). In this chapter, we will examine not just the forms and terrains of struggle in the workplace, but the intersections of local knowledge and local community resources with workers' shop-floor networks.

I now turn for an in-depth look at the subaltern life of the maquila workers. The focus is on the major forms and terrains of struggle: What are the tactics and strategies of resistance? What are the objectives of struggle? The so-called restriction of output, which is a basic expression of resistance against assembly-line speedup, is a major focal point of my discussion. But there are also a variety of other collective actions such as wildcat strikes and other work stoppages, protests, and efforts to establish independent worker coalitions. These struggles sometimes represent the beginnings of more developed organized resistance and formal political organization. Before turning to these struggles, I will present a brief description of the workers who were the focus of this study.

PROFILE OF A PERFECT, DOCILE WORKFORCE?

Most of the 223 workers originally interviewed for this study were employed in electronics assembly plants (70 percent); another much smaller proportion worked in apparel factories (20 percent); and about 10 percent worked in automotive-parts assembly (mainly electronic components). Most of the workers were women (about 98 percent of the respondents). The workers had an average age of 22.3, and generally workers in the electronics sector were younger than those in apparel plants. The respondents averaged an educational attainment of 8.05 years. Workers in the consumer-electronics sector had higher level of educational attainment than those in apparel plants. (See table 9.)

About three fourths (74 percent) of the workers were single, 17 percent were married, almost 5 percent were in common-law relationships,

Table 9. Select Demographic Characteristics
of Maquila Workers

	number	frequency
Age Groups[a]		
under 18	15	6.7
18 to 20	62	27.8
21 to 23	67	30.0
24 to 26	40	17.9
27 to 29	24	10.8
30 & over	15	6.7
Educational Attainment[b]		
6 years or less	74	33.2
7 to 11	138	61.9
12 or more	11	4.9
Marital Status[c]		
single (never married)	153	74.3
married	35	17.0
divorced	2	1.0
common-law marriage	10	4.8
widowed	6	2.9
Migratory Origin[d]		
ejido	13	10.1
ranch	8	6.2
small village	51	39.5
medium city	31	24.0
large city	11	8.5
state capital	14	10.9
other	1	.8
Prior Job in Maquiladoras[e]		
yes	58	26.5
no	161	73.5

a. Mean = 22.30, mode = 23.00, median = 22.17.
b. Mean = 8.05, mode = 6.00, median = 8.05.
c. Missing cases = 17.
d. Ninety-four cases were born in Ciudad Juárez.
e. Missing cases = 4.

nearly 4 percent were widowed or divorced. The origins and backgrounds of respondents were consistent with demographic trends documented by other researchers.[21] It has generally been found that large numbers of maquiladora workers have migratory backgrounds. Fifty-eight percent of the respondents in this survey were born in a place other than Ciudad Juárez. Most of the workers with migratory backgrounds came from rural areas (56 percent). Prior research also indicates that most maquila workers are working in an industrial setting for the first time.[22] The majority have no prior employment experience in maquiladoras or other factories.[23] Only 26 percent of the respondents in this survey had prior experience working in the maquilas.

In general, the workers in the sample were young, educated, and single. However, I do not wish to imply that all maquila workers share these characteristics. In fact, there is a great deal of diversity in the maquila workforce.[24] There are also married and single mothers, older women with little formal education, and women living in common-law relationships. Many of the workers in my 1981–83 sample came from migratory backgrounds, and they tended to originate in rural areas. Most of them were engaged in wage labor for the first time and had no prior experience in industrial settings. These workers would appear to fit management's ideal profile of the docile, quiescent, and highly productive employee. But demographic characteristics can be misleading: however young they may be, these workers can quickly become seasoned veterans of shop-floor struggle. Although they originate in rural areas, these workers can adapt very quickly to their urban surroundings. And although inexperienced, these workers can learn very quickly to survive the vicissitudes of employment in the maquilas by becoming full participants in the subaltern life of the shop floor.

Tortuguismo: The Struggle against Speedup

Elisa Gamboa is a five-year veteran of a major electronics assembly plant in Juárez that specializes in the production of precision surgical instruments. She describes the struggle against speedup in matter-of-fact terms:

> The standards are the main problem we struggle with. The supervisors are constantly raising the standards. On the switch assembly line I was first assigned to, they started us off at 150 units per hour. Each switch has five parts. After one month, they raised it to 200. Three weeks later to 250. Then two weeks up to 300 and 340. And finally they started doing time studies and they demanded 21 more per hour [361]. I was the fastest on

the line, so they picked me to time. They took me to the engineering office and filmed me. I thought to myself, if I work fast I'll screw everyone up. So, I worked at a normal pace, really a kind of slow pace. As it turned out, they didn't raise the standard to 361 per hour. (Interview, Ciudad Juárez, December 1981)

Another worker, Ramona Torres, who was once employed by a manufacturer of color television sets, describes the struggle against speedup as an effort to limit exploitation:

Q: What type of work do you do?
A: Electrical tests for quality control. I test the control panel on the chassis.
Q: Which part is that again?
A: The control panel, you know, for the adjustments . . . the horizontal and vertical holds, brilliance, and sound controls. From my test it goes to the final quality control and then to final packing.
Q: In the survey interview you indicated that you sometimes work slower than expected. Can you tell me more about this? How do you organize this resistance? What motivated your resistance?
A: What motivated me? Well, alright. When I see that they are about to increase my standard when they feel like it, that motivates me. I accumulate units without testing them.
Q: Do you hide them?
A: Not precisely. Rather, I always have some pretext on hand. Sometimes I'll break the *escantillón*,[25] or I'll take the fuses off the visual [*sic*].
Q: Little acts of sabotage, eh?
A: Yes, a little bit, that's correct. That is what counts because that is what you can get away with, little acts of sabotage, not enough to irritate, just enough to slow the work down.
Q: How do you avoid getting caught?
A: The supervisors and line chiefs never notice. The only ones that could possibly notice are the technicians [in final quality control], and they have never noticed either.
Q: What does this form of resistance signify for you?
A: Well, it's just a way of not letting them make you work more.
(Interview, Ciudad Juárez, July 1982)

Previous studies of Fordism demonstrate that the assembly line is characterized by high levels of absenteeism, sabotage, work slowdowns (output restriction), and wildcat work stoppages.[26] My survey research on informal networks and shop-floor dynamics among workers in thirty-five Juárez-area maquiladoras produced information on output restriction, and unexpected results (see table 10). A remarkable 62 percent of the respondents said they participated in output restriction.[27] This is an extraordinarily high level of informal struggle, particularly considering that the general prognosis of scholars has been a lack of struggle and a persistence of "labor quiescence."

Motives for output restriction among these workers varied along two dimensions. A small number of workers restricted output due to a variety of administrative, technical, or health-related reasons. Among these were conflicts over bureaucratic rules and regulations. Of the rest, 40 percent reported lack of incentive pay as the underlying motive for restricting output. However, the largest proportion of cases (60 percent) identified resistance to speedup as a motive for output restriction.

Maquiladora workers refer to output restriction as *tortuguismo* (literally, working at a turtle's pace or working stubborn as a turtle).[28] Further analysis reveals that workers subjected to speedup are more likely to

Table 10. Output Restriction

	number	frequency
Worker Restricts Output[a]		
yes	136	61.8
no	70	31.8
not line worker	14	6.4
Motives for Output Restriction[b,c]		
lack of incentive pay	45	40.2
resistance to speedup	67	59.8

Crosstab of Output Restriction & Production Speedups[d,e]

	Output Restriction	
	yes	no
Production Speedup		
yes	121 (73.3%)	44 (26.7%)
no	15 (37.5%)	25 (62.5%)

a. Missing cases = 3.
b. Missing cases = 2.
c. Twenty-two cases reported other motives, including illness, lack of raw materials, and problems with machinery or tools or both.
d. Missing cases = 18.
e. Chi-square (Pearson's value) = 21.56146, 2 df, $p < .001$, G = .60516.

engage in output restriction than are workers who do not undergo speedup. Of the 165 respondents who reported speedup, over 73 percent were involved in output restriction. In contrast, among the forty respondents who did not report speedup, only 37 percent restricted their output. The speedup, a prominent feature of capitalist control in the maquilas, appears to generate the sharpest, most consistent opposition from workers.

Like any form of technical control, speedup does not operate in an organizational or sociopolitical vacuum. Productivity supervision engenders intense social relations. Recent research suggests that higher levels of supervision may be closely related to conflict between workers and management. Shop-floor conflict, especially output-restriction struggles, is strongly associated with regimes of high-productivity and intense supervision.[29] Workers have been shown to restrict output in response to increased supervision, speedup, and other forms of intensification of work. In the maquilas, the struggle against speedup centers largely around the relationships between group chiefs and first-line supervisors.

Many workers have described the ease with which they can sabotage or slow down production. Management's efforts to disrupt primary work-group networks do not always succeed. Workers in Juárez have given numerous examples of tactics they used to overcome productivity supervision, particularly time and motion study and other managerial efforts to increase output. Verónica Rivera, a worker at a plant that assembles car stereos, described the struggle against time and motion study:

Q: Are there ever informal agreements among the line workers to restrict output?

A: Many, yes. In reality the standards are much too high. We agree on this and promise not to surpass the standards. This is especially true when they are observing and timing us. We have told the managers to count all the movements and not just those involved in actual assembly. Sometimes they don't count having to pick up parts or packing parts inside fixtures or boxes. We have had arguments over this.

Q: How do you arrive at these agreements to restrict output?

A: When we see an engineer with watch in hand we already know what to do through experience. We discuss tactics on the line as long as we are not overheard. If one worker is going fast and is being timed, we'll go over later and cuss her out. We'll tell her that if they raise the standards, she'll be alone in meeting them. When they fix the standards and the supervisor asks why we can't meet them, we answer that we don't all have the same capacity, the same speed or ability. They have never been able to prove otherwise with their clocks. Like right now, our current supervisor is demanding that we turn in the same level of production during our rest periods as during our regular work periods. You see, at two o'clock we get a ten-minute rest break when we can slow down or stop working altogether. She is trying to take this away from us. We only get ten minutes for breakfast and a half hour for lunch as it is. We are not paid for time off the line. I always tell the supervisor to get someone else to work, I'm not giving up my rest period.

(Interview, Ciudad Juárez, July 1982)

Maquila workers clearly engage in the old practice of "binging" (i.e., use of informal sanctions or threats against rate-busters) in order to control output levels and preserve the solidarity of primary work groups. Use of verbal admonishments serves to restrain rate-busters from surpassing standards during time and motion study and speedups. In this regard, the dynamics of informal networking and struggle among shop-floor groups in the maquilas develop along lines similar to those documented among workers in the mass-production industries of the United States, Britain, and Italy.[30]

The evidence suggests that output restriction is fairly common: it occurs in Fordist organizational settings regardless of national location or cultural context. But in the maquiladoras, output-restriction struggles operate in a context involving other, cross-cultural mechanisms of managerial control. In the maquilas, the difficulties are not so much related to technical control as to informal social regulation. Because workers can circumvent both assembly-line speedup and bureaucratic regulation (including time and motion study and quality-control procedures), maquila management ultimately resorts to informal tactics to control productivity and sabotage on the shop floor. This type of control largely relies on the relationships between first-line supervisors and group chiefs.

ROMPECOLAS AND FRIENDSHIPS: FIGHTING INFORMAL CO-OPTATION

There are two different types of workers directly involved in productivity supervision in the maquilas: group chiefs and first-line supervisors. The group chief is a regular assembly-line operator selected by management as a group leader on the basis of performance and behavioral standards. Group chiefs are selected from among the assembly operators who consistently produce at higher levels compared to other workers. Among industrial sociologists, these workers are known as rate-busters because they surpass the productivity standards informally set by the primary work groups.[31] In the maquilas, these rate-busters are derisively called *santanitas,* presumably in reference to the Mexican dictator General Santa Anna. Others refer to them as *rompecolas,* literally "ass busters," and yet others call them, simply, *traicioneras* (traitors).[32]

However, in addition to rate-busting, group chiefs are also recruited on the basis of demonstrated loyalty to the company and subservience to male supervisors. Group chiefs function as the first level of control over productivity standards, that is, as informants and as leaders of output rates; their loyalty is thus critical in managerial efforts to exercise informal control. Group chiefs receive economic and noneconomic incentives for their co-optation: for example, bonuses, gifts, tolerated absenteeism or tardiness, and after-hour entertainment hosted by male supervisors.

Verónica Rivera, the worker who deceived the time-and-motion-study engineers, described the roles of rate-busters and first-line supervisors in the battle over productivity:

> But then there were workers who had a fast pace, finishing with one half hour to spare. They wanted to rest so I can't really blame them. But you have to do it more carefully. In this case, the supervisor saw that these girls could finish faster. So, she personally raised the standard! To 410! She said we all could do 410 an hour, which is ridiculous. We agreed among ourselves not to meet the standard. . . . The managers got very angry . . . and reassigned us, breaking up the group. (Interview, Ciudad Juárez, July 1982)

And another worker, Carlota Fríaz, who worked at an automotive parts assembly plant, explained the conflict between the *rompecolas* and the other line workers:

> Anabel was always the one who worked faster and better than the rest of the group. She really made trouble for us by always producing above the standard. I guess she thought the benefits were worth the trouble and no one in the group liked her very much, so . . . she must have been doing this to get back at us. Eventually, the managers promoted her to group chief and in time she even made it to supervisor. We tried to talk some sense into her, to get her to see things our way. . . . Our way? Well, you know that the wages are low, the benefits are not that great, and no matter, the conditions are lousy in our plant. Why should we bust our tails? Anabel was a *rompecolas* . . . you know, someone who works faster than the rest . . . and the managers gave her gifts, bonuses, things like that. . . . They bought her loyalty, and pretty cheaply too, I might add. We fought her every step of the way, telling her that we would get her after work, that she would be alone in meeting the standards. We never meant to get her, and I guess we should have kept our word. Instead, she saw us as mouthing off idle threats,

and this just got her to be even meaner. She started reporting problems and insubordination to the engineer in our section. Before long, the managers were dragging us away to other positions. (Interview, Ciudad Juárez, August 1989)

Many other workers expressed similar concerns over the co-optation of lead operators, and they described efforts to prevent this from happening. Juana Ortega was perhaps exceptionally effective at preventing co-optation:

It has to do with how the group works together, whether or not the group has a sense of solidarity, a feeling that, hey, we are all in the same position here, no one has an unfair advantage. . . . I think the key to keeping the standards under control, and to keeping the members of the group loyal to each other, is the manner in which the members support one another on the line. A good worker will help another with her job after she is done with her own, instead of keeping up the pace and then exceeding the standards. . . . But even more important is whether or not we are friends after work. This is really the key. If you don't get together socially after work, what is to prevent someone from selling out the others? Our favorite thing was to go dancing at Cosmos Disco. We would dance with each other and with men as well. This really helped us establish a sense of belonging to a group that was not just a work-type situation, but a friendship thing as well. . . . Every so often someone would almost violate this trust and solidarity . . . not on purpose, but because we sometimes let our guard down. . . . I remember two things that happened that almost destroyed the solidarity of the group. One was when the managers came and performed a new series of time and motion studies in order to increase the standards and improve efficiency. . . . We had to be careful to make certain none of us did the best we could. . . . One of us, Sara, almost blew it [*ya mero la fregaba*]! But we created a diversion, a fake accident, that got the engineers off her. While they saw to the "accident," I went over and reminded her that she was obligated to the group, to keep a slower pace, and then she did. . . . There was also this supervisor. He was young, handsome, and Mexican. Josefa was attracted to him and she wanted to have a thing with him, you know? Well, we took her out one night and gave her a long lecture. . . . She was ready to sell us out for the sake of a sexual relationship with this man. In the end, it worked out, and he even got in trouble for harassing her. (Interview, Ciudad Juárez, March 1982)

This account makes clear the importance of friendship networks in the subaltern life of the factory, particularly as a tactic for maintaining the solidarity of the primary work groups so essential in sustaining informal struggle. But it also illustrates the constant threat to these friendships posed by the informal surveillance and harassment machine of productivity supervision.

The informal social control of productivity on the shop floor involves efforts by management to co-opt group chiefs and to suppress or disrupt the formation of primary work-group networks. For management, first-line supervisors, who are predominantly male, are the key to this process. Males who assume first-line supervisory positions are either promoted from the ranks of line workers, technicians, and quality-control inspectors or they are recruited into the positions, usually right out of engineering schools. Few female workers break into the first-line supervisory ranks. Given the highly gender-stratified division of labor in the maquilas, in which a predominantly female workforce is supervised by a predominantly male force of production supervisors and managers, the initial contact point between workers and management is that between group chiefs and first-line supervisors.

PATRIARCHY ON THE SHOP FLOOR

Because of the numbers of workers involved, it is next to impossible for first-line supervisors to keep close track of the entire assembly line. Thus, first-line supervisors rely heavily on the group chiefs to exert control. This produces a patriarchal system of informal social regulation in which control over work rules, evaluation, and discipline is exercised by males indirectly through control of group chiefs.[33] Male first-line supervisors use various forms of sexual and sexist harassment to manipulate group chiefs into conforming with the expected informant and rate-busting roles. Once group chiefs have been selected, sexual and sexist harassment can play a critical role in keeping them under the control of male supervisors. Essential for success in managing the productivity of female line workers, then, is participation by male supervisors in after-hours events, such as parties, dinners, and dances. Many maquiladora managers seem to believe that women will work harder for young and handsome Mexican supervisors who lavishly entertain the workers after hours.[34] In fact, wage hierarchies in the maquilas are also partly established on the basis of male manipulation of social and friendship networks. Women who join supervisors for entertainment and who actually "put out" on the shop floor are rewarded with wage increases, bonuses, vacations, and the like. Women who resist the "seduction" are ostracized and threatened with termination.

Sexual harassment is therefore a fundamental aspect of informal social control that maquila workers must learn to resist. Chela Delgado, a former group chief at an electronics assembly plant in Juárez, describes her experiences with this problem:

> There were two young Mexican men who were hired as supervisors. They were assigned to our line, which was charged with assembling the circuit boards for a color television set. . . . At first, they were very kind, always asking how the work was going, asking if we needed any help. They asked a group of us out to dinner, supposedly to celebrate their first month at work and the fact that we had broken the previous month's production records. Pretty soon, these men were hanging around us all the time, making suggestions about how good-looking we were and how much they would like to take one or the other of us out alone to dine and dance. I was one of the faster workers, a sort of group leader, and so Eduardo, the youngest of the two, started paying a lot of attention to me. He asked me out, saying that if I dated him he could get me a raise and some extra vacation time. He also said that I could get promoted if I would help him keep track of the workers on the line. He said, "Help me control them and I will make sure you get a supervisory or technical job." It was then that I realized, "Hey, this guy is a sexist lout [*un macho malcriado*]." I told him that I already had a friend and that I wasn't interested in a relationship with him. . . . He kept insisting and he became much more aggressive about it. . . . He started fondling me, at first making it look like it was an accident, you know, brushing his hand across my breasts. Then he started grabbing me from behind . . . one time I almost cut my fingers on the belt, he startled me so. Finally, one night as I was leaving the plant . . . he grabbed me in the parking lot and kissed me. He said something like, "If you don't give it to me, I'll make sure you never work in Juárez again." I pushed him away and ran off. The next day I complained to the personnel manager. It didn't make any difference. In fact, he became even more persistent. . . . So I eventually left my job. (Interview, Ciudad Juárez, August 1989)

By exerting pressure on a group chief to conform to the male-dominated supervisory system, first-line supervisors expect to gain control over the entire group of assembly-line operators without resorting to direct contact with all of them. Group chiefs thus find themselves in a "buffer space" between female line workers and male supervisors. Group chiefs are caught in a contradictory position. On the one hand, they are treated as assembly-line workers and must interact with co-workers daily to keep production running. On the other hand, group chiefs are used as a sort of proletarianized technical or supervisory class of workers and thus must interact daily with male management under a set of expectations that requires that they accept male authority and the objective of control over the labor of women workers.

This contradictory location in the constellation of shop-floor networks produces conflicted, erratic expressions of linkage between group chiefs and both co-workers and management. There are indications, in the context of a gender-stratified division of labor, that group chiefs and line workers form specific and temporary linkages in order to cooperate over matters related to productivity and shop-floor organization. Group chiefs do not always succumb or submit to male demands. Group chiefs often cooperate with line workers in matters related to output restriction and other forms of resistance. Oral histories revealed that group chiefs are sometimes participants in the informal shop-floor networks that facilitate output restriction. As Guadalupe Rodríguez, a veteran of a strike at Electrocomponentes, once explained:

> Elisa is an old friend of mine. We both started work at Electrocomponentes in 1978. In 1979, she was promoted to group chief because she was always very good about meeting standards. Then, in 1981, there were some very bad problems with the quality-control supervisors. They accused her of being sloppy with her unit. The truth is that they had consistently raised the standards until she decided it had gone far enough. She helped us to organize ways of getting around the standards . . . by working slower, damaging components, and hiding pieces. Eventually, management caught on to what we were doing. They fired several workers and demoted her back to the soldering line. (Interview, Ciudad Juárez, September 1983)

The process of linkage building on the shop floor proceeds on the basis of friendship networks. But the formation of these networks depends as much on factory-based work groups as on social groups in the workers' communities.[35] Management tries to disrupt shop-floor groups through line and workshift reassignments or the co-optation of lead operators. Workers must often resort to community-based social networks in order to counterbalance the effects of this informal social regulation.

Subaltern Counterplans: Circulating Struggle beyond the Shop Floor

Management often responds to output restriction by imposing line and workshift reassignments. These tactics are buttressed by informal surveillance and harassment. Informal manipulation of shop-floor groups must be understood in this political light: It is an attempt to break down the unity of primary work groups in order to disrupt communication and coordination within shop-floor networks. This amounts to interference in the workers' production of a subaltern culture of resistance—a sort of low-intensity, counterinsurgency combat strategy for the shop floor. Maquila workers respond to disruption by conducting "counterplanning" activities both inside and outside the factory. Juana Martínez, a leader of the well-known Acapulco Fashions strike,[36] explained this to me:

> From the start the group was clandestine. Our actions in the factory were invisible until the time we hit with the walkout and sabotage. Sometimes it was necessary to meet after work since they closely watched over us. . . . We made little groups [*bolitas*], had dinners and parties. We talked about the problems and made plans for the next day at work. (Interview, Ciudad Juárez, December 1981)[37]

Martínez further explained the advantages of clandestine organization and the workers' effective use of community kinship and friendship networks to organize and sustain strikes:

> The clandestine group existed for fear of dismissals. The firm does not know, cannot know, who is stirring the waters, it only knows that there is a group that resists [*que ya no se deja*]. . . . In September 1978 there was an outbreak of spontaneous action. We said: "We are so many who walked out and we know that the supervisors have our names." If we already agreed on this, the only thing remaining was to unite in struggle. And like that, they [the supervisors] knew all of the ones who had walked out. They called us to the office of [the plant manager], but all of us spoke out, and they could not figure out who was leading the group. We then spoke with other workers on the shop floor, but again clandestinely. I feel more free in a coalition than in a trade union. I feel more satisfied doing things in a clandestine manner than formally. . . . Our experiences during 1978, leading up to the full-blown strike and the formation of the independent union, were based on the effectiveness with which we could strike at the firm clandestinely . . . . This was totally possible because of the way in which we came together as a social group. Many of us were from the same neighborhood [*colonia*], our parents and husbands were friends. Some of us grew up together. We had a place to go to after work. We don't come from just nowhere. Every one of us has a personal history, and a sizable set of relations, relatives I mean, in the community. They are also a source of support. . . . Who feeds you in the middle of a strike? It sure as hell is not the CTM or the CROC. All they are good for is creating *zafarranchos* [quarrels or melees]. . . . It wasn't like the group work ended when we got off our shift. In many ways, that was when our real work began, the work of resisting in a more powerful manner. . . . Our ability to get together after our shift was over, to draw from our base in the community, this was the decisive factor in building a coalition and in conducting the strike. . . .

Without our community, we could not have built or sustained an independent union. (Interview, Ciudad Juárez, December 1981)

The strike at Acapulco Fashions demonstrates that workers shared information outside the factory. This was critical to the development and sustenance of the struggle. The solidarity initially established inside the factory was sustained by means of friendship and social networks in the community. In the maquilas, this type of social networking seems to occur whenever management threatens workers with wage cuts or layoffs or when subaltern struggles over speedup develop into more collective organization and wildcat work stoppages that require additional resources available in the workers' residential communities.

FROM GO-SLOWS TO WORK STOPPAGES
AND POLITICAL PROTESTS

Occasionally, informal resistance by individuals or small groups on the shop floor develops and matures into higher states of confrontation with management, trade unions, arbitration boards, and other organizations that intersect with the maquiladora industry. When this happens, we might describe it as involving a process of "political recomposition."[38] Workers recompose their relationships by moving beyond tactics that tend to be erratic and limited to individuals or isolated groups. This recomposition involves a shift to more collective forms of direct action when workers actively seek to create more explicitly political forms of struggle. As long as resistance is limited to the shop floor, and especially to output restriction, it remains ultimately an ineffectual "game," because it cannot challenge or transform the formal and informal hierarchies that sustain the relations of domination at the point of production.[39] Such battles yield temporary victories against the imposition of speedup, but they do not significantly alter the production regime.

Political recomposition is associated with the emergence of new organizational forms, the development of broader terrains of struggle, and the establishment of links among an expanding group of workers and their community support networks. What factors explain the emergence of new organizational forms and broader political relationships among workers? What leads to the shift from individual and small-group resistance to collectively organized direct action? Why do workers increase the level of confrontation from a mostly hidden battle with management on the shop floor to struggles that openly challenge the system of domination itself?

Over the years, I have documented a total of thirty-three strikes involving conflicts that originated in resistance against speedup.[40] In all these cases informal worker coalitions initiated the process of resistance on the shop floor, and in four cases *charrista* unions were present as an additional threat. In two thirds of the cases, the coalitions evolved into independent unions, although most were short-lived. However, my survey provided useful additional data on the development of broader terrains of struggle among maquila workers. To assess the transition from *tortuguismo* to work stoppages, I interviewed workers to gauge their knowledge of or attitude toward organizational issues, working conditions, and networking activities.

Organizing Perspectives & Militancy. Respondents were asked a series of questions related to the organization of struggle (see table 11). This allowed me to determine the level of "militancy" in the sample.[41] I asked workers if participating in strikes was a better way to defend their rights. I asked if maquila workers should attempt to unite with the struggles of other workers. I asked if maquila workers should make demands for improving living conditions in the community and not just the workplace. I asked if participating in an independent union was the best way to defend workers' rights. I asked if maquila workers should join independent unions instead of the CTM, CROC, or CRT.[42] And I asked if they agreed with the principle of workers' control of production. These topics turned out to be quite helpful in indicating the ideological persuasions of workers. Presumably, workers who agreed with the importance of using strikes, achieving unity, improving community conditions, joining independent unions, and establishing workers' control can be considered as "more militant." As it turns out, these "more militant" workers are more likely to participate in output restriction and work stoppages.

Workers who supported independent unionism and who thought independent unions were the most effective form of struggle were more likely to have restricted output in response to production speedups. Those workers who rejected independent unions, or who supported the CTM, CROC, or CRT, were less likely to have restricted their output. Likewise, the more militant the workers, the more likely they were to have participated in work stoppages. Workers who strongly supported the principle of workers' control were more likely to have a history of participation in work stoppages. However, the output restrictors who had no experience with work stoppages were not always supportive of strikes, unity, community issues, or workers' control. In other words, the

Table 11. Summary of Chi-Square and Gamma for
Output Restriction and Work Stoppages, Controlling
for Worker-Militancy (Attitudinal) Variables

	chi-square	df	G
Output Restriction			
Control Variables			
favor use of strikes	5.68059	2	.53676
value unity	6.83030	2	.56188
favor community development	8.36242	2	.54759
favor independent unions	19.50421	2[a]	.73994
favor workers' control	3.54386	2	.04167
Work Stoppages			
Control Variables			
favor use of strikes	31.57348	4[b]	.81343
value unity	33.64008	4[b]	.79618
favor community development	47.62432	4[b]	.71352
favor independent unions	13.31996	2[b]	.83478
favor workers' control	22.64040	4[b]	.63102

a. Significant at $p < .001$.   b. Significant at $p < .01$.

respondents who were involved in work stoppages were more militant than those who were only involved in output restriction. I am particularly intrigued by the fact that the principle of workers' control was very important to those who were involved in work stoppages but not to those who were only involved in output restriction. Apparently those workers who believe in self-management of production are willing to engage management in broader terrains of struggle.

Attitudes toward Working Conditions. I was also interested in determining if specific attitudes toward working conditions were associated with the shift from output restriction to work stoppages. I asked workers if they were satisfied with wages, job tenure, and policies related to promotions and seniority (see table 12). Workers who report dissatisfaction with working conditions will presumably be more likely to participate in both output restriction and work stoppages. I found that those workers who were dissatisfied with working conditions were more likely to participate in militant actions. Dissatisfaction with wages was particularly prevalent among those workers who had a history of involvement in work stoppages. In

Table 12. Summary of Chi-Square and Gamma for
Output Restriction and Work Stoppages, Controlling
for Job-Satisfaction (Attitudinal) Variables

	chi-square	df	G
Output Restriction			
Control Variables			
satisfied with wages	9.08817	2[a]	.54577
satisfied with job tenure	4.59121	2	.49669
satisfied with seniority	19.43939	2[b]	.67936
satisfied with promotions	16.03394	2[b]	.74954
Work Stoppages			
Control Variables			
satisfied with wages	66.49610	4[a]	.48039
satisfied with job tenure	36.21338	4[a]	.45912
satisfied with seniority	29.56611	4[a]	.49408
satisfied with promotions	23.96969	4[a]	.63327

a. Significant at $p < .01$.   b. Significant at $p < .001$.

contrast, dissatisfaction with seniority and promotions figured prominently among the workers engaged in output restriction. This suggests
that the more militant workers tend to be dissatisfied with working conditions and act on their discontent. It also suggests that economic issues
(i.e., wages) are more likely to result in work stoppages than simply in
output restriction.

Networking Activities. I was also interested in determining whether workers involved in networking activities would display more militancy (see
table 13). I asked respondents if they participated in shop-floor conversations. I asked them to describe the topics of those conversations. I then
selected the cases that reported work-related topics and asked if they participated in informal group meetings. I asked if they participated in
group discussions, and I asked them to describe the topics of informal
group meetings. Presumably, those workers involved in networking will
be more likely participants in output restriction and work stoppages.

I was not surprised to find that workers who engaged in networking
activities were also more likely to have participated in output restriction
or work stoppages. Workers with the highest level of participation in
shop-floor conversations were also the most likely to have engaged in go-
slows. However, for workers involved in work stoppages, participation in

Table 13. Summary of Chi-Square and Gamma for
Output Restriction and Work Stoppages, Controlling
for Networking Variables

	chi-square	df	G
Output Restriction			
Control Variables			
shop-floor conversations	23.23376	2	.68391
shop-floor topics	2.60372	2	.58042
group meetings	13.49539	2[a]	.62484
group discussions	11.62676	2[b]	.57421
group topics	.21672+	—	.56522
Work Stoppages			
Control Variables			
shop-floor conversations	75.27039	4[a]	.57589
shop-floor topics	27.10665	4[a]	.44531
group meetings	58.01666	4[a]	.68235
group discussions	42.12720	4[a]	.54350
group topics	.06364	1	.11111

a. Significant at $p < .001$.   b. Significant at $p < .01$.

shop-floor conversations was not the only significant factor. These workers were also more likely to be involved in informal group meetings and
discussions. Those workers who limited their resistance to output restriction were not as likely to be involved in informal groups, meetings, or
discussions.

NETWORKS, MILITANCY, AND THE
POLITICIZATION OF STRUGGLE

From the perspective of political recomposition, the shift from output
restriction to work stoppages is an important dynamic because it represents a transition to a qualitatively higher level of resistance and confrontation. With work stoppages, the terrain of struggle can expand to include the workers' communities, unions, political parties, and the state.
Workers involved in go-slows are generally more militant than other
workers, particularly in terms of their dissatisfaction with working conditions. However, workers with a history of participation in work stoppages are even more outwardly politicized than the turtles on the line. In
other words, when workers take struggle to the level of full-blown work

stoppages (i.e., strikes), they are more likely than the output restrictors to be involved in subaltern shop-floor networks. The restriction of output tends to be limited to individuals or smaller groups of workers; in fact, it can be successfully articulated by a handful of workers. In contrast, work stoppages must involve the majority of the workers in a given assembly plant.

The factors that explain this shift include not just ideological components (i.e., more militant attitudes), but also certain organizational dynamics that are not present in the resistance to speedup. Participation in group meetings and group discussions are critical elements of this transition to higher levels of struggle. When Juana Martínez, with the Acapulco Fashions strike coalition, spoke of the "real work" of building social solidarity, enlarging the clandestine group, and establishing links with the community, she was describing this process of political recomposition. But almost every case of informal work stoppages that I have documented also involved an escalation in the level of managerial reprimands: workers were fired or threatened with layoffs as managers retaliated against the strikers. Thus, the shift to work stoppages involves increased networking by workers as well as increased managerial harassment of the insurgents through the imposition of harsher working conditions or through reprisals, including political violence.

Once workers develop struggle to the level of a work stoppage, they are in a position to seriously challenge the regime of managerial control over production. Strikes are after all the refusal of work, and nothing is more crippling to capitalist production than the conscious and absolute withdrawal of labor power. Strikes, and especially wildcats, have the potential to transform the relations of production and to challenge the conditions of domination and exploitation. Of particular significance in such cases is the increasingly political character of the strikers' demands. Further analysis of wildcat work stoppages in Juárez maquiladoras revealed that the insurgents usually made demands not just for wage increases and the reinstalling of terminated workers, but also for workers' control, democratization of the workplace, or other major changes in the organization of production.[43] Chela Delgado, a woman with a long history of participation in wildcat strikes, expressed this more radical set of demands in no uncertain terms:

> When I was at SESA [Subensambles Electrónicos] and we went on strike our struggle was not so much over wages and benefits—you have to understand that we were limited in what we could demand by the law. . . . There were instead some very serious problems with the way production

was organized. Three things were the main problems. First, the hazards. Not just toxic chemicals and vapors, but the way the lines were set up . . . well, it was conducive to accidents happening. We wanted to eliminate certain procedures, and we insisted that proper ventilation systems be installed, especially in the soldering-deck area. We also wanted management to implement constant testing of worker health and to establish a special fund for sick and injured workers. We thought that some of the chemicals could be eliminated, especially the more dangerous ones. . . . Second, we wanted more input on decisions. The most important issue was who was to determine production standards. We were against the continued use of time and motion study and insisted that workers alone should determine quotas [*estandards*]. And third, we wanted an independent union, one that would truly represent our interests and not the union the company wanted to impose. . . . We had political objectives that I can now describe, five years later, as involving a desire for more democracy in the factory, more power for the workers. (Interview, Ciudad Juárez, August 1989)

Since 1979, wildcat strikes at Acapulco Fashions, RCA, SESA, Electrocomponentes, Texscan, AAMSA (Autopartes y Arneses de México), AMF, Tonka, and Florex, to name a few, have involved informal coalitions or independent unions articulating demands of a similar political nature. Calls for workers' control and other workplace democratization demands were consistently articulated during these strikes. For example, during the 1986 wildcat strike at RCA, workers demanded the removal of the union leadership and the establishment of an independent democratic union. The strike was primarily motivated by the fact that the official union, the CROC, had accepted a 21.9 percent wage increase when the workers had demanded 50 percent. Workers also decried "internal repression" at RCA in press coverage. This strike actually started as an informal fifteen-minute work stoppage by twenty workers on July 15, 1986. By October the struggle had circulated to encompass close to two thirds of the entire workforce. On October 25, almost three thousand out of the RCA–Juárez workforce of 5,100 went on a wildcat strike.[44]

In reaching higher levels of struggle, workers use the media to appeal to a broader base of supporters. The staging of political protests in public settings, including blockades and demonstrations, also becomes an important tactic of struggle. Another aspect involves links between worker coalitions and community-based organizations. The relationship between the Acapulco Fashions strike coalition and Despacho Obrero or between COMO and striking workers at Electrocomponentes, Texscan, and RCA are some examples of such linkage. When this circulation of struggle occurs, workers develop a struggle over ideology as well as autonomous forms of organization. The creation of autonomous organizations is the most political form of struggle among maquila workers. Autonomous organizations are independent of the established power structure, including labor unions. The ideologies they articulate represent oppositional alternatives to the dominant discourse. I now turn to a brief overview of ideology and autonomy in the circulation of maquila workers' struggle.

Ideology, Struggle, and Autonomous Worker Organizations

> The Center for the Orientation of Women Workers (COMO) unites with the struggle of our colleagues, the Workers' Coalition of Texscan. We support the struggle for: social justice, respect for the dignity of the worker, better working conditions and job security, the organization of the workers. We reject violence and repression as methods for resolving the conflict. We urge dialogue as the road to a just negotiation.

This announcement was signed by Guillermina Valdés de Villalva, Jesús Montenegro, Margarita Ishida, and other organizers from COMO. It was published in the Juárez daily newspaper *El Fronterizo* on April 10, 1986. Five workers from Texscan, three women and two men, had just initiated a hunger strike to support the independent workers' coalition and its demands for negotiations with management over wages, working conditions, and organizational recognition. Throughout the 1980s, a period characterized by the arbitration and conciliation board in Juárez as involving "too much labor conflict,"[45] maquila workers developed a political movement by circulating their struggles out of the shop floor and into the community where they articulated both reformist and revolutionary demands. Border studies and maquiladora scholars have generally ignored this movement, despite the fact that it involved dozens of major strikes, tens of thousands of workers, and the establishment of several important autonomous organizations such as COMO and Despacho Obrero, and more than a dozen independent unions and worker coalitions.

In a July 1989 interview, Guillermina Valdés described the ideological nature of the struggle unfolding in the maquilas:

> You are aware . . . of the history of struggle in the maquilas. You know that we have a history of continuous resistance and organized struggle. [Since 1984] many things have developed. One of the most exciting aspects is the development of a clear ideological perspective shared by the workers and the independent organizations that represent their interests. . . . The expe-

rience with COMO since 1984 is one in which the cooperatives, with the exception of one, continued to thrive and became more independent of COMO, more self-sustaining. The cooperatives demonstrated the possibility of an alternative to employment in the maquiladoras. Workers saw what we were doing . . . our successes. . . . From COMO, the workers learned more than just self-esteem. What good is pride when you are going hungry or you are being slowly poisoned and overworked to death? You died with a smile on your face? A lot of good that will do you. Workers learned the value of self-organization. They learned that there are other ways to organize production, more just and humane ways, more democratic. And they found ways to express this theoretical understanding in practice. By organizing independent unions . . . or coalitions, yes; by joining forces to establish or support cooperatives and by seizing center stage in the public discourse, these workers asserted both a new vision and a new practice. . . . We now have the independent organizational resources to combat management and the state by presenting our case before a public forum. This has made a big difference—the newspapers can no longer get away with presenting just one side of the story. (Interview, Ciudad Juárez, July 1989)

Self-esteem and self-organization are principles underlying the development of a political ideology among activist maquila workers. But self-organization, at least as practiced at COMO, has itself two other fundamentals: the self-management of labor as basic to workplace democracy, and the use of counterhegemonic discourse by women workers in reclaiming the public sphere and especially the political debate surrounding the maquiladoras. I will revisit the role of COMO in a variety of struggles in subsequent chapters.

Why should we be concerned with ideology? Ideology as a category in social theory has a complex and troubling history. Among social theorists, ideology has too often been rendered as "false consciousness," thanks in part to a serious misreading of arguments originally posed by Marx and Engels in *The German Ideology*.[46] Agreeing with Clifford Geertz, I am more interested in the role of ideology as a force capable of promoting or inhibiting social change.[47] From the vantage point of maquila workers' struggles, ideology can be a powerful tool for promoting social change, both at the level of the individual and within the broader community or society. As Ramón Saldívar has argued:

One particularly salient way of conceiving ideology is to think of it as the ways a culture links social action with fundamental beliefs, a collective identity with the course of history. Basically, ideology functions as a unifying social force. . . . An ideology as such is not necessarily good or evil, true or

> false. We can set aside crude notions of "false consciousness." . . . No cul-
> ture is ideology-free. . . . [Ideological] narrative presents subjects acting . . .
> in active resistance to the existing material apparatus.[48]

Understood as a type of "oppositional consciousness,"[49] ideology can be viewed as an important tool of struggle. Seen in this way, ideology is a force for both social control and social change. In either case, ideological conflict takes place as a struggle to control the terrain of public discourse, to define what the "real" is.

The construction of a public-relations image of the maquiladoras by the media, government officials, management, and even scholars imposes the dominant ideological view: maquilas are good for Mexico and the United States—they create jobs, increase Mexico's foreign-exchange earnings, offer training opportunities and technology transfers, and integrate third-world women more fully into meaningful and gainful employment. And when workers rebel by conducting wildcat strikes and other struggles, the media, government officials, and industry representatives tend to depict them as irrational, irresponsible, and even criminal deviants who are endangering the economic future of Mexico. The Association of Maquiladoras (AMAC), representing the industry, has denounced strikes most often by suggesting that workers "are being misled by unethical lawyers."[50] In other words, workers really have nothing to complain about, and if not for a handful of unscrupulous lawyers labor peace would surely prevail.

But strikes continue to occur. If anything, strikes in Juárez have become more frequent and have involved larger numbers of workers during the late 1980s and early 1990s compared to the period prior to 1984. Even RCA, that bastion of "labor peace" that was without a serious strike until 1986, has since had its share of workers' struggle. Such a level of insurgency, at times involving thousands of workers, cannot be contrived by a handful of allegedly manipulative lawyers. Efforts to discredit and delegitimize these struggles have failed to prevent workers from conducting strikes. And increasingly, the ideological position of the dominant groups is being challenged by articulate workers and organizers. Chela Delgado explained the role of ideology in the struggle to support strikes:

> The press depicts us as hooligans. . . . We are accused of being a threat to
> development. One journalist reported that we were endangering economic
> development by going on strike and that we should gratefully accept our
> jobs at whatever pay we received. What? Are we supposed to take our ex-
> ploitation lying down with our legs open? It's bad enough that we are un-
> derpaid and overworked. But how do you compensate workers for sexual

abuse and harassment? How do you compensate a worker who has ovarian cancer from working with toxic chemicals in the workplace? . . . When you conduct a strike there are two things you must constantly nurture: the solidarity of the workers' organization and public opinion. . . . Public opinion can destroy a strike, especially if it gets so negative that it demoralizes the workers. We cannot ignore managers and [government] officials pontificating about how good they are and how bad we are. . . . During our strike, we managed to get a few good reporters, Lau and Galarza, to cover the dispute. They did a fair job of giving us access to the newspaper. The reports they wrote on violence against women and on, what did Galarza call it, the neocolonialism of the maquilas, these helped us set the tone of the public discussion. It generated considerable support for our strike.[51] (Interview, Ciudad Juárez, August 1989)

The development of this ideological warfare would not be possible without the existence of autonomous organizations willing and able to articulate workers' demands and perspectives. Having friends in the print media is nice but by itself cannot be relied on to sustain a discourse capable of challenging the dominant ideology. This, perhaps more than anything else, is why the establishment of COMO, Despacho Obrero, Solidaridad Obrera, and other independent worker organizations was so critical. These organizations provided a safe haven for workers to gather, organize, and plan their struggles. Some provided legal assistance (e.g., Despacho Obrero) while others focused on fund-raising and media campaigns (e.g., COMO and Solidaridad Obrera).

In their search for autonomy—for independence from the established institutions of the power structure, including *charrista* unions—maquila workers circulated their struggles from the shop floor to broader political institutions and the community. The necessity of generating support in the community was their mother of invention. My colleague Beatriz Vera once told me that the maquilas were contributing, inadvertently, to the development of a feminist movement in the border region. Her idea was that the industry brings women together under shared material conditions in such large numbers that they cannot help but learn to resist and organize. It would seem that our ghostly pranksters eventually develop their own homes to haunt. In chapter 5, I will examine this process of autonomous organization further by focusing on the history and struggles of COMO.

5

The Mirror of Exploitation

COMO was a mirror for us. El espejo de la doble explotación *[the mirror of double exploitation]. At COMO I came to understand my exploitation as a woman and as a worker. And if what you saw in the mirror was ugly, then you had to take the responsibility, and you had to improve your methods of resistance, in challenging the exploitation.*
— Former General Electric worker and student at COMO (Ciudad Juárez, 1984)

The Refusal of Development

In 1971, when Donald Baerresen published his plant-location guide for investors curious about the Border Industrialization Program (BIP), it was widely presumed that Mexico's maquiladora workers would be a reliable source of cheap, quiescent, productive, and apolitical labor.[1] Instead, over the years, tens of thousands of workers have participated in organized struggle. And they have done so in a manner wholly antagonistic to and independent of the "logic" of the global assembly line and the systems of labor control that perpetuate the terror of the machine.[2]

In seeking alternatives to the dominant institutions, maquila workers have invented new organizations and ideologies. In the process, they have discovered a new awareness of their own "agency," that is, of their ability to transform the world, however real or illusory that ability may turn out to be. The dynamic subjectivity of maquila workers, their conscious militancy, is nevertheless associated with myriad forms of subaltern struggle: go-slows, work stoppages, political protests, and autonomous organizing. In creating this subjectivity—a consciousness of themselves as agents of history if not as owners of their own destiny—Mexican working-class women are reappropriating the right to self-activity and developing a social-change orientation. Mexican women workers are redefining the nature of development itself by assuming a more active role in social and political change. In the process, they are also redefining their identities as members of a broader, historically located community.[3]

These struggles and organizations are not new in the history of working-class insurgency in general. Indeed, these women workers are perhaps just examples of what Marx called a "class-for-itself." However, in the context of the border region, these struggles and organizations are a quantum leap forward in the political life of Mexican women industrial workers. It makes, as Chela Delgado once told me, quite a difference to go from being a household servant to being an industrial laborer and then an agitator for workers' rights. Restriction of output, sabotage, work stoppages, political protests, and the establishment of independent organizations are all indicative of an ongoing process of political recomposition among maquila workers. Drawing from their experiences in the industrial workplace, women workers are inventing new organizational forms by circulating their struggles beyond the confines of the shop floor back to their families and communities. Maquila women workers are challenging established ideologies, attitudes, relations of power, and orientations to family and community.[4]

But these are more than just ideological challenges to the dominant discourses and values. Maquila workers have established independent unions, student-worker-peasant coalitions, legal-aid centers, and other autonomous organizations intended to redirect the path of development in the border region. Experimenting with new forms of organization, including self-managed cooperatives, women workers are refusing development as defined by the imperatives of collective global capital. The subjectivity of maquila workers is increasingly antagonistic toward the terror of the machine. Capital's pretensions of possessing universal models of development are being challenged by the fierce refusal and unbounded creativity of third-world women.[5]

In searching for alternatives to maquiladora industrialization, a knowledge of the history of COMO is fundamental. This organization, more than any other in the border region, has consistently articulated a set of unique struggles and demands over a quarter century of social-justice and labor activism. COMO gained prominence as a gathering point of struggle by committing itself to directly involving maquila workers in self-managed cooperatives, radical pedagogies and alternative education, participatory democracy, and autonomous organizing efforts on the shop floor and in the working-class community of Ciudad Juárez. An important aspect of this struggle is the establishment of worker-owned, self-managed cooperatives. These cooperatives, many of which are still economically viable, are prototypes of alternatives to global Fordism.

Workers have struggled to redefine attitudes and ideologies, alter political power relations, and strengthen their roles in the workplace and community. In so doing, they have created a collective identity that corresponds to the emerging cooperative forms of education, health, housing, and work. By examining the construction of this new subjectivity, and the organizational forms it produced, I hope to shed light on the prospects for workplace democracy, feminist organization, and sustainable development in the U.S.–Mexico border region.

A History of COMO

The history of COMO spans more than two decades. Since its humble beginning in 1968, the women's center has gone through six stages of development, each one with different organizational forms, changing ideological outlooks, and expanding constituencies. The center's formative phase was the period between 1968 and 1975. The second phase, between 1975 and 1977, involved the consolidation and formalization of the center. The third period, from 1978 to 1983, witnessed the emergence of *autogestión* (self-management) as its basic organizational principle. This period also witnessed the growth of rank-and-file initiatives, as workers brought their own struggles to COMO.[6] Between 1983 and 1985 the organization experienced a period of retrenchment initiated after a series of internal and external evaluations. During this fourth period, a funding crisis occurred, and the center briefly functioned as a volunteer organization with a more limited political agenda.

The fifth phase, 1985 to 1990, witnessed the departure of Guillermina Valdés de Villalva from the directorship of COMO. Dr. Valdés became an administrator for the Colegio de la Frontera Norte (COLEF, College of the Northern Border). This phase also saw the development of new relationships with striking maquila workers (especially at Texscan and RCA). Given COMO's reputation as a sanctuary for insurgents, workers sought the assistance of the center. Since 1991 and the death of Dr. Valdés, the center has been reorganized under the leadership of her daughter, Luchi. COMO is once again supporting independent worker coalitions and offering alternative education programs.

ORIGINS AND FORMATION: 1968–1974

In 1967, María Villegas was a nurse-practitioner at the sprawling RCA factory complex in Bermúdez Industrial Park on the eastern edge of Ciudad Juárez. At that time, Guillermina Valdés was a member of a philanthropic organization, Grupo Damas. The "Women's Group" was made up of middle-class professionals who were interested in solving the problems that faced working women in Juárez. María Villegas was struggling with RCA management over health issues affecting the workers. At the time, the RCA plant was among the largest on the border, with close to three thousand regular, full-time workers. In an interview I conducted with Villegas in 1983, she recalls the events that led her to develop what she characterized as "working-class consciousness":

> When I started working as a nurse in 1967 at RCA, I had a totally different mentality. I believed my work consisted solely in making sure the workers got sick less. Well, the indoctrination [*el coco-wash*] did not last for long. I began to realize workers often came to my nursing station only to relieve themselves from the tensions of the [assembly] line. It occurred to me that there were many social problems, promiscuity, health problems. After observing the production line it occurred to me that the working conditions and working materials . . . caused many of these problems. I began to ask management for things to protect the health of the workers. They told me I was being stubborn [*necia*], and that the things I was asking for were not needed. It was over a period of one to three years, my transition to . . . working-class consciousness. (Interview, Ciudad Juárez, January 1983)

At RCA between 1967 and 1969, María Villegas actively pressured management to adopt policy changes that would protect worker health and safety. She began by asking RCA management to conform with federal regulations on occupational safety and social security. Her efforts then turned to organizing self-help groups of RCA workers, which held meetings inside the plant and after work. These groups had informal discussions on occupational health and safety, stress, and sexuality. About this time, Villegas first met Guillermina Valdés. In an interview, she recalled the circumstances surrounding their first meetings and her idea of what an organization such as COMO might be like:

> I tried to find people who . . . shared my concerns. I found out about Guillermina through the newspapers. I made an appointment with her. She came to the plant. They [RCA management] had a psychologist present, presumably to counteract my influence on the workers. After I spoke with Guillermina, she went to speak with the personnel manager. The information she sent me never got to me. There were some discussions at the 20/30 Club. . . . I was not invited. But I went anyway. At the moment of debate I criticized them. They spoke of family life . . . but it was a middle-class view. I told them that that sort of discussion did not focus on the more dignified aspect of reaching out to the workers. The

third discussant was the RCA psychologist, a member of the Christian Family Movement. She refused to talk because I was present. The organizers of the seminar called Guillermina to tell her a bothersome person was disrupting their meeting. Guillermina asked if I wanted to talk. It was then that I told her that I dreamed of a group that would orient women workers, not help them like the boss, but rather in their self-orientation. I mean an intrinsic or integral orientation. We had to recognize that workers carried strong values. . . . The workers only had their labor power, but that has a lot of value. Guillermina agreed . . . she is very intuitive, she has a tremendous ability to synthesize and adapt. But it was a unity of upper- and working-class interests. It was an incredible unity based on a common, deeply held concern for the women of the plants. (Interview, Ciudad Juárez, January 1983)

During this formative period, COMO's ideological leanings tended toward an emphasis on *beneficiencia,* or *asistencialismo. Beneficiencia* involves a philosophy of "interpersonal helping." The center's formative ideological outlook was as much reflective of Guillermina Valdés's affinity for the teachings of Erich Fromm and Paolo Freire as of María Villegas's working-class perspective and experience at RCA.[7] Villegas's perspective emphasized an awareness of the systemic causes of problems faced by workers.

The formation of COMO was also strongly influenced by Valdés's theoretical knowledge. As a university-educated middle-class woman, she had experience in dealing with public forums, organizing research, and generating resources. She never exploited this advantage for the sake of personal gain, and instead tirelessly dedicated herself to generating support for and directing resources to the establishment of an independent center for working women. Initially, while COMO attempted to gain a beachhead in the maquilas, Valdés emphasized a philanthropic orientation and *beneficiencia.* She conceived of this in terms of social-casework intervention designed to improve human relations through personal change and development of self-esteem. Over time, she came to understand this in more profoundly ideological and political ways as well.

As a result of this initial perspective, COMO developed a collaborative relationship with management in order to carry out its mission of serving maquila workers. With the approval and consent of maquila management, the center for a brief time offered "promotional courses" inside the assembly plants. This work largely focused on presenting a more positive social image of the Mexican working-class woman and on understanding social problems such as drug abuse, alcoholism, and marital conflict. The courses also encouraged discussion of physical and mental hygiene. Five factories contracted with COMO to teach these courses.[8] But the basic organizational nucleus during this period was drawn from RCA and Grupo Damas. The latter group published a magazine called *La Mujer,* in which it sought to promote a positive image of working-class women in the border region. Many of the articles focused on topics such as assertiveness, consciousness-raising, stereotypes, and social problems (drug and alcohol abuse, promiscuity). COMO also organized the Casa para Jóvenes, an educational youth hostel where classes and seminars were held for adolescents and young adults in Juárez.

During its formative years, COMO emphasized helping individual women adjust to their new roles as industrial workers. In later years, it would focus on providing women workers with the skills and ideologies necessary for them to alter and take control of their own productive and political lives. The problems initially voiced by María Villegas would lead Guillermina Valdés de Villalva to develop a more radical curriculum for the center that involved a remarkable adaptation of the methodologies of Freire for self-education (*autodidáctica*) through critical social-problem solving.[9] The influence of Villegas and other maquila workers would also eventually lead COMO to undertake a rigorous struggle for economic democracy and sustainable development through worker-owned, self-managed cooperatives and other forms of community organizing.

In 1973, the women's center received a public building located in Colonia Exhipódromo, a lower-middle- and working-class neighborhood in south-central Ciudad Juárez. This building became COMO's permanent headquarters and greatly enhanced the organization's further development independently of the maquila industry and its proponents. Edificio COMO is a large concrete-block and white-stucco building. It has a set of office suites, classrooms, a library and archive collection, a general assembly room, a kitchen area, and several conference rooms—some of which were eventually converted into production areas for an apparel workers' cooperative named "Guille" (which is short for Guillermina). A smaller wooden A-frame building houses additional classroom and childcare space. After COMO moved into the Exhipódromo building, Guillermina Valdés, María Villegas, and other organizers established their first contacts with the garbage dump workers (*pepenadores*). The squatters from the garbage dump were among the first to participate in the establishment of the worker-owned, self-managed cooperatives that became the hallmark of COMO's accomplishments after the mid 1970s (see chapter 7).

Toward the end of this formative period, COMO's relations with maquila management became strained. The organizers found themselves increasingly at odds with managers, and open hostilities emerged. Maquila managers were apparently dismayed by what they perceived as increasing militancy on the part of the women's center. In fact, Valdés and Villegas became much more concerned with advising workers about health hazards in the workplace than with improving their self-image. But COMO did more than just inform workers about workplace conditions. Instead, the organizers began pressuring management to improve working conditions, especially with regard to health hazards and medical services. Over the years, management became increasingly antagonized by the center's pathbreaking research and public-advocacy programs that dealt with the adverse working conditions and social problems facing maquila workers.[10] This constituted a critical turning point in the relationship between the organization and maquila workers. Freed of managerial constraints and influence, the center became increasingly receptive to the rank-and-file initiatives of assembly-plant workers. The maquila workers circulated struggle to COMO and in the process radicalized the organization even more.

CONSOLIDATION AND FORMALIZATION: 1975–1977

The period between 1975 and 1977 witnessed the consolidation and formalization of the center's organizational structure and staff. Importantly, during this period former maquila workers moved into direct administrative, support, and organizing staff positions at COMO. Various international, national, and local events influenced the organization's increasing militancy: Mexico was in the grips of a deep recession dating back to 1973; the International Year of Women in 1975 led to a Mexico City conference that was attended by COMO staff; 1976 brought a *peso* devaluation and an exodus of capital from Mexico partly fueled by Echeverría's lame-duck attempts at agrarian and political reforms. The economic and political climate during this period strengthened COMO's activist orientation. The number of maquila workers in Juárez increased from 3,800 in 1968 to more than twenty thousand in 1976, in effect greatly expanding the center's chosen constituency.

During this period, COMO established its first two worker-owned, self-managed cooperatives: Guille and SOCOSEMA (Sociedad Cooperativa de Seleccionadores de Materiales). Guille is an apparel cooperative originally organized by COMO and seamstresses laid off from their jobs in the private maquila sector.[11] SOCOSEMA is a garbage recycling and recovery operation collectively owned and managed by dump workers and their families. An anthropologist who was a guest researcher at the center during the late 1970s described the significance of these efforts:

> For the first time, COMO successfully transferred its learnings obtained by workers during their employment in the factories to the experience of cooperative formation. Mass production, fragmentation of labor processes, quality control, were all criteria implanted by [Guille] in the organization of its work.[12]

Was COMO merely reproducing the terror of the machine in its cooperatives by adopting the principles of Fordist mass production? I interviewed a former Guille worker in July 1989. Hortencia Hernández, who worked at Guille for thirteen years before retiring, had this to offer about her experience in the cooperative:

> Sure, we produced big quantities of the same product. For example, several thousand uniforms for RCA workers or a thousand dolls. And we had a division of labor. But things were totally different compared to working in the private maquilas. . . . I was fired from a company that was a subcontractor. In the maquila, our jobs were never secure because it was never assured that the sales manager had received a work order. He was a rather irresponsible type. Work came and went. It was very inconsistent. And if you did not work, you did not get paid. Nothing for nothing. . . . The pay was by piece rate [*a destajo*], and that also made things tough because the standards were high. It seemed like when the work finally came around we did it so fast it was over before you knew it and then, there you go again without any work to do. . . . At Guille things were better organized. We were careful to spread our work out evenly over the year so that there was always plenty to do. . . . We also produced more than just one thing, and we changed the product lines from time to time. . . . We also decided things for ourselves. I mean the administration of the cooperative. Everything was in our hands. Who to sell the products to. Who to go to for supplies, work materials. How to organize the work. Figuring out the members' shares in profit. How much to invest back into production. Defining our benefits and so on . . . You could switch jobs if you got bored or tired. And if you had trouble with your task there was no one around to scream at you or threaten you. Instead, someone would always be there to help you get the job done. This reduced our stress and made working at Guille a joy, a thing you looked forward to. . . . It was just a much healthier environment to work in.[13] (Interview, Ciudad Juárez, January 1982)

Other members of Guille felt that a job in the cooperative was better than working in the maquilas because "you don't get sexually harassed and you have a large community of women around you that makes you feel safer."[14]

The establishment of the first two cooperatives was another important turning point in COMO's development. From 1975 forward, the center focused much of its efforts on linking factory struggles with community organizing, drawing largely from its experiences with Guille and SOCOSEMA. During this period, COMO not only promoted cooperatives, but itself took the first steps toward a self-managed organizational form. Maquila women workers began to develop their own initiatives and utilized the center as a place to strengthen their own networks or as a source of political and economic support. Moreover, the ideological perspective of the organization shifted away from philanthropy and *beneficiencia* to community organization and development. This shift was to a large extent the result of maquila management's rejection of COMO, but the organization nevertheless shrewdly managed to establish a beachhead in the industry.

Between 1975 and 1977, the educational program was reorganized and formalized. Prior to 1975, courses at COMO were for the most part informally organized, often spontaneous, and covered largely unrelated subjects ranging from consciousness-raising to weaving and other handicrafts. Curriculum development after 1975 incorporated areas of concern and interest expressed by maquila workers. Course offerings came to include English, psychology, library science, typing and other clerical skills, weaving, and even yoga. Additionally, a variety of experimental training programs in nursing, social work, public education, personnel management, and secretarial work were initiated.

Thus, the period between 1975 and 1977 involved integration of maquila workers as the core constituency of COMO. This integration signified acceptance of the center by workers. The period also witnessed the first, albeit limited, response to layoffs in the maquilas with the establishment of the Guille co-op. COMO also took steps toward formalizing the organization by preparing for incorporation as a "civil association." The center revamped its curriculum and instituted a larger capacity for training. This period led to acceptance of the center by public-health organizations—for example, the Secretaria de Salubridad y Asistencia.[15] The period also witnessed the development of the first links with the so-called marginalized communities of Ciudad Juárez (the principal example of these being SOCOSEMA).

SELF-MANAGEMENT AND COMMUNITY
AND LABOR ACTIVISM: 1978–1983

From 1978 through 1983, COMO underwent major changes in its scope of activities, political agendas, organizational structure, and funding base. Formal incorporation was completed in January 1978. The center was recognized by UCECA (Unidad Coordinadora para el Empleo, Capacitación y Adiestramiento),[16] a federal agency that promotes on-the-job training for industrial workers. Formal incorporation and recognition by UCECA were indicative of COMO's legitimacy as a viable community-based organization. In addition, for the first time the center received funding from the Inter-American Foundation (IAF), in 1978 and 1980.[17] A key development throughout the period of 1980 to 1983 involved the establishment of a program of *promotores externos,* student-workers acting as community organizers and labor activists. The significance of the *promotores* program was twofold. On the one hand, it formalized the role of maquila women workers as agents of community organizing, self-management, and labor struggles. On the other hand, it provided a stable vehicle for the elaboration of links between factory and community struggles.

It was largely through the organizing activities of *promotores* that COMO asserted and maintained its presence in the working-class community. The *promotores* were the key to supporting the cooperative movement, circulating solidarity among different sectors of the Juárez working class, and developing outreach in the form of intensive basic education centers (CEBIs, Centros de Educación Básica Intensiva).[18] *Promotores* provided ongoing advice, counseling, and logistical support to farmworkers and farmers (*ejidatarios*) in the Juárez Valley, to worker cooperatives, and to maquila workers' independent unions and coalitions. This organizing strategy provided maquila workers with an opportunity to begin redefining their social roles and attitudes, and the very nature of community development in Juárez. As María P. Fernández-Kelly, a former guest researcher at the center, observes:

> It is COMO's intent to provide women with information and ethical guidelines which will transform them into "social promoters" capable of bringing about and mediating constructive change. In doing this, COMO opens economic and political alternatives for women who are seldom noticed or appreciated in their full potential.[19]

The desire to encourage "social promotion" required a more systematic educational program, and this led to the establishment of a critical, neo-Freirean curriculum.[20] In 1979, COMO began developing and implementing a new educational program. The program offered *certificados de auxilio* (auxiliary certificates endorsed by UCECA) in four main areas: public education (principally the training of literacy instructors for the CEBIs), personnel management (discontinued in 1982), public-sector nursing, and social work. Before pursuing specialized training in one of the four areas, all student-workers attended the *tronco común,* a six-month-long promotional course focusing on consciousness-raising, critical analysis of the maquiladoras, study of transnational capitalism, and workers' recognition of their history-making and social-change capacities.

A related innovation during this period involved the *brigadas de investigación* (research brigades). The *brigadas* provided a vehicle for student research in their own communities and factories. *Brigada* research was linked to a variety of other activities and struggles—for example, to the *autodidáctica* (self-teaching) activities of the student-workers. The entire learning process unfolded in dialectical fashion: concepts and problems were collectively identified in class; groups split up into collaborative teams that designed and conducted field research; the teams returned to class and assessed research findings in collective discourse, criticizing earlier views and perspectives; then, the teams returned to their communities or factories in an attempt to apply their research findings.

The praxeological unity between external promotion, the *tronco común,* and the *brigadas* represented an immense leap forward in COMO's organizational diversity, networking capacity, and ability to conduct field-based research. During this period, the center blended self-management, self-directed and social-problem-solving education, and "change agent" principles.[21] Workers' autonomy and community self-organizing were increasingly important as guiding principles. The role of COMO in the CEBI educational outreach centers demonstrates this search for unity among external promotion, training, and research activities.

In 1980, COMO was contracted by the Comisión Nacional de Fomento Educativo (CONAFE, National Commission for Educational Development) to participate in the CEBI project. The CEBIs, as mentioned earlier, are outreach education centers that provide literacy instruction to children, adolescents, and adults living in "marginalized" communities. Collaborating with CONAFE and the National Polytechnic Institute (IPN), COMO staff and *promotores* conducted research, developed training guidelines, and contributed to teaching methods and the curriculum as part of the effort to establish CEBIs in some of the most impoverished areas of Ciudad Juárez.

In the course of conducting research, external promoters utilized a tactic referred to as "socially relevant activity." Through this tactic, members of a particular targeted community participated in the research and planning process. One COMO *promotora* summarized the political bonding and reciprocity of this approach as it occurred in 1982:

> [T]hrough us, people in the community can pool together knowledge of their own communities. . . . We serve as a local nucleus for meetings and discussions. . . . Even in the Colonia Libertad CEBI, the children we teach get involved in researching the problems of the community. I remember one time we had asked the children to go out and learn about the housing in the area. These kids . . . are eleven, twelve—sometimes younger or older. But they can do these things very well, they are very eager. A few of them came back and told us that they had found some houses that looked like fire hazards. The children's discovery did not go unnoticed. It led to agitation for building materials and better fire protection. (Interview, Ciudad Juárez, February 1982)

As CEBI instructors, *promotores* circulated struggle by sharing the problem-solving skills that they learned at COMO and in the maquilas. The *promotores* also participated in collective actions with self-organized groups in the Juárez working-class community. Through *autodidáctica* and *autogestión,* the external promoters became agents of social change and community organizing and thus redefined their own political roles.[22] The pedagogy of socially relevant problem solving became a vehicle for community organizing and individual change.

By 1981, the majority of *promotores* and students associated with COMO were former maquila workers. Juárez assembly plants had over forty thousand employees, but there had been periods with major layoffs, plant closings and relocations, violence against striking workers, and wage reductions (especially between 1974 and 1975 and between 1976 and 1980). Of course, there was also the incessant speedup of the Fordist assembly lines. Many of the workers who were laid off by plant closings, who left the plants exhausted by productivity pressures, or who were terminated for their militancy came to COMO as students, as volunteer or paid staff members, or as drifting activists.

Workers' lived experiences in the factories had a definite impact on their development as social promoters and labor activists. Many of the women maquila workers who joined COMO in 1980 and 1981 had participated in output-restriction networks or had been active in rank-and-file "grievance groups," independent unions, and informal worker coalitions.[23] One former maquila worker, who to this day continues her involvement with farmer cooperatives in the Juárez Valley, noted the importance of her experiences on the assembly line:

> As much as I hated my job in the factory, I have to admit that I learned a lot. . . . I learned that workers can do a lot of self-organizing. Maybe it's the way the plant itself is organized [shades of Austin Lewis?]. I mean, here you have this immense place, with assembly lines running up and down the length of the building. And while it may seem somewhat chaotic, there was a lot of order, a lot of interdependency. (Interview, Ciudad Juárez, February 1982)

COMO provided an atmosphere that encouraged the development of a critical, ideological view of the possibilities for change. But workers' experiences in the maquilas also influenced the organization to focus on systemic change in the workplace *and* community. Continuing struggles against layoffs and antistrike violence shaped the center's agenda throughout this period. Rising food, utility, and rental prices, access to adequate housing and potable water in marginal *colonias,* the survival of *ejido* farm cooperatives in the Juárez Valley, and the forced relocations of squatter communities were also major concerns of the student-workers and staff.

Juárez has a remarkably persistent history of confrontations between "popular sectors" and *charrista* unionists, military and police forces, and maquila management. It is a history marked also by manipulation or suppression of popular movements through graft, patronage, violence, and harassment.[24] Some of these popular organizations include the Comité pro Defensa Popular (CDP), the students of ESAHE (Escuela Superior de Agricultura Hermanos Escobar), the Acapulco Fashions independent union, the cotton farmers of the Juárez Valley, and myriad smaller groups, including self-help and legal-aid organizations (e.g., Despacho Obrero) and informal coalitions of maquila workers.[25]

While not directly involved in any of these organizations, COMO shared in many of these struggles. The center's *promotores* became directly involved in many of these organizations by promoting solidarity networks and circulating information and resources. During this time, street protests, bridge and road blockades, spontaneous work stoppages and wildcat strikes, and land occupations all became commonplace in Juárez. Maquila workers were involved in many of these protests. Moreover, former maquila workers headed the establishment of labor law and occupational health and safety study groups both within COMO and in other organizational settings.

To an extent, the traditional differences that divided the popular sector from other sectors of the Juárez working class were overcome through the social-problem-solving activities of student-workers and *promotores*. Between 1968 and 1981, all sectors of the Juárez working class experienced "generalized austerity and marginality."[26] Maquila workers shared a similar set of experiences involving difficulties with subsistence, housing, and health. They articulated these as a common set of demands and struggles in order to unite the various sectors into one mass movement. COMO's strength during this period resided in the resilience, autonomy, creativity, and linkage-building capacities of its external promoters, the former maquila workers. Maquila workers and other groups not formally affiliated with the center circulated the struggle *through* the organization. In other words, COMO—particularly between 1979 and 1983—became a nerve center for the self-organizing activities of maquila workers, farmers and farmworkers, *colonos* and squatters, and progressive educators, researchers, and lawyers.

By 1981, activities focused on building links with other sectors of the working class. An estimated four thousand maquila workers had by then participated in educational, outreach, and external promotion programs while another two thousand persons in several hundred families had worked with the organization in establishing self-managed cooperatives. Hundreds of maquila workers had participated in *brigada* research projects, and equal numbers were members of the informal self-help groups that gravitated to COMO. These rank-and-file initiatives had a profound impact on the organization's development. The activity of maquila workers at a number of Juárez assembly factories circulated struggles to the center, increasing the organization's involvement in industrial conflicts. For example, in 1980 a series of worker-management confrontations at Convertors (a subsidiary of American Hospital Supply Company) pulled COMO deeper into the self-organizing efforts of its student-workers. Relations were also established with the independent unions involved in the protracted strikes at Acapulco Fashions and Electrocomponentes. The center provided logistical support and tactical advice, raised funds, promoted self-help and solidarity networks, and issued press proclamations and denunciations.

Throughout the 1981–83 period, rank-and-file activity at COMO also directly contributed to transforming its curricular subject matter and training priorities. The *tronco común* shifted emphasis toward a range of shop-floor–oriented problem-solving projects.[27] Action-oriented projects developed independently by student-workers became the core experiential activity. During this period, the *tronco común* still focused on critical analysis of the internationalization of capital. But the *brigadas* pursued some new concerns, which included the political and wage effects of "deskilling"; defining strategies for industrial apprenticeship programs and self-managed, community-based cooperatives; exploring the possibilities for north-to-south technology transfers; and gaining recognition for deskilled labor's inventive force.[28] Discussions in the *tronco común* also focused on the history and forms of capitalist labor-process organization; on labor struggles in Mexican history, with an emphasis on the contributions of women; and on new forms of working-class organization. These student-workers were redefining the nature of development in the border region by pointing toward self-managed cooperative organizational forms. Meanwhile, the politics of production in the maquiladoras became a major focus of *brigada* research projects. The character of the changes in the relationship between COMO and its maquila-worker constituency was indicative of a type of organizational change that was largely initiated by the workers' autonomous research activities and workplace struggles. The center provided the ideological and analytical resources for the development of these initiatives. As one former RCA worker observed:

> The struggles were germinating [*brotando*] because we were working in two spaces, the factory and COMO. It was like living a double life. But we had the benefit of a place where we could critically discuss and analyze the problems that we confronted in the factory. COMO was a mirror for us. *El espejo de la doble explotación* [the mirror of double exploitation]. At COMO I came to understand my exploitation as a woman and as a worker. And if what you saw in the mirror was ugly, then you had to take the responsibility, and you had to improve your methods of resistance, in challenging the exploitation. (Interview, Ciudad Juárez, July 1984)

"Germinating" their militancy in individual, usually isolated acts of resistance and sabotage, and then moving to informal shop-floor group actions (work stoppages), maquila student-workers at COMO were gradually transformed into full-fledged organizers. Of the sixty student-workers I interviewed in 1981–82, over 30 percent were members of informal shop-floor networks—compared to only 15 percent for the total sample of 223.[29] Such workers were more active as external promoters or in the multitude of other roles available at the center.

Ideologically, COMO's orientation in 1981–83 was the culmination of a transition that began in 1977, a transition from a focus on community organization and development to a renewed emphasis on the "politicized" individual woman. It may seem somewhat contradictory that this shift in educational philosophy came at a time when the links between students and the diverse sectors of the Juárez working-class community were expanding and solidifying. However, COMO's return to an apparently individualist focus was politicized—its starting point being the collectively defined priorities and experiences of its organizers, students, *promotores,* and cooperative members.

An internal evaluation, prepared in 1981 by center staff and participating students, listed the following accomplishments: restructuring of the educational program (principally due to worker-initiated changes in the *tronco común*), entry of students into new labor markets (especially in nursing, social work, and public education), and acceptance of COMO by UCECA and CONAFE. The underlying current during this period involved activities by *promotores* and *brigada* research teams, which promoted solidarity among the various sectors of the Juárez working-class community. Toward the end of 1981, COMO was receiving considerable international visibility and recognition by scholars, researchers, and foundations in the United States, West Germany, Canada, and France, as well as in Mexico and other Latin American countries. For example, the Friedrich Ebert Foundation of West Germany, an organization dedicated to promoting and funding women's grassroots development organizations in the third world, accepted a proposal for the study of industrial apprenticeship and appropriate technology transfers.

CRISIS AND RETRENCHMENT: 1983–1985

Since 1978, COMO had established close relations with scholars from the United States, Mexico, Canada, and Western Europe. But in 1981–82, the center increased its capacity to undertake independent research projects with an aim toward social action. Important advances were made in terms of methodological rigor, funding, policy relevance, and linkage with other researchers.[30] These advances were exemplified by COMO's first, and unfortunately last, major sponsored research project: its capstone study of industrial apprenticeship in the maquiladoras.[31] This research project was critical to the development of what Guillermina Valdés called a "transference methodology." This was a plan for transferring maquila workers' tacit skills and working knowledge to other branches of production and to community organizing efforts. Research would contribute to the "transference" of skills through an "inductive apprenticeship" in industrial production:

> The results of the project would permit COMO and the female working-class sector to offer to the public, academic, and private sectors information and statistics that present the reality of the woman worker and her

crossroads, and that could counteract the many investigations that have superficially concluded that the woman worker—having been educated by her relatives and country exclusively for the purpose of complying with the requirements of . . . transnational corporations that demand sixth-grade completion and secondary or its equivalent, and who within a labor experience has been deskilled—does not possess any knowledge transferable to other branches of production or the national economy.[32]

The transference methodology challenged the conclusions of most researchers, who depicted maquila workers as "unskilled" or "deskilled." It revalued the knowledge and skills of the industrial worker. And it explicitly linked industrial apprenticeship with the formation of worker-owned and self-managed cooperatives:

The systematization of this knowledge, linked to an adequate methodology that complements what the workers already know . . . would permit groups of women workers to establish their own companies, taking advantage of . . . the national conjuncture that has pushed cooperative societies as a form of creating employment.[33]

This strategy for worker-directed development issued a serious challenge to transnational corporations operating maquilas in the border region.[34] The transference methodology challenged the dominance of the export-oriented development model. It was designed to empower workers in confronting the major problems posed by the dominant model: extremely dangerous productivity pressures and other hazards, high turnover rates, and a refusal by management to recognize skilled labor.

Throughout this period, COMO's strategy for autonomous development was based on the principles of workers' self-organization and community self-reliance, confronting policies seen as fetters to economic democracy and social justice:

[T]he woman worker will count with a tool, a weapon that will permit her to demand that the development policies of the border zone are not focused exclusively on promotion and attraction of transnational firms or on exportation, but rather on an authentic industrialization of the zone, coherently linked to the national economy. At the same time, the demand could be made for the removal of the fiscal restrictions that impede border production, and with national support promote . . . those companies in the hands of the workers . . . so that they [the companies] can satisfy without intermediaries . . . the necessities in basic consumer goods required by the workers and marginalized groups.[35]

This strategy redefined the development process in the border region by first of all questioning the wisdom of export-led industrialization. The maquilas were problematic not just because the jobs they offered were low waged and hazardous. The transnational corporations did not produce for the national market, and especially not for the subsistence needs of the border working class. The point was for the workers to control their own production systems and produce for their own communities. COMO thus focused oɪ̩ what it defined as the major barrier in linking the industrial and the popular sectors of the border working class: the struggle over basic necessities. The women's center envisioned a project that would eliminate dependence on transnationals for employment and on local intermediaries for basic goods. The key to self-reliance and economic democracy lay in developing worker- and community-owned cooperatives as centerpieces of a grand experiment in *autogestión*.

By 1983, COMO had arrived at a critical crossroads. Its capacity for community organizing and research and development activities had matured. *Promotores* had increased their level of participation in the struggles of *colonos* for potable water supplies, street improvements, adequate housing, and education for marginalized children, adolescents, and adults. Some of the external promoters and students from COMO collaborated with the farmers from the Juárez Valley. They participated in road and bridge blockades and called for federal price supports and credits to assist *ejidatarios* in dealing with the crisis in the domestic cotton market. Student-workers and external promoters continued collaborating with SOCOSEMA, which was under attack by local politicians wishing to reprivatize and "industrialize" recycling operations at the municipal dump. The rest of COMO's cooperatives survived the effects of a protracted Mexican economic crisis (more *peso* devaluations, continued inflation, and unemployment). The organization continued its work with the CEBIs and served hundreds of illiterate children, adolescents, and adults through its *primaria abierta* (open primary) and *secundaria* (secondary) education programs. *Promotores* continued to play critical roles in public meetings, protests, and other organizing initiatives among maquila workers.

However, serious problems faced the organization toward the end of 1983. In an internal evaluation prepared by COMO, staff members identified a number of central problems: (1) rejection of COMO by the maquiladoras, (2) continuing limits on job opportunities for graduates, (3) insufficient funding and overdependence on volunteers, (4) a lack of administrative experience in organizing and maintaining the cooperatives, (5) ineffective acceptance by UCECA, (6) little development of the personnel-management training program, and (7) the decline of the workers' council (*consejo obrero*) that had been established in 1981 to formalize worker participation in the center's administration.

Among these problems, the lack of administrative skills and the decline of the workers' council stood out. Lack of administrative skills created problems for COMO in its efforts to assist cooperatives, particularly in dealing with banks and federal agencies. The decline of the workers' council was a setback to a more substantive self-managed organizational structure. Nevertheless, the continuing presence and participation of maquila women workers (as external promoters, organizers, researchers, and students) suggests a de facto, if less obvious, persistence of rank-and-file autonomy within the organization. The decline of the workers' council limited only the *formal* participation of workers in direct administration of the organization. But COMO, like the maquilas, had a subaltern life of its own, and informal networks and self-help groups continued to flourish both within and through the organization. The mirror of exploitation was not shattered by the collapse of the workers' council.

The critical turning point came between 1982 and 1984, when the organization was subject to internal and external evaluations. The internal evaluation provided an important opportunity for critical self-reflection and reorientation. Internal evaluation led to a restructuring of relationships with visiting researchers. It also led to a revamping of the *tronco común,* a streamlining of specialized training programs (including the elimination of the personnel-management track), and greater administrative independence for the affiliated cooperatives. However, the external evaluation proved cumbersome and somewhat damaging. The IAF, as COMO's main source of funding, directed the external evaluation, which began in 1982 and ended in 1984.[36] The IAF evaluation concluded that the organizational structure, while "flat" and lacking hierarchy, was too dependent on its director (Guillermina Valdés), particularly in the areas of information and communication. This evaluation, however, assumed that the core group of twenty-two paid staff members was in fact the organizing nucleus of the organization. This assumption was unwarranted in light of my research, which demonstrates the independence of maquila student-workers in relation to the staff and director.

The evaluation ignored the subaltern life of the organization, very likely because the evaluators did not spend enough time observing the dynamics of small groups and informal networks and instead focused on executing a formal evaluation design. The student-workers from the maquilas and other groups from the Juárez working-class community used COMO as a "liberated political space" for self-organizing struggles. The consistent appropriation by the student-workers of the learning and networking resources available at the center was completely overlooked by the evaluation team.[37] These subaltern and sub-rosa dynamics were by their nature not self-evident; they remained hidden as intimate whispers and off-the-record conversations workers shared between classes or on the way back home or to work. These were "personal narratives" and could not have been detected through formal interviews or discussion sessions with the staff and director.[38]

I am reminded here of Renato Rosaldo's critique of classic norms in anthropology, namely the objectivist model of "distanced normalizing description." As Rosaldo eloquently states:

> Although personal narratives often appear in ethnographies written in the classic mode, they usually have been relegated quite literally to the margins: prefaces, introductions, afterwords, footnotes, and italicized small-print case histories. In fact, the classic norms usually achieved their authority at the expense of personal narratives and case histories. Yet the latter forms often facilitate the analysis of social processes that have proven difficult to perceive through distanced normalizing discourse.[39]

It is clear to me that the reports by the external evaluation teams were examples of distanced normalizing discourse; that is, attempts at "objectivity," at detached observation and analysis. It was a case of the worse pretensions that we have in the social sciences today, where the analysts imitate the objectivist norms of the natural sciences. This is why the team was so intent on doing things like "pre-tests" and "post-tests" armed with a battery of culturally biased questionnaires that sought to measure the "empowerment" and "ideological transformation" of the student-workers at COMO on the basis of Western feminist values.

Unfortunately, the IAF evaluation produced serious political problems in Washington, D.C. Some COMO student-workers and staff interpreted the external evaluation as a political effort by unknown opponents to undermine the organization's already fragile economic base.[40] In fact, after the election of Ronald Reagan in 1980, the IAF board of directors was reorganized to include a number of new political appointees. Among the new appointees was Thomas Enders, a hawkish anticommunist from the State Department and a frequent, hostile opponent of funding for self-management and alternative-development projects in Latin America.[41] By the end of March 1984, the IAF had terminated funding for COMO. If I may indulge in some speculation: It may very well be that the "transference methodology" was the real reason that the IAF terminated funding. The project was perhaps just too radical for the right-wingers in the Reagan IAF to stomach. Imagine Enders in a meeting somewhere going on about how COMO was the seed for another "Evil Empire," this one in "America's Backyard," as Mexico is often described by those imperialists with a nostalgia for the good old days when the "little brown people" stayed happily in their place.

Another aspect of organizational crisis during the 1983–84 period had to do with the declining and less direct role of the center's staff in industrial workers' struggles. For a time, the core staff group became somewhat ambivalent and restrained about direct involvement in the struggles of industrial workers.[42] This was not a consequence of co-optation or a less militant stance. There were historical reasons. After 1981, the core staff increasingly shifted focus from supporting labor struggles in the maquilas to promoting cooperative economic development. However, the defeat of the Acapulco Fashions independent-union strike left many former student-workers who had been active in that struggle feeling frustrated. They may have misread the center's intentions and strategies. In any event, by the end of 1984 fewer rank-and-file activists were gravitating to COMO. Fewer informal groups and coalitions were meeting there to network. In a word, the prominence of rank-and-file activity was waning. The number of students in the *tronco común* declined. Moreover, the general climate of industrial relations in the maquilas as a whole had shifted: there were fewer slowdowns, walkouts, and wildcat and legal strikes in Juárez in 1984 and 1985 than in 1979 to 1983. This is not to deny the profound impact the center had on several thousand maquila workers who studied there and who have continued their activism after leaving the organization. After 1984, the cooperative societies affiliated with COMO became increasingly independent, particularly in terms of administrative and planning functions. This autonomy was all the more important with the funding and staffing of the organization deteriorating as it did between 1984 and 1985. The claim by the IAF evaluation teams that the survival of the co-ops would be jeopardized by overdependence on COMO for administrative and technical direction proved erroneous.

Late in September 1984, COMO had exhausted funding resources. It was forced to operate with a significantly reduced, all-volunteer staff. From this time until the spring of 1985, liaison with the co-ops had been all but eliminated. The organization was in a period of retrenchment. The cooperatives continued to function as economically viable and independent entities. SOCOSEMA survived a particularly difficult period of political attacks by corporate and governmental powers, including a threatened takeover of the municipal dump by a proposed consortium of

Mexican and U.S. investors. The Guille co-op also survived, and to this day remains a profitable enterprise under complete worker ownership and self-management. The various farm co-ops also survive, despite continued problems with access to fertilizer and equipment credits and accounting battles with Rural Bank (Banrural) officials. The damage that NAFTA may inflict on the farm co-ops remains to be seen. And despite the end of COMO's involvement with the CEBI training programs, a former *promotora* continues to direct nine CEBI projects in Ciudad Juárez.

Beyond the loss of paid staff and students, the main casualty of the crisis was the *tronco común*. Reduced in scope and then discontinued during the fall of 1984, the promotional course had been an important source of rank-and-file activity between 1979 and 1983. The *tronco común*, through the formation and activities of the research brigades, had undoubtedly increased the level of autonomous struggles circulated by the student-workers. Unfortunately, without funding and adequate staff, the struggles associated with rank-and-file research and self-organizing efforts would no longer be mobilized by COMO. A wonderful "liberated political space" had been severely damaged.

DEPARTURES, NEW LINKS, TWO COMOS? 1985–1990

A former staff member of the IAF describes the situation after 1985 as involving the co-optation of COMO by the PRI (Partido Revolucionario Institucional).[43] The PRI and the Education Ministry had earlier approached the center with promises of financial support, but the offers were always firmly rejected. In mid 1985, after Guillermina Valdés resigned from the COMO directorship and assumed a full-time position with CEFNOMEX (later COLEF, Colegio de la Frontera Norte), the Mexican government provided a six-month, $50,000 grant to fund a program for Juárez working-class men and women. By the summer of 1986, COMO was apparently back on track with a full-time, paid staff of eight and seven part-time teachers on contract.[44]

This turn of events led some observers to conclude that the PRI had co-opted COMO because it expected the organization to deliver the "women's vote" at a time when a major opposition party, the PAN (Partido de Acción Nacional), was ascendant in Juárez and other northern border cities.[45] This interpretation overlooks several key factors. Throughout this period, COMO renewed its links with maquila workers. In fact, between 1985 and 1989 the center supported a variety of independent workers' unions and wildcat strikes. The 1986 RCA strike, involving more than three thousand workers, was strongly supported by the center.[46] It must be remembered that by 1985 the PRI was a staunch supporter of maquiladora industrialization. Why would the party support an organization with a consistent legacy of opposition to maquilas and a strong record of organizing support for militant independent workers' groups? If it hoped to co-opt the organization, it certainly did not accomplish this by imposing a more moderate or even pro-maquila stance. If the PRI believed COMO would "deliver the women's vote," it certainly misjudged the organization's willingness to act as an influential force in local *electoral* politics. The co-optation argument seems too simplistic.

A more intriguing argument is offered by the Canadian political scientist Kathryn Kopinak.[47] In 1988, Kopinak interviewed Guillermina Valdés de Villalva and concluded that, after 1985, there were in reality "two COMOs." As Kopinak states:

> Villalva says that now there are two COMOs. Men are the visible leaders
> of the government-funded COMO, and it serves young men who work in
> the informal sector as well as women and men maquiladora workers. . . .
> I believe the second COMO she spoke of is the one described in the video-
> tape [*Pepenadores: Down, but Not Out*], the one which the Church asked
> Guillermina to form, and with which she developed her own religious po-
> liticizing process. The second COMO is the St. John the Baptist Commu-
> nity. . . . Villalva says that it was the economic crisis and the political stress
> it has caused in Mexico since 1986 which has created the separation and
> distance between the two COMOs.[48]

Kopinak argues that Guillermina Valdés utilized her contacts and experience in the religious community to organize the "new" COMO. Valdés, in fact, did have a long-standing relationship with the more progressive segments of the Charismatic Catholic movement in Juárez dating back to the early 1970s.[49] Again, Kopinak:

> Villalva was an intellectual who had a lifelong commitment to social jus-
> tice; while she herself was an atheist, she had been intellectually interested
> in how U.S. Blacks and Chicanos had used religion in their respective civil
> rights movements. She was socially involved in her community giving lec-
> tures from a Marxist perspective in the technical schools and colleges on
> issues such as Mexican migrant labourers to the U.S., commuting workers,
> etc. Her work with priests who were also committed to reducing the sense
> of anomie in Juárez led to discussions about whether the holy spirit could
> be seen as the new person who needed to emerge in order to deal with so-
> cietal changes.[50]

In March 1984, after the IAF had terminated funding, Guillermina Valdés was stricken with a serious illness. She was hospitalized in Houston, Texas. During the illness she experienced a second "religious conversion," which led her to forge a more intimate relationship with the St. John the Baptist Community. Many of Valdés's closest professional colleagues were privately dismayed by this conversion. They viewed her renewed religiosity with skepticism. But as Kopinak argues:

> Since Villalva was already deeply involved in building COMO when she underwent her [first] conversion, she began to link the religious and the political in her work there, developing a systematic leadership training process which incorporated both. This was a female leadership because women were more likely to be maquiladora workers and to be religious. When I interviewed her in 1988, she said that she did not agree with Mother Teresa that one should follow people to the grave without political support and help. Villalva considered it naive to think that religious ideas do not have political ramifications.[51]

I agree with Kopinak that after 1985 and COMO's temporary retrenchment Valdés began to more earnestly search for alternative ways of organizing working women and marginalized communities. Many of the members of SOCOSEMA were also involved in the St. John the Baptist Community.[52] It is not surprising that Valdés continued her activist work through religious organizations.

When I was at COMO between 1981 and 1984, Valdés and I had several lengthy discussions about religion and politics. We both shared an interest in liberation theology. I recall telling her that the Virgen de Guadalupe had been an important symbol in the Chicano farmworkers' struggle during the 1960s and 1970s. She responded that perhaps it was time to invent new symbols for the struggle. I also told her about the role of the New Mexican *penitentes,* a folk religious brotherhood, in the struggles of Chicanos against the theft of land grants, and she said that religious organizations had always played a role in politics and that grassroots groups of a religious nature were particularly potent forces for promoting working-class struggle. Valdés was never one to accept the idea that the meek shall inherit the earth.

AN UNTIMELY DEATH, NEW POLITICAL AGENDAS: 1991–1992

In September 1991 a Continental commuter flight from Laredo to Houston crashed, killing all on board. Guillermina Valdés was among the ill-fated passengers. Her death is one of the most profound losses in recent memory for those of us committed to workplace democracy and environmental justice. Valdés did not create the struggle, but she channeled and sustained it. She did not invent the pedagogy of the oppressed, but she made it relevant to the working women of Mexico's *frontera*. She did not create theories of workplace democracy and sustainable development, but in her practice she was the definitive champion of both. She did not invent liberation theology, but she blended religious conviction with political commitment in a manner few are capable of emulating.

No gravestone could be large enough to hold the epitaph that would do justice to Guillermina Valdés and her legacy. I can offer the last words she said to me during an interview in July 1989:

> The maquilas are constantly changing. They always have. And they have always had the necessity of changing—a necessity . . . that is born of the workers' resistance. This presents a special challenge for us. We too must change, adapting our struggles, our organizations and ideologies, to counteract the capitalist strategy. . . . I predict that by the year 2000, there will be thousands of maquilas with more than a million workers. What will our border be like then? It is already burdened with too many people, too much pollution, too many factories, too much of everything except hope. And, to answer your question about my future direction. . . . This is what I see myself directing my work to, creating hope. But not without action. Hope without action is, well, hopeless. But to resort to action without hope is to indulge the worst of human impulses: the idea that we can act in the world without values, orientation, or a view of what the good life should be, *must* be. (Interview, Ciudad Juárez, July 1989)

Since Valdés's death, the two COMOs continue to be active, viable organizations. The St. John the Baptist "COMO" maintains its relationship with the worker cooperatives. This will remain the case as long as the co-op members remain committed to religious life and as long as these experiments in workplace democracy are economically stable. The official COMO was for a short time directed by an ex-*obrera*. A group of workers and staff members asked Guillermina Valdés's daughter, Luchi (Luz María) Villalva, to assume the directorship, which she did in late 1991.[53] The *tronco común* has been reactivated with the familiar emphasis on the activities of the research brigades. This is not surprising, given the historically salient role of the *brigadas* in COMO's research and organizing programs.

But new problems and issues define the center's political agenda. Of particular importance are environmental problems related to maquila industrialization and the North American Free Trade Agreement (NAFTA).

From what I have gathered, COMO has yet to articulate an official position on free trade. On environmental issues, the center has long taken public positions critical of the impact of maquiladoras, particularly in terms of worker health and safety and the toxic contamination of water, air, and soil in the communities surrounding industrial parks and individual plants (many of which are located in residential zones). The concern for worker health and safety as an environmental policy issue has long been a fundamental aspect of COMO's political agenda. It can be expected that the center will continue to embrace these concerns in its research and advocacy programs.

On the problem of NAFTA, according to my sources in Juárez,[54] before Luchi Villalva assumed the directorship, some staff members had internally debated the issue and arrived at four alternatives: (1) support NAFTA if certain environmental-protection and labor-rights standards are incorporated into the final agreement, (2) support NAFTA regardless of how it deals with environmental-protection and labor-rights issues with an understanding that the "system integration" process may eventually result in the upgrading of standards on the Mexican side of the border, (3) reject NAFTA under any circumstances as a threat to national sovereignty, working-class autonomy, and environmental integrity, and (4) take no stand. The largest group in COMO seems to favor the more moderate stance: support NAFTA, then work to improve standards and hope integration helps the process along. The understanding in 1990–91 was that the Mexican government would not accept anything but approval of NAFTA and that the best COMO could hope for was to position itself to pressure for the improvement of standards over time, once integration took place. But there are those who are opposed to "integration" in principle and resist even partial endorsement of NAFTA. This debate is still being sorted out within the organization.

COMO has consistently survived crises; in fact, it is probably safe to say that no developmental stage in the organization's history was free of some type of crisis. As long as maquila and other workers experience conflict and exploitation in their workplaces there will be a need for an organization such as COMO to step into the breach caused by the corruption of official unions and arbitration boards and the ineffectiveness of legal strikes. With the emergence of Luchi Villalva as director, workers will continue to circulate their struggles to the women's center out of necessity and because they recognize and value the legacy left by a spirited and imaginative organizer who spoke directly to their needs and strategies.

From the Factory to the Community:
Native Ethnographies

This history would remain incomplete without hearing more from the former maquila workers who became activists and organizers at COMO. What follows are lengthy excerpts from two of the five oral histories I conducted with members of the staff between 1981 and 1984. These narratives tell us much about the circulation of struggle from the factory to the community. They speak to the creativity and inventiveness of the workers, students, and staff at COMO. And they indicate the changing identities and alliances crafted by former maquila workers in circulating the struggle and creating a bit of history themselves.

MARISA TORRES

Born in Allende, Durango, Marisa Torres is a former maquila worker who was with COMO throughout the late 1970s and 1980s as a liaison to the farm cooperatives in the Juárez Valley. She migrated to Ciudad Juárez with her mother, two brothers, and a sister. She was but five months old when her family moved to live and work in Juárez. Torres was twenty-seven years old when I interviewed her at COMO in 1982. I asked her about her experiences as a maquila worker.

> I started way back in November 1969 at RCA. The plant had just opened.
> It was the first plant at Bermúdez [Industrial] Park. Back then it was a
> pretty small operation. . . . RCA was the only plant I ever worked at. I quit
> in July 1978 . . . because I became involved with COMO. I never really
> liked my factory job. I started as a line worker but was eventually pro-
> moted to group chief. It was as group chief that I was involved in some
> struggles. You see, by that time [1977] RCA had three different plants at
> the park. The group chiefs from two of the plants drafted a set of de-
> mands. Some of these demands were quite petty, the others were good.
> The group chiefs from plants one and two wanted recognition as group
> chiefs. For them this included the right to get to work tardy and the right
> to leave early if they so desired. They also wanted better and different uni-
> forms from the rest of the workers, made of finer materials, something to
> distinguish themselves. They also wanted parking spaces with their names
> on them. The group chiefs from plant three, of which I was sort of infor-
> mal leader, refused to go along with the demands. We suggested that we
> first sit down and review the demands. That way we could decide which
> were useful. (Interview, Ciudad Juárez, March 1982)

Marisa Torres's characterization of the group chiefs' demands as "quite petty" is interesting because it brings into sharp relief the possible co-optation of rate-busters. Torres frowned on the idea that "privilege" meant getting a parking space with your name on it. She was also critical of the demand for new uniforms to "distinguish" some workers from others, seeing this as ultimately divisive. The group she belonged to articulated what she saw as a more radical set of demands:

> The managers were surprised by our refusal to accept . . . these demands. So they called us in and asked why we didn't want to go along. We told them the demands were a farce, they were cosmetic issues. . . . We were more interested in long-term problems. Most important for us was the wage question. We told the managers that if they were serious . . . then they should begin with the wage question. We demanded . . . a wage increase. Better yet, we asked for the minimum professional wage. This would force them to recognize us as professional, technical workers. We also made the demand for the establishment of a fellowship program. We wanted money to go to school, to study. The idea was to get training to become technical workers. This would mean more income. It would also open up the possibility of promotions to higher levels. Group chief was the highest promotion women could get under the RCA system. In response, they offered to establish some courses . . . dealing with human relations. They thought we would be thrilled by the prospect of learning more about how to manipulate line workers, which is what "human relations" are really all about. Our demands were not resolved. The internal divisions were bad you know, between us and the other group chiefs. They were threatened by the militancy of our demands, maybe embarrassed at the pettiness of their own demands. . . . We returned to the managers with the same set of proposals and they turned us down again. The managers said they could not support a higher wage and less so a fellowship, since there were too many limitations. One of the managers told us that since we were women, after age twenty-three we would all get married, have children, and start missing work and stop going to classes. He said, "If we give you fellowships you won't finish." He thought that we would either get bored or married, so that the investment on their part was not worth the risk. This really angered us. We organized a work stoppage [*paro*]. This went on for a whole day but in the end we were defeated. Some of us were fired, others were reprimanded. The threats were heavy and it pretty much shook up the organizers. You know, it is more difficult to organize and struggle in a transnational firm than in a national company. It will never be possible to really win struggles in the maquilas. (Interview, Ciudad Juárez, March 1982)

Torres's experiences were similar to those of other COMO staff members and students. While working in the maquiladoras she had to confront a patriarchal system, a workplace characterized by a gender-based division of labor and atrocious sexism on the part of managers and supervisors. In the process, she became involved in many struggles, experiencing what she describes as increasing militancy. In fact, some of the demands articulated by the network of group chiefs she belonged to struck at the core of some critical contradictions in the maquilas. The technical and skilled nature of much of the work performed by assembly-line workers is legally and managerially defined as deskilled, or unskilled. This justifies a lower wage regime for most maquila workers. Arguing for a transition to a higher (technical labor) wage regime was a radical demand because it challenged management's definition of maquila work as deskilled and thus low-waged (see chapter 6 for further discussion). But her experience with continuous defeats at the hands of management give an edge of cynicism to her view of the prospects for workers' struggles in the maquilas.

Marisa Torres's experience was typical of many of the student-workers I interviewed. Even before she came to COMO, the workplace was a setting that fomented her participation in self-organizing and encouraged a heightened awareness of class conflict and sexism. Her affiliation with the women's center strengthened her organizing skills and an ability to work with other groups of workers. Torres described her experiences at COMO:

> As I said, 1977 was my first year. This first year I spent as one of the first students to attend courses at COMO. . . . I was studying in the area of personnel management. This first year, the course was really a lot of self-directed study. It was a time of discovery and searching. I was living a certain reality but was not really aware of it. You know how sometimes you live through something without recognizing it for what it really is. It was like that with me then. Involved but somewhat unaware of the meaning of what I was doing. . . . In 1978, I became a *promotora* at COMO. We were trying to organize a workers' council. My tasks were to promote COMO internally and externally. We organized seminars dealing with issues affecting maquila workers. That was one of the purposes of the council, to promote knowledge and information among maquila workers. . . . Toward the end of 1978, I left RCA and became a full-time COMO staff worker. . . . In 1979, I became more involved in specific COMO projects. I started to help . . . with the SOCOSEMA project. . . . In the afternoons I helped with personnel management classes. (Interview, Ciudad Juárez, March 1982)

Marisa Torres's initial experiences at COMO, like those of other maquila workers, involved a transformation; that is, consciousness-raising, the development of an awareness of her own agency and capacity for practice. Torres eventually came to play a critical role in establishing and strengthening the farmer cooperatives that COMO started promoting in the late 1970s. She was directly involved in the establishment of Vado de Cedillos, one of the first farm co-ops affiliated with the women's center.[55] She recalled her experiences as a farm co-op promoter:

> At the beginning of 1979, that is when the farmers first came to COMO looking for help. Guillermina asked me if I wanted to work with them. I was scared, for I did not know the first thing about farmers. I had grown up in a city and was very unfamiliar with the rural way of life. The farmers are a very special people, yet they have very traditional views of women. They still think that a woman should stay in the home, raising children, keeping the house, not wearing pants, you know, the traditional male view of things. So, I had to break through this in order to work with them. It was not easy at first but soon it all worked out. When the farmers came to COMO they were facing some real serious economic and political problems. As a cooperative, the farmers' organization had been misused by others for political self-interests. A federal congressman [*diputado federal*] had exploited them for his own political purposes. This had caused many legal problems. These problems were totally new to me. At first, it was a struggle to gain acceptance of the group and for me to understand the situation at their workplace, the *ejidos*. I had to study hard on my own to gain an understanding of agriculture, cooperative laws, and the agricultural institutions the farmers deal with. By the end of 1979, the group pretty much had accepted me, and we began to initiate some activities and projects that have carried over to the present. . . . Let me tell you that many of the projects were delayed by the lack of staff—it was a genuine human-resource problem. This cooperative society is a strong organization. It has one hundred and ten *ejidatarios*. In the Juárez Valley [where the co-op operates], the current president . . . is a very highly respected man. He is a real politician. He really helps his people and does not bathe them in a bunch of rhetoric. . . . Unfortunately, prior political problems, including various cases of fraud against the co-op, resulted in a loss of interest on the part of . . . members. They were seriously demoralized. The cooperative also suffered from a lack of capital, seeds and equipment mostly. So, we had to find a way of reorganizing the members, of rekindling the members, of rekindling their interest and morale. We also had to find a way of generating capital. These were the two principal projects. (Interview, Ciudad Juárez, March 1982)

Torres's early experiences as a farm co-op promoter involved a struggle for acceptance. This struggle had to confront the traditional views that male farmers had of women's roles, as well as the farmers' skepticism toward outsiders and toward city people. But acceptance came quite quickly. The farmers were ready to accept help, and the gender of the *pro-motores* was less problematic than would seem to be the case.

Once Marisa Torres gained initial acceptance, she engaged in a long and difficult period of self-directed study to expand her knowledge of agricultural science, cooperative law, and the workings of the various federal banks and agencies charged with administering farm co-ops. During this period of self-study, Torres developed new skills in accounting that she then transferred to the farmers. She explained her efforts to liquidate the debt of the cooperative:

> Most *ejidos* do not keep records of the credit or money they receive from the Banrural. They also do not keep track of their harvest. . . . This was a real problem. The Banrural administers credit through an *ejido* commissioner. The commissioner . . . is seldom an honest man . . . behind him is the entire corrupt bureaucracy of the bank. . . . Banrural did not keep records itself! So, we taught the farmers the necessity of record keeping. . . . We taught them all the basic aspects of accounting. . . . By the end of the first year of dealing with the Banrural [1980], we had developed a good system of accounting. . . . The bank was surprised to find out that we had developed our own internal accounting system. In fact, the bank was very angry because it had never maintained records on money outflows. One reason for [this] was that they could refuse to liquidate our *ejido* debts. . . . We documented our end [and] they were . . . forced to liquidate our credit obligations. This resulted in an increase of 450,000 *pesos* of profit for the co-op in that first year. This really solidified our relationship with the farmers, for after all the early complaints about my being a woman, they were finally seeing the fruit of our common efforts. (Interview, Ciudad Juárez, March 1982)

I asked if she thought her experiences as a maquila worker had increased her ability to learn new things. Torres explained that the organization of the maquila workplace taught "self-organizing" and "interdependency." She further explained this process: "You work the lines, and as a group chief you get to know more about other areas of the plant. Roaming around, I got to learn that way. That is what I think got me to view the world as I do now . . . it really opens up your eyes." The knowledge, skills, and inquisitive character that Torres developed in the maquilas were transferred to her activities as a farm co-op promoter. She spoke of her efforts to get capital credits for the cooperative:

At the start of 1980, the only real alternative was to get the group credit to buy seeds, equipment, fertilizer, and pesticides. Only then could we get production going again. . . . In February 1980, we solicited the Banco Rural for credit. We were turned down. They explained that as reconstituted the co-op would lead to the disintegration of the *ejidos* since they were aided by outsiders [i.e., by COMO]. This was a dubious explanation. . . . In March of 1980, we organized a protest at the Banrural offices in Chihuahua. We wrote letters to Mexico City, to the Ministry of Agriculture and the president's office. By the time we returned from Chihuahua, the credit had been granted. . . . They were perhaps trying to avoid a larger confrontation. There was no doubt that . . . the co-op could have mobilized the entire valley. (Interview, Ciudad Juárez, March 1982)

Marisa Torres noted that the struggles she experienced at RCA long ago convinced her of the need to keep agitating until the opposition surrenders. Torres feels that she has fulfilled the promise of what it means to be an external promoter: women (and men) in positions that enable them to create and mediate individual and group change. Her experiences also capture the dynamics at work in the circulation of struggle from the factory to the rest of the working-class community. When asked about the significance of the links between COMO and the farmers, Torres had this to say:

The link will strengthen because agriculture needs more attention to its industrial aspects. Maquiladora workers are learning about the organization of industrial processes. Therefore, they will be able to help the farmers. . . . We will see greater cooperation in efforts involving rural development, especially those requiring the maquila workers' knowledge. . . . Maquila workers have few alternatives for struggle. The transnationals can always leave if we get well organized. So, maquila workers can seek out the support of farmers and others. . . . Urban workers here are the weak sector. Especially the maquila workers because of the transnational companies. Struggles in national firms, including cooperatives, are easier to win and more fruitful. The two must link. The farmers could support maquila workers through acts of solidarity and through combined economic development efforts. If the maquila workers are given an opportunity to express their technical capacity, their country will have to recognize it. If the farmers acknowledge this force, the government may have to as well. (Interview, Ciudad Juárez, March 1982)

Marisa Torres's experiences demonstrate that maquila workers can become effective and imaginative organizers. She is an example of how COMO empowered maquila workers to circulate struggle from the factory to the community. Her inventiveness is obvious in her ability to master new skills, such as accounting, which she then transfers to other sectors of the Juárez working-class and farming communities.

LUPE VALLES

Guadalupe Valles migrated to Ciudad Juárez from a rural community in central Mexico. She was born in Chalchihuites, Zacatecas, and came to Juárez in 1969 to join four of her sisters. Lupe Valles also worked in the maquilas, first at a glove factory in 1973 and then at Comunicaciones Banda Grande (CBG),[56] between 1974 and 1979. She was thirty-two when she came to work at COMO in 1979. She described her experience at CBG:

> Look, for some time during the recession in 1975 I was laid off at CBG. In 1979, I had problems at the plant. I was very familiar with labor law and I tried to orient the women about it. Personnel management . . . was bothered by this. It was not a daily thing, but the pressure for me to leave was there. So, I voluntarily quit. Who knows what they have listed as my reason for not working there [*this said jokingly, referring to records kept by the local arbitration and conciliation board*]. There was some pressure, mainly a lot of vigilance. Really, they were overly vigilant, always on the look for something to hang me on. (Interview, Ciudad Juárez, February 1982)

Like many other maquila workers, Lupe Valles felt that the working conditions in the plants were problematic. She also felt it was difficult to engage in successful struggle against transnational companies with maquilas in Ciudad Juárez. Nevertheless, she felt that her experience in the maquilas had been a valuable lesson in organizing struggle.

Valles first heard about COMO in 1972. It was in 1976 that she first went to the women's center, with hopes of becoming involved in organizing work. She had long been active in the church and later joined Guillermina Valdés and others at the St. John the Baptist Community. In 1976 she moved to another area of Juárez far from her congregation. Soon after this, she decided to study at COMO.

> I felt like I was not doing anything so I decided to take some English classes. I immediately liked it here. I felt the people gave you something without you having to ask for it. I took various classes: the biology and psychology of sexuality, human relations, social work, and English. These courses helped me a lot. They . . . oriented me, opened up the possibility of having a clearer vision of society, myself, and my family. (Interview, Ciudad Juárez, February 1982)

Lupe Valles became involved with COMO's first special-education program for youth (*creatividad infantil*, children's creativity). She taught the children of maquila workers and co-op members painting, crafts, theater, and gymnastics. Between 1977 and 1979, she was involved in the educational programming activities that led to the development of the *tronco común* and the four areas of specialized training eventually adopted as the core of the center's curriculum. Her own specialization was social-work education. During this period she was also a liaison to UCECA and to this day has pursued a research interest in the agency. But Valles's most significant work, in her own estimation, was with the CEBI project:

> CONAFE asked for a study of the marginal areas to see if CEBIs were needed and feasible. The first study was in 1980. We used the same techniques of the *brigadas de investigación*. In fact, during the *tronco común* that same year we got the students involved in assisting us with the research in three different *colonias*. We had very positive results, identifying a need for the program in all three of the communities. (Interview, Ciudad Juárez, February 1982)

Prior to her involvement with the Juárez literacy campaign, Valles worked with the National Polytechnic Institute (IPN) in the Mexico City CEBIs. After returning to COMO, she found that CONAFE had established a national program to promote CEBIs in marginalized areas. Valles and other staff members were approached by CONAFE to provide planning and research support. The principles of self-management and self-directed learning utilized by COMO in its educational programs were adopted by the national CEBI project, largely as a consequence of Valles's own efforts. She explained her understanding of these principles:

> For me, self-management means you are conscious of what you are doing. The same holds for the children we teach in the CEBIs, not just us the promoters, the teachers. The right to protest, to speak out and question things in order to arrive at collective action. To let the people achieve realization of their basic needs, and to express the ideals that shape their lives. This is what self-management in the CEBIs is all about. This also implies responsibility for your own actions, that not all of your decisions will work. You have to take that risk in order to work with your own communities. (Interview, Ciudad Juárez, February 1982)

Lupe Valles is a very religious person. But she is also the type of person whose beliefs and actions repudiate all of the stereotypes about Mexican religiosity. Like Guillermina Valdés, Valles is not one to uphold the ideal of quiescence captured in the adage about the meek, who shall inherit the earth. She wants justice now, on this earth, and not later in some ideal heaven. She thus upholds the idea that self-management is about the "right to protest, to speak out and question things in order to arrive at collective action."

The transference of COMO's socially relevant and problem-solving pedagogy to the CEBIs resulted in numerous community-organizing and -development activities. When I first interviewed her in 1982, Valles explained the role of the CEBIs in this process of community organizing:

> The CEBIs do have various other functions. Given the methods used in instruction, the CEBIs should have more projection into the community. The socially relevant activity makes this projection possible. Students constantly study problems in the community. There is a very intimate communication between CEBI staff and the community. Our goal is to transform the CEBIs into informal centers of community organizing. We are presently arriving at such a point. For example, there is the problem of the water supply to these marginal zones. During the summer, water shortages and contamination are common. The children and their parents researched the problem. Soon, they were agitating the local government to meet their water needs. They have done the same thing with the price of housing. The children went to the INFONAVIT [Instituto para el Fomento Nacional de la Vivienda de los Trabajadores][57] housing developments, asking questions about the price of apartments, the building materials, and so on. They realized that they will probably never be able to afford such housing, and that raises their awareness of the way the world is run. These tasks are efforts to get the children and their parents to think in more logical ways. We seek to help them develop a critical analytical capacity. (Interview, Ciudad Juárez, February 1982)

It is clear from Valles's account that the CEBIs were not just part of a literacy campaign, but a powerful tool for community organizing and consciousness-raising. But Valles's work with the CEBIs also provided an opportunity to do something that was uniquely meaningful to her, to organize struggles that would improve living conditions in the marginalized and working-class areas of Ciudad Juárez. In 1984, after COMO's funding crisis, Valles was placed in charge of coordinating the CEBI projects for Juárez as a whole. She worked in this capacity for several years. In 1988, she joined Guillermina Valdés as a staff research associate at CEFNOMEX. Today, she remains active as a researcher with COLEF and as a member of the St. John the Baptist Community.

Many of the workers who left their jobs in the maquilas to join COMO as promoters, teachers, social workers, and organizers had to endure a real economic sacrifice. As one CEBI instructor explained:

> The CEBIs represent a cherished ideal for us. It's not the money, it's too little, the money is clearly not enough to survive on. I like working in the CEBI because it gets my attention, my commitment. Working with children is a beautiful experience. It's an ideal to work in such a school. It doesn't matter that you hardly make a living. All that is important is that we share our knowledge with them. It is difficult because once you make a commitment to change this society you have to see it through.[58]

One does not become a CEBI instructor if the goal is to earn more money. Many literacy instructors make less than the minimum wage, despite a working week that is often longer than forty hours. Some of these instructors are probably making less money than they earned in the maquilas. What motivates these young women to sacrifice income is their persistent desire to challenge the status quo and to pursue the development of their own working-class and marginalized communities. And while former maquila workers are willing to make economic sacrifices, they have long-term objectives and community interests in mind. Another CEBI instructor told me: "Sure, we give up income for a time. But we are building for future struggles. Educated children will go further than us in gaining access to life's basic needs: food, homes, and a richer cultural existence."[59] "Building for future struggles" through the education of children was a commonly held belief among CEBI instructors when I was at COMO. I believe this is indicative of the extent to which the instructors valued the interests of the entire community over their own personal financial advancement. Adopting these values meant that the instructors were crafting new identities that nevertheless drew from the knowledge and experiences they had as maquila workers. After all, it was in the maquilas that these workers first encountered the necessity of resisting speedup through *tortuguismo*—a struggle that was also based on oppositional identities (see chapter 6).

COMO and Sustainable Development on the U.S.–Mexico Border

The narratives in this chapter provide intriguing glimpses of what is perhaps the most important organization that has organized among women workers in the maquiladoras. These narratives suggest a rejection of development as defined by the imperatives of collective global capital. Many of the women workers in Juárez who became students at COMO during the late 1970s through the early 1980s redefined their political identities by actively participating in the circulation of struggles from the factory to the community, and by experimenting with alternatives in community development and self-organization. I want to suggest that the alternative forms of struggle and organization created by maquila workers constitute a refusal of capitalist *mal*development. The subjectivity of maquila workers, as members of a socially constituted and historically located community, was channeled through COMO in an increasingly antagonistic relation to the "objectivity" of transnational capitalist accumulation. Capital's pretensions at possessing universal models of development, especially in the organizational form of the maquiladoras, were challenged by the refusal of Mexican working-class women to acquiesce in the reduction of their lives to mere cogs in assembly lines.

A community of women workers, activists, and organizers opposed and *separated* itself from capital's twisted concept of development. This involved not just the establishment of autonomous organizations such as COMO but the development of oppositional identities. When workers in Ciudad Juárez sought to be something other than exploited labor in transnational factories, they crafted a separate, independent mode of economic and cultural existence. The separatist-identity politics of maquila workers consisted of a rejection of maldevelopment and especially of the reduction of their lived experiences to mere exploited labor power. Workers rejected the dehumanization that comes with the terror of the machine.

These struggles and forms of organization may seem reformist in their outlook. The rejection of maldevelopment and the emergence of separatist identities both imply the existence of an organized radical opposition. It matters little that these activists and organizers were not a "representative majority" of maquila workers, as more strict empiricists might insist. What matters is that these oppositional tendencies exist. On the one hand, there is capital seeking to impose "abstract labor"; that is, trying to reduce humans to interchangeable and substitutable units of labor time. On the other hand, there is the multiplicity of the needs individuals and social groups seek to fulfill in the course of their lifetimes. Capitalist development imposes a homology between economic value and workers' needs. The rupture of this homology consistently informed the class politics that circulated struggle to and through COMO during the late 1970s and early 1980s.

Because of the way COMO and the workers redefined "development," their perceived social needs were bound to conflict with capital's reduction of the human being to mere labor power. Working for maquilas, assembling gadgets for the universal market, increasingly interfered with the ability of many of these workers to fulfill self-defined needs in the context of the living conditions in their own communities. The primacy of fulfilling individual and community needs was therefore a counterpoint to the dictates of capitalist accumulation. This was the significance of COMO's "transference methodology" as we will see in the subsequent chapter. Struggles that seek to meet these needs are revolutionary not because they are championed by "leftist vanguards," but rather because they are collectively articulated in the community as autonomous forms of self-development and self-valorization.[60] Maquila women are not just redefining needs, they are outlining the blueprints of alternative economic and political institutions to fulfill those needs. And perhaps most importantly, they are organizing in a space separate from the delusive universe of capitalist values.

The history of COMO suggests that there are alternatives in the border region to maquiladora industrialization. The establishment and longevity of the worker-owned, self-managed cooperatives is one indication of what these alternatives might look like. Despite the temporary fragmentation of COMO after 1985, the cooperatives continue as viable examples of creative working-class autonomy. As alternatives to the maquilas, these cooperatives offer a blueprint for future experiments in workplace democracy and sustainable development. However, the political and economic climate in Mexico as a whole, and specifically in the U.S.–Mexico border region, is once again experiencing turbulent change. The election of President Salinas de Gortari signaled a willingness on the part of the corporatist Mexican state to implement a radical restructuring of the economy that is more conducive to investments by foreign, transnational capitalist interests. The laws that promoted cooperative ownership, especially during the de la Madrid *sexenio,* have been weakened by a shift toward a more open foreign-investment policy and long-term cutbacks in the social sector (education, housing, health care, and environmental protection). These changes are significant and merit further examination on their own. In the final chapter I discuss the implications of NAFTA for the future of the working class in the U.S.–Mexico border region.

That the cooperatives can function profitably is not in doubt if we focus on their internal characteristics. But these cooperatives, and organizations such as COMO, do not exist in a political economic vacuum. National and, increasingly, international market dynamics impinge on the ability of the cooperative sector to survive. This is not a question of protectionism or unfair competition, so much as the more problematic political issue of which model Mexicans adopt to guide their development policies. Transnational capital can easily outproduce and outcompete the cooperatives. But it fails miserably as a model of workplace democracy and sustainable development.

The prospects for workplace democracy and sustainable development in the U.S.–Mexico border region do not seem very bright at this point. NAFTA will likely diminish these prospects. Mexico, like the maquila workers who struggled through COMO, is at a critical crossroads. It must decide if it wants to succumb to the delusive seductions of free trade, with all its attendant social and environmental problems. Or, it can emulate the creativity and inventiveness of maquila workers, and choose the equally difficult path of cooperative development, a path that may at least strengthen the prospects for workplace democracy and environmental protection. The key lesson to be learned here is that economic development is a political process, and there are no inevitable paths or results. But to expect the "Colossus of the North" to provide appropriate models of development is like asking a drug addict to look after the pharmacy. The United States is addicted to capitalism and a consumerist ethic; Mexico increasingly so. These addictions are destroying the ecological and cultural diversity of the planet. Mexico should think twice before blindly following the United States down the path of further environmental destruction and workplace tyranny. There are alternatives, and the history of COMO provides many insights on some of the features for other, more sustainable paths. Guillermina Valdés once said: "It is simply a matter of appreciating the value of your own culture enough to see that it provides plenty of creative possibilities for a more just, more humane future."

Part Three

MOTHERS OF INVENTION

6

Mexican Thinkwork

Think the same, remain the same.
— Octaviana Medrano, electronics-assembly technician
(Ciudad Juárez, 1989)

Sometimes you play dumb and sometimes you don't. But in either case, you better make sure the engineer doesn't figure out your little game.
— Juana Ortega, maquiladora worker (Ciudad Juárez, 1982)

We must defend the fact, we must legitimize the idea, that scientific knowledge is not the exclusive province of experts, engineers, and trained scientists.
— Guillermina Valdés (Ciudad Juárez, 1989)

Think Carefully
— A sign in the Dale Electronics assembly plant (Ciudad Juárez, 1982)

Knowledge, Power, and the Politics of Deskilled Labor

[S]elves are crafted in processes of work and within matrices of power, and . . . categories such as personal and political, experiential and theoretical, personal and social are persistent North American narrative conventions unable to fully account for the complexities and ambiguities of everyday life.[1]

In 1974, Harry Braverman published his account of the destruction of craft skills under twentieth-century monopoly capitalism.[2] His "deskilling thesis" initiated a debate within Marxist labor-process theory and the sociology of work that continues through the present day. At the heart of Braverman's argument is the idea that the technological, managerial, and sociological changes that occurred in the twentieth-century workplace degraded skilled labor. Mechanization, managerial tyranny, and changes in the demographic composition of the workforce undermined the intellectual basis of workers' skill—craft knowledge. Prior to monopoly capitalism and mass production, craftwork was the "chief repository of scientific production technique."[3] But monopoly capitalism begets the degradation of labor. Capital uses science to destroy workers' knowledge of production by appropriating and transferring skill to management through technological innovation. The deskilled worker on the mass-production assembly line is ultimately a laborer without knowledge. The degradation of skill is thus associated with the separation of planning from execution, with the imposition of an absolutely impermeable boundary between mental and manual labor. Braverman asks us to remember F. W. Taylor's prime directive: Managers think, workers follow orders.

There have been many different criticisms of Braverman's theory in the course of the deskilling debate. One major contested problem is the extent to which the degradation of labor is experienced by different workers over time and in varying occupations.[4] How widespread and irreversible is deskilling? Another major point of debate is the extent to which deskilling is associated with alienation and powerlessness.[5] Does deskilling turn workers into unhappy, unthinking, and disenfranchised automatons, trapped in the rut of "preconceptualized" labor?[6] Some argue that Braverman failed to provide genuine historical examples of deskilling and that his arguments rely on spurious claims and a "generic" definition of the concept.[7] Gender and ethnic differences in deskilling have also been explored and debated.[8] One study suggests that white men have more opportunities to learn skills compared to white women or people of color.[9]

Another facet of the debate deals with the concept of "tacit" skill. Is there some routine "experiential knowledge" that workers learn to use in the workplace?[10] This perspective emphasizes the capacity of workers for self-awareness and working knowledge. It significantly revises the concept of skill to involve much more than the usual repertoire of technical and manual tasks narrowly predefined by science or managerial convention.[11] Skill is not reducible to instrumental technique or established convention. It is also working knowledge—in the sociological sense of a complex and evolving set of predispositions, attitudes, beliefs, and thinking reflexes.[12] Skill emerges from active learning in social context—in this case, in the context of the social relations of production and their corresponding cultural and technical practices.[13] A related approach posits the view that workers "import" their own forms of consciousness into the workplace. Consciousness affects the politics of production, as in the case of the "manufacture of labor's consent" to the degradation of skill.[14] Another criticism of the deskilling thesis is that it ignores the micropolitics of "workplace oppositional cultures."[15] Forms and tactics of resistance and struggle are also skill. Learning to fight a system of production implies a working knowledge of how the system operates; otherwise, the struggle would be ineffective and could not be sustained over time. In this view, working knowledge can lead to counterplanning on the shop floor.[16]

Labor-process theorists have long argued that the definition of skill involves much more than just an inventory of "objective" criteria established a priori by the mechanisms of a scientifically ordered internal labor market. From the perspective of managerial ideology, skill is defined through the use of supposedly neutral technical criteria: the "pure" scientific measurement and organization of work tasks down to the minutest detail. This is presumably a matter of efficiency and nothing more. Politics has nothing to do with it. However, most scholars involved in the *sociological* debate scoff at such a simplistic view of deskilling, given the ever-changing historical context of a *highly politicized* workplace such as one governed by the principles of Fordism or any other capitalist organizational system. The tumultuous and changing political character of the workplace renders the issue of a neutral constant such as efficiency irrelevant. There is nothing neutral about the use of production technologies that degrade human skill and thereby undermine the political power of labor in the workplace.[17] Thus, what is most interesting about this facet of the labor-process debate is that the question of skill is viewed not as a technical but as a political problem.[18]

Of interest to me are those approaches emphasizing workers' production of knowledge discourses and the role of workplace oppositional cultures in the struggle to define labor as skilled or deskilled.[19] Maquila workers have taught me over the years that knowledge is power, and that if you "think the same" you will "remain the same"—that is, in a subjugated and exploited location. The subjectivity of workers—their contextual self-awareness and capacity to think, reflect, and act—is only problematic because so many of us (authors) have assumed that workers are really incapable of thought, especially intellectual or scientific thought.[20] Henry Ford may not have been the first to express this view, but he was certainly among the first who set out to put it into practice. After the terror of Ford's machine, science and technology are ruthlessly deployed to achieve political control of the workplace through divisions of labor based on "skill."[21] The imposition of machine systems combined with bureaucratic control also augments preexisting wage-and-skill hierarchies. But this does not necessarily mean that the technological and bureaucratic assaults reduce workers to unthinking, inarticulate dupes. That is perhaps the most serious error committed by Braverman and his disciples: a tendency to favor a technologically determinist slant (discourse) on workers as nothing *but* deskilled, exploited, and subjugated labor power. This is too close to Ford's own view of the worker wanting a job in which "he does not have to think."

Both Marxist and non-Marxist labor-process theorists have slipped into the framework of a correspondence theory of skill and deskilling. Scholars have presented their knowledge as representing something that is assumed to exist independently of the texts they themselves generate as theorists. Like managers, who contrive gradations of skill to keep wages low, theorists construct deskilling as a nearly absolute state of ignorance. But politically, skill and deskilling do not exist independently of the knowledge discourses that define, constrain, and invent them. This is why my own approach to the study of skill in the maquilas relies on reading worker and managerial narratives as textual representations for which multiple correspondences exist—depending on the power relationships of the subjects and authors. I realize this is a controversial shift to take in the study of workplace politics. For instead of focusing on the materialist concept of the production of commodities and the political uses of the technological and bureaucratic divisions of labor, I focus on the construction and deconstruction of working knowledge through a reflexive analysis of emic workplace narratives.

KNOWLEDGE, POWER, DISCOURSE, AND SKILL

The social construction of knowledge as power is for me the axis around which rotates the political problem of skill. Like Michel Foucault's study of knowledge and power in various domains of human life, my work is concerned with the genealogy of truth claims.[22] Here, I rely on the techniques of site ethnography to analyze knowledge claims in the context of maquila workplace politics.[23] I am concerned with examining truth claims about the nature of the workplace, especially as these are articulated through the personal narratives of workers and managers. It is important that we (social theorists) acknowledge that workers and managers are just as capable of constructing and deconstructing texts. They too will "argue" over truth as long as they remain conflicted participants in a matrix of relationships sharply stratified by power. In the workplace, differences in power are often articulated as hidden dimensions of everyday labor experience.[24] For example, the deployment of technology can obscure the human bases and dimensions of domination on the shop floor—the engineer is always one step removed from labor's experience with the mechanical despotism of the flow line. But the contradictory and ambiguous narratives of differently empowered subjects can also make domination more transparent, and thus have a more direct impact on material conditions and power relations in the workplace, as well as on people's perceptions of these phenomena.

This basically means that instead of treating the narratives as if they correspond to some objective reality that can be located "somewhere out there" (by me as the analyst), I approach them as discursive practices that are very much a part of the unfolding, site-specific power struggles that workers and managers engage in when dealing with the conditions of labor in the workplace. What people say here is not presented as "verifiable truth" in support of some theory or another. Instead of searching for absolute truths, I read the narratives as an integral part of the struggle over truth claims in maquila milieux. Workers and managers construct identities when defending their interests in the power struggle over truth; they are no different than us (academics) in that regard. I am not suggesting, however, that we reduce human agency (action) to discursive practice.[25] Nor am I suggesting that we take these narratives to be the only focal point for the analysis of the forms of everyday life in the workplace. I am also not suggesting that everyone entirely abandon survey research and other etic methods in the study of maquila workplace politics.

In this chapter my analysis of the politics of knowledge in the maquilas consists primarily of a series of ethnographic vignettes of power relations in the workplace. For example, the politics of knowledge in the maquilas is expressed through the argumentative narratives that workers and managers articulate when they define, redirect, and constrain discourses related to the status and conditions of "deskilled" labor. I am especially concerned with workers' narratives that redefine deskilled labor as "inventive force," with how workers see themselves as "mothers of invention." Identity narratives are thus also of concern because I see these as related to the discursive practices that workers and managers invoke when they are involved in struggles over the "crafting of selves" in the workplace. That is, to study the politics of skill you may also have to study the even more ambiguous politics of identity. These identity narratives therefore figure prominently in my analysis of struggles over unpaid technical work in the maquilas.[26]

It is here that I am greatly indebted to the work of Dorinne Kondo. Her book, *Crafting Selves: Power, Gender, and Discourses of Identity in a Japanese Workplace,* led me to make extraordinary changes in my approach to the study of workplace politics in the maquilas. For some time I have been intrigued by identity as a category in the study of workplace politics. But before reading Kondo, I had never really made a conceptual link between the uses of autobiographic and ethnographic narratives and the actual construction of power matrices in the workplace. In her book, Kondo experiments with multiple, shifting voices to focus on

> the ways that people construct themselves and their lives—in all their complexity, contradiction, and irony—within discursive fields of power and meaning, in specific situations, at specific historical moments. Surely, investigations of "crafting selves" in the domain of work cannot ignore the fields of power, hierarchy, and discipline within which people struggle over the meanings of "company," of "family," of what it means to work in a . . . factory, . . . of what we might call "class," of artisanship, and of the conventions surrounding the construction of gender.[27]

Throughout this book, I too have used multiple voices—recall the Ford and Ortega epigraphs in the opening chapter. I have done so for several reasons. Like Kondo, I am concerned with understanding how people construct identities. The best way I know to do this involves using case-study and ethnographic methods to collect first-person narratives. Along with Rosaldo and Kondo, I want to minimize the position of the detached observer (myself as author) and instead place the workers' narratives at the center of the text, and not somewhere in the margins in parenthetical statements, endnotes, or appendices. This is an exercise in the negation of the canon. And it is also an epistemological counterpoint aiming to empower unheard voices. Centering the text on the workers' narratives is itself an act of resistance because it places me, the author, and you, the reader, in direct contact with the discursive practices of the workers. The narrative forms expressed by workers deserve to be recognized as discourses of the will to power as much as do the analytical pirouettes of the students of workplace politics.[28]

I agree with Kondo that we cannot ignore "fields of power," hierarchy, and discipline as integral parts of everyday lived experience in the workplace. In fact, Kondo's "fields of power" are precisely what I mean by "terrains of struggle." But my concern here is not so much with how people struggle over the meanings of "company," "family," or "class." Instead, my focus is on how workers and managers struggle over the meanings of "skill," "engineering knowledge," "science," "wage," and other concepts related to the structuring of power relations in cross-cultural and Fordist milieux. I am also interested in how gender and class identities shape and constrain these discursive practices, an interest shared by Kondo. And finally, also like Kondo, I am concerned with relating these workplace practices to a specific and dynamic historical and cultural context.

DISCURSIVE PRACTICE, SCIENCE, AND SKILL

There is a tendency in Fordist managerial discourse to equate skill with performative mastery of routine, narrow, fragmented, and predefined tasks.[29] Students of the labor process, unfortunately, sometimes equate this *discursive* tendency with actual practices. We have seen Marxists argue that capital constructs a hierarchical division of labor by using science and technology to impose an impermeable boundary between "mental" and "manual" labor. Hierarchy is control, and deskilling is the technological strategy that management uses to achieve control by separating workers from the production of "scientific" knowledge.

Management wants to constrain and obscure truth claims about the actual nature of skill and working knowledge. So it is important to recognize how workers constantly construct their own definitions, which they derive from lived experiences and discursive practices in the workplace. Workers' lived experiences with labor involve activities that lie outside the parameters of the narrow technical criteria contrived by management for the sake of defining job descriptions. It must be understood that job descriptions and definitions of skill are political. Job descriptions are political if we read them as narratives of power that management constructs to define skill on the basis of presumably neutral criteria. The rank-ordering of wage gradations on the basis of spurious time and motion studies corresponds with the reification of skill. The "scientific" measurement of work is misrepresented as derivative of neutral and inherent properties of jobs.[30] This is an example of the political economic sleight of hand that takes place when managers make use of these practices we call "administrative" and "engineering" sciences. Job descriptions remain political not because they actually correspond to lived experiences in the workplace. It is their misrepresentation by management as examples of neutral science that makes them a political problem. In other words, management uses politically charged criteria to define jobs and skill every time it tries to describe what it means by "fair pay" and "a fair day's work" for a given job. And this obscures the working knowledge of labor, because it defines skill on the basis of a purely political and ideological convention that masquerades as neutral technical criteria. Management is using a discursive trick to justify its fetish for "efficiency," which is not grounded so much in "science" as in political desires and objectives. This tactic can result in occupational differentiation, or the rationalization of job tasks down to their minutest details (as per the standard deskilling argument). But it does not prevent workers from acquiring and exercising working knowledge of production systems.[31] Under the critical scrutiny of workers, these managerial practices acquire a certain degree of transparency, even if few scholars recognize the deceit. The boundary between "mental" and "manual" labor is not as impermeable as the deskilling theorists or managerial conventions would have us believe. Despite management's desire to separate planning from execution, lived experience in the workplace includes workers' discursive practices articulated when they acquire working knowledge of production regimes and construct oppositional identities.

The discourses of skill in a given factory are thus constrained and reshaped by the workplace oppositional cultures that workers create to articulate demands and challenge managerial power. Workers experience the workplace through their own site-specific knowledge. This knowledge can become a source of resistance and counterplanning on the shop floor. Is it possible for workers to subvert the power matrices of the workplace by appropriating the working knowledge that is supposed to be held exclusively in the minds of the engineers in lab white? What makes this working knowledge a source of power?

We must first understand that working knowledge includes empirical, anecdotal, and metaphorical stories of lived experiences in the workplace. This is local, situated knowledge—specific to the gender, class, ethnic, technical, and idiosyncratic locations of the worker.[32] This knowledge—a dynamic by-product of workers' shifting subjectivity—is social, cultural, and technical in nature. And we must not forget that this "subjectivity" includes shifting discursive practices, full of contradiction, irony, and ambiguity. Workers, like managers, engineers, or social theorists, are perfectly capable of creating and articulating their own discourses on moral rights and deconstructions of the will to power on the shop floor.

Social skills such as the ability to communicate orally and through body language are important forms of tacit knowledge, without which the individual worker can neither perform production tasks nor participate in informal networks. Culturally specific resources such as the use of metaphorical language and aphorisms to transmit information or preferences for cooperative association and mutual aid are also forms of tacit knowledge, the stuff that makes for the "imported consciousness," or shifting identity constructions of workers.[33] Then there is the working knowledge of production techniques, accumulated by workers over time in a strictly empirical manner—that is, based on direct observation and experimentation. Together, these different forms of tacit knowledge constitute the labor subjectivity of workers. Workers' narratives on the politics of deskilled labor and working knowledge can therefore be read as dynamic aspects of the intellectual qualities and ideological ambiguities that emerge in the course of everyday lived experience in the workplace. It is precisely these "subaltern narratives" that have been all but ignored by the few case studies and ethnographies that have been written in the course of the maquila and Marxist labor-process and deskilling debates.[34]

Is the working knowledge of third-world assembly-line workers science? And what have we to gain by insisting so? Other than perhaps contributing to a badly overdue *Methodenstreit,*[35] any focus on the status of workers' knowledge is clearly an argument in favor of the politics of empowerment. The answer to the question—is it science?—in part depends on what is meant by scientific knowledge and how exclusive a definition is adopted. Sandra Harding provides a starting point to answer this question by reminding us that "many scientific and technological innovations that people of European descent tend to assume are uniquely their inheritance have been made independently in the Third World—sometimes far earlier than in the West." Harding notes that Westerners "need to rethink their stereotypes of 'primitive cultures,' which are associated with the assumption that all sciences deserving the name have been developed in the West." The third world can take credit "for helping to make possible the sciences and technologies of the North Atlantic."[36]

Harding's point is directed at a general tendency of knowledge production and truth claims in vastly different, and decidedly abstract, cultural domains. Can the same be seen to operate in a more focused setting involving the production of local knowledge? Might we insist, for example, that a crucial mistake to avoid is to assume that only engineers, scientists, and managers have "scientific" knowledge of maquila labor processes and that these "experts" have somehow created an impermeable boundary between "mental" and "manual" labor? And what can we gain from seeing whether the actual, lived permeability of the boundary is constantly traversed by maquila workers to gain working knowledge of production? The workers' narratives examined later in this chapter suggest that no form of knowledge is impermeable. This points precisely to the error committed by most students of the deskilling debate. We can avoid Braverman's mistake of equating writings on scientific management with actual practices, by first of all eschewing concepts of deskilled labor that equate managerial rationalizations with absolute hegemony over the working knowledge of labor. Indeed, conflating managerial theories with actual managerial (and worker) practices can create the worst nightmares for social theorists interested in the politics of knowledge in the workplace. The starting point has to be the workers' and managers' own narratives of power, in this case as they are centered on the politics of working knowledge and deskilled labor.

The knowledge that maquila workers acquire of industrial production and engineering techniques is "experiential." By this I simply mean that it is immediately empirical: it involves "firsthand" or "direct" observation. Such knowledge is scientific in the sense that it involves an analytical process joining observation with manipulation. Science can thus be defined in this context as a mode of analytical inquiry involving experimental manipulation of the conditions that are observed in order to exercise functional control over those same conditions. This involves a search for predictable outcomes in order to reduce the complexity of the processes that are observed. When maquila workers use inductive rationality to solve mechanical problems, they employ precisely this type of reductionist scientific logic. This suggests, perhaps to the dismay of some feminist and Marxist epistemologists, that members of dominant social classes (engineers, scientists, managers, etc.) do not in fact have a monopoly on the methods and logic of reductionist science.[37] Guillermina Valdés makes a case for this view with regard to maquila workers' creativity:

> [T]he women workers who lived the experience of production in daily reality determined that an inductive apprenticeship exists; inductive because it has never been acquired through training or formal education. To continue to consider the maquila workers, especially the assembly-line workers and group chiefs, as unskilled manual labor, is to not recognize their creativity and remain blind to the skilled activities that these workers realize.[38]

Whether or not the working knowledge of maquila workers is "skilled" and "scientific" is clearly then not so much a technical as it is a political problem. That workers construct "scientific" discursive practices related to maquila labor processes is really not the issue here. On the other side, the political power of capital is exercised through managerial definitions and imperatives, and this too must remain open to further critical scrutiny. Maquila management uses its power to deny the existence of the workers' inventive force, but simultaneously uses this knowledge to increase productivity and profits. Thus, the conflicting constructions of skill and knowledge in the maquiladora workplace are fundamentally political problems. This is not just an ideologically motivated denial either: the discourse involves a strategic effort on the part of management to prevent workers from justifying and demanding higher wages for the unpaid technical work that they perform, and an equally strategic effort by workers to counteract the imposition of managerial imperatives.

DESKILLING IN THE MAQUILADORAS

The deskilling of labor in the maquiladoras has also been at the center of much debate and controversy. Many researchers have focused attention on the minimal training received by maquila workers.[39] One influential study characterizes maquila jobs as "hyperspecialized."[40] Some researchers argue that maquilas have failed to provide adequate skills that can be transferred to other jobs. The failure of maquiladoras to promote technology transfers has also been noted. These same studies suggest that employability in other sectors of the economy does not necessarily increase for those who have worked in the industry.[41] Some scholars have focused on the relationship between deskilling, employee turnover, and managerial control of production.[42] For example, one study suggests that maquila workers are routinely terminated by management before they reach the age of thirty. After years of eye-straining work, individual worker productivity declines. So older—more tired and less productive—workers are dismissed, and normally without even severance pay or advance notice. And the deskilled character of most jobs in the maquilas makes replacement of workers that much easier.[43] Deskilling is thus explained as a managerial control strategy based on constant renewal of the workforce, with the ultimate goal of preventing seniority and the formation of workers with union consciousness.[44] This strategy presumably reflects management's understanding that "the greater the worker seniority, the greater their nonconformity."[45]

Deskilling in the maquilas has been described by researchers mostly in terms of the nature and length of training, without reference to the substance and content of jobs. One study notes that training for maquila jobs involves nothing more than getting workers to utilize sensory-motor coordination skills to the fullest extent possible. Maquila job tasks are characterized as "hyperspecialized," in reference to the monotonous, repetitive, and mechanically simplified nature of assembly-line work.[46] Accordingly, hyperspecialized jobs require relatively little skill or training, thereby augmenting capital's ability to replace or renew its workforce at will. Jorge Carrillo, a leading expert on labor-management relations in the maquilas, argues that training in the industry is a farcical imitation of apprenticeship:

> The training received by workers throughout their productive life . . . may be reduced to an apprenticeship in work discipline. . . . If we take into account the hyperspecialization that [workers] acquire through a specific activity in the total process of production, . . . then the only real training they get is the internalization of work discipline.[47]

Job training in the maquilas therefore basically involves workers learning and accepting a regimented and hierarchical system of order giving and taking. Capital controls the command structure of the labor process, and workers—because they are deskilled—are passive victims of an authoritarian managerial regime. This perspective views deskilling as the underlying principle that makes capitalist control in the maquilas possible. Deskilling allows management to impose strict labor discipline, planned turnover, and ideological manipulation. This, presumably, is always an effective strategy to combat worker insurgency and prevent workers from establishing informal shop-floor networks.

However, others have argued that maquiladora workers are engaged in numerous skilled activities for which they have not been formally trained and for which they are not paid.[48] This type of skilled labor is a source of what Guillermina Valdés calls "technical surplus value" (*plusvalía técnica*).[49] Management in the maquilas is generally aware of this activity and does much to encourage it. But this awareness does not easily translate into official recognition, since that would imply acceptance of a higher-wage regime for the entire industry workforce, and would in fact undermine the political basis for defining maquila labor as deskilled. The managerial construction of skill is a political act used to structure and maintain low-wage–high-productivity regimes. But again, workers have their own discourse on skill and continuously struggle with management to overturn the political definition of their labor as deskilled. Maquila management may perhaps best be characterized as an authoritarian regime that utilizes deskilling to control workers, but this does not necessarily imply that workers passively accept the arrangement or that they absolutely lack working knowledge of production systems as a direct and unavoidable consequence of managerial intentions.

Mothers of Invention: Working Knowledge, Discourse, and Gender in the Maquilas

The last place we might think to look for evidence of skill and creativity is on the typical assembly line in a Mexican maquiladora. After all, maquila workers are supposedly so thoroughly deskilled as to be terrorized into submission. But the politics of knowledge in production, as well as the politics of the production of knowledge, is a much more complex affair than that posited by the standard deskilling models. My own research in the maquilas has produced five primary insights: (1) Job positions are deskilled by design and for a variety of reasons and purposes, including the existence of efficiency cults and managerial control imperatives. (2) Official training for most jobs in the maquilas is minimal, but labor processes can be used by workers as an informal inductive apprenticeship in industrial engineering and work organization. (3) Workers in maquila jobs are not themselves necessarily deskilled in some absolute sense and in fact have demonstrable working knowledge of production systems and techniques. (4) The working knowledge of maquila workers is associated with both self-exploitation and resistance. (5) Finally, working knowledge is sometimes combined with local knowledge, especially when workers articulate identity narratives to redefine and defend their positions in power relations and struggles with management.

During 1981 and 1982, a group of COMO staff members and I interviewed more than two hundred maquila workers in Juárez. During 1989 and 1990, we conducted another survey, and I report on those findings later, in chapter 8. In the original survey, we found nearly half of the workers (45 percent) routinely performing "skilled" tasks.[50] Our definition of skill referred to worker involvement in methods and process engineering; repair and maintenance activities; job setups and modifications to components, tools, or machinery; and outright inventions. The activities had to be performed by assembly workers, although these were not necessarily limited to workers on conveyor-belt positions. Nearly half the workers in the survey (48 percent) reported knowledge of engineering activities. Twenty-nine percent confirmed repairing and maintaining tools or machinery to continue working. Another 23 percent routinely completed job setups and almost 8 percent performed time and motion studies. About 3 percent respecified or recalibrated raw materials or components or both. Forty-three percent of the workers reported making inventions, including modifications to tools and machinery (38 percent) and to production processes (26 percent). Twenty percent of the workers reported making modifications in product or component designs, while 14 percent reported combinations of two or more activities.[51]

In a study conducted during 1982 and 1983, COMO also extensively documented the working knowledge learned and applied by maquila assembly workers to solve problems at the point of production.[52] Both the 1984 COMO report and the research I conducted during and subsequent to 1981 and 1982 include hundreds of substantive worker descriptions of modifications made to production instruments, components, and end products. The modified production instruments that workers described included soldering machines and exhaust systems, wiring bobbins, frame molders, lathes and jig borers, drill presses, sorting devices, frequency test equipment, circuit-board engravers, microscopes, and conveyor belts (*bandas*). Workers also described modifications to a wide range of components, including integrated circuit boards for television sets, surgical instruments, and other electronic equipment; wire-harness systems for automotive dashboards; and cabinetry for a variety of consumer electronic products.[53]

Managers, of course, are interested in knowing what factors motivate workers to conduct these activities. Workers are interested because this working knowledge can help them generate struggles to redefine and defend labor against managerial policies. Melina Ochoa, an electronics maquila worker on a wiring-bobbin machine, describes her motive for this activity: "Sometimes the wiring bobbin breaks down. It jams up. I suppose that I could wait for the mechanic to come by and fix it. But if I wait too long, I'll fall behind in my production. That could be a serious thing. For if I fall behind and fail to meet my daily standard I could be punished for it." Workers often make their own repairs to keep pace with production quotas. Sometimes mechanics and other repair and maintenance personnel are in short supply. In the absence of such personnel, assembly-line workers simply repair their own instruments of production. Zulema Gutiérrez, another electronics assembly worker, reiterates this view:

> I work with a machine that makes engravings on the circuit board. These steps are necessary prior to the soldering operation. Often the machine breaks down. The switch that turns the perforation point gets stuck or the perforation point does not follow the necessary pattern. I have observed that if I recalibrate the perforation point with my screwdriver the problem is solved. Now, I do this because it makes the machine work smoothly and makes things easier for me. If I don't fix it, then I'll be there waiting too long for the mechanic or engineer to show up. I cannot afford to wait, so I do it myself. There is really not that much to it. . . . I don't think we really

need all these mechanics and engineers. We can do these things ourselves. Too bad they don't pay us extra for this work. (Interview, Ciudad Juárez, May 1984)

Management may design maquila jobs with hyperspecialization in mind, but workers remain involved in a wide range of activities beyond the limited tasks they have been officially trained and positioned to do. They succeed in breaking through the impermeable boundary that allegedly exists between mental and manual labor; they defy the deskilling of their labor as "preconceptualized" by Fordist managerial conventions. Oral histories I collected in Juárez over a whole decade (1981–1990) revealed many aspects of the hidden dimensions of everyday labor experience in the maquilas. These narratives confirm the existence of an amazing variety of activities involving considerable working knowledge of production and engineering techniques. The accurate technical detail and tense political ambiguity present in these narratives of working knowledge are perhaps ultimately the best gauge to use in assessing the significance of the inventive force.

There are two main types of activities described in these narratives: modifications to machinery, tools, and components; and modifications to the labor process itself. But throughout the narratives, these technical descriptions are interlaced with expressions of the contradictory, ironic, and ambiguous beliefs that workers construct about the political and cultural nature of lived experience and working knowledge in the maquilas.

MODIFYING MACHINERY, TOOLS, AND COMPONENTS

When I interviewed Emilia Zamora in 1982, she had been working at RCA–Juárez for three years. She started as a component assembler but was soon promoted to group chief. During her third year at RCA she was promoted to the position of repair technician: she became a shop-floor troubleshooter.[54] She spoke of numerous occasions when engineering personnel were unavailable to redesign troublesome circuit boards or deal with bottlenecks in the flow line. The workers, facing the possibility of temporary layoffs as a consequence of these production problems, often took matters into their own hands. In one case, workers redesigned the circuit boards and conducted time and motion studies to improve line flows and output rates. For example, between 1979 and 1980, a group of assembly workers, group chiefs, and technical troubleshooters redesigned an entire circuit board for a color television set that eventually made the RCA best-seller list.[55]

During our many interviews, Zamora spoke with ease about *gráficas de eficiencia* (efficiency graphs), *cartas de trabajo* (job orders), and other terms that are part of the shop-floor engineering vernacular. She possessed substantive knowledge of engineering terminology and methods. She recalled one incident when engineers proved incapable of modifying machinery. The incident involved a group of wiring-bobbin operators. Workers, she recalled, were having some difficulty meeting new productivity standards because the bobbins vibrated too much at higher speeds. The imposed higher speed made more troublesome the task of rolling and cutting wire for specific components in preparation for soldering and circuit-board stuffing operations. Engineers examined the bobbins and concluded that no improvements were feasible or necessary. Yet, they insisted that the new quotas were attainable and that workers who failed to meet them should be terminated.

Facing an unbearable situation, the workers experimented with various sizes of rubber gaskets that they slipped onto the bobbin shafts to provide a buffer against friction with the troublesome drive-gear and spinning-shaft casings. This reduced the vibrations, making it at least possible for workers to meet the standards. Innovations like these, as simple as they might appear to the engineer or technologist, are indicative of the type of working knowledge maquila workers employ to solve production problems. Emilia Zamora provided critical assistance to the bobbin operators in this effort, and she then used the experience to challenge management's definition of the workers as deskilled. Also interesting about her story is that the workers came up with a solution that apparently eluded the engineers and mechanics.

> How is it that we, who are the unskilled operators, we who are at the very bottom of the pile, how is it that we can solve these problems while the engineers walk away scratching their heads? I'll tell you why. It's because the engineers are not close enough to the job at hand. We have to use these machines every day and we really know how they work. The engineers and managers understand all this in theory. We understand in theory *and* in practice. We are closer to the job. No one knows how to fix something better than the person that is right there in front of the problem every day. . . . After we solved the bobbin problem—and it was not the only one we worked on—we called for a meeting with the production superintendent and the personnel manager. They are always happy to meet with us [technicians and group chiefs] to get our input because they know how valuable our skill is. I went in with three other technicians and we asked [the plant manager] to increase the wages for the work group that fixed the wiring jobs. We said, "Look, you cannot treat people like they know noth-

ing. We deserve better. Give us a pay raise." The production engineer said that what we had done was part of our job and that it was not so unusual that it merited higher pay. [The plant manager] agreed and he said, "Thanks for being good workers. It will go on your record as an excellent accomplishment. That is your reward." . . . I think they treat us this way because most of us are women. They figure they can get away with it because we don't always protest. And they know how difficult it is for us to change the way things are organized. (Interview, Ciudad Juárez, October 1982)

Zamora's experience at RCA taught her that workers were being manipulated to perform tasks beyond the call of their job descriptions. She believed that the reason workers were able to solve problems that eluded the engineers was that, by being the closest to their machines, workers had a clearer understanding of production technique. Emilia Zamora privileges the knowledge of the workers over that of the trained engineers and technicians. She does not suspect engineers might choose not to do the work because they know the workers will do it for them. As someone who was sensitive to being "at the bottom of the pile," Zamora struggled to increase the workers' wages. The lack of a corresponding wage upgrade in return for the workers' inventiveness troubled her to no end. Her explanation for the treatment of the workers by managers in refusing to grant them a wage upgrade rests on the belief that gender plays a big role in the problem. She thinks that management refuses the wage increase because the workers are women, and that as women, the workers are too disempowered to "change the way things are organized."

MODIFYING LABOR PROCESSES

Workers' innovations are not limited to modifying equipment, components, or products. Often, workers experiment with new methods of production. They alter the sequence of tasks for a particular job, develop new motions for certain tasks, or modify the process of assembly through their own time and motion studies. My research suggests that many of these activities involve job setups that engineering staff refuse to do. Interestingly, interviews with labor lawyers, engineering personnel, and workers indicate that Mexico's technological dependency itself may discourage applied engineering at the point of production. Mexican engineers, at least in the maquilas, often function more in an administrative capacity than in a technical one. This may be due also to management's customary cost-saving practice of employing engineering students instead of fully trained and accredited personnel.[56]

In the case of job setups, workers routinely utilize their working knowledge to solve fine-tuning problems, such as those involved in optimizing the technical functioning of equipment. Workers at one maquila—a subsidiary of a U.S.-based corporation—that is involved in military-spec assembly of semiconductor devices commonly perform their own job setups in the wiring-harness subdepartment. According to workers at this plant, wire harnessing involves various mathematical calculations to determine the appropriate megahertz specifications for each wiring job.

In the next narrative, Rosario Menchaca, the chief technical troubleshooter for the subdepartment, describes how workers acquired this knowledge. She also notes changes made in setting up wiring jobs and reflects on the results of this activity:

> I first learned how to do this from the production engineer when we were having some problems with personnel. There were not enough technicians around to do the job, and so management decided to teach [the wire-harness machine operators] how to do it. Before, we basically started the machine and watched over it. We watched and made sure the wire was sorted, cut, and fed into the machine and then resorted and pretested for assembly. From watching, I already knew how to do the setup, but the engineers did it for us anyway. I was one of the three operators selected for the extra training. It was easy to learn the math part. The calculator is an interesting tool, one that allows you to work with your mind and not just your hands. It's all about matching the numbers in the production superintendent's manual with your wire selection. But to really do the job right you have to develop a feel for the material. It is not enough to do the right calculations for the width and length of the wire. What you have to figure out is something the tools can't do. This is the tension of the wire [for a particular job]. It's important for the long-term performance of the component. What is the relationship between the width, the length, and the tension that the wire will be exposed to over time? And this is the part that the engineers were having trouble with. . . . Down the line these components have to go through the quality-control tests. . . . That is done by a computer. Before we got on the job, the rejects were pretty high: about 20 to 30 percent. The engineers had set it up so that the speed of the machine, the bobbin, you see, was the same for all the jobs. (They can be so foolish, so inept.) But that doesn't work all the time because of the tension. The same speed makes the tension wrong for some of the wire, and we figured out which cut needed more speed and which less speed. . . . I am glad that I learned this job because now I am less bored. But this really doesn't change very much. Our pay is pretty much the same, but the year-end bonus is a little higher, I have noticed. I can't say that we are better off because of it.

It's like we are only helping the company make money but we don't share in it that much. (Interview, Ciudad Juárez, August 1989)

The ability to make calculations and set up the job, to work the mind a little as it were, is important to Rosario Menchaca because she has acquired a skill. But it is also important to her because she learned a way to avoid boredom. Like Emilia Zamora, she feels that a wage increase is justified, but remains frustrated and ambivalent when confronted with the fact that management chooses not to concede an upgrade to the workers. In the end, she feels self-exploited and realizes "this . . . doesn't change very much."

But in her working knowledge of the wiring bobbins, she demonstrates an ability to solve a variety of technical problems employing methods that management and trained engineers cannot or will not use. Menchaca and her workmates have invented a new way to deal with the specification of wiring jobs, as a result of an inductive apprenticeship in industrial engineering. This seems to have been accomplished because she and her co-workers understand that mathematical calculations are only part of the process. The workers, she says, "develop a feel for the material," and this goes beyond the knowledge of the engineers, who only understand the mathematical part. Like Zamora, Menchaca privileges the knowledge of the workers over that of the engineers. These workers have technically redefined the deskilling of their labor, even if they have failed to challenge the political structure of the wage imposed by managerial authority. Thus, she is angry that management continues to rob the workers by appropriating the fruits of their inventive force while at the same time maintaining the regime of unpaid technical work. She is left only with her ambiguous victory against the "impermeable" boundary between mental and manual labor, a victory that allows her to privilege her knowledge and to taunt the engineers for being foolish and inept.

Another type of skilled activity in the maquilas involves worker-administered time and motion study. This activity often leads to changes in the organization of the labor process, changes that are often formally adopted by management after considerable worker experimentation. Juana Ortega described time and motion study to me over the years, noting how different workers arrived at the technique and how they did not always share the results with supervisors or engineers:

The job is ready for you, because the engineer tells you how to do it. You step in and do what he tells you. He says, okay, this first step, where you pick up the tweezers, that should take two seconds. You pick the tweezers up with your hand and you position it at this angle over the circuit board. The second step is, you take the tweezers and twist the wires on the capacitor or whatever with a half-circle motion of your wrist. And that takes five seconds or less. The third step, and so on. . . . Well, that is not necessarily the best way to do it. . . . But you can't tell the engineer who is timing the operation. You have to wait and experiment later, when he is gone. There is always a better way to do it. Sometimes you play dumb and sometimes you don't. But in either case you better make sure the engineer doesn't figure out your little game. (Interview, Ciudad Juárez, August 1989)

Over the years, Juana Ortega readily performed time and motion studies and changed the sequences and timings of her tasks in several different jobs. The changes made her work not just faster but easier, especially less straining on her fingers and wrists. But she did not necessarily share this knowledge with the engineers. Instead, she used it to her own advantage, to make work less hazardous and increase output rates. But she also did not always share the increased output with management. She accumulated units and hid them as "booty" (*tesorito,* she called it), to be turned in on other jobs. Or sometimes she shared the "excess" with slower workers, especially when their jobs were threatened for failure to meet production quotas.[57] Ortega's innovations resulted from an informal, inductive learning process. But again, the attainment of a skill—in this case, the use of conceptual techniques such as time and motion study—was not the end result of an informal apprenticeship in industrial engineering. Ortega, like other workers, used her knowledge to construct argumentative narratives. She then used this discourse in a struggle against managerial authority and control. Ortega used "language games" to construct arguments for worker solidarity and conserve the identities of the workers as a distinct social group.

Deskilling, Self-Exploitation, and Workplace Oppositional Cultures

Maquila workers increase their productivity by utilizing their own working knowledge, and they often do so without an increase in pay. However, sometimes workers use this knowledge to their own advantage in order to make their jobs easier, less tedious, or less hazardous. This knowledge can also be used by informal shop-floor networks—for example, when workers deny management access to their information and abilities, or when they directly appropriate the knowledge to make their struggles against managerial control more effective. The dynamics of informal shop-floor relations are infinitely complex, and it is unwise to determine or assume the existence of universal circumstances that lead to acquiescence or resistance. Nevertheless, worker and manager narratives can provide valuable insights into the dynamics of self-exploitation and the ambiguities and contradictions that surface in the struggle over deskilled labor's inventive force.

WORKING KNOWLEDGE AND SELF-EXPLOITATION

A former plant manager at RCA–Juárez once observed that

> [maquila] workers are very creative. They make changes in components, machinery, tools, and in the assembly process itself. These are activities one comes to expect from engineers or technicians. But the line operators also make contributions. We would have a more difficult time without all this activity. (Interview, Ciudad Juárez, July 1983)

Despite their official status as low-waged, deskilled labor, maquila workers can continuously challenge Fordist conventions that presume a deficit in labor's creativity. Most of the time, when workers fix and modify the instruments of production or make changes in the production process itself they are engaging in self-exploitation. But it is equally clear that they most often do this out of self-preservation in the face of managerial threats, especially the threat of layoffs or reprimands. The primary motive for inventive activity remains the need to maintain pace with exceedingly high production quotas.[58] Many workers fear losing their jobs if they fail to keep their productivity standards at levels that meet or exceed managerial expectations. Melina Ochoa best described the dilemma facing maquila workers: "If I wait too long, I'll fall behind in my production [and] that can be a serious thing. For if I fall behind and fail to meet my daily standard I could be punished for it." Failure to meet production quotas is statistically the most frequent reason reported by workers for terminations and reprimands.[59]

For managers, the identification and appropriation of engineering, repair, and other skilled activities by assembly workers yields tremendous cost savings. The threat of layoffs or reprimands is used to subtly solicit compliance with organizational goals. Various informants over the years have recalled incidents in which the threat of layoffs was contrived by management in an effort to maintain productivity at steady levels in the midst of real or contrived personnel shortages. Rogelio Madruga, a former production superintendent at an automotive electronics assembly plant, explains this managerial tactic:

> There were times when we were a little short on mechanics. We lacked a number of repair and maintenance staff, beyond levels we are comfortable with, you see? For some time we had observed that many of the line operators could repair their own tools. What's more, they had contributed some important modifications in our conveyor-belt systems. They were capable and we knew it. So we told the operators that the plant was going to close down temporarily for lack of personnel and that we did not have anyone to repair the machinery or maintain the tools. Immediately, just as we expected, the best operators came forward and volunteered to do the work until we could find the appropriate personnel. . . . And you know what, they did as good a job as the skilled mechanics. Even better because we paid them less. [*He suppresses a chuckle.*] The best troubleshooter is a proud, hardworking, dedicated line operator. . . . Eventually, we promoted a few of these operators, and when I left the plant they were still on the job. (Interview, Ciudad Juárez, August 1989)

Here finally is a manager admitting to the contrived, political nature of wage regimes and occupational hierarchies that management manipulates to exploit the unpaid technical work of assembly "operators." This tactic usually involves temporarily allocating job setups, repair and maintenance activities, and quality-control tasks to assembly workers during periods of (real and contrived) high turnover among engineers, technicians, and inspectors. On occasion this has led to promotions for assembly workers, but most of the time this type of "job enlargement" is used to cut costs and maintain low wages without sacrificing high production quotas. Managers readily recognize the inventive force, but will not officially acknowledge its existence.

Workers obviously have their own perspectives on this issue. Paulina Guerra, a former electronics assembly worker, describes the problem of self-exploitation in no uncertain terms:

> One of my companions was on a sorting machine and she had a standard of thirty-five hundred pieces. When the machine broke down she would lose time, and since the majority of the occasions the mechanic took too long to arrive, she had to figure the problems out herself [*ingeniárselas*]. Okay, it's a situation where you can't win because the engineers won't fix the machines but they also will not let up on the standards. They want you to maintain the standards one way or another so most of the time you have no choice but to do the work yourself. . . . Yes. Of course I think this

is unfair! They are not paying us at the rate for engineers or repair technicians. So why should we do it? . . . We may be exploiting ourselves here, right? But what would you do? It's either get the job done or don't get paid and workers can even get fired if they don't make the standard. . . . You can say we are exploiting ourselves but it's better than not having a job. (Interview, Ciudad Juárez, July 1989)

The narrative practices that managers and workers construct ultimately do not always obscure the political nature of the regime. Threats to job security are clearly the primary motive underlying these activities, and both workers and managers recognize this as a political and not a technical construct. There may be other factors involved in the dynamics of unpaid technical work that have less to do with discursive practices and more to do with the imposition of unstated expectations that management has for certain types of workers. As the 1984 COMO report on skill in the maquilas points out,

> The job order [*carta de trabajo*] also predetermines the "standard," or what is thought to be producible in a certain amount of time. Nevertheless, it is against this standard that the worker has to compete daily to conserve her employment. . . . The necessity of conserving employment and the creative ability of the worker make possible a continuous process of innovation in the daily work routine.[60]

There are interesting parallels here to the informal shop floor relations that management uses to control output restriction and other types of worker resistance. As we saw in previous chapters with the case of the battle over *tortuguismo*, managers rely on group chiefs to solicit unpaid technical work from assembly workers. Juana Ortega recalls her role as a group chief and the pressures she was subjected to by a supervisor as a result of his efforts to exploit her work group's inventive force:

> I was promoted because I was the fastest worker. In the early days, before I got over my brainwashing, I always exceeded the standard. But my supervisor wanted more than high quotas. He constantly pressured me to get the workers to do things that were really not part of our jobs. He would say, "Look, I know you all can fix the conveyor belt, so why don't you just ask the girls to do it?" One time we were having problems with the conveyor belt on the . . . board-stuffing line. There was a shudder. The belt and the components on it vibrated too much. This happened whenever the engineers increased the speed. The problem was the speed of the belt, and there was really no reason to expect that anyone could fix it. But we had done some other things. You recall? It was really too bad. We were too

ignorant. In the early years [1979], we came up with the idea of installing the stop-start button [see chapter 3]. The engineer came and asked that we fix the vibration. I refused, and he threatened me by saying that I would no longer enjoy certain privileges . . . you know, what he thought were privileges, like being excused for getting to work late, or getting invited to dinner parties, things like that. It always made me angry that he saw these things as privileges. (Interview, Ciudad Juárez, July 1989)

Ortega is one of the most politicized maquila workers that I have ever spoken to over the course of ten years of field research in Juárez. This narrative captures the political character of her identity. The statement conveying anger because the supervisor "saw these things as privileges" reveals disdain for the sex-typed conventions that inform the attitudes of the males she worked under. Over the years, Ortega was also sexually harassed, an experience that reinforced her tendency toward militancy and struggle. She became increasingly wary of the dangers posed to worker solidarity by group chiefs who encouraged their primary work groups to comply with managerial expectations.

The COMO study further documented the role of group chiefs in promoting these activities among assembly workers. According to that study, the division of labor in the maquilas informally delegates primary responsibility for work organization to the group chief:

> For the corporation, the capacity to organize production personnel is normally . . . expected of the group chief; it is the group chief who has the responsibility of organizing the line [group] so that it will comply with the goals of production. It is the group chief that receives the job order and who has the direct responsibility to make sure that the instructions are followed so that the operations will comply with the production goals. Approximately 10 percent of the workers in the maquila export industry acquire the labor experience of group chief, and they are the real link between the company and the production line worker, given that the line engineer has as an exclusive function the supervision of the worker group chief, and it is not rare that an engineer first-line supervisor will not pass even one hour of his working day truthfully working close to the production line.[61]

These informal relationships—between first-line supervisors and group chiefs and between these and assembly workers—can generate intense micropolitical conflicts over the exploitation of the women's working knowledge of production techniques. And it is here, in the micropolitics of working knowledge, that maquila workers generate an entire array of informal shop-floor networks and narrative arguments that sustain workplace oppositional cultures.

WORKING KNOWLEDGE AND OPPOSITIONAL CULTURES

Managers pressure group chiefs to secure worker compliance with organizational goals. But this pressure does not always go unopposed. The situation can in fact produce struggles over the loyalty of the group chiefs when line workers move to prevent the co-optation of their immediate production leaders by subverting the power narratives of deskilling. While workers often rely on working knowledge of production to comply with managerial demands and protect their jobs, they sometimes use this knowledge to empower themselves in daily shop-floor confrontations with management. Or sometimes they *refuse* to use working knowledge to comply with managerial dictates—they subvert the stereotype of the "dumb Mexican worker" and do precisely that: they play "dumb." The working knowledge of maquila workers can thus be associated with workplace oppositional cultures, or what I might call subaltern networks of resistance. Juana Ortega's refusal to subordinate herself to managerial authority through time and motion studies is an example of this type of oppositional tendency.

Other workers have over the years described similar struggles to me with a profound sense of irony and conscious resistance. For example, Alicia Vargas, a former repair technician and group chief at Subensambles Electrónicos (SESA) who was also a student at COMO during the early 1980s, spoke of the struggle over unpaid technical work in an interview conducted in 1989:

> Did we always comply with the supervisor's desires? Do I have a head on my shoulders? Of course, we always had our own ideas about right and wrong and what we could get away with. Our position of advantage was the fact that the engineers and supervisors seldom came into contact with us on the line. We could get away with a lot because of this. If you can get the group chief over to your side, or better never let her cross the line . . . then there is no way for the managers to lock in on every single worker every hour of every shift. They depend on group chiefs doing these things for them . . . you know, organizing repairs, drawing up quota schedules, maintaining output charts, and monitoring these things for the supervisor or engineer. The engineers want to take advantage of us [*quieren abusar de nosotros*], but it sort of backfires on them. This situation gives us access to information because the group chief is not just responsible to management . . . we had to look out for our own also, watch over our sisters. *La que es verdadera amiga, no es espía* [The one who is a true friend isn't a spy]. . . . At SESA, the group of us that studied at COMO, we found a new understanding of our work. At COMO we learned we had a value that was

not just in the labor we performed, but in our value as dignified human beings. And what we found out was that the understanding we had of our own work, of the different organizations of work in the plant, was the most valuable thing we had . . . because we could use what we learned to struggle. (Interview, Ciudad Juárez, August 1989)

In this narrative, working knowledge of production undergoes a metamorphosis and reemerges as a source of resistance—a fountain that workers draw from to construct oppositional practices in the workplace. In Alicia Vargas's case, the narrative has moved beyond the privileging of workers' knowledge to the actual use of knowledge in struggle. This is perhaps the most significant aspect of the working knowledge that maquila workers produce on the line, despite the political chimeras and technical contrivances of management. This knowledge production, or creative praxis, is utilized and organized by apparently "deskilled" workers to circulate and escalate struggles within the workplace and community. Workers challenge management with wage demands for unpaid technical work; they design better ways to get the job done and to protect their health; they link their skills with struggles in the community. Workers produce and share knowledge with each other in ways that can subvert and undermine managerial imperatives.

But the knowledge produced by maquila workers in the context of the workplace is not limited to technical know-how derived from firsthand observation of labor processes. Much of their "technique" is also combined with other forms of knowledge, especially local knowledge and associated tacit social and cultural skills. Local knowledge, when coupled with the inventive force of working knowledge, can engender the circulation of struggle, promoting discourses that link with the activities of informal shop-floor networks and other organizational forms. This link occurs because the discourses provide a common cultural framework for collaboration in struggle. Juana Ortega's experiences with time and motion study are illustrative here: she not only modified her jobs, she shared the results with other workers to empower them vis-à-vis the struggle over productivity standards.

Clashes over identity figure in this process whenever workers consciously vie with management to win the hearts and minds of the other workers. In 1989, Juana Ortega and I revisited many of her ideas about the nature of workplace politics in the maquilas:

Yes. [To win,] I had to do two things. First, I learned the system—the work organization—better than the managers and engineers. That way they can't deceive you but you can fool them. Second, I had to get as many of the workers to cooperate (one sellout [*vendida*] was about all it took). And that was a lot harder than learning the job. The only way to maintain solidarity is by sharing the results of your own work. That way you can share responsibility. That makes it harder for any one person to get caught in the act. Everyone does it and it's harder to get caught. Too many hands in the process really messes up things. It drives the engineers crazy. My own way was always to make sure that, well, that the fact that I was faster and that I produced more never meant that anyone else was going to be punished by having to match my output curve. Instead of being greedy, I shared my output. When that was not possible, then I had to say: "Okay, companion, you know this condition here hurts us. I will back you up to fight the managers in order to make it better even if it doesn't affect me directly." Which it does anyway. *Lo malo para una es malo para todas, ¿verdad?* [An injury to one is an injury to all, right?] . . . I believe if we workers [*obreras*] are to maintain solidarity, we cannot be confused about who we are. If one worker thinks she is in the same class with the manager then we are really in trouble. There can be no struggle. . . . How did we maintain a common identity as workers? I don't think that was it at all. Much of that was already established, since we shared the same experiences, the same conditions—you know, the same hazards, pressures, and problems inside the factory. It was not hard to see how your life was different from the managers and engineers. When you left work and got into that crowded bus or *rutero* [passenger-van taxi], while the manager drove off in his nice brand-new car, you knew the difference. Unless you were blind. . . . But what you call the identity came from our friendship and not just from our being workers. It's silly to see it that way. That's not all we had in common. We had to keep together after work, and that could be difficult. It was a hard thing, because family responsibilities took many of us away from each other. For those of us who didn't have families, especially the unmarried women, well, the only friends you had were often your co-workers. It was hard to see us go our own separate ways after work so often. . . . Were we women changing history? That's sort of a joke because it . . . well . . . let me just say that history means that a lot of things are possible, and all we can do is just push it a little bit over in another direction. Okay, I suppose . . . yes, there we were, industrial women workers who refused old ways by not getting married and having children. [*She laughs, for I am clearly the butt of the joke for asking these questions.*] You know, all that made me age too quickly. [*She chuckles again.*] The changes did not mean we had it better. For some, instead of marriage and motherhood making us old, the assembly line did that just about the same and faster if you are a working mother. [*A sadness creeps into her eyes; tears well up.*] . . . My partner, you know? She helped a lot with these problems over the years. All my women worker friends, every one of them helped through hard times—two pregnancies and a divorce—talk about something that can really mess up your attitude about fighting the authority of the supervisors. It [the struggle against managerial authority] could get a little intimidating for me when I was depressed. My friendships provided an anchor, a sense of comradeship with other workers. And sometimes all we had to show for our work were the same problems like in the factory or at home. (Interview, Ciudad Juárez, August 1989)

Ortega's narrative strikes at the heart of the dynamics that workers use to define and redefine the lines of solidarity in workplace oppositional cultures. These are the narratives of power struggles over the definition of class and gender identities. These discourses of identity are part of the working knowledge created by workers such as Ortega. In her case, the formation and free expression of an emergent lesbian identity provided her with yet another basis for establishing friendships and promoting relationships of solidarity with co-workers. In her narrative, I see a particular type of identity construction at play, one that is derived from the multiple, shifting positions she occupies, not just as a worker but as a single working mother with a newly defined lesbian identity. Ever modest, Ortega remained equally wary of my own feeble attempts to draw some historical significance from her story. She thinks my questions are a joke because I am inflating the significance of her words and actions. Ortega conveys what for me is an "affirmative" postmodern attitude toward human agency in history. Her view that "history means that a lot of things are possible and all we can do is just push it a little bit over in another direction" is consistent with the postmodern position of multiple meaning, local truth, and the limited possibilities of collective human action.[62]

In the context of the history and sociology of industrial work organizations, workplace oppositional cultures are really not that unusual. What is intriguing in the specific case of these Juárez-area maquilas during the 1980s is how some workers actively created and defended identities that they consciously located outside the parameters of conventional gender-typed expectations—women do not work in factories; women are supposed to get married, have children, and stay at home; women should not become lesbians. I recognize this as constitutive of a form of knowledge—social, tacit knowledge—that is born of a situation involving not just the tactical search for solidarity on the shop floor but also the formation of identities that allow workers to negotiate their positions in a search for conviviality in everyday life outside the factory gates. And this, fortunately, is the one aspect of the workers' everyday lived experience that management perhaps will never conquer. These discursive practices can assist workers in breaking through managerial contrivances in order to reach one another. These practices remain just beyond the reach of managerial despotism, and can empower workers to create and protect the vital autonomous spaces necessary for the reproduction of workplace oppositional cultures. In these identity narratives, workers recognize the importance of friendship in the struggle against productivity drives. But narratives of identity and power are also important when workers struggle to protect themselves from managerial attempts to appropriate and control subaltern working knowledge of production systems. The narratives are thus a fundamental part of identity politics because workers use them to reshape the content, intensity, inclusiveness, and direction of struggle.

Working Knowledge and COMO's Transference Methodology

The so-called discovery of deskilled labor's inventive force led COMO to develop a strategy for transferring the working knowledge of maquiladora workers to other branches of production. Specifically, between 1982 and 1985 there was a concerted effort to harness this inventive force in the service of worker-owned, self-managed cooperatives. Finding alternatives to employment in the maquilas was always important to COMO's political agenda, and many of the organizers and teachers there believed such alternatives could be fomented by linking the workers' inventive force with organizing and educational resources available at COMO. This was a project that I personally participated in, and so much of what I have to say derives from my own experience in the struggle.

REDEFINING DESKILLED LABOR AS UNPAID TECHNICAL WORK

COMO's transference project essentially revolved around efforts to redefine deskilled labor by carefully documenting the innovations and inventions of maquila assembly workers. The crux of this strategy involved efforts to equate workers' lived experience and working knowledge of production with unpaid technical work, or technical surplus value. It was a conscious effort to politically, and not just technically, redefine the labor of maquila workers as skilled. In a 1989 interview, Guillermina Valdés recalled this struggle in the following terms:

We must defend the fact, we must legitimize the idea, that scientific knowledge is not the exclusive province of experts, engineers, and trained scientists. This was the fundamental notion that guided our work. At COMO, we focused on documenting the inductive apprenticeship, the creativity of the workers. For most observers it was difficult to accept that theirs was, and is, a scientific type of knowledge. And it was certainly not just the managers who resisted this fact. The academics also resisted the idea and continue to depict the workers as unskilled know-nothings. . . . We demonstrated through the project not only that the workers had this knowledge, but that it could be effectively transferred to other branches of production. The task, the unfinished task, has to do with the ideological front, with the political problem of legitimizing this knowledge and using the power of the workers' self-organization to redefine the labor of the entire industry as technical skilled labor. This is the only strategy that gives us at least a remote opportunity to transform the maquila wage structure in a fundamental and enduring way. . . . The other task was to transfer this creativity to the community, where it could be put to use in the development of the cooperatives and in satisfying the unmet social needs of the so-called marginalized communities, the *pepenadores* [garbage dump workers], for example. That, as you know, led to mixed results, but it is also an evolving process. It's far from over, this matter of inventing new work, new organizational forms. (Interview, Ciudad Juárez, August 1989)

In July 1982, preliminary results generated by my dissertation survey research provided evidence of extensive working knowledge and skilled activities among maquila assembly workers. I immediately brought the results to Valdés's attention. A series of meetings was held shortly thereafter, and then a number of us designed a preliminary model for a more comprehensive survey of skill in the maquilas, utilizing a larger sample of workers. Guillermina Valdés, Jesús Montenegro, and I, along with several COMO students (maquila workers), contributed to the first draft of a proposal that was eventually submitted to and approved by the Friedrich Ebert Foundation of West Germany.

The urgency (for us) of the project must be understood in the historical context of the times. A series of *peso* devaluations, initiated by the Mexican government in 1981, substantially increased the wage-bill savings for transnational corporations involved in the maquiladora Border Industrialization Program (BIP). At 1983 exchange rates, the maquila workers were averaging a daily wage of approximately $3.00 (not including benefits).[63] This compared with a high of $9.19 a day in January 1981. In the period from January 1981 through March 1983, maquila workers experienced a threefold decrease in their wages expressed in terms of the devalued exchange rate (see table 14). Workers' wages were also affected by inflation and the not uncommon imposition of fixed wage rates for extended employment periods. Wages were also being affected by the sporadic and seasonal character of production schedules in many of the maquilas.[64] Many maquila workers at the time experienced numerous weeks of unemployment or reduced work schedules due to fluctuations in international and U.S. markets. This tendency was quite evident in 1982 and 1983, when several Juárez-area maquilas implemented large-scale layoffs, furloughs, or staggered workshifts for reasons misleadingly attributed by some managers to the recessionary condition of the U.S. economy.[65]

Critics of the maquilas were justified in bringing attention to the wage issue. Van Waas had already documented the link between wages and productivity and concluded that the maquilas were superexploitative propositions at best.[66] From a theoretical point of view, maquiladoras represent a strategy used by transnational corporations to maximize profit rates by combining low-wage regimes with high-productivity regimes

Table 14. Average Daily Wages, Juárez Maquiladoras, Select Years, 1969–1983

Year	Daily Wage[a]
1969	2.80
1972	4.00
1974	4.80
1975	5.76
1976 (June)	6.64
1976 (Aug.)[b]	4.43
1977	4.88
1978	5.43
1979	6.21
1980	6.25
1981 (Jan.)	9.19
1981 (Dec.)[c]	7.81
1983 (March)[d]	3.00

Source: de la Rosa (1982); except for 1983, *El Paso Times* (1983).

a. In U.S. dollars.

b. After 1976 *peso* devaluation.

c. After 1981 *peso* devaluations.

d. After 1983 *peso* devaluations.

(workers in Mexico are not just cheaper but more productive than comparable U.S. workers).[67] A Fordist organization can constantly drive productivity up by increasing the speed of the assembly line. This, combined with depressed wages in the postdevaluation period, is what increased the rate of exploitation in the maquilas.[68]

At COMO, we knew that workers were having great difficulty making ends meet with the reduced purchasing power of their wages. Many workers, students at COMO during the early 1980s, complained that they could no longer purchase staple items such as milk, eggs, and ground beef. Many were forced to move in with other workers under increasingly crowded housing conditions. Estela Romero, a former COMO student and electronics worker, recalls the situation as it was in 1981–1983:

> Before the devaluations, I could help my mother and father with the food. We could enjoy a good meal every day. We could even purchase meat at least twice a week. Eggs, milk, bread—all these were readily available in our home. But after the devaluations, especially the last ones this year [1983]—well, it really hurt us. We could no longer purchase meat, except maybe once or twice a month; it was a real luxury. Even milk and eggs were hard to get with any regularity, so we were eating *fideos* [vermicelli], beans, rice, and tortillas. That was bad enough, but even worse was the fact that we could not heat our homes during the cold winter months. The entire situation worsened, and it made everyone in the family sick. (Interview, Ciudad Juárez, October 1983)

These were the same workers who as students at COMO were busy at the time detailing the inventive creativity that we sought to politicize. It did not seem fair to us, nor to the workers, that they should starve while the corporations reaped the benefit of their working knowledge. The time to challenge managerial avarice had arrived. The definition of maquila workers as deskilled labor had to be politically, and not just technically, deconstructed.

COMO AND THE TRANSFERENCE METHODOLOGY

Our analysis at COMO led us to new theoretical insights about deskilled labor's inventiveness. The issues revolving around unpaid technical work were not limited to problems of self-exploitation. Deskilled labor's creativity in the maquilas raised important theoretical and political questions that we felt had not been sufficiently addressed by researchers, organizers, or policymakers. Worker innovations and other skilled activities were a new additional source of surplus value for transnational capital that went beyond the usual unequal exchange relations that produced a depressed Mexican wage regime. This activity involved a newly created sector of workers in restructured transnational labor processes. Maquila workers were contributing to capitalist restructuring by providing an un-fathomable source of unpaid technical work and not just "cheap labor." In contrast, we knew that workers in the United States had become noto-rious (at least among management) for their being uninterested in their work. They were more likely to sabotage their equipment than to fix it.[69] Capital's search for a malleable and cooperative workforce had brought the maquilas to the Mexican border.[70] Workers were inadvertently col-laborating by voluntarily providing unpaid technical work. We felt that this inventive force could just as well serve the interests of the workers and their communities. Our goal at COMO was to find a method for transferring the working knowledge of maquila women to experiments in worker-owned, self-managed cooperatives and other community de-velopment projects.

ORGANIZING THE INDUCTIVE APPRENTICESHIP

The transference methodology developed at COMO was summarized in a series of three diagrams that accompanied its 1984 report on creativity and innovation in the maquilas. These diagrams outline the three facets of the methodology: (1) identifying the tacit and potential skills of ma-quila workers and verifying their embeddedness in the industrial work organizations of the factories, (2) documenting the process of informal inductive apprenticeship, and (3) systematizing this working knowledge in a reflexive manner to allow for the transference of skills to other work-place settings.[71]

Identifying Tacit & Potential Skills. The starting point of the transference methodology was to identify the potential and tacit skills of the workers. COMO categorized these into affective, intellectual, mechanical, psycho-logical, and psychomotor skills. Workers were seen as utilizing these skills upon their introduction to industrial work in the maquiladoras. This in-volved two aspects: direct contact of the worker with the production pro-cess, and the self-directed integration and adaptation of the worker to a "productive labor environment." Further formal training increased the workers' familiarity with equipment, component parts, and the overall workplace setting. Training also allowed workers to elaborate products and acquire working knowledge of the products. The COMO model posited a direct link between industrial work processes and the ability of the worker to learn concepts and acquire working knowledge in manufacturing engineering, including production planning and the use of job orders (outlining actual production processes). Subsumed under engineering was time and motion study, which workers also acquired through informal practice and formal training.

Documenting the Inductive Apprenticeship. Engineering knowledge was seen by COMO as directly linked to what was called *la tecnología interna de la obrera* (the internal technique of the worker). This internal technique was posited as a tacit skill that allowed workers to engage in the informal inductive apprenticeship. Efforts to describe this inductive apprenticeship led us to document working knowledge in several areas:

1. modification of pre-established systems (including the reduction of times and motions and a better distribution of work materials)
2. improvement of production processes (including innovations in products, machinery, tools, and the workplace setting)
3. reduction of the waste of materials and tools
4. acquisition of quality-control criteria (including quality control of assembled products and damaged materials)
5. understanding of the functioning of equipment (including a decrease in wasted time and the ability to fix and maintain machinery and tools in general)
6. organization and reorganization of production processes (including the creation of small lines for the repair of certain products, the creation of lines for the recycling of production materials, and the reassignment of certain operations in the absence of particular workers)
7. self-organization and self-management of personnel
8. self-management of production reports
9. self-organization of materials inventories
10. understanding of physical-chemical properties and processes related to the products (e.g., soldering and fluxsilicon)

The inductive apprenticeship, moreover, was seen as leading directly to the development of skills that could then be transferred to other branches of production.

Transference of Skills through Reflexive Methods. The final step involved "systematizing the working knowledge to make it reflexive and transferable." Several neo-Freirean pedagogical (or social problem-solving) models would be utilized by accessing educational resources available at

COMO. The transference would then be effected by immersing workers in self-learning projects designed to help them (1) apply and critically reflect on the acquired knowledge in practice sessions, (2) further their understanding of industrialized production processes through work with the cooperatives, (3) develop an awareness and understanding of the concept of *plusvalía tecnológica* (technological surplus value), (4) develop familiarity with the history of corporate versus cooperative organizational forms, (5) learn formal concepts in design engineering, (6) learn formal concepts in manufacturing engineering, and (7) learn formal concepts in quality-control engineering.

Once funding was secured in 1983 from the Friedrich Ebert Foundation, COMO implemented the transference-methodology project. Eventually, over three hundred maquila workers participated in the training program. From the start, the goals of the project were twofold: first, to document the inventive force and working knowledge of the maquila workforce and use the resulting data to pressure the industry into accepting a higher-wage regime; and second, to develop strategies and programs to transfer this skill to other branches of production, especially to the developing worker-owned, self-managed cooperatives that had been promoted since the mid 1970s. This approach allowed the women's center to make use of its expertise and resources in alternative education for women workers and to rely on its capacity to promote community organizing through existing and extensive activist, kinship, and friendship networks.

WORKING KNOWLEDGE, SOCIAL ACTIVISM, AND COMMUNITY ORGANIZING

Over the course of the project, COMO linked the creativity of maquila workers with projects involving the promotion of worker-owned, self-managed cooperatives, educational and health outreach programs, and other community organizing efforts (see chapter 5). The working knowledge of maquila workers was thus transferred not just to other workplaces, but to more general efforts aimed at improving the working and living conditions of so-called marginalized communities. In a word, working knowledge was effectively linked with social activism and community organizing.

But COMO's interface with maquila workers could not have automatically led to activism among the students were it not for the types of knowledge claims and discursive practices that some of the workers had

previously articulated and developed as members of workplace oppositional cultures. Clearly, not every maquila worker was subversive or active in struggle. Nor was every actively struggling worker engaged with
the organization as a student. Activist workers who were also COMO students underwent training in the inductive apprenticeship. Additionally,
through the core curriculum (*tronco común*) these workers gained exposure to studies in the history of worker and capitalist organizational forms
and community organizing. Many of them were thus empowered to draw
on their own resources to articulate identity narratives and forms of
working knowledge that they first acquired in the maquila milieux to escalate struggles in the larger political terrain of the community as a whole.

The next chapter outlines one important case in which COMO staff
and students, many of them former maquila workers, joined with a community of marginalized dump workers in a struggle to establish a worker-
owned, self-managed cooperative. In the SOCOSEMA struggle, the most
"marginalized of marginals" articulate narratives of moral rights and obligations. The following story of the *pepenadores* of SOCOSEMA is not
just a site ethnography of power relations; it is a marginal's morality play.

7

Marginality as Inventive Force

Badly clothed, living in holes
Under the eaves, in the ruins
with the owls and the thieves
Companions of the shadows.
—Pierre Dupont ("Le chant des ouvriers," 1846)[1]

The struggle is an invention of the people.
—Wall slogan in a "squatter" community
(Colonia Libertad, Ciudad Juárez, 1981)

The pepenadores? *We were the original recyclers.*
—Isabel Robles, founding member of SOCOSEMA
(Ciudad Juárez, 1989)

Companions of the Shadows

Most of us had houses of wood and cardboard and some of wood with tin and some caves in roofed-in cliffs [*barrancos techados*]. Okay, like who says to not be outside in the cold or the heat? . . . We did not earn enough to eat. Wore clothes that came out of the dump. Ate also in the dump. . . . One or another good thing.[2]

This chapter tells the story of several hundred squatters who settled by the Juárez municipal waste dump during the 1950s and 1960s. At first, these homeless individuals and families lived in cardboard boxes and the lucky ones in single-room adobe sheds or shanties constructed from recycled pieces of lumber and rubber tires. Others lived in caves with rickety tin roofs. There was no electricity or running water. Sanitation was nonexistent, and the human waste surrounding the shanties made everyone sick. People drank water from drainage ditches, or rainwater captured in discarded metal barrels that had once contained toxic industrial chemicals. They scavenged in the trash heaps for food, clothing, and the makings of shelter.

Some of the "luckier" ones worked for a local businessman who controlled the private concession for recycling garbage at the dump. These dump workers, or *pepenadores,* worked twelve to fifteen hours a day and were paid by piece rate. Tons of garbage had to be sorted, selected, and carried for wages as low as a dollar per day. Most of the families were from displaced rural peasant communities. Most were illiterate and without formal education. The children were not in school and ran barefoot in the trash, trying to enjoy the few moments they could glean for childhood games. Numerous children became ill from the lack of clean drinking water, and some died from the dehydration that accompanies untreated diarrhea or dysentery. The cold winters made everyone—young and old, weak and strong—ill and distraught. There was no sense of community, no neighbors or pleasant talk. Even the children lacked the time to be obstinate, as children are when they have a safe environment to play in. There was no time for rest. There was no reason or place to celebrate life. But the powers that be in Ciudad Juárez refused to acknowledge their existence. The media also ignored the presence of starving families and dying children. The squatters were truly "companions of the shadows."

In 1975, with the assistance of COMO, the *pepenadores* organized themselves into a cooperative society. Within ten years, the dump workers developed a vibrant, self-sustaining community. The recycling cooperative, SOCOSEMA (Sociedad Cooperativa de Seleccionadores de Materiales),[3] gave them not just employment and housing but collective empowerment and a chance to build an intentional community. The *pepenadores* redefined their place in the political economy of the Mexican border not by remaining hapless victims and therefore passive, expectant recipients of humanitarian goodwill (which can never be enough no matter how well intended), nor by becoming integrated into the transnational economy of the border as cheap wage labor. Instead, they invented a new organizational form linking their needs for housing, clean water, basic health care, education, and food with a bold experiment in workplace democracy, ecological sustainability, mutual aid, and community revival.

The establishment of the SOCOSEMA cooperative is a watershed in U.S.–Mexico border economic and social history that has been almost universally overlooked in the contemporary discourse on border regional development.[4] At our collective peril, scholars and policymakers have largely ignored SOCOSEMA's significance to the history and future of economic development in the region. The peril is that, as Mexico, the United

States, and Canada implement the North American Free Trade Agreement, sustainable and culturally appropriate options for economic development and community revitalization are being closed off or ignored.

To this day, SOCOSEMA thrives as a grassroots sustainable-development organization and as a viable, intentional community because it successfully joined strong spiritual traditions with mutual-aid practices, reciprocity networks, cooperative work organization, and ethnoscience. The dump workers' co-op is a living example of sustainable alternatives for Mexican border regional development. As an alternative to mass production and environmental degradation, SOCOSEMA provides a sharp contrast to the rapidly expanding and destructive hubs of the maquiladora industry. Moreover, the history of the co-op calls into question many of the assumptions and generalizations made by sociologists, media pundits, and policymakers about the characteristics of the so-called urban underclass.

SOCIOLOGICAL MISCONCEPTIONS OF MARGINALITY

Popular and sociological conceptions of marginality are today dominated by depictions of social misfits and pariahs. One persistent image, both in popular ideologies and in social research, is that of the marginal person as an isolated outcast.[5] According to this perspective, marginals are in such severe social isolation as to remain completely incapable of interacting with mainstream society. They are also assumed to exist in a state of normlessness that leads to a predictable pattern of individual dysfunction and "criminality."[6] The lack of values is said to permeate the entire psychological fabric and social life experiences of these isolated and powerless individuals. Marginality is thus commonly defined as "individual social pathology." Ultimately, the urban underclass has only itself to blame for its woes.

The culture-of-poverty view is also very much alive as an ideology among social scientists who have written about "collective" marginality.[7] The conservative sociological and public discourse represents marginality as at best a state of wretched powerlessness. But sociologists *mis*define the "underclass" by obscuring the subjectivity of marginalized communities and assuming that all "marginals" exist in a condition of anomie. Lacking the capacity for ethics or common values, marginals are simply presumed incapable of sustaining a sense of community or articulating discourse. This is perhaps why so much of the marginality literature is *just* theory: analytical pirouettes and fancy logical language games disengaged from the lived experiences and discourses of marginalized others. Ungrounded theory notwithstanding, marginals have their own stories to tell. Guillermina Valdés, in the prologue to a historical essay written by Isabel Robles, warns that

> [w]hen we are accustomed to reading history written by observers, academics, or novelists, it is easy to forget that the people write their own history with blood and sweat. . . . We have also fallen into the trap of believing that history is exclusively written by the educated expert and that it is more true if recounted by an intellectual. . . . Now, finally, Isabel silences us all and proclaims the truth, because it is his experience, his life, his history, and not ours. Isabel speaks to us with brutal honesty but with his heart in hand; he begins to teach us how to write history.[8]

The dominant sociological discourse ultimately constructs a false image of marginality in which the companions of the shadows are not only deviant and powerless, but also mute. They cannot possibly have anything important to teach us, and if they did they would not possess the intellectual resources to express themselves to us; we have to do it for them. By definition, the sociological discourse assumes that marginals lack the values, skills, and resources to come together with others to form a community. Marginality is also defined as a state of social disorganization. The conflict-theory sociologist Randall Collins, for example, defines marginality as isolation from social networks.[9] The marginal person is the ultimate loner. Such isolated individuals are presumed incapable of effectively participating in human organizations or contributing to the process of social change.

Our inarticulate companions of the shadows presumably have no role to play in history. They are the contemporary "people without history," to borrow a phrase from Eric Wolf.[10] Their history, presumably, must be constructed by outsiders, as when they come under the rational gaze of the sociologist or when their life stories are subjected to the literary manipulations of novelists. But the history of SOCOSEMA demonstrates that these popular and sociological depictions of marginality are more the ideological constructions of theorists and media pundits than accurate renditions of the everyday lived experiences of marginalized others.

There is another view, however. In 1928, Robert Park, the renowned Chicago-school sociologist, published an article on marginality in the *American Journal of Sociology*. He wrote of "marginal man" as a source of inventiveness and "the hope of civilization."[11] This idea has been largely undeveloped in contemporary sociological and anthropological discourse on marginality. Park's original notion of "inventive" marginals seems to have faded with time. The voices of the margins have been muted by the canons of scholars who are guilty of establishing a sort of intellectual apartheid that privileges the white, male scientific voice over other kinds of voices. The idea of marginals as transformers and bearers of civilization has been buried under problematic, negative constructions of marginality. Homeless bag ladies, sexual perverts, merciless serial killers, and insane street derelicts are the mute character types that haunt the discourses of popular lore and sociological theory.[12] Rejecting such negative constructions, I return to and extend Park's concept of marginality as inventive force. In this chapter, marginals present themselves as agents of social and cultural change and inventors of political struggle. This is a less problematic construction of the marginal as sojourner. I view marginals as liminal beings full of creative and transformative potential. They are fully capable of expressing their own voices and in doing so can challenge and undermine dominant views and ideologies. In the words of the urban squatters of Ciudad Juárez: "Struggle is an invention of the people."

And this itself is worth noting: the language of the *pepenadores* is compact and dense. It is not long-winded, overly ornate, or obscure like the skeptical, pastiche-like narratives of postmodern deconstructionists. This is a precise, fragmented, and yet "deep" language. It is brutally honest in its humility and its utter lack of pretension and is therefore scornful of "surface" meanings. Multiply layered empirical observations are laced with dense strings of moral aphorisms that invoke mutual respect and ritual kinship. As we will see, this ability to produce their own language games has been utilized effectively by the *pepenadores* to produce intense social solidarity and to circulate struggle.

From this standpoint—that of the *pepenadores'* autoconstruction of meaning and history—marginality is not the "social problem." Instead, the *political* problem is the domination implied by the fact that the discourse of the marginals, the language of the edges, has been suppressed by the gatekeepers of the canon. Contemporary discourses on marginality are predominantly framed by a view that grants an unstated primacy to the values and worldviews of "mainstream" cultures and social systems.[13] Parsonian sociologists are particularly guilty of taking the dominant values for granted. Prevailing values become hidden assumptions and immutable (nay, sacred) normative expectations against which people are ultimately judged. This has the effect of enshrining the "expert" voices of those who seek a universal truth while dismissing the "untrained" voices of local knowledge as illegitimate and irrational. The time has come to relocate the voices of the margin to the center of new discourse about ecologically sustainable and socially just development.

The Original Recyclers: SOCOSEMA, COMO, and the Politics of the Excluded

> Let them read this, but I am only writing truths, nothing more. How it was learned through our innocence. . . . We were like seeds without products.[14]

RECLAIMING LOST CHILDHOODS

The quote above is from Isabel Robles's historical essay on SOCOSEMA. The idea that truth is something one learns through innocence is explored in this chapter.[15] That innocence, if I may venture, is something that frames the experiences of many *pepenadores* who grew up in the garbage dump as children and are now young-adult workers. Rufino Santos has been with the dump workers' co-op since he was fifteen. He is now approaching thirty-two and has this to recall about the family's experiences before their arrival on the edges of a sprawling borderlands metropolis:

> I was twelve when my family moved to Juárez. Like many other families, my brother, who also lost land. They say, "El que se deja, nada deja" [He who allows himself to be dominated leaves nothing behind]. There were the big farmers and banks who rob the people. Really, if truth is known, federal politicians are behind those things. . . . All the political maneuvering we could not comprehend. My brother, nearly all of us unschooled and illiterate. To defend ourselves properly, no . . . God help us. Not possible to plant crops—no water, no seed, only the blowing dust. I know this now. To recall father's suffering. He grew food, and then he could not. On the *ejido*. That is how our people were forced off the land. (Interview, Ciudad Juárez, July 1989)

Displaced from their *ejido* of five generations, Rufino Santos's family moved to Juárez. According to him, the family walked half the distance to Juárez from their *ejido* west of the city of Chihuahua. He describes what it was like when the family first arrived on the border:

> We had no money. No food or clothes. Some of us without shoes. Everyone cold. No coats, two sweaters to share. My mother got sick soon, from the water I think. My youngest sister also sick. She was three years old. Almost died. . . . This in 1973. . . . First we lived north of the dump . . . west side of the city. Like this into the mountain inside a gulch. Rain, a big

storm came. Our camp, the shanties, the water flooded there. My brother, everything [*he waves his hands*] destroyed. Living through that, we thank God for our survival. (Interview, Ciudad Juárez, July 1989)

Leaving the dusty, flashflood-prone *arroyos* on the west side of Ciudad Juárez, the Santos family joined hundreds of other families already living farther south down the mountain range, at the municipal dump. Employment could be found there with a private businessman who was the concessionaire for garbage selection and sorting. Wages were extremely low, less than a dollar a day. The work was difficult, and pay was determined by a piece rate based on tons of garbage collected and sorted each day. Santos recalls his experiences as a teenager working and living in the dump, with no hope for the future:

Mother and sister got sick. I had a lot of fear. All of us were going to die. I thought, hunger will kill us. If not, the [drinking] water or cold weather. I always feared dying in the cold. We all have that in common, no? *La muerte hace mismo de todos, rico o pobre* [Death makes the same of everyone, rich or poor]. . . . Conditions at the dump? Not good to work in. Dirty, smelly things in the air all the time. Insects, flies, mosquitoes, ticks, fleas everywhere. Cut your feet on a broken bottle, a thing to avoid. My brother, imagine living in garbage. I now know that is why everywhere was much sickness. This is how it was before *la doctora* ["the doctor," in reference to Guillermina Valdés] and COMO, before they came to help us. . . . Working garbage is one thing, living in it is another. It is bad for people's health. . . . I didn't see a future. . . . My mother once said: "If we ever build a real home we will all be healthy and happy again." She was right. *Con techo 'sta hecho* [With a roof (over your head), it's done]. Young, I did not understand my beloved mother. My father believed this also. (Interview, Ciudad Juárez, July 1989)

Rufino Santos painfully recalls the changes his father was forced to endure in making the transition from being an independent peasant farmer, to being a homeless dump worker, and finally to becoming a member of the SOCOSEMA cooperative:

In his heart he always knew. Life will never be like before. On the *ejido* . . . for him it was all planting crops. This was his way. Not any more. This makes him sad. Not growing food to feed us. Imagine, my brother, his pain. He cannot feed us from the land—you know, directly. I think he is happier, now with the cooperative. But also sad for some time. . . . I think he will die, God bless him, dreaming of land to work. . . . It hurts him to have to live by turning garbage. My brother, it hurts the soul. (Interview, Ciudad Juárez, July 1989)

For Santos, and others who scratched a below-subsistence livelihood from the dump work, hope for a better future came in the form of COMO organizers and teachers. The organizing struggle undertaken by the Santos family and other families created a more secure future for the child laborers of the dump. The older generations have endured the loss of a cherished original livelihood and have been forced into a new urban home. But out of the ruin, hardships, and sacrifices of the older generations, the dump workers have created new opportunities for the young. Santos says, "I lost my childhood in that dump. I also found my personhood. My dignity as a human being. My brother, we are all children of God."

ORIGINS OF THE COOPERATIVE

Isabel Robles came with his family to Juárez from central Mexico because of a drought.[16] He writes the history of SOCOSEMA with the certitude and insight of someone who has lived his own struggle. He also writes with the confidence of someone who has participated in making a bit of history. In his essay, Robles vividly recalls the handicap of illiteracy and the continuous struggle of the dump workers for higher wages and access to recyclables for self-help:

> The work was by piece rate. . . . We had no benefits—not even our own materials. We had nothing. The truth is, a person who is educated knows more than an illiterate and in everything they beat us. If we complained about the lack of money for our materials they got angry. And since they were the learned ones they always won against the complainers and they got nothing. And they had a watchman posted where the people entered and exited the dump. That watchman searched all the people [dump workers]. If they had a knife or spoon or glass or plate he took them away. To take something bigger, we had to go out through the mountain as if it were stolen. And if he saw us he would chase after us until he caught up with us and took it away. And we were left sad looking at that person who took our thing.[17]

The formation of SOCOSEMA was the culmination of a long struggle by the dump workers to challenge exploitation and their treatment as thieves. The *pepenadores* had worked the dump long before the appearance of concessionaires. They had established a practice of appropriating recyclable goods from the dump for use in self-help construction of homes and for other purposes. After businessmen took over the dump this activity was forbidden. Struggles with concessionaires over the use of recyclables created an ambience of resistance. The seeds of an oppositional consciousness were sown. While the struggle focused on bread-and-butter issues such as the equitable share of profits and access to recycled materials, the origin of SOCOSEMA was also shaped by the articulation of a marginal's morality play. The difference between humiliation and humility was not lost on Isabel Robles and the other members of SOCOSEMA, and they used this understanding to launch a very effective ideological discourse. Robles thus invokes the following maxim as a principle underlying the struggle for community: "The higher we find ourselves situated, the more humble we should be."

Who are the *pepenadores*? Most are members of squatter families with origins in peasant communities from rural areas of northern and central Mexico.[18] In most cases, their communities of origin experienced significant political, economic, and environmental changes after 1950.[19] Changes in land tenure and property ownership accelerated as Mexican and U.S. agribusiness interests converted vast tracts of land in northern Mexico (Chihuahua, Coahuila, and Durango) and central Mexico (the Bajío area) from family subsistence to large-scale commercial farming and ranching.[20] Large-scale irrigation projects flooded *ejido* lands, while mechanization increased unemployment, spelling doom for the communities of origin of the displaced families. Lack of access to credit, seeds, machinery, and conservation resources led to the abandonment of numerous *ejidos*. Soil erosion and drought contributed to displacement pressures in many of their communities of origin.[21] Forcibly separated from their traditional land base, many peasant families and single individuals relocated to the periphery of Ciudad Juárez, in an area in and around the municipal garbage dump. The availability of land for a shantytown in the area encouraged squatting there. Their decision to locate in the dump was also based on the need to carve out a niche in the local economy. At the time of the arrival of the first families in the 1950s, no other group was involved in systematically "scavenging" the garbage dump. So the peasants decided to become *pepenadores* for a livelihood. By 1975, over two hundred families were firmly settled in the area.

A sizeable squatter community began to take shape as the early self-help shanties were constructed. Built from recycled cardboard, aluminum cans and metal canisters, wood scraps, sheet metal, concrete brick pieces, adobe, and rubber tires, the original one-room shanties had dirt floors and no plumbing, heating, electricity, or running water. The less fortunate among the *pepenadores* dug caves and holes to live in.[22] But the inadequate housing, lack of health care, and exploitative working conditions were not the only reasons the *pepenadores* were ready to pursue an organizing campaign. Political problems also arose in 1975 when the municipal government threatened to remove squatters throughout Juárez under pressure from private businessmen, some of whom wanted to "rationalize" and "modernize" the management of the garbage dump.

During the same period (1968–1975), a group of social workers, community organizers, and former maquila workers were busy establishing COMO. The working women from the transnational maquiladoras, as we have seen, participated in the center's educational programs, labor and social advocacy services, and community and cooperative development projects. Under COMO's guidance and support, the maquila workers transferred their extensive knowledge of production to cooperative development projects, and learned new skills in areas such as social work, public education, and public-health nursing. Many former maquila workers left the factories and went into working-class and marginalized communities as teachers, social workers, nurses, and organizers. Providing assistance to SOCOSEMA was one of the most important projects at COMO. The objective was to assist marginalized communities in developing cooperative alternatives to employment in the transnational or informal sectors. The cooperative linked the knowledge of former maquila workers and community organizers with the knowledge of displaced peasants.

Together, COMO and SOCOSEMA challenged the municipal government's "rationalization" policy. The proposed policy supported the concessionaire's plan to "industrialize" the garbage dump while continuing to employ the families at below-subsistence piece rates. The resistance campaign involved three strategies: a media "blitz" to generate community support for the families, an educational program designed to provide literacy and organizing skills for the families, and the development of a plan for establishing a cooperative society that the families would join to "develop" the garbage dump.

By the time of COMO's involvement in the struggle, seven different municipal administrations in Juárez had controlled the city dump through concessionary agreements with private business interests. And despite the presence of two rival unions, the interests of the *pepenadores* were consistently neglected. In March 1975, the concessionaire announced that "recyclables" would be limited solely to cardboard and other paper products. Glass, aluminum, tin, and other recyclable metal and plastic products would no longer be allowed. This amounted to a 50 percent wage cut.

COMO stepped up the media campaign and the pressure on the municipal administration. Proclamations and denunciations were published and circulated. Mass meetings, protests, and news conferences were held. Armed with careful research on the working and living conditions of the dump workers, COMO successfully mobilized public opinion in favor of the squatter families. By mid March 1975, the municipal president had conceded operation of the city dump to the workers with the condition that they organize themselves into a cooperative. However, the administration refused to grant workers concessionary rights over the recycling of cardboard and other paper products, the most profitable materials in the dump. On April 4, 1975, Guillermina Valdés and Francisco Villarreal published an important denunciation in local newspapers that rallied further political and church support to the cause.[23] As a result, the municipal president came under increasing criticism from various sectors of the civic and religious communities. A few days later, the municipal administration ceded control of all recycling operations at the dump to the workers. By mid May the *pepenadores* registered with the Ministry of Industry and Commerce as a worker-owned and self-managed cooperative society.[24]

Several factors contributed to the success of the *pepenadores* in this organizing campaign. First, COMO did not originate the struggle but rather strengthened and channeled it onto broader terrains of struggle. No matter how downtrodden the dump workers might have appeared, they never once accepted their exploitation as an inevitable given. They were already inclined to resist and organize by the time Guillermina Valdés and COMO came along to assist the families. Isabel Robles's descriptions of the struggles to appropriate the materials of the dump for auto-construction of homes and other purposes is evidence of this original and enduring oppositional identity among the dump workers. Without it, the women's center could not have mobilized the squatter community in a concerted struggle against the municipal government and private business interests.

Second, COMO provided advice and logistical support to the workers at a critical formative stage in their own struggles. The organization's ability to conduct research in support of the struggle proved particularly important. Together, the co-op and the women's center researched the working and living conditions of the *pepenadores*. Low wages, lack of health care and adequate housing, high rates of illiteracy and mortality, and the absence of educational opportunities for both young and old were carefully documented. During the struggle to gain the concession for the recycling operation, SOCOSEMA and COMO jointly prepared a research document outlining their findings and strategies for action. The research document described the sociological characteristics of the *pepenador* as "classic features of 'generational marginalization.'"[25]

The majority of the workers were found to be living in "subhuman conditions" similar to those their parents had lived in. Half of the workers were found to be completely illiterate; 30 percent could write but not read; and 10 percent could read but not write. Less than 2 percent had any formal education, and these averaged one to two years of primary-level instruction. Nearly all the workers (90 percent) were rural migrants, and 20 percent had more than fifteen years of residence in the Juárez area. Their participation and interaction with the local urban environment was found to be extremely limited. Only fifteen persons among the adult population of 224 were familiar enough with such public services as schools, transportation, and health centers to actually use them at some point in their lives.[26] Further, the transgenerational character of this marginalization was visible among the children between the ages of twelve and eighteen. Ninety-five percent of these children were illiterate. These children were found to have histories of sporadic school attendance in schools far removed from the community, and many had deserted the schools altogether before completing two years of primary.[27] This research document became a primary tool in the ideological effort to win the public discourse over the fate of the municipal dump.

Underlying the COMO–SOCOSEMA research program was an empowerment pedagogy that engaged the *pepenadores* in their own problem-solving education. This is the third factor that contributed to the success of the organizing campaign. Jesús Montenegro, a former coordinator of external projects at COMO and a major figure in the reorganization of the cooperative society, had this to recall about the role of self-education at the literacy school, CEBI Libertad:[28]

> Since that time [1974–75], the cooperative has . . . developed two different sides: educational and organizational. The dump workers undertook an experiment in *autodidáctica* [self-education], drawing on the support of COMO and its methods. The goal all along has been to enable the members of the co-op to analyze their problems systematically and critically, always moving toward concrete solutions they themselves develop. . . . By learning to read and write, the dump workers and their families—women, men, and children alike—were enabled to do research for themselves to solve the problems of housing, health care, drinking water, and work organization. . . . This also had the benefit of making them more articulate speakers in public meetings. They had their own rich voices to use now. No one had to speak for them, and the results were that the media and

politicians could no longer ignore their plight and rights. They were empowered to be directly responsible for their own solutions and to create their own alternatives by directly confronting the opposition. (Interview, Ciudad Juárez, June 1982)

Working with COMO's earliest teams of "social promoters," SOCOSEMA embarked on an intensive effort to develop educational resources. The self-management of the literacy component of the organizing campaign proved critical not just in the initial struggle over the rights to the recycling operation, but in establishing a solid educational resource for meeting the long-term needs of the entire community. With 430 school-age children, the task was a formidable one. These efforts began in 1974 and culminated in 1980 with the establishment of CEBI Libertad. Staffed by former maquila workers retrained as schoolteachers, the literacy school played a critical role in the organizing work of SOCOSEMA and in the continuing education of children and adults.

But perhaps the most important factor underlying the success of the campaign was the ability of the *pepenadores* to establish an enduring, cooperative relationship with COMO. Isabel Robles notes that the dump workers and the CEBI instructors and other organizers had complex, intimate relationships. Ties extended beyond the realm of schoolroom activities and into the cultural, political, and religious life of the cooperative members. Robles also describes the changes that came with the establishment of SOCOSEMA:

> And now we directly receive the value of our materials without intermediaries. And now all the jobs are occupied by our co-op members. We can decide the price of our materials. Many of us know how to read. . . . And many of the members now have one or two trucks and houses of block or adobe. But of cardboard and tin now no one. Medicines, bathrooms, hospitals, and funerals all on the part of the cooperative. And we know of our money integral to our work without intermediaries. And of the dry seed that was SOCOSEMA. That seed has blossomed. And it came forth from the land [*Salió a flor de tierra*]. And we expect to see it flourish in the future.[29]

CREATING WORKPLACE DEMOCRACY

Prior to 1975, when the garbage recycling operation was controlled by private businessmen, more than two thirds of the profits went to the concessionaires. On April 4, 1975—as mentioned above—Guillermina Valdés (representing COMO) and Francisco Villarreal Torres (representing SOCOSEMA) published a proclamation in the Juárez daily newspaper *El Fronterizo*. The proclamation was headlined "An Injustice That Must Be

Made Public." It closed with the motto "Let the garbage be exploited, not those who work the garbage dump."[30] The authors noted that the work of the *pepenadores* was producing 110,000 *pesos* a week in recycled goods sold at market value. Of this amount, the concessionaire received 80,000 *pesos* (6,400 in 1975 U.S. dollars) and the workers received 30,000 *pesos* (2,400 in U.S. dollars). With more than two hundred workers to share this amount, each *pepenador* received an average of 136 *pesos* a week, or less than seven dollars a week. However, since pay was based on piecework, some of the workers received as little as five dollars a week (around 62 *pesos*).

The organizing struggle that led to the establishment of SOCOSEMA focused on creating an alternative system of work organization that would correct this injustice by giving workers complete control over the process of production and the distribution of profits. However, economic democracy aside, the organization of production was itself designed to reduce the hours that each member was obligated to work on a given day. In fact, under SOCOSEMA the *pepenadores* reduced their working time from an average of thirteen and a half hours a day to less than six hours a day.[31] They maximized earnings through collective profit sharing and minimized working time by reducing workloads for everyone and allowing families to continue to work, albeit to a lesser degree, as a group. This reduction of what Marx called "socially necessary labor time" continues to be one of the most fundamental principles governing cooperative work organization in SOCOSEMA's version of workplace democracy. The benefits charter for the co-op reads as follows:

> The benefits received by the workers of SO.CO.SE.MA. are these: medicines, hospitalization, sanitary facilities, disability compensation, profit sharing, loans by the cooperative, and help to the worker to make work lighter [*como se hace más liviano el trabajo*]. And on the part of our advisors we have the assistance for when a member is in jail, they will go arrange for bail.[32]

Work schedules were modified to allow co-op members more time away from the dump to pursue other activities (among them literacy classes and workshops on craftwork or cooperative organization). The reduction in the amount of time spent working in the garbage dump was critical since the members needed more free time to develop other aspects of their lives. Harry Cleaver describes this alternative form of workplace democracy in the following terms: "What is fascinating about this economy is . . . how little work it takes many people to make a living in it, and how much free time they have carved out to build a community around other kinds of activities."[33]

In SOCOSEMA, free time has been created through a combination of innovations in work organization, economic democracy, and small-scale mechanization. For example, the large family size characteristic of many of the co-op members allows everyone to work for less time each day and still earn sufficient income for the group. Workloads can be shared, with the proceeds of that work going to families as a unit. There is always enough income for the group without any one individual having to work themselves into exhaustion or tedium. Each individual member of the family thus enjoys greater freedom from work and more time to spend on leisure and other activities. Furthermore, the equitable distribution of profits, instituted after the establishment of the co-op, more than doubled, and eventually quadrupled, everyone's income without increasing individual member's work time.[34]

Rufino Santos fondly recalls changes in work organization that occurred after the establishment of SOCOSEMA:

> I started and work was all day and all night. From five in the morning until dark, nothing but work—hard, long work. One had to work long hours—not enough money otherwise. But never enough, no matter how much the work. Too little money, never enough to eat fresh food. Had to eat from the garbage. All my family was tired and hungry. . . . Then we go into the cooperative. This is the way for poor people, you know? Work together, not with bosses taking everything. . . . What I like about the co-op? My brother, like this, much better. Now I only work five, six, maybe seven hours. Never work on Sundays. Some Wednesdays are holy days—no work then either. . . . I feel free, more free than ever before. As God is my witness, the work is more dignified now. . . . I am important and I get to vote. My vote is my strength. No more bosses screaming and hitting and stealing. We decide in the assembly, and this is right. My brother, the poor people also have rights. . . . With free time? I learned to read and write. I like to study. Find my poet's voice. Do you know? . . . I grow roses and other flowers. My mother helps. . . . I go to church and meetings at COMO. Time to rest, play, or talk—simple things. There is more time to go to meetings. SOCOSEMA must have direction. We all do this part. The general assembly. All this, directing SOCOSEMA. (Interview, Ciudad Juárez, July 1989)

Liberated from excessive, imposed work, the *pepenadores* used free time to expand and enrich their lives through a broad network of relationships tied to all sorts of cultural, social, political, and religious activities. *Pepenadores* such as Santos embrace their free time with enthusiastic and sustained creativity. Learning to read and write, even growing a lush flower garden in a dusty alley, are activities that make the person whole.

SOCOSEMA's organizational structure is actually reminiscent of that of the worker factory councils of Antonio Gramsci's Italy. The governing body of the cooperative is the general assembly, constituted by the members (*socios*) of the society. The assembly elects the president of the cooperative and the chair and members of the Consejo de Vigilancia (Council of Vigilance, an accountability board). The assembly also elects the treasurer, secretary, chief of production, and shop stewards (*vocales*). The comptroller has authority to appoint an accounting secretary and an administrative assistant from among the ranks of *socios*. Two official advisors to the assembly are appointed in consultation with COMO.[35]

Democratic decision making for most aspects of the cooperative takes place in the context of general-assembly meetings. Since 1981, I have observed more than a dozen meetings of the general assembly. What impresses me the most about these meetings is the atmosphere of conviviality that prevails during the long hours of debate, discussion, and voting. I cannot help but wonder why the faculty meetings at my college lack this kind of excitement and collegiality. At these general-assembly meetings, I have observed participatory democracy at work. I have seen the enthusiasm, dedication, and inventiveness of the *socios* slowly blossom.

However, in a self-managed workplace democracy, the participation of workers must be sustained over time if the cooperative form is to survive the inevitable generational transitions. SOCOSEMA endures because of the enormous responsibility that all *socios* assume for decision making in several key areas of policy. These include decisions related to production organization, election of officers, administrative directives, formulation of wages and benefits, approval of contracts, terminations and admonishments, and external relations (for example, policies governing use of CEBI Libertad and local media). Very few important decisions are left for the exclusive consideration of elected officers. The structure of authority within SOCOSEMA is horizontal, not vertical.

COMMUNITY REVIVAL

The reduction of working time made possible by the reorganization of the dump work after 1975 created the political and cultural spaces necessary to support a community revival. Guillermina Valdés, Isabel Robles, and others always recognized that the revival of a sense of community was essential to the survival of the co-op over time. The entire SOCOSEMA project can perhaps be viewed as an experiment in the creation of an "intentional" community.[36] The use of kin networks made lighter workloads possible, relieving individuals from having to seek employment outside the community. Every member of the co-op that I have spoken with over an eleven-year period mentions the importance of a shorter working day. They inevitably explain that it gives them more time to spend with family and friends. The idea that people should work twelve or more hours a day seems to them excessive and immoral. Candelaria Santos, Rufino's sixty-three-year-old mother, expressed this view in an ironic rhetorical question she once posed to me as we discussed the workweek at SOCOSEMA. "My son," she said pointedly, "is it a family if no one is ever home?"[37]

Pepenadores I have spoken to also mention being able to work and live in the same place as a major benefit of their association with SOCOSEMA. Herbert Gans's idea of "urban villagers" seems to have some validity here, since the merging of workplace and residence is characteristic of Mexican peasant lifestyles.[38] This lifestyle is reflected in the *pepenador* adage "We work to live, we don't live to work." Seen in this cultural context, it seems hardly surprising that people spend more time socializing in the streets or homes than working to make more money. To an extent, some of the dump workers and their families remain committed to SOCOSEMA because it respects their right to choose a livelihood based on voluntary simplicity.

Indeed, excessive consumption, so prevalent in mass consumer culture, and the cooperative form of organization do not appear to mix well. Obviously, the cooperative would not have the material resources necessary to provide every household with a TV and a VCR. But it is possible to have audiovisual electronic equipment for use in a communal fashion, which is exactly the case at CEBI Libertad. In other words, voluntary simplicity is not deprivation. The cooperative is based on the reduction of work. It is also based on maintaining low levels of consumption among the members. Yet this is much more than just "survival" or "subsistence"—terms that have been themselves tainted by the colonizing discourses of Western developers who misdefine subsistence lifestyles as poverty.[39]

A sense of community is created and maintained through the activities of the general assembly that oversees the operations of SOCOSEMA. But many other activities offer opportunities for conviviality as well. Social events and gatherings such as prenuptial parties, wedding dinners, *quinceañeras* (a rite of passage for adolescent girls on their fifteenth birthday), births, baptisms, and daily visits with friends and family are important aspects of community life. Two other important sources of community are the activities associated with the literacy school and the close ties between SOCOSEMA members and the St. John the Baptist Community (see section "A Liberation Spirituality," later in this chapter).

MAKING ETHNOSCIENCE: SOCOSEMA AND APPROPRIATE TECHNOLOGY

Among the first projects undertaken by SOCOSEMA was the development of a production schedule that greatly reduced the hours of work for the cooperative's members. But other changes in work organization followed. In 1981, the co-op received a contract to "industrialize" the recycling operations. This project involved making appropriate technological choices and implementing technical innovations in the existing systems of production. A variety of appropriate technologies were purchased or developed to make the work of recycling cardboard and other "wastes" more efficient. Eventually, the co-op opened a $2.5 million (U.S.) recycling plant and acquired a fleet of twenty large trucks.[40]

The most important changes in work organization at SOCOSEMA involved a search for access to appropriate technologies. This had been a long-term concern of Guillermina Valdés and COMO organizers. Their experience with maquila workers suggested that an untapped reservoir of tacit skills and working knowledge existed among the lowest-ranking assembly-line operators. Maquila workers' inventions and modifications to the labor process were carefully documented by the center beginning in 1982. The results of this research were published in a monograph in 1984.[41] COMO utilized this research to promote what it called a "transference methodology" (see chapter 6). Guillermina Valdés once described this as

> a fact, an actual activity, that is based on the scientific and mechanical knowledge of the workers. We have to recognize this creativity; the managers don't or won't. But we can organize this knowledge to promote the development of appropriate technologies in the other worker-owned cooperatives.[42]

The project had identified maquila workers who were involved in developing small lines for recycling some of the damaged components and wastes from electronics assembly work. These workers joined with the *pepenadores* in an effort to develop a similar process for dump work. SOCOSEMA thus became the first field site where COMO experimented with the transference methodology. Valdés describes the significance of this link between SOCOSEMA and the transference methodology:

SOCOSEMA represents a rare opportunity for us to collectively develop an appropriate technology, and we are, for example, experimenting there to mechanize the packing and processing of paper products. Through this type of activity, we can empower the working women of the maquila to make practical use of the inductive apprenticeship and promote sustainable community development at the same time. (Interview, Ciudad Juárez, June 1983)

Some of the technical innovations pioneered at the dump were direct by-products of the workers' own ideas. For example, the workers developed a variety of handheld tools to make the work of sorting, selecting, and carrying recyclables easier. The *gancho* (hook) was one of these inventions. The *gancho* is a metal tube with two points at the end. It is enclosed by a rubber sheath, for a better grip and safety. This tool eliminated the traditional practice of sorting garbage with bare hands, which often resulted in injuries and was considered unhygienic. Other changes were more technologically sophisticated and required advice from industrial and mechanical engineers. For example, in 1983, SOCOSEMA designed and experimented with a cardboard and paper-product packing machine drawing on the assistance of student-workers from COMO and some students from the regional engineering school.

In either case, simple or sophisticated, the workers participated in all aspects of research, testing, evaluation, and implementation of new technologies. This guaranteed that the *pepenadores* would ultimately define what was considered an appropriate technology. Technologies were rejected if workers were uncomfortable with the tools or techniques, or if they felt the changes would diminish the quality of work or the control they had over the process of production. These principles, which in the language of the modern technologist are known as "ergonomics" and "span of control," meant that the workers would not be displaced or otherwise adversely affected by the technological changes.

One unforeseen consequence of the campaign for appropriate technology was the enthusiasm of children and adults alike for the study of mathematics and science at the literacy school. Eulalio Medrano, a forty year old who, like Rufino, grew up in the dump, explains this fascination with science among the *pepenadores:*

School is not just to read and write. Math is important. That way no one can cheat you. . . . But my favorite is science. I enjoy learning things that show about how the world works. Why things work the way they do. Few are the mysteries in the universe, really. . . . This opens up a new view. I also realize that science is a great responsibility—not that hard, really, the part that deals with how to do it. The hard part is getting respect for us plain, everyday people. We can know the sciences like anyone else. Better is that we can make our own science. A science that helps us live better. And we don't have to stop being good to each other because of it. (Interview, Ciudad Juárez, July 1989)

Abdón García, another member of the co-op, expresses a similar view when he states: "My hope, though, is the recycling plant we are planning to build. You can't get ahead in this world without technology or education. The plant will create jobs. It is a future for our children."[43] The transference methodology initiated by COMO through its experiments at SOCOSEMA produced practical technologies and innovations in the technical organization of work. But it went beyond that in creating a cultural milieu that nurtured a science of and for the people. CEBI Libertad thus became a center not just for a literacy campaign but for a grand experiment in science for and of the people. The members of the co-op were not the only ones to benefit from this education: spouses and children also participated in the effort.

This "new" science—or better, ethnoscience—was based on empirical observations that the *pepenadores* accumulated over years of practical experience in the workplace. But, as is apparent in Medrano's narrative, this is a science with very specific social ethics. It is not the science of domination, but of liberation from toil. This is science that respects human dignity, and does not force one into a detached pseudo-objectivity: "We don't have to stop being good to each other because of it." This is not dissimilar from the observation offered by Frances Densmore, an authority on American Indian ethnoscience, who argues that "the essential differences between primitive and scientific thought lay not in the logical mechanism, but in the difference of the premises, the interests, the values, which are differences in degree not in kind."[44]

MUTUAL-AID AND RECIPROCITY NETWORKS

Beyond literacy and organizing skills, other basic needs of the *pepenadores* centered around adequate shelter, safe drinking water, and basic health services. Over the years, SOCOSEMA successfully expanded its markets by gaining customers for recycled products in the United States and by solidifying its relations with other Juárez-area worker cooperatives.[45] But this type of market integration did not necessarily lead to the adoption of purely individualistic, market-oriented logic. More profits for the co-op enterprise led to more than wage increases. In keeping with the mutualist ideals of the co-op, SOCOSEMA established a housing fund and other development funds. Over the years, these funds have been used by the *socios* for home-improvement and construction projects. In 1975, before the co-op had been organized, fifty out of the two hundred families working in the dump were also living there. Only twenty-three families had shanties with more than one room.[46] By 1984, none of the families were living in the dump, and over half had three- and four-room concrete block and adobe homes.[47] By 1990, nearly 90 percent of the families had new, autoconstructed homes, and many others had additional rooms built. These new homes were collectively designed and built by the *pepenadores,* in a manner reminiscent of Amish barn raising.

Another area in which mutual-aid traditions are important is health services. Of particular importance here are the prenatal and postnatal needs of women in the community. Prior to 1975, health services in general were practically non-existent, and prenatal care was completely unavailable. Only two of the women, out of more than two hundred, had ever seen an obstetrician-gynecologist, and none had ever had cervical screenings (Pap smears), breast exams, or other types of health-care services that most Western women consider routine. Mortality data for the *pepenadores* prior to 1975 are not available, but oral testimony indicates that at least eight women died during childbirth between 1955 and 1975.[48] This educational strategy wisely drew from preexisting reciprocity networks constructed by the women of the community. These mutual-aid networks circulate information and provide assistance in getting women to utilize services more consistently. This is where CEBI Libertad proved invaluable as a resource used to mobilize the networks.

The mutualist tradition is a familiar one to the *pepenadores,* especially the older males who were once members of peasant cooperatives, irrigation-ditch associations, or mutual-aid societies. Women are also familiar with mutualist practices, since many have had experiences with *comadre* (godmother) networks. The reinvention of mutualist practices through SOCOSEMA is, therefore, hardly surprising. Moreover, in the absence of material resources, the *pepenadores* and their families must rely on each other for survival. Scarcity of material resources breeds intense social solidarity and inventiveness. Mutual-aid practices are normal consequences of political, economic, and cultural milieux bordering on material deprivation. This social ethic must also be reproduced over time if the cooperative is to endure. The problem-solving educational models introduced by COMO at CEBI Libertad engaged the children of

SOCOSEMA in mutual-aid behavior. This process reproduced a social ethic of cooperation that is indispensable to the transgenerational development and survival of intentional community.

CRAFTING ECOLOGICAL SUSTAINABILITY

In the United States, recycling has clearly emerged as the "environmentally correct" behavior of the 1990s. The work of recycling, however, is no longer the province of grassroots organizations; it has become a multi-billion-dollar industry. It seems ironic that Mexico, which is seen by many critics as inept in the area of environmental protection, would provide a social and political milieu for the emergence of an organization such as SOCOSEMA, a prototype of ecological sustainability. Recycling is a much older practice, especially in the third world, where situations of resource and job scarcity have long led to the intense utilization of wastes by both rural and urban poor.[49]

While recycling is a consumer-oriented activity in the United States, in third-world countries such as Mexico recycling has roots in productive work. The *pepenadores* do not work in recycling because they want to offer an ameliorative, Band-Aid solution for the excesses of U.S. mass consumerism. To the contrary, their experience with recycling comes precisely from their location outside the consumer markets and logic of capitalism. Recycling is not something one does to rationalize or diminish the harmful effects of excessive consumption. For the dump workers, recycling *is* productive consumption. It produces shelter, clothing, tools, and even food; it creates employment and generates other forms of social wealth. This is why most of the *pepenadores* view SOCOSEMA as sustainable in two ways: it helps to deal with the wastes of mass consumer markets, and it strengthens the low-consumption lifestyle of the squatter families.

For the *pepenadores,* however, the co-op addresses environmental issues in ways that go well beyond the immediate benefits of recycling. More significantly, the co-op organized efforts to deal with environmental problems in the living and work spaces of the community. For example, the lack of potable drinking water and basic sanitation in both the dump and homes were environmental problems that the cooperative confronted early in its existence. Health and safety hazards in the workplace also drew the immediate attention of the cooperative. Elena Alvarado, a key COMO organizer and former maquila worker who was involved with SOCOSEMA from the start, has this to say about the nature of environmental problems on the border and the approach of the coop-erative in seeking solutions:

> Most people don't even think about where their garbage goes. They don't care. Talking of ignorance, you look across the border and see all that wealth, but where are they going? What are they producing? And how? Where does it end up? Pollution does not respect borders. Dirty air and water don't stop to check in at the customs inspection station. . . . For the workers, development often means we are stuck with the wastes generated in producing someone else's goods. The wealthy get the products, and all we get is the refuse. . . . It was something else, really, to turn this on its head. To take our resources from the wastes of the world's richest and big-gest economy. But the recycling was not the thing that really distinguished SOCOSEMA. Although that is certainly a point to remember. What is it Isabel says about the *pepenadores*? "We were the original recyclers." Our approach has always been to emphasize the lifestyle as less wasteful, more beneficial for the person and the planet. Our approach emphasizes this point about, well, if the poorest of the poor can be responsible with what little they have, how come the rich over there can't? (Interview, Ciudad Juárez, March 1984)

WOMEN AND SOCOSEMA

Women played a major role in the organizing campaign to establish SOCOSEMA. They have figured prominently in its administration, work organization, and educational efforts from the beginning. By 1984, only twenty-eight out of the 203 members (*socios*) of the co-op were women. However, all twenty-eight were very active in various aspects of the coop-erative. Women have been elected officers of the co-op. For example, Catalina Martínez was the first elected chair of the Consejo de Vigilancia. Several women have served as secretary or as a member of the account-ability board. The spouses of male members have also played a key role in the organization.

An intriguing aspect of the history of SOCOSEMA is that women ac-tivists and social promoters from COMO organized a predominantly male group of workers. As was the case in Vado de Cedillos, the farm-worker co-op (see chapter 5), the women organizers and teachers had to break through gender barriers. Elena Alvarado explained this to me in very explicit terms: "Many of the men thought we were just stupid women, with no skills that could be of use to them." Some of the CEBI instructors felt that at first the CEBI schoolroom was an awkward social context for male-female collaboration. One former teacher said, "It was like they did not know how to relate to a woman unless it had to do with cooking a meal or cleaning house." Some of the men apparently found being cast in the role of male student of a female teacher embarrassing. Over time, especially as progress for the cooperative became apparent, the initial perceptions and hesitation gave way to mutual trust and respect. This change in male perceptions and attitudes was largely the result of the increased visibility that the women of the community gained through participation in various CEBI-initiated projects, such as a study group established to secure safe drinking water.[50]

Those women of the SOCOSEMA community who did not regularly work in the dump were the ones who pursued the issue of health care at the literacy school. With free time, and the instructional resources offered by COMO, the women began to study the health needs of the community. Following the problem-solving, self-education model, they designed several projects to find solutions to common problems such as the lack of prenatal and postnatal care, alcoholism among males, and drug abuse among adolescents.[51] In the area of women's health-care needs, the cooperative developed a strategy that advocated utilizing the services of traditional practitioners—such as *parteras* (midwives)—as well as of state-run clinics and hospitals.

A LIBERATION SPIRITUALITY

From the start, religion played a key role in the struggle to organize the cooperative. Many of the *pepenadores* were from very religious families. But Guillermina Valdés's own links with progressive religious communities in Juárez greatly influenced the development of SOCOSEMA, both in terms of ideology and organizing strategies. As members of the co-op joined the St. John the Baptist Community, a Charismatic Catholic group in Juárez, religion played an even more central role in the organizing work of the co-op and the community life of the *socios*.[52]

In fact, one of the benefits of the reduction of working time was that members now had more time to spend on activities such as participating in religious groups. The role of religion as a principal organizing tool in the SOCOSEMA struggle must not be overlooked. To maintain solidarity in the face of powerful, hostile forces, the *pepenadores* needed a focal point around which both the workers and their families could gather. The literacy school and shared religious activities provided that focus. Here were two tools, literacy and religion, that could be harnessed to mobilize groups, provide support and networking opportunities, raise funds and other resources, and, above all, provide a context for the development of a sense of community. The religious life of the community provided a ritual context for the development of personal empowerment and spiritual insight—processes that contributed to the opening of new possibilities for collective political action.

Marginality as Inventive Force: A Theoretical Exegesis

Images of powerlessness, isolation, exclusion, anomie, and social pathology are persistent in the academic discourses on third-world marginality.[53] These are typical images in the work of social scientists whose interpretations equate subsistence lifestyles with poverty, and poverty with "economic marginality." Too much of this theorizing takes the form of an ethnocentric discourse that posits marginality as a problem of control over so-called underdeveloped areas and peoples.[54] This assumption cuts across diverse ideological and theoretical persuasions, and informs the scholarship of many theorists working with social-ecological, ethnographic, sociopsychological, modernization, dependency, structuralist, and even world-system models.[55] The possibility that marginals may respond to their integration in such a way as to make their adaptation less reactive and more proactive is antithetical to the predominant conceptualizations of third-world marginality.

One important exception to this ethnocentric discourse is the work of Larissa A. Lomnitz.[56] Lomnitz offers the following relevant commentary, drawing from research on reciprocal exchange networks among Mexican shantytown dwellers:

> Latin American marginality represents a successful evolutionary response of traditional populations to the stresses of rapid urbanization and industrialization. The marginals have carved out an ecological niche within the urban milieu, one that provides for their basic survival needs. . . . The economy of the marginals has proved efficient in two respects: (1) the utilization of social resources for economic ends, and (2) the recycling of surplus and waste materials toward their maximum utilization.[57]

In other words, marginal lifestyles are ecologically sustainable, and may actually offer the Western world glimpses of the social, cultural, and technical innovations necessary for life on a planet increasingly characterized by both politically contrived and real scarcity.

Therefore, social and cultural change can flow from margins to center. The margins are inventive forces. Sylvere Lotringer and Christian

Marazzi call this "marginality at the center." This refers to the struggles of marginals to remain marginal, to remain outside the circuits of capitalist production, global Fordism. Marginals become the center of an alternative "subeconomy" that functions independently of the core economy. Marginals invent a subeconomy (*lavoro nero*, as the Italians say) for purposes of "self-valorization"—that is, fulfilling self-defined needs. Lotringer and Marazzi elaborate:

> [T]oday, in Italy, well over one-third of an active population of 21 million work part-time, off-the-books, etc. . . . What the Bolognesi call "marginality at the center" is precisely the critique of all attempts to subordinate this *invention force,* that is, the creativity and productivity of the struggle and of the life-styles developed by the so-called "marginals." These recently formed "social subjects" are productive workers in a double sense: they produce wealth and they produce struggles. Thus they are at the center, or at any rate rightfully belong there.[58]

Marginality as a state of powerlessness and exclusion certainly exists. But to assume that powerlessness is static and lacking permutation, that marginality exists only as an extension of the dynamics of "cores," or that the political behavior of marginals always involves a linear pattern of reaction to external forces—all seem to be serious interpretive errors. What is interesting about the case of SOCOSEMA is that this invented subeconomy evolved into a formal, yet autonomous, worker-controlled organizational form.

Another misconception in the discourse on third-world marginality is the view that the powerlessness of marginal groups renders them inconsequential to history and social change. Marginals can be integrated into the political life of third-world nation-states, but they are not generally viewed as capable of significantly affecting the evolution of nation-states or of determining the nature of their mode of "integration" into the so-called world system.[59] Thus, marginalized peoples are generally held to exist not only in isolation from the social system, but also on the margins of the historical processes of state formation and social change as a whole. Marginality is political and ideological impotence, since marginals are presumed to be permanently located outside the core intellectual and ideological discourses *about* marginality. They are not "allowed" to exercise *their* subjectivity, and thereby enter the hermeneutic circle. To the extent that marginals are mainly constructed as "reactive social subjects," they are not seen as capable of creating their own history. Rather, marginals are seen as victims of history and social change, swept along and overwhelmed by the currents, actions, and transformations induced by the true change agents of history, the various dominant social groups associated with "core" societies. Such constructions are obviously ethnocentric and reflect the ideological presuppositions of the dominant social classes. In contrast, Lomnitz's stance recognizes that the political and cultural traditions of marginal groups are not based exclusively on adaptive necessity. Instead, these traditions and struggles can derive from autonomous innovations in lived experiences and can be mobilized in building alternatives to mainstream integration. Moreover, these traditions can secure continuity in the transmission of indigenous culture and knowledge.[60]

Mutualist work networks and communal kin structures, such as those underpinning SOCOSEMA, in effect provide alternatives to employment in the segmented labor markets that are endemic in Fordist industrial organizational forms. The core system's work organizations are characterized by the predominance of industrially integrated, white male norms and value structures. In contrast, in SOCOSEMA we witness the power of informal networks in providing for the production and distribution of subsistence (use) and exchange value. But these networks also provide a means for institutionalizing "marginal" values and norms, *outside* the boundaries of the core system. These alternative organizational forms and networks represent a "refusal of development," in the sense that their modus vivendi is a deliberate rejection of a mode of subordinate integration posed by the dictates of core-directed modernizing elites in any given "developing area."

The organizational forms and traditions of "excluded" groups are not limited to reactive efforts aimed at negotiating the terms of integration with the mainstream. For most ethnic, third-world communities, integration means "death" as a culture. Rejecting modernization (total integration), marginals struggle for their own autonomous "space." The social structures of marginalized groups also include completely autonomous domains in which cultural as well as technical invention can develop free of core hegemonic intrusions.

Marginality as inventive force involves a quest for autonomy, and this is especially apparent in the *pepenadores'* identity narratives. Mutualist support systems provide a material basis for the survival of alternative subeconomies and local subcultures. But to get there, maquila workers and *pepenadores* must first learn to articulate oppositional identities and the inversion of dominant, or "core" values. While the core demands acceptance of a high-productivity regime and strict "labor discipline," the maquila workers engage in output restriction and other forms of sabotage.[61]

While the core demands acceptance of poverty and subemployment at below-subsistence wages, the *pepenadores* espouse communal values and the development of a cooperative way of work. Both of these "social subjects" invert the values of the core system in struggling toward an autonomous path for development. Victor Turner notes that the power of marginals springs from a "profound immersion in humility."[62] This "immersion in humility" strengthens cooperative and communalistic values. "Humility" as a common denominator in the lived experience of marginality is expressed by the *pepenadores* in their adage "Cuanto más altos estemos situados, más humildes debemos ser" (The higher we find ourselves situated, the more humble we should be).[63]

The intense social solidarity of maquila workers and *pepenadores* is a by-product of the "humility" both experience as exploited marginals. Their solidarity and common struggle are born of the necessity to join together as equals, as communities equally subject to domination and exploitation by the core, and capable of espousing a joint vision of "alternative" community based on oppositional social ethics. Instead of accepting degradation and powerlessness as exploited marginals, COMO organizers (qua former maquila workers) join with the *pepenadores* in search of an autonomous alternative.

The technical, cultural, and organizational innovations that went into the development of the SOCOSEMA cooperative are exemplary of an alternative to integration into core-dominated socioeconomic institutions. The cooperative came to represent an "antistructure," an autonomous social and economic space arrived at through the *pepenadores'* transformation from peasants, to landless squatters, to members of an intentional community. The *pepenadores* express this in their statement "El poder más grande está en el cerebro, no en el bolsillo" (The greater power is in the mind, not in the pocketbook).[64] This statement captures the character of the *pepenadores* as liminal inventors. For indeed, their creativity is based on an inversion of values that rejects the materialistic orientations of the core, and embraces the more "spiritual" or interpersonal orientations of the margin. Marginals are alleged to exist in *isolation* from social relational networks, or at any rate in positions isolated from the "center" of such networks.[65] However, in the case of the *pepenadores* we find the development of an intentional community characterized by very intensely personal, reciprocal, and egalitarian social networks. Margins construct networks. More importantly, these networks serve as "countercenters" to the expansionist and enveloping tendencies of Western core systems.

The alternative standpoint epistemology of the *pepenadores* is perhaps, in the final analysis, the most intriguing dimension of inventive
marginality. The more the core tries to homogenize and colonize indigenous and tribal life-worlds, the more these communities resist, diversify,
and mutate. In so doing, they are presenting alternatives to the development models heretofore embraced by the core. Nowhere is this made
clearer than in the contemporary rush by Western scientists (such as
botanists, ecologists, and hydrologists) to preserve the ethnoscientific
knowledge base of indigenous peoples the world over. These efforts are
being undertaken under the sponsorship of core institutions, such as
museums, science foundations, and research centers. The desire to preserve the "wisdom of the folk," in regions as far-flung as Brazil's Amazonia, Mexico's Lacandón, the Balinese islands, and Four Corners in the
southwestern United States, is motivated by the understanding that the
survival of the core may depend on the folkways and lifeways of the margins.[66] Larissa Lomnitz captures this best when she observes the contrast
between

> the successful adaptation of the marginals to a situation of scarcity of re-
> sources, generating mechanisms of social solidarity and methods of in-
> tense utilization of waste, and the crisis of Western industrial societies at-
> tributed precisely to a lack of social solidarity and a wasteful utilization of
> dwindling resources. The reciprocity networks [of Mexican shantytown
> residents] may well prove to be a prototype for the social structures
> needed for the survival of mankind.[67]

The alternatives developed by the *pepenadores* through SOCOSEMA
were the results of an inventive force that emerged from struggles against
pauperization and exploitation. Their experiences provide lessons that
core societies and cultures might do well to learn if we are all to survive,
preserving the ecological and cultural diversity of the planet. It is time
social scientists took another cue from natural scientists. This time, instead of flirting with the exclusionary dictates of the positivist canon, social scientists need to embrace the humility exhibited by botanists and
ecologists who have come to recognize the power of marginals as inventors of creative, sustainable local lifeways.

Part Four

BACK TO THE FUTURE

8

Mexico in the Fast Lane?

When you go to a woman, don't forget the whip.
—Attributed to Friedrich Nietzsche

"When work itself is simple and repetitive, it is easy to identify parasitical and superfluous persons (oneself included)."
—T. Shimizu, citing Toyota sources[1]

Let us remember that the automatic machine ... is the precise economic equivalent of slave labor. Any labor which competes with slave labor must accept the economic consequence of slave labor.
—Norbert Wiener (*The Human Uses of Human Beings: Cybernetics and Human Beings*, 1950)

Ten Years After (1982–1992)

What happened to Juana Ortega? I lost track of her after my last extended fieldwork trip to Juárez. When I spoke with her in early August 1989 outside the COMO building, she was unemployed, back in school, and debating the possibility of a move to Los Angeles or Tucson. She said she had lost her job at RCA to automation in 1987. Other companies had refused to hire her, even at starting "apprentice" wages. She speculated about being blacklisted or "too old" at thirty-eight. I wonder: Did maquila management decide Juana Ortega was one of Shimizu's "parasitical and superfluous persons"? Was she a victim of Wiener's automatic slave-labor machines?

When I last visited with Ortega, she was in school studying for a degree in personnel management. This was an effort that she believed allowed her to build on skills she learned in the maquilas and COMO. Forty years old in 1989, Ortega was a divorced mother of three children. She was having health problems, which she attributed to her twelve years as a maquila worker. She described how she had come out as a lesbian during her years at COMO in the mid 1980s. Her partner was also a

245

former RCA worker. By 1989, the two had been in a relationship for more than three years. Her relatives had rejected the open couple, and so Ortega was living with her three children and her lover, who was supporting the entire family on a single income, from a job in a Juárez maquila. Is Juana Ortega somewhere in the United States today? Is her family still together? Perhaps she has a job in some California electronics sweatshop? It troubles me to no end to have lost contact with a person who contributed so much to my understanding of the maquilas.

Starting in 1985, RCA–Juárez, like many other maquila operations, underwent a new wave of technological change. Ortega's job was among thousands that were eliminated by the unforgiving mechanical hand of incessant corporate rationalization. During the late 1980s, board-stuffing assembly lines throughout the maquila electronics industry were reorganized.[2] In some cases hundreds, perhaps thousands, of workers were displaced by Japanese-made automated component-insertion (ACI) machines. These were among the first quasi-robotic devices used in the industry, and their increasingly common deployment during the mid through late 1980s eliminated significant numbers of assembly positions in the consumer-electronics sector of the maquilas. I wonder, did long-standing patterns of "induced failures" by workers such as Juana Ortega precipitate this brutal technological path? Whip them into submission or drive them out seems to have been the robo-Nietzschean position of maquila management.

Beyond restructurings of the machine, the maquilas have experienced many other important changes over the past decade. A substantial shift in the demographic composition of the workforce has occurred. Larger numbers of male workers are now employed in assembly-line jobs, and while women are still the majority, men are now visibly established as a significant part of the industry workforce. Another important change is that there are now greater numbers of Japanese transnational corporations operating maquilas in the U.S.–Mexico border region. Still relatively small in numbers, the Japanese maquilas are located principally in Tijuana, Baja California.[3] There has also been an extraordinary growth of the automotive assembly industry in Mexico over the past five years, with an increasing number of maquilas supplying a variety of processed components to companies such as Ford, Chrysler, General Motors, Honda, and Nissan.[4]

Recently, environmental problems have figured more prominently in research activities and policy debates on the maquilas, as well as in labor activism in the maquilas. Occupational health hazards in the maquilas have long been of concern to some researchers, organizers, public-health activists, and unionists.[5] Industrial work accidents have also remained a subject of inquiry since at least 1985.[6] However, the past five years have brought increasing awareness of and concern for environmental issues on both sides of the border. In fact, a burgeoning environmental movement is active both within Mexico and in the U.S.–Mexico border region.[7] Activists and researchers are documenting the environmental effects of the maquila industry. Research clearly links the industry with damage to the ecology of the border.[8] Toxic wastes, heavy metals, and other contaminants that maquilas, in an almost unregulated manner, are releasing into the water, soil, and atmosphere may be associated with a variety of public-health problems.[9] For example, researchers in South Texas are currently documenting higher rates of anencephaly (brain-structure diseases) among infants born to residents of neighborhoods adjacent to maquila industrial facilities on both sides of the border (see chapter 9).[10]

Finally, with approval of the North American Free Trade Agreement (NAFTA) many scholars are debating the future of the maquiladora industry. In the United States, the oppositional discourse is led by a wide variety of groups, including grassroots people of color environmental justice organizations, progressive rank-and-file labor activists, and even mainstream "Group of Ten" environmentalists.[11] There is also considerable organized Mexican opposition to NAFTA involving small and medium-sized farmers and ranchers, environmental and feminist groups, indigenous communities, the leadership of industrial unions and opposition political parties, and left-leaning intellectuals and researchers.[12] The debate over free trade is thus associated with a renewed interest in the maquilas, since their numbers will probably increase significantly under the conditions induced by NAFTA.

These issues pose challenging questions about the evolving character and impact of the maquiladora industry in the context of the political ecology and economy of Mexico in a post-NAFTA era. Have technological and organizational changes in the maquilas driven the ghosts out of the machine? Alternatively, are workers still resisting productivity drives by practicing *tortuguismo?* Are informal shop-floor networks still a part of maquila workplace politics? Are workers still circulating struggle from the factory to the community? Has the addition of male workers eliminated sex-typed divisions of labor and improved working conditions for all workers? Is sexual harassment still a problem in the maquilas? What has happened to skill—are maquila workers still acquiring working knowledge as an inventive force? Has the growing role of the Japanese changed the nature of industrial relations and labor-management conflicts in the maquilas? Has the growth of automotive assembly within Mexico affected the demographic composition of maquila workforces? Has it induced further technological restructuring? To what degree and in what manner are maquilas still hazardous to workers' health and safety? What are the other environmental impacts of maquilas? Are maquilas a type of "disturbance regime," and if so, how will that affect an assessment of their nonsustainability? How will these conditions be transformed by NAFTA? Are there viable, ecologically sustainable alternatives to maquila-style rapid industrialization? What are these alternatives, and what are the possibilities and challenges involved in seeking to implement them? These are some of the key questions that are important to me as I survey the changes that have occurred in the maquilas between 1982 and 1992. In the final two chapters I seek to answer these and other related questions. But before doing so, I owe some words as a kind of *homenaje* (homage) to my former mentor and colleague in struggle, the late Guillermina Valdés.

During our last interview, in Juárez, July 1989, Dr. Valdés formally agreed to serve as coauthor of the last two chapters of this book. We spent considerable time before, during, and after that interview discussing and negotiating the focus of our collaboration. She suggested that we focus on five critical issues to guide our joint assessment of changes in the state of the maquila industry since 1982: (1) changes in the demographic composition of the workforce, (2) changes in technology, (3) changes in the extent and focal points of worker resistance, (4) unresolved problems in comparative maquila research, and (5) the future of the maquilas in a post-NAFTA context.

With regard to the first question, Valdés argued in favor of the possibility that an increasing number of male workers in the maquila industry did not necessarily guarantee significant improvements in working conditions for workers of either gender. Both male and female workers were still subjugated in a production system that remained largely exploitative, dangerous, and degrading. On the second issue, she felt that we should not limit our study of technological change in the maquilas to an analysis of how management introduced automation and other types of mechanization and computerization to control labor. She believed that the technology used by the industry in the future would be qualitatively different from previous labor-intensive regimes. Valdés agreed that the assembly flow lines we grew accustomed to during the early to mid 1980s had been radically restructured before the turn of the decade. Maquila production layouts, especially in consumer electronics, today still often follow the characteristic pattern of the Fordist regime. That is, they are still based on the flow-line principle because they involve the imposition of performance-based quota standards linked to daily minimum wages— precisely the sort of low-wage and high productivity regimes that were predominant in the maquilas prior to 1985.

However, Guillermina Valdés went further in her analysis by suggesting that after 1985 one could see signs of major changes to come, which she characterized as a problem of scale combined with one of disrespect for ecological and cultural appropriateness.[13] Future development in the maquilas could mean we will experience a larger scale of environmental and cultural degradation. This will be caused by the presence of even more plants, and by the technological systems being developed, and their inherent spatial, physical, and chemical properties. Everything points to ecological disaster and an equally destructive homogenization of culture. On this issue, I regard Valdés as nothing short of prescient: the maquilas in a post-NAFTA era might very well engender a qualitative and quantitative leap forward in both ecological and cultural disruptions. Maquilas might just make ethnocide a permanent servant of ecocide.

On the third issue, Valdés viewed the forms of worker resistance and struggle through the same activist lens that led her to observe what she took to be the evolving and inherently political properties of the workplace. She suggested that we should examine the possibility that technology evolved through changes in the material and political conditions of production, and so too the workers' desires and forms of struggle.[14] She suggested that, while job security and turnover would remain central concerns of workers, environmental problems were becoming, and would continue to become, more important than ever as organizing issues among workers and their communities. Valdés had previously participated in the development of ecological awareness when COMO worked with *pepenadores* in establishing SOCOSEMA and with student-workers in confronting RCA with occupational health hazards during the late 1970s. Now, she was witnessing how maquila workers and organizers were themselves increasingly focused on understanding and solving the environmental and occupational health problems generated by the politics of social choice in the design of maquila workplace technologies. This was, I believe, one of the primary unstated political objectives that guided

Valdés and COMO in their work with the transference methodology (see chapter 6). For Valdés, a fundamental aspect of the workers' inventive force was a concern with the possibility of finding ways to avoid the ecological and cultural destruction spawned by the maquiladora program.

On the fourth issue, Valdés agreed that the increasing variety of maquiladoras merited further comparative inquiry, because a better understanding on our part of differences in organizational forms and working conditions could strengthen our political practice. She did not think the establishment of Japanese maquiladoras would trigger many significant changes in worker-manager relations or in the mediation of industrial conflicts. However, she believed that the Japanese would eventually pose a challenge to U.S. hegemony within the various maquiladora trade associations. She doubted that I would find significant differences between Japanese- and U.S.-owned maquilas, or at least she suggested that such differences would be sectoral rather than gender related or culturally embedded.

Finally, Valdés thought that NAFTA had to be critically analyzed and challenged, if not opposed. She remained, at least until 1989, somewhat ambivalent about a concept that had not yet been publicized much—but in our discussions it was obvious that her good standing within the left spectrum of the PRI meant she had access to insider information early on in the process. Late in 1990, she privately expressed concern that progress on environmental and labor standards on both sides of the border might be forestalled or compromised by any NAFTA-like arrangement. She also expressed concern with the implications of a political framework in which the de facto economic annexation of Mexico might be transformed into the de jure annexation of Mexico's national economy by transnational corporate interests. Like other Mexican "leftists," Valdés feared the worst scenario: a relapse into a nightmarish neo-Porfirian regime. Throughout our discussions, Valdés remained privately skeptical of efforts to formally incorporate Mexico into a continental trade market. She believed that—under the constraints of a continent-wide production and trade apparatus that would be inevitably based on unequal exchange relations between differently empowered partners—Mexico's potential for autonomous development might well be subordinated to U.S. corporate interests. She suggested that we examine the possibility that formal incorporation into a "free trade" zone could compromise Mexico's ability to improve environmental and labor standards in the maquila industry. She further suggested that we examine the possibility that incorporation would impose limits on public discourse in pursuit of alternatives that could better guide the nation as a whole in the direction of more earth- and worker-friendly forms of development.

Much of what is argued in this chapter is thus actually ghostwritten by Guillermina Valdés. Her insights and contributions (albeit incomplete) to this work remain guiding forces underlying my analysis of the changing maquila phenomenon. By focusing on the composition of the workforce, changes in technological systems, the national origins of management, environmental issues, and the implications of NAFTA, I hope to pursue some of the ideas that deeply concerned Guillermina Valdés just prior to her untimely and tragic death in 1991.

Ghosts in Evolving Machines

During 1989 and 1990, Dr. Valdés and I jointly coordinated a new study of maquila workers in which we interviewed one hundred respondents.[15] This study confirmed many of Valdés's predictions and some of our earlier research findings.[16] Briefly stated, the most recent findings indicate that vast technological restructuring is occurring in the maquilas. Despite this restructuring, or perhaps in part because of it, both male and female workers continue to face considerable dangers and problems in the workplace. Sexual harassment is still pervasive; exposure to toxic chemicals and dangerous machine systems remains prevalent; turnover and short-lived tenure are still endemic; conflicts over productivity standards persist; workers continue to restrict output and sabotage equipment; the political constructions and deconstructions of skill still generate struggles over unpaid technical work; and many workers are still circulating struggle by participating in work stoppages and other informal, spontaneous acts of resistance. In short, there seem to be plenty of ghostly pranksters in the stubbornly evolving machines.

TECHNOLOGICAL RESTRUCTURING AND
CYBERNETICS ON THE FLOW LINE

The potential for technological change has always been at the heart of the maquiladora production strategy. The global assembly line is a dynamic organizational form, still the offspring of a revolutionary Fordist progenitor. Maquiladoras have continuously experimented with new technology in an effort to maintain "efficiency," defend daily quota standard regimes, and reinforce other managerial imperatives characteristic of Fordist organizational forms. Since the start of the BIP, transnational corporate managers have demonstrated a willingness to deploy techno-logical advances in the Mexican maquilas. This is not new. Our research verifies two persisting tendencies in the technological choices made by maquila management: the continuing incorporation of recent advances in robotics and other automation systems, and an increasing reliance on computer-aided design, manufacturing, and testing systems—that is, greater use of CAD/CAM/CAE hardware and expert systems.[17]

However, we have also detected a qualitative shift in production lay-out that involves redeployment of intensive-labor operations in a system that now ties assembly workers to emergent cybernetic technologies lo-cated *directly on* the flow line. This signals a continued willingness on the part of management to incorporate technological advances in the ma-quila organizational environment whenever this serves the command and control imperatives of capital. Automatic machine systems are in-creasingly common in the maquilas. We do not, however, find significant evidence of technology anchorage in the maquilas—a finding that con-firms the results of at least one astute observer.[18] This seems equally true of U.S. and Japanese operations. Despite endemic technological restruc-turing, maquilas do not appear to function much as sites for technology research and development—at least not formally.[19] Nor is technological restructuring common in all sectors of the industry.

At least one production engineer has observed that "the level of skill in electronics-sector maquiladora plants has increased with the addition of new technologies." An increasingly common example involves the ad-dition of "computerized production instruments" that "require technical operatives" who understand "computing languages and expert systems."[20] Research by Grupo Bermúdez[21] indicates that the percentage of "techni-cians" (*técnicos*) in the industry as a whole increased between 1980 and 1987, from 9 percent to over 12 percent.[22] Similar data for 1990 indicates that the percentage of workers who are classified as technicians is now more than 14 percent.[23] But the percentage of technicians is not evenly distributed across all the sectors. For example, nearly 16 percent of all workers in the consumer-electronics sector in 1987 were classified as "tech-nicians."[24] In contrast, maquilas in the service sector averaged less than 5 percent, and those in the food-processing sector less than 6 percent. So the plants in the consumer-electronics sector that are my primary re-search focus have averaged at least three times the number of technical workers than other types of maquilas.

This technological shift actually involves something more than what may now be considered routine microelectronics computerization. The introduction of *cybernetic* production instruments on the assembly line itself is of a different order altogether, even if such technology is still based on microprocessing chips.[25] While workers have long been deployed in large numbers alongside automated conveyor-belt systems, direct automation of instrumentation on the flow line itself remained, at least until 1985, relatively static and undeveloped. The capacity was clearly there but the process, methods, and systems engineering had probably not yet been debugged. As we saw in chapter 3, since at least the early 1980s, workers and managers have been describing automated component-insertion devices, semiautomated testing and monitoring equipment, and other interactive microelectronics-based processing equipment connected to assembly-line work. These include the obvious examples of microscopes for use in circuit microassembly tasks or the more sophisticated Zehntel monitor stations for use in quality-control testing and repair.

However, what we are now seeing is the use of devices with cybernetic feedback capabilities that are located directly alongside or above workers positioned on conveyor-belt assembly lines. Theoretically, cybernetic technologies are self-enclosed, zero-discharge, continuous-process production systems with built-in human "feedback loops" and multiple redundancies.[26] Examples of cybernetic technology systems include petrochemical cycle plants, nuclear power stations, the space shuttles, and the enclosed cyanide leach vats used in the industrialized milling and processing of gold, silver, and other heavy metals.[27] In a way, the old stop-start mechanism developed and used at RCA–Juárez during the early 1980s was a precursor of this cybernetic shift. But in that case the feedback loop was not automated, and its reliability as a control mechanism over productivity depended almost entirely on the quality of informal relationships between rate-busters and novice assemblers.

Today, cybernetic instrumentation in the maquilas more likely involves the installation of workstations based on microelectronic processors—these are electronic feedback loops used not just by workers but more insidiously by engineers and managers to gather information about the status of production on the shop floor. It appears that much of this silicon-based technology functions primarily as an electronic surveillance, accounting, and measuring expert system that can be used to exert greater levels of control over productivity regimes. Similar technologies were pioneered in the early 1980s at the Ford Motor Company in the form of computer-based "management information systems" (MIS). The MIS, as well as a more advanced version, the "total operations planning system" (TOPS),[28] allows managers or engineers to instantaneously and electronically supervise the shop floor from their desktops. In the maquilas, the MIS technology is most frequently used as a set of computerized expert systems and workstations that link production workers to management via an electronic feedback loop.[29] To the extent that these instruments are also used by workers in the process of assembly itself, managers are simultaneously provided with a surveillance feedback loop to the desktop. This portends ever increasing opportunities for management to use microprocessor technology as a surveillance tool that displaces group chiefs from long-established roles as primary access points for monitoring and controlling labor activity on the flow line. It appears that these automatic machines, "the economic equivalent of slave labor," as Norbert Wiener said, have made a permanent intrusion into the maquila workplace, with startling consequences for workers' ability to struggle collectively.[30]

The addition of cybernetic instrumentation, or even just the application of the hardware and software of expert systems, increases the number of on-line "technical operatives." But sometimes it also involves enlarged job responsibilities for both technical and assembly workers. This is consistent with the patterns of unpaid technical work documented in my research over a period of ten years. However, the rationalization strategy applied by maquila management during the mid to late 1980s may have also involved efforts to reduce the span of control that workers, and especially group chiefs, had over their own immediate work environment. The introduction of MIS applications and the automation of other flow-line instruments have been, and will continue to be, major aspects in the redesigning of maquila assembly-line layouts.

The cybernetic character of automation in the maquilas will probably generate the most formidable challenges and intense struggles during the mid to late 1990s. As technical operators develop working knowledge of MIS and other computer-based information systems, as they begin to shift their identities and establish relations of solidarity with other line workers, the character of workplace politics in the maquilas is likely to undergo another major transformation. The new generation of on-line technicians may yet emerge as a major force capable of catalyzing new forms of struggle. This is exactly what occurred with the TOPS at the Ford assembly plant in Batavia in the late 1970s.[31] And although that case involved highly skilled diemakers, there is no reason to suspect that the maquila technicians and other workers will take less "pride" in defending their skills and labor conditions against automation.

Full-scale cybernetic technologies will also be more commonplace along the U.S.–Mexico border. Maquilas in the chemical sector are one example of full-scale cybernetic systems. Química Flor de México in Matamoros, a cybernetic petrochemical cycle plant, is one already controversial case. That particular plant has been at the center of an environmental and public-health controversy for some time now, and medical researchers have linked extraordinarily high rates of anencephaly in Brownsville-Matamoros with toxic wastes from that and other maquilas in the same area.[32] In the last chapter, I will more closely examine the environmental problems posed by full-scale cybernetic industrial plants, which are precisely the types of production systems Guillermina Valdés warned about. For now, I turn to the emergence of temporary-personnel services and their use by maquila management.

"MAQUILA TEMPS" AND INFORMAL NETWORKS

Guillermina Valdés was the first person to alert me to this problem in 1985. I have yet to see a published study of temporary-personnel services and their use by maquila management. In conversations over the past five years with temporary workers, labor organizers, first-line supervisors, and personnel managers, I have learned that during the mid 1980s several Juárez businessmen established temporary-personnel companies to provide management with alternatives in dealing with the high rates of employee turnover that characterized the industry then, as they do now. I also remember viewing some ads for the services in Valdés's office at the Colegio de la Frontera Norte (COLEF) in 1989. In a brief, and tense, telephone interview I conducted in 1990, a maquila personnel manager explained this development in glowing terms:

> This was the best thing to happen around here in a long time. You see, the idea is rather simple, yet very efficient. Why not spin out some of the recruitment and screening of employees? These temporary-personnel services provide greater capability at lower cost for the psychological screening and adaptation of employees before they even set foot in our plant! This means we don't have to build a huge organization around recruitment and training. . . . Is this related to [control over] strikes, unions, and things like that? Is that what you mean? Well, the truth is, this is an excellent way to find better workers, and that is the only thing that really matters to us. . . . How are they better? Well . . . okay. Is it because they are more efficient? Yes. Is it because they resist the learning curve less? Yes. Is it because they have a more cooperative psychological profile? Yes. But this does not mean we

are opposed to labor rights. . . . Are you implying that? If you are, then I strongly disagree, because the level of job satisfaction increases whenever we manage the profile better . . . you see? (Telephone interview, June 1990)

Did I ever! The personnel manager's allusion to the "learning curve" is a thinly veiled criticism of workers who restrict their output. Of course, our obdurate managerial informant openly proffers the need for efficiency as the only real motive for the use of these services. He becomes defensive and abrupt when asked if this is a strategy for labor control. Immediately he turns the control issue into a question of rights, and he assures me that, of course, management supports labor rights. Support for labor rights in his view means "managing the profile better" to increase "job satisfaction." I wonder if he equates job satisfaction with worker acquiescence?

What effects did the use of "temps" actually have on the informal dynamics of maquila workplace politics? I cannot provide a carefully documented analysis, but there are indications that the use of temporary personnel caused at least some disruptions in the processes that lead to the formation of shop-floor networks and the emergence of oppositional identities. Contrast the following two views of the "maquila temp" experience—the first expressed by a young temporary worker and the second by an older and more seasoned veteran:

> I like working in different plants because it gives me more opportunities to advance myself. I am assigned to a new job every two or three days and sometimes for a whole week. . . . I enjoy meeting new people and learning new jobs. This is a good opportunity for me to develop a career in the electronics industry. I am getting a lot of good training and I also appreciate the way the plant managers treat me. They are very friendly, kind, and will assist you with any problems. I hope to get married to an engineer I met at my first job this year. It's nice how my company got me a job and maybe even a husband! (Interview, Ciudad Juárez, August 1989)

In vivid contrast, the veteran observes:

> These part-time newcomers can be a lot of trouble. They have no loyalty to their peers, their work companions [*compañeras del trabajo*]. They come and go pretty fast and you can hardly get to know them before they're gone. . . . The longer I stay on the job, the more I learn about my work companions. At this plant, eighteen months I have been there. The longer I am there I become closer to my work companions. . . . [We] start agreeing on things more often and you gain a lot of trust. You become an old hand. . . . This trust is missing with part-timers because they have no idea of the need for workers to fight together. (Interview, Ciudad Juárez, August 1989)

This managerial tactic may disrupt the dynamics of shop-floor networks simply because temporary workers are not in the same plant very long. They do not have enough time to establish knowing, trusting friendships with the "permanent" plant workers. This may even generate some internal divisions—horizontal power struggles—among the workers. For example, the "old hands" may pit themselves against the "part-time newcomers." Might the "old hands" construct a stereotype of temporary workers as untrustworthy minions of managerial authority? Judging from the old hand's comments, the full-time workers can develop a deep-seated suspicion of the part-timers. Might this younger temporary worker fit the psychological profile, preferred by management, of the quiescent and satisfied conformist? Judging from her own narrative, it appears that temporary-personnel services sometimes do a very good job of psychologically screening and adapting workers to an identity built around conformity. The younger worker is glad to have found "career opportunities" and "maybe even a husband." Perhaps the younger worker is dealing with her own "survival strategy" and does not have "time" to espouse a cause or construct an alternative identity?

Might the "maquila temp" represent a hegemonic identity readily constructed and imposed on unsuspecting workers by these service companies through the crafty use of industrial and social psychology? I have several reasons to suspect that the use of temporary-personnel services will not be a very effective long-term strategy for labor control, and will decline over time. The providers of this service cannot count on remaining effective all the time, because temporary workers tend to develop shifting identities and loyalties.[33] If these companies do experience a long-term inability to "craft the identities" of temporary workers, then it is likely that their services will not effectively help managers keep pace with persistently high rates of turnover in the maquilas.[34] Management will then probably just go back to building large organizations around the recruitment and training of workers (to paraphrase our personnel manager).

DEMOGRAPHIC RESTRUCTURING AND SHIFTING CONSTRUCTIONS OF GENDER

Recent data on the demographic composition of the maquila workforce indicate that the proportion of males in the industry as a whole has increased dramatically since about 1983. These changes have led to a renewal of debate over the "sexual division of labor" in the maquilas.[35]

Leslie Sklair reports that in 1975 nearly 80 percent of maquila "operatives" were female. Ten years later (in 1985), only 69 percent of the operatives were female, and by 1988 the percentage had dropped further, to a low of 64 percent.[36] More recent estimates place the industry-wide average of female assembly operatives at 62 percent in 1990.[37] However, there are some significant sectoral differences that merit discussion. Counting the total sector workforce and not just operatives, in 1987 the maquila garment industry had the highest percentage of women workers, with almost 79 percent. In contrast, the furniture assembly sector had the highest percentage of men workers, nearly 72 percent. In the consumer-electronics sector, females constituted nearly 74 percent of the workforce.[38]

The maquila industry still reflects a pattern of general occupational segregation by gender, much like the rest of Latin America and even the United States. For example, women are 76 percent of the total workforce in service-sector maquilas, and nearly 77 percent in food processing. The chemical sector of the maquila industry has a surprisingly even distribution of male (50.8 percent) and female (49.1 percent) workers. These patterns are familiar to students of gender-based occupational segregation in Latin America and the United States. If we consider occupational distributions within the internal labor markets of the maquiladoras, we are likely to find even more pronounced evidence of gender-based divisions of labor. For example, within a given factory in the consumer- or automotive-electronics sector, the division of labor by gender will tend to segregate women and men even more. It is difficult to locate official published data on gender distributions for plant-specific occupational categories in the maquilas. On the basis of research conducted in 1981–83, Peña and Cárdenas report that 80 to 95 percent of assembly-line operative positions and 100 percent of the soldering operative positions were held by women. In contrast, the eight highest-ranking positions in production (from repair mechanic through plant manager) were held exclusively by males.[39] More recent data suggests that assembly-line operatives are 65 to 70 percent female, a noticeable decline since 1983. More men are also now found as soldering operatives, the lowest paid and one of the most hazardous job positions in the electronics sector. However, even here I have verified the existence of at least seven plants in Juárez where the soldering decks are still operated entirely by all-female work groups.[40]

The findings further suggest that many of the males who entered the workforce since 1983 are disproportionately present in technical, repair, maintenance, group-chief, and supervisory positions. And engineering, supervisory, and managerial positions are overwhelmingly held by males. The distribution of respondents in the 1989–90 survey indicates the existence of gender segregation in the internal labor markets of the plants we studied: 89 percent of the women are assembly operatives, none are group chiefs, one is a supervisor, 4 percent are quality-control inspectors, and another 4 percent are technicians. In contrast, only 67 percent of the male respondents are assembly operatives, 4 percent are group chiefs, 8 percent are quality-control inspectors, one is a supervisor, and 12 percent are technicians. One of the more interesting contrasts is the relative percentage of women and men who are technicians: 4 percent of all females compared to 12 percent of all males.

Additional findings from another source indicate that of forty-five establishments surveyed in Juárez in 1990, only two plant managers were women and less than 2 percent of the engineering and supervisory jobs were held by females.[41] It is probably pointless to dwell on these statistics very long. The data basically indicate a significant shift in the demographic composition of the total maquila workforce, and this is primarily a consequence of the growth of those sectors with predominantly male sex-typed occupations (for example, in furniture-making and non-electronic transport equipment assembly plants). A continuing gender-based division of labor within factories in other sectors is also indicated, particularly in consumer and automotive electronics assembly. The findings suggest that males have been prime beneficiaries of an increase in the number of technical operative positions available to workers in the consumer and automotive electronics assembly maquilas. Ultimately, this type of evidence tells us very little about the impact these demographic changes have had on workplace politics. To get at the impact of these changes on informal shop-floor networks, we have to go back to the workers' narratives.

By 1987, Rosario Menchaca found herself working alongside greater numbers of male employees. In her work as a repair technician for a manufacturer of military-spec semiconductor devices, she had always interacted with male supervisors, inspectors, mechanics, technicians, or engineers. But after 1987, she noticed more men among the group chiefs and assemblers. In Menchaca's mind, this changed the character of relationships within the work groups. She attributed the change to the use of male group chiefs:

> It just wasn't the same working with men. I mean, they do not seem to understand the problems the same way the women do. I don't believe it has to be this way either. But it was like they were really just competing with

the women. Trying to work faster and better. It was awful. But, well ... it's like they don't even notice the same things that we [the women workers] notice. ... One thing, for example, was all the chemicals used in the plant and especially in our work area. The men didn't seem to care about it that much. But it affected all of us in the [integrated circuit-board preparation] area. The fumes and the splashes. My eyes burned. My throat was always sore. ... I think some of the men wanted to prove they were tough. They didn't have to complain about the chemicals because they were tough. But I could tell they were also getting sick. ... One day, the group stopped working. For like twenty minutes we stopped. All of us, women and men alike. But then the group chief came over and he ignored the women. Just totally ignored us. He only spoke to the men. ... I said, "You have to listen to all of us. This affects everyone, not just the men." But he continued to ignore us, and the other men stopped complaining. Beto, the lanky one I told you about. He was always trying to be the toughest one in the group, and he said something to Reynaldo [the group chief] about it only being the women and that there was no problem at all. (Interview, Ciudad Juárez, July 1989)

I could sense the frustration Menchaca felt as she described her battle for solidarity in a mixed-gender work group. The demographic shift in the maquilas appears to have had some impact on the dynamics of informal shop-floor relations, at least in the case of Menchaca's work group. The addition of male assembly-line workers and group chiefs may introduce yet another positioned subjectivity that workers must negotiate in constructing identities and loyalties within the immediate work groups. Demographic restructuring basically involves a more frequent occurrence of mixed-gender assembly-line work groups. This change may introduce new dynamics—as when male and female co-workers engage in argumentative discursive practice with each other—that may result in shifting constructions of gender.

I have scant ethnographic evidence with which to explore this problem, but the results of the 1989–90 survey suggest certain intriguing possibilities. For example, almost 46 percent of the women worker respondents believe the production quota levels to be too high. In contrast, only 36 percent of the male workers think quotas are unreasonably high. Even more fascinating is that 57 percent of the women worker respondents restrict their output, compared to only 40 percent of the men. The women worker respondents in our survey are more likely than the men to find quota levels unreasonable and to restrict their output. It is tempting to invoke the specter of *machismo* to explain these differences, but if toughness is what it is all about, then why don't the men "toughen up" by struggling in solidarity with the women? Would not that seem the more *macho* thing to do? Maybe some of the men are quiescent because they have less seniority than the women. A chi-square test of the data suggests that, when controlling for job tenure, women and men with equal seniority come closer to each other in viewing quotas as unreasonably high and in restricting output. Thus, the longer persons are on the job, male or female, the more likely they are to exhibit oppositional tendencies.

However, one other aspect of the survey data merits discussion here. Nearly 70 percent of the women worker respondents believe that their jobs expose them to occupational health hazards, compared to just under one third (31 percent) of the male worker respondents.[42] Either women are concentrated in the more hazardous positions within the plants,[43] or there are significant differences in how the two genders perceive workplace hazards, or both. It is difficult for me to invoke "essentialist" arguments that refer to "women's innate biological characteristics" in order to account for gender differences of this type. Some might argue that women are more aware of and sensitive to the dangers posed by environmental degradation because various forms of such degradation directly affect their reproductive systems.[44] But men also have reproductive organs and, presumably, some awareness of their bodies' biological characteristics and vulnerabilities. It is also possible that social constructions of gender identity in the context of the U.S.–Mexico border render men less concerned than women with the links between workplace environmental hazards and occupational health and safety.[45]

Whatever the case may be, the introduction of greater numbers of men in direct assembly-line positions has apparently altered some of the dynamics of informal shop-floor relations. It should be noted that male respondents in our 1989–90 survey were almost as likely as females to report membership in informal networks and to converse with other workers over workplace-related problems. But the nature of this active participation in informal networks by male workers is not something I can comment on with much confidence. Future research on workplace politics might focus on determining whether there are in fact any significant gender-based differences among maquila workers. My own limited account here suggests that there are some differences, but whether these are attributable entirely to gender or to other factors as well (such as seniority) is something I am not prepared to resolve at this point. Students of maquila workplace politics would do well to design future survey and ethnographic research projects with this problem in mind: it is important that we select equal numbers of male and female respondents in future studies. To continue to ignore male workers is to risk misunderstanding and misrepresenting the nature of the shifting constructions of gender in maquila workplace politics.[46]

TORTUGUISMO REVISITED

In my original 1981–82 survey sample, almost 62 percent of the respondents were restricting output, and most of these identified assembly-line speedup as the primary motive for their resistance. In the 1989–90 sample, almost 47 percent of the respondents were engaging in *tortuguismo,* and again workers reported speedup as the primary motive for restricting output (53 percent). One third (33 percent) reported other motives, including occupational health and safety hazards. Obviously, the data indicate that output restriction is a persisting feature of maquila shop-floor politics. You could extrapolate these findings and argue the existence of a significant, steady decline in the percentage of workers restricting output (from 62 to 47 percent). However, this difference does not concern me that much at all. Whether at 60 or 40 percent, the frequency of *tortuguismo* in the maquilas remained high from 1981 through 1990. But I am also convinced that the level of informal struggle in the maquilas is too dynamic and cyclical a phenomenon to be effectively gauged solely through survey techniques. As I have argued elsewhere in this book, the workplace politics of the maquilas are such that there is a constant ebb and flow in the pattern of labor-management conflicts: sometimes managers have the upper hand and things "settle down," while at other times workers are involved in more intense resistance. What impresses me most about the survey data is the consistent association over time between output restriction and assembly-line speedup; not much changed in this important regard over the ten-year period of my field research.

The more recent findings on work stoppages also indicate the continuation of a pattern I first documented in 1981–82. More than 30 percent of the 1989–90 respondents report participating directly in work stoppages lasting longer than five minutes. This is similar to the 31 percent reported in the 1981–82 sample. Output restriction is often limited to actions by individual operatives or small groups. In contrast, work stoppages involve the coordination and participation of large numbers of workers and sometimes of the entire assembly-line workforce in a given plant. It is, in short, a more intense and more collective form of struggle. This form of struggle seems to have remained consistent over the decade.

Besides some differences related to gender discussed earlier, there are other aspects of informal oppositional shop-floor cultures that continue to exert influence on the dynamics of output restriction and work stoppages in the maquilas. Those workers expressing more militant attitudes toward labor rights and self-organization continue to be more likely participants in *tortuguismo* networks or work stoppages. Workers expressing higher rates of dissatisfaction with wages and other working conditions are still more likely to participate in both forms of struggle. Those workers who are dissatisfied with the level or nature of productivity supervision are still more likely to resist by restricting output or participating in work stoppages. And finally, those workers reporting membership in informal networks are also more likely to engage in acts of resistance and sabotage.

A glimpse at workers' narratives may capture some of the complexities and ambiguities surrounding output restriction and other forms of struggle in the maquilas in the 1990s. Manuela Peña, one of four respondents in the 1989–90 survey sample who agreed to a more lengthy, semi-structured interview, spoke about her experiences in a plant that assembles circuit boards and other components for automotive onboard computers. She had already identified herself as a participant in go-slows:

> What I learned quickly is that you have to resist the time-study engineer. I always work slower when the engineer is timing my operations. . . . Yes, sometimes I have problems with the group chief. She is not a good co-worker . . . because she pushes the group too hard. She wants to keep the standards too high. And she is always buddying up with the engineer and supervisors. I hear she is finally getting a promotion. Some big-time position as a repair technician [troubleshooter]. More pay and better working conditions. . . . No, honestly, I would reject a promotion. They may pay you more, but what is the point? You are still under pressure all the time, even more. You are also subject to the personal whims of the supervisors. I'd like to see that woman when she comes crying back to us because some manager or engineer pressured her to have sex with him. Then we'll see whose side she's on. Then we'll see what she is made of. (Interview, Ciudad Juárez, August 1989)

All four workers interviewed in 1989 described similar situations involving conflicts with group chiefs, supervisors, engineers, and other assembly-line operatives over productivity standards and time studies. In Peña's case, she is angry with what she perceives as the co-optation of the female group chief by management. She clearly disapproves of the group chief's behavior. Will Peña express sympathy for the group chief should she turn to the workers for help in the event of an experience with sexual harassment? Peña herself remains ambiguous about the prospect, preferring instead to question the quality of the group chief's integrity. Perhaps she is merely affirming her loyalty to the work group by contrasting her own personal integrity with what she sees as the less desirable, individualistic orientation of the group chief?

Whatever the consequences of technological and demographic restructuring in the maquilas over the past decade, the extinction of *tortuguismo* and other forms of struggle is not among them. Nor have the most fundamental aspects of informal shop-floor networks changed that much. Workers are still restricting output by forming oppositional shop-floor cultures of resistance and by developing distinct identity narratives in order to articulate and define struggles against managerial power and authority. Technological restructuring in the maquilas has not entirely driven the ghosts out of the machine. I cannot say with certainty if management responded to specific struggles during the late 1980s and early 1990s with the same technical, bureaucratic, and social-control strategies discussed in detail earlier in chapters 3 and 4. I was not in the field long enough to document specific cases. I suspect that the pursuit of managerial control in the maquilas during the late 1980s and early 1990s involved continuity in the standing search for hybrid strategies that combine technology, bureaucracy, and informal social regulation. That much seems apparent from the evidence of the 1989–90 survey and ethnographic narratives.

INVENTIVENESS REDUX

What has happened to the inventive force in the maquilas? Are women assembly workers still engaged in skilled activities for which they are untrained and unpaid? Are they still generating working knowledge of production systems? Do workers still confront management with wage demands for unpaid technical work? Do they prevent management from gaining access to their working knowledge? How do they use this working knowledge and toward what aims?

As we saw in chapter 6, over 45 percent of the respondents in 1981–82 were involved in repair and maintenance activities, over 48 percent in engineering activities, and close to 44 percent in modifications and inventions. The 1989–90 survey has 24 percent of the respondents repairing or maintaining their production tools, 22 percent performing engineering activities, and 20 percent making modifications or inventions. None of the

1989–90 respondents received remuneration for these activities—their inventive force remains unpaid technical work. The level of unpaid technical work in the maquilas has dropped off significantly since 1983–85. The workers' inventive force has not disappeared but is apparently not as widespread as it was during the early to mid 1980s, the heyday of COMO's transference methodology.

Lacking substantial ethnographic evidence, I can only speculate about the significance of these data. There are two main possible factors that could help account for these remarkable changes. First, since the level of automation on the flow line in the maquilas has increased, and this presumably corresponds with an increase in the number of "technical operatives," it may be that fewer assembly workers are engaged in activities that lie beyond the limits of their job descriptions. These activities may now be part of the "normal" job descriptions for a new generation of (mostly male) technical operatives whose numbers increased after 1985. Workers may no longer view this as unpaid technical work, and in fact may correctly consider such activities to be consistent with expectations outlined in their official job descriptions.

Second, again given the increasing level of on-line automation of production instruments, it may be that the boundary between "mental" and "manual" labor has become somewhat "impermeable" for assembly operatives over the past five to seven years. A more polarized technical division of labor could now be in place. Some workers, the predominantly male technical operatives, are perhaps now routinely expected to use cognitive as well as psychomotor coordination skills. In contrast, the predominantly female assembly operatives may now be more thoroughly deskilled, in the sense that the physical layout of production instrumentation reduces their opportunities to gain substantive working knowledge beyond formally designated, hyperspecialized tasks. A third, and less likely, possibility is that workers are refusing the informally enlarged job responsibilities that assembly workers willingly accepted and performed during the early to mid 1980s; workers may no longer be voluntarily providing management with easy access to unpaid technical work.[47]

My own best guess is that maquila management, perhaps partly in response to the challenges posed by the COMO transference methodology, "rationalized" the inventive force. Technological and demographic restructuring in the maquilas occurred simultaneously. Perhaps the addition of new technologies, combined with an increasing number of new, upgraded skilled positions (e.g., technical operatives), was intended to subordinate and diminish the struggle over unpaid technical work? Why not introduce new, cybernetic technology, place its use in the hands of more highly paid, openly skilled male technicians, and then rob the remaining, predominantly female assembly operatives of opportunities to develop working knowledge of production? I have but one interview from 1989 that suggests that this is precisely what happened:

> Yes, I remember. In 1988, the managers shut the plant down for two whole months. When we came back, everything had changed. There were these new computer machines . . . like television sets with all these numbers and other little figures in them. They had keyboards and they were connected to the conveyor belt. Some of us [assembly operatives] asked if we were going to be trained to use the new machines. My supervisor laughed, and he said that new employees had already been hired and trained. . . . Who were they? Mainly men who were trained on the computers. I really do not understand enough to tell you. All I know is that these changes made things harder on us [the women workers]. . . . It was harder because we had many problems with the new [computer] technicians. (Interview, Ciudad Juárez, July 1989)

Throughout the history of capitalist workplace restructuring, there are many cases in which the technical upgrading or mechanization of jobs resulted in the displacement and exclusion of women from certain occupational categories.[48] It would appear that a similar process has occurred in the maquilas since about 1983. The addition of male technicians working with cybernetic instruments on the flow line in the maquilas may have come at the expense of women assemblers, who lost opportunities for training and promotion into upgraded technical operator positions. The demographic shift that brought a higher percentage of male workers into the industry workforce as a whole during the mid to late 1980s may have also created a much larger cadre of male technical operatives in consumer and automotive electronics assembly maquilas. If this was the case, women in these two sectors lost several types of opportunities. By not receiving training and promotion into technical and supervisory ranks, they were obviously denied opportunities to break through the glass ceiling that restricted nearly 90 percent of them to assembly operator positions in our 1989–90 survey sample. More importantly, women workers in this sector were perhaps also denied the opportunity to articulate discursive practices that would allow them to oppose the political and technical definition of their labor as deskilled.

Restructurings of maquila labor processes resulted in the addition of a larger number of higher-waged, technical operative positions (recall an increase from 9 to 14 percent). But these positions were predominantly occupied by male workers (in our sample, 75 percent of the technical operators were male). The deployment of these male technicians on *flow-line* cybernetic instruments may have been part of a managerial strategy to increase control over productivity. But this may have also been a logical response to any long-term threat posed by an "idea" such as COMO's transference methodology—because the strategy also destructured the shop-floor context of informal relations that supported the struggle against unpaid technical work. For now, it may be that combined technical and demographic restructuring can at least somewhat depoliticize the context that encourages assembly workers, male or female, to articulate wage demands for unpaid technical work. Whether or not the women assembly workers eventually break through the glass ceiling and are more equitably distributed within technical and supervisory positions remains to be seen. And whether or not such "mobility" results in new forms of struggle will probably depend on how the workers' identities and loyalties shift once they regain access to lived experiences with which to generate new forms of working knowledge of production and workplace politics.

Nihon no Kaisha: Osaka on the Border

The establishment of Japanese maquiladoras immediately caught the attention of journalists, business leaders, government officials, and unionists on both sides of the border.[49] The arrival of Japanese transnationals on the border was seen by many observers as part of the efforts by the Big Four Japanese automakers (Honda, Nissan, Mitsubishi, and Toyota) to position themselves more favorably in relation to U.S. trade barriers.[50] Since the early 1980s the Japanese have operated automotive assembly plants in the United States and Mexico, with Honda and Nissan leading the way. The development of supplier networks in closer proximity to these assembly plants was a logical next step. The border beckoned. By 1987, Japanese interests had purchased at least $14.2 million in Mexican properties, primarily in the Tijuana area.[51] Suppliers for the Big Four automakers were among the first Japanese maquilas established.[52] By 1986, Japan ranked first and Mexico second as sources of 806/807 imports into the United States.[53] One observer commented that Japan's lead in this category of imports from Mexican maquilas was due almost entirely to the success of Japanese automobiles in the U.S. market. In 1987, vehicle parts assembled in maquilas and destined for use as production inputs in Japanese automotive assembly plants in the United States accounted for a considerable proportion of 806/807 imports.[54]

The earliest Japanese maquilas opened during the mid to late 1970s and were primarily concentrated in the consumer-electronics assembly sector. For example, in 1979 Matsushita opened a new color television assembly plant in Ciudad Industrial Nueva Tijuana (CIN), an industrial park developed by the government of Baja California Norte to attract foreign investments.[55] The Sony Corporation subcontracted assembly work to Cal Pacífico in the mid 1970s, terminated its operations in Mexico in the late 1970s, and then established its own maquila operations in the Tijuana area in 1987.[56] Between 1987 and 1992, at least forty new Japanese maquilas were established along the U.S.–Mexico border.[57]

Has the arrival of Japanese companies, *Nihon no kaisha,* led to any significant changes in maquila labor-management relations? Are Japanese maquilas free of *tortuguismo,* work stoppages, and other forms of informal struggle? Are workers in Japanese plants also developing the inventive force? What is the nature of Japanese organizational forms in the maquila workplace? Before answering these questions, it will be useful to examine the debate surrounding the comparative study of Japanese and American workplace organizational forms.

FORDISM, TOYOTISM, OR FUJITSUISM?

In 1983, Satoshi Kamata published his book *Japan in the Passing Lane: An Insider's Account of Life in a Japanese Auto Factory.* Kamata, a journalist, was employed as a part-time seasonal assembly worker at Toyota. His book sparked a fierce debate about the nature of Japanese workplace organization and politics that continues to the present day. It was Kamata's critical view of Japanese managerial practices and technological systems that led to the controversy. Many American and British scholars and automotive "experts" had over the years constructed numerous idealized views about *Nihon no kaisha,* and Kamata exposed them as myths. Kamata's ultimate indictment of the Japanese workplace is expressed in a sentence toward the end of the book in which he observes: "Every man is beaten down and his pride broken into pieces."[58]

For many "Nipponologists" this was an outrage! American (and British) observers had spent considerable energy during the 1970s and early 1980s trying to meet the "Japanese Challenge" by first constructing an idealized image of "corporate paternalism," of the Japanese corporation as based on an organizational structure that mimicked the "family." Automotive experts visited Japanese automakers in search of the "secrets" of their success. These experts concluded that the "Japanese edge" was not in automation or other manufacturing technologies, or in innovative engineering. Instead, it was the management system that made the difference. The Japanese management system was touted as a new, alternative organizational paradigm that could, and should, be adopted by American and British automakers to meet the challenge.[59] The proponents of Far East managerialism were hoping to convince U.S. and British corporate executives and workers to emulate this system as closely as possible in order to compete more effectively against the Japanese.[60] They began to preach the merits of "quality circles" and group technologists,[61] and they called for the creation of "corporate work cultures" to encourage cooperative labor-management relations. According to this view, the organizational paradigm in Japanese auto companies was characterized by lifetime employment, a hierarchy based on ascribed status, wage rates that have family allowance as the basic element, welfare schemes, and a familial ideology in labor-management relations (what some called "groupism").[62] The Japanese were beating the pants off their competitors because their workers were part of "one big happy family."

However, Kamata's book revealed that lifetime employment and *nenkō seido* (seniority-based wage system) were the privilege of a minority of workers within Japanese internal labor markets.[63] His book described a Japanese version of the terror of the machine. He detailed technological and managerial abuses of workers on the assembly line. He described wage regimes as sharply stratified and insufficient in meeting the needs of workers or their families. If the Japanese paradigm was a mimicry of family structure, then the family involved was seriously dysfunctional. In Kamata's narrative, the one characteristic that conformed with the ideal type was the existence of factory dormitories, which part-time and seasonal workers were required to live in as long as they worked for the company.[64]

The debate stirred by Kamata's findings has more recently focused on discussions related to the uniqueness, sophistication, and transferability of the Japanese organizational paradigm.[65] This has led to arguments over whether the Japanese paradigm involves "Toyotism," "neo-Fordism," or "post-Fordism." Knuth Dohse, Ulrich Jürgens, and Thomas Malsch make the case for Toyotism:

> While the Japanese organization of the labor process differs from that of the U.S. and European automobile industries, it is not a basic alternative to fordism, as is commonly believed. "Toyotism" is simply the practice of the organizational principles of fordism under conditions in which management prerogatives are largely unlimited. . . . It functions with so little

difficulty because Japanese management has been able to use the peer group as a control instrument. This control is based on the organization of strong competition between individual workers who lack effective *collective* means of resistance.[66] (Emphasis added)

Others have argued for a view of the Japanese paradigm as an example of "post-Fordism," or Fujitsuism. Toyotism is dismissed as a relic of more dated, presumably to be superseded, mass production industries. For example, Martin Kenney and Richard Florida argue:

> The social organization of Japanese production has overcome many of the institutional rigidities associated with fordism. Self-managing teams, just-in-time production complexes, and learning-by-doing have replaced functional specialization, deskilling, and linear production lines of fordist mass manufacturing. . . . The institutional contours of postfordist Japan establish an organizational context uniquely equipped to cope with the current round of restructuring based on new, information-intensive technologies. . . . [T]hese new institutional arrangements—which we refer to as *fujitsuism*—represent a qualitative break with fordism and a best-practice frontier for information-intensive production.[67]

Kenney and Florida concede, however, that Fujitsuism is limited to "self-contained innovation complexes" that "exist parallel to the prevailing system of mass production and thus have little transformative impact on Fordist industry."[68] It is not at all certain that Fordism will be superseded by the innovation complexes of Fujitsuism. It would appear that in actual *practice* post-Fordism is not the "prevailing system," or dominant paradigm, in Japan. Kenney and Florida also argue that the contemporary Japanese political economy is characterized by "segmented labor markets" in which women, less-educated, and older workers are confined to the peripheral or secondary labor market.[69] They note:

> The Japanese political economy, like those in the United States and Western Europe, is characterized by uneven social relations and in particular by segmented labor markets. Workers and managers in large corporations, roughly one-third of the labor force, comprise the core of the Japanese economy in the [*nenkō seido*] accord. Surrounding the core is a continuous gradient of workers employed by suppliers or subcontractors or large companies and a sizeable group of part-time and temporary workers, especially women, who make up the periphery of the Japanese economy. . . . The Japanese labor market is characterized by gender segmentation and discrimination. Women receive significantly lower wages than do males across every category of firm size and industrial branch.[70]

Finally, others have argued that the Japanese workplace paradigm is more of a hybrid, neither Toyotist nor post-Fordist. Michel Aglietta was an early proponent of this view, which he derived from a "regulation" theory of political economy. Phil Blackburn, Rod Coombs, and Kenneth Green are the more recent, major proponents for "neo-Fordism."[71] This perspective argues that neo-Fordism involves the use of new technologies (especially CAD/CAM/CAE and other cybernetic flow-line instrumentations) within the general context of Fordist managerial conventions and social regulations. Technological advances are routinely combined with bureaucratic and social-control strategies, which are the continuing legacies of Fordism (see chapter 2).

Several points of criticism can be directed at the participants in this debate. Dohse, Jürgens, and Malsch do not fully consider the possibility that "peer groups" can also play a role in informal shop-floor struggles. They ignore the dynamics of subaltern oppositional workplace cultures. There is no reason to assume that the peer group always, everywhere, functions effectively as a "control instrument." Kamata's lived experience in the Toyota factory and the maquila site ethnographies presented throughout this book amply demonstrate this point. Kenney and Florida can be criticized for assuming that Fordism (and by implication Toyotism) is riddled with "institutional rigidities." The continuous prevalence of technological and demographic restructuring at the Ford Motor Company since the earliest days of the old River Rouge Complex roundly contradicts their assumption.[72] Kenney and Florida overlook Henry Ford's advocacy and practice of a constant revolution in methods engineering and deployment of automated technology, a continuous search for managerial innovation through social regulation, and a never ending flexibility in personnel policies to accommodate and manipulate changing demographic compositions of the workforce.[73] Fordism is not solely based on the mechanical despotism of the flow line. From the start, Fordism relied not only on mass-production assembly but also on the five-dollar day (bureaucratic control) and the social department (social control).

Kenney and Florida can also be criticized for implying that "learning by doing" is unique to Fujitsuism. They fail to consider the implications of deskilled labor's inventive force, of the tacit and working knowledge that assembly workers in mass-production industries acquire and utilize. These qualities of the workers are amply demonstrated in the site ethnographies presented earlier, in chapter 6. Kenney and Florida also have an uncritical view of what they call "information intensive" production. They appear to associate its use with innovation complexes and the reskilling and upgrading of labor processes. They applaud its role in constructing a "best-practice frontier" for Fujitsuism. But the application of "information intensive" technologies basically involves the MIS and TOPS strategies criticized by Harley Shaiken and others as actually constituting a potential deskilling of "intellectual" work.[74]

However, Kenney and Florida's observations regarding segmented labor markets are quite significant. Gender-based segmentation and discrimination are also prominent features of the Toyotist mass-production regimes that, by Kenney and Florida's own admission, still prevail in Japan. It is this system, and obviously not the Fujitsuist paradigm, that has been exported to Mexico. In fact, the global assembly line from Japan is no different from the U.S. model in basic technological and engineering practices. As we will now see, in the case of Japanese-operated maquilas organizational forms are perhaps best understood as simply a case of "hyper-Toyotism."

HYPER-TOYOTISM

Is workplace politics in Japanese maquilas significantly different from that in American-owned plants? The 1989–90 survey provides some interesting results. Nearly 48 percent of the respondents working in Japanese maquilas report output restriction; this compares with 44 percent of respondents in U.S. maquilas. Close to 35 percent of Japanese maquila respondents report work stoppages compared to 32 percent of workers in U.S. plants. This suggests that output restriction in 1989–90 was more common in Japanese maquilas, but the frequency of work stoppages remained about the same for both U.S. and Japanese plants. The Japanese have clearly not been any more effective than the Americans in driving the ghosts from the machine.

In the area of unpaid technical work, the survey data again provide some interesting results. For example, while more than 57 percent of U.S. maquila workers in the sample report engineering activities, only 43 percent of Japanese plant workers do so. Data on inventions (modifications to equipment or processes, etc.) reveal an even greater disparity. Close to 32 percent of workers in U.S. maquilas report inventions, compared to less than 14 percent of workers in Japanese plants. Again, none of the workers in either Japanese or U.S. plants report remuneration for these activities. It is also interesting to note that nearly 84 percent of the inventions reported by Japanese maquila workers involve modifications to machinery and tools. In contrast, 33 percent of worker inventions in U.S. maquilas involved modifications to machinery and tools, nearly 7 percent involved modifications to product or component design, and 40 percent involved modifications to the flow-line labor process. None of the workers in Japanese maquilas report modifications to product/component design or flow line. The range of inventive activity in Japanese maquilas is clearly much more restricted and is for the most part limited to modifications of machinery and work tools.

Finally, the data also indicate some differences in the types of engineering activities. Workers in Japanese maquilas are more likely to report doing their own job setups (50 percent compared to only 23 percent) and time and motion studies (10 percent compared to none). However, workers in U.S. maquilas are more likely to report fixing equipment or work tools to keep pace with production quotas (69 percent compared to 30 percent).

What factors might explain these differences? One possibility lies in the different managerial systems used in organizing the activities of primary work groups. Many Japanese corporations have transferred so-called quality circles to Mexican maquiladoras. At Tasiho in Juárez, quality circles are the primary mechanism used in organizing the activities of work groups. But it appears that instead of hiring "group technologists" (i.e., "experts" in human relations), the Japanese maquilas have enlarged the responsibilities of on-line technical operators. This is evident in the following worker narrative:

> [O]ur problems started when the computer technicians took over the quality-control tests right there on the line. . . . Yes, next to us. There was one of them for every twenty of us [assemblers]. The problems were over rejects. These technicians sure harassed us a lot more than the group chiefs did in the old days. They forced us to meet with them constantly. I don't really mind having a meeting. But it is not always necessary. And sometimes it makes it even harder to meet your quota. Too much time spent in meetings and not enough time spent working. At first, we could not meet the standards. But after a while we complied most of the time. (Interview, Ciudad Juárez, July 1989)

This narrative presents an example of the displacement of group chiefs by a new generation of technical operatives with supervisory responsibilities. But it also suggests that some of the Mexican workers view the quality circles as intrusive, as a form of harassment: "They forced us to meet with them constantly." This worker is not convinced that the quality circles are a good idea. She would prefer to spend more time on assembly work and less time talking about it. It is worth noting that few (less than 6 percent) of the workers in the Japanese maquilas attempt to sabotage quality control on the line. In contrast, close to 15 percent of the workers in U.S. maquilas report sabotage of quality control. Despite the worker's negative view of quality circles, this managerial strategy to control rejects remains largely successful.

A worker in a Japanese maquila that assembles automotive electronics parts for a Japanese autoplant inside Mexico describes a struggle involving *tortuguismo*. García was herself a former employee of a Juárez General Electric plant where she had experience with a work stoppage.

> There are only three Japanese in the plant. . . . The plant manager, Mr. H., is Japanese and so is the production superintendent. The chief production engineer is also Japanese, and he is the one I have had some trouble with. . . . One time my group was working on a template that is used for etching the patterns on a circuit board . . . for the instrument panel. We were trying to change some things that didn't work, and he got so angry. I thought we were all going to be terminated. He told us not to mess with the components, to do only as we were instructed. Nothing more, nothing less. Okay. So we stopped trying to fix the problem. . . . The result was that, well, we decided to slow down, to bring the quotas down. They were too high to begin with. . . . It [the slowdown] didn't last long, about one hour, not even that. . . . See, the computer checks our output every fifteen minutes or so. The engineer, the supervisor, even the superintendent came down to see what was happening. It was very confusing and there was a lot of shouting and arguing. María, my closest friend, started crying. The engineer was really upset. But the superintendent was very nice. He hugged María and said not to worry, that the engineers would fix the problem. He instructed the engineer to look into the problem and so he did. A week later the problem was fixed and everything was back to normal again. (Interview, Ciudad Juárez, July 1989)

Marta García's narrative indicates that a different sense of the technical division of labor is held by some Japanese engineering staff in the maquilas. The engineer in this plant seems less tolerant than would be a U.S. maquila manager of situations in which workers exceed the activities outlined in their job descriptions. He expects the workers to strictly follow instructions and do "nothing more, nothing less." García's narrative also indicates that this managerial inflexibility, somewhat surprising given the context, can generate output-restriction struggles. However, the use of computer-based management information systems (MIS) means that the workers' *tortuguismo* is somewhat short-lived. The electronic surveillance machines can detect the activity in an automated fashion. The resulting managerial intervention is instantaneous.

But there is one other element in this narrative that strikes me as significant. Notice how everyone, not just the supervisor, but also the chief engineer and even the departmental superintendent, personally responded to the *tortuguismo*. I have never really witnessed that kind of reaction in the U.S. maquilas, nor has such a reaction ever been described to me by workers in those U.S. plants I have surveyed. In the U.S. plants, not even the supervisors come around very often, much less the chief engineers or departmental heads. The management style is decidedly different here, with the Japanese managers and engineers seeming more likely to want direct contact with the workers on the shop floor, perhaps even if the MIS makes that somewhat unnecessary.

JAPANESE MAQUILAS AND THE FUTURE OF INDUSTRIAL RELATIONS ON THE U.S.–MEXICO BORDER

My research on Japanese maquilas indicates that the industrial work organizations, technologies, and managerial practices that have been transferred to the border region are really an exaggerated case of Toyotism. This "exaggeration" is evident in several ways: (1) the "sexual" division of labor in the Japanese maquilas is even more pronounced; (2) management has a tendency to rely on quality circles even if the cultural context makes their effectiveness somewhat suspect; and (3) management tends to rely on direct contact with workers on the shop floor in order to control productivity regimes.

The survey results for 1989–90 indicate that 97 percent of the women in Japanese maquilas are segregated to assembly-operative positions. This is a much higher incidence than the 78 percent for female respondents in U.S. maquilas. Both U.S. and Japanese maquilas are gender segregated, but the results clearly indicate a more exaggerated regime in the *Nihon no kaisha*. Among the respondents working in Japanese plants, there were no women group chiefs, quality-control inspectors, or supervisors, and only one female technical operator. The glass ceiling in the Japanese maquilas seems to be even lower than the one in the U.S. plants. Quality circles also seem to be associated with certain exaggerations of basic features of Toyotism. Japanese managers, engineers, and supervisors invest an extraordinary amount of time directly interacting with workers on the shop floor. This is not just the result of a workplace culture built around quality circles. In fact, despite the existence of quality circles, conflicts can spill out beyond the ranks of the primary work groups and result in the intervention of even the higher levels of production management. The MIS provides an instantaneous managerial link to the shop floor, and chief engineers and departmental heads readily respond to the electronic eye.

For Dohse and his collaborators, Toyotism is an essentially Fordist regime with the added feature of a sociopolitical environment that allows management enormous leeway in the mediation of industrial conflicts. In the Mexican context, these "unlimited managerial prerogatives" become even more extreme. Management can get away with more abuse of power because the legal and political systems allow it to do so. A major case in point is the Mexican tripartite corporatist system of industrial mediation and arbitration (see chapter 4). This system offers advantages not readily available in either the Japanese or U.S. political economic contexts. The arbitration system can be used to prevent or break strikes, deny terminated workers reinstatement or severance pay, and reinforce managerial decisions over working conditions and benefits. I am only speculating, but I suspect that the Japanese are as adept as the U.S. managers in making use of this form of state-mediated power and control over disaffected labor. Differences in the patterns and results of arbitration involving Japanese and U.S. maquila employees is a major question deserving of more study.

Instead of adapting the Toyotist regime to cross-cultural dynamics, Japanese transnationals with Mexican maquilas have integrated their production strategies, in basically unmodified form, into a structure that gives management enormous leeway in the mediation and control of industrial conflicts and the micromanagement of shop-floor struggles. This is what I have called hyper-Toyotism, because it involves a strategy that exaggerates tendencies already found in the historical Japanese context. My results are exploratory, and I am sure they raise more questions than are answered. But there are definite indications of significant differences between Japanese and U.S. management systems in the maquilas. Future research could focus on the extent of differences in gender segregation, occupational hazards, and direct contact on the part of managerial and engineering staff with workers on the shop floor. However, it does not appear that the growing number of Japanese maquilas has resulted in very many significant changes in the technologies and demographics of the industry as a whole. The major differences are likely confined to managerial strategies for the control of the productivity and informal resistance of workers. One thing is certain: the *Nihon no kaisha* will continue to increase their presence in the maquila industry. Most observers agree that NAFTA will contribute to the establishment of more Japanese maquilas. Given the rules of regional origin set in the free-trade agreement, it can be expected that the Japanese will increase the proportion of maquila-assembled components in their automotive assembly plants in all of North America.[75]

9

Promised Land or Wasteland?

We don't have the complexion for protection.
—Southwest Organizing Project (Albuquerque, 1992)

Dirty air and water don't check in at the customs inspection station.
—Elena Alvarado, COMO staff member (Ciudad
Juárez, 1984)

Free trade? . . . Out there on the streets—the ambulantes *[street
vendors]. Now, that's free trade!*
—Luis Herrera, lawyer (Ciudad Juárez, 1992)

A Mexican Bhopal?

The extraordinary growth of the maquiladoras during the past decade
has led to serious concern with the environmental impacts of the industry on both sides of the border. Toward the end of 1992 there were more
than 2,080 maquilas in Mexico and most of these were located in the
northern border region. From 1975 to 1987, the industry grew at an average annual rate of 8 percent. Since 1987, it has expanded at an average
annual rate of 15 percent.[1] Maquilas now employ more than one-half
million workers.[2] The size of the workforce has increased at even faster
annual rates, ranging from 14 percent between 1975 and 1987 to 20 percent since 1987. Many expect this expansion to continue and even accelerate after NAFTA.

A critic of the maquila industry, John Cavanagh of the Institute for
Policy Studies in Washington, D.C., expresses the major concerns shared
by many researchers, community organizers, and border residents: "Lack
of adequate housing, exposure of workers to dangerous toxic substances,
and contamination of drinking water with industrial pollutants have
turned the Mexican side of the border into an environmental wasteland and industrial slum."[3] The National Toxics Campaign calls the U.S.–
Mexico border "a two-thousand-mile Love Canal."[4] The U.S. side of the

border is also affected by the maquilas. As Elena Alvarado says, "Dirty air and water don't check in at the customs inspection station." The border is no barrier to pollution.[5] Pollution pervades the border because the so-called twin cities are built in extremely close proximity and because industrial parks and support facilities are primarily located in areas with high population densities. The twin cities are "functionally integrated," as Ellwyn Stoddard points out.[6] This integration means that the twin cities on the border function as single entities and therefore must share the problems caused by pollution, though not always in their resolution.

Toxic substances in the workplace are not the only dangers workers are exposed to. The terror of the machine does not need to rely on industrial chemicals to harm workers: speedup, the mechanical despotism of the flow line, is itself enough. And workers may not be the only ones whose health is affected. During a fourteen-month period ending in October 1992, at least fifteen cases of anencephaly were diagnosed within a five-square-mile area in the Texas-Mexican border cities of Brownsville and Matamoros.[7] Anencephaly is a neural-tube birth defect: infants are born with missing or seriously deformed brains. In an October 24, 1992, newspaper story, the president of the maquila trade association in Hermosillo, Luis Alfonso Lugo Páez, stated that the extraordinarily high incidence of anencephaly in the border region was due to malnutrition among pregnant mothers, and not to industrial wastes generated by maquilas.[8] The Chicano mayor of Brownsville, Texas, expressed a similar view a few days later at a press conference, saying that anencephaly was "a genetic defect that we Mexicans naturally have."[9]

As if timing had little to do with it, on October 22, 1992, SEDESOL, the Mexican Ministry of Social Development,[10] imposed heavy fines on four maquiladoras in Matamoros for "poor management of toxic residues."[11] The four plants involved were Rimir, Deltrónicos, Metales Federados, and Victoreen. Two of these, Rimir and Deltrónicos, are owned and operated by General Motors.[12] A few weeks later, on November 7, a Mexico City daily, *La Jornada,* ran a news item about the Weaver Electrical Company, which is based in Denver. The company admitted to illegal dumping of toxic wastes in El Paso. The dumping reportedly involved 575 electrical capacitors and 226 barrels of polychlorinated biphenyl (PCB), a highly toxic carcinogenic and mutagenic chemical associated with diseases of the nervous and respiratory systems. The U.S. Environmental Protection Agency imposed a one-half-million-dollar fine on Weaver.[13]

A week later, on November 14, these reports were followed by yet another newspaper story announcing a "hard line" (*mano dura*) against maquilas found violating Mexico's environmental laws. The head of the newly created Attorney General's Office for Environmental Protection, Santiago Oñate, made the announcement. He reminded maquila management that the plants "do not exist on the margins of society or their geographic locales, but rather form part of them and as such they have to be established in specific urban conditions, and they are obligated to respect them."[14] Between July and October 1992, SEDESOL inspected more than four hundred maquila plants on the border. The field enforcement team found violations in about 90 percent of the inspected plants.[15] The ensuing enforcement actions led to numerous plant closures. In Tamaulipas, eight maquilas were forced to close permanently, three were forced to relocate, and 102 were issued technical citations. In Coahuila, eighty-five inspections yielded four plant closings and seventy-nine technical citations. And in Baja California, at least half of the two hundred inspected plants had violations serious enough to result in partial or complete closures. Alfredo Rich, president of the Western Maquiladora Trade Association, attributed the problem to the "overreaction" of inexperienced field inspectors.[16] What troubles me is that less than 20 percent of the existing maquilas were inspected during 1992. Even with the addition of two hundred new inspectors, SEDESOL, by its own admission, is having difficulty keeping track of all the plants on a regular basis. It may also be that stricter enforcement of environmental laws is a temporary strategy designed to weaken U.S. and Mexican opposition to NAFTA. Some fear that NAFTA will allow for a return to business as usual, to more negligent, lackadaisical enforcement and bureaucratic stalling.[17]

In 1983, Mexico and the United States signed a bilateral accord known as the La Paz Agreement.[18] Under the terms agreed to at La Paz, all companies that import hazardous chemicals into Mexico for use in the maquilas and other border industries must ship the resulting toxic wastes back to the country of origin. La Paz also mandated the EPA and SEDUE to cooperate in enforcing laws that regulate transboundary hazardous waste shipments.[19] In 1989, the EPA reported that only about 1 percent of maquilas were in strict compliance with environmental regulations governing the transboundary shipment, use, and disposal of toxic substances and hazardous wastes.[20] After the 1991–92 crackdown by SEDESOL, 30 percent of the plants were reportedly in compliance.[21] In October 1988, Reagan signed the Rio Grande Pollution Control Act (PL 100-465), a bill authorizing the U.S. Secretary of State, through the International Water and Boundary Commission (IWBC), to conclude environmental agreements with the Mexican Ministry of Foreign Relations.[22]

Inside Mexico, the federal government has delegated primary responsibility for the environmental regulation of maquiladoras to SEDESOL. This legal authority dates back to March 1983 and the establishment of the General Law of Ecological Equilibrium and Environmental Protection, Mexico's equivalent of NEPA (the U.S. National Environmental Policy Act of 1969).[23] The law dealing specifically with maquilas was published in the *Diario Oficial* on August 15, 1983, and is known as the Decree for the Promotion and Operation of the Maquiladora Industry for Exportation.[24]

Many critics remain skeptical of these efforts, and they question the adequacy of the legal foundations and fiscal authorizations thus far established to support environmental regulation and cleanup in the border region. For example, while Bush and Salinas pledged $1 billion for environmental cleanup along the border,[25] critics argue that effective cleanup will require an investment of at least $18 billion.[26] Even the pro-NAFTA, pro-maquila Border Trade Alliance (BTA) puts a price tag of $5.5 billion on the cleanup.[27] Despite presidential pledges, the EPA requested only $240 million in funding from Congress in fiscal year 1993. Mexico claimed it could not afford to spend more than $460 million over the three-year period from 1993 to 1996.[28] Such has been the magnitude of the border environmental dilemma in a *pre*-NAFTA context.

Have the maquilas turned the border into an environmental wasteland? What is the nature of the environmental impact of maquila industries? Are workers being slowly poisoned to death along with residents of neighborhoods adjacent to the maquila industrial parks? Is the Mexican government finally serious about enforcing federal environmental laws? Is bilateral management of transboundary hazardous wastes adequate and effective?[29] Will implementation of NAFTA strengthen or weaken environmental enforcement standards and practices along the U.S.–Mexico border? Will NAFTA reinforce the tendency toward an "experts only" bureaucratization and "professionalization" of environmental assessment, and thereby reduce direct citizen participation in the politics of environmental regulation? The environmental issues raised by the spectacular expansion of the maquiladoras are endless. The dangers posed by their continued growth in a post-NAFTA scenario are nothing if not ominous.

In this final chapter I focus on developing an ecosystems approach for evaluating the nature of environmental degradation associated with the rise and expansion of the maquila industry on the U.S.–Mexico border. I also examine the political-ecological and political-economic implications of NAFTA, focusing especially on issues raised by opposition groups in the context of a broader criticism of the so-called neoliberal reforms championed by the Mexican federal government during the Salinas *sexenio* (six-year presidential administration). Finally, I recast the entire debate over the future of maquiladoras in the context of a broader oppositional discourse dealing with free trade and sustainable development, and I offer a vision of alternative futures.

Maquilas and Environmental Degradation

Like a death in the family, the issue of environmental degradation provokes powerful emotions. This is probably what leads conservative media pundits to ridicule environmentalists by portraying them as irresponsible alarmists.[30] The "greens" are said to be a bunch of fuzzy-headed Chicken Littles. For my part, I simply find it very difficult to accept or ignore the wanton destruction of our planet. The stark reality of ecocide and ethnocide causes me great distress, and even an occasional bout of contempt for some members of my own species. I was a Cuban-missile-crisis adolescent. And now that the cold war appears to have subsided, I certainly do not need another dire threat to upset me with new visions of apocalypse. But I cannot ignore the signs of ecological and cultural devastation that surround me. The point, however, is to go beyond the critique of domination, to a vision of reconstruction.

I have personally witnessed the potential for devastation in the threatened destruction of the oldest water rights in Colorado by an industrial strip-mine operation. Since 1988, I have been involved in the struggle against Battle Mountain Gold (BMG) in San Luis, Colorado, a Chicano land-grant community founded in 1851. The BMG operations in San Luis include a mile-long, five-hundred-foot-deep strip mine and a cyanide leach-vat gold mill. These operations are located in the Rito Seco watershed and threaten the headwaters for thirty-five *acequias* (irrigation ditches) that are virtually the lifeblood of Chicano family farms in the microbasin.[31] These families have lived in San Luis for six generations. And their future is now threatened by an overzealous pursuit of gold, an enterprise that will last a mere seven years and leave a permanent two-hundred-acre toxic site, laden with heavy metals, cyanide, and other hazardous wastes.[32] Everywhere I go, I find local cultures and their natural homelands threatened by the forces of capitalist industrialization.[33]

I mention my experiences with BMG because it was in that struggle that I received my initial training in the environmental sciences. Of necessity, I gained new knowledge in areas such as hazardous-waste management, surface and subsurface hydrology, and mined-land reclamation. And while ecocide and ethnocide evoke strong emotions, those emotions do not necessarily cloud one's thinking on these issues. I do not accept the positivist separation of "facts" from "values."[34] Nor do I accept the conventional disciplinary boundaries sociologists habitually impose on themselves when framing investigation and discourse. Instead, I remain committed to specific social ethics that I have derived from certain emotional, cultural, and political lived experiences. My commitment to social justice for Chicanos leads me to use working knowledge of environmental sciences not just to explain ecological destructiveness in theory, but to challenge it in practice. It is here that ecology, specifically restoration ecology and ecosystems theories, proves invaluable to my work on the maquilas. The field of conservation biology, which deals mainly with wildlife populations, is, ironically, also relevant. I have sought to put this knowledge to use in analyzing the maquilas as ecological "disturbance regimes."

THE ECOLOGY OF DISTURBANCE REGIMES

Mainstream environmentalists tend to separate "wilderness" and "civilization," "nature" and "culture."[35] As a consequence, they usually focus research and advocacy in defense of nature as represented in rural or relatively undeveloped areas (forests and wildlife habitats, for example). Within the mainstream green movement, this focus has led to enormous neglect of environmental degradation in urbanized, developed areas.[36] Urbanized and industrialized areas are at one end of a spectrum of "anthropogenic habitats."[37] Anthropogenic habitats are natural environments that have been subjected to human-induced change. Most of the planet has been transformed by human activities over the past ten thousand years.[38] Cities are at one extreme in a continuum of natural environments that have been affected by human activity. The other extreme is what some call "wilderness" areas, but there are actually very few places on Earth that remain totally untouched by human activity.[39]

We must avoid thinking of cities and their industries as somehow existing above or separate from the laws of ecology—that is, as purely artificial human constructs, independent of their ecosystemic contexts. A city, what the geographers like to call a "built environment," does not form a self-enclosed environment. It is part of a preexisting and dynamically evolving ecosystem.[40] The biotic communities (flora and fauna), watersheds, landforms, and geochemical properties of an area do not altogether vanish just because humans build cities and factories. Thinking in terms of anthropogenesis, of human-effected changes in the natural environment, frees us from the constraints of the wilderness-civilization, nature-culture dichotomy. Instead, the rules that are seen to apply to "natural" ecosystems are also seen to apply to the interface between built environments and nature.[41] The issue is not the separation of humans from nature in order to protect nature. The real issue is that some built environments, and the cultures that construct them, are sustainable in relation to nature, while others are not.[42] This basic insight guides my application of ecological principles to a critical analysis of the environmental consequences of maquilas. Cities and their many built environments do not exist in biological vacuums. For me, nowhere is this made clearer than along the Texas-Mexican border from El Paso–Juárez to Brownsville-Matamoros, where the Río Bravo del Norte (also known as the Rio Grande) is home to a complex of diverse ecosystems and is also an international boundary punctuated by an increasing number of urbanized and industrialized zones.

The growth of urban-industrial zones underlies the basic problems of ecosystemic disruption and habitat fragmentation that characterize most of the biogeographical subregions along the two-thousand-mile border.[43] Research on transboundary ecosystems in the U.S.–Mexico border region is, unfortunately, also framed by the division posited between culture and nature. There is a tendency in the discourse toward specialization and focus on environmental problems only as they affect humans in urban areas, resulting in a growing body of studies that focuses on occupational health hazards and environmental health problems in the U.S.–Mexico border region. But research has largely neglected the intrinsic, underlying biogeographical aspects of environmental degradation in the region. For example, few researchers have explored the links between rapid industrialization and urbanization, ecosystemic disturbances, and the viability of the populations of various species along the border.[44]

In conservation biology and ecosystems theory, several concepts play a foundational role. Ecology posits that the first law of ecosystems is interconnection. Every part, every niche, every species is interconnected to form a whole. Ecosystems are communities of life-forms in interaction with their geophysical and geochemical environments. A second principle of ecosystems, which derives from the first, is that of equilibrium. The balanced interconnection of landforms, watersheds, geochemical properties, and life-forms is what creates the conditions that sustain life within the ecosystem.[45] A third principle, which is also related to the first two, is that of diversity. The biodiversity of ecosystems is essential to the health and equilibrium of the whole community of life-forms. This implies a fourth principle, that disruptions and disturbances of one element or niche will have repercussions, usually unanticipated and somewhat unpredictable, throughout the entire ecosystem.[46] It must be noted that ecological disruptions and the disturbance regimes that produce them are not intrinsically destructive or negative; this is a peculiarly human judgment call. In fact, the natural history of the planet prior to the appearance of human beings manifests numerous episodes in which disruptions of ecosystems and habitats over the long term increased biodiversity and contributed to the evolution of new ecosystems and life-forms.[47] However, the past five hundred years of *human* history have given rise to increasingly destructive anthropogenic disturbance regimes that rob nature of parity, that is, of the ability to regenerate its life-sustaining diversity.[48]

Conservation biologists and ecosystem theorists define disturbance regimes primarily by reference to their *stochastic,* or random, quality. They view disturbance regimes as events and processes that introduce "uncertainty" into ecosystems. This includes genetic, demographic, environmental, and catastrophic uncertainty.[49] In turn, this uncertainty can lead to disruptions and imbalances that over time—in the context of conservation biology—produce fragmented habitats and reduce the viability and diversity of species populations. The land organism as a whole becomes "sick," as Aldo Leopold might say.[50] There is a qualitative difference between naturally occurring and human-induced disturbance regimes. The results of natural disturbances—for example, fires, floods, volcanic eruptions, and the like—contribute to the evolution of a multiply layered and patchy landscape mosaic. We might think of natural disturbances as the forces that shape and reshape the "macro-niches" of the biosphere. But human disturbance regimes, cities and industrial zones among them, not only introduce higher rates of habitat fragmentation, but they can also permanently interrupt the natural evolution of ecosystemic complexity, that is, the essential qualities of natural-habitat "patchiness" and "edginess."[51]

MAQUILAS AS DISTURBANCE REGIMES

There are several ways to consider maquilas as serious factors in human-induced disturbance regimes. They can contribute to the threatened or endangered status of wildlife species. They can contribute to the pollution of surface and groundwater aquifers and watersheds with startling consequences for the long-term health and viability of both nonhuman and human populations. Maquilas can also contribute to the degradation of air and soil quality, with long-term consequences for the health of all life-forms and the ability of adjoining landforms and air and water basins to support diverse populations or agricultural activities. The establishment of maquila industrial parks involves vast investments in infrastructure. These industrial parks and their associated infrastructures can fragment wildlife habitats and impinge on biological corridors. They can also degrade rural built environments that are often more compatible with ecosystemic integrity (such as farmsteads and orchards). Cybernetic technologies such as petrochemical cycle plants pose additional, catastrophic-scale risks for the natural and built environments in the border region. Finally, the maquiladora industry is linked to resource extraction and exploitation in many other areas of Mexico and the world, since the inputs of Fordist and hyper-Toyotist mass production are globally dispersed.

Threatened, Endangered, & Extinct Species in the Borderlands. A comprehensive natural history of the U.S.–Mexico border region is not readily available. One must examine thousands of separate primary and secondary sources to reconstruct that history.[52] This is a task I have recently initiated as part of another research project.[53] I have only scratched the surface of the environmental history of the borderlands, but what I have learned is a source of a growing concern with the biogeographical consequences of border industrialization and urbanization. I would first like to offer a few examples of endangered, threatened, or extinct species in the border region before discussing the threats posed by the maquilas.

During the 1950s, Aldo Starker Leopold conducted extensive research documenting species diversity among Mexican mammals.[54] His work and more recent work by Ticul Álvarez Solórzano and Manuel González Escamilla in the *Atlas cultural de México: Fauna* provide the baseline data for exploratory assessments of the distribution and viability of certain aquatic, avian, mammalian, and reptilian wildlife populations in various biogeographical subregions of the borderlands.[55] I note before proceeding that Mexico is recognized as one of the three most biologically diverse regions on Earth—the other two being the Amazonian watershed and the Malesian rainforests.[56] And while the majority of Mexican species diversity is concentrated in the humid rainforests of southeastern Mexico (in Veracruz and the Lacandón region, for example), the northern borderlands as a whole have also long sustained large and diverse populations of mammals and other wildlife. That is, until recent times.

The decline of species diversity in the borderlands has not been the focus of much research on either side of the international boundary.[57] Nonetheless, according to the World Environment Center,

[h]abitat preservation and protection of biodiversity is one of the most critical issues along the Rio Grande/Rio Bravo. Ninety-five percent of the region's native habitat on the U.S. side has been lost to agriculture and development. Wildlife in the area is severely threatened. The region is home to 115 vertebrate species that are listed as endangered, threatened, or at the periphery of their range. One-hundred-forty-five of the 700 vertebrate species inhabiting the Matamoran District of the Lower Rio Grande Valley have been identified by the U.S. Fish and Wildlife Service as in need of immediate protection. And there is a lack of wildlife travel corridors between the disappearing habitat areas. Endangered animal species include the jacarundi and the ocelot, while threatened plant species include the palmetto, the baretta tree, Johnston's frakenia, and ashy dogwood. About three dozen species of fish may already be extinct in the lower areas of the Rio Grande due to saltwater intrusion and pollution.[58]

At this stage in my own research, I have gathered detailed information on at least six species that are now listed as endangered, threatened, or extinct in significant portions of their range. The six species are (1) the Lower Rio Grande alligator gar (*Lepisosteus osseus*), or *catán;* (2) the common brown pheasant, also called Mexican pheasant (*Ortalis vetula*), or *chachalaca común;* (3) the Mexican gray wolf (*Canis lupus*), or *lobo mexicano;* (4) the Mexican ocelot (*Felis pardalis*), or *gato moteado;* and (5 and 6) two species of spotted big-horned toad (*Phrynosoma cornutum* and *Phrynosoma coronatum*), or *camaleón cuerno grande.*

In the case of the *catán,* Álvarez and González list three species as endangered nationwide and one, *Lepisosteus osseus,* as most likely extinct in many parts of the Lower Rio Grande River in South Texas and northern Tamaulipas.[59] The *chachalaca* is considered a threatened species in the subtropical marshlands, tidal basins, and riparian woodlands surrounding the mouth and meanders of the Río Bravo del Norte up- and downstream from Brownsville-Matamoros. With regard to the wolf, Álvarez and González note that it has been exterminated, as a threat to livestock, in most parts of Mexico and is now considered endangered.[60] The Mexican government has considered a bilateral accord with the U.S. Fish and Wildlife Service (USFWS) in order to implement an endangered-species recovery plan for *Canis lupus.*[61] Álvarez and González consider the ocelot to be extinct in most of the *seno mexicano.*[62] The ocelot is endangered in all other Pacific and Atlantic watershed habitats. Finally, in the case of the *camaleón cuerno grande,* Álvarez and González describe the two species as endangered in most of their native northern Baja California.[63]

Álvarez and González emphasize three factors in their brief discussion of the causes underlying the changing and uncertain status of these species. They attribute the near-extinction of the Mexican wolf to long-standing federal government policies (on both sides of the border), which until recently treated wolves as pests, as livestock predators.[64] In the case of the *chachalaca* and *camaleón cuerno grande,* fragmented habitat is the primary suspect in their threatened and endangered statuses, respectively. Of particular concern in the case of the *chachalaca* and the *catán* is the destruction of the oxbow lakes that are a favored habitat for these species in the region downstream from Brownsville-Matamoros. Another source suggests that a horned toad species in South Texas, locally known as *el torito de la virgen,* has been driven to the brink of extinction by DDT contamination of vital habitat.[65] The extinction of the alligator gar in certain border water courses may be due to several risk factors, including the dumping of raw, untreated sewage and toxic industrial wastes in the Río Bravo del Norte downstream from Eagle Pass–Piedras Negras, Laredo–Nuevo Laredo, McAllen-Reynosa, and Brownsville-Matamoros. The construction of dams and reservoirs, such as Lake Amistad, may also have been a contributing factor farther upstream in the Del Rio area. Finally, the case of the ocelot involves a combination of hunting pressures and habitat fragmentation.[66] A reduction in the availability of adequate prey populations may also be implicated in the ocelot's decline.

Major factors affecting habitat include the intrusive patterns of urbanization, industrialization, suburbanization, and subdivision. The clearing of land for large-scale agriculture on both sides of the border is another principal factor underlying habitat fragmentation for all species.[67] The major factors in the contamination of aquatic habitats include untreated raw sewage and runoff from urban areas; toxic chemical spills, point source discharges, and illegal dumping by industry; and nonpoint sources of nitrates, pesticides, herbicides, and other chemicals from agribusiness operations. I have found no published evidence that directly ties problems of wildlife species viability to the effects of rapid maquila industrialization.[68] However, further investigation reveals that all of the listings (threatened, endangered, or extinct) for the six species discussed above postdate the establishment of the first maquilas in 1967.[69] Moreover, the Finsa industrial park in Matamoros clearly involves expansion of maquila-related infrastructure into the known habitat of several wildlife species (the *chachalaca* and *catán* among them).

The threats posed by maquila industrialization to species diversity and viability remain virtual terra incognita. There is a tremendous need for rigorous population viability studies and research on species diversity in rapidly changing transboundary ecosystems. Comprehensive baseline biogeographical research on habitat fragmentation is also urgently needed. These studies should target industrial and urban zones and not just existing patches of habitat (although the impact on the latter should also be studied). Little is actually known about the habitat requirements and changing biological statuses of most species in the region. Only those species with official recovery plans are likely to receive the meticulous attention they deserve from conservation biologists.[70] Research on the risk factors introduced by urban and industrial development is also of critical importance. Such work could study the effects of intrusive development on existing wildlife habitats and biological corridors. The resulting databases would be of use to citizen groups active in regional environmental planning and wildlife advocacy along the border. And finally, research on the impact of these risk factors on migratory species could lead to a better understanding of possible links between borderland habitats and the viability of continental population source pools.

I recognize that island biogeography as a theory within conservation biology is controversial.[71] The industrial and urban development of the northern borderlands can be conceptualized as a two-thousand-mile-long, one-hundred-mile-wide anthropogenic disturbance regime. The international boundary system implies the existence of "attraction pole" forces that operate through the workings of the sprawling twin cities and their vast physical infrastructures. These poles of attraction generate physical disturbance regimes capable of altering the biogeographical integrity of ecosystems along the entire length of the border.[72] The borderline itself, because it politically bisects naturally interconnected biomes, may encourage landscape fragmentation patterns that could cause disruptions in the continental source pools and migratory corridors of numerous species. Future research will have to consider these possibilities in more depth than I currently can. Several dissertation topics urgently beckon.

Degradation of Surface & Groundwater Aquifers & Watersheds. While the maquilas are not the original or even the primary cause of the degradation of surface and subsurface waters in the border region, they have exacerbated preexisting conditions and radically altered the quality of the damage and therefore the nature of and prospects for remediation.[73] For at least three decades, the twin cities in the U.S.–Mexico border region have experienced the usual water quality and supply problems that are associated with growing populations and urban expansion.[74] Bilateral conflicts involving the adjudication and delivery of water rights in the upper Rio Grande area date back at least to the 1890s. One historical example involves conflict over shortfalls in deliveries made to Mexico from the Elephant Butte Reservoir in south-central New Mexico.[75] Water-quality issues have also had a long history. In the lower Colorado River basin, binational conflicts have occurred because upstream agribusiness practices and large-scale hydraulic projects (e.g., dam building) in the United States increased the salinity and turbidity of deliveries made to fulfill Mexican water rights in Baja California and Sonora. These conflicts date back at least to the 1940s.[76]

More recent times have witnessed conflicts over the dumping of untreated sewage into water courses in Tijuana, Ciudad Juárez, Nuevo Laredo, and Matamoros.[77] The contamination of the Tijuana and New Rivers are well-known cases. The first involves twelve million gallons of raw sewage flowing daily into the river from Tijuana. The river is unfit for any use and has been linked to outbreaks of hepatitis, vibrio cholera, amoebic dysentery, encephalitis, and malaria. Wildlife along most parts of the river is either completely absent or severely threatened; the river is virtually dead from a biological viewpoint. The second case involves a toxic brew of sewage, agricultural, and maquila industrial discharges that has turned the New River through and downstream from Mexicali into the most hazardous waterway in all of North America, the Grand Mexica Drainage Canal of Mexico City notwithstanding.[78] The New River is not biologically dead, even if it is bereft of fish and bird life. According to the EPA, its "waters" carry almost every known viral and bacterial microorganism fatal to human beings in the Western Hemisphere.[79]

The growth of the maquila industry poses additional threats to drinking and irrigation water supplies throughout the border region, but especially in the California–Baja California, Arizona-Sonora, Texas-Chihuahua, and Texas-Tamaulipas watersheds. The maquila impact must be understood as involving changes in both the scale and quality of the threat. There are numerous documented cases of point-source pollution from maquilas. The addition of wastes from the assembly plants obviously increases the overall volume of pollution in watersheds. Maquilas generate at least one third of the total waste discharge flowing into some border waterways. This is the case with the New River and with the Rio Grande downstream from El Paso, Laredo, and Brownsville. Raw sewage and nonpoint sources account for most of the remaining two thirds of these total discharges.[80] Moreover, pollution from the maquilas introduces new chemicals that had not been present in the toxic brew. For example, the case of Rimir (a GM automobile-trim plant in Matamoros) involves a point-source discharge of 2.8 million parts per billion of xylene. These levels are so toxic that point-source samples used to determine contamination from Rimir are considered hazardous wastes. Xylene is a solvent associated with respiratory irritation, brain hemorrhage and other internal bleeding, and lung, liver, and kidney damage.[81] This case obviously represents a change in the scale and quality of potential and real damage to water-quality standards and public health.

Traditionally, water-pollution problems in the border region were for the most part related to agricultural nonpoint sources (runoff from fields sprayed with fertilizers and other agroindustrial chemicals) or multiple point sources such as sewage drainage and seepage.[82] With the maquilas there is a new dimension involving increased contamination of subsurface or groundwater aquifers.[83] Research by Benjamin Goldman indicates that violations of surface- and groundwater quality are concentrated in the northeast (primarily Pennsylvania and New England) and in the border counties of California, Arizona, and Texas.[84] Goldman includes Cameron County in South Texas in a list of the top fifty counties in the United States that subject minority populations to acutely hazardous waste exposures.[85] The twin cities of Brownsville-Matamoros are located in this county.

The challenge of groundwater contamination is that it develops slowly and is more costly to clean up. For example, the migration of heavy metals in groundwater aquifers is usually a slow process, unless the toxic plume is accelerated by the typical cones of depression induced by the operation of agricultural center-pivot irrigation or even of domestic water wells.[86] Unlike fecal coliform bacteria in surface water courses, which can theoretically be remediated within a few years or even months, contamination from heavy metals and synthetic organic chemicals is much more difficult to correct, especially after contaminants concentrate in sediment deposits, perched aquifers that lie below the soil horizon, or recharge zones for entire microbasin watersheds. Merely pinpointing the sources of groundwater pollution is a complicated and costly affair. The cleanup of subsurface toxic wastes is a technical quagmire, limited to highly expensive and somewhat unreliable technologies.[87]

It is at this stage difficult to predict what long-term effects maquilas will have on the water quality in subsurface aquifers and recharge zones—this type of damage is gradual and incremental. There is mounting evidence of contamination of irrigation and domestic water wells by hazardous wastes associated with maquilas.[88] Evidence of illegal transboundary shipment and dumping of hazardous wastes in unregulated and clandestine Mexican sites is an additional concern. The previously mentioned case of Weaver Electrical only hints at the magnitude of this problem. Humberto Ramos, a researcher with the Colegio de la Frontera Norte (COLEF), cites the case of El Rancho Félix, a hazardous-waste dump in Tecate, Baja California.[89] This illegal dump lacks even the barest minimum of safety features such as double-lining of disposal sites with compacted clay and a polyurethane lens to contain seepage. Wastes in this dump are seeping into area groundwater aquifers and soils, posing a threat to surrounding water-rights users, residents, and wildlife. It can be argued that maquilas introduce genetic and environmental uncertainties into the natural and built environments of the border region. At a minimum, the maquilas spawn numerous stochastic effects that can seriously and perhaps irreparably damage the health of human and nonhuman populations and permanently disturb the regenerative properties of regional ecosystems. Maquila industrialization does not just degrade the health of all life-forms; it may also undermine life-support systems in many areas of the northern borderlands.

The Varied Impacts of Infrastructure. The infrastructure supporting maquilas would probably exist to some reduced extent in the absence of the global assembly-line factories. But there is little doubt that the maquilas have had a major impact in accelerating the expansion of overall physical infrastructure in border twin-city subregions. Maquilas are associated with increased demand for and construction of superhighways, reservoirs, water aqueducts, sewage and hazardous-waste treatment facilities, fossil-fuel pipelines and storage and transmission facilities, electrical generation and transmission facilities, warehouse districts, and customs installations. The impact of transport facilities alone boggles the mind. Maquilas have had to invest millions of dollars to help cover miniscule portions of the gargantuan costs involved in the construction of special load-bearing bridges, wider, more modern highways, and other types of transport infrastructure.[90]

A primary effect of expansive infrastructure, and perhaps one of the most easily overlooked, is the fragmentation of wildlife habitats. I addressed this issue earlier. Another overlooked effect is the diminishment and degradation of rural landscapes, especially agricultural districts. This can have long-term consequences by reducing the diversity of regional landscapes and economies. This reduction makes subregions more dependent on nonagricultural activities and thus more sensitive to external investment decisions. The decline of diverse rural landscapes can also contribute to the degradation of ecosystems, especially since some farmlands (those with sustainable practices) may double as relatively safe biological corridors and buffers for migrating and resident wildlife species.[91] The decline of rural areas is closely associated with the growth of urban enclaves and industrial activities.[92] In this manner maquilas may impose demographic and environmental uncertainties on changing transboundary rural and urban landscapes.

The Catastrophic Threat of Cybernetic Technologies. The lethal release of methyl isocyanate gas (MIC) in the Union Carbide accident in Bhopal, India, focused attention on the catastrophic risks posed by cybernetic production systems.[93] Dupont operates a petrochemical cycle plant in Matamoros known as Química Flor de México which is similarly located in a densely populated area. The technology in the Matamoros plant is the same as that in a Texas City Dupont facility that suffered a chemical-release accident that resulted in the hospitalization of more than one thousand workers and residents.[94]

The dangers of cybernetic technologies involve questions of design and scale. Fail-safe features in these technologies, the feedback loops and multiple redundancies, are not infallible. Despite multiply redundant safety features, these technologies can, and do, often fail. The scale of potential devastation is usually more extensive than that involving noncybernetic systems. Beyond Union Carbide–Bhopal, some recent examples of catastrophic cybernetic failure include Three Mile Island, Chernobyl, PEMEX–San Juan Ixhuatepec, and the space shuttle *Challenger* disasters.[95] While the hazards of assembly-line work are many, the dangers posed by cybernetic maquilas are even greater, having the potential to kill thousands of humans and nonhumans all at once. There are at least twelve major maquila-type petrochemical cycle plants along the U.S.–Mexico border; this figure does not include numerous gasoline refineries and related storage and distribution nodes.[96]

If cybernetic technologies are theoretically failure-proof, then why do they fail in practice? The answer is simple: human error. The human interface with feedback loops is inherently and randomly problematic—a failure is always possible from the viewpoint of simple probability. Humans are ultimately the sole random factor in cybernetic systems theory.[97] This is why some critics of the maquilas argue that we are engaged in a waiting game with catastrophe: a failure will occur somewhere sooner or later.[98] It can be safely claimed that at a minimum these cybernetic technologies introduce the certainty of eventual catastrophe to the densely populated border regions. I believe this was the qualitative shift in maquila technologies that so concerned Guillermina Valdés as early as 1989. As factors in a border-long disturbance regime, maquilas impinge on and disrupt ecosystems in transboundary landscapes. The effects in the case of cybernetic technologies could be lethal to all life-forms within many square miles of habitat surrounding these types of installations. But a Mexican Bhopal may already be occurring: a catastrophic event is not necessary for catastrophic effects to accumulate over time. And here, the maquilas and their toxic wastes may already be affecting human and nonhuman health. Traces of toxic wastes in the air and water are more silent, but no less lethal.

Maquilas & Global Resource Extraction. The global assembly line is part and parcel of a globe-trotting, land-devouring machine run amok. A global ecological perspective on the maquilas leads to the inescapable conclusion that these industries are contributing to the ravages of natural-resource extraction in many parts of Mexico and the rest of the world. The sources of inputs for maquila production are dispersed throughout the globe. For example, the aluminum, copper, tin, steel, ceramics, and plastics contained in maquila assembly components come from mining, milling, and fabrication operations in North America, Indonesia and other parts of Southeast Asia, Africa, and South America. A production superintendent at GTE–Juárez once told me that the parts for a color television set, counting the chassis and mounting frames, came from fifty-four countries.[99] The same holds true for automotive parts assembly components: one Toyota Company brochure claims that resources from ninety-two countries are involved in producing one automobile.[100] One need only recall the Ford Escort, touted as the "World Car," to get the point.[101]

In 1988, Mexican maquilas consumed at least $802 million in U.S. inputs (mainly components and raw materials).[102] The maquila industry could eventually constitute a two- to four-billion-dollar market for what amounts to global production inputs—ranking among the top twenty manufacturing branches in North America. If maquilas are counted with other export-processing industries in third-world countries, then the total value of production inputs for the global assembly line could easily surpass $40 billion.[103] In today's international economy, that can buy a good bit of environmental destruction. By themselves, maquilas have a

noticeable impact on resource depletion; combined with global assembly-
line factories across the world, the impact they have is staggering. The
multiplier environmental effects of the maquilas remain to be thoroughly
researched. Again, several dissertations beckon.

OCCUPATIONAL HEALTH HAZARDS IN THE MAQUILAS

Since the early to mid 1980s, researchers on both sides of the border have
conducted studies related to occupational health hazards in the maquilas.
Jorge Carrillo of COLEF–Tijuana is a leading authority in this complex
and controversial field.[104] A basic research finding is that work-related
health risks increased in the border states by more than 45 percent between 1976 and 1980.[105] This corresponds with the consolidation and
growth of the maquila industry, which Carrillo identifies as a primary
factor in the dramatic increase of jobs that can be defined as high risk.[106]
In pioneering studies, Carrillo and Mónica Jasís found that the ratio of
industrial accidents in the maquilas was marginally higher than the national average (11.9 versus 11.8 cases per 100 workers).[107] However, rates
varied by sector. Some maquila sectors have notoriously higher rates of
exposure to occupational health and safety risks: chemical production at
60 risks per 100 workers, furniture production at 37 per 100.[108] This can
result in higher rates of industrial accidents and work-related illnesses.
For example, in furniture production the rate of industrial accidents per
100 workers in 1981 was 28.8, in non-electronics assembly 65.3, and in
metal fabrication 31.8.

Carrillo's findings are a cause for concern. In the case of Baja California Norte, he documents an increase in the number of industrial accidents from 10,867 in 1976 to 17,536 in 1982.[109] The total number of "occupational disease" cases also increased between 1976 and 1982 (from 8
to 30 cases). The average number of risks for each exposed worker remained fairly steady throughout this period (11.4 in 1976 and 11.9 in
1982). The average number of workplace accidents per 100 workers also
remained steady (11.0 in 1976 and 11.3 in 1982). The ratio of workers
who developed occupation-related diseases increased slightly from 0.8 to
1.9 per 10,000 cases. If we kept this ratio constant for all sectors, locations, and years, then we would expect no more than 95 cases of occupational illness among 500,000 maquila workers in 1993. This is a statistically insignificant number, except, of course, to those workers who happen
to get sick. Obviously these are not valid assumptions to make in approaching the data. When we break down the data by sectors, the results

can be quite different. For example, the rate of accidents in the furniture sector in 1981 was 29 per 100 workers (rounded). With 60,000 furniture workers in 1987, we would expect no less than 17,480 accidents in that sector border-wide.

In presenting data on occupational accidents and diseases in the maquilas of Baja California, Carrillo follows federal classifications and uses three main categories: (1) work-related accidents, (2) in-transit accidents, and (3) work-related diseases. Utilizing these categories, he was surprised to find that the occupations that exposed workers to a higher number of risks (electronics assembly and chemical production, for example) were not necessarily the most hazardous as measured by the ratios for occupational accidents and diseases. Some disagreement is possible over the manner in which workplace-related accidents and diseases in Mexico (and the maquilas) are classified and enumerated. Carrillo makes the key point that all occupations are rated by the government according to the number of risks posed per worker (*número de riesgos*). The methods of official data collection very likely lower the ratios for the incidence of occupational disease. The ratio of 1.9 per 10,000 workers is probably too low, perhaps by as much as a factor of ten.

This is evident if we consider data collected at the plant-specific level as Carrillo and I have done. In a study of the Solidev electronics assembly plant in Tijuana, Carrillo focuses on three main "risk factors," which he identifies as (1) instruments of production, (2) physical plant conditions, and (3) psychosocial conditions.[110] Risk factors associated with the instruments of production include direct use of toxic chemical substances, continuous use of high-powered microscopes and other tools, and elevated levels of noise and vibration caused by the poor state of machinery. Carrillo identifies several risk factors in the physical plant conditions, including poor lighting and inadequate ventilation, contamination of the workplace atmosphere by vapors and smokes from soldering decks, and the use of acids to wash and clean components and machinery. Among the risk factors in the psychosocial conditions are monotonous and repetitive movements combined with elevated production standards, inadequate spatial positioning of jobs, and constant supervision of production.[111] This is a good start, because it indicates some of the aspects we need to examine to move beyond the limits of official data and to capture the nuances of workplace health and safety hazards in the maquilas.

Carrillo found a wide variety of symptoms among the fifty-four workers he interviewed at Solidev in 1983. Nearly eight in every ten of the respondents reported eye irritations, by far the most common ailment.

Thirty-five percent reported depressive episodes during work hours, back pains, visual disorders, and skin rashes. Similar proportions reported mouth and throat irritations, headaches, nervousness and irritability, and other apparently work-related maladies.[112] Also important in these findings are data related to the causes workers believe underlie these symptoms. Carrillo found that economic pressures, noise, and voices were the most frequent risk factors cited by workers (55 percent for each category). Sexual-harassment problems were reported by more than 44 percent of the respondents, and nearly 41 percent reported vibrations.[113] This research strongly supports the argument that the rate of occupational diseases in the maquilas is much higher than that reported by the Mexican government. The rate of general illnesses among the respondents was quite elevated, at more than 31 percent. But Carrillo links four of the eleven general illnesses to occupational risk factors. Over 31 percent of the respondents in Carrillo's survey reported hyperallergic reactions; slightly more than 11 percent reported hypertension; 9 percent reported kidney disease; and another 9 percent arthritis. All these are health problems associated with work-induced pathologies.[114]

With Carrillo, I suspect that the Mexican government is grossly miscalculating actual rates of accidents and disease by overlooking important risk factors. In remaking this methodology, I remain interested in the workers' own definitions. Maquila worker co-investigators have defined five principal conditions that pose threats to their health and safety.[115] These are remarkably similar to the categories used by Carrillo. The workers' list of risk factors includes (1) direct contact with toxic chemicals and wastes, (2) inhalation of toxic fumes and vapors, (3) exposure to and direct use of dangerous machinery (including conveyor belts), (4) exposure to dangerous methods and processes (for example, assembly-line speedup, inappropriate time and motion sequences, and intense managerial supervision of productivity standards), and (5) exposure to abusive managerial behavior. There are several expected risk factors on this list: for example, toxic chemicals, dangerous machinery, speedup, and constant productivity supervision. But there are also some surprising categories: for example, managerial abusiveness.

The workers' own categories are interesting for being absent from official studies. Official record keeping does not legally have to count many of them as risk factors. Official versions of occupational epidemiology do not classify sexual harassment, for instance, as a work-related health hazard. But ask any woman maquila worker who has been sexually harassed, and she will explain how the experience resulted in psychological and even physical health problems. Speedup and sexual harassment have been cited elsewhere as contributing factors in operator nervousness and associated psychogenic illnesses.[116] The frequencies and ratios for work-related health and safety problems reported by the government are probably seriously underestimated, because the methodology used excludes many potential risk factors and overlooks different symptomologies— perhaps especially those that are important from the woman worker's point of view.

Carrillo found that, according to government data, the hazards of electronics assembly, while dangerous, were less threatening to worker health and safety than those of the chemical and furniture sectors. However, as Carrillo knows, many problems associated with the use of toxic solvents and other chemicals in electronics assembly have longitudinal aspects not easily detected by a methodology relying on one-time, fixed counts. The more deleterious, life-threatening effects of long-term exposure to toxic chemicals are slow in developing. For this reason, work-related diseases are notoriously difficult to pinpoint using the methods of conventional epidemiology.

The 1989–90 survey data that Guillermina Valdés and I collected from 100 workers in Juárez and Tijuana complements many of the findings reported by Carrillo. Nearly 48 percent of the workers reported workplace hazards (although women were more likely to do so than men—see chapter 8). The largest proportion of cases (about 18 percent) reported direct contact with toxic chemicals and fumes. Another 16 percent reported dangerous machinery, while 7 percent reported dangerous labor processes, including speedup and inappropriate time and motion sequences. Only 15 percent of the respondents said that management had corrected the problems; close to 22 percent said that the problems had not been corrected; and 52 percent were uncertain that the problems had been adequately corrected. Only 4 percent of the respondents received medical attention due to work-related injuries or illness. This suggests either that workers are underutilizing medical care or that management is not readily providing access to it.

Our survey results did not include data on specific job-related illnesses. However, in a 1989 informal survey of thirty workers from RCA–Juárez I generated the following list of possible job-induced pathologies: hypertension (5 cases), optical nerve disorders or astigmatism (10), menstrual irregularities and external vaginal bleeding (3), skin rashes and sores (8), miscarriages (1), persistent migraines and nosebleeds (2), and chronic coughs and sore throats (6). Surely these maladies are also present in the general population. But the concentration of so many problems (a total of 35) among such a small group of workers is certainly troubling.[117] Thirteen of the thirty workers reported multiple symptoms, a tendency not so likely to be found among the general population and typical of occupationally linked pathologies that are aggravated by synergistic combinations of toxins and job-related stress.[118]

Whatever the actual extent of dangers posed by workplace organization and physical conditions in the maquilas, workers find it difficult to effectively confront the problems of occupational health and safety. It is difficult for maquila workers to organize around workplace hazards for a variety of reasons. In situations involving large groups of sick workers, managers are prone to mislabel mass toxic poisonings as incidents of "collective hysteria."[119] The case of Comunicaciones Banda Grande (CBG) in Juárez is one familiar to me. In 1981, shortly after first arriving at COMO, I interviewed seven workers from CBG. They related the problems that followed a chemical spill in the plant, which had made several dozen workers ill. CBG management dismissed the women as hysterical and denied many of them access to medical attention. Shortly thereafter, management posted signs with the warning: "Workers Who Contact Unions Will Be Fired." Clara Elena Torres, a former CBG assembler, summarized the problems faced by the workers who confronted management over workplace hazards:

> You have to understand that the managers view this only as a cost issue. To protect us, they should make an investment in special uniforms, masks, emergency respirators, ventilation fans and chutes to get rid of vapors, things like that. But they don't have to make the investment. Not by law nor by their good graces. . . . One time the supervisor told us it was up to us to buy the protection we wanted. That we could get cheap cotton masks across the border in El Paso. But how are you going to do that on a pittance of a wage? And those cotton masks won't really protect you. It is just a pretense. If they want to eliminate the problems they will have to find a way of eliminating the chemicals, or at least reduce our exposure. But if you complain you can get fired. And if you contact a union or a lawyer, the same. (Interview, Ciudad Juárez, October 1983)

Torres's narrative strikes at the core of the problem: The greatest threat to workers' health and safety is management's refusal to install a bare minimum of safety equipment and implement procedures to protect employees. Combined with managerial intolerance for union or legal intervention, this neglect greatly limits the ability of workers to deal effectively with occupational health and safety hazards.[120]

These difficulties are compounded by the scant and vague legal protections afforded to Mexican workers. For example, sexual harassment was not considered an offense in Mexico until 1988, and civil penalties have yet to be enacted.[121] Going back to the problem of maquila noncompliance, recall that in 1989 only 1 percent and in 1992 only 30 percent of inspected plants were strictly abiding by Mexican regulatory standards. Recall also that during 1991 and 1992, SEDESOL issued hundreds of technical citations to inspected plants during an opportunistic crackdown. What all this means, in many instances, is that containers for toxic chemical substances used in production are not appropriately labeled with warnings or handling procedures, that workers are not trained in the safe handling of toxic chemical substances and associated hazardous wastes, that the use of chemicals in production is exposing workers to levels exceeding regulatory standards.[122] Maquilas increase the environmental uncertainty workers face at the point of production. This uncertainty may augment synergistic effects among various risk factors, with resulting cumulative increases in the ratios of long-term occupationally induced pathologies. A veritable worker and public environmental health emergency may be in the making.[123]

MAQUILAS AND ENVIRONMENTAL HEALTH PROBLEMS

It is difficult enough to precisely describe the link between occupational risk factors and higher disease rates among exposed workers. It is even more difficult, from an epidemiological standpoint, to connect maquilas to degraded health conditions in the general population. I have already noted the controversy surrounding the high incidence of anencephaly in the Brownsville-Matamoros area. Another maquila-related controversy in the Brownsville-Matamoros area involves sixty-seven children with mental retardation and brain deformities. The mothers of many of these children worked at the same maquila, Mallory Capacitors, during their pregnancies.[124] There are further indications that the mismanagement of hazardous wastes by maquilas is associated with general public outbreaks of liver and pancreatic cancers, chronic pulmonary infections, and other diseases of the respiratory and lymphatic systems among border residents.[125] Water pollution is an old problem. But the more recent types of hazardous wastes introduced into the ecosystem by production activities in many sectors of the maquiladora industry further increase uncertainty about the short- and long-term safety of drinking water supplies for hundreds of thousands of affected border residents.

The difficulties with the measurement of environmental health problems are primarily threefold. First, the time between exposure and disease effects can be very lengthy; it sometimes takes decades (and even generations in the case of mutagenic pathologies) for the more lethal symptoms to appear. Given the geographical mobility of humans, it is next to impossible to accurately track specific populations over time. Second, there are many synergistic effects involving exposure to more than one chemical. It is difficult to predict which combinations are dangerous and what the long-term effects are. Finally, there are predispositional factors involved in most environmental health problems. Many epidemiologists argue that genetic predispositions can result in varying rates of pathology among different subpopulations. We all may get sick from environmental risk factors, but some of us get sick more often or experience more serious, life-threatening effects.

There are other conditions that may predispose certain subpopulations to experience higher rates of environmental diseases than other subpopulations.[126] Poverty is one such factor that can make persons more sensitive to environmental disturbances. In the case of the U.S.–Mexico border, high poverty rates may augment the effects of the environmental health threats posed by the maquilas. Widespread poverty conditions are associated with higher general rates of illness, which weaken the body's immune system and detoxifying defense mechanisms. Toxicity is cumulative, and a sick and weak body is less able to defend itself against the effects of environmental hazards. Poverty is also associated with a lack of access to medical care, including preventive care, to the further detriment of exposed populations. Perhaps even a factor such as malnutrition may heighten the effects of exposure to hazardous wastes among the poor. This means that poverty has a synergistic relationship with such environmental risk factors as the disturbances introduced by maquilas.

The fields of environmental health and environmental preventive medicine are relatively recent developments (in the United States dating back to the late 1960s, prior to the passage of the Occupational Health and Safety Act). On the Mexican side, the undeveloped state of these fields is even more striking, as Carrillo suggests. This means that the entire debate over the public-health effects of maquila-induced environmental degradation is as yet based only on scattered empirical evidence. However, in no way should this be taken to imply that such problems are nonexistent or exaggerated. The pioneering research by Carmen Rocco, Sylvia Herrera, and Gregoria Rodríguez in the Brownsville-Matamoros area should go far in addressing the substantial gaps in our knowledge. One main point to keep in mind is that the proponents of maquila industrialization use the "objectivist semantics" of epidemiology to obscure the links between environmental degradation and occupational as well as public health problems.[127] Despite the obscurantist rhetoric of pro-maquila special interests, a significant environmental-justice movement is emerging along the entire length of the U.S.–Mexico border. This movement is challenging the hegemony of managerial and governmental imperatives, and in some cases is effectively pressing for positive change to protect the health of workers, residents, and ecosystems. I now turn to an overview of this important development.

MAQUILAS AND THE ENVIRONMENTAL-JUSTICE MOVEMENT

As Robert Bullard notes, the U.S. environmental-justice movement grew out of civil- and labor-rights struggles among working-class people of color.[128] Much of the original impetus for the consolidation of this new social movement came from studies indicating that race and ethnicity are factors in the differential distribution of environmental health hazards in the United States.[129] Researchers found that people of color are disproportionately affected by the location of uncontrolled toxic-waste sites and other sources of environmental degradation in their workplaces and residential communities.[130] Distinct from mainstream environmentalism in its concern for the human consequences of ecological degradation (instead of just the human causes), the environmental-justice movement has grown into a continent-wide struggle involving Native Americans and Pacific Islanders, Chicanos and other Latinos, African Americans, and Asian Americans. A recent directory of environmental groups of people of color lists more than 205 grassroots organizations.[131]

In states along both sides of the border, numerous organizations have emerged as part of the wider environmental justice movement. In the United States, these include the Southwest Organizing Project (SWOP), the Southwest Research and Information Center (SRIC), the Water Information Network (WIN), and the Tonantzin Land Institute, all based in Albuquerque. The Southwest Network for Environmental and Economic Justice (also called simply the Southwest Network) includes member groups from Arizona, California, Colorado, Nevada, New Mexico, Texas, and Utah. The Coalition for Justice in the Maquiladoras (Coalición para Justicia en las Maquiladoras, also called the Coalition for Justice) is a nationwide network of local offices affiliated with the American Friends

Service Committee (AFSC) and similar groups in Mexico.[132] United Farmworkers of America has launched a national pesticide campaign with implications for farmworkers and consumers in the border states.[133] There are numerous local and regional groups such as the Border Ecology Project (mainly active in southern California), La Mujer Obrera (El Paso), Fuerza Unida (San Antonio), the Labor-Community Strategy Center (Los Angeles), and COMO (Juárez). In 1991, the Southwest Network was instrumental in confronting the EPA with charges of "environmental racism" for persistent agency patterns of enforcement and regulatory neglect in predominantly ethnic communities, including neighborhoods in twin cities along the U.S.–Mexico border.[134]

From October 24 to 27, 1991, more than 350 activists and organizers representing several hundred organizations from the Arctic to the Andes met at the First National People of Color Environmental Leadership Summit in Washington, D.C.[135] The 1991 summit meeting culminated in the adoption of seventeen "Principles of Environmental Justice."[136] These principles are interesting from a philosophical vantage point—they contribute to the revival of a biocentric environmental ethic based on the unity of culture and nature.[137] But they also have practical importance as guiding principles for the hundreds of local, regional, national, and multinational organizations active in the fight for environmental justice, including groups in the border region struggling over issues related to maquilas, free trade, and environmental degradation.

Six of these seventeen principles are particularly relevant to the struggle against environmental degradation caused by the maquilas. These six principles involve:

1. Universal protection from extraction, production, and disposal of toxic and hazardous wastes that threaten the fundamental right to clean air, land, water, and food

2. Cessation of the production of all toxins, hazardous wastes, and radioactive materials, with strict accountability of all past and current producers for detoxification and containment at the point of production

3. The right of all peoples to participate as equal partners at every level of decision making, including needs assessment, planning, implementation, enforcement, and evaluation

4. The right of all workers to a safe and healthy work environment, without being forced to choose between an unsafe livelihood and unemployment, and the right of those who work at home to be free of environmental hazards

5. The rights of victims of environmental injustice to receive full compensation and reparations for damages as well as quality health care
6. Urban and rural ecological policies to clean up and rebuild cities and rural areas in balance with nature, honoring the cultural integrity of communities, and providing fair access for all to the full range of resources

The Coalition for Justice in the Maquiladoras and the Southwest Network have been at the forefront of efforts to bring these principles to bear on governmental and corporate policies and practices in the border region. For example, in the Rimir and Deltrónicos point-discharge case, efforts by these organizations eventually resulted in a pledge by General Motors to invest close to $20 million in waste treatment facilities at thirty-one of its maquiladora plants in Mexico.[138] This is an important case, because the treatment and containment of wastes *at the point of production* is a major underlying principle of environmental justice. These organizations have not been the only ones to oppose the maquilas' destructive production practices. Resistance is also developing within the plants themselves, as workers risk their jobs by becoming involved in struggles related to occupational and environmental health issues. For example, in the case of the GM plants in Matamoros, former and current workers have joined with the Coalition for Justice in an effort to pressure management to observe regulations and practices related to occupational health and safety, especially the exposure of workers to hazardous chemical substances and the handling and disposal of toxic wastes.[139]

SWOP, the Southwest Network, and Fuerza Unida have also led the environmental-justice movement's opposition to NAFTA by drawing attention to the environmental, labor, and social costs for workers and communities on both sides of the border. Fuerza Unida in San Antonio, for example, unites a workforce of predominantly Chicano and Mexican seamstresses against a Levi Strauss plant closing and relocation.[140] This case is similar to others in Texas, New Mexico, Arizona, and southern California—all involve plant closings and relocations to Mexico.[141] The instances of economic blackmail of communities by corporations seeking wage, environmental, and other concessions are too many to mention here. But the use of geopolitical mobility by capital against struggles by working-class communities of people of color has generated some of the most intense struggles in the environmental-justice movement.

Other environmental-justice activists have demanded that public-health agencies provide quality health care and that the judicial system provide financial reparations for damages sustained by the victims of the mismanagement of hazardous wastes.[142] Several court cases involving class-action lawsuits in Brownsville-Matamoros and Tijuana–San Ysidro are anticipated, and these must be closely monitored to see if the judiciary opens a wider aperture for greater citizen scrutiny and greater account-ability on the part of corporations and government agencies. Others in the environmental-justice movement emphasize the search for sustainable local alternatives to capitalist industrialization.[143] These activists cham-pion strategies that connect restoration ecology, cultural autonomy and renewal, sustainable economic development, worker self-management, and political self-determination. The objective in these cases is to experi-ment with bioregional alternatives for economic development.[144]

THE POLITICS OF ENVIRONMENTAL ASSESSMENT

One final set of comments is appropriate here with regard to what Gre-goria Rodríguez calls the "objectivist semantics" of official epidemiology and environmental risk assessment. The ideological discursive practices of the scientific community at once create and obscure the political character of existing regulatory regimes on both sides of the border. The emergence of "environmental impact assessment" (EIA) as a "scien-tific profession" was largely a political response to ecological and social-justice struggles. As Les Levidow argues,

> In response to community struggles against environmental degradation,
> a profession of "impact assessment" has arisen to provide supposedly neu-tral expertise on proposed waste dumps, dams, mining, military exercises
> and other projects. . . . Through "impact assessment" both human and
> environmental costs become reified as rationally calculable things, whose
> magnitude can be variously minimized, or traded for other things.[145]

Conventional approaches to EIA have been significantly influenced by the U.S. Army, which regularly cosponsors the annual meetings of the In-ternational Association for Impact Assessment.[146] The dominant EIA paradigm is an exercise in market logic, values, and language. It treats ecosystems—air, land, water, and even the health and viability of life-forms—as "non-priced natural resources." One proponent of this ap-proach defines natural resources as "strategic environmental commodi-ties" and advocates treating nature as "capital stock" in a system of "tradable development damage permits."[147] This is reminiscent of the se-mantic and discursive tricks used by maquila managers and engineers to define workers as "deskilled" labor in the struggle over unpaid technical work (see chapter 6).

The environmental-justice movement offers a basis for a radical departure from the business-as-usual, nature-as-commodity approach to EIA. Indigenous (and ethnic) local cultures provide a strong basis for resisting the universal logic and predominance of market values.[148] Grassroots citizen organizations are challenging bureaucratic rationality by directly confronting corporate nonaccountability and resisting the usual governmental complicity and goldbricking that characterize the politics of EIA. Grassroots resources such as information clearinghouses; training workshops in community organizing, hazardous-waste management, water quality, and EIA; networking and conferencing; independent research programs; and citizen review boards authorized by local self-government statutes are some of the strategies currently being developed to more effectively negotiate the contested terrain of environmental regulatory politics.[149]

Another key point is that all this activity involves fundamental shifts in the principles that underlie regulatory theory and practice. There are widespread calls by citizens' groups for democratic participation at all levels and in all aspects of policy and decision making, planning, enforcement, and evaluation. Environmental-justice activists also favor a shift from strategies that emphasize cleanup after the fact (what the experts like to call mitigation or remediation) to strategies that focus on prevention and restoration.[150] Preventing environmental degradation is advocated as a better long-term strategy for ecological, social, cultural, medical, and even economic reasons. Many in the environmental-justice movement see the restoration of damaged ecosystems as essential to strategies designed to protect the long-term viability of all life-forms and the sustainability of human landscapes.[151]

This oppositional discourse embraces a set of noninstrumentalist values that correspond to a preference for ecologically sustainable development strategies. The environmental-justice movement calls for a shift from anthropocentric (or human-centered) values to biocentric (or Earth-centered) values as guiding principles of environmental regulation and economic development.[152] To overcome the increasing levels of ecosystemic damage occasioned by anthropogenic disturbance regimes, communities will have to find ways to transcend the anthropocentric values that drive the machinery of destruction. And the necessary transformation is not limited to changing values in the form of individually or collectively held attitudes, norms, beliefs, and ideologies. The struggle involves fundamental modifications to value systems as they are codified in environmental laws, land- and water-use policies, regulatory statutes, and discretionary bureaucratic decision making. As Levidow argues,

> At stake in impact assessment is a particular development model, legitimated through the "public interest" and in turn by [contrived, constrained, and manipulated] public participation. If the latter disputes costings rather than values, and means rather than ends, then the predominant institutional power will impose its model by default. It remains for oppositional movements to challenge market language and to counterpose different purposes; only then can intangible [noncommodified] meanings of the environment be validated as a contending rationality, demanding a substantive participation.[153]

Environmental justice offers alternative, Earth-centered values to contest the overbearing presence and influence of the objectivist cult of expertise and its market-driven ethos. The environmental-justice movement focuses precisely on redefining the values, purposes, and organization of political-ecological and political-economic institutions. By forming citizen and labor coalitions, environmental justice activists open new possibilities for more substantive participation by workers and residents in the politics of environmental regulation and impact assessment, but also in the movements for sustainable *and* equitable development alternatives.

Maquilas and Free Trade versus Sustainable Development

What changes will occur in the process of maquila industrialization in a post-NAFTA scenario? Will free trade bring us a promised land of prosperity and improved standards of living? Will the wealth generated by five thousand maquilas find its way back to the land and water in the form of investments in environmental protection? Or will it bring us a Conradesque heart of darkness—a veritable environmental wasteland? It is certain that the number of maquiladora plants will increase dramatically in the coming decades. Will the environmental impacts of these factories also increase in scale and severity? What of the rights of labor? Will NAFTA strengthen or further weaken labor rights and occupational health and safety standards in Mexico and the United States? Are there politically and economically viable alternatives for sustainable development in the border region? What impacts will NAFTA have on local rural cultures and indigenous nations? These are questions of utmost importance to anyone concerned with preserving and promoting sustainable alternatives to "free trade." Before answering these questions and looking at some alternatives, it is necessary to first outline NAFTA.[154]

THE NORTH AMERICAN FREE TRADE AGREEMENT

NAFTA is designed to facilitate liberalized trade and deregulated investments in Canada, Mexico, and the United States. It establishes a trilateral, continent-wide economic and trading bloc to "meet the challenge" of European unification (the EU) and growing Pacific Rim competition in global markets. In Mexico, NAFTA is known as the Tratado de Libre Comercio (TLC).[155] There are twenty-four key provisions in the negotiated agreement.[156] Here I will elaborate only those provisions that are most likely to have a direct bearing on the future operation and impact of the maquilas. These include provisions dealing with rules of origin, textiles and garments, automotive products, investments, and environmental regulation.[157]

Rules of Origin. The NAFTA rules of origin eliminate most tariff barriers to free trade for goods originating in Canada, Mexico, and the United States. The regional-origin content is set for most goods at 60 percent. A commercial good is defined as originating within the trilateral bloc if all its components were produced in North America, or if components and inputs from outside North America have been effectively transformed in the process of production or assembly.[158] The rules of origin promote the reduction of administrative obstacles for exporters, importers, and producers engaged in commercial activities under the terms of the agreement. Moreover, the rules of origin may not strictly apply to transboundary free trade in specific types of manufactured products (for example, textiles and automotive products).

Textiles & Garments. NAFTA ties the three countries to a ten-year program for the elimination of all tariff and nontariff barriers to free trade in textile fibers, fabrics, and garments produced in North America. One clause requires the United States to eliminate quotas on textile goods imported from Mexico, including those that do not strictly meet the rules of origin requiring 80 percent regional content for most textile raw materials. The provisions also call for the elimination of import tariffs on garments manufactured in North America from textiles produced outside the trading bloc.

Automotive Products. NAFTA eliminates tariff barriers for automobiles, trucks, buses, and auto parts. It also eliminates remaining investment restrictions in the sector, particularly within Mexico. Specific clauses require the United States to immediately eliminate tariffs on passenger cars imported from Canada or Mexico. Other clauses require the United States to reduce tariffs on light trucks by 10 percent immediately and to eliminate such tariffs totally within five years. Under other provisions, Mexico is required to reduce tariffs on passenger cars imported from Canada and the United States by 50 percent immediately and to phase out these tariffs within ten years. Mexico is also required to reduce tariffs on light-truck imports from Canada and the United States by 50 percent immediately and by 100 percent within five years. And finally, Mexico is required to eliminate all remaining tariffs on other automotive products within ten years. The same liberalized trade standards apply in trilateral fashion to the automotive-parts industry, a sector with a strong maquila presence. The agreement also mandates the elimination of all remaining Mexican restrictions on foreign investments in the automotive sector within five years. Regional content under rules of origin for automotive production is set at about 62 percent.

Investments. The trade agreement eliminates most barriers and restrictions on foreign investments, makes certain guarantees to foreign investors, and establishes an internal and secret mechanism for the resolution of commercial disputes. Expropriations of foreign investments are expressly prohibited, except in cases of overriding "public interest." In such cases, expropriated properties and other investments are to be priced for indemnification at fair market values. A final clause establishes that no country may reduce its environmental standards in order to attract investments. Ongoing consultations will define implementation of this particular clause.

Environmental Protection. The NAFTA text outlines seven basic principles in support of environmental protection and sustainable development:[159]
  1. The obligations of trading-bloc member nations related to international conventions on endangered species, ozone-depleting chemical substances, and hazardous wastes are not nullified by the terms of the trade agreement. However, the text declares it necessary to minimize the incompatibility of these conventions with respect to the terms of the trade agreement.
  2. Each signatory retains the right to establish its own levels of protection and to define the levels considered adequate for environmental, human, animal, and plant health.

3. To guarantee adequate levels of protection, each member nation retains the right to adopt and maintain sanitary and phytosanitary norms, even if these are stricter than international standards.[160]

4. The three countries are to cooperate to improve the level of protection of the environment and the life and health of humans, animals, and plants.

5. No member nation may reduce its level of environmental protection to attract investment.

6. In the case of commercial controversies related to the norms of a given country and having environmental implications, that country has the option to submit disputes for consideration under mechanisms established by NAFTA for conflict resolution. Any of the three signatories can opt to use the tribunals established by NAFTA as a substitute for existing institutional procedures governing the resolution of commercial disputes.

7. The dispute-resolution tribunals established to deal with NAFTA-related controversies can solicit the advice of scientists, including environmental scientists or those who have expertise in the norms and practices of environmental impact assessment.

NAFTA SUPPLEMENTAL AGREEMENTS

Environmental Cooperation. Under the Clinton administration, the Office of the U.S. Trade Representative was instructed to develop a supplemental agreement in the area of environmental cooperation. Opposition to NAFTA within the environmental community was strong and the Clinton administration sought to enlist support by outlining the terms for environmental cooperation.[161] In essence, the supplemental agreement created a trilateral commission composed of environmental ministers and a nominally independent secretariat. Responding to criticisms on the lack of mechanisms for public participation in the dispute-resolution process, the supplemental agreement establishes that "[t]ransparency is the hallmark of the agreement, and citizens of all three countries will be free to make submissions to the commission on their concerns related to the full range of environmental issues."[162]

Labor Cooperation. Like the agreement outlining environmental cooperation, the NAFTA supplemental agreement on labor cooperation established a trilateral commission composed of cabinet-level labor ministers from all three countries. This agreement was a response to strong criticism of NAFTA by U.S. and Canadian labor unions. The new Commission on Labor Cooperation has "a broad mandate to work cooperatively on labor issues, including occupational health and safety, child labor, benefits for workers, minimum wages, industrial relations, legislation on formation and operation of unions and the resolution of labor disputes."[163]

MEXICAN OPPOSITION

Diverse social forces are present in the organized opposition to NAFTA in Mexico. The opposition includes leaders in left-of-center political parties; labor, peasant, small-business, and popular organizations; academics and intellectuals; ecology groups; feminists; and indigenous nations. Two of the principal concerns voiced by the Mexican opposition are the accelerating rate of environmental degradation forecast by critics and the erosion of labor rights and occupational health and safety standards. These critics fear the ecological consequences of a wave of rapid industrialization and a weakening of regulatory regimes on both sides of the border under NAFTA. The erosion of labor rights will result from attacks on so-called nontariff barriers to free trade. Critics say that the trilateral negotiators have apparently agreed to allow free exercise of administrative discretionary power, which could be invoked to interpret certain environmental protection standards and labor rights as constituting a type of "nontariff barrier to free trade."[164] Transnational corporations may use the dispute tribunals to effect such deregulatory reforms over time. The rules of origin mandating the reduction of administrative obstacles could also be used by transnational corporations to weaken the definition and enforcement of regulations designed to protect the health and safety of the workforce.

In Mexico, some opposition groups have coordinated their activities through the Red de Acción Frente al Libre Comercio (Action Network on Free Trade).[165] The Red de Acción represents a coalition of independent small and medium-sized businesses, some opposition unions, and some leftist intellectuals and academics. In November 1992, the Red de Acción released a comprehensive analysis of NAFTA. The coalition faults the agreement for failing to consider the use of "redistributive mechanisms" to secure the benefits of economic growth for labor and small and medium-sized industry. NAFTA is "designed to benefit the industrial and financial elite" of transnational corporations.[166] These critics charge that the trade agreement's most significant flaws lie in provisions dealing with foreign investments. These provisions allow for the treatment of foreign investors on the basis of the principle of parity with national capital. Besides violating the Mexican constitution, this would allow transnational investors to circumvent traditional requirements such as "technology transfers, reinvestment of profits, preferences for national production inputs including percentage-based host-nation origin rules, and preservation of the environment."[167] These are all issues raised in long-standing criticisms of the maquilas which are seen as failing to effect adequate technology transfers, reinvestment of profits, increased Mexican production inputs, or environmental protection.

Some argue that the most severe problems presented by NAFTA derive from the framers' unquestioning acceptance of a regime based on rapid, export-led economic expansion.[168] The unstated priority given to economic growth as the key to development and trade will overload the physical infrastructure capacities of the nation, and especially of industrializing zones in the northern border region. This means the "social sector" stands to lose the most from the deregulation of foreign investments, since most economic expansion is likely to employ capital- and not labor-intensive strategies. Nor will the concentration of foreign investments in high-technology sectors benefit the small and medium-sized industries, because the demand for production inputs manufactured by national capital will decline in the absence of the older origin rules requiring minimum Mexican content.[169] Infrastructure will grow, but it will serve the same capital-intensive investments and benefit few in the excluded sectors of the working and small and medium-sized business classes. Workers left out of the new, more narrowly defined, job-growth sectors will find it increasingly difficult to meet their own social needs. The result will be an increasing polarization between a minority of workers with access to adequate medical care, housing, education, nutrition, and recreation and an underserved majority of unemployed and subemployed masses. This is one reason why the Red de Acción calls for the creation of a new unemployment insurance fund to cushion the transition to a continental free-market regime.[170]

The Grupo de Cien (Group of One Hundred) and the Movimiento Ecologista Mexicano (MEM) are Mexico's most visible and perhaps most influential environmental organizations.[171] They too have developed a critical analysis of NAFTA. Many Mexican environmentalists take issue with the negotiators' failure to provide substantive definitions of such key concepts as "sustainable development" and "environmental protection."[172] Some go further and question the compatibility of free trade and sustainable development, pointing to the maquilas as a primary example of nonsustainable practices and ecological destructiveness.[173] Environmentalists also worry that the tribunals will be manipulated to circumvent the existing regulatory regimes, which they view as in need of serious overhauling. Along with other critics, they are concerned that capital will use the NAFTA tribunals to challenge environmental standards as nontariff barriers to free trade. The further erosion of environmental standards as a consequence of the "harmonization" of trilateral regimes is another concern. Instead of pushing Mexican standards closer to still-inadequate U.S. and Canadian levels, the tribunals may decide to make regulatory regimes more "compatible" by lowering standards in all three countries. This could effectively cut citizens and workers out of dispute resolution and environmental assessment. Some have described these tribunals as yet another example of neoliberal trickery, an administrative reform aimed at preventing organized citizens and workers from asserting themselves as an effective force for social justice in the politics of environmental regulation.[174]

Mexican ecofeminists criticize NAFTA as a strategy for the continued exploitation of third-world women workers by transnational capital.[175] They consider maquilas to be examples of unsustainable development based on patriarchal capitalist values, examples of the exploitation and control of women and nature through androcentric (male-dominated) political and economic institutions. They criticize the increasing ties between maquilas and the production of environmentally destructive military technologies. Other feminists focus on sexual and state-sanctioned political violence against women workers.[176] They see NAFTA as strengthening an international sexual division of labor that devalues women's work and degrades the personal integrity and safety of all working people. Feminists fear that the free-trade agreement will increase the degradation of women's work by restricting most of the female labor force to a rapidly growing number of deskilled jobs in the maquilas. In short, feminists argue that NAFTA will augment gender segregation in Mexico's internal labor markets and occupations.[177]

Indigenous nations within Mexico have also articulated a unique set of criticisms emphasizing sovereignty, cultural integrity, environmental protection, and intellectual property rights.[178] They are concerned with the expropriation of indigenous ethnoscientific knowledge, especially information related to landraces (native crop species) and genetic and biological diversity. Biotechnology firms, international seed companies, and corporate agribusinesses represent a growing threat to the sovereignty of

Indian nations, the integrity of Mexican ethnoscience, and the survival of traditional sustainable practices.[179] The effects of accelerating exploitation of "natural resources" in traditional indigenous homelands are a fundamental concern. The displacement of indigenous communities by extractive industries (mining, petroleum, timber) and public infrastructures (dams, canals, highways, ports, power plants, etc.) is likely to intensify as a consequence of NAFTA-induced economic expansion.[180]

Peasant and other independent agricultural producers have also expressed concerns over NAFTA. Even the Confederación Nacional Campesina (CNC, the peasant wing of the ruling PRI) has criticized the absence of provisions establishing standards and rules for the protection of international migratory farmworkers.[181] Hugo Andrés Araujo, national director of the CNC, argued that the election of Clinton could be seized as an opportunity to recast the negotiations to include discussion of the rights of undocumented and guest workers and the strengthening of environmental protection. Instead, we have been given Proposition 187 and the 1996 welfare bill. Araujo views the privatization of the *ejido* as an additional and related concern that requires more effective organization of peasant and farmworker groups. Mexican pork producers also expressed reservations about NAFTA, which they believe encourages unfair intrusions by U.S. competitors. And at least one researcher has evidence indicating NAFTA-induced impacts on four to five million small-grain producers.[182]

Finally, Mexican agroecologists and proponents of sustainable rural "ecodevelopment," or *ecodesarrollo,* have also been at the center of the struggle against NAFTA. Iván Restrepo, David Barkin, and the Centros para Ecodesarrollo in Mexico City and Morelia have long organized to promote sustainable agricultural institutions and to resist the intrusion of development practices serving the interests of transnational agribusiness corporations. The modernization and rationalization of the rural Mexican economy has been going on for some time, has been accelerating under the *salinista* neoliberal reforms, and is likely to accelerate even more under NAFTA. David Barkin observes that the displacement of local peasant communities has been accompanied by the transference of rural productive resources (land and water) to transnational capital. This has given rise to an enormous informal sector in overcrowded cities that are incapable of absorbing the migrants expelled from the countryside. As Barkin writes, "The accelerated development of the Mexican economy set the stage for a new and more terrible social polarization of the country, the loss of food self-sufficiency, and ecological crisis."[183]

José Luis Calva, who is associated with the agricultural student movement at Chapingo, argues that NAFTA will undermine the many remaining subsistence communities throughout rural Mexico.[184] It is completing the conversion by rural agricultural producers to crops that no longer serve the self-sufficiency requirements of the Mexican population. For Calva, the loss of *autosuficiencia alimentaria* (food self-sufficiency) is among the most serious implications of NAFTA. Already most Mexican farmers are producing mainly for the cash nexus, that is, for commercial sales to the market. By 1975, more than 86 percent of the agricultural output of the *ejidatarios* was destined for national and international market sales; less than 14 percent was destined for self-subsistence use in the *ejidos* or local areas.[185] Policies in place since at least the Cárdenas *sexenio* have promoted the transformation of Mexican agriculture from self-sufficiency in basic staples to the production of cash crops destined for exportation from the rural areas. NAFTA is already accelerating this process even more and could result in an increasing dependency of Mexicans on U.S. imports for meeting their basic needs in food staples such as grains (including *maíz* and wheat). The loss of this capacity to produce for *autoconsumo* (local consumption) could have troubling long-range consequences for the survival of rural farm communities and local cultures throughout Mexico. The path to self-sufficiency in food production may be permanently obstructed by the changes that could occur after NAFTA.

On October 24, 1992, over three hundred representatives of more than twenty Mexican, Canadian, and U.S. oppositional labor, social, human rights, and political party organizations met in Juárez to establish a Pact of International Solidarity against NAFTA.[186] This was an important turning point in the organization of a multilateral opposition group. From north of the U.S.–Mexico border, the solidarity pact includes representatives from Common Frontiers (a Canadian labor coalition), Unión de Trabajadores Agrícolas Fronterizos, Congreso Chicano, Brown Berets, Servicios Diocesanos (a Catholic Church charity group serving migrants and refugees), and La Mujer Obrera. From south of the border, the pact includes representatives from Convergencia Democrática, Centro de Información y Estudios Migratorios, Coordinadora de Resistencia Obrera, Partido Revolucionario de Trabajadores (PRT), Partido de la Revolución Democrática (PRD), and Despacho Obrero. María Elena Rodríguez of the Unión Nacional de Trabajadores summarizes the main points of opposition to NAFTA in Mexico:

[NAFTA] is against all Mexican workers, whose wages have been reduced by more than one third over ten years, and who must now confront environmental degradation, an increase in labor-law violations, and accelerated unemployment that affects 1.4 million workers who have been fired by the largest corporations in the country such as PEMEX, Volkswagen, Ford, General Motors, the textile industries, mining, and others.[187]

Cindy Melon, representing Common Frontiers, warns that Canada has already lost 550,000 jobs as a direct result of the U.S.–Canada Free Trade Agreement (FTA).[188] Since 1989 and the signing of the Mulroney-Bush accord, Canadian unemployment has increased to 11 percent, while 22 percent of the workers are now employed in part-time jobs. Of the five hundred largest corporations operating in Canada, 286 are now 100 percent foreign-owned. The Canadian experience may portend similar structural adjustments and displacements in Mexico. Indeed, such changes have already taken place with dramatic effect under the so-called neoliberal reforms championed by President Salinas since 1988.

U.S. OPPOSITION

The opposition to NAFTA within the United States is also quite diverse and includes labor and human-rights activists, environmental-justice and mainstream environmental organizations, agroecologists, alternative rural environmental planning groups, social-justice advocates, local community-based citizens' groups, and a variety of radical and progressive intellectuals and leftist academics. Like their Mexican counterparts, U.S. opponents of NAFTA are concerned with the further erosion of standards that protect the environment and labor. As noted earlier, SWOP, the Southwest Network, the Pact of International Solidarity, and Fuerza Unida are among the environmental-justice movement organizations opposed to NAFTA in the United States. These groups have been instrumental in drawing attention to the disproportionately high impact that NAFTA will have on working-class communities of people of color: the bulk of job loss will be concentrated in the labor-intensive sectors these workers tend to be segregated in. This, plus economic blackmail, or "jobmail," will strengthen corporate efforts to lower wages and environmental protection standards in the secondary labor market occupations even more.[189]

One of the most astute critical analyses of NAFTA has come from the U.S. Citizens' Task Force on NAFTA (CTF). The "U.S. Citizens' Analysis of NAFTA" is one of the most comprehensive written documents produced by the U.S. opposition.[190] It addresses all the provisions in NAFTA and offers broad and detailed critical analyses of their environmental, labor, social, and political implications. The CTF position against NAFTA was unequivocal: the "agreement must either be rejected or fundamentally recast."[191] Like their Mexican counterparts, U.S. opponents call for

> a more democratic process through which the people of the United States, Canada, and Mexico can engage their governments in the search for equitable and sustainable solutions to the profound problems related to the economic integration that is currently underway. These include declines in wages and employment levels, a diminishing of labor rights and standards, environmental degradation, dislocations in rural communities, massive migration, and human rights violations.[192]

Among the key findings of the CTF is that the trade agreement "lacks the funding mechanisms to ensure that a sufficient share of the wealth it may generate will go toward improvements in infrastructure and the strengthening of environmental clean-up and oversight."[193] This is similar to criticisms raised in Mexico by the Red de Acción and many ecologists.

The U.S. Citizens' Task Force is also concerned with the impact of NAFTA tribunals for dispute resolution, fearing that under NAFTA "a dispute panel, meeting in secret and heavily biased in favor of free trade to the exclusion of all other concerns, will judge whether or not the challenged regulation represents an unfair trade barrier."[194] This is likely to result in the lowering of environmental- and worker-protection standards in all three countries. Moreover, the "energy chapter of the NAFTA fails to include conservation and resource efficiency goals and timetables."[195] The development of renewable energy resources will also be sidestepped by NAFTA.

The CTF also cites studies showing that up to 500,000 U.S. jobs could be lost over the next ten years as a result of shifting investments and plant relocations.[196] Furthermore, workers in peripheral or secondary labor markets are bearing the brunt of industrial restructuring via plant closings and relocations. As the CTF analysis states,

> NAFTA could cost U.S. workers up to $320 billion over the next decade in lost jobs and lower wages. Liberalizing trade and facilitating the shift of investment from the United States and Canada to Mexico will put downward pressure on U.S. and Canadian wages without necessarily pulling Mexican wages up. Median wages for U.S. workers, especially those lacking a high school degree, have fallen dramatically in the last decade. This suggests that workers at the bottom of the wage scale have borne the brunt of

the "globalization" of the U.S. economy, though all workers have felt its impact. Recent immigrants, [white] women, and people of color are disproportionately concentrated in some of the labor-intensive industries that may be the most vulnerable to wage erosion and job loss due to NAFTA.[197]

Thus the CTF position complements those taken by Mexican oppositional unionists, left-of-center political parties, ecologists, and feminists. Of particular concern on both sides of the border is the impact of free trade on those sectors where white women and people of color are concentrated.

An additional concern raised by the CTF is the role of state governments in regulating food purity and other environmental health standards. This is an important issue because some state regulatory regimes are stricter than federal standards.[198] NAFTA could still result in the "preemption of state law" if implementing legislation passed by Congress encourages the erosion of states' rights to substantively regulate environmental, consumer, or public health.[199] Finally, the CTF closes with an analysis of the Enterprise for the Americas Initiative (EAI) championed by Bush during 1992. Bush's proposal involves a "free-trade zone stretching from Anchorage to Tierra del Fuego."[200] Like the *proyecto salinista* (Mexico's neoliberal project), the EAI involves the "implementation of a structural adjustment program, programs that have resulted in falling wages, increased poverty, environmental degradation, and the weakening of unions and other organizations representing the interests of working-class people."[201]

This brings us to the issue of the so-called neoliberal reforms promoted by the Mexican government since the inauguration of the Salinas administration in 1988. It is precisely the "implementation of a structural adjustment program" that is at the center of the forces in Mexico driving the transition to a continental "free trade" regime. I now turn to an overview of the Mexican critique of neoliberalism to clarify the concept of sustainable development as an alternative paradigm offered by opponents of the NAFTA and EAI models.

SUSTAINABLE DEVELOPMENT AND THE CRITIQUE
OF THE NEOLIBERAL PROJECT

The anti-NAFTA discourse is part of a broader oppositional critique of the neoliberal reforms implemented by the Mexican government during the Salinas *sexenio*. The *proyecto salinista* involves several key reforms:

(1) privatization of the state enterprise sector (the *paraestatales*), (2) termination of the agrarian reform and privatization of the *ejido*, (3) rationalization and modernization of the agricultural sector, (4) elimination of all restrictions on foreign investments, (5) long-term reduction of social-sector funding for education, housing, and health care, and (6) rationalization and streamlining of environmental regulatory regimes. In short, the *proyecto salinista* is a Mexican version of Thatcherist and Reaganite political-economic policy. U.S. and British neoconservatism is reincarnated in Mexican neoliberalism.

The dismantling and privatization of the *paraestatal* sector is at the heart of recent neoliberal restructuring. This policy has resulted in the sale, transfer, merger, or liquidation of most of the 612 state-owned enterprises that existed when Salinas was elected. Of these, 152 have been sold to private investors (about 90 percent Mexican capital), 125 have been liquidated, 41 have been dismantled, and 16 have been transferred to 9 states.[202] This leaves 221 *paraestatales* in operation and 57 in different stages of transformation or elimination. Between 1988 and August 1992, more than 87,400 workers were terminated from their jobs in the public industrial manufacturing sector.[203] Many of these *paraestatales* have been the locus of considerable worker resistance and organized struggle. State-sector workers have led historic oppositional movements such as the Tendencia Democrática and the workers' unions at SICARTSA and DINA.[204] The neoliberal reforms thus target not just a particular sector of state-owned capital, but one of the most militant, and traditionally most powerful, sectors of the Mexican working class.

The neoliberal reforms terminate the agrarian reform program that was initiated at the end of the Mexican Revolution in Article 27 of the 1917 Constitution. Not only are land-distribution programs finished, any irregularities "left over" from the complex historical adjudication of land claims and illegal expropriations will no longer be addressed by the federal government. The book is basically closed on future land transfers to an increasingly dispossessed and dislocated peasantry.[205] The other aspect of neoliberal restructuring of agrarian policy in Mexico involves the privatization of the *ejido*.[206] The reforms to Article 27 represent radical transformations in the legal status of and political regulations governing the *ejido*. Peasant landholdings will no longer be treated as a type of usufructuary common property. Individual peasants are receiving private title for their lands and can now sell, lease, or transfer *ejidal* properties to other persons. In a word, international free-market capitalist rules now govern the economic and political life of the *ejidos*.[207]

A related development is the promotion of policies designed to ratio-nalize and modernize the entire Mexican agricultural sector. Liberalized investment policies, the consolidation of landholdings, increasing mech-anization of production, control of germ plasm by transnational agri-businesses, and environmental deregulation are transforming most of rural Mexico into a nationwide version of Sinaloa's Culiacán Valley.[208] Peasants are increasingly being converted into migratory waged labor for transnational agribusiness, and the already dismal protection agricultural workers can claim is being further eroded. These developments have led one U.S. critic of neoliberalism to ask,

> How can Mexico compete now? There are three ways the Mexican govern-ment and its international creditors consider viable. One is to lower wages more, along with lowering social expenditures for such things as educa-tion, housing, and medical care. The second is to open the country wider to foreign investment by regulating it less and taking a smaller cut for so-cial needs and the requirements of the state. Nationalized firms are to be sold to private investors. The currency is to be devalued even further . . . to encourage exports. Licensing and patent requirements are to be liberalized to the advantage of foreign investors, and environmental or social legisla-tion to regulate corporate activities is to be de-emphasized. The third is to sell the products of Mexico's natural environment at the cheap prices the international market will bear. The prices of mineral and tropical agricul-tural products have in general declined for about fifteen years as country after country has experienced the same problems as Mexico and must sell its natural endowment at bargain basement prices for the same reasons Mexico must.[209]

The *proyecto salinista* has clearly opted for all three strategies: the neolib-eral reforms in agriculture are lowering wages and social expenditures for the rural social sector; liberalized foreign-investment policies and re-duced environmental regulation are in place; and the continuing devalu-ation of the *peso* is encouraging higher exports at lower prices. A note of clarification: Salinas increased short-term expenditures in the social sec-tor (including environmental protection).[210] The Mexican government financed this increase through funding generated from the sale and dis-mantling of the *paraestatales*. But this is a one-time bonanza. With the dismantling of the state-owned sector, no further funding will be avail-able for increases in social-sector programs.

Agroecologists on both sides of the border have criticized NAFTA and neoliberalism for opening the gates to transnational agribusiness tech-nologies and practices that will accelerate environmental degradation due to soil erosion, mining and contamination of groundwater aquifers, decline of crop biodiversity (and the extinction of endangered land-races), increasing mechanization, and increasing reliance on large quantities of agroindustrial chemicals (fertilizers, pesticides, herbicides, fungicides, etc.).[211] The work of Restrepo, Barkin, and Calva, among others, is particularly important because it offers models for sustainable agro-ecological development that would protect local farming communities, encourage self-sufficiency in food production, and preserve the traditional, ecologically sound practices of Mexican peasant and indigenous ethnoscience.[212]

We have already seen how NAFTA liberalizes policies governing foreign investments. This has already taken effect in most sectors of the Mexican economy under Salinas's neoliberal project. For example, in the transport sector General Electric and Union Pacific have already invested heavily in Ferronales (Mexican national railways). Ferronales is undertaking a project to build a rapid train linking Monterrey, Nuevo León, and San Antonio, Texas.[213] The loosening of restrictions on foreign investments applies not just to the agriculture, manufacturing, telecommunications, transport, mining, timbering, and real estate sectors, but to financial services and banking as well. The reprivatization of the banks involves considerable foreign takeover and control of credit, lending, and mortgage services.[214] The privatization of the nation's port facilities will follow the pattern adopted for the Mexican telecommunications giant, Telmex.[215]

In the area of environmental protection, we have seen how NAFTA proposes to replace existing regulatory mechanisms with internal dispute-resolution tribunals. This move was also anticipated in the neoliberal project. (The 1991–92 SEDESOL crackdown on maquila environmental violations can be seen in this context as an opportunistic attempt to gain support for NAFTA in the U.S. Congress.) The neoliberal reform has prevented indigenous and peasant communities from gaining control of forestry planning and management in areas that have been considered common property resources in practice.[216] (While there has been a tremendous problem with clandestine timber operations throughout Mexico, these cannot be attributed to indigenous or peasant abuse of traditional usufructuary norms governing the use of common-property resources.)[217] Peasant communities and indigenous nations are demanding a direct role in the management of forestry and other resources. And there is growing evidence to support these communities' claim that they have generations of experience in sustainable stewardship of their own homelands.[218] But the neoliberal reforms are designed to expand and modernize the timber industry by encouraging a shift to the technologies and management systems of transnational corporations.

We must not lose sight of the fact that the neoliberal project anticipated many of the policies that have been subsequently integrated into NAFTA. For example, by 1989, Salinas had relaxed foreign-investment regulations and liberalized commercial-trucking laws to promote transboundary trade at the border.[219] The same principles are being applied at a continental level through NAFTA. As Guillermina Valdés once observed, NAFTA converts the de facto economic integration of the United States and Mexico achieved by neoliberalism into a multilateral de jure regime with startling consequences for the political autonomy of workers and small-business groups in each country. Neoliberalism in Mexico and NAFTA suppress the assertion of "nationalist" (qua protectionist) impulses. All these changes have led to criticism of Mexican neoliberalism as a new "form of colonialism."[220]

But ecologists in Mexico go a step further in linking the colonial dimensions of NAFTA and neoliberalism to environmental degradation by arguing that the free-trade political strategy derives from an "antinature economic rationality."[221] It is not just Mexico as a nation that is being exploited and degraded, but also Mexico as a complex of diverse ecosystems. Furthermore, the neoliberal reform affects political institutions by limiting the prospects for and effectiveness of citizen participation in regulatory politics and the management of natural resources. NAFTA will accelerate these processes and thereby increasingly extend unregulated control over the exploitation of nature to transnational capital, which can then extract natural resources with even more destructiveness.

The Mexican ecologist Enrique Leff offers the following key criticism of the neoliberal project underpinning NAFTA:

> The progressive development of the productive (and destructive) forces guided by the objective of maximizing profits in the capitalist economies . . . has generated, along with an increase in production and consumption, an unprecedented destruction of the resource base of humanity, as well as ecological disequilibriums at a planetary scale and processes of environmental degradation that threaten sustainable development, equitable and sustained by the community of nations.[222]

This important critique points to the threat of NAFTA as a strategy by transnational capital to subordinate ecological principles to economic expansion and profiteering. But Leff's other key point is that the "margins" of society, the groups that have been the most excluded and segregated, are producing new social movements that articulate novel ecological,

324 The Terror of the Machine

social-justice, and political demands. The margins generate new "political cultures" guided by what Leff calls a *racionalidad ambiental* (environmental rationality). These local political cultures generate new forms of self-organization and experiments in sustainable development. I believe that SOCOSEMA in Juárez is one example of the kind of local political cultures that Leff describes.

Many critics of NAFTA focus on the incompatibility of free trade and sustainable development. For example, Carlos Martínez de la Torre argues that the maquilas and NAFTA are not sustainable because they embrace development strategies based on mass-production industries that are intrinsically hazardous to human health and the environment.[223] Likewise, the "U.S. Citizens' Analysis of NAFTA" concludes that the "resulting agreements would severely limit future governments' abilities to implement industrial policies, sustainable-development programs, or other alternative economic programs."[224] But the environmental-justice movement is not concerned so much with protecting the state's ability to implement sustainable development as with building sustainable alternatives now in grassroots efforts at the local and regional level. As Víctor M. Toledo, a leader in MEM, argues,

> As a countercurrent to the dominant views of the neoliberals who seek the liquidation of the Mexican peasantry, the most effective and only realistic strategy for long-term preservation of biodiversity in Mexico requires the participation of the peasant in two senses: as coparticipant in the management of protected natural areas and as preserver of traditional, nondestructive systems of production who can act as a protector and steward of natural areas and in turn contribute to the maintenance of the genetic diversity of cultivars and domesticated animals.[225]

The defense and protection of peasant and indigenous ethnoscientific knowledge is emerging as a central issue in the search for sustainable alternatives to "free trade." The search for these alternatives is therefore a worthy focus with which to end this book.

Ancient Futures for Sustainable Development

I learned long ago from Guillermina Valdés de Villalva and the student-workers at COMO that the struggle against domination is pointless without a feasible alternative. As Valdés once told me, "Hope without action is, well, hopeless." For many of us, the imposition of NAFTA must seem like yet another milestone in an inevitable and long journey down into the "heart of darkness." But the struggles that workers engage in as they go about their everyday lives and the alternative organizations they create to channel their resistance and inventiveness should be recognized as starting points for the renewal and reconstruction of our communities and ecosystems. As Isabel Robles teaches us, "The people write history with their own sweat and blood." Rapid industrialization, mass production, and environmental degradation need not be accepted as faits accomplis. Alternatives exist everywhere around us. In Juárez–El Paso—to cite one border community—COMO, SOCOSEMA, Vado de Cedillos, Mujer Obrera, Unión de Trabajadores Agrícolas Fronterizos, and Despacho Obrero are a few important examples. To treat these groups as isolated anomalies is to ignore the possibility that change can flow from the margin to the center. It may be that marginality *is* the center (of inventiveness), or, at any rate, rightfully belongs there, as Sylvere Lotringer and Christian Marazzi have argued.[226]

I consider the search for sustainable development a struggle to protect the local against the intrusions of the global; to protect the diverse against the homogenizing. As Helena Norberg-Hodge argues,

> Without retreating into cultural or economic isolationism, we can nourish the traditions of our own region. A true appreciation of cultural diversity means neither imposing our own culture on others, nor packaging, exploiting, and commercializing exotic cultures for our own consumption. One of the most effective ways of reviving cultural differences would be to lobby for a reduction in unnecessary trade. At the moment our taxpayers' money is going to expand transport infrastructure and to increase trade for the sake of trade. . . . What we should be doing instead is reinforcing and diversifying local economies. . . . What exactly is "local," and what is "necessary" as opposed to "unnecessary" trade, are issues that cannot be defined in absolute terms. But the crucial point is that the *principle* of heavily subsidized international trade is one that needs critical reassessment. . . . It is in robust, local-scale economies that we find genuinely "free" markets; free of corporate manipulation, hidden subsidies, waste, and immense promotional costs that characterize today's global market.[227]

We must reconsider NAFTA and the maquilas from the point of view of the concept of sustainable development. To do so, we must be very clear about what we mean by sustainability. Indeed, even NAFTA is touted by its framers and supporters as a vehicle for sustainable development. But the only things that will be sustained are the profit rates of transnational corporations and the acceleration of environmental destruction. Capitalism is inherently incompatible with sustainable development.[228] The transition to a "steady-state economy" is of paramount importance in defining sustainable alternatives.[229] Thus, the unending, unrestrained expansion of international trade that drives the engine of capitalist economic growth is not compatible with a steady state of any kind.[230]

DEFINING SUSTAINABLE DEVELOPMENT

My working definition of sustainable development is not derived only from extensive knowledge of the academic and scholarly discourse. It is mostly drawn from the workers' perspectives I have been exposed to over the course of more than ten years of field research and consultancy with COMO and other grassroots organizations on both sides of the border.[231] What I say here is not so much a personal theory as a set of principles drawn from my observation of practices in actual struggles. This definition of sustainable development emphasizes seven interrelated principles: (1) long-term ecological integrity, (2) steady-state economies, (3) political decentralization and democratization, (4) a shift to nonpatriarchal and biocentric values, (5) the preservation of local knowledge and ethnoscience, (6) voluntary simplicity, and (7) the protection and reconstruction of bioregional communities.

1. Long-Term Ecological Integrity. Gaian biogeochemistry holds that the earth functions as a living organism, one live cybernetic system in which the solar wind, oceans, atmosphere, land masses, flora, fauna, and microbes all interconnect to create the conditions that make life on the planet possible.[232] The local, regional, national, and global disturbance regimes spawned over the past five hundred years by colonial and capitalist expansionism, conquest, war, and "development" are disrupting the Gaian feedback loops. For example, as deforestation, desertification, air and water pollution, and other forms of environmental degradation expand, species biodiversity declines. Gaian theory holds that the decline of biodiversity extinguishes nature's ability to regenerate ecosystems and to make them fit for habitation. Other species are driven into extinction while humans uncomfortably settle into a highly degraded anthropogenic landscape full of genetic, environmental, and other uncertainties. Biogeochemistry is a paradigm shift with profound implications for the politics of sustainable development. The principle of sustainability must conform to the biocentric ethos of radical Gaian biology. Development must sustain all life-forms, not just humans. There should be no "costs" that reduce life's diversity or viability. Development is sustainable when it respects the regenerative processes of life, that is, ecosystemic integrity.[233]

2. Steady-State Economies. This brings me to a second principle of sustainable development: steady-state economies. According to ecofeminists, the development of steady-state economies is possible only with a complete conversion of human production systems from militaristic and mass production and consumption norms and objectives.[234] There is a vast literature on economic conversion, but we are only now beginning to explore the links between conversion and the transition to steady-state economies.[235] Key elements of a steady-state economy include

- an emphasis on small-scale technologies and production systems
- a preference for regional inputs and outputs, including soft energy paths derived from locally available sources (sun, wind, methane, etc.)
- a renewal of labor-intensive agroecological and handicraft productive techniques; a preference for the production of goods destined for use in the local and regional social sector (education, housing, preventive and holistic health, nutrition, recreation, etc.)
- reliance on productive techniques involving the elimination of wastes through recycled and reduced production inputs[236]
- a propensity toward higher levels of "prosumption" (local production for local consumption)[237]

3. Political Decentralization & Democratization. With a transition to small-scale appropriate technologies and regional markets, sustainable development can increasingly rely on decentralized planning and policy-making. Political decentralization can emerge from regional steady-state economies because the need for widely dispersed production inputs (and decision making) is greatly reduced. In the absence of mass-production industries and international markets, local and regional steady-state economies can rely less on centralized bureaucracies to regulate and coordinate human use of productive technologies and resources. The "watershed commonwealths" envisioned long ago by John Wesley Powell are more feasible if the production apparatus has been decisively downscaled from a global assembly-line model to regional agroecological or handicraft productive techniques. Likewise, the liberation of regional resources from the grasp of the military-industrial complex will create leeway for transferring investments to productive activities that meet social needs (education, housing, health care) without the intervention or control of centralized bureaucracies.[238] This decentralization implies the democratization of policy- and decision-making in the workplace and in the larger bioregional community as well.

4. Nonpatriarchal, Biocentric Values. Sustainable development requires a values transformation from norms, attitudes, beliefs, and ideologies that embrace the domination and exploitation of nature, women, people of color, and workers.[239] The maquilas are a perfect example of a synthesis of science, technology, and capital in the service of patriarchal systems of domination and exploitation. The terror of the machine, hierarchy and absolute male managerial authority, gender occupational segregation, abuse of workers and sexual and sexist harassment, and environmental degradation are joined together in one fell swoop in the organization of maquila workplaces. The alternatives are found in organizations like COMO, SOCOSEMA, Mujer Obrera, and hundreds of other self-help and self-managed cooperatives in Mexico and the border Southwest region. The values of mutual aid and reciprocity, nonhierarchical forms of decision making, and voluntary simplicity are consistent not just with ecofeminist principles but with the practices and worldviews of border worker cooperatives like the *pepenadores.* Women and men alike can participate in remaking economic, political, and social institutions on the basis of biocentric and communitarian values.

5. Local Knowledge & Ethnoscience. Elsewhere I have outlined the connection between environmental degradation and the destruction of local cultures.[240] I have argued that the extinction of local cultures means that people of color are also an endangered species. I have further argued that the loss of local cultures hastens the erosion of ethnoscientific knowledge bases that are critical in moving toward ecologically sustainable forms of economic development. There are many viable indigenous communities on the U.S.–Mexico border: the Kickapoo and Tigua in Texas, the Tohono O'Odham (Sand Papago) in Arizona and Sonora, and the various Mission Indians of southern California, to name a few. These communities still offer alternative methods for sustainable agroecological development that must be protected and renewed.[241]

The preservation and promotion of ethnoscientific knowledge is clearly indispensable to the transition to sustainable development. However, to avoid the exploitation of indigenous knowledge we must find ways to protect ethnoscience as intellectual property. This is obviously a problem in light of NAFTA. As Darrell Posey argues,

> The indigenous peoples should possess sources of economic well-being, and if these are the conservation of the land, their people and cultures, then traditional understanding must be compensated in an economic manner. In not doing so, indigenous communities will see themselves

driven closer to the brink of ecological destruction, and their knowledge bases will atrophy.[242]

6. Voluntary Simplicity & Mutualism. One critical aspect of building sustainable communities is "voluntary simplicity," or "right livelihood." This principle affirms the protection of alternative lifestyles that are not built around excessive levels of consumption and generation of wastes. Voluntary simplicity, combined with economic conversion, holds the promise of a fuller transition to steady-state economies. Mutualist traditions in Mexico and among Mexicans and Chicanos in the United States remain strong and can be found in nearly every community that has formal and informal voluntary associations. Mutualism is ecologically sustainable because it encourages self-reliance and low levels of consumption of market-driven goods and services.

7. Bioregionalism. A good description of a bioregional community was long ago offered by Powell when he characterized the Pueblo, Mexican, and Mormon *acequia* communities of the intermountain West as "watershed commonwealths."[243] What is a bioregion? The environmental sociologist and "deep ecologist" William DeVall emphasizes four qualities: (1) a common watershed, (2) biotic and (3) cultural distinctiveness, and (4) a spirit or sense of place.[244] Julian Steward anticipated this approach to the study of nature and culture when he pioneered the field of "cultural ecology."[245] The ecological study of culture examines the "relationship between a people's system of economic production and their physical environment."[246] For Steward the "cultural core" consists of those material practices related to the technologies human groups develop to exploit chosen resources. However, distinct environmental contexts impose limits on the types of technologies that can be used without degrading the ecosystem. I believe this is why Powell admired Chicano *acequias,* because as technology they respect the limits of their ecological locales— more, they actually increase biodiversity instead of reducing it.[247]

This is a central principle in bioregional sustainable economics: The productivity of development is measured not by the quantity of outputs but by contributions to biodiversity and ecosystemic integrity.[248] A mode of production that respects the integrity of the ecosystem is more conducive to human and nonhuman health and well-being in the long run.[249] As Donald Worster argues, "Humans are animals with ideas as well as tools."[250] Perception, ideology, and values also play a critical role in the nature-culture dialectic. Bioregional cultures are distinctive in their sense of place, their attachment to locality.[251] This attachment also teaches respect for the place, with the implicit command that the land be well and lovingly used, as Wendell Berry has so eloquently suggested.[252] But intrusive, expanding, or colonizing cultures do not have the same sense of place or respect for the limits of ecosystems. The cross-cultural production of knowledge is a complex affair, and I do not mean to overgeneralize, but it seems clear that some cultures are predatory while others are symbiotic in their relationships with the physical environment.[253]

This leads me to add two other dimensions to the definition of a bioregional community: (1) local knowledge and ethnoscience (including the production of ritual and religious practices), and (2) the conflict between local cultures and intrusive capitalist modes of production.[254] Cultures and ecosystems are not static entities. Even biomes in a state of homeostasis experience a considerable amount of systemic flux and change. The point is that the ecosystemic integrity of bioregions is everywhere threatened by the disrupting environmental changes wrought by five hundred years of expanding capitalist development. A defense and reconstruction of endangered bioregional communities is thus of fundamental importance in the struggle for sustainable development. The ecological integrity of ecosystems can best be attained and maintained by organizing at the bioregional level and by linking distinct bioregional communities through cooperative exchange networks. The contributions of bioregionalism to restoration ecology could be put to use in reclaiming the health and viability of our ravaged and overdeveloped homelands. The process of reinhabitation, championed by certain North American bioregionalists, could guide ecological restoration by targeting specific watersheds and the communities within them for focused action campaigns.[255]

❖

The search for alternatives in sustainable development requires not just the practice of the principles I have outlined above. It involves recognizing that the search will most likely bring us back to our own homelands and communities where alternatives have deep, ancient roots. As Norberg-Hodge notes,

> Around the world, in every sphere of life, from psychology to physics, from farming to the family kitchen, there is growing awareness of the interconnectedness of all life. New movements are springing-up, committed to living on a human scale, and to more feminine and spiritual values. The numbers are growing, and the desire for change is spreading. These trends are often labeled as "new," but, as I hope Ladakh has shown, in an important sense they are very old. They are, in fact, a rediscovery of val-

ues that have existed for thousands of years—values that recognize our
place in the natural order, our indissoluble connection to one another and
to the earth.[256]

It is in the search for "ancient futures," I believe, that we will find the
keys to a revolutionary transformation of the culture-nature relationship.
I will now close with some brief reflections on tiny bits of the ancient-
future wisdom created and sustained by the workers and organizers of
Juárez, Mexico, lessons I have had the privilege of learning over the past
thirteen years.

REMEMBERING LESSONS FROM THE MARGINS

In chapter 7, I traced the history of SOCOSEMA and the struggle of the
pepenadores to overcome their oppressed and exploited condition. Agreeing with Larissa Lomnitz, I also argued that the *pepenadores* remain marginal even if they have effectively dealt with their oppression. They represent an alternative not just to exploitation but to total integration with
the existing transnational mode of production. In their refusal to remain exploited, the *pepenadores* demonstrated the value of political self-
determination and mutual aid. In their refusal to become cheap labor for
transnational capital, they demonstrated the value of workplace democracy and sustainable development. But SOCOSEMA is more than just
a case of self-organization and cooperative workplace democracy. We
should remember the inventiveness of the dumpworkers' co-op, for their
struggle is also a lesson in the virtues of voluntary simplicity and ecological sensibility. SOCOSEMA is an alternative paradigm, a model of emergent identity politics derived from nonanthropocentric values. The *pepenadores* are an example of the type of local political culture described
by Leff as based on a new "environmental rationality." I would argue,
though, that this new rationality is actually quite old. Ancient sources of
ecological wisdom have reemerged and merged with other social movements for workplace democracy and human rights.

COOPERATIVE WORKPLACE DEMOCRACY

Another critical element in the struggle for sustainable alternatives
involves a shift toward cooperative (community-based) ownership of
the means of production. There is growing evidence of the positive effects of cooperative workplace ownership and organization.[257] Workplace
democracy tends to be associated with lower levels of occupational health

and safety problems, reskilling and integration of the working knowledge that workers bring to the labor process, reduced turnover and job-related stresses, and environmental protection. The important example of SOCOSEMA brings this into sharp focus: people in cooperative workplaces liberate themselves from the imposed, stressful conditions of too much work and create considerable free time, which they then use to enjoy the full richness of community social life. The reduction of working time made possible through democratically administered workplaces increases the overall well-being and diverse life experiences of humans.

BORDER ENVIRONMENTAL RESTORATION
AND BIOREGIONALISM

Finally, I return to the challenges posed by the U.S.–Mexico borderline as a two-thousand-mile-long, one-hundred-mile-wide anthropogenic disturbance regime. I have long viewed the border as a political fiction. I still do, but now I realize that despite the fictive character of this international boundary, the borderline generates an amazing variety of enormously destructive patterns of environmental degradation. We will have to find a way of uniting ecological, labor, and alternative community development groups on both sides of the border to initiate a strategy for environmental restoration based on bioregional principles. The border region consists, above all else, of unified, but highly endangered, biotic communities. The birds and the bees as well as many humans do not stop to check in at the customs inspection station. The reality of transboundary ecosystems, of unified biomes, compels us to construct alternatives that respect the basic biological, cultural, and topographical realities of the borderlands. Rivers should bind and not divide us. The pioneering example of the Arizona Farmworkers Union's Cooperativa sin Fronteras (Cooperative without Borders) provides one intriguing example of the possibilities for transboundary sustainable development.[258]

(In)Conclusion

Mexico may be on the fast lane to economic growth and industrialization—now more than ever under NAFTA. But it is also on the inside, passing lane to environmental, cultural, and political disruptions, the likes of which the U.S.–Mexico border region has never experienced. This is not about proffering knee-jerk doomsday scenarios. The environmental, cultural, and political repercussions of unrestrained "free trade" already exist—we don't have to invent them. And the severity of their impact is no figment of overly alarmist imaginations. Maquilas are intimately associated with great ecological, cultural, social, and political changes in the border region. Much of this change has been harmful, but some of it has engendered new struggles and possibilities for empowering communities to construct ecologically sound, democratic alternatives. I believe the resilience of local cultures will eventually prevail—perhaps even more so in the binational, pluricultural context of the U.S.–Mexico border. Jorge Bustamante states that NAFTA will not destroy *mexicanidad*.[259] It may homogenize many aspects of the surface features of both Mexican and U.S. cultures. But this process involves a two-way flow of cultural influences and information. Moreover, there is no one essential Mexican (or U.S.) identity. And the myriad, shifting identities of borderlanders are a source of an incredible amount of creativity and inventiveness. People are constantly renewing themselves through multicultural productions of meaning and identity, especially in the border region.[260]

In retrospect, I now realize that I grew up in the midst of many environmental hazards. I was raised in the South Texas border city of Laredo about three miles from the Río Bravo, in a *barrio* known as El Three Points. The Chacón Creek, a tributary of the river, was a block from my house. I can recall the smell that came from the Chacón. My grandmother Margarita always warned me to stay away from the dirty water. I now know that it was contaminated with raw sewage. I also remember that we lived about a hundred yards from a major natural gas transfer pump station. The damn valves would break frequently and shake our home violently. I recall this happening mainly at night while we were asleep. We were all afraid of being blown to bits by a natural gas explosion. I never became inured to that fear.

The tracks for the Texas-Mexican Railway were also located about three blocks north of our home. Next to the tracks was an old cotton gin. The noise and rattling in our home from both of these sources was also quite unbearable. I remember as a child having terrible nightmares about the cotton gin and the train. In one dream, I was walking across the tracks. I looked up suddenly, and the cotton-gin machine came alive. Tearing itself from the building, the funnel headed toward me on steel-clad stilts, razor-sharp and gleaming in the dusky moonlight. I tried to run away, but my feet sank into the ground, which turned to quicksand. The harder I tried to run, the faster the bellowing and clanking machine moved toward me. I would wake up crying, and my dear *abuelita* would come and comfort me. Finally, one day when I was about ten, Margarita grabbed me by the hand and led me to the tracks. The cotton gin was operating, and the noise and dust spewing from the funnel were unbearable. We stood there for some time and waited for the train to come by. The train appeared, and my grandmother picked up a rock from the ground. She put it in my hand and said, "Defend yourself. Don't be afraid of that train. Here, throw rocks at it and defend yourself!" I did. She applauded my newfound courage as I confronted my own worst fears. Perhaps now you may understand why I feel such an affinity for Juana Ortega. Her nightmare was different: her monster was the assembly line. But in our own ways we both learned to resist the terror of the machine. Ortega and I are not technophobes. I believe we both share a conviction that an Earth-friendly technology is not only desirable but necessary in building a better human future.

The road to free trade and the road to environmental justice go two separate ways. The first path leads to an environmental wasteland wrought by capitalist maldevelopment. To a world deficient in biological and cultural diversity. This is a place in the heart of darkness. It is a free-trade netherworld, lethally contaminated by toxic wastes and the garbage of self-indulgent lifestyles. This is a world born of a ruthless, globe-trotting search for material wealth violently extracted from nature, woman, worker, and colony. Postmodern satanic mills dot this infernal Dantean landscape. This is a concrete, steel, and barbwire world, an antihabitat. It is a place where the broken bodies of homeless workers pass the days bound to the task of creating wealth for the acquisitive few who are animated by ruthless greed. The second path leads perhaps to a promised land where ecological integrity, social justice, economic democracy, community empowerment, and cultural diversity are practiced and celebrated. This is a world where rivers that never wanted to be borders are restored to ecological balance. This is a place of safe homelands and refuge, where the mixed communities of humans and nonhumans can once again truly prosper and flourish, where the life of the earth is reclaimed as sacred and the specter of the power of money no longer haunts the land and the people in a nightmare called the terror of the machine.

Notes

1. "NO TERRORS, TO A CERTAIN KIND OF MIND"

1. Ford 1922: 102–103.

2. There have been numerous sociological studies of the Ford Motor Company. Critical studies include Gambino 1972, Gartman 1979, Clawson 1980, Meyer 1981, Hounshell 1984. See also Edwards 1978, 1979; Littler 1982; Burawoy 1979, 1985; Hirszowicz 1982; Piore and Sabel 1984.

3. Frederick Winslow Taylor was a turn-of-the-century industrial engineer who is credited with the development of "scientific management." Taylor is said to have led one of the first systematic assaults on craft-labor skills through the development of time and motion studies and the imposition of the nefarious piece-rate system. See Taylor 1903, 1991. See also Braverman 1974, Nelson 1980, Fischer and Sirianni 1984. I discuss Taylorism further in chapter 2 of this work.

4. See Gartman 1979; Hounshell 1984: 11, 238–239, 244, 256–259; Sward 1948: 50–80.

5. On the struggles at Highland Park, Dearborn, and River Rouge, see Sward 1948, Gartman 1979, Hounshell 1984.

6. An interesting history of engineering innovations at the Ford Motor Company is offered by two engineers who worked with the company during the 1930s and 1940s; see Arnold and Faurote 1972.

7. For more on the establishment of the BIP, see Bustamante 1975; Peña 1980; Sklair 1994: 26–47.

8. The reference here is to the "dark Satanic mills" in William Blake's poem *Milton*. In volume 1 of *Capital*, Karl Marx quotes from the poem to describe the textile factories of Lancashire.

9. In an unpublished study called "The Organization of the Unskilled," Austin Lewis, the legendary labor lawyer and organizer for the Industrial Workers of the World (IWW), stated that

> [t]he machine industry compels the mass of unskilled proletarians. It drives them to work together in unison. It forces them to keep step with the industrial machine and in so doing teaches them the goose step of industrial organization, for organization by the employer is the first step to the organization of the employed. . . .
> Facts themselves force him [the proletarian worker] to revolt. Facts also teach him the method of revolt. (1913: 178)

Marx, of course, originally made this argument in *Capital* when he observed:

> [W]ith ... this process of transformation, the mass of misery, oppression, slavery, degradation and exploitation grows; but with this there also grows the revolt of the working class, a class constantly increasing in numbers, and trained, united and organized by the very mechanism of the capitalist process of production. (1977: 929)

10. Between 1811 and 1817, the so-called Luddites resisted the mechanization of the hosiery and lace industries and the introduction of machine power in the textile mills. The resistance came in the form of episodes of machine breaking and sabotage. These struggles were particularly fierce in Lancashire. According to Dinwiddy (1987), their name was derived from a legendary youth named Ludlam who broke a knitting frame. The Luddites signed their proclamations "General Ludd," "King Ludd," or "Ned Ludd." For further discussion, see Marx 1975a: 553–554; Jones 1982: 20–21. A comprehensive historical study of Luddism is Thomis 1970; for a more contemporary view of mechanization and resistance, see Noble 1993.

11. The original three-year study was conducted from 1980 to 1983. For the results of that study, see Peña 1983, especially chapter 7.

12. The term "subaltern," especially in the context of British colonial history, has strong imperialist connotations. After all, subalterns were the infantry-level troops of the British armed forces, which were virulently racist in their behavior toward so-called colonial subjects. The infantry soldiers were the lowest-ranking members of the British military, hence "subaltern." (Gwyn Kirk, notes to author, April 1993.)

However, more recently, such radical Indian historians as Ranajit Guha and Gayatri C. Spivak have appropriated the term to refer to their particular brand of critical, revisionist Indian history as a type of "subaltern studies," that is, the study of the hidden, everyday resistance of the marginalized classes in India. My use of the term is consistent with theirs, and refers to the sub-rosa, everyday resistance of colonized and marginalized ethnic populations. See Spivak's "Subaltern Studies: Deconstructing Historiography," in Guha and Spivak 1988.

13. North American Congress 1975; Peña 1979, 1980.

14. On environmental hazards and problems of maquiladoras, see, for example, Carrillo 1989b; Carrillo and Jasís 1983, 1991; Center for Investigative Reporting 1990; Greenpeace 1988, 1989; Kam and Gregory 1988; Pearson 1987; Sánchez 1989a, 1990a, 1990b; Valette 1989. See also chapters 3, 4, and 8 of this work.

15. See Stavrianos 1981. I use the term "third world" with hesitation because it assumes a certain degree of homogeneity among regions and cultures that is simply not there. For further discussion, see Shiva 1988, Minh-ha 1989.

16. See Van Waas 1981, Nash 1983.

17. The classic statement on modernization theory is Huntington 1968; but see also Kerr, Harbison, Dunlop, and Myers 1960. For a concise critique of Huntington, see Leys 1982.

18. For a discussion of racist constructions of the third world, see van Dijk, who notes:

> In sum, Third World peoples, like minority groups in Western countries, are portrayed as follows. . . . 1. Homogeneous: They are all the same. 2. They are different from us. 3. They are poor, helpless, hence in need of our aid. 4. They are illiterate and dumb, hence in need of our instruction and education. 5. They are primitive, backward, or underdeveloped, and hence in need of our technology. 6. They are passive or happy-go-lucky: They should adopt our diligence. 7. They are politically backward: They need "our" democracy, instead of their dictators. (1993: 232–233)

19. See chapter 9 of this work for a lengthy discussion of NAFTA.

20. See Shiva 1988.

21. Shiva 1988.

22. For further discussion, see García 1988, Guha 1989, Peña 1992a.

23. See the discussion of "Western" and "non-Western" rationality in *Z Papers* (vol. 1, no. 4 [1992]).

24. See chapters 5 and 7 of this work for discussion of worker-owned, self-managed cooperatives in Juárez.

25. As quoted in Mamozai 1982: 212.

26. On Mexican women and labor history, see, for example, a thematic issue of *Historia Obrera* (1975). See also Arizpe 1977, Elmendorf 1977, Acuña 1981.

27. On the concept of situated knowledge, see Haraway 1991: chap. 9. For relevant and useful discussions of "truth" in the social sciences, see also Rosaldo 1989, Roseneau 1992.

28. Other critical aspects of the epistemological debate concerning the nature of knowledge and truth claims are discussed in Harris 1980; Rosaldo 1989; Haraway 1991; Harding 1986, 1991.

29. See especially Rosaldo 1989: chaps. 1, 2, 3.

30. On the "emic-etic" dichotomy, see Harris 1980. See also Peña 1989a. Briefly, "emic" truth claims are generated by the community of participants in a given social event. "Etic" truth claims are generated by the community of experts. Thus, emic truth claims may be thought of as an open circle, while etic truth claims can be seen as articulated from within an enclosed hierarchy. Etic truth privileges the perspectives of "experts," while emic truth privileges the perspectives of everyday participants in situated contexts.

31. Rosaldo 1989.

32. For critical reviews of the state of maquiladora research during the early to mid 1980s, cf. Peña 1983, especially chapter 2, and Stoddard 1987. For more recent assessments, see also Sklair 1994, Stoddard 1990.

33. See, for example, Stoddard 1987, 1991.

34. For annotated bibliographies on social-scientific studies of the maquilas, see Peña 1981, Sklair 1988.

35. Among the recent books and anthologies are Fernández-Kelly 1983b; Ruiz and Tiano 1987; Stoddard 1987; Carrillo 1989d; Sklair 1989, 1994.

36. At the heart of the debate is the Tariff Schedule of the United States (TSUS), particularly items 806.30 and 807.00, which promote offshore production processing by U.S. corporations. These regulations greatly reduce the costs of and simplify the export, processing, and reentry of products assembled abroad. Thus, U.S. unions argue that the provisions encourage the exportation of American jobs to the third world. See Bustamante 1975; Peña 1980; Peña 1983: chap. 1; Sklair 1994: 8–16.

37. Center for Investigative Reporting 1990.

38. In addition to *Global Dumping Ground,* there are two other significant film documentaries, *A Small World* and *Global Assembly Line.*

39. See Hirszowicz 1982. For the classic statement on "plant sociology," see Kerr and Fisher 1957.

40. See Burawoy 1985.

41. See, among others, Carrillo 1980, 1985, 1989a, 1989c, 1989d; Carrillo and Hernández 1982, 1985; de la Rosa Hickerson 1979; Escamilla and Vigorito 1978; Fernández-Kelly 1980, 1983b, 1987; Gambrill 1980, 1982, 1984; Hernández 1980; Peña 1980, 1983, 1984, 1986, 1987; Sklair 1994; Stoddard 1987, 1991, 1992a, 1992b; Tiano 1984, 1985, 1987a, 1987b; Van Waas 1981.

42. See, for example, Carrillo 1980, 1985, 1986, 1989c, 1989d; Carrillo and Hernández 1982; de la Rosa Hickerson 1979; Escamilla and Vigorito 1978; Fernández-Kelly 1983b; Hernández 1980; Stoddard 1987, 1991; Van Waas 1981.

43. Nathan Shefferman led the way in getting management to take into account "clandestine groups" on the shop floor. A self-described union buster, Shefferman founded Labor Relations Associates in Chicago in 1939. Sears and Roebuck was his first major customer. Over the years, many other "corporate social research consultants" have developed successful organizations that provide services to corporations in the areas of union-management relations, employee social control, and corporate culture. For further discussion, see Baritz 1967, Cooley 1980, Kassem 1976, Grenier 1988.

44. The classic statement on scholarly collaboration with management is Baritz 1967. See also Kassem 1976, Grenier 1988.

45. In the field of maquila research, scholarly collaboration with management is exemplified by Lucker and Álvarez (1984, 1985) and Lucker (1984).

46. Saldívar 1990: 207.

47. Even the postmodern social theorist David Harvey is guilty of perpetuating the stereotype of helpless, vulnerable, and disorganized third-world women workers. See Harvey 1989: 153–154.

2. FROM DARK, SATANIC MILLS TO MAQUILAS

1. Hyman 1975: 12. See also Hirszowicz 1982.

2. My thinking on these issues has been influenced particularly by the feminist critique of Western philosophies of science and technology. The feminist critique of science and technology emphasizes the links between class, patriarchy,

and science in the domination of nature, women, and colonies. See, for example, Haraway 1989, 1991; Harding 1986, 1990; Merchant 1980, 1989, 1993; Shiva 1988.

3. The feminist critique of Western philosophy and science identifies the androcentric (or male-centered) perspective as a major factor in the domination of nature. Merchant (1980, 1989), Keller (1987), Shiva (1988), and Biehl (1991) have made particularly important contributions to the feminist critique of androcentric science. Shiva calls this Western philosophical tradition "reductionist science" and attributes the following qualities to it:

> Exclusion of other traditions of knowledge by reductionist science is threefold: (i) ontological, in that other properties are not taken note of; (ii) epistemological, in that other ways of perceiving and knowing are not recognized; and (iii) sociological, in that the non-specialist and non-expert is deprived of the right both to access to knowledge and to judging claims made on its behalf. All this is the stuff of politics, not science. Picking one group of people [white male experts], who adopt one way of knowing the physical world (the reductionist), to find one set of properties in nature (the mechanistic) is a political, not a scientific mode. (1988: 30)

4. The so-called Scientific Revolution, beginning with Descartes and Bacon, was characterized by a language of domination based on explicit sexual metaphors. In the feminist critique, the Scientific Revolution is the ultimate accomplishment of an androcentric epistemology. Elizabeth Fee notes that

> the language and metaphors of the scientific revolution were clear: sexuality was the metaphor for a mediation between mind and nature. Mind was male, Nature was female, and knowledge was created as an act of aggression—a passive nature had to be interrogated, unclothed, penetrated, and compelled by man to reveal her secrets. (1986: 44)

5. See Merchant 1980, Shiva 1988. Shiva describes the struggle between a feminine science (identified in the hermetic tradition of Paracelsus) and a masculine science (identified in the mechanical tradition of Bacon) at the time of the emergence of industrial capitalism. As Shiva notes,

> With the formation of the Royal Society and in the context of emerging industrial capitalism, the contest between mechanical and hermetic traditions was won by the masculine project which was the project of a particular class. . . . Paracelsus and Bacon did not merely differ in their ideology of gender and science; they were also differently rooted in the politics of class, with Bacon committed to middle class values . . . and identifying with capitalists, merchants and the State in his scientific project, and Paracelsus, on the side of the peasants in their uprising in the Tyrol. (1988: 20)

6. For elaboration, see Rosenberg 1981.

7. See especially Marx 1973: 584–594, 702–710. Whether we thus judge Marx guilty of anthropocentrism is a matter reserved for another time. For relevant commentary, see Levidow and Young 1981, Rosenberg 1981, Peña 1989b. See also the useful ongoing discussion in *Capitalism, Nature, Socialism: A Journal of Socialist Ecology.*

We find in Marx an anticipation of the political ecology of capitalism. He expressed concern over the depredation and exhaustion of both workers and nature. Peña (1989b: 8–10) quotes passages from *Capital* in which Marx discusses the destruction of the "deer forests" of the Gaels, a process that degraded both natural and human ecology. Of course, in those sections of *Capital* that deal with the transition from handicrafts to large-scale industry, Marx also prophetically denounced the occupational health hazards and environmental risks experienced by workers in the "satanic mills." His use of the English Factory Inspector Reports is truly a pioneering example of environmental epidemiology (see Peña 1989b). That we may consider Marx too much of a technological determinist does not detract from the enduring value of his pioneering contribution to the development of the ecological critique of capitalist exploitation of nature and labor as commodities.

8. For commentary on the role of the Lancashire witch trials in the Scientific Revolution and the emergence of industrial capitalism, see Merchant 1980, Shiva 1988. The feminist critique treats the witch trials as an attack on the autonomy of women as scientists and healers.

9. The original data and research findings of the so-called Hawthorne Studies are outlined in Roethlisberger and Dickson 1939.

10. Cooley 1980: 17.

11. For more on these questions, see Nandy 1992, Ellis 1992, Marglin 1992, Chomsky 1992, Ehrenreich 1992.

12. For elaboration of this point, see Mies 1987, Peña 1989a, Shiva 1988.

13. Marx discusses the Luddite struggles against the introduction of ribbon looms, wind-driven sawmills, the Everett wool-shearing machine, and Arkwright's scribbling mills and carding engines. On the struggles of the Industrial Workers of the World (IWW), see Bock, Carpignano, and Ramírez 1976. On workers' struggles in Red Emilia and the Fiat workers' protest at Piazza Statuto, see Potere Operaio 1970, Red Notes 1979, Sabel 1984. On the student and worker revolt of 1968, see Katsiaficas 1987.

14. See Cleaver 1979, 1988; Merrington and Marazzi 1971.

15. Cleaver 1988: 1.

16. As von Werlhof points out,

the proletarian wage labourer is a minority phenomenon. . . . Today, only a small percentage of the world population belongs to this category and it has never been more. The "prototype" of the free wage labourer—male, white and over 21 years-old urban industrial worker—is even rarer. Eighty to ninety percent of the world population consists essentially of women, peasants, craftsmen, petty traders and such wage labourers whom one can call neither "free" nor proletarian. (Mies, Bennholdt-Thomsen, and von Werlhof 1988: 171)

17. Admittedly, I cannot present in detail this history of resistance and struggle; I refer readers to such excellent works as Burawoy 1985; Brecher 1978; Brighton Labour Process 1978; Conference of Socialist Economists 1976; Micro-

electronics Group 1980; Coriat 1982; Edwards 1978, 1979; Fennell 1976; Gordon, Edwards, and Reich 1982; Gorz 1977; Gramsci 1971; Levidow and Young 1981; Negri 1980; Watson 1971; Zerowork 1975, 1977. One of the earliest studies of informal struggle by a U.S. social scientist is Mathewson 1931.

18. For an elaboration of the critique of orthodox Marxism, see especially the articles in *Zerowork: Political Materials I* (Zerowork 1975) and *Zerowork: Political Materials II* (Zerowork 1977). See also Cleaver 1979.

19. On the enclosure movement, see Marx 1977: 879, 885–889.

20. See Marx 1977, especially part 8.

21. Primitive accumulation should not be misconstrued as an event at some distant point in history but rather should be understood as a process unfolding through the present day. One can find throughout the history of capitalism examples of the struggle of land-based communities against the violent appropriation of natural-resource bases that make possible a livelihood that is not dependent on wage labor. There are thousands of historical and contemporary examples of struggles by peasant and indigenous peoples against the primitive accumulation.

The Rhineland peasantry undertook the so-called Wood Theft Wars during the 1600s in order to reclaim access to timber (see Linebaugh 1976); there have been similar struggles by other peasant cultures involving so-called forest crimes (see Scott 1985, Peña 1992b). Mexicans waged the "El Paso Salt War" to defend common-property resources in borderland West Texas during the 1890s (see Acuña 1981). There were similar episodes in the upper Rio Grande watershed of southern Colorado (see Peña 1992b). The Lacandón Maya in Mexico's rain forests are engaged in various ongoing revolts in defense of their homeland (see Caufield 1984), as is the Kayapo tribe in the Xingu watershed of Amazonia (see Posey 1983, 1987; Taylor 1990). Various Chicano agropastoral communities are struggling for the restoration of ancestral land grants (see Peña 1992a, 1992b, forthcoming). The traditional Hopi and Navajo tribes of Black Mesa in northeastern Arizona are fighting against relocation by multinational energy development corporations (see Matthiessen 1994, Weiss 1984, Hall 1992). And Marx, of course, wrote about the struggles of the Gaelic peasantry in the Scottish Highlands (Marx 1977: part 8).

22. Beyond Marx, among the more notable historians of the English Industrial Revolution are Hobsbawm (1964, 1969) and Wolf (1983). For more recent accounts of revolutionary industrial and technological change in North America, see Edwards 1979, Piore and Sabel 1984.

23. The reference here is to Marx's discussion of the steam engine as a "power inimical" to the worker, as a weapon to break down strikes and other forms of struggle. See Marx 1977: 562–563.

24. Marx 1977: 412–413.

25. See Montgomery 1976, 1979.

26. Marx 1977: 450.

27. Marx 1977: 457.

28. Marx describes specialization in the following terms:

[T]he interdependence of work . . . creates a continuity . . . and an intensity of labor, quite different from that found in an independent handicraft or even in simple cooperation. (1977: 464–465)

29. For discussion of the wage hierarchy, see Marx 1977: 469–470.

30. Marx 1977: 333–338. The English manufacturers used Professor Senior's polemic to argue against the ten-hours legislation on the grounds that it would eliminate the "last hour" of the working day, which, it was claimed, was the only time when they could make a profit.

31. Marx 1977: 319. This, ironically, sounds amazingly similar to Ford's own description of the introduction of labor-displacing technology in his automobile plants more than a half century later.

32. Marx argued this point at length, and then concluded:

In the background lurked the intention of using the children to force the working day of the adult males up to 15 hours. . . . The experience of the three years which followed [the Act of 1850] demonstrated that such an attempt was bound to fail in the face of the resistance of the adult male workers. (1977: 407–408)

33. For a discussion of Taylor's personal life, see Andrew 1981: 56–72.

34. Among Taylor's leading supporters in the American Society of Mechanical Engineers were Frank and Lillian Gilbreth; see Gilbreth 1911. See also Nelson 1975, 1980.

35. Taylor 1903: 30.

36. See Taylor 1903, 1911.

37. See Braverman 1974: 99–100.

38. The principle of absolute managerial control over the knowledge base corresponds to the separation of mental and manual labor that Marx criticized some sixty years before Taylor outlined his plan for the further deskilling of labor. As Taylor states,

[t]he managers [must] assume . . . the burden of gathering together all of the traditional knowledge which in the past has been possessed by the workmen and then of classifying, tabulating, and reducing this knowledge to rules, laws, formulae. . . . All possible brain work should be removed from the shop and centered in the planning or laying-out department. . . . The work of every workman [must be] fully planned by management in advance. (1911: 36–38)

39. There has been considerable debate about the adoption of the Taylor system by American management since Braverman offered one of the first extended critiques of Taylorism. Much of this debate focuses on determining the extent to which Taylorism was actually incorporated into workplace organization by capitalist corporations in the United States. Edwards (1979) criticizes Braverman for accepting writings on management theory as evidence for actual developments on the shop or office floor. But there is also a considerable body

of research that documents the use of Taylorist principles in factories and other work settings. See, for example, Baldi 1972, Palliox 1976, Sohn-Rethel 1976, Aglietta 1979, Coriat 1979, Zimbalist 1979, Littler 1982.

In Taylor's day, acceptance of the principles of scientific management was limited by union opposition. In time, however, the principles of scientific management were incorporated into the university curriculum as part of the academic training of a variety of engineers and social scientists. The further development of actual managerial practices did not necessarily incorporate Taylor's specific plans, but this is due to the particular requirements of each factory setting and its political-economic context. Nevertheless, the U.S. managerial tradition did incorporate and experiment with the underlying principles of time and motion study, deskilling, and piece rates. For elaboration, see Nelson 1975, 1980. My own research on the maquilas documents the continuing influence of Taylorist principles on the capitalist control of production.

Subsequent developments in machine technologies, methods-and-design engineering, and modern personnel administration have, at any rate, increased the capacity for labor control first envisioned by Taylor and his followers. Even if the designs given to us by the straitjacketed engineer seem anachronistic in an age of microelectronics, robotics, and flexible production, the quest for a monopoly over knowledge by the methods-engineering profession remains very much a part of the organization of modern assembly-line factories in the third world today.

40. Gartman 1979: 197.

41. Arnold and Faurote 1972.

42. See Sohn-Rethel 1976.

43. Blauner 1973: 98–99.

44. Baldi 1972.

45. Gartman 1979.

46. The following excerpts from Ford's autobiography provide ample evidence for the operation of the principles of division of labor, accuracy, and continuity in the Ford Motor Company:

> The radiator is a complex affair and . . . used to be a matter of skill. . . . Now it is all done by a machine . . . no tinsmith work and no skill are required. . . . We used to rivet the crank case, using pneumatic hammers. . . . It took six men to hold the hammers and six men to hold the casings. . . . Now one automatic press operated by one man, who does nothing else, gets through five times as much work in one day as those twelve men did. . . . In the Piquette plant . . . [t]here is no manual handling of material. There is not a single hand operation. . . . If a machine can be made automatic, it is. . . . Dividing and subdividing operations, keeping work in motion—these are the keystones of production. But also it is to be remembered that all parts are designed so that they can be most easily made [and interchanged]. (1922: 89–90)

See also Hounshell 1985.

47. For an extended discussion of the evolution of technological and engineering innovations at Ford, see Hounshell 1985. Hounshell offers a limited treatment of the Ford social department, which was notoriously intrusive in the immigrant workers' private lives during the first two decades of the Ford Motor Company. Some of the activity of the Ford "sociologists" focused on gaining control of high turnover rates. Sward (1948) offers a more interesting, if less critical, history of the Ford Motor Company that draws heavily on Ford's own book, *My Life and Work* (1922). But Sward does not examine Ford's policies on gender beyond mentioning the work of the Ford social department. Gartman (1979) does not discuss the issue of gender much, choosing to focus instead on the dynamics of resistance without accounting for the demographic composition of the workforce. Ford (1922) himself probably provides the best description of company policy regarding women workers.

48. Ford 1922: 128–129.

49. Ford 1922: 129.

50. Ford 1922: 111.

51. See Grenier 1988.

52. Ford 1922: 126.

53. Ford states that in 1919, eighty-two women were discharged because their husbands were working (1922: 111).

54. This is evident from a more recent study of wildcat strikes at Ford during the 1960s; Linebaugh and Ramírez (1975) note the changing demographic composition of the Ford Motor Company (increasing numbers of white women and ethnic minority workers).

55. See Aglietta 1979, Cleaver 1979.

56. Ford 1922: 129.

57. Mayo's 1933 book, *The Human Problems of an Industrial Civilization*, initiated the discourse and posited conformity and spontaneous collaboration as underlying principles of group consensus and social equilibrium in industrialized society. See also Whitehead 1938. The discourse was revived by Roethlisberger and Dickson and Homans. See Roethlisberger and Dickson 1939, Committee on Work in Industry 1941, Homans 1950.

58. Carey (1967) was the first to develop the term "managerial sociology" to describe the political orientations of human relations theory.

59. Mayo believed that workers could form a social code at a lower level in opposition to the economic logic of management, and thus posited workers as semiautonomous subjects. See Mayo 1933: chap. 7.

60. The original empirical foundations of managerial sociology lie in the infamous "Hawthorne Works" research studies conducted at a Western Electric Company factory outside Chicago. The results of these studies were first published by Mayo in 1933. The Hawthorne studies were originally begun as attitudinal surveys devised to improve the supervision of workers.

Researchers sought to understand employee opinions concerning such things as job tasks, working conditions, and supervision. The managerial sociologists developed what they called the "analysis of complaints" in order to get at the underlying causes of worker discontent and provide management with information for training and planning. The results of the original studies led the researchers to a more detailed analysis of what Homans called "social sentiments" in the workplace. This involved the so-called Bank Wiring Observation Room and Relay Assembly Test Room experiments, which focused on the analysis of informal social organization on the shop floor. The goal was to gather more data on informal shop-floor networks, since these networks were thought to govern the formation of social sentiments and to influence worker behavior in the workplace. For detailed commentary on these studies and experiments, see Carey 1967; Braverman 1974; Peña 1983: chap. 3.

61. Output restriction was found to be organized in two major ways. Often, the group standard of production was below "bogey," that is, below the fixed upper limit on each worker's output chart. To the surprise of the researchers and the chagrin of management, output restriction was caused by "binging." In binging, the person with consistently higher output curves is admonished and ridiculed by co-workers. Informal sanctions, usually in the form of verbal warnings or the threat of physical punishment and exclusion, were identified as the major cause of output restriction. See Roethlisberger and Dickson 1939: 422–423. See also Dalton 1950; Roy 1952a, 1952b, 1953, 1954, 1958.

Sometimes punishment included a slap ("bing") to the head of the "rate-buster" (quota violator). A second, more sophisticated form of output restriction involved the distortion of departmental output records. Cooperation with low-level supervisors was necessary for this tactic to succeed. The researchers at Hawthorne discovered that such cooperation was not difficult to secure. See Roethlisberger and Dickson 1939: 426–428, 445–446.

The earliest North American study of output restriction that I have identified is Mathewson 1931. For a review of this literature, see Peña 1987.

62. Roethlisberger and Dickson 1939: 525, 567–568.

63. Shefferman as quoted in Friedman and Weir 1982: 47. See also Shefferman 1955.

64. See Edwards 1979 for relevant discussion.

65. The leading advocates of this view are Argyris (1964) and his disciples in "personality and organization" theory. This view is actually much older and can be found in the "shop-floor sociology" pioneered by Donald Roy and Melville Dalton during the late 1940s and early 1950s. For further discussion, see Peña 1983: chap. 3.

66. The most recent incarnation of personality and organization theory is the so-called humanistic-management model developed over the past two decades and popularly known as the Quality of Working Life (QWL) movement. The "alphabet soup" managerial theorists have made perhaps the most significant contributions to this discourse because they developed their perspectives in

the context of work as consultants with corporate managers. The alphabet-soup theories include the "X and Y Dichotomy" (McGregor 1961), the "T-Groups" (Argyris 1964), and "Theory Z" (Ouchi 1982).

Grenier (1988) suggests that post-1970s managerial sociology embodies the strategy of the "de-bureaucratization of control." The key to the supposed dismantling of the corporate bureaucracy is the "personalization of authority." This is a management "style" in which the supervisor plays the empathic role of another subjugated worker. Management must adapt a human face and free itself from dependence on the despotism of machine pacing to achieve its goals. Instead of advocating the inflexible work rules of the classic Fordist bureaucracy, the new managerial theories emphasize that "rules be created [only when] threats to control arise."

This model also requires that workers participate in Quality of Working Life (QWL) circles. But quality circles are based on the separation of decision making from the implementation of policy. Workers may participate in decision-making debates, but management reserves the authority to implement policy. This is precisely the hopeless debate "over the color of the bars" ridiculed by Mike Cooley (1980) in *Architect or Bee?*

Humanistic managerialism incorporates peer pressure as a control mechanism by promoting an ethic of worker responsibility for the attitudes and behavior of peers. Instilling loyalty to corporate ideals is essential if workers are to become, in effect, snitches against their colleagues' alleged deviance. The new managerialism promotes loyalty by resorting to a "rhetoric that de-emphasizes power differences between workers and managers and emphasizes the common purpose of all and the uniqueness of the corporate culture" (Grenier 1988: 131).

67. See Maccoby 1981.

68. Howard 1985: 122–123.

69. For the parallels, see Foucault (1977), who argues persuasively that the rise of the factory and the prison occurred simultaneously and involved exchanges between the two in the development of technologies of discipline and control.

70. Kassem 1976: 55.

71. On cybernetics (the theory of continuous process, self-regulating systems with built-in multiple redundancies and human "feedback loops"), see Wiener 1948, 1950; Blauner 1973. On CAD/CAM, see Cooley 1980. On flexible specialization, see Piore and Sabel 1984. On robotics, see Conference of Socialist Economists 1976, Microelectronics Group 1980, Levidow and Young 1981. Norbert Wiener, the inventor of cybernetic-systems theory, entitled his book *The Human Use of Human Beings*. For a recent study of the so-called Cybernetics Group, see Heims 1993.

72. This is the argument made by Sabel 1982 and Piore and Sabel 1984.

73. See Hirschhorn 1987.

74. Piore and Sabel 1984.

75. For related commentary, see Bluestone and Harrison 1980, Bluestone 1982, Harrison and Bluestone 1988.

76. For relevant commentary, see Goldhaber 1980; Lipietz 1982; Negri 1980, 1984.

77. See Harvey 1989: chap. 9.

78. In the context of the Mexican automotive assembly industry, the shift toward "flexible specialization" is documented in Carrillo 1989a, 1989c.

79. On postmodern social theory, see Haraway 1991, Peña 1989a, Roseneau 1992.

80. See, for example, Carrillo 1980; Carrillo and Hernández 1982, 1985.

81. For relevant commentary, see Braverman 1974.

82. Stoddard 1991: 23–50.

83. See, for example, Sabel 1982, Piore and Sabel 1984, Kenney and Florida 1988.

84. For discussion, see Gambino 1972; Tagliazucchi 1982; Shaiken 1982, 1984.

85. See Lucker 1984; Lucker and Álvarez 1984, 1985.

86. Not because these efforts actually help plant managers control the political character of the workforce, but because the measurement of "job satisfaction" is a discursive act aiming to legitimize managerial imperatives as natural, immutable givens. Job-satisfaction studies are political constructs with which the managerial consultants hope to create a workplace culture of conformity. But the pursuit of labor conformity through the "objective" measurement of "job satisfaction" is an ineffective fantasy bred of a concept of workplace politics that freezes workers into a rigidly exact and immutable position. This concept obviously fails to take account of the shifting loyalties, identities, and experiences of workers. Nowhere is this made clearer than in the case of Cupones de Oro, a coupon-sorting factory in Juárez that used psychological screening mechanisms and job-satisfaction surveys in an attempt to shape a compliant workforce, only to find itself under siege as workers went on strike to protest wages and working conditions. See Centro de Orientación 1989a.

87. See Lewis, Kaltofen, and Ormsby 1991: 1–8; Barry and Sims 1994: 57–68.

88. As reported in Barry and Sims 1994: 59–60.

89. Peña 1980, 1983; French 1993.

90. Barry and Sims 1994: 60.

91. As reported in Barry and Sims 1994: 61.

3. (MIS)MEASURING THE IGNORANT

1. Among the leading critics of the maquilas are Bustamante 1975; Carrillo 1980, 1983, 1984, 1986, 1989b, 1989c; Carrillo and Hernández 1982, 1985; Carrillo and Jasís 1983; Fernández 1977; Fernández-Kelly 1983b, 1983c, 1987; Gambrill 1981, 1982, 1984; Iglesias 1983, 1985a, 1985b; Mungaray 1983; Peña

1980, 1983, 1984, 1985, 1986, 1987; Peña and Gettman 1986; Peña and Cárdenas 1988; Sklair 1994; Tiano 1984, 1985, 1987a, 1987b; Valdés de Villalva 1981, 1985; Van Waas 1981; Young 1986, 1987.

2. See, for example, Peña 1980, 1983, 1986.

3. See, for example, Carrillo 1980; Carrillo and Hernández 1982, 1985; Fernández-Kelly 1983b; Peña 1980, 1983, 1987; Peña and Gettman 1986; and Peña and Cárdenas 1988.

4. Peña 1989b, 1990b; Barry and Sims 1994.

5. See, for example, Lucker 1984; Lucker and Álvarez 1984, 1985; Stoddard 1987.

6. For example, Stoddard 1987, 1991; Lucker 1984.

7. See, for example, Stoddard 1987.

8. See Sklair 1994 for discussion.

9. Anderson and de la Rosa (1989) found that wages were less than adequate to meet needs. See also Sklair 1994.

10. Anderson and de la Rosa 1989: 8–10.

11. See Carrillo 1989b, Carrillo and Jasís 1983, Peña 1983.

12. See, for example, Center for Investigative Reporting 1990; French 1993; Sánchez 1987, 1990a, 1990b.

13. For example, Química Flor, a subsidiary of Union Carbide, operates a hydrofluoric acid chemical complex in Matamoros. Fearing another Bhopal, Mexican officials have established Mexico's first "Intermediate Safeguard Zone" within a one-and-one-quarter-mile radius of the plant. See McDonnell 1991b. A recent University of Texas study found higher-than-average levels of liver and gallbladder cancers in the thirty-three counties that line the Rio Grande.

14. See Carrillo 1989b; Carrillo and Jasís 1983, 1991. Also cf. Instituto Mexicano del Seguro Social 1981.

15. See Howard 1985.

16. I am, therefore, greatly indebted to the pathbreaking work of Richard Edwards (1979), who was among the first labor process theorists to conceptualize the transformation of capitalist control in the context of the American workplace.

17. This layout includes (1) mini-stack (supplies), (2) large-parts assembly table, (3) primary-assembly table with automated conveyor belt, (4) automated solderer, (5) holding-fixture tables for follow-up soldering, (6) preliminary quality-control inspection station, (7) automated quality-control test, (8) repair workstation, (9) final cable soldering, (10) intermediate frequency-test work stations, (11) power-test and adjustment workstations, (12) power-test quality-control workstation, (13) prepackaging, and (14) final packing. This schematic was prepared with assistance from an electronics engineer working at a maquila in Juárez.

18. See chapter 4 of this work for a discussion of workers' responses to this strategy.

19. See Cooley 1980, Hales 1980.

20. For similar approaches to the analysis of capitalist control strategies, see, for example, Burawoy 1979, 1985; Edwards 1978, 1979; Zimbalist 1979.

21. Fernández-Kelly 1983b, for example.

22. One former superintendent at a car-seat assembly plant addressed this point:

> The apparel industry here is, in my opinion, too relaxed about recruiting. They do not even have a screening interview, although most use perfunctory manual-dexterity tests. Some of these plants evaluate on the floor; it is there they can see if the employee has the endurance and strength to do repetitive work. . . . In automotives, especially if we are talking about the type of assembly-line work you are interested in, we are much more precise about our recruitment. . . . We have a reputation. Maybe part of it is that we are American based. This seems attractive to the workers. We advertise . . . and [rely on] worker contacts also. . . . But the key to our recruitment is two things: one, we subject every prospective employee to a battery of tests, for dexterity, but also psychological profiles . . . and two, outstanding employees who bring other exemplary prospects are rewarded with bonus pay. But if you bring a poor employee, then that does not reflect well on your record either. (Interview, Ciudad Juárez, March 1982)

23. For other examples of "personnel selection" strategies in coupon-sorting maquilas, see Lucker 1984; Lucker and Álvarez 1984, 1985.

24. This is not to deny that sexism is an intrinsic part of Mexican culture. But it is important to note that the history of gender roles in Mexico is much more complex than the stereotypical image of *machismo* suggests. For further discussion, see Rascón 1982, Carrillo 1986.

25. For relevant commentary, see Kanter 1977.

26. Most maquiladoras operate on either a two- or three-shift system. The two-shift system includes *matutino* (morning) and *vespertino* (afternoon) shifts. The three-shift system adds a *nocturno* (night) shift.

27. For related comments, see Fernández-Kelly 1980, 1983b.

28. Marx observes that "in the history of capitalist production, the determination of what is a working-day, presents itself as the result of a struggle between . . . the class of capitalists, and . . . the working class" (1975a: 235).

29. There are some problems with the accuracy and reliability of these data. First, quota levels are in a state of constant flux and readjustment. Second, the different types of product or component being assembled will entail different levels of skill and concentration and different numbers of tasks and parts. Obviously, there are differences between the difficulty and complexity of the job tasks involved in, say, sewing precut pockets on men's denim jeans and those involved in assembling six components on an integrated circuit (IC) board. Both jobs require considerable effort; both involve repetitive tasks that cause fatigue. However, some jobs require less expenditure in terms of physical effort and concentration. Third, the data also indicate that a substantial number of workers participate in output restriction (see chapter 4 of this volume). Thus the quota

levels reported above may deviate, positively or negatively, from a worker's "normal" performance level.

30. See Peña 1980, Carrillo and Hernández 1982, Van Waas 1981.

31. Another plant manager remarked that productivity rates are doubled every six to eight weeks in the Mexican plants, a feat he characterized as impossible in the United States (interviews, Ciudad Juárez, March–June 1992).

32. On a visit to one plant in March 1982, I noticed a large bulletin board on the wall facing workers on the primary assembly line. The bulletin board had a roster of all workers, to document their performance. Gold stars next to the workers' names traced increased output for the week. The bulletin board carried the following reminder: "Yesterday's output goal was 550 units. Today, let us reach 600! Performance is the key to Quality!"

33. Compare this view with Burawoy 1985.

34. According to managerial interviews collected during 1981 and 1982. This was verified by observation of plants visited over a ten-year period.

35. Compare this with Grenier 1988.

36. Of those who reported reprimands, the largest group (about 39 percent) stated that the method of reprimand involved criticism by the group chief or first-line supervisor. Another 20 percent stated that a report on their performance was prepared; these workers had to read and sign the report. Slightly more than 10 percent reported that they were required to visit the personnel office (table 8). A visit to the personnel office is feared by most workers, since it is often the first step toward termination.

37. For excellent summaries of the research on turnover in the maquilas, see Stoddard 1987, Sklair 1994.

38. See North American Congress 1975, de la Rosa Hickerson 1979, Peña 1980, Van Waas 1981.

39. See, for example, Stoddard 1991.

40. Approximately 20 percent of the workers in our sample stated that management intrudes on their personal and social lives. See also Carrillo and Hernández 1982, Fernández-Kelly 1983b.

41. See especially Carrillo 1980, Carrillo and Hernández 1982.

42. Carrillo 1980: 53 (my translation).

43. Peña 1983: 317–318.

44. Peña 1983.

45. Peña 1983: 318.

46. Peña 1983: 315.

4. LIKE TURTLES ON THE LINE

1. The term "dead labor" has commonly been used since Marx to refer to the instruments of production (machinery and other technology) that are produced by living labor in previous labor processes.

2. Ong (1987) uses the term "spirits of resistance" in reference to the informal shop-floor struggles of Malaysian factory workers. "Specter of autonomy" is a reference to the Italian extraparliamentary movement known as *autonomia*.

3. See, for example, Baerresen 1971, López 1970, Camarena 1970, Van Waas 1981, Lucker 1984, Stoddard 1987. Even Fernández-Kelly (1983b), Carrillo (1980), and Carrillo and Hernández (1982) in earlier works presented a rather one-sided view of capitalist control coupled with relative labor quiescence.

4. There have been some important exceptions: for example, Unión de Trabajadores Agrícolas Fronterizos and the Arizona Farmworkers' Union (AFW) have actively organized among Mexican female farm laborers. La Mujer Obrera in El Paso has actively organized among Mexican and Chicana seamstresses and other female factory workers.

5. López 1970.

6. See, for example, Bustamante 1975, Escamilla and Vigorito 1978, Fernández 1977. The leftist view of workers as subordinate labor power, as victims of exploitation, is really not all that different from management's wishful view of workers as simply another, albeit more troublesome, factor in production. Thus many critics and most managers seldom see workers in their multiplicity as human beings, as active agents of social change and struggle endowed with their own values and situated knowledges. One predominant tendency in the discourse of leftist intellectuals emphasizes capitalist control strategies and portrays workers as passive or, at best, reactive victims. It is easy to see why writers approaching the maquiladoras from this perspective would ignore the subaltern dimension of maquila industrial relations.

7. See chapter 3 of this volume.

8. See, for example, de la Rosa Hickerson 1979; Carrillo 1980, 1983, 1984, 1985, 1986; Carrillo and Hernández 1982; Gambrill 1984, 1989; Peña 1980, 1983.

9. See the pioneering research by de la Rosa Hickerson (1979), Carrillo (1980), Carrillo and Hernández (1982), and Gambrill (1980, 1989).

10. See Peña 1979; Peña 1983: 28–36.

11. See Carrillo 1983, 1984; Gambrill 1984, 1989.

12. See Scott 1985.

13. See, for example, North American Congress 1975; Peña 1979, 1980, 1986, 1987; Baird and McCaughan 1979; Gambrill 1980, 1989. The "plant-specific ethnographies" include Fernández-Kelly 1983b and Arenal 1986.

14. For a borderwide inventory of major strikes between 1974 and 1979, see Peña 1979, 1980. On the major strikes in Ciudad Juárez between 1979 and 1987, see Centro de Orientación 1989a, 1989b.

15. Despacho Obrero was established in 1978 by Gustavo de la Rosa Hickerson, a Juárez labor lawyer, to provide technical assistance to workers involved in organizing struggles or engaged in arbitration proceedings. The Coalition for Justice in the Maquiladoras was established by the American Friends Service Committee and operates on both sides of the border as a research, advocacy,

and lobbying organization. The group Solidaridad Obrera is a spin-off from COMO and includes a number of former maquila workers and labor organizers who actively support strikes and other political protests. A full history of COMO is provided in chapter 5 of this volume.

16. See Centro de Orientación 1989a, 1989b; Carrillo 1984; Gambrill 1989.

17. De la Rosa Hickerson 1979, Gambrill 1989, Van Waas 1981.

18. On violence against striking maquila workers in Juárez, see de la Rosa Hickerson 1979; Centro de Orientación 1989a, 1989b; Peña 1983.

19. See de la Rosa Hickerson 1979; Carrillo and Hernández 1982; Gambrill 1980, 1989. See also records in the COMO archives (Centro de Orientación 1989a, 1989b). Newspaper articles collected in the COMO archives suggest that a common outcome for workers involved in unofficial work stoppages is termination without indemnification. Carrillo and Gambrill have conducted the most comprehensive research with official data from the local and state labor arbitration and conciliation boards; they too have found that workers seldom win in the tripartite system of arbitration and conciliation. See Carrillo 1983, 1984, 1985, 1986; Gambrill 1984, 1989. See also La Botz 1992. Some of the plants in Juárez that have shut down or relocated during strikes and other labor conflicts are Acapulco Fashions, Mattel, Muebles Mexicanos, Sarkes-Tarzian, Solidev, Tonka, and Zaragoza Casting.

20. Compare this with Burawoy's (1979) idea of "imported consciousness."

21. See, for example, Fernández-Kelly 1983b; Centro de Investigación 1981; Carrillo and Hernández 1982; Gambrill 1980, 1982.

22. See Centro de Investigación 1981, Gambrill 1981.

23. Generally, most maquila workers have little prior work experience in any occupation. However, those workers with prior work experience tend to come from private-household, food-service, and retail-sales occupational backgrounds. See Gambrill 1981, 1982; Carrillo and Hernández 1982, 1985; Fernández-Kelly 1983b.

24. For further discussion, see Tiano (1990), who criticizes the "young, single, and educated" profile as stereotypical. It is important to briefly note that there are important sectoral differences. In my own samples, the workforce in the apparel manufacturing includes greater proportions of older women, married and single mothers, and workers with less education. The workforce in consumer-electronics assembly tends to be single, young, and educated— although even this sector has a great deal of diversity. The main point here is that there is no one essential type of maquiladora worker: the maquila workorce is increasingly heterogeneous in terms of age, gender, and marital status.

25. The *escantillón* is the template used to inscribe the positions of pathways and components on the integrated circuit board prior to assembly.

26. See, for example, Braverman 1974, Burawoy 1979, Cleaver 1979, Lamphere 1979, Shapiro-Perl 1979, Ong 1987.

27. The sample for this study is by no means representative of the entire ma-

quila workforce. Thus, I would caution against overgeneralization regarding the high level of output restriction among the cases in the sample. For more discussion, see Peña 1983: 377–378.

28. See Arenal 1986, Peña 1987.

29. See, for example, Burawoy 1979, Lamphere 1979, Shapiro-Perl 1979.

30. See Roethlisberger and Dickson 1939; Roy 1952a, 1952b, 1953; Burawoy 1979; Lamphere 1979; Shapiro-Perl 1979; Cavendish 1982; Gambino 1972; Potere Operaio 1972; Negri 1980.

31. Cf. Roethlisberger and Dickson 1939; Roy 1952a, 1952b.

32. According to several oral histories collected in 1981–82 and 1989.

33. Cf. Hartmann 1978.

34. Three managers mentioned this as a deliberate policy in the selection of shop-floor (production) supervisors. A production superintendent, who was fired from his job for questioning management at a plant assembling car seats and dashboard harnesses, remarked:

> At first, the plant manager hired *gringo* men for the foreman positions. But this was trouble. Mainly, some of the supervisors were overly militaristic, and this caused a considerable amount of disenchantment. . . . Being Mexican, I understood this. So I recommended that the management have a policy of hiring younger Mexican males, with a different, more personal style. . . . There was a change in the middle 1970s, not just at our plant, toward the "Mexicanization" of middle management and production supervision. (Interview, Ciudad Juárez, February 1983)

35. Cf. Cavendish 1982, Ong 1987.

36. The definitive study of the Acapulco Fashions strike is de la Rosa Hickerson 1979.

37. See Cavendish 1982 for a similar account of informal organization in a British automotive-parts assembly plant.

38. For conceptual discussions of the theory of political recomposition, see Cleaver 1979, Merrington and Marazzi 1971. See also Peña 1983: chap. 4.

39. For relevant discussion, see Burawoy 1979, Shapiro-Perl 1979.

40. I documented these strikes through oral interviews conducted between 1981 and 1984 and research at the archives of COMO. These archives, which are a rich and largely untapped source for labor studies, primarily consist of newspaper reports on strikes and other protests, and additional documents collected by COMO students and research staff. I documented some of these cases with the assistance of Gustavo de la Rosa Hickerson, director of Despacho Obrero, and Luis Trujillo Herrera, a labor lawyer in Juárez. Other cases were documented during the 1989–90 field research project.

41. For a detailed description of the methodology of this aspect of the original study, see Peña 1983: 398–410.

42. These are longstanding Mexican labor unions: Confederación de Trabajadores Mexicanos (CTM), Confederación Regional de Obreros y Campesinos (CROC), and Confederación Revolucionaria de Trabajadores (CRT).

43. See Peña 1983: chap. 1. Further data on wildcat strikes was collected in 1989 from the COMO archives.

44. For coverage of this remarkable strike, see *El Fronterizo* 1986a, 1986b, 1986c, 1986d, 1986e, 1986f, 1986g; *El Universal* 1986c, 1986d, 1986e, 1986f; *El Diario de Juárez* 1986a, 1986b, 1986c, 1986d; Lau 1986.

45. *El Universal* 1986b.

46. An interesting and refreshing discussion of the concept of ideology, particularly as it relates to the production of narrative, is Saldívar 1990: 208–215. See also Eagleton 1991.

47. Geertz 1973: 203.

48. Saldívar 1990: 209–213.

49. See also Haraway 1991: chap. 9.

50. See, for example, *El Universal* 1986a.

51. Delgado is referring to Rubén Lau and Judith Galarza Campos, frequent contributors to two of Juárez's daily newspapers, *El Diario de Juárez* and *El Fronterizo*, respectively. See especially Galarza's article "Maquiladoras: Neocolonialismo" appearing in the September 12, 1986, issue of *El Fronterizo*.

5. THE MIRROR OF EXPLOITATION

An earlier draft of this chapter was prepared for the Silicon Valley Research Group's Workshop Series on Women, High Technology, and Society, University of California, Santa Cruz, June 1985.

1. See Baerresen 1971. For another example of this view, see Greater Laredo Development Foundation 1976. The foundation published a handbook in which it touted the advantages of operating assembly plants in the border region under the heading "Low Wages Await You in Laredo." For further discussion, see Peña 1983: chaps. 1, 2.

2. See Peña 1983, 1984, 1986, 1987.

3. For more on these questions, see Staudt 1987, Young 1987.

4. For more on these questions, see Staudt 1987, Young 1987.

5. For more on these questions, see Andreas 1985, Development Alternatives for Women 1985, Shiva 1988, Leonard 1989.

6. We must avoid confusion regarding the use of the terms *autogestión* (self-management) and *autonomía* (autonomy). My use of *autogestión* in this chapter is consistent with COMO's usage; that is, it refers to the principles associated with self-management models of labor-process organization in which immediate producers (workers) have complete, democratic control over decision making in the workplace. My use of the term *autonomía* follows that of Cleaver (1979) to refer to extraparliamentary (i.e., noninstitutionalized) rank-and-file actions as aspects of working-class self-activity. My use of the term *autonomía*, or autonomy, should not be construed as referring to the specifically Italian "autonomous left," which has no perfect parallel in the Mexican context. *Autonomía* is for present purposes rendered simply as "rank-and-file autonomy."

7. Guillermina Valdés did postgraduate work at the University of Michigan during the 1960s. She described this work to me as involving the study of "the pedagogy of Fromm and Freire in the psychosocial reality of contemporary Mexico." Her research, as I understand it, was a sophisticated, incisive, and focused critical reading of Fromm's theory of psychoanalysis and Freire's theory of pedagogy. Valdés synthesized these theories with the objective of uniting "self-concept" and "self-help" as principles for organizing alternative educational strategies. To my knowledge, she never finished writing this work. But perhaps more importantly, she left a legacy of practices that, in my opinion, hold the kernel of a genuinely alternative model of development for the Mexican border working-class community.

8. See Fernández-Kelly 1982: 21–22; Yudelman 1987: chap. 1; Kopinak 1989.

9. For the original statement on this problem-solving pedagogy, see Freire 1971. See also Fernández-Kelly 1983a.

10. See *El Fronterizo* 1979, *El Diario de Juárez* 1980, *El Correo* 1980, Flores Simenthal 1981.

11. Most of the original members of Guille were workers fired from their jobs due to "declining productivity." They were older than the average maquila worker and were more likely to have children. Early on, COMO established child care for members of the cooperatives as well as the student-workers who were attending classes. See Sociedad Cooperativa 1975; *El Fronterizo* 1980; Fernández-Kelly 1982, 1983b; Peña 1983: chap. 8.

12. Fernández-Kelly 1982: 24–25.

13. My observations of labor-process organization at Guille from 1981 to 1983 lead me to believe that the cooperative was very adept at implementing a variety of job-rotation schemes that lessened stress and boredom. The degree of democratic decision making also created a relaxed, almost jovial, atmosphere in the work areas. But could this be simply a case of self-exploitation as self-management? It is worth noting that the workweek for members of the Guille cooperative averaged 38 hours, much lower than the average of 45–48 hours for maquila workers. I never witnessed speedup or rate-busting at Guille. The absence of wage or supervisory hierarchies also clearly reduced work-related stress and conflict at Guille.

14. Former Guille worker. Field journal entry, 23 July 1989.

15. The SSA is Mexico's national public-health secretariat. It certified COMO as a training center for nursing assistants in 1977.

16. UCECA, Coordinating Unit for Employment, Training, and Instruction, is Mexico's equivalent of the U.S. Manpower and Training Administration.

17. The IAF was established by Congress in the 1960s to promote cooperation and development projects in Latin America. The 1973 Percy Amendment to the Foreign Assistance Act mandated the IAF to integrate women's concerns into its development-assistance planning. The 1978 IAF grant to COMO was for $182,000 and the 1980 grant was for $160,500. Yudelman 1987: 6, 22–23.

18. The CEBIs (Centers for Intensive Basic Education) were the front line in Mexico's efforts to reduce illiteracy. CEBI projects were established in "marginal" areas, for the most part in urban settings, although more recent efforts have involved outreach to rural areas.

19. Fernández-Kelly 1982: 27–28.

20. COMO's pedagogy incorporated the work of Freire (1971) in its training and educational programs for maquila workers. Through the capable intervention of Guillermina Valdés, COMO developed a unique approach that blended Freire's techniques of dialogic interaction and socially relevant, experiential learning with Fromm's principles of self-actualization and autonomy. This synthesis was the direct result of Valdés's postgraduate research at the University of Michigan (see note 7 of this chapter).

21. The concept of the change agent derives from traditions in social-work practice that involve intervention by case workers in the resolution of problems facing individuals. One of the central debates in the social-work profession centers on the nature of the relationship between the problems of the individual and the social, political, and historical milieux. The tendency in recent times has been to separate the "clinical" practice aspects of social work (that is, psychotherapeutic interpersonal helping) from its community-organizing and social-change aspects. In both Mexico and the United States, this separation is reflected in the organization of MSW academic programs in which two major, distinct specializations are the norm: clinical practice, and administration and planning. The "old" community-organizing curriculum is virtually absent from most programs, which generally limit themselves to paying lip service to Saul Alinsky in a few introductory classes. Critics of this dichotomy point to the transformation of social workers from agents of individual and social change to agents of social control. For the classic statement on the differing roles and functions of the change agent, see Perlman 1959. Attempts to overcome the dichotomy have been made within the liberal-welfare tradition of mainstream social work. For critical commentary and alternative approaches, see Galper 1975, Corrigan and Leonard 1978, Bailey and Brake 1976, Tudiver 1982, Gettman 1983, Withorn 1983, Peña and Gettman 1986. After 1978, COMO shifted from a focus on individual-change strategies to more systemic and structural approaches to social change.

22. Fernández-Kelly also discusses the *promotores'* role in social change (1982: 39–41).

23. Of the sixty student-workers at COMO who were part of my 1981–82 survey study, 80 percent had participated in slowdowns and more than 70 percent had participated in work stoppages, including full-blown wildcat strikes.

24. During the period that I was at COMO, from 1981 through 1984, there were repeated bridge and road blockades by cotton farmers, student occupations of buildings at the regional agricultural college, and protest marches by land squatters (*paracaidistas*) and maquila workers. Some of these protests trig-

gered violent responses from the police and military forces. For some earlier accounts of land occupations in Juárez, see *El Paso Herald Post* 1963; on the recent struggles of farmers in the Juárez Valley, see *El Fronterizo* 1981. See also Martínez 1978, which describes the actions of the squatters as "traumatic."

25. The CDP (Committee for Popular Defense) was established to defend land occupations and *colono* struggles throughout the state of Chihuahua and especially the region around Ciudad Juárez. Currently, it receives minimal PRI (Partido Revolucionario Institucional) support as an opposition group to the emergent rightist municipal governments in Juárez, headed by the PAN (Partido de Acción Nacional). The students at ESAHE have been involved in a protracted struggle to gain federal-university status. The struggle at ESAHE focuses on nonpayment of faculty salaries, lack of laboratory equipment, and a general lack of funding for academic and extracurricular programs. Despacho Obrero (Labor Office) was founded in 1979 by Gustavo de la Rosa Hickerson, a labor lawyer, scholar, and activist in Ciudad Juárez. The Despacho has provided years of assistance to maquila workers involved in arbitration conflicts and strikes.

26. This is according to an unpublished history of the period prepared by COMO for its archives during an internal evaluation in 1981.

27. Between 1981 and 1983, I was a guest researcher, lecturer, and technical consultant at COMO. Guillermina Valdés asked me to teach classes in the *tronco común* during the 1981 and 1982 fall semesters. My work as a lecturer in the *tronco común* led to my direct participation in the *brigada* research projects of the student-workers. As a consequence, I became directly involved in the shop-floor struggles of workers at several electronics assembly plants in Juárez. My own small, personal victory against the terror of the machine came when workers at one plant, utilizing problem-solving techniques they developed through *brigada* research activities, undermined management's use of a "stop-start" mechanism to control productivity rates on an assembly line.

28. For further discussion of "deskilled labor's inventive force," see Centro de Orientación 1984, Peña 1984. See also chapters 6 and 7 of this volume.

29. Peña 1983: 455.

30. Fernández-Kelly 1982: 37–38.

31. For the research reports generated by this project, see Centro de Orientación 1984, Peña 1984, Valdés de Villalva 1989.

32. Centro de Orientación 1982: 12 (my translation).

33. Centro de Orientación 1982: 12 (my translation).

34. For extended discussion of skilled activity in the maquilas, see Peña 1984. See also chapter 6 of this volume.

35. Centro de Orientación 1982: 12 (my translation).

36. María P. Fernández-Kelly (at the time with the Center for U.S.–Mexican Studies at the University of California, San Diego) conducted the first stage of the evaluation in March 1982. Martín de la Rosa, director of the Instituto Mexicano de Investigación Social (IMISAC, Mexican Institute for Social Research),

conducted the second stage of the evaluation in July 1982. The final evaluation was conducted by Beatriz Vera (former codirector of COMO and a social researcher) and Gay Young (at the time assistant professor of sociology at the University of Texas at El Paso). The final evaluation was conducted between September 1982 and September 1983. See Fernández-Kelly 1982, Vera and Young 1984, Yudelman 1987.

37. The limited exception to this was Yudelman, who some years later wrote a book that included a chapter on COMO. But Yudelman relegated the autonomous activity of the workers to a small-print endnote in which she states that the workers' council was disbanded because two members of the COMO staff disagreed with the council's "increasingly independent stance" and militant activism inside the factories. See Yudelman 1987: 32 (n. 19).

38. I recorded these "personal narratives" in a field journal based on participant observations made between 1981 and 1984. I did not try to detect the subaltern life of COMO by resorting to formalized interviews with ready-made questionnaires.

39. Rosaldo 1989: 60.

40. I base this statement on conversations I had with former student-workers and COMO staff in 1983, 1984, and 1989.

41. Enders, a self-proclaimed expert on Latin American politics, was appointed in 1982, after COMO had received both of its IAF grants. My own confidential sources in Congress told me that Enders in fact opposed COMO because he viewed it as a "philanthropic organization that had gotten out of control."

42. Vera and Young 1984: 53–54. I should note that this certainly was not the case with everyone on the staff. It was my experience that the staff that worked on María Villegas's projects was not ambivalent about directly participating in these struggles.

43. See Yudelman 1987: 28. See also Kopinak 1989. The PRI (Institutional Revolutionary Party) has been the dominant political force in Mexico over the past seventy-five years, during which it has had an almost uncontested hold over the presidency.

44. Yudelman 1987: 28.

45. See, for example, Yudelman 1987: 28.

46. See chapter 4 in this volume. During this period, COMO also supported wildcat strikes at Texscan, Electrocomponentes, and Florex.

47. See Kopinak 1989.

48. Kopinak 1989: 233.

49. The St. John the Baptist Church in Juárez is the center of the Charismatic Catholic community in that city.

50. Kopinak 1989: 229.

51. Kopinak 1989: 231.

52. A Charismatic Catholic organization; see Kopinak 1989.

53. I spoke with Luchi Villalva in February 1992 in Juárez after a memorial

panel held in honor of her mother during the annual meeting of the Association for Borderland Scholars. Much of what I have to say here is based on that conversation.

54. This information is drawn from interviews with Jesús Montenegro and María Villegas (January–February 1992).

55. Vado de Cedillos produces cotton and other natural fibers. It was established, as a co-op, in 1975 and has been affiliated with COMO since 1979.

56. CBG (Wide-Band Communications) is a maquila with some eight hundred workers (in 1978). It is a subsidiary of Sylvanna's CATV (cable TV) division. It has a history of poor working conditions, including a number of incidents in which workers were exposed to toxic chemicals and fumes. One such incident resulted in the hospitalization of workers and a number of fetal miscarriages.

57. INFONAVIT, Institute for the National Promotion of Workers' Housing.

58. Field journal entry, 23 March 1983.

59. Field journal entry, 23 March 1983.

60. This opposition between working-class self-valorization and capitalist valorization is outlined in Negri 1984.

6. MEXICAN THINKWORK

I use the title for this chapter with apologies to Mike Hales, author of the 1980 book *Living Thinkwork: Where Do Labour Processes Come From?*

1. Kondo 1990: 300.

2. See Braverman 1974.

3. Braverman 1974: 131.

4. For arguments on "deskilling" and "reskilling," see Noble 1979, 1984.

5. For a classic Marxian argument on deskilling, alienation, and powerlessness, see Blauner, who notes:

> The automobile worker has very little control over the technological environment in which he works. The assembly line's inexorable control over the pace and rhythm of work is most critical; it is largely responsible for the high degree of pressure, the inability to control the quantity of work, and the lack of freedom of movement. The extreme rationalization of work organization results in the lack of freedom to determine the techniques of work. (1964: 106)

See also Monthly Review Press 1976, Hales 1980. Much of the sociological discourse is mired in a pointless debate over "worker job satisfaction," an obvious neo-Parsonian euphemism for the absence or presence of worker estrangement.

6. See Hales 1980.

7. Elger 1982: 52. See also Littler 1982: 27–34.

8. See, for example, Beechey 1982, Crompton and Reid 1982.

9. Gordon, Edwards, and Reich 1982.

10. See, for example, Lee 1982, Manwaring and Wood 1984, Juravich 1985.

11. Hales (1980) argues that modern labor processes are completely "precon-ceptualized." The "dead labor" of design engineers dictates the terms and condi-tions of the manual workers' "living labor" processes. I read this as neo-Marxist shorthand for the old Taylorist formula that calls for the absolute separation of planning from execution. Hales apparently does not envision how workers "punch" through the permeable boundary separating mental and manual labor.

12. See Harper 1987 for a fascinating rural case study that focuses on the concept of working knowledge and relates skill to social, cultural, and local con-text. Harper argues that working knowledge, in interaction with community discourses, can affect the evolution of skill over time, creating conditions that allow for the survival of older forms of craft knowledge despite the predomi-nance of Taylorist and Fordist regimes in the surrounding urban areas.

13. For a relevant discussion of science as socially produced knowledge, see Longino 1990, especially chapters 9 and 10.

14. Burawoy (1979, 1984) argues for the "imported consciousness" of work-ers by describing its role in obscuring, securing, or subverting the manufacture of consent on the shop floor.

15. Aronowitz (1978) developed the concept of workplace oppositional cultures.

16. See Watson (1971), who first used the term "counterplanning on the shop floor" to refer to workers' knowledge and practice of sabotage.

17. See Cooley 1980 for an important argument on technology, deskilling, and the political disempowering of labor.

18. For an extended discussion of technical versus political divisions of labor, consult Peña and Cárdenas 1988.

19. The most significant study in this regard is the trailblazing research by Kondo (1990) on power, gender, and discourses of identity in the Japanese workplace. See also, of course, Foucault 1977, 1980.

20. See the relevant commentary in Harding 1991, especially chapters 8, 9, and 11.

21. Marx certainly anticipated the use of skill as a political division of the working class (i.e., as a "divide and conquer" strategy). He included divisions of skill in a historical analysis of the political composition of the working class in England. See especially the chapters on the struggle for a normal working day and the rise of large-scale industry in volume 1 of *Capital.* See also chapter 2 of this volume.

22. Foucault 1980.

23. On site ethnography as a methodology for the study of site-specific power relations, see Dorst 1989. See also Rodríguez, who makes the following relevant observation:

> I want to propose, therefore, that not only should informants *not* be disposed of in intensive Site ethnography, they should be investigated as potential sources of counterhegemonic resistance, as well as living, breathing loci of commodified—

or "commodifying"—subjectivity. In other words, one would expect at least some informants to embody contests between hegemonic and potentially counterhege-monic discourses. Such individuals become walking battlefields—as they become agents, enemies, cynics, beneficiaries, casualties, or dupes of the process of . . . Site reconstruction. (1990: 553)

See also Peña 1992b, which provides a site ethnography of the enclosure of common property resources in the Upper Rio Grande (the Sangre de Cristo land grant in southern Colorado's San Luis Valley).

24. See Burawoy 1979.

25. For a useful elaboration of this point, see Eagleton 1991.

26. For theoretical views of discourse and power that informed my own approach, see Foucault 1980; Kondo 1990: 33–53.

27. Kondo 1990: 43–44.

28. See Rosaldo 1989, Kondo 1990.

29. See Ford 1922, Sward 1948, Hounshell 1985. Also cf. Littler 1982, Sabel 1982.

30. This is not unlike the conflating of intelligence with IQ scores, which proponents of "scientific racism" have touted for too long. See Gould 1981.

31. I appreciate Rubén Martínez's suggestions on efficiency cults and occupational differentiation.

32. Haraway (1991) provides a relevant critical discussion of feminist "standpoint epistemologies" and argues for locating truth claims about knowledge in the multiple identities of "cyborgs"—a wonderfully appropriate metaphor for the fragmented nature of third-world women workers' identity politics in multicultural, transnational sites such as the maquiladoras along the U.S.–Mexico border. For further discussion of "poststructural feminist" theories, see Butler and Scott 1992.

33. I place "consciousness" in quotation marks because I do not agree with Burawoy that this is an effective, nonessentialist way of expressing the dynamics of working knowledge. I prefer to focus on "identity constructions" that are understood to be both "imported" and "emergent" features of workplace lived experiences. I believe this avoids some of the more static aspects of such a concept as "consciousness." See Burawoy 1979, 1984. Cf. Eagleton 1991, Haraway 1991.

34. Exceptions would include Juravich 1985, Harper 1987, and Kondo 1992, although the latter two are not directly concerned with the deskilling debate.

35. That is, an epistemological (and ontological) debate. See Peña 1989a.

36. Harding 1991: 235, 241 ff. Also cf. Goonatilake 1985, Shiva 1988.

37. This is not to argue that workers are just as reductionist as managers, engineers, or scientists. But scientific knowledge is not produced only by means of discursive practices that are grounded in reductionist epistemologies. Science can also be thought of as generated in an interactive manner, through the use of forms of rationality that are not ethically or metaphysically grounded in an obsession with the pursuit of control and command objectives—a problem that is

characteristic of Cartesian epistemologies. In nonreductionist forms of knowledge, the logic of control and command objectives is replaced by a preference for nondualistic, complementary, and holistic interaction. This is what Shiva (1988) calls "ethnoscience." Instead of the Cartesian dualism undergirding reductionist empiricism, the epistemology of ethnoscience calls for local, situated, mutable, and interconnected knowledge. This is the traditional-standpoint epistemology of ethnoscience, and it embraces an understanding of human knowledge as deriving from lived experiences that are ecologically and culturally grounded. While reductionism seeks universal truths, ethnoscience embraces local truths. Ethnoscience is thus interactive "emic" knowledge produced by people through lived experiences and is distinct from the "etic" narratives articulated by experts in lab white. Ethnoscience involves a "decentered knowing subject." This implies the "disappearance" of control and command imperatives as ethical or metaphysical foundations of human knowledge. See Shiva 1988; Haraway 1989, 1991; Harding 1991; Peña 1992a. For an interesting perspective on the articulation of reductionist and nonreductionist scientific logic, see Cini 1992.

38. Valdés de Villalva 1989: 5–6 (my translation).

39. For example, Fernández-Kelly 1980, 1983b; Van Waas 1981; Carrillo 1980, 1985; Carrillo and Hernández 1982, 1985; Peña 1983.

40. Carrillo and Hernández 1982.

41. For example, Bustamante 1975; Fernández 1977; König 1979; Carrillo and Hernández 1982, 1985.

42. For example, Peña 1980, 1983; Peña and Cárdenas 1988; Carrillo 1985; Carrillo and Hernández 1985; Fernández-Kelly 1983b. For criticism of this research, see Stoddard 1987. See also the useful commentary in Sklair 1994.

43. Carrillo 1980: 44–45.

44. Carrillo 1980: 45. For a critique of this perspective, see Stoddard 1987. For an extremely useful commentary, please see Sklair 1994: 173, 174–175, 209, 215, 217–218.

45. Carrillo 1980: 45 (my translation).

46. Carrillo 1980: 46–47.

47. Carrillo 1980: 47–48 (my translation).

48. See Centro de Orientación 1984; Peña 1983, 1984, 1985; Valdés de Villalva 1989.

49. Centro de Orientación 1984. See also Valdés de Villalva 1985.

50. Peña 1983: chap. 6; Peña 1984; Peña 1985.

51. For the original data, see Peña 1983: tables 6.57–6.60; Peña 1985.

52. See Centro de Orientación 1984: 46–65. The COMO monograph includes fourteen pages of drawings sketched by workers to describe their innovations. See also Valdés de Villalva 1989.

53. These are just a few of the modifications and inventions documented in oral histories that I collected from workers face to face in Juárez and by tele-

phone during 1981–84, 1985–86, and 1989–92. Some published examples can be found in Centro de Orientación 1984; Peña 1984, 1985; Valdés de Villalva 1989.

54. This turned out to be important to Zamora's work group because the promotion provided her with greater physical mobility in comparison to the majority of workers, who were positioned in stationary jobs on the conveyor belts. Zamora was free to roam the plant, and she used this privilege to learn more about the layout of the plant as a whole and about the various production systems and their interfaces. Such site-specific knowledge figured prominently in subsequent informal group struggles in her area of the plant.

55. This fact was verified by the plant manager at RCA–Juárez during a plant visit I conducted in the winter of 1982.

56. One of my informants, a male engineering technician, stated that over half of the engineering staff in Juárez maquilas are students, while another one fourth are uncertified graduates (*pasantes*).

57. This is similar to a tactic described by Roy (1952a, 1952b, 1954) and Burawoy (1979). In the case Roy describes, the hidden units were called "kitty." See also Peña 1983: 113–117.

58. For further evidence, see Peña 1984, 1985; Centro de Orientación 1984.

59. See chapters 3 and 4 of this volume. See also Centro de Orientación 1984: 49.

60. Centro de Orientación 1984: 24–26 (my translation).

61. Centro de Orientación 1984: 30 (my translation).

62. For relevant commentary, see Roseneau (1992), who makes a distinction between "skeptical" and "affirmative" postmodernists. The skeptical postmodernists reject truth, abolish the knowing subject, and so eschew agency. The affirmative postmodernists reject "universal" truth (i.e., "master" narratives, single true stories) and embrace "local," "situated" truth (i.e., local knowledge). They decenter the subject while remaining committed to the possibility of agency, but only within fields of discursive practices, which they see as constituting an important part of shifting, multiple locations and subjectivities. In this sense, I would place myself and Juana Ortega in the affirmative postmodern camp.

63. *El Paso Times* 1983: 1-G.

64. The garment industry has remained particularly susceptible to seasonal fluctuations in market demand, with the bulk of sales concentrated around the new spring and fall fashion seasons. The *peso* devaluations may have had an adverse impact on the garment-industry maquilas, since many of their products were sold in retail outlets on the U.S. side of the border, often to maquila workers. The case of consumer-electronics maquilas merits more careful scrutiny. Some of the plant managers I interviewed blamed the layoffs and furloughs on the U.S. recession, but this seems unlikely given the steady growth of consumer-electronics sales in the United States at the time. It seems more likely that the period was one in which temporary closings, layoffs, and furloughs were a prelude to major technological rationalizations in the plants (see chapter 8 of this volume).

65. Among the plants implementing layoffs, staggered workshifts, and two-week furloughs were RCA, Subsensambles Electrónicos (SESA), General Electric, Electrocomponentes, General Instruments, Spectronics, TDK, and Allen Bradley. See *El Diario de Juárez* 1982. During the period between January and March 1982, close to five thousand Juárez maquila workers were affected by the layoffs, furloughs, and staggered workshifts.

66. Van Waas 1981. See also Peña 1983: chap. 2.

67. Van Waas (1981) and de la Rosa (1982) made the earliest attempts to examine the link between historic fluctuations in wage levels and productivity in the maquilas. See the important discussion of Van Waas and the wage issue in Sklair 1994: 37–41.

68. Compare this with the hourly wage data reported in South for 1980–89 (1990: table 2). According to South, in 1980 "hourly compensation costs" were $1.42, and in 1987 the figure was pegged at $.84 (1990: 554). Comparable hourly wages for U.S. manufacturing workers were $9.84 in 1980 and $13.46 in 1987. South also notes that on January 1, 1989, the minimum wage in Mexico was 8,640 *pesos* per day ($3.75 per day at an exchange rate of 2,300 *pesos* to the dollar). See also Hayes 1987 for data indicating an hourly wage of $.60 after the *peso* devaluations through the end of 1987.

69. See Demac and Mattera 1975. See also Sprouse 1992.

70. Peña 1980 offers an early analysis of the relationship between workers' struggles in the U.S. textile and consumer-electronics sectors and the incidence of plant closings and relocations to the border.

71. See Centro de Orientación 1984: diagrams 1–3.

7. MARGINALITY AS INVENTIVE FORCE

1. As quoted in Marx, *Capital,* volume 1. The original French reads:

Mal vêtus, logés dans des trous
Sous les combles, dans les décombres
Nous vivons avec les hiboux
Et les larrons, amis des ombres.

2. Robles 1984: 1 (my translation).

3. This translates to English as "Cooperative Society of Material Selectors."

4. One of the few published studies of SOCOSEMA is Magee 1983.

5. See Collins 1975.

6. Images of the so-called black underclass are particularly frequent examples of this ideological perspective. For commentary, see Marable 1983.

7. For example, see Merton and Nisbet 1971, Gilder 1982. A more recent example of the "culture of poverty" redux argument is Harrison (1992), who declares:

There's nothing intrinsic or immutable about culture. It is transmitted and received. And it changes while genes do not. . . . [A cultural interpretation of ghetto conditions] is not blaming the victim, it is a way of understanding a grave problem that may contribute to the solution. (As quoted in Germani 1992: 7)

According to Harrison, the "erosion of U.S. values" (i.e., white, middle-class values) parallels underdevelopment, poverty, and marginal status. Harrison also argues that "some cultures are superior to others." In his book *Who Prospers? How Cultural Values Shape Economic and Political Success,* he targets blacks and Latinos for particular criticism as belonging to cultures that are corrupt, fatalistic, lacking a work ethic, nepotistic, and rigidly authoritarian. The same is the case with *all* Latin American cultures, which he views as backward and undeveloped.

8. This essay by Isabel Robles was the first to be published in the COMO series Folletos de Solidaridad Obrera (Labor Solidarity Monographs). The title of the monograph is *Para que no olvidemos: SOCOSEMA.* See Robles 1984. (My translation.)

9. See Collins 1975.

10. See Wolf 1982.

11. Park 1928. However, Park also believed that over time, through acculturation, groups of marginal people tended to break down, succumbing to the culture of the center. (I thank my colleague Robert Dunne for pointing this out to me.)

12. This is particularly true of the sociological literature on "deviance," as Margi Duncombe suggests (conversation with author, Colorado Springs, Colo., May 1990).

13. Again, Harrison 1992 exemplifies this continuing approach in the dominant discourse. See also Gilder 1982. For relevant critical commentary on racist discourse in the social sciences as an aspect of the sociopolitical construction of elite ideologies, see van Dijk 1993, Wetherell and Potter 1992.

14. Robles 1984: 10–11 (my translation).

15. Most of this section is based on field notes and interviews collected between 1981 and 1983 in Ciudad Juárez during the time I was conducting research for my doctoral dissertation on the struggles of women maquiladora workers. Additional interviews were collected in August 1989 and February 1992. The key informants included Guillermina Valdés de Villalva, María Villegas, Jesús "Chuy" Montenegro, Guadalupe Valles, Isabel Robles, and Luchi Villalva.

16. Magee 1983: 6.

17. Robles 1984: 1 (my translation).

18. According to Guillermina Valdés, six of every ten families were displaced *ejidatarios* (conversation with author, Ciudad Juárez, June 1983).

19. For a relevant study on the displacement of peasant communities as a consequence of environmental degradation and political and economic factors, see García, García, and Álvarez 1991. See also Wright 1984, 1990.

20. See Wright 1990, Calva 1988.

21. Of the five families I interviewed, all mentioned problems with droughts and soil erosion.

22. Magee 1983, Sociedad Cooperativa 1975.

23. See Valdés de Villalva and Villarreal Torres 1975.

24. Sociedad Cooperativa 1975: 1–2. Incorporation of SOCOSEMA was official on May 16, 1975.

25. Sociedad Cooperativa 1975: 4 (my translation).

26. Sociedad Cooperativa 1975: 4.

27. Sociedad Cooperativa 1975: 4.

28. CEBI Libertad was the outreach literacy school established by COMO under the guidance of Guillermina Valdés in order to provide educational services to the *pepenadores*. See chapter 5 of this volume.

29. Robles 1984: 11 (my translation).

30. Reproduced in Sociedad Cooperativa 1975.

31. Field journal notes, Ciudad Juárez, February 1992.

32. Robles 1984: 24 (my translation).

33. Cleaver 1987: 3.

34. After SOCOSEMA was organized, weekly income increased dramatically for everyone. A modest wage hierarchy remained in effect, although it was subject to changes over time. The lowest-paid workers averaged between 250 and 500 *pesos* weekly (about thirty workers were in this category in September 1975). The largest number of workers (close to ninety) earned between 1,000 and 1,500 *pesos* weekly, an increase of almost 1,000 percent over the pre-SOCOSEMA average of 136 *pesos*. See Sociedad Cooperativa 1975. By 1983, the *pepenadores'* wages had increased from $7 a week to over $25 a week (Magee 1983: 2).

35. See the "Organigrama General" in Sociedad Cooperativa 1975.

36. On intentional communities, see Bey 1992.

37. Field journal entry, Ciudad Juárez, August 1989.

38. See Gans 1962.

39. See Shiva 1988.

40. Magee 1983: 2.

41. See Centro de Orientación 1984.

42. See Centro de Orientación 1984 (my translation).

43. Quoted in Magee 1983: 9.

44. Densmore 1929: 86–87. See also Shiva 1988, Kidwell 1985, Peña 1992.

45. Compare the annual reports of Sociedad Cooperativa (1975, 1980, 1981, 1988, 1990).

46. Sociedad Cooperativa 1975: 25.

47. Guillermina Valdés, conversation with author, Ciudad Juárez, June 1984.

48. From a discussion with two members of the Santos family, Ciudad Juárez, August 1989.

49. See Schmink 1989: 139–162. See also Ortiz Monasterio, Mena, and Pa-

rada 1983. In chapter 6 of this volume, I also note that maquila workers developed small lines to recycle damaged components and wastes generated by assembly work in Juárez-area electronics plants.

50. Schmink, in a study of a waste-recycling cooperative in Mexico City (the SIRDO, Sistema Integrado para el Reciclo de Desperdicios Orgánicos, or Integrated System for the Recycling of Organic Wastes), makes a similar observation:

> SIRDO users also point out that the system has brought about more unity and communication among residents of the experimental block than had previously existed. Solidarity has been fostered by their everyday communal labor, their work on the commissions, and their weekly meetings. SIRDO and its related activities have greatly increased women's visibility within the community and their confidence in handling community affairs. While men continue to dominate formal decision-making positions in the community, women have increased their power through informal pressure groups, such as the water commission. . . . [T]he women . . . are emerging as a political force through their involvement with the SIRDO. (1989: 156)

51. During the 1980s, the most serious drug abuse problem among the adolescents of SOCOSEMA families was the inhalation of paint thinners and airplane glues.

52. For a more detailed discussion of the role of clergy in the SOCOSEMA struggle, see Magee 1983, Kopinak 1989.

53. For summaries and critiques of this literature, see Lomnitz 1977, Vélez-Ibáñez 1983.

54. Vélez-Ibáñez 1983, Shiva 1988.

55. A significant recent departure from this ethnocentric stance is the work of the world-system theorist Tom D. Hall. His study of the historical sociology of the Comanches in the Southwest is based on a dialectical model that focuses on the dynamics of resistance and integration in the periphery. Thus, groups at the margins are posited as significant social actors with the capacity to enact transformations in the process of sociohistorical change. See Hall 1989.

56. See Lomnitz 1977.

57. Lomnitz 1977: 212–213.

58. Lotringer and Marazzi 1980: 15. See also Philip Mattera 1985 for comparative views of the subeconomy in the United States, Western Europe, and Japan; March and Taqqu 1986 on third-world women and the "informal sector"; and Kurtz 1973 on the rotating credit association as an adaptation to urban poverty.

59. The world-system approach of Immanuel Wallerstein and his protégés is exemplary of this perspective.

60. For more on these questions, see Scott 1985, Shiva 1988, Guha and Spivak 1988. The eight case studies in Leonard 1989 provide further evidence of the organization and preservation of indigenous culture and knowledge among marginalized third-world women workers.

61. In my own sample of 226 maquila workers (interviewed between 1981 and 1983), over 65 percent reported participation in output-restriction struggles (*tortuguismo;* see chapter 4 of this volume). These struggles exist because the workers reject the speedup inherent in the Fordist organizational form that characterizes the maquiladoras. They are rejecting what they define as an irrational rate of productivity, which they rightly perceive as a threat to their health and autonomy.

62. Turner 1969: 105. Turner also argues that marginality reinforces *communitas.* For Turner, liminal entities (inventive marginals)

> are persons or principles that (1) fall in the interstices of social structure, (2) are on its margins, or (3) occupy the lowest rungs. . . . [C]ommunitas has an existential quality; it involves the whole man in his relation to other whole men. . . . [C]ommunitas . . . is the product of peculiarly human faculties, which include rationality, volition, and memory, and which develop with experience of life in society. (1969: 125–126)

63. Robles 1984: 26.

64. Robles 1984: 26. This saying also indicates a very different conceptualization of power as "power within" instead of the core definition of "power over." One might say that the lococentric (or *communitas*-based) ontology of the *pepenadores* reinforces a concept of power that is more diffuse and undifferentiated (all persons in the community have the power to think and therefore to invent).

65. I am grateful to Robert Dunne for this clarification of a key sociological perspective.

66. See, for example, Altieri 1987; Burger 1990; Caufield 1984; Cockburn and Hecht 1989; *Vanishing Forest* 1986; Linden 1991; Luhnow 1992; Maybury-Lewis 1992; McNeely 1990; Norberg-Hodge 1991; Peña 1992a, 1993a, 1998a, forthcoming; Posey 1983, 1987; Shiva 1988; Taylor 1990; Toledo 1987, 1992; Wright 1990.

67. Lomnitz 1977: 213. Posey eloquently describes the significance of the destruction of cultural diversity through the attack on tribal and other indigenous peoples:

> With the decimation of each indigenous group, the world loses thousands of years of accumulated knowledge of adaptation to tropical ecosystems. Such precious information is overlooked without the least consideration: the rapid pace of economic development cannot be halted long enough to take note of what it is about to destroy. Amerindian cultures offer a rich and untapped source of information on the natural resources of the Amazonian Basin. Transformation of this knowledge into modern technological know-how can open new perspectives for ecologically sound development in Amazonia. (1987: 13)

Newsweek (March 6, 1989) reported on the case of the rice farmers of Bali. Two U.S. scientists, the anthropologist Stephen Lansing and the ecologist James Kermer, learned that the ancient irrigation rites of Agama Tirtha ("the religion of the holy water") constitute integral parts of a holistic, ecologically sustainable system for rice cultivation. The Balinese ritual system was not only culturally appropriate, it was also more productive than the Western techniques that the Asian Development Bank sought to impose on the natives. See also Peña 1992a.

8. MEXICO IN THE FAST LANE?

A special debt of gratitude is owed Mary Dodge, who prepared the survey research results for this chapter.

1. As cited in Dohse, Jürgens, and Malsch 1985. See Shimizu 1977; Sugimori et al. 1977: 543–553.

2. Interview with Jaime de Arce, former repair technician and troubleshooter at RCA from 1983 to 1988, Ciudad Juárez, 9 July 1989. See Carrillo 1989c.

3. Sklair 1994. On Japanese investments in Mexico, see Unger 1989. On Japanese investments in the maquila industry, see Ocaranza and Kerber 1989. In a paper presented at the seminar "Mexamérica: Empleo, Migración y Movimientos Sociales en los Ochenta," Cristina Taddei Bringas provides data giving the name of the maquila company; the name of the parent company; the location; the number of workers, technicians, and administrative staff; the amount of investment capital; and the types of products involved. By November 1989, according to Taddei Bringas's data, there were fifty-two Japanese-owned maquilas (Taddei Bringas 1989).

4. See Carrillo 1989c. See also Baker 1991, Taddei Bringas 1989.

5. For a listing of the major environmental and public-health organizations active in the border region, see World Environment Center 1992.

6. See, for example, Cleary 1981; Jasís 1983; Carrillo and Jasís 1983, 1991; Venegas and Barrera 1985; Carrillo 1989b.

7. See Peña 1988, 1993c.

8. See, for example, Sánchez 1987, 1989a, 1990a, 1990b; Tomaso and Alm 1990.

9. For general overviews and sources, see Lewis, Kaltofen, and Ormsby 1991, Ortman 1992, Leonard and Christensen 1992. Sánchez (1989a, 1990a, 1990b) provides some of the most significant findings to date on the health and environmental risks associated with maquiladoras. See also Tomaso and Alm 1990.

10. See Rodríguez 1993, *Latinos and the Environment* 1993.

11. See, for example, Bullard 1993; Cavanagh et al. 1992; Grossman 1992; Peña 1993b, 1993c. Mander 1992 reproduces the "U.S. Citizens' Analysis of NAFTA: An Introduction," a document that includes joint analysis and criticism by representatives of the Sierra Club, UAW, Fair Trade Campaign, Institute for Policy Studies, National Lawyers Guild Free Trade Task Force, Greenpeace USA, Development Group for Alternative Policies, International Labor Rights Education and Research Fund, Economic Policy Institute, Institute for Agriculture and Trade Policy, and Public Citizen. In the case of the Citizens' Analysis group, conspicuous by their absence are representatives of the grassroots people-of-color

and multiethnic organizations that are at the heart of the environmental justice movement (for example, Southwest Organizing Project, Southwest Network for Environmental and Economic Justice, Labor-Community Strategy Center, Southern Labor Organizing Committee, Commission for Racial Justice, Earth Island Institute, National People of Color Environmental Leadership Summit, etc.).

12. On Mexican opposition to NAFTA, see Peña 1993b, 1993c. See also chapter 9 of this volume.

13. I never had an opportunity to pursue this matter further with Valdés, and I am still searching for that flash point that apparently led her to a profound, visionary insight. I suspect that she was referring to her experience with SOCOSEMA, which she viewed as an example of a development model that was based on respect for local cultural integrity and on an espousal of ecological awareness.

14. See also Peña 1983: chap. 3.

15. Fifty of the respondents were employed in Japanese and fifty in U.S. maquiladoras. Half of them were women and half were men. Half the respondents were in Tijuana and the other half in Juárez. In addition, oral histories of four of the survey participants were collected in July and August 1989 and August 1990, Ciudad Juárez.

16. See Peña 1983, 1984, 1986, 1987; Centro de Orientación 1984; Valdés de Villalva 1985, 1989.

17. *CAD* stands for "computer-aided design," *CAM* for "computer-aided manufacturing," and *CAE* for "computer-aided engineering." Expert systems are software programs used for diagnosis and other analytical processes.

18. Sklair 1994: 211–213.

19. Of course, for us the workers' inventive force, or working knowledge, retains the potential for generating emically grounded technological and scientific discursive practices and innovations. See chapter 6 of this volume.

20. The source of these phrases is an unidentified production engineer quoted in notes taken by a student of mine who attended a Tijuana seminar on CAD/CAM/CAE systems, organized by the American Chamber of Commerce of Mexico and a coalition of local trade associations, November 8–10, 1990. The student's interest in expert systems led to an independent study project at Colorado College that involved attendance at various seminars and conferences in Tijuana, Tucson, and Denver. The student plans to undertake field studies on this topic and prefers to remain anonymous since the research will involve a participant-observation project in a multinational assembly-line factory.

21. Grupo Bermúdez was established in the 1960s by one of the wealthiest and most influential Mexican families on the border. Antonio J. Bermúdez, the patriarch of the family, became a millionaire in the construction business and was involved in the development of the Programa Nacional Fronterizo (PRONAF) during the late 1950s and early 1960s. PRONAF sought to improve the appearance of the border cities by promoting infrastructure development and tourism in the border region. In 1966, the Bermúdez family established the Antonio J.

Bermúdez Industrial Park in Ciudad Juárez to promote the maquiladora industry. In 1967, RCA was among the first transnational corporations to establish a
maquila at the Bermúdez Industrial Park. See Martínez 1978: 103, 109, 132–136;
Sklair 1994: 110–114. Grupo Bermúdez also runs a research and information
clearinghouse that regularly publishes statistical data on the state of the maquila
industry. The data is intended primarily for the benefit of business executives.

22. Grupo Bermúdez 1989: 67.

23. Grupo Bermúdez 1991: table 6.0.2.b.

24. Grupo Bermúdez 1989: 73.

25. In Valdés's and my 1989–90 sample, fifteen workers identified "computerized production instruments" as familiar tools they work with.

26. See Wiener 1948, 1950. See also Cooley 1980, Hirschhorn 1984, Jones
1982. Norbert Wiener is considered the "father" of cybernetics. The concept of
the feedback loop is critical in cybernetic theory. The loop links humans with
the autonomously self-regulated processes of the system. An example of a "primitive" feedback loop is the automobile speedometer. The loop provides instantaneous information on the conditions and parameters of the cybernetic system
processes. Other examples include the water-level and pressure gauges and me-
ters in nuclear power plants.

27. Hirschhorn 1987. See also Peña 1993a.

28. For a critical analysis of TOPS, see Shaiken 1984: 190–216.

29. On the Ford Motor Company's MIS, see Shaiken 1984: 174–190.

30. See also Levidow 1981, Jones 1982, Solomonides and Levidow 1985. Levidow's case study of the Grunwick strike in England deflates common arguments that modern computer technology will eliminate "autocratic management
practices." As Levidow notes,

> At Grunwick the truly docile "dead labour" of modern science and technology
> joins with work discipline and management attitudes . . . to decompose the work-
> ing class as a class, politically fragmenting its collective relations of production into
> purely market relations among different[ly] [skilled] workforces, each subordinat-
> ing its internal production relations to market competition. (1981: 159–161)

31. Shaiken 1984: 174–178, 190–216.

32. Rodríguez 1993, *Latinos and the Environment* 1993.

33. Other studies suggest that even these attempts (the use of industrial and
social psychology) lead to transparent results. See, for example, Grenier 1988.
Workers are not so easily "indoctrinated" into identifying their life chances ("ca-
reers") or opportunities for the good life with company expectations and definitions. Witness, for example, Juana Ortega's view of her politics after she got over
"brainwashing." (See chapter 6 of this volume.)

34. See the relevant commentary by Kondo 1990: 45–46. For some interesting commentary on turnover in the maquilas, see Moffett (1984), who quotes
the complaint of a maquila manager: "They come and go so fast, you've got to
be hiring workers in pairs."

35. See Sklair (1994: 167–180) for an excellent discussion of the debate over the sexual division of labor in the maquilas. Also cf. Peña 1983: chap. 2; Peña and Cárdenas 1988; Ruiz and Tiano 1987; Stoddard 1987.

36. Sklair 1994: 167.

37. Instituto Nacional de Estadísticas 1991: table 2.

38. Grupo Bermúdez 1989: 71.

39. Peña and Cárdenas 1988: 95. See also Peña 1983; chapter 3 of this volume also discusses this data.

40. According to information gathered by COMO in 1990 and transmitted to me by Elena Alvarado.

41. Telephone survey conducted by me in October 1990.

42. The chi-square test (Pearson value) for "hazards × gender" is significant at the $p > .0005$ level with 2 df.

43. Actually, this probably depends on the sector. If we compare our findings with Carrillo's important contribution on occupational health hazards and industrial accidents in the maquilas (1989b), then we can extrapolate that the majority of endangered workers in the furniture-making, machine-tool, non-electrical equipment, and chemical sectors of the BIP are male. In contrast, women are probably in the majority among the workers at risk in the consumer-electronics, auto-parts (including electronics), and garment-assembly sectors.

44. See, for example, Nelson 1990, Hamilton 1990, Bagby 1990.

45. On differences in health-care utilization among Chicanos, see Estrada, Treviño, and Ray 1990, Marks, García, and Solís 1990.

46. Again, see the useful commentary by Sklair (1994: 167 ff.).

47. Finally, a fourth and highly unlikely possibility is that the original (1981–82) and the more recent (1989–90) samples were not representative of the population of maquila workers. I suspect this was not the case given the experience we had with the transference methodology at the Centro de Orientación de la Mujer Obrera during the early to mid 1980s.

48. See, for example, Braverman 1974, Levidow 1981. The reverse is also often the case when job positions are degraded and men are increasingly replaced with women. Davies (1982), for example, documents changes in the history of office work from 1870 through 1930, and concludes that prior to deskilling, clerical work was a predominantly male occupation.

49. See, for example, Besher 1987, *Business Japan* 1983, Flynn 1986, Golden 1987, Golden and Funabiki 1987, Hawkins 1987, Jacobson 1987, Otani 1987, Peterson and Yoshihara 1987, Rohter 1987.

50. See, for example, Golden 1987, Golden and Funabiki 1987, Rohter 1987. Kaoru Hayama of the Bank of Tokyo predicts that NAFTA will convert Mexico into one of the most important manufacturing bases for Japan. See *Uno Más Uno* 1992a.

51. Besher 1987: 31.

52. For example, Yazaki, a large transnational corporation headquartered in

Osaka, opened an electrical wire and cable assembly plant in Tijuana in 1983. In the Yazaki product line are wire-harness systems destined for use in the dashboards of Japanese automobiles assembled in Mexico and the United States. See *Business Japan* 1983. Additional information was gathered through a telephone interview with a Yazaki receptionist in San Ysidro, California, June 1990.

53. The Tariff Schedules of the United States (TSUS) provide for nearly tariff-free importation of products assembled abroad. There is only a nominal tariff on the "value added," which—in the case of maquila 806/807 imports—is an assessment based solely on the labor costs for assembling the imported products. (The term "806/807" refers to the Tariff Schedules' items 806 and 807, which detail the provisions allowing for duty-free imports.) For discussion, see Sklair 1994: 10–13.

54. Sklair 1994: 22 (n. 13). See also Bennett 1986.

55. Sklair 1994: 82.

56. Sklair 1994: 84.

57. United States and Foreign Commercial Service Office, Rochester, N.Y. Telephone interview, December 1992.

58. Kamata 1983: 191.

59. Dohse, Jürgens, and Malsch 1985: 116–117. See, for example, Cole 1971, Dore 1973, Crawcour 1977, Cole 1979, Hazama and Kaminski 1979, Vogel 1980, Ouchi 1982, Pascale and Athos 1981, Dore 1983. Contrast these with Dohse, Jürgens, and Malsch 1985, Kondo 1990.

60. Many American scholars argued that Japanese superiority in the market was due to special management systems, not to technological fixes. For example, Abernathy, Harbour, and Henn state:

> In fact, the Japanese are of the opinion that management is the key to productivity, and that until Detroit changes its management system, increased capital investment [technological restructuring] on the part of the American firms does not bother them. (1981: 44)

Cf. Dohse, Jürgens, and Malsch 1985.

61. They did so, in my opinion, as if quality circles and the use of group technologists were uniquely Japanese innovations. These practices were actually American managerial *conventions* championed during the late 1930s and 1940s at such assembly factories as the Western Electric Company's famed Hawthorne Works. See Roethlisberger and Dickson 1939. See also chapter 2 of this volume. For a recent critique of the quality-circles mania, see Parker 1985.

62. Littler 1982: 155–156.

63. See also Totsuka 1981.

64. The dorm system had roots in the early industrialization of Japan in the 1920s and was primarily designed to prevent women who worked in textile plants from escaping or being abducted. See Harada 1928; Mears 1976; Littler 1982: 148–151.

65. Compare Dohse, Jürgens, and Malsch 1985 with Kenney and Florida 1988.

374 *Notes to pages 270–280*

66. Dohse, Jürgens, and Malsch 1985: 141.

67. Kenney and Florida 1988: 145.

68. Kenney and Florida 1988: 145. The authors also view *fujitsuism* as similar to the "rise of innovation complexes, most notably California's Silicon Valley and Route 128 in the Boston area." These U.S. innovation complexes are also post-Fordist. For a similar view, see Sabel 1982, Piore and Sabel 1984.

69. Kenney and Florida 1988: 129–130.

70. Kenney and Florida 1988: 129–130.

71. Aglietta 1979, Blackburn, Coombs, and Green 1985.

72. See Shaiken 1984: 175. See also chapter 2 of this volume.

73. See chapter 2 of this volume. See also Shaiken 1984.

74. Shaiken 1984.

75. One report in the *Economist* makes the following point:

> The newest argument against maquiladoras is that they offer a back-door entry route into the American market for the Japanese. Japanese firms that assemble in maquiladoras still face tariffs; but because their products come from Mexico, they are not blocked by import quotas. (1989: 82)

See also Baker, who predicts growing investments in the maquilas by the Japanese, Taiwanese, South Koreans, and Chinese (1991: 43).

9. PROMISED LAND OR WASTELAND?

I am indebted to Kathy Kaylan of the Colorado College Southwest Studies Program for providing critical assistance in the library research for this chapter.

1. Grupo Bermúdez 1989: iv.

2. *El Nacional* 1992b. Citing INEGI data, this report also confirms that more than 84 percent of the maquilas are in the northern border region.

3. Cavanagh 1992: 8.

4. As quoted in Greider 1992: 32. For more on water pollution and other types of environmental degradation along the U.S.–Mexico border, see Eaton and Anderson 1987, LaFranchi 1987, *Time* 1986, Davis and Altamirano 1993, *International Environmental Reporter* 1991. For a general critique of state control of environmental policy in Mexico, see Barkin 1991b. On toxic wastes and environmental hazards in general, see Davis 1993.

5. Transboundary environmental problems along the U.S.–Mexico border date back at least to the turn of the century and the conflicts between the United States and Mexico over the adjudication and appropriation of water rights in the Upper Rio Grande Basin. The transboundary impacts of Mexican sewage have also long been a source of bilateral conflict and cooperation. See Barry and Sims 1994: 29–44.

6. Stoddard 1978.

7. See Rodríguez 1993. See also Adler and Annin 1992.

8. *Excélsior* 1992c.

9. As quoted by Gregoria Rodríguez. Telephone interview, 14 January 1993.

10. On the recent reorganization of Mexican environmental protection agencies and the evolution of their legal underpinnings, see Carmona Lara 1992, Mumme 1992a, Mumme and Nalven 1988. SEDESOL (Secretaría de Desarrollo Social) has a much wider sphere of operations and responsibilities than SEDUE (Ministry of Urban Development and Ecology), Mexico's earlier attempt to institutionalize environmental policies at the federal level. SEDESOL includes an Office of the Attorney General for Environmental Protection, which has the authority to prosecute violators of federal laws and regulations. I thank my colleague Leslie Sklair for bringing these changes to my attention.

11. *La Jornada* 1992a.

12. For an overview of GM operations in Mexico, see Ebersole 1992.

13. *La Jornada* 1992b.

14. As quoted in *El Nacional* 1992c (my translation).

15. *Mexico City News* 1992.

16. Oñate, attorney general for environmental protection, rebuked Rich, saying that "the SEDESOL inspectors were fully aware of Mexico's regulations and had taken 20 U.S. EPA training courses." See *Mexico City News* 1992.

17. For critical perspectives on transboundary environmental-management systems along the U.S.–Mexico border, see, for example, Conchello 1992, Selcraig 1992, Mander 1992, Texas Center for Policy 1992.

18. For important, critical commentary on the La Paz Agreement and related problems in transboundary environmental regulation, see Mumme 1988, 1992a, 1992b. The more recent transboundary environmental management plan is in the Environmental Protection Agency's *Environmental Plan for the Mexican–U.S. Border Area: First Stage, 1992–1994* (Environmental Protection Agency 1992).

19. Lewis, Kaltofen, and Ormsby 1991: 68. The La Paz treaty, officially known as the Border Environmental Cooperation Agreement (BECA), was signed by Presidents Reagan and de la Madrid in August 1983. For critical commentary, see Texas Center for Policy 1992, Solís 1993. See also Council on Scientific Affairs 1990: 3318. There were antecedents of bilateral environmental cooperation between the United States and Mexico. During the 1970s, the International Water and Boundary Commission (IWBC) established bilateral procedures to deal with "border sanitation." See Warner 1991: 245; Lloyd 1984: 215–227. See also Mumme's (1992a) extensive bibliography. One major criticism of BECA was its exclusion of local governments, nongovernmental organizations, and academic institutions from participation in the working-group structure of the agreement. See Mumme 1992a: 547.

20. Lewis, Kaltofen, and Ormsby 1991: 68.

21. Martínez de la Torre 1992: 2.

22. Council on Scientific Affairs 1990: 3319–3321; Warner 1991: 245.

23. The general law for the environment was published in the *Diario Oficial* of March 1, 1988. See *Ley General de Equilibrio Ecológico* 1988; Davis and Altamirano

1989: 1209; Ranger 1991. NEPA is the enabling legislation for the EPA and also establishes the foundational mandates and regulatory guidelines for the procedure of the environmental impact statement (EIS). The EIS, of course, is at the heart of environmental regulation in the United States, and a similar assessment process has been developed for Mexico (see Ranger 1991). For further discussion of NEPA, see Peña 1992a.

24. See Davis and Altamirano 1989: 1209.

25. Environmental Protection Agency 1992: 4.

26. See, for example, Cavanagh et al. 1992, Mander 1992.

27. See Old, Baker, and Walker 1992: 31.

28. Old, Baker, and Walker 1992: 31.

29. For a perspective on the problems posed by global hazardous-waste transfers, see Yakowitz 1989: 510–511. See also Center for Investigative Reporting 1990. On the specific case of the U.S.–Mexico border, see Sánchez 1990b.

30. See, for example, Baker 1992. See also Salinas-León (1993), who argues that only "trade liberalization" can protect the environment and portrays environmental opposition to NAFTA as consisting of just so many "green herrings." For a comprehensive critique of anti-environmental rhetoric, see Ehrlich and Ehrlich 1996.

31. See Peña 1993a.

32. See Peña and Gallegos 1993. On the environmental attitudes of Chicanos and the struggle against toxic wastes and industrial mining in southern Colorado, see Peña, Martínez, and McFarland 1993.

33. See Bullard 1993.

34. See Gouldner 1970, Peña 1989b.

35. See Peña 1992a.

36. Bullard 1993.

37. McNeeley 1990.

38. As Jeffrey A. McNeeley (chief conservation officer of the International Union for the Conservation of Nature and Natural Resources) states,

> Conservation is linked in the public mind with wildlife. But humans have occupied this planet very thoroughly for thousands of years. Instead, the Planet Earth consists of a number of more-or-less anthropogenic habitats, originally occupied by people who have developed cultural approaches to managing resources of their local ecosystems in a reasonably sustainable fashion. (1990: 1)

39. See McNeeley 1990. For an excellent critique of the wilderness conservation movement from a third-world perspective, see Guha 1989. See also Peña 1992a.

40. On the need for sustainable cities, see Munro and Holdgate 1992: chap. 12; United Nations Centre 1990. For useful case studies and perspectives in planning for sustainable cities, see Gordon 1990. For further commentary, see Bookchin 1990.

41. See Lovelock 1979, 1988, 1991.

42. See Peña 1992a, forthcoming.

43. See, for example, Herzog 1986, World Environment Center 1992.

44. One useful approach, although its focus is more general and does not deal directly with the U.S.–Mexico border region, is that of Odum 1971. Odum makes the intriguing argument that ecosystems theory allows us to view exchanges between humans and nature as "life-support systems and supplies." While I do not entirely agree with his approach, I believe it is a good step in the direction of a perspective that sublates the culture-nature dichotomy. My views have also been strongly influenced by the work of Merchant (1980, 1990), Shiva (1988), and Lovelock (1979, 1988, 1991).

45. I am drawing here on the pioneering work of Lovelock and Margulis, the principal proponents of the "Gaia" paradigm shift (Lovelock and Margulis 1973; Lovelock 1979, 1988, 1991). Lovelock summarizes this paradigm shift in the following way:

> We have since defined Gaia as a complex entity involving the Earth's biosphere, atmosphere, oceans, and soil; the totality constituting a feedback or cybernetic system which seeks an optimal physical and chemical environment for life on this planet. The maintenance of relatively constant conditions by active control may be conveniently described by the term "homeostasis." . . . If Gaia exists, the relationship between her and man, a dominant animal species living in the complex living system, and the possible shifting balance of power between them, are questions of obvious importance. (1979: 11–12)

46. This is a summary of principles I have gleaned from a reading of Leopold (1949), Lovelock (1979, 1988), Grumbine (1992), and many others. For an overview of the concept of ecology, see Dobson 1991: 1–3.

47. See Lovelock 1988, Grumbine 1992.

48. For a useful introduction to the field of environmental history, see Worster 1988. See also Blaikie and Brookfield 1987.

49. Shaffer 1981. See also Grumbine 1992: 32.

50. Leopold 1949.

51. See Grumbine 1992: 22–63.

52. For an initial annotated bibliography of studies dealing with the ecology and cultural ecology of the Rio Grande watershed, see Peña and McFarland 1989. On the life zones of the border region, see Gelbach 1991. Among the more useful syntheses of the environmental history of the upper Rio Grande is Van Ness 1987. See also deBuys 1985, Peña 1992a.

53. The Rio Grande Bioregions Project, Hulbert Center for Southwestern Studies, Colorado College.

54. Aldo Starker Leopold is not to be confused with Aldo Leopold of *Sand County Almanac* fame. Aldo Starker was born in 1919 and Aldo in 1887. See Leopold 1965.

55. Leopold 1965. In addition, I have consulted Álvarez and González 1987: 12, 58–59, 110, 159, 168, 179–182.

56. See Leopold 1965; Caufield 1984; Álvarez and González 1987; Rzedowski and Equihua 1987: 212–217. See also Embassy of Mexico 1992: 6. Mexico has twelve of the fourteen major ecosystems in the world.

57. The Texas Parks and Wildlife Service and the U.S. Fish and Wildlife Service have published some results from population and habitat studies for a few native and migrating species along the Rio Grande. It is a disappointment that the major published study on transboundary environmental problems along the border, Herzog 1990, does not address the impact of urban and industrial development on wildlife habitat and biodiversity. Two other major studies of environmental issues in the border region, Applegate and Bath 1974 and Bath 1986, do not focus on wildlife either. On the status of programs to protect biodiversity in the Texas-Mexican border region, see Texas Center for Policy 1993.

58. World Environment Center 1992: 144–145.

59. Álvarez and González 1987: 180.

60. For a critique of "Animal Damage Control" programs affecting eagles, coyotes, and mountain lions in Texas, New Mexico, and Mexico, see Schueler 1991.

61. U.S. Fish and Wildlife Service, Denver. Telephone interview, January 1993.

62. The *seno mexicano* is a subtropical gulf-coast bioregion originally composed of vast salt marshlands, tidal pool grasslands, and related riparian woodlands. It encompasses an area lying several hundred kilometers south and north from its geographic center at the mouth of the Río Bravo. Much of the bioregion north of the river's mouth, including the barrier islands along the Texas coast from Brownsville to Baffin Bay, has experienced considerable commercial, industrial, and residential development. The same is increasingly true of the bioregion south of the river all the way toward Tampico, where major port facilities and petrochemical complexes are located.

63. See also Ortiz Monasterio et al., who provide the following breakdown of endangered species in Mexico as a whole: mammals, 92 endangered species; birds, 155; reptiles, 11; amphibians, 48; fish, 52; and invertebrates, 21—for a total of 379 endangered species (1987: 284).

64. See also Schueler 1991: 230–266.

65. Víctor Nelson Cisneros, conversation with author, Colorado Springs, Colo., 19 January 1993. Mario Montaño provided me with the name *torito de la virgen* (which translates as "the Virgin's little bull").

66. Álvarez and González 1987: 180–182.

67. See Schueler 1991.

68. Although the Texas Parks and Wildlife Service has periodically published accounts of threatened and endangered species in the borderlands, the maquilas are never mentioned as a source of risks and uncertainty for the viability of these populations.

69. United States Fish and Wildlife Service, Denver. Telephone interview, January 1993.

70. The most celebrated example is *Canis lupus.*

71. I thank Patricio Sandoval for his suggestions on these issues. The controversy stems from a debate between those who remain skeptical of the idea of the "biological corridor" as a tool for linking habitat "islands" to increase the viabil-

ity of isolated wildlife populations. Given the fragmented nature of wildlife habitat in today's highly anthropogenic landscapes, many propose using these corridors to increase the opportunities for species' genetic and demographic diversity. But critics argue that such corridors are a bad idea, since most would not meet the criteria of "edginess" needed to protect isolated populations from stochastic disturbances due to encroachment by other competing species or pathogenic habitat conditions imported from other ecotopes. See Grumbine 1992, Noss 1990, Lansky 1992, Hudson 1991.

72. See Hansen 1981, Ranfla González 1989.

73. See Sánchez 1987.

74. See Stoddard 1979. See also Metzner 1988, Mumme 1988.

75. On Elephant Butte, see Dunbar 1983: 142–145, 192–193. See also Stoddard 1979.

76. On problems and conflicts related to salinity in the Lower Colorado River, see Moberly 1964; Oyarzabal-Tamargo 1976; Reisner 1990: 44, 58–59, 77, 79, 127–128; Stoddard 1979; Getches 1992.

77. See Stoddard 1979.

78. On the main drainage canal in Mexico City, see Ortiz Monasterio et al. 1987. The drainage canal is so contaminated with industrial wastes that it has on occasion burst into flames, leading to the adage "In Mexico, the rivers burn." See also Peña 1988.

79. Lewis, Kaltofen, and Ormsby 1991: 69–70. The New River is part of a watershed that drains out of Mexico northward across the border into the United States, where it empties into the Salton Sea in southern California. The pollution has caused massive fish and bird kills in the Salton Sea Wildlife Sanctuary. This is part of a more generalized problem in Mexico involving the toxic contamination of rivers and other watershed systems by industrial activities. Contamination in Mexico is in some watersheds so extreme that riparian ecosystems and water courses in them are rendered biologically dead. Ortiz Monasterio et al. provide startling evidence of the magnitude of this problem. They report on the twenty most contaminated rivers in Mexico. The Río Bravo (Rio Grande) is among them and is listed as contaminated by wastes from cellulose and paper mills, cannery and other food-processing industries, textile operations, mining, and carbon-production facilities (see Ortiz Monasterio et al. 1987: 278–279). Ninety-eight percent of all the rivers in the state of Mexico are classified as biologically dead (with the exception of certain microorganisms such as viruses and bacteria). See also Peña 1988.

80. I base these estimates on data provided by Goldman 1990 and World Environment Center 1992.

81. Lewis, Kaltofen, and Ormsby 1991: 69.

82. There are some documented cases of nitrate pollution of groundwater aquifers in South Texas, Big Bend, southern California, and other regions. See Committee on the Role of Alternative Farming 1989: 98–119.

83. See also Tolan 1990. Tolan used independent lab analysts to verify the presence of toxic chemicals commonly used in the maquilas in samples taken from water courses and drainages in the area of the Nogales Industrial Park on the Arizona-Sonora border (1990: 31, 40). Tolan quotes Enrique Medina, an environmental scientist with Industrial Ecology International of San Diego, as stating that the lab analysis "definitely indicates an illegal handling of volatile chemicals" by the maquilas (1990: 40). For a broader perspective on the destruction of groundwater aquifers in the Southwest, see Bowden 1977. For detailed discussions of problems and strategies in groundwater protection, see Jorgensen 1989.

84. Goldman 1990: 256–257.

85. Goldman calculates the mortality rates due to acutely hazardous exposures. In Texas, Cameron County has a rate of 20 male minority deaths per 100,000 and Presidio County a rate of 380 female minority deaths per 100,000 (1990: 149–150).

86. See Chow 1964. For more on "perilous plumes" (migrating toxic wastes in groundwater), see Stewart 1990: 35–48, 54–74, 171–184.

87. See Chow 1964 for an elaboration of the basic principles of hydrology relevant to any discussion of the potential and actual impacts of maquila toxic wastes on groundwater aquifers, recharge zones, and watershed microbasins. See also Jorgensen 1989: 230–247; Stewart 1990: 29–48, 129–145. For a useful discussion of the technological and scientific limits of environmental remediation and restoration, see Cohen and O'Connor 1990: 269–306.

88. Ortman 1992: 70–71.

89. Ramos 1989. For a general view of the problem of toxic-waste dumps in Latin America, see Benesch 1991, Center for Investigative Reporting 1990, Maguire and Brown 1986.

90. Stoddard 1979.

91. For related commentary from the perspective of rural environmental planning, see Sargent et al. 1991.

92. See Blaikie and Brookfield 1987, Field and Burch 1989, Sargent et al. 1991, Peña and Gallegos 1993.

93. For an early analysis of cybernetic production technologies, see Blauner's (1964) study of a petrochemical plant. On the Bhopal accident, which resulted in more than two thousand deaths and some one hundred thousand permanent injuries, see Weir 1987; Cohen and O'Connor 1990: 109, 135–137.

94. Gregoria Rodríguez. Telephone interview, 14 January 1993.

95. On the PEMEX disaster in San Juan Ixhuatepec, see Ortiz Monasterio et al. 1987: 290. In the United States, according to limited EPA data, there have been at least 6,928 accidents (as of 1985), resulting in 135 deaths, 1,500 injuries, and more than 200,000 evacuated residents. See Cohen and O'Connor 1990: 135.

96. My assessment is based on a reading of Mitchell's 1990–91 directory of maquiladoras.

97. See Hirschhorn for a description of chemical plants as the first cybernetic industry (1987: 41–47, 153) and for discussion of cybernetic-systems failure and human error (1987: 1–2, 12, 28, 31, 46–47, 71–73, 75–86, 150).

98. Domingo González, conversation with author, Albuquerque, January 1993.

99. Telephone interview, Ciudad Juárez, October 1983.

100. *The Legendary Toyota: A Global Partnership in Resource Management* (no date or publisher provided).

101. See Shaiken 1982.

102. INEGI figures as reported in Elizalde 1992. See also Baker, Vogel, and Bard 1988: 102.

103. I have extrapolated these figures from Kamel 1990 and the TSUS 806/807 data reported in Sklair 1989. Thus, the estimate is likely conservative because it includes only the top ten countries that export assembled products to the United States under the existing tariff regime.

104. See, for example, Carrillo 1984, 1989b; Carrillo and Jasís 1983, 1991. See also Cleary 1981, Jasís 1983, Venegas and Barrera 1985, Álvarez and Mungaray 1986. The pioneering study of occupational health hazards in Mexico as a whole is Laurell and Márquez 1983.

105. Carrillo 1989b: 279. During the same period, the national average increased by only 39.6 percent.

106. However, as Carrillo notes, the Mexican federal government only recently (in 1976) began systematically collecting data on industrial accidents and occupational epidemiology. The IMSS (Mexican Social Security Institute), through the Sistema Nacional de Vigilancia Epidemiológica, is charged with maintaining statistics.

107. Carrillo 1989b: 318.

108. Carrillo 1989b: 318.

109. Carrillo 1989b: 310–311.

110. Solidev was at the heart of an intense labor struggle during the late 1970s and early 1980s. For more on the Solidev struggle, which focused on fighting toxics in the workplace, see Sindicato de Empleados de Industria 1979. See also Peña 1983: chap. 1. For a useful perspective on political and occupational hazards to worker health, see Diamond 1982.

111. Carrillo 1989b: 322 ff.

112. Carrillo 1989b: 327.

113. Carrillo 1989b: 329.

114. My only comment here is that the cases reported by Carrillo as "arthritis" may be more accurately diagnosed as complying with the symptomology of "carpal tunnel syndrome," an occupational illness involving injuries caused by repetitive hand and wrist motions. For further discussion of workplace toxins and other hazards (including carpal tunnel syndrome), see Goldman 1990: 216–228. Goldman lists two Texas border counties among the top fifty-nine nationwide in the rates of illegal occupational exposures involving workplace toxins:

El Paso County is ranked 19th on the list (at 60 per 1,000 workers) and Cameron County is ranked 59th (at 30 per 1,000) (1990: 225). I have not been able to locate comparable data for *municipios* on the Mexican side of the border.

115. These co-investigators are the maquila workers who assisted Guillermina Valdés and me with the construction of the survey interview schedules and oral-history instruments used in our participatory research projects during 1981–83 and 1989–90.

116. For further discussion, see Peña and Gettman 1986.

117. Interviews gathered outside RCA–Juárez, July–August 1989.

118. For a summary of this research, see Peña and Gettman 1986.

119. See also Sklair 1994: 105, 115 (n. 7).

120. For more on the nature and politics of occupational hazards in the maquilas, see Sklair 1994: 95, 115 (n. 7), 168, 209, 216; La Botz 1992: 166–168, 174, 178, 183. See also Cleary 1981, Jasís 1983, Venegas and Barrera 1985.

121. La Botz 1992: 27.

122. La Botz 1992: 21–25, 185. It should be further noted that these standards may not be adequate and may expose workers to high levels of risk even under conditions of compliance. Cf. Laurell and Márquez 1983.

123. This is exactly the argument that Guillermina Valdés made in our last interview, in 1989.

124. Greider 1992: 32–33.

125. For more information on environmental health problems in the U.S.–Mexico border region, see Cavanagh et al. 1992, Greider 1992, World Environmental Center 1992. On the environmental health problems posed by pesticides to farmworkers in an international context, see Perfecto 1990.

126. For further discussion, see Committee on Environmental Epidemiology 1991.

127. See Rodríguez 1993.

128. See Bullard 1989, 1993.

129. See Commission for Racial Justice 1987; Bullard 1990, 1993; Lee 1990, 1993a, 1993b; Russell 1989; Peña, Martínez, and McFarland 1993.

130. See, for example, Bullard 1990: 35–38; Commission for Racial Justice 1987; Goldman 1990: 281–318; Lapin and Hoffman 1981; Lee 1990: 22–25; Lee 1993a, 1993b; Mann 1990; Mann et al. 1991; Truax 1990: 19–21; U.S. General Accounting Office 1983.

131. Bullard 1992.

132. Brecher and Costello 1992: 122.

133. On the early UFW pesticide campaign, see Pulido 1996. On the recent campaign, see the video *The Wrath of Grapes.*

134. SWOP, led by Richard Moore and Jeane Gauna, wrote a letter addressed to the EPA director William Riley in June 1990. The letter charged the EPA with environmental racism in its enforcement and hiring practices; see *Dallas Morning News* 1992: 3-A; Suro 1993. A similar letter was sent to the "Big Ten" envi-

ronmental organizations (Audubon Society, Sierra Club, Wilderness Society, Nature Conservancy, Environmental Defense Fund, Greenpeace, Friends of the Earth, National Parks and Conservation Society, League of Conservation Voters, and Ducks Unlimited). For further discussion of the EPA enforcement controversy, see "Unequal Protection" 1992, Bullard 1993. The EPA responded to these pressures by establishing a task force to increase ethnic diversity within the agency and to assess questions of inequity in enforcement activities by the agency. In June 1992, the EPA published a two-volume report entitled *Environmental Equity: Reducing Risk for All Communities* (Environmental Equity Workgroup 1992). The report includes criticism and correspondence from SWOP and Dr. Robert Bullard; see also Environmental Protection Agency 1992, "United States, Mexico to Clean up Border" 1992. For further discussion of environmental racism, see Bullard 1990, 1993; Bryant and Mohai 1992; Bryant 1995; Hofrichter 1993; Petrikin 1995.

135. Bullard 1993 is an anthology of studies generated by participants in the first national summit. The proceedings of the summit are in Lee 1993b. For commentary on the summit and the white media response to the charges of environmental racism, see Grossman 1992: 28–35.

136. See Bullard 1992. The principles were adopted on October 27, 1991.

137. For further discussion, see Peña 1992a, 1998a.

138. Domingo González, conversation with author, Albuquerque, January 1993. See also Old, Baker, and Walker 1992: 31. This is a critical case to follow, not just because GM has a poor track record of keeping its pledges, but because this case involves the world's largest, most important transnational manufacturing corporation with maquila plants. And it involves a corporation that has recently been restructuring global operations by eliminating more than two hundred thousand jobs in several dozen U.S. permanent plant closures.

139. Domingo González, conversation with author, Albuquerque, January 1993.

140. See, for example, Contreras 1992: 16–17.

141. Mann et al. 1991.

142. For example, Dr. Carmen Rocco and Gregoria Rodríguez in Brownsville-Matamoros.

143. See Peña 1992a, Peña and Gallegos 1993.

144. The examples here are numerous and though not all of them are located strictly within the border region, most are actively pursuing research and advocacy activities related to the greater U.S. Southwest and northern Mexico bioregions. Among these are Ganados del Valle–Tierra Wools (Los Ojos, New Mexico); SWOP, WIN, and Tonantzin Land Institute (Albuquerque); Costilla County Committee for Environmental Soundness (San Luis, Colorado); and the Rio Grande Bioregions Project—a comprehensive watershed research and advocacy project that focuses on finding and developing agroecological alternatives for regenerative agriculture in the Rio Grande basin. The Bioregions

Project is a program of the Baca Projects Office, Hulbert Center for Southwestern Studies, Colorado College (in Colorado Springs). For discussion of the Ganados de Valle–Tierra Wool case, see Peña 1992a, Sargent et al. 1991, Pulido 1996. See also Peña forthcoming. On sustainable agroecological alternatives for the aridlands of the intermountain West, see Peña 1993a.

145. Levidow 1992: 117–118.

146. The World Bank has also taken a "fragmented, reductive approach toward 'mitigating' the destruction that it encourages" (Levidow 1992: 118–119).

147. Levidow 1992: 121–122. See also Rodd 1991.

148. Levidow 1992: 123. See also Peña 1992a.

149. For case studies in such local environmental organizing, see Bullard 1993.

150. SWOP has been a leading advocate of such changes in New Mexico; the Coalition for Justice and the Southwest Network have done the same in Texas and California. For relevant discussions of preventive and restorative approaches to environmental management, see Berger 1990, Sargent et al. 1991.

151. Domingo González, Sylvia Herrera, and Gregoria Rodríguez, conversation with author, Albuquerque, January 1993.

152. See the preamble and principle 1: affirming the sacredness of the earth, ecological unity and interdependence of all species, and the right to be free from ecological destruction; principle 2: affirming the right to ethical, balanced, and responsible uses of land and renewable resources in the interest of a sustainable planet for humans and other living things; and principle 3: opposing military occupation, repression, and exploitation of lands, peoples and cultures, and other life-forms. For perspectives on Chicano environmental ethics, see the collection of essays in Peña 1998b.

153. Levidow 1992: 123. See also Gismondi and Richardson 1991: 43–66; Edelstein 1988.

154. At the time of writing, this was difficult because the negotiations were cloaked in secrecy and the actual document is more than two thousand pages long; most of the text consists of obscurantist rhetoric that veils the underlying free-trade metaphysics of the document.

155. An executive summary published by the Mexican Ministry of Trade and Industrial Development (SECOFI, Secretaría de Comercio y Fomento Industrial) defines the objectives of the TLC:

> [to] eliminate trade barriers, promote conditions for fair competition, increase opportunities for investment, establish adequate protection for intellectual property rights, establish procedures for the application of the TLC and solutions for controversies, and promote trilateral, regional, and multilateral cooperation. (Secretaría de Comercio 1992: 1 [my translation])

156. These provisions deal with (1) rules of origin, (2) customs administration, (3) commodity import rules, (4) textiles and garments, (5) automotive products, (6) energy and basic petrochemicals, (7) agriculture, (8) sanitation and phytosanitation, (9) technical norms, (10) emergency measures, (11) anti-

dumping rules and compensatory rates, (12) public-sector purchases, (13) trans-boundary commercial services, (14) ground transport, (15) telecommunications, (16) investments, (17) competition, monopolies, and state enterprises, (18) financial services, (19) intellectual property rights, (20) temporary entry of business persons, (21) institutional procedures for dispute resolution, (22) administration and legal procedures, (23) exemptions, and (24) environmental rules and regulations. Mander 1992 notes that NAFTA is over two thousand pages long and filled with ambiguous "legalese."

157. What follows is a brief summary of those provisions with significant implications for the future of the maquilas, environmental protection, and labor rights in the border region. I will also consider the implications of NAFTA for indigenous nations and agricultural communities, since both of these are relevant to an understanding of sustainable alternatives anywhere within Mexico. Much of my summary of the NAFTA provisions is based on documents published by the Mexican Ministry of Trade and Industrial Development (SECOFI); see Secretaría de Comercio 1992. I have also drawn on the "U.S. Citizens' Analysis of NAFTA" as reported in Mander 1992, and on Cavanagh et al. 1992. Additional sources include a variety of articles published in Mexican and U.S. newspapers, journals, and magazines in 1991 and 1992. These are cited at appropriate points.

158. Secretaría de Comercio 1992: 1–2. NAFTA has a *de minimis* clause that requires that no more than 7 percent of the total value of the materials that go into producing a good originate outside the trading bloc.

159. Secretaría de Comercio 1992: 21.

160. Phytosanitation refers to the purity and cleanliness of food supplies, including fresh and processed fruits, vegetables, meats, poultry, and fish.

161. The supplemental agreement on environmental cooperation is outlined in U.S. Office of the Trade Representative 1992a. For commentary, see Bradsher 1992b.

162. U.S. Office of the Trade Representative 1992a: 2.

163. U.S. Office of the Trade Representative 1992b: 4.

164. Cuauhtemoc Cárdenas of the Partido de la Revolución Democrática (PRD) is among those who have made this criticism. See Cárdenas's inaugural address before the Twenty-Seventh Plenary of the National Council of the PRD (Cárdenas 1992).

165. See Muñoz Ríos 1992.

166. Muñoz Ríos 1992 (my translation).

167. Muñoz Ríos 1992 (my translation). For a critique of NAFTA as an anti-democratic treaty, see García 1992.

168. See Martínez de la Torre 1992.

169. Muñoz Ríos 1992.

170. Muñoz Ríos 1992.

171. For more on Mexico's environmental movement, see González 1979, 1985, 1992; Kurzinger-Wiemann 1990; Leff 1977, 1984, 1986, 1988, 1990, 1991;

Maihold and Meza 1989; Moguel and Velázquez 1991; Mumme and Nalven 1988; Mumme 1992b; Ortiz Monasterio et al. 1987; Quadri 1990; Wibo 1991. The Group of One Hundred, which includes such renowned scholars and authors as Carlos Fuentes, Carlos Monsiváis, and Octavio Paz, came into prominence through its leadership in the struggle against the Laguna Verde nuclear reactor in Veracruz. See McFarland 1992, Peña 1988. For an exhaustive listing of Mexican ecologists, environmental scientists, and research centers involved in Mexico's green movement, see González Jácome 1991.

172. See Leff 1986, 1988; Martínez de la Torre 1992; Alfie 1992.

173. For example, Martínez de la Torre 1992.

174. For example, Leff 1988.

175. For example, Mexican ecofeminists associated with the working-group project Triángulo Verde (Green Triangle) in Mexico City.

176. Grupo Fem has played a leading role in the campaign to confront violence against women in Mexico.

177. Lourdes Arizpe, Marta Lamas, Carmen Lugo, and Elena Poniatowska have been among the leading Mexican feminists advancing this critique.

178. For example, a conference held in Mexico City in November 1992 brought together indigenous peoples, environmentalists, and ethnobotanists for a discussion of the role of indigenous knowledge in building sustainable alternatives to biotechnology and corporate agribusiness. See Luhnow 1992. For more on biotechnology in Mexico, see Arroyo 1989. For biotechnology in other third-world countries, see Kloppenburg 1988. See also Allen and Sachs 1991. For a critical analysis of the "Green Revolution" in Mexico, see Wright 1984, 1990.

179. See, for example Posey 1983, 1987, 1992; Peña 1992a.

180. For more discussion, see Ortiz Monasterio et al. 1987, Peña 1988. There are numerous cases in Mexico of the displacement of indigenous populations by extractive industries, infrastructure, and even tourism. The Laguna Verde nuclear power plant in Veracruz, dams and reservoirs in the Río Usumacinta and Río Pánuco watersheds, and the Bajío de Huatulco tourism development all dislocated Indian and peasant communities. On Laguna Verde, see García Michel 1988, Arias and Barquera 1988, McFarland 1992. On the impacts of large-scale dams and tourism (resort) developments, see Peña 1988. The research on the displacement of indigenous nations is quite extensive. See the bibliographies in Wright 1990; Leff 1992; Toledo 1987, 1992; Madrid 1992.

181. Rojas 1992.

182. On the pork producers, see Pérez U. 1992b. In the case of small grain producers, I refer to research by Gustavo Esteva, author of *The Struggle for Rural Mexico* (Esteva 1983).

183. Barkin 1991: 33. See also Toledo et al. 1985; Calva 1988, 1992.

184. See Calva 1992.

185. Calva 1992: 64 (n. 40).

186. Ibarra 1992.

187. As quoted in Ibarra 1992 (my translation).

188. Ibarra 1992.

189. See Contreras 1992: 16–17.

190. See the executive summary in Mander 1992. The U.S. Citizens' Task Force includes representatives from Sierra Club, United Auto Workers (UAW), the Fair Trade Campaign (FTC), Institute for Policy Studies (IPS), National Lawyers Guild Free Trade Task Force, Greenpeace USA, Development Group for Alternative Policies, International Labor Rights Education and Research Fund, Economic Policy Institute, Institute for Agriculture and Trade Policy, and Public Citizen. See also Orme 1991: 10–19; Davidson 1991: 20; Gershman 1992; Cavanagh and Gershman 1992; Cavanagh et al. 1992.

191. Mander 1992: 2.

192. Mander 1992: 2.

193. Mander 1992: 2.

194. Mander 1992: 2, 6.

195. Mander 1992: 3.

196. Mander 1992: 3. See also Cavanagh et al. 1992. Bluestone and Harrison provided evidence of the unemployment effects of global industrial restructuring by U.S. corporations (Bluestone and Harrison 1980, Bluestone 1982).

197. Mander 1992: 3.

198. Mander 1992: 6. For example, the California environmental-protection laws are stricter than U.S. EPA statutes; likewise, Colorado mined-land reclamation standards are higher than U.S. federal standards under the Mining Act of 1872.

199. The CTF is careful to note that the final draft of NAFTA uses less explicitly "preemptive" language than the earlier draft of the agreement prepared during the Dallas round of the negotiations.

200. Mander 1992: 7.

201. Mander 1992: 8.

202. *La Jornada* 1992a.

203. Lomas 1992.

204. See Cockcroft 1983.

205. See Araujo et al. 1992: 39–48; Wright 1990.

206. Araujo et al. 1992.

207. There is a debate within Mexican intellectual and academic circles over the long-term consequences of *ejido* privatization. See Araujo et al. 1992.

208. On agribusiness in the Culiacán Valley, see Wright 1990.

209. Wright 1990: 229–230.

210. See Salinas's Fourth State of the Union Address in Salinas de Gortari 1992.

211. Wright 1990. See also Hobbelink 1992, Allen 1992, Altieri 1988.

212. See Calva 1992. See also Hobbelink 1992; Allen 1992; Peña 1993a, 1993c.

213. See *El Nacional* 1992b.

214. See *Uno Más Uno* 1992b: 13. There are eighteen major Mexican banks involved in reprivatization (with the new private investors and holding companies in parentheses): MMM (Probursa), Banpaís (Mexival), Cremi (Empresarios de Jalisco), Confía (Abaco), Banorie (Margen), Bancrecer (Roberto Alcántara), Banamex (Accival), Bancomer (Vamsa), BCH (Cabal), Serfin (Obsa), Comermex (Inverlat), Somex (Inverméxico), Banco del Atlántico (GBM), Promex (Finamex), Banoro (Grupo Estrategia Bursátil), Mercantil del Norte (Roberto González and Alberto Santos), Banco Internacional (ditto), and Banco del Centro (Prime Multiva). There are 130,000 individual investors involved in these transactions and more than forty trillion *pesos* in assets.

215. Cardoso 1992. The *paraestatal* scheduled for liquidation and privatization in this case is Puertos Mexicanos and the National Fund for Port Development. All these cases of privatization involve U.S. and Canadian investors. For example, I know that Colorado College owns several hundred thousand shares of common stock in Telmex (from information available to the All-College Committee on Socially Responsible Investments, on which I served).

216. On the new *ley forestal* (forestry law), see Ortega R. 1992: 26; Pérez U. and Camacho 1992. For criticism of the forestry law, see Pérez U. and Rojas 1992: 15; Sierra Valencia 1992; Toledo 1992: 2–3. A major proponent of this view is the Red de Organizaciones Forestales (ROF); see Pérez U. 1992a: 15. For the position of the PRD, see Pérez U. 1992c. On deforestation in Mexico, see Ortiz Monasterio et al. 1987, Vargas Márquez 1984.

217. On clandestine timbering operations in Mexico, see Pérez U. 1992a: 18; Lozano 1992.

218. See, for example, Toledo 1992: 1–3; Caballero 1992: 4; Carrillo Trueba 1992: 5–6; Scholtes 1992: 6; Posey 1992: 7; Madrid 1992; Allen 1992; Hobbelink 1992; Peña 1992a.

219. Nauman 1989: 15.

220. This was the position stated by the Bishop of Colón, Panama, on October 24, 1992 (Aponte and Román 1992). It is interesting to note that a new version of the Catholic litany treats greed, profiteering, and environmental destruction as mortal sins. At the Fourth Conference of the Latin American Episcopate (CELAM), the "Declaration of Santo Domingo" also criticizes neoliberalism as a source of increasing immiserization, marginality, and impoverishment of the masses, arguing that it is based on "a mentality and lifestyle that is consumerist and selfish" (*El Nacional* 1992a).

221. Leff 1992: 47 (my translation).

222. Leff 1992: 47 (my translation).

223. See Martínez de la Torre 1992. See also Leff 1992.

224. Mander 1992: 8.

225. Toledo 1992: 3. See also Toledo 1987, García, García, and Álvarez 1991, Linden 1991, Brown 1985, Caballero 1987.

226. Lotringer and Marazzi 1980.

227. Norberg-Hodge 1991: 183.

228. See Martínez de la Torre 1992, O'Connor 1991.

229. See Daly 1973, Daly and Townsend 1993.

230. The most comprehensive statement on steady-state economics is Daly 1973.

231. The scholarly discourse on sustainable development is quite vast. A good introduction to this literature would include Shiva 1988, Merchant 1990, Holmberg, Bass, and Timberlake 1991, Dover and Talbot 1987, Munro and Holdgate 1992, Poore 1989, Peña 1992a, Leff 1992. I am thankful to Joe Gallegos of the Costilla County Committee for Environmental Soundness in San Luis, Colorado, for his long conversations with me on the nature and prospects of sustainable development in the upper Rio Grande watershed. I also thank my colleagues Reyes García and Gwyn Kirk for extending to me the privilege of similar lengthy conversations.

232. See Lovelock 1976, 1989. See also Silver and DeFries 1990: 15–60; Earth System Sciences 1988.

233. Vandana Shiva (1988) is a major proponent of this view.

234. See Benería and Blank 1989.

235. For an exploratory approach, see Benería and Blank 1989, Development Alternatives for Women 1990. See also Miller 1991: 63–69.

236. I have derived most of these principles from my observations of SOCOSEMA operations. See also Daly and Townsend 1993.

237. See Argüelles et al. 1984.

238. See Benería and Blank 1989.

239. Shiva 1988.

240. Peña 1992a.

241. See Bowden 1977, Berry 1981. For relevant perspectives, see Norberg-Hodge 1991.

242. Posey 1992: 7 (my translation).

243. I thank Clay Jenkinson for bringing this to my attention. See Powell 1892.

244. See DeVall 1988, Sale 1985, Peña 1992a.

245. See Steward's (1955) *Theory of Culture Change.* See also Worster 1988: 299–302.

246. Worster 1988: 300.

247. See Peña 1993a, 1998a.

248. The concept of productivity in feminist ethnoscience is described in great detail by Shiva in her study of the Green Revolution in India and the struggles of women in land-based communities. Shiva defines productivity as

> built on the continued capacity for nature to renew its forests, fields, and rivers. These resource systems are intrinsically linked in life-producing and life-conserving cultures, and it is in managing the integrity of ecological cycles in forestry and agriculture that women's productivity has been most developed and evolved. . . .

"Productivity," "yield," and "economic value" are defined for nature and for women's work as *satisfying basic needs through an integrated ecosystem managed for multi-purpose utilisation.* Their meaning and measure is therefore entirely different from the meaning and measure employed in reductionist masculinist [science]. . . . [I]n reductionist [science] overall productivity is subordinated to . . . industrial and commercial biomass. (1988: 45, 64–65)

This is really a biogeochemical definition of productivity in which the energy circuits of the community of species in the ecosystem must be conserved to maintain homeostasis and secure long-term stability and viability of the life-support system. See Lovelock 1979, 1988.

249. For more on these questions, see Daly 1973.

250. Worster 1988: 302.

251. See Peña 1992a for further discussion.

252. Berry 1990: 153 ff.

253. There is a vast discourse on this issue of cultural differentiation in relation to the human interface with physical environments. See Maybury-Lewis 1992 for a good start. See also Mies 1987: 44–73; Peña 1992a. The work of Yi-Fu Tuan on "topophilia" has also influenced my view of cross-cultural environmental ethics. Tuan makes the following relevant observation:

The group, expressing and enforcing cultural standards of society, affects strongly the perception, attitude, and environmental value of its members. Culture can influence perception to the degree that people will see things that do not exist: it can cause group hallucination. Where sex roles are distinct, men and women adopt different values and perceive different aspects of the environment. The perception and environmental judgements of natives and visitors show little overlap because their experiences and purposes have little in common. . . . Attitude to environment changes as mastery over nature increases and the concept of beauty alters. . . . The world views of nonliterate and traditional societies differ significantly from those of modern men who have come under the influence . . . of science and technology. (1990: 246–247)

254. Peña 1992a: 86–88.

255. On the concept of reinhabitation, see Andruss et al. 1990: 100–129. For a Mexican perspective on bioregionalism, see Aguilar and Bozzano 1989.

256. Norberg-Hodge 1991: 191–192.

257. On the positive effects of workplace democracy and cooperative ownership, see Zwerdling 1980, Lindenfield and Rothschild-Witt 1982.

258. See Barry 1978.

259. As quoted in Orduña 1992.

260. Anzaldúa 1987.

References

Abernathy, William J., James E. Harbour, and Jay M. Henn. 1981. *Productivity and Comparative Cost Advantages: Some Estimates for Major Automotive Producers*. Report to the Department of Transportation. Cambridge, Mass.: Transportation Systems Center.

Acuña, Rodolfo. 1981. *Occupied America: A History of Chicanos*. 2d ed. New York: Harper & Row.

Adams, Richard. 1974. "Harnessing Technological Development." In *Rethinking Modernization: Anthropological Perspectives,* edited by John J. Poggie Jr. and Robert N. Lynch. Westport, Conn.: Greenwood Press.

Adler, Jerry, and Peter Annin. 1992. "A Life and Death Puzzle." *Newsweek,* 8 June.

Aglietta, Michel. 1979. *A Theory of Capitalist Regulation*. Translated by David Fernbach. London: New Left Books.

Aguilar, Margot, and Julia Bozzano, eds. 1989. *El bioregionalismo: Una propuesta de vida*. Mexico City: Editorial GEA.

Alfie, Miriam. 1992. "En busca de un desarrollo sustentable dentro del Tratado de Libre Comercio." *El Cotidiano* 8 (47): 76–81.

Allen, David. 1990. "Preventing Pollution." In *Fighting Toxics: A Manual for Protecting Your Family, Community, and Workplace,* edited by Gary Cohen and John O'Connor. Washington, D.C.: Island Press.

Allen, Patricia L. 1992. "La agricultura sostenible en la encrucijada." *Ecología Política* 4: 73–88.

Allen, Patricia L., and Carolyn E. Sachs. 1991. "The Social Side of Sustainability: Class, Gender, and Race." *Science as Culture* 2 (13): 4.

Altieri, Miguel A. 1987. *Agroecology: The Scientific Basis of Alternative Agriculture*. With contributions by Richard B. Norgaard, Susanna B. Hecht, John G. Farrell, and Matt Liebman. Boulder, Colo.: Westview Press.

Álvarez, Juan, and Alejandro Mungaray Lagarda. 1986. "Maquiladoras, política económica y medio ambiente en la frontera norte de México." In *Ecología y frontera,* edited by Juan Álvarez and Víctor M. Castillo. Tijuana: Universidad Autónoma de Baja California.

Álvarez Solórzano, Ticul, and Manuel González Escamilla. 1987. *Atlas cultural de México: Fauna*. Mexico City: Secretaría de Educación Pública and Grupo Editorial Planeta.

Anderson, Joan, and Martín de la Rosa. 1989. "Estrategias de sobreviviencia entre las familias pobres de la frontera." In *Memorias de fronteras iberoamericanas ayer y hoy.* Mexico City: Instituto Histórico, Universidad Nacional Autónoma de México y Universidad Autónoma de Baja California, Tijuana.

Andreas, Carol. 1985. *When Women Rebel: The Rise of Popular Feminism in Peru.* Westport, Conn.: Lawrence Hill.

Andrew, Ed. 1981. *Closing the Iron Cage: The Scientific Management of Work and Leisure.* Montreal: Black Rose Books.

Andruss, Van, Christopher Plant, Judith Plant, and Eleanor Wright, eds. 1990. *Home! A Bioregional Reader.* Philadelphia: New Society Publishers.

Anzaldúa, Gloria. 1987. *Borderlands/La Frontera: The New Mestiza.* San Francisco: Aunt Lute Books.

Aponte, David, and José Antonio Román. 1992. "El neoliberalismo: Una forma de colonialismo." *La Jornada,* 25 October.

Applegate, Howard G., and C. Richard Bath, eds. 1974. *Air Pollution along the United States–Mexican Border: The First Binational Symposium on Air Pollution Held on the Campus of the University of Texas at El Paso, September 27–28, 1973.* El Paso: Texas Western Press.

Aragonés C., Ana María. 1992. "Migración de trabajadores en el TLC." *Ciudades* no. 15: 15–19.

Araujo, Hugo Andrés, Roberto Cabral, Rolando Cordera, Diego Fernández de Cevallos, Gustavo Gordillo, Margarito Montes, and Luis Téllez. 1992. "¿Es o no es viable el campo mexicano? Un debate." *Nexos* 15 (179): 39–48.

Arenal, Sandra. 1986. *Sangre joven: Las maquiladoras por dentro.* Mexico City: Editorial Nuestro Tiempo.

Argüelles, Lourdes, Larry Hirschhorn, Devon G. Peña, and Gloria Romero. 1984. "A Guide to the Implementation of a Working-Class, Ethnic Women–Led Economic Conversion Project in Pomona, California." Unpublished manuscript. Institute for Policy Studies, Washington, D.C.

Argyris, Chris. 1964. *Integrating the Individual and the Organization.* New York: Wiley.

Arias, José, and Luis Barquera, eds. 1988. *¿Laguna Verde nuclear? !No, gracias!* Mexico City: Claves Latinoamericanas.

Arizpe, Lourdes. 1977. "Women in the Informal Labor Sector: The Case of Mexico City." *Signs* 3: 1 (autumn): 25–37.

Arnold, Horace, and Fay Faurote. 1972. *Ford Methods and the Ford Shops.* New York: Engineering Magazine Co., 1915. Reprint, New York: Arno Press.

Aronowitz, Stanley. 1978. "Marx, Braverman, and the Logic of Capital." *Insurgent Sociologist* 8: 2–3 (fall): 124–146.

Arroyo, Gonzalo, ed. 1989. *La biotecnología y el problema alimentario en México.* Mexico City: Plaza y Valdés Editores.

Arteaga, Arnulfo, and Jorge Carrillo. 1988. "Automóvil: Hacia la flexibilidad productiva." *El Cotidiano* 4 (21): 79–88.

Baerresen, Donald W. 1971. *The Border Industrialization Program of Mexico.* Lexington, Mass.: Heath-Lexington Books.

Bagby, Rachael L. 1990. "Daughters of Growing Things." In *Reweaving the World: The Emergence of Ecofeminism,* edited by Irene Diamond and Gloria Feman Orenstein. San Francisco: Sierra Club Books.

Bailey, Roy, and Mike Brake, eds. 1976. *Radical Social Work.* New York: Pantheon Books.

Baird, Peter, and Ed McCaughan. 1979. *Beyond the Border: Mexico and the U.S. Today.* New York: North American Congress on Latin America (NACLA).

Baker, C. Edwin. 1992. "Apostles of Modern-Day Environmentalism Worship at the Altar of Fatalism and Despair." *Rocky Mountain News,* 12 December.

Baker, George. 1991. "Mexican Labor Is Not Cheap." *Río Bravo Journal* no. 1 (fall): 7–26.

Baker, Stephen. 1991. "Assembly Lines Start Migrating from Asia to Mexico." *Business Week,* 1 July.

Baker, Stephen, Todd Vogel, and Adrienne Bard. 1988. "Will the New Maquiladoras Build a Better Mañana?" *Business Week,* 14 November.

Baldi, Guido. 1972. "Theses on the Mass Worker and Social Capital." *Radical America* 6 (1): 3–21.

Baritz, Loren. 1967. *Servants of Power: A History of the Use of Social Science in American Industry.* New York: Wiley.

Barkin, David. 1991a. "About Face." *NACLA Report on the Americas* 24 (6): 30–38.

———. 1991b. "State Control of the Environment: Politics and Degradation in Mexico." *Capitalism, Nature, Socialism* 2 (1): 86–108.

Barry, Tom. 1978 (August). "The Impossible Strike." *Nuestro* 2 (8): 23–25.

Barry, Tom, and Beth Sims. 1994. *The Challenge of Cross-Border Environmentalism: The U.S.–Mexico Case.* U.S.–Mexico Border Series, no. 1. Albuquerque: Resource Center Press.

Bartz, Diane K. 1989. "Trashing the Third World Is No Longer a Neat Trick." *In These Times,* 29 March–4 April.

Bath, C. Richard. 1986. "Environmental Issues in the United States–Mexico Borderlands." *Journal of Borderlands Studies* 1 (1): 49–72.

Beechey, Veronica. 1982. "The Sexual Division of Labour and the Labour Process: A Critical Assessment of Braverman." In *The Degradation of Work? Skill, Deskilling, and the Labour Process,* edited by Stephen Wood. London: Hutchinson.

Benería, Lourdes, and Rebecca Blank. 1989. "Women and the Economics of Military Spending." In *Rocking the Ship of State: Toward a Feminist Peace Politics,* edited by Adrienne Harris and Ynestra King. Boulder, Colo.: Westview Press.

Benesch, Susan. 1991. "Latin America: Toxic Waste Dump." *Rocky Mountain News,* 22 February.

Bennett, Douglas. 1986. "Regional Consequences of Industrial Policy: Mexico and the United States in a Changing World Auto Industry." In *Regional Impacts of U.S.–Mexican Relations,* edited by Ina Rosenthal-Urey. Monograph Series, no. 16. La Jolla: Center for U.S.–Mexican Studies, University of California, San Diego.

Berger, John J., ed. 1990. *Environmental Restoration: Science and Strategies for Restoring the Earth.* Washington, D.C.: Island Press.

Berry, Wendell. 1978. *The Unsettling of America: Culture and Agriculture.* San Francisco: Sierra Club Books.

——. 1981. *The Gift of Good Land: Further Essays, Cultural and Agricultural.* San Francisco: North Point Press.

——. 1990. *What Are People For? Essays.* San Francisco: North Point Press.

Besher, Alexander. 1987. "Japanese Manufacturers Setting up Shop in Mexico." *San Francisco Chronicle,* 3 August.

Bey, Hakim. 1992. *T.A.Z., the Temporary Autonomous Zone: Ontological Anarchy and Poetic Terrorism.* Brooklyn, N.Y.: Autonomedia.

Biehl, Janet. 1991. *Rethinking Ecofeminist Politics.* Boston: South End Press.

Blackburn, Phil, Rod Coombs, and Kenneth Green. 1985. *Technology, Economic Growth, and the Labour Process.* New York: St. Martin's Press.

Blaikie, Piers, and Harold Brookfield. 1987. *Land Degradation and Society.* London: Methuen.

Blauner, Robert. 1964. *Alienation and Freedom: The Factory Worker and His Industry.* Chicago: University of Chicago Press.

Bluestone, Barry. 1982. *The Deindustrialization of America: Plant Closings, Community Abandonment, and the Dismantling of Basic Industry.* New York: Basic Books.

Bluestone, Barry, and Bennett Harrison. 1980. *Capital and Communities: The Causes and Consequences of Private Disinvestment.* Washington, D.C.: Progressive Alliance.

Bock, Gisela, Paolo Carpignano, and Bruno Ramírez. 1976. *La formazione dell'operaio massa negli USA, 1898–1922.* Milan, Italy: Feltrinelli Editore.

Bookchin, Murray. 1990. *Remaking Society: Pathways to a Green Future.* Boston: South End Press.

Bowden, Charles. 1977. *Killing the Hidden Waters.* Austin: University of Texas Press.

Bozzano, J., and G. Maihold, eds. 1990. *Hacia una cultura ecológica.* Mexico City: Editorial CCYDEL-DDF-FES.

Bradsher, Keith. 1992a. "Global Issues Weigh on Town as Factory Heads to Mexico." *New York Times,* 1 September.

——. 1992b. "Side Agreements to Trade Accord Vary in Ambition: Unions Are Dissatisfied." *New York Times,* 18 September.

Braverman, Harry. 1974. *Labor and Monopoly Capital: The Degradation of Work in the Twentieth Century.* New York: Monthly Review Press.

Brecher, Jeremy. 1978. "Uncovering the Hidden History of the American Workplace." *Review of Radical Political Economics* 10 (4).

Brecher, Jeremy, and Tim Costello. 1992. "Global Village vs. Global Pillage: A One-World Strategy for Labor." In *Trading Freedom: How Free Trade Affects Our Lives, Work, and Environment,* edited by John Cavanagh, John Gershman, Karen Baker, and Gretchen Helmke. San Francisco: Institute for Food and Development Policy.

Brighton Labour Process Group. 1977. "The Capitalist Labour Process." *Capital and Class* no. 1 (spring): 3–26.

Brown, Cecil H. 1985. "Modes of Subsistence and Folk Biological Taxonomy." *Current Anthropology* 26 (1): 43–53.

Brown, F. Lee, and Helen M. Ingram. 1987. *Water and Poverty in the Southwest.* Tucson: University of Arizona Press.

Bryant, Bunyan, ed. 1995. *Environmental Justice: Issues, Policies, and Solutions.* Washington, D.C.: Island Press.

Bryant, Bunyan, and Paul Mohai, eds. 1992. *Race and the Incidence of Environmental Hazards: A Time for Discourse.* Boulder, Colo.: Westview Press.

Bullard, Robert. 1990. *Dumping in Dixie: Race, Class, and Environmental Quality.* Boulder, Colo.: Westview Press.

———. 1992. "Principles of Environmental Justice." In *People of Color Environmental Groups: Directory.* Riverside: Department of Sociology, University of California, Riverside.

———, ed. 1993. *Confronting Environmental Racism: Voices from the Grassroots.* Boston: South End Press.

Burawoy, Michael. 1979. *Manufacturing Consent: Changes in the Labor Process under Monopoly Capitalism.* Chicago: University of Chicago Press.

———. 1985. *The Politics of Production: Factory Regimes under Capitalism and Socialism.* London: Verso Books.

Burger, Julian, ed. 1990. *The Gaia Atlas of First Peoples.* New York: Anchor Books.

Business Japan. 1983 (August). "Yazaki Bridges Border for Joint U.S.–Mexican Production."

Bustamante, Jorge. 1975. "Maquiladoras: A New Face of International Capitalism on Mexico's Northern Frontier." Paper presented at the Seventh National Meeting of the Latin American Studies Association, March, Atlanta.

Butler, Judith, and Joan W. Scott, eds. 1992. *Feminists Theorize the Political.* New York: Routledge.

Caballero, Javier. 1992. "El Tercer Congreso Internacional de Etnobiología." *La Jornada del Campo* no. 9 (10 November).

Cabral, Luis, and Martín de la Rosa. 1980. *Empresa forestal comunal Santa Cruz Tanaco: Una empresa hacia la autogestión.* Mexico City: Taller de Impresiones Populares de SEPAC.

Calderón Salazar, Jorge A. 1992. *El TLC y el desarrollo rural.* Mexico City: Centro de Estudios del Movimiento Obrero y Socialista.

Calva, José Luis. 1988. *Crisis agrícola y alimentaria en México, 1982–1988.* Mexico City: Fontamara.

———. 1992. *Probables efectos de un tratado de libre comercio en el campo mexicano.* Mexico City: Fontamara.

Camarena, Porfirio. 1970. "The Runaways: Multinational Corporations of the Mexican Border." *American Federationist* 77 (November): 2–6.

Cárdenas, Cuauhtémoc. 1992. "Un rumbo estable para la nación: Democracia, honestidad, crecimiento, justicia." *La Jornada,* 16 November.

Cardoso, Víctor. 1992. "El proceso no tiene ni pies ni cabeza." *La Jornada,* 22 October.

Carey, Alex. 1967. "The Hawthorne Studies: A Radical Criticism." *American Sociological Review* 32 (2).

Carmona Lara, María del Carmen. 1992. "SEDESOL: Reestructuración de la autoridad ecológica." *Ecológicas: Sociedad y medio ambiente* 3 (2): 6–8.

Carrillo, Jorge. 1980. "La utilización de la mano de obra femenina en la industria maquiladora: El caso de Ciudad Juárez." Unpublished report. Centro de Estudios Sociológicos, Colegio de México, Mexico City.

———. 1983. "Crisis y sindicatos en la frontera norte." *Coyoacán* no. 16: 51–68.

———. 1984. "La frontera norte y el movimiento obrero en la industria maquiladora." Paper presented at the Reunión Estados Unidos y México: Conferencia en la Movilidad Internacional del Capital y Organización Binacional de Trabajadores, July, Mexico City.

———. 1985. *Conflictos laborales en la industria maquiladora.* Tijuana: Centro de Estudios Fronterizos del Norte de Mexico.

———. 1986. "Conflictos laborales en la industria maquiladora de exportación." *Comercio Exterior* 36 (1): 46–57.

———. 1989a. "La Ford en México: Reestructuración industrial y cambio en las relaciones sociales." Ph.D. diss., Centro de Estudios Sociológicos, Colegio de México.

———. 1989b. "Maquiladoras, industrialización fronteriza y riesgos de trabajo: El caso de Baja California." In *Reestructuración industrial: Maquiladoras en la frontera México–Estados Unidos,* edited by Jorge Carrillo. Mexico City: Consejo Nacional para la Cultura y las Artes and Colegio de la Frontera Norte.

———. 1989c. "Reestructuración en la industria automotriz en el norte de México: Impacto de la tecnología en las relaciones sociales." Paper presented at the annual meeting of the Association of Borderlands Scholars, April, Albuquerque.

———, ed. 1989d. *Reestructuración industrial: Maquiladoras en la frontera México–Estados Unidos.* Mexico City: Consejo Nacional para la Cultura y las Artes and Colegio de la Frontera Norte.

Carrillo, Jorge, and Alberto Hernández. 1982. "La mujer obrera en la industria maquiladora: El caso de Ciudad Juárez." Professional thesis, Facultad de Ciencias Políticas y Sociales, Universidad Nacional Autónoma de México.

———. 1985. *Mujeres fronterizas en la industria maquiladora.* Mexico City: Secretaría de Educación Pública and Colegio de la Frontera Norte.

Carrillo, Jorge, and Mónica Jasís. 1983. "La salud y la mujer obrera en las plantas maquiladoras: El caso de Tijuana." *Enfermería Hoy,* June.

———. 1991. "La salud de la mujer obrera en la industria maquiladora." In *Medio ambiente en la frontera México–Estados Unidos,* edited by Colegio de la Frontera Norte. Mexico City: Secretaría de Educación Pública and Colegio de la Frontera Norte.

Carrillo Trueba, César. 1992. "Memoria y saber: Una defensa del conocimiento campesino." *La Jornada del Campo* no. 9 (10 November).

Caufield, Catherine. 1984. *In the Rainforest.* Chicago: University of Chicago Press.

Cavanagh, John, and John Gershman. 1992. "Free Trade Fiasco." *Progressive,* February.

Cavanagh, John, John Gershman, Karen Baker, and Gretchen Helmke, eds. 1992. *Trading Freedom: How Free Trade Affects Our Lives, Work, and Environment.* San Francisco: Institute for Food and Development Policy.

Cavendish, Ruth. 1982. *Women on the Line.* London: Routledge & Kegan Paul.

Center for Investigative Reporting. 1990. *Global Dumping Ground: The International Traffic in Hazardous Waste.* Washington, D.C.: Seven Locks Press.

Centro de Estudios Históricos del Movimiento Obrero Mexicano. 1975. *Historia Obrera* 2: (5).

Centro de Investigación y Docencia Económica (CIDE). 1981. "Los límites del programa de industrialización fronteriza para el abatimiento de las tasas de desocupación y la calificación de la fuerza de trabajo." Unpublished report prepared for CIDE by José Luis Fernández and Bertha Elena de Buen. Mexico City.

Centro de Orientación de la Mujer Obrera (COMO). 1979. "Efectos del trabajo en las industrias de maquiladoras sobre la salud obrera." Unpublished report. Ciudad Juárez.

———. 1981. "Estudio económico y social de la industria maquiladora en Ciudad Juárez." Unpublished report. Ciudad Juárez.

———. 1982. "Propuesta para una investigación del aprendizaje industrial en las maquiladoras." Unpublished proposal. Ciudad Juárez.

———. 1984. *Primer taller de aprendizaje en la producción y transferencia de tecnología en la industria de maquila de exportación.* Ciudad Juárez: COMO and Fundación Friedrich Ebert.

———. 1989a. Conflictos laborales, 1985–1986. COMO newspaper archives. Ciudad Juárez.

———. 1989b. Conflictos laborales, 1987–1989. COMO newspaper archives. Ciudad Juárez.

Chane, George W. 1942. *Motion and Time Study.* Rochester Technical Series. New York: Harper & Brothers.

Chilcote, Ronald H., ed. 1977. Women and Class Struggle. Special issue. *Latin American Perspectives* 4 (1, 2).

Chomsky, Noam. 1992. "Rationality/Science." *Z Papers* 1 (4): 52–57.

Chow, Ven Te. 1964. *Handbook of Applied Hydrology: A Compendium of Water Resources Technology.* New York: McGraw-Hill.

Cini, Marcello. 1989. "Continuity and Discontinuity in the Definition of a Disciplinary Field: The Case of Twentieth Century Physics." In *Imre Lakatos and Theories of Scientific Change,* edited by Kostas Gavroglu, Yorgos Goudaroulis, and Pantelis Nicolacopoulos. Dordrecht, Netherlands: Kluwer.

Clawson, Dan. 1980. *Bureaucracy and the Labor Process: The Transformation of U.S. Industry, 1860–1920.* New York: Monthly Review Press.

Cleary, Amity. 1981. "A Comparative Analysis of Occupational Health and Safety Issues in the Electronics Industry: Silicon Valley, California, and Ciudad Juárez, Mexico." Senior thesis, University of California, Santa Cruz.

Cleaver, Harry. 1979. *Reading Capital Politically.* Austin: University of Texas Press.

———. 1987. "The Uses of an Earthquake: Tepito, Mexico." Unpublished manuscript. Department of Economics, University of Texas at Austin.

———. 1988. "Letter to George Rawick on the Argentine Gauchos." Unpublished manuscript. Department of Economics, University of Texas at Austin.

Cockburn, Alexander. 1989. "Trees, Cows, and Cocaine: An Interview with Susanna Hecht." *New Left Review* no. 173 (January–February): 33–46.

Cockburn, Alexander, and Susanna B. Hecht. 1989. *The Fate of the Forest: Developers, Destroyers, and Defenders of the Amazon.* London: Verso Books.

Cockcroft, James D. 1983. *Mexico: Class Formation, Capital Accumulation, and the State.* New York: Monthly Review Press.

Cohen, Gary, and John O'Connor, eds. 1990. *Fighting Toxics: A Manual for Protecting Your Family, Community, and Workplace.* Washington, D.C.: Island Press.

Cole, Robert E. 1971. *Japanese Blue Collar: The Changing Tradition.* Berkeley: University of California Press.

———. 1979. *Work, Mobility, and Participation: A Comparative Study of American and Japanese Industry.* Berkeley: University of California Press.

Collins, Randall. 1975. *Conflict Sociology: Toward an Explanatory Science.* New York: Academic Press.

Commission for Racial Justice. United Church of Christ. 1987. *Toxic Wastes and Race in the United States: A National Report on the Racial and Socioeconomic Characteristics of Communities with Hazardous Waste Sites.* New York: United Church of Christ.

Committee on Environmental Epidemiology. National Research Council. 1991. *Environmental Epidemiology: Public Health and Hazardous Wastes.* Washington, D.C.: National Academy Press.

Committee on the Role of Alternative Farming Methods in Modern Production Agriculture. Board of Agriculture. National Research Council. 1989. *Alternative Agriculture.* Washington, D.C.: National Academy Press.

Committee on Work in Industry. National Research Council. 1941. *Fatigue of Workers: Its Relation to Industrial Production.* Report prepared by George Homans. New York: Reinhold.

Conchello, José A. 1992. *El TLC: Un callejón sin salida.* Mexico City: Grijalbo.

Conference of Socialist Economists, ed. 1976. *The Labour Process and Class Strategies.* London: Stage One.

Contreras, Roberto. 1992. "NAFTA: Who Gains, Who Loses?" *Voces Unidas,* December.

Cooley, Mike. 1980. *Architect or Bee?: The Human/Technology Relationship.* Boston: South End Press.

Corcom, S.A. n.d. *Manual para empleados.* Ciudad Juárez: Corcom.

Coriat, Benjamin. 1982. *El taller y el cronómetro: Ensayo sobre el taylorismo, el fordismo y la producción en masa.* Mexico City: Siglo Veintiuno.

Corrigan, Paul, and Peter Leonard. 1978. *Social Work Practice under Capitalism: A Marxist Approach.* London: Macmillan.

Council on Scientific Affairs. 1990. "A Permanent U.S.–Mexico Border Environmental Health Commission." *Journal of the American Medical Association* 263 (24): 3319–3321.

Coyle, Laurie, Gail Hershatter, and Emily Honig. 1979. *Women at Farah: An Unfinished Story.* El Paso, Tex.: Reforma (El Paso chapter).

Crawcour, E. Sydney. 1977. *The Japanese Employment System: Past, Present, and Future.* Canberra: Australian National University.

Crompton, Rosemary, and Stuart Reid. 1982. "The Deskilling of Clerical Work." In *The Degradation of Work? Skill, Deskilling, and the Labour Process,* edited by Stephen Wood. London: Hutchinson.

Dale Electronics. 1983. *Newsletter,* March.

Dallas Morning News. 1992 (14 September). "Bias in EPA Penalties Alleged: Polluters' Punishments Softer in Minority Areas."

Dalton, Melville. 1950. "Unofficial Union-Management Relations." *American Sociological Review* 15 (October): 611–619.

Daly, Herman E. 1977. *Steady-State Economics: The Economics of Biophysical Equilibrium and Moral Growth.* San Francisco: W.H. Freeman.

———, ed. 1973. *Toward a Steady-State Economy.* San Francisco: W.H. Freeman.

Daly, Herman E., and John B. Cobb Jr. 1989. *For the Common Good: Redirecting the Economy toward Community, the Environment, and a Sustainable Future.* With contributions by Clifford W. Cobb. Boston: Beacon Press.

Daly, Herman E., and Kenneth N. Townsend, eds. 1993. *Valuing the Earth: Economics, Ecology, Ethics.* Cambridge: MIT Press.

Davies, Margery W. 1982. *Woman's Place Is at the Typewriter: Office Work and Office Workers, 1870–1930.* Philadelphia: Temple University Press.

Davis, Allyn M., and René Altamirano Pérez. 1989. "Hazardous Waste Management at the Mexican–U.S. Border." *Environment, Science, Technology* 23 (10): 1208–1210.

Davis, Charles E. 1993. *The Politics of Hazardous Waste.* Englewood Cliffs, N.J.: Prentice-Hall.

deBuys, William. 1985. *Enchantment and Exploitation: The Life and Hard Times of a New Mexico Mountain Range.* Albuquerque: University of New Mexico Press.

de la Rosa, Martín. 1982. "Estructura de los salarios en la industria maquiladora de exportación y la devaluación del peso." Unpublished report.

de la Rosa Hickerson, Gustavo. 1979. "La contratación colectiva en las maquiladoras." Professional thesis, Escuela de Derecho, Universidad Autónoma de Ciudad Juárez.

del Castillo, Adelaida R., and Magdelena Mora, eds. 1980. *Mexican Women in the United States: Struggles Past and Present.* Los Angeles: Chicano Studies Research Center, University of California, Los Angeles.

Demac, Donna, and Philip Mattera. 1975. "Developing and Underdeveloping New York: The 'Fiscal Crisis' and the Imposition of Austerity." *Zerowork: Political Materials* no. 2 (fall): 113–140.

de Montmollin, Maurice. 1974. "Taylorisme et anti-Taylorisme." *Sociologie du Travail* 16 (4): 374–382.

Densmore, Frances. 1928. *Uses of Plants by the Chippewa Indians.* Forty-Fourth Annual Report of the U.S. Bureau of American Ethnology. Washington, D.C.: GPO.

DeVall, Bill. 1988. *Simple in Means, Rich in Ends: Practicing Deep Ecology.* Salt Lake City, Utah: Peregrine Smith Books.

Development Alternatives for Women Now. 1985. *Development, Crises, and Alternative Visions: Third World Women's Perspectives.* Prepared by Gita Sen and Casen Grown. New Delhi: Institute of Social Studies Trust.

Devine, James, and Michael Reich. 1981. "The Microeconomics of Conflict and Hierarchy in Capitalist Production." *Review of Radical Political Economics* 12 (4): 27–45.

Diamond, Steve. 1982. "Political and Occupational Hazards to Occupational Health." *New Labor Review* 4 (fall): 34–50.

Dinwiddy, John R. 1987. *From Luddism to the First Reform Bill: Reform in England, 1810–1832.* Cambridge: Blackwell Publishers.

Dobson, Andrew, ed. 1991. *The Green Reader: Essays toward a Sustainable Society.* San Francisco: Mercury House.

Dohse, Knuth, Ulrich Jürgens, and Thomas Malsch. 1985. "From 'Fordism' to 'Toyotism'? The Social Organization of the Labor Process in the Japanese Automobile Industry." *Politics and Society* 14: 2 (June): 115–146.

Dore, Ronald. 1973. *British Factory, Japanese Factory: The Origins of National Diversity in Industrial Relations.* Berkeley: University of California Press.

———. 1983. Introduction to *Japan in the Passing Lane: An Insider's Account of Life in a Japanese Auto Factory,* by Satoshi Kamata. New York: Pantheon Books.

Dorst, John. 1989. *The Written Suburb: An American Site, an Ethnographic Dilemma.* Philadelphia: University of Pennsylvania Press.

Dover, Michael J., and Lee Merriam Talbot. 1987. *To Feed the Earth: Agro-Ecology for Sustainable Development.* Washington, D.C.: World Resources Institute.

Dunbar, Robert G. 1983. *Forging New Rights in Western Waters.* Lincoln: University of Nebraska Press.

Duncan, Mike. 1981. "Microelectronics: Five Areas of Subordination." In *Science, Technology, and the Labour Process,* edited by Les Levidow and Bob Young. Marxist Studies, vol. 1. London: CSE Books.

Eagleton, Terry. 1991. *Ideology: An Introduction.* London: Verso Books.

Earth System Sciences Committee. NASA Advisory Council. 1988. *Earth System Science: A Closer View.* Boulder, Colo.: University Corporation for Atmospheric Research.

Eaton, David J., and John M. Andersen. 1987. *The State of the Rio Grande/Río Bravo: A Study of Water Resource Issues along the Texas-Mexico Border.* Tucson: University of Arizona Press.

Ebersole, Phil. 1992. "GM's Jobs in Mexico Are Hot Topic." *Rochester Democrat and Chronicle,* 4 March.

Economist. 1989 (16 September). "Manufacturing in Mexico: On Uncle Sam's Coat-Tails."

Edelstein, Michael. 1988. *Contaminated Communities: The Social and Psychological Impacts of Residential Toxic Exposure.* Boulder, Colo.: Westview Press.

Edwards, Richard. 1978. "The Social Relations of Production at the Point of Production." *Insurgent Sociologist* 8 (2–3): 109–125.

———. 1979. *Contested Terrain: The Transformation of the Workplace in the Twentieth Century.* New York: Basic Books.

Ehrenreich, Barbara. 1992. "Truth, Justice, and the Left." *Z Papers* 1 (4): 58–64.

Ehrenreich, Barbara, and Jon Ehrenreich. 1981. *Between Capital and Labor: The Professional-Managerial Class.* Boston: South End Press.

Ehrlich, Paul, and Anne Ehrlich. 1996. *Betrayal of Science and Reason: How Anti-Environmental Rhetoric Threatens Our Future.* Washington, D.C.: Island Press.

El Correo. 1980 (19 June). "Las maquiladoras utilizan compuestos químicos dañinos."

El Diario de Juárez. 1980 (3 August). "Tóxicos y ruidos en maquiladoras afectan el aparato reproductor humano."

———. 1982 (30 May). "Desempleo masivo en maquiladoras: Paulatinamente reducen las jornadas de trabajo."

———. 1986a (25 October). "Se inconforman contra líder sindical en la RCA."

———. 1986b (26 October). "Paros: Indebida forma de presión, dice Vidal Quiñones."

———. 1986c (27 October). "Trabajadores de RCA piden reunión sindical."

———. 1986d (28 October). "Conatos de choque en RCA al parar obreros."

Electronics Committee on Safety and Health (ECOSH). 1980. *You Are Not a Hypochondriac.* Mountain View, Calif.: ECOSH.

El Fronterizo. 1979 (26 August). "Largo camino ha recorrido el COMO en sus diez años de vida: Una mujer nueva para un mundo cambiante."

———. 1980 (8 May). "Operan dos cooperativas en el Centro de la Mujer Obrera."

———. 1981 (27 October). "Dañó el bloqueo de campesinos."

———. 1986a (25 October). "Paro obrero en la RCA."

———. 1986b (26 October). "Irreal demanda obrera en RCA, dice la CROC."

———. 1986c (27 October). "La CTM merece ser rebasada: Izquierda Unida."

———. 1986d (27 October). "Es inconveniente un aumento del 50 por ciento: Isela Torres."

———. 1986e (28 October). "Miles de obreros de RCA paran."

———. 1986f (28 October). "Nuevo paro hoy en maquiladora RCA."

———. 1986g (29 October). "Censura Isela a golpeadores en conflicto de RCA."

Elger, Tony. 1982. "Braverman, Capital Accumulation, and Deskilling." In *The Degradation of Work? Skill, Deskilling, and the Labour Process,* edited by Stephen Wood. London: Hutchinson.

Elgin, Duane. 1981. *Voluntary Simplicity.* New York: Morrow.

Elizalde, Triunfo. 1992. "Adquirieron 450 mil millones en México." *La Jornada,* 30 October.

Ellis, Kate. 1992. "Life without Father: A 'Postmodern' Political Practice." *Z Papers* 1 (4): 5–12.

El Nacional. 1992a (29 October). "Concluyó la cuarta conferencia del CELAM: La política neoliberal de AL profundiza su pobreza."

———. 1992b (29 October). "Ya comenzaron a invertir en talleres y almacenes."

———. 1992c (14 November). "La procuraduría será inflexible, advierten en Ciudad Juárez."

El Paso Times. 1983 (3 October). "Maquiladora Wages Down: Peso Devaluation Impacts Labor Costs."

El Universal. 1986a (19 June). "En peligro de despido veinte empleados de RCA que pararon labores quince minutos."

———. 1986b (7 August). "Emplazaron a huelga una coalición de trabajadores, a la maquiladora AAMSA."

———. 1986c (25 October). "Se le voltearon obreros de RCA a su líder: Anuncian un paro el lunes."

———. 1986d (27 October). "Amenaza el paro de labores hoy en la RCA: La policía a la expectativa."

———. 1986e (28 October). "Paro en la RCA: Amenazan con otro hoy."

———. 1986f (30 October). "Fin al lío de la RCA: Depuesto líder sindical y pérdidas por $320 millones."

Embassy of Mexico. 1992. *Mexico Environmental Issues: Fact Sheets.* Washington, D.C.: Office for Press and Public Affairs, Embassy of Mexico.

Environmental Equity Workgroup. Environmental Protection Agency. 1992. *Environmental Equity: Reducing Risk for All Communities.* 2 vols. Washington, D.C.: GPO.

Environmental Protection Agency. 1992. *Environmental Plan for the Mexican–U.S. Border Area: First Stage, 1992–1994.* Washington, D.C.: GPO.

Escamilla, Norma, and María A. Vigorito. 1978. "Consideraciones sociológicas del trabajo femenino en las maquiladoras fronterizas." Unpublished report. Escuela de Ciencias Sociales y Políticas, Universidad Autónoma de Baja California, Mexicali.

Esparza, Lourdes. 1992. "Operan en México 2,080 industrias maquiladoras: Emplearon a 590 mil personas de enero a julio." *El Nacional de Guanajuato,* 21 October.

Esteva, Gustavo. 1983. *The Struggle for Rural Mexico.* South Hadley, Mass.: Bergin & Garvey.

Estrada, Antonio L., Fernando Treviño, and Laura A. Ray. 1990. "Health Care Utilization Barriers among Mexican-Americans: Evidence from HHANES, 1982–84." *American Journal of Public Health* 80 (December): 27–31.

Excélsior. 1992a (19 October). "Inversión extranjera: Reubicará Japón dos plantas en México."

———. 1992b (21 October). "Se trasladarán de EU a México dos fábricas de Corea del Sur."

Fee, Elizabeth. 1986. "Critiques of Modern Science: The Relationship of Feminism to Other Radical Epistemologies." In *Feminist Approaches to Science,* edited by Ruth Bleier. New York: Pergamon Press.

Fennell, Dodee. 1976. "Beneath the Surface: The Life of a Factory." *Radical America* 10 (5): 21–41.

Fernández, Raúl. 1977. *The United States–Mexico Border: A Politico-Economic Profile.* South Bend, Ind.: Notre Dame Press.

Fernández-Kelly, María Patricia. 1980. "'Chavalas de Maquiladora': A Study of the Female Labor Force in Ciudad Juárez' Offshore Production Plants." Ph.D. diss., Rutgers University.

———. 1982. *The Centro de Orientación de la Mujer Obrera.* Program evaluation report prepared for the Inter-American Foundation. La Jolla: Program in United States–Mexican Studies, University of California, San Diego.

———. 1983a. "Alternative Education for Maquiladora Workers." *Grassroots Development: Journal of the Inter-American Foundation* 6 (2), 7 (1).

———. 1983b. *For We Are Sold, I and My People: Women and Industry in Mexico's Frontier.* Albany: State University of New York Press.

———. 1983c. "Mexican Border Industrialization, Female Labor Force Participation, and Migration." In *Women, Men, and the International Division of Labor,* edited by June Nash and María Patricia Fernández-Kelly. Albany: State University of New York Press.

———. 1987. "Technology and Employment along the U.S.–Mexican Border." In *The United States and Mexico: Face to Face with the New Technology,* edited by Cathryn Thorup. New Brunswick, N.J.: Transaction Books.

Field, Donald R., and William R. Burch Jr. 1988. *Rural Sociology and the Environment.* New York: Greenwood Press.

Fischer, Frank, and Carmen Sirianni, eds. 1984. *Critical Studies in Organization and Bureaucracy.* Philadelphia: Temple University Press.

Flores Simenthal, Raúl. 1981. "La industria maquiladora: Falsa alternativa al desempleo y la marginación del hombre." *Diario de Juárez,* 8 July.

Flynn, Julie. 1986. "Some Japanese Labels Now Say: Made in Mexico." *Business Week,* 21 April.

Ford, Henry. 1922. *My Life and Work.* Garden City, N.Y.: Garden City Publishing.

Foucault, Michel. 1977. *Discipline and Punish: The Birth of the Prison.* Translated by Alan Sheridan. New York: Pantheon Books.

———. 1980. *Power/Knowledge: Selected Interviews and Other Writings, 1972–1977.* Edited and translated by Colin Gordon. New York: Pantheon Books.

Foy, Nicole. 1992. "EPA Chief, Senators Clash on Free-Trade Pact: Reilly Says U.S. Can Make Mexico Conform to Strict Environmental Standards." *Dallas Morning News,* 17 September.

Freeman, H. W. 1981. "Millions Lost through 'Time Theft.'" *El Paso Times,* 29 November.

Freire, Paolo. 1971. *Pedagogy of the Oppressed.* London: Herder & Herder.

French, Hilary F. 1993. "Reconciling Trade and the Environment." In *State of the World, 1993: A Worldwatch Institute Report on Progress toward a Sustainable Society,* edited by Lester R. Brown. Washington, D.C.: Norton.

Friedman, Sam, and Stan Weir. 1982. "Informal Work Groups: Invisible Power in the Workplace." *Against the Current* 1 (4): 45–48.

Fröbel, Folker, Jürgen Heinrichs, and Otto Kreye. 1980. *The New International Division of Labour: Structural Unemployment in Industrialised Countries and Industrialisation in Developing Countries.* Translated by Pete Burgess. Cambridge: Cambridge University Press.

Galarza Campos, Judith. 1986. "Maquiladoras: Neocolonialismo." *El Fronterizo,* 12 September.

Galper, Jeffry H. 1975. *The Politics of Social Services.* Englewood Cliffs, N.J.: Prentice-Hall.

Gambino, Ferruccio. 1972. "Workers' Struggles and the Development of Ford in Britain." Unpublished manuscript.

Gambrill, Mónica Claire. 1980. "La fuerza de trabajo en las maquiladoras: Resultados de una encuesta y algunas hipótesis interpretativas." In *Lecturas del CEESTEM: Maquiladoras.* Mexico City: Centro de Estudios Económicos y Sociales del Tercer Mundo (CEESTEM).

———. 1981. "Composición y conciencia de la fuerza de trabajo en las maquiladoras." In *La frontera del norte: Integración y desarrollo,* edited by Roque González Salazar. Mexico City: Colegio de México.

———. 1982. "Empleo vía maquiladoras: El caso de Tijuana." In *Primer encuentro sobre impactos regionales de las relaciones económicas, México–Estados Unidos. The First Conference on Regional Impacts of United States–Mexico Economic Relations.* Vol. 2. Mexico City: Primer Encuentro sobre Impactos Regionales de las Relaciones Económicas México–Estados Unidos.

———. 1984. "El sindicalismo en las maquiladoras de Tijuana." *Campo Libre* 2 (1–2): 119–132.

———. 1989. "Sindicalismo en las maquiladoras de Tijuana: Regresión en las prestaciones sociales." In *Reestructuración industrial y maquiladoras en la frontera México–Estados Unidos,* edited by Jorge Carrillo. Mexico City: Consejo Nacional para la Cultura y las Artes and Colegio de la Frontera Norte.

Gans, Herbert. 1962. *The Urban Villagers: Group and Class in the Life of Italian-Americans.* New York: Free Press.

García, Reyes Roberto. 1988. "A Philosopher in Aztlán: Studies for Ethnometaphysics in the Indo-Hispanic (Chicano) Southwest." Ph.D. diss., University of Colorado, Boulder.

García Barrios, Raúl, Luis García Barrios, and Elena Álvarez-Buylla. 1991. *Lagunas: Deterioro ambiental y tecnológico en el campo semiproletarizado.* Mexico City: Colegio de México.

García Michel, Hugo. 1988. *Mas allá de Laguna Verde.* Mexico City: Editorial Posada.

García Urrutia, Manuel. 1992. "Impactos democráticos en el proceso de integración del continente americano: El TLC en México." *El Cotidiano* 8 (47): 72–75.

Gartman, David. 1979. "Origins of the Assembly Line and Capitalist Control of Work at Ford." In *Case Studies on the Labor Process,* edited by Andrew Zimbalist. New York: Monthly Review Press.

Geertz, Clifford. 1973. *The Interpretation of Cultures: Selected Essays.* New York: Basic Books.

———. 1983. *Local Knowledge: Further Essays in Interpretive Anthropology.* New York: Basic Books.

Gelbach, Frederick. 1991. *Mountain Islands and Desert Seas.* College Station: Texas A&M Press.

Germain, Carel. 1973. "An Ecological Perspective in Casework Practice." *Social Casework* 54 (June).

Germani, Clara. 1992. "Culture as the Cause of Underdevelopment." *Mexico City News,* 8 November.

Gershman, John. 1992. "Privileged Paradise: Free Trade in North America." *Active for Justice* 5 (3): 1–2.

Getches, David H. 1989. "The Threatened Water Supply of the West: The Colorado River and Its Binational Views." Paper presented at the Thirty-First Annual Conference of the Western Social Science Association, April, Albuquerque.

Gettman, Dawn. 1983. "A Proposal for a Cross-Cultural Study of Women and Mental Health in the Workplace." Unpublished prospectus. School of Social Work, University of Texas at Austin.

Gilbreth, Frank B. 1911. *Motion Study: A Method for Increasing the Efficiency of the Workman.* New York: D. Van Nostrand.

Gilder, George. 1981. *Wealth and Poverty.* New York: Basic Books.

Gismondi, Michael, and Mary Richardson. 1991. "Discourse and Power in Environmental Politics: Public Hearings on a Bleached Kraft Pulp Mill in Alberta, Canada." *Capitalism, Nature, Socialism* 2 (3): 43–66.

Golden, Arthur. 1987. "Japan Goods from Mexico Spared Tax." *San Diego Union,* 4 April.

Golden, Arthur, and Jon Funabiki. 1987. "Japan-Owned Maquiladoras Called No Threat." *San Diego Union,* 13 September.

Goldhaber, Michael. 1980. "Politics and Technology: Microprocessors and the Prospect of a New Industrial Revolution." *Socialist Review* 10 (4): 9–32.

Goldman, Benjamin A. 1990. *The Truth about Where You Live: An Atlas for Action on Toxics and Mortality.* New York: Random House.

González, Alfonso M. 1979. *Crisis ecológica, crisis social: Algunas alternativas para México.* Mexico City: Editorial Pax.

———. 1985. "¿Por qué las luchas ecologistas?" *Revista Comunidad* no. 52: 13–19.

———. 1992. "Las luchas ecológico-sociales en México: ¿Hacia dónde?" *Ecología Política* no. 3: 35–50.

González Jácome, Alba, ed. 1991. *Directorio de ecólogos.* Mexico City: Departamento de Ciencias Sociales y Políticas, Universidad Iberoamericana.

González Salazar, Roque, ed. 1981. *La frontera del norte: Integración y desarrollo.* Mexico City: Colegio de México.

Goonatilake, Susantha. 1985. *Aborted Discovery: Science and Creativity in the Third World.* London: Zed Books.

Gordon, David, ed. 1990. *Green Cities: Ecologically Sound Approaches to Urban Space.* Montreal: Black Rose Books.

Gordon, David, Richard Edwards, and Michael Reich. 1982. *Segmented Work, Divided Workers: The Historical Transformation of Labor in the United States.* Cambridge: Cambridge University Press.

Gorz, André. 1977. "The Tyranny of the Factory." In *The Division of Labor,* edited by André Gorz. Atlantic Highlands, N.J.: Humanities Press.

Gould, Stephen Jay. 1981. *The Mismeasure of Man.* New York: Norton.

Gouldner, Alvin. 1970. *The Coming Crisis of Western Sociology.* New York: Basic Books.

Gramsci, Antonio. 1971. *Selections from the Prison Notebooks of Antonio Gramsci.* Translated by Quintin Hoare and Geoffrey Nowell Smith. New York: International.

Greater Laredo Development Foundation (GLDF). 1976. *Low Wages Await You in Laredo.* Laredo, Tex.: GLDF.

Greenbaum, Joan. 1976. "Division of Labor in the Computer Field." *Monthly Review* 28 (3): 40–55.

Greenpeace. 1988. *Greenpeace Waste Trade Update* 2 (1).

———. 1989. *Greenpeace Waste Trade Update* 3 (2).

Greider, William. 1992. "How We Export Jobs and Disease." *Rolling Stone,* 3 September.

Grenier, Guillermo J. 1988. *Inhuman Relations: Quality Circles and Anti-Unionism in American Industry.* Philadelphia: Temple University Press.

Grossman, Gene M., and Alan B. Krueger. 1991. *Environmental Impacts of a North American Free Trade Agreement.* Working Paper, no. 3914. Cambridge, Mass.: National Bureau of Economic Research.

Grossman, Karl. 1992. "From Toxic Racism to Environmental Justice." *E: The Environmental Magazine* 3 (2): 28–35.

Grumbine, R. Edward. 1992. *Ghost Bears: Exploring the Biodiversity Crisis.* Washington, D.C.: Island Press.

Grupo Bermúdez. 1989. *La industria maquiladora de exportación en México: Compendio estadístico histórico.* Ciudad Juárez: Grupo Bermúdez.

———. 1991. *La industria maquiladora de exportación en México: Compendio estadístico, 1989–1991.* Ciudad Juárez: Grupo Bermúdez.

Guerrero Chiprés, Salvador. 1992. "Se mostró escéptico respecto de las elecciones de mañana." *La Jornada,* 7 November.

Guha, Ramachandra. 1989. "Radical American Environmentalism and Wilderness Preservation: A Third World Critique." *Environmental Ethics* 11 (1): 71–83.

Guha, Ranajit, and Gayatri Chakravorty Spivak, eds. 1988. *Selected Subaltern Studies.* Oxford: Oxford University Press.

Gutiérrez, Carlos Antonio. 1992. "INEGI: Creció 10 por ciento la ocupación en maquiladoras." *La Jornada,* 22 October.

Hales, Mike. 1980. *Living Thinkwork: Where Do Labour Processes Come From?* London: CSE Books.

Hall, Kathy. 1992. "Changing Woman, Tukunavi, and Coal: Impacts of the Energy Industry on the Navajo and Hopi Reservations." *Capitalism, Nature, Socialism* 3 (1): 49–78.

Hall, Thomas D. 1989. *Social Change in the Southwest, 1350–1880.* Lawrence: University Press of Kansas.

Hamilton, Cynthia. 1990. "Women, Home, and Community: The Struggle in an Urban Environment." In *Reweaving the World: The Emergence of Ecofeminism,* edited by Irene Diamond and Gloria Feman Orenstein. San Francisco: Sierra Club Books.

Hansen, Niles. 1981. *The Border Economy: Regional Development in the Southwest.* Austin: University of Texas Press.

Harada, Shuichi. 1928. *Labor Conditions in Japan.* New York: Columbia University Press.

Haraway, Donna. 1989. *Primate Visions: Gender, Race, and Nature in the World of Modern Science.* New York: Routledge.

———. 1991. *Simians, Cyborgs, and Women: The Reinvention of Nature.* New York: Routledge.

Harding, Sandra. 1986. *The Science Question in Feminism.* Ithaca, N.Y.: Cornell University Press.

———. 1991. *Whose Science? Whose Knowledge? Thinking from Women's Lives.* Ithaca, N.Y.: Cornell University Press.

Harper, Douglas. 1987. *Working Knowledge: Skill and Community in a Small Shop.* Berkeley: University of California Press.

Harris, Larry D. 1984. *The Fragmented Forest: Island Biogeography Theory and the Preservation of Biotic Diversity.* Chicago: University of Chicago Press.

Harris, Marvin. 1980. *Cultural Materialism: The Struggle for a Science of Culture.* New York: Vintage Books.

Harrison, Bennett, and Barry Bluestone. 1988. *The Great U-Turn: Corporate Restructuring and the Polarizing of America.* New York: Basic Books.

Harrison, Lawrence E. 1992. *Who Prospers? How Cultural Values Shape Economic and Political Success.* New York: Basic Books.

Hartmann, Heidi. 1978. "Capitalism, Patriarchy, and Job Segregation by Sex." In *Capitalist Patriarchy and the Case for Socialist Feminism,* edited by Zillah R. Eisenstein. New York: Monthly Review Press.

Harvey, David. 1989. *The Condition of Postmodernity: An Enquiry into the Origins of Cultural Change.* Oxford: Blackwell.

Hawkins, Steve. 1987. "Tokyo Opens a Southern Trade Route." *U.S. News and World Report,* 3 August.

Hayes, Thomas G. 1987. "Plunging Peso Has Benefits: Foreign-Owned Plants Attracted by Cheap Labor." *New York Times,* 29 November.

Hazama, Hiroshi, and J. Kaminski. 1979. "Japanese Labor-Management Relations." *Journal of Japanese Studies* 5 (1).

Heims, Steve Joshua. 1993. *Constructing a Social Science for the Postwar America: The Cybernetics Group, 1946–1953.* Cambridge: MIT Press.

Hernández, Alberto. 1980. "Política y práctica laboral en la industria maquiladora: El caso de Ciudad Juárez." Preliminary report. Centro de Estudios Sociológicos, Colegio de México.

Herzog, Lawrence A. 1986. "Transboundary Ecosystem Management in the San Diego–Tijuana Region." In *Across Boundaries: Transborder Interaction in Comparative Perspective,* edited by Óscar J. Martínez. El Paso: Texas Western Press.

———. 1990. *Where North Meets South: Cities, Space, and Politics on the U.S.–Mexico Border.* Austin: Center for Mexican American Studies, University of Texas at Austin.

Hirschhorn, Larry. 1984. *Beyond Mechanization: Work and Technology in a Postindustrial Age.* Cambridge: MIT Press.

Hirszowicz, Maria. 1982. *Industrial Sociology: An Introduction.* New York: St. Martin's Press.

Hobbelink, Henk. 1992. "La diversidad biológica y la biotecnología agrícola: ¿Conservación o acceso a los recursos?" *Ecología Política* no. 4: 57–72.

Hobsbawm, E. J. 1964. *Labouring Men: Studies in the History of Labour.* London: Weidenfeld & Nicolson.

———. 1969. *Industry and Empire: An Economic History.* Harmondsworth, England: Pelican.

Hofrichter, Richard, ed. 1993. *Toxic Struggles: The Theory and Practice of Environmental Justice.* Philadelphia: New Society Publishers.

Holguín, Samuel. 1982. "Motivating Factors in Spectronics." Internal corporate report. Spectronics/Honeywell Optical-Fibers and Optico-Electronics Division. Ciudad Juárez.

Holmberg, Johan, Stephen Bass, and Lloyd Timberlake. 1991. *Defending the Future: A Guide to Sustainable Development.* London: Earthscan.

Holusha, John. 1992. "Trade Pact May Intensify Problems at Border." *New York Times,* 20 August.

Homans, George. 1950. *The Human Group.* New York: Harcourt, Brace & World.

Hounshell, David A. 1984. *From the American System to Mass Production, 1800–1932: The Development of Manufacturing Technology in the United States.* Baltimore: Johns Hopkins University Press.

Howard, Robert. 1985. *Brave New Workplace.* New York: Viking.

Hudson, Wendy, ed. 1991. *Landscape Linkages and Biodiversity.* Washington, D.C.: Island Press.

Huntington, Samuel P. 1968. *Political Order in Changing Societies.* New Haven, Conn.: Yale University Press.

Hyman, Richard. 1975. *Industrial Relations: A Marxist Introduction.* London: Macmillan.

Ibarra, Rodrigo. 1992. "Acuerdan varios grupos un pacto internacional contra el Tratado." *La Jornada,* 25 October.

Iglesias, Norma. 1983. "El empleo de mujeres en la industria maquiladora." *Boletín Informativo sobre Asuntos Migratorios y Fronterizos* 5 (1).

———. 1985a. *La flor más bella de la maquiladora: Historias de vida de la mujer obrera en Tijuana.* Mexico City: Secretaría de Educación Pública and Centro de Estudios Fronterizos del Norte de México.

———. 1985b. "Las mujeres somos delicadas y pacientes." *Fem* 39 (April–May): 52–54.

Il Manifesto. 1977. "Challenging the Role of the Technical Experts." In *The Division of Labor,* edited by André Gorz. Atlantic Highlands, N.J.: Humanities Press.

Instituto Mexicano del Seguro Social (IMSS). 1981. *Reglamento para la clasificación de empresas y determinación del grado de riesgo del seguro de riesgos de trabajo.* Mexico City: Jefatura de Servicios Técnicos, Subdirección General de Servicios Institucionales, IMSS.

Instituto Nacional de Estadísticas, Geografía e Informática (INEGI). 1991. *Estadística de la industria maquiladora de exportación, 1985–1991.* Mexico City: Secretaría de Programación y Presupuesto.

International Environmental Reporter. 1991 (4 December). "Hazardous Waste from U.S.-Owned Plants in Mexico Dumped Illegally, Panel Told."

Jacobson, Gary. 1987. "Mexican Border Lures Japanese." *Journal of Commerce and Commercial,* 9 January.

Jasís, Mónica. 1983. "La maquiladora electrónica y la salud de la mujer obrera: Un estudio de caso en Tijuana, Baja California." Thesis, Universidad Autónoma Metropolitana, Xochimilco.

Jones, Barry. 1982. *Sleepers, Wake! Technology and the Future of Work.* Melbourne: Oxford University Press.

Jorgensen, Eric P., ed. 1989. *The Poisoned Well: New Strategies for Groundwater Protection.* Washington, D.C.: Island Press.

Juravich, Tom. 1985. *Chaos on the Shop Floor: A Worker's View of Quality, Productivity, and Management.* Philadelphia: Temple University Press.

Kam, Dick, and Michael Gregory. 1988. "Hazardous Material Inventory of Agua Prieta, Sonora, Maquiladoras." Unpublished manuscript. Border Ecology Project, Tucson.

Kamata, Satoshi. 1983. *Japan in the Passing Lane: An Insider's Account of Life in a Japanese Auto Factory.* Translated by Tatsuru Akimoto. New York: Pantheon Books.

Kamel, Rachael. 1990. *The Global Factory: Analysis and Action for a New Economic Era.* Philadelphia: American Friends Service Committee.

Kanter, Rosabeth Moss. 1977. *Men and Women of the Corporation.* New York: Basic Books.

Kassem, M. Sami. 1976. "Organization Theory: American and European Styles." *International Studies in Management Organization* 6 (3): 46–59.

Katsiaficas, George. 1987. *The Imagination of the New Left: A Global Analysis of 1968.* Boston: South End Press.

Keller, Frances Fox. 1985. *Reflections on Science and Gender.* New Haven, Conn.: Yale University Press.

Kenney, Martin, and Richard Florida. 1988. "Beyond Mass Production: Production and the Labor Process in Japan." *Politics and Society* 16 (1): 121–158.

Kerr, Clark, and Lloyd Fisher. 1957. "Plant Sociology: The Elite and the Aborigines." In *Common Frontiers of the Social Sciences,* edited by Mirra Komarovsky. Glencoe, Ill.: Free Press.

Kerr, Clark, Frederick Harbison, John Dunlop, and Charles Myers. 1964. *Industrialism and Industrial Man: The Problems of Labor and Management in Economic Growth.* New York: Oxford University Press.

Kidwell, Clara Sue. 1985. "Science and Ethnoscience: Native American World Views as a Factor in the Development of Native Technologies." In *Environmental History: Critical Issues in Comparative Perspective,* edited by Kendall E. Bailes. Lanham, Md.: University Press of America.

Kirk, Gwyn. 1998. "Ecofeminism and the Chicana/o Environmental Movement: Bridges across Race and Gender." In *Chicano Culture, Ecology, Politics: Subversive Kin,* edited by Devon G. Peña. Tucson: University of Arizona Press. Forthcoming.

Kloppenburg, Jack Ralph. 1988. *First the Seed: The Political Economy of Plant Biotechnology.* Cambridge: Cambridge University Press.

Kondo, Dorinne K. 1990. *Crafting Selves: Power, Gender, and Discourses of Identity in a Japanese Workplace.* Chicago: University of Chicago Press.

König, Wolfgang. 1979. "Efectos de la actividad maquiladora fronteriza en la sociedad mexicana." Paper presented at the Simposium Nacional sobre Estudios Fronterizos, January, Universidad Autónoma de Nuevo León, Monterrey.

Kopinak, Kathryn. 1989. "Living the Gospel through Service to the Poor: The Convergence of Political and Religious Motivations in Organizing Maquiladora Workers in Juárez, Mexico." *Socialist Studies/Etudes Socialistes: A Canadian Annual* 5: 217–245.

Kurtz, Donald V. 1973. "The Rotating Credit Association: An Adaptation to Poverty." *Human Organization* 32 (1): 49–58.

Kurzinger-Wiemann, Edith, ed. 1990. *Política ambiental en México: El papel de las organizaciones no gubernamentales.* Mexico City: Instituto Alemán de Desarrollo.

La Botz, Dan. 1992. *Mask of Democracy: Labor Suppression in Mexico Today.* Boston: South End Press.

LaFranchi, Howard. 1988. "On Rio Grande, Pollution Knows No Borders." *Christian Science Monitor,* 12 December.

La Jornada. 1992a (16 November). "Cumplen funciones sociales y productivas: Sólo quedan 221 paraestatales en operación, indicó la SECOGEF."

———. 1992b (17 November). "Llegó Nissan al millón y medio de autos fabricados en México."

Lamphere, Louise. 1979. "Fighting the Piece-Rate System: New Dimensions of an Old Struggle in the Apparel Industry." In *Case Studies on the Labor Process,* edited by Andrew Zimbalist. New York: Monthly Review Press.

Landsberger, Henry A. 1958. *Hawthorne Revisited. Management and the Worker: Its Critics, and Developments in Human Relations in Industry.* Ithaca, N.Y.: Cornell University Press.

Lansky, Mitch. 1992. *Beyond the Beauty Strip: Saving What's Left of Our Forests.* Gardiner, Maine: Tilbury House.

Latinos and the Environment. 1993. Special issue. *Race, Poverty, and the Environment* 4 (3).

Lau, Rubén. 1986. "La protesta obrera." *El Diario de Juárez,* 27 October.

Laurell, Asa Cristina, and Margarita Márquez. 1983. *El desgaste obrero en México: Proceso de producción y salud.* Mexico City: Ediciones Era.

Lee, Charles. 1990. "Toxic Waste and Race in the United States." In *The Proceedings of the Michigan Conference on Race and the Incidence of Environmental Hazards,* edited by Bunyan Bryant and Paul Mohai. Ann Arbor: School of Natural Resources, University of Michigan.

———. 1993a. "Beyond Toxic Wastes and Race." In *Confronting Environmental Racism: Voices from the Grassroots,* edited by Robert Bullard. Boston: South End Press.

————, ed. 1993b. *Proceedings of the First National People of Color Environmental Leadership Summit.* New York: Commission for Racial Justice, United Church of Christ.

Lee, David. 1982. "Beyond Deskilling: Skill, Craft, and Class." In *The Degradation of Work? Skill, Deskilling, and the Labour Process,* edited by Stephen Wood. London: Hutchinson.

Leff, Enrique. 1984. "Racionalidad ecotecnológica y manejo integrado de recursos: Hacia una sociedad neguentrópica." *Revista Interamericana de Planificación* 18 (69).

————. 1986. *Ecología y capital: Hacia una perspectiva ambiental del desarrollo.* Mexico City: Universidad Nacional Autónoma de México.

————. 1988. "El movimiento ambientalista en México y en América Latina." *Ecología: Política/Cultura* 2 (6).

————. 1991. "Tecnología, cultura y recursos: Hacia una perspectiva no economicista del desarrollo." In *México ante la crisis: El impacto social y cultural,* edited by Pablo González Casanova and Héctor Aguilar Camín. Mexico City: Siglo Veintiuno.

————. 1992. "Cultura democrática, gestión ambiental y desarrollo sustentable en América Latina." *Ecología Política* 4 (September): 47–55.

————, ed. 1977. *Ecodesarrollo: Memoria del primer simposio.* Mexico City: Asociación Mexicana de Epistemología.

————, ed. 1990. *Medio ambiente y desarrollo en México.* 2 vols. Mexico City: Miguel Ángel Porrúa.

Leonard, Ann, ed. 1989. *Seeds: Supporting Women's Work in the Third World.* New York: Feminist Press.

Leonard, Rodney, and Eric Christensen. 1992. "Lax Enforcement of Environmental Laws in Mexico." In *Trading Freedom: How Free Trade Affects Our Lives, Work, and Environment,* edited by John Cavanagh, John Gershman, Karen Baker, and Gretchen Helmke. San Francisco: Institute for Food and Development Policy.

Leopold, Aldo. 1949. *A Sand County Almanac, and Sketches Here and There.* New York: Oxford University Press.

Leopold, Aldo Starker. 1965. *Fauna silvestre de México: Aves y mamíferos de caza.* Mexico City: Editorial Pax.

Levidow, Les. 1981. "Grunwick: The Social Contract Meets the Twentieth Century Sweatshop." In *Science, Technology, and the Labour Process,* edited by Les Levidow and Bob Young. Marxist Studies, vol. 1. London: CSE Books.

————. 1992. "The Eleventh Annual Meeting of the International Association for Impact Assessment." *Capitalism, Nature, Socialism* 3 (1): 117–124.

Levidow, Les, and Bob Young, eds. 1981. *Science, Technology, and the Labour Process.* Marxist Studies, vol. 1. London: CSE Books.

Lewis, Austin. 1913. "Mass Action" and "The Organization of the Unskilled." Archival manuscripts. Syndicalism and Political Socialism, Austin Lewis Papers. Bancroft Library, University of California, Berkeley.

Lewis, Sanford J., Marco Kaltofen, and Gregory Ormsby. 1991. *Border Trouble: Rivers in Peril.* Report on water pollution due to industrial development in northern Mexico. Boston: National Toxics Campaign.

Ley General de Equilibrio Ecológico y Protección Ambiental. Diario Oficial de la Nación. 1988 (1 March). Mexico City: Gobierno Federal de la República Mexicana.

Leys, Colin. 1982. "Samuel Huntington and the End of Classical Modernization Theory." In *Introduction to the Sociology of "Developing Societies,"* edited by Hamza Alavi and Teodor Shanin. New York: Monthly Review Press.

Linden, Eugene. 1991. "Lost Tribes, Lost Knowledge." *Time,* 23 September.

Lindenfeld, Frank, and Joyce Rothschild-Whitt, eds. 1982. *Workplace Democracy and Social Change.* Boston: Porter Sargent.

Linebaugh, Peter. 1976. "Karl Marx, the Theft of Wood, and Working Class Composition." *Crime and Social Justice* 6 (fall): 5–16.

Linebaugh, Peter, and Bruno Ramírez. 1975. "Crisis in the Auto Sector." *Zerowork: Political Materials* no. 1 (December): 60–84.

Lipietz, Alain. 1982. "Towards Global Fordism?" *New Left Review* no. 131: 33–47.

Littler, Craig R. 1982. *The Development of the Labour Process in Capitalist Societies: A Comparative Study of the Transformation of Work Organization in Britain, Japan, and the USA.* London: Heinemann Educational Books.

Lloyd, William J. 1984. "Growth of the Municipal Water System in Ciudad Juárez, Mexico." In *The U.S.–Mexico Border Region: Anticipating Resource Needs and Issues to the Year 2000,* edited by César Sepúlveda and Albert E. Utton. El Paso: Texas Western Press.

Lomas, Emilio M. 1992. "87,405 despedidos en el sector industrial paraestatal de 1988 a agosto de 1992: SEMIP." *La Jornada,* 3 November.

Lomnitz, Larissa Adler de. 1977. *Networks and Marginality: Life in a Mexican Shantytown.* Translated by Cinna Lomnitz. New York: Academic Press.

Longino, Helen E. 1990. *Science as Social Knowledge: Values and Objectivity in Scientific Inquiry.* Princeton, N.J.: Princeton University Press.

López, David. 1969. "Low-Wage Lures South of the Border." *American Federationist* 76 (June): 2–3.

López, Martha Olivia. 1992. "Multa la SEDESO a cuatro maquiladoras por mal manejo de residuos." *La Jornada,* 22 October.

Lotringer, Sylvere, and Christian Marazzi. 1980. "The Return of Politics." *Semiotext(e)* 3 (4): 8–21.

Lovelock, James. 1979. *Gaia: A New Look at Life on Earth.* Oxford: Oxford University Press.

———. 1988. *The Ages of Gaia: A Biography of Our Living Earth.* New York: Norton.

———. 1991. *Healing Gaia: Practical Medicine for the Planet.* New York: Harmony Books.

Lovelock, James, and Lynn Margulis. 1973. "Atmospheric Homeostasis by and for the Biosphere: The Gaia Hypothesis." *Tellus* 26 (2).

Lozano, Macario. 1992. "Para abatir la tala ilegal se generarán más empleos en el agro, anuncia Colosio." *Uno Más Uno,* 25 October.

Lucker, George W. 1984. "The Hidden Costs of Worker Turnover: A Case Study in the Maquiladora Industry." *Journal of Borderlands Studies* 2 (1): 93–98.

Lucker, George W., and A. J. Álvarez. 1984. "Exploitation or Exaggeration? A Worker's Eye View of 'Maquiladora' Work." *Southwest Journal of Business and Economics* 1 (2): 11–18.

———. 1985. "Controlling Maquiladora Turnover through Personnel Selection." *Southwest Journal of Business and Economics* 2 (3): 1–10.

Luhnow, David. 1992. "Environmental Solutions Sought in Practices of the Third World." *Mexico City News,* 11 November.

Maccoby, Michael. 1981. *The Leader: A New Face for American Management.* New York: Simon & Schuster.

Madrid, Javier E. 1992. "Medios de comunicación y formación de una nueva cultura ecológica: Información, cultura y realidad." *Excélsior,* 25 October.

Magee, James R. 1983. *Life in the Juárez Dump.* Border Perspectives, no. 1. El Paso: Center for Inter-American and Border Studies, University of Texas at El Paso.

Maguire, Andrew, and Janet Welsh Brown, eds. 1986. *Bordering on Trouble: Resources and Politics in Latin America.* Bethesda, Md.: Adler & Adler.

Maihold, Gunther, and Leonardo Meza. 1989. *Ecología: Motivo de solidaridad.* Mexico City: Editorial FES.

Mamozai, Marta. 1982. *Herrenmenschen: Frauen im deutschen Kolonialismus.* Reibeck, Germany: Rororo Frauen Aktuell.

Mander, Kai. 1992. "U.S. Citizens' Analysis of NAFTA: An Introduction." Internet file.

Mann, Eric. 1990. "Lighting a Spark: L.A.'s Smogbusters." *Nation,* 17 September.

Mann, Eric, with the Watchdog Organizing Committee. 1991. *L.A.'s Lethal Air: New Strategies for Policy, Organizing, and Action.* Los Angeles: Labor/Community Strategy Center.

Manwaring, Tony, and Stephen Wood. 1984. "The Ghost in the Machine: Tacit Skills in the Labor Process." *Socialist Review* no. 74: 57–86.

Marable, Manning. 1983. *How Capitalism Underdeveloped Black America: Problems in Race, Political Economy, and Society.* Boston: South End Press.

March, Kathryn S., and Rachelle L. Taqqu. 1986. *Women's Informal Associations in Developing Countries: Catalysts for Change?* Boulder, Colo.: Westview Press.

Marglin, Stephen. 1992. "Why Is So Little Left of the Left?" *Z Papers* 1 (4): 13–16.

Marks, Gary, Melinda García, and Julia M. Solís. 1990. "Health Risk Behaviors of Hispanics in the United States: Findings from HHANES, 1982–84." *American Journal of Public Health* 80 (December): 20–26.

Martínez, Óscar J. 1978. *Border Boom Town: Ciudad Juárez since 1948.* Austin: University of Texas Press.

Martínez de la Torre, Carlos. 1992. "Medio ambiente y libre comercio: ¿Compatibles?" *Dos Mil Uno,* 19 November.

Marx, Karl. 1969. *Pre-Capitalist Economic Formations.* New York: New World.

———. 1973. *Grundrisse: Foundations of the Critique of Political Economy.* Translated by Martin Nicolaus. New York: Vintage Books.

———. [1887] 1975a. *Capital: A Critical Analysis of Capitalist Production.* Vol. 1. Translated by Samuel Moore and Edward Aveling. London: S. Sonnenschein, Lowrey. Reprint, New York: New World.

———. [1887] 1975b. *Capital: A Critical Analysis of Capitalist Production.* Vol. 2. Translated by Samuel Moore and Edward Aveling. London: S. Sonnenschein, Lowrey. Reprint, New York: New World.

———. 1977. *Capital: A Critique of Political Economy.* Vol. 1. Translated by Ben Fowkes. New York: Vintage Books.

Mathewson, Stanley. 1931. *Restriction of Output among Unorganized Workers.* New York: Viking Press.

Mattera, Philip. 1985. *Off the Books: The Rise of the Underground Economy.* New York: St. Martin's Press.

Maybury-Lewis, David. 1992. *Millennium: Tribal Wisdom and the Modern World.* New York: Viking.

Mayo, Elton. 1933. *The Human Problems of an Industrial Civilization.* New York: Macmillan.

McDonnell, Patrick. 1991a. "Border Boom Feeds Hazardous Waste Ills." Part 1. *Los Angeles Times,* 10 September.

———. 1991b. "Border Boom Feeds Hazardous Waste Ills." Part 2. *Los Angeles Times,* 11 September.

McFarland, Louis. 1992. "Laguna Verde Nuclear Power Plant: Mexican Hope or Exploitation?" Unpublished research report. Department of Sociology, Arizona State University, Tempe.

McGregor, D. 1960. *Handling Personality Adjustments in Industry.* New York: Wiley.

McNaughton, Wayne L. 1945. *Industrial Economy and Labor Control.* Los Angeles: Golden State.

McNeely, Jeffrey A. 1990. "An International Perspective on Conserving Cultural Diversity: How the Variety of Human Experience Can Help Promote Sustainable Forms of Using Natural Resources." Paper presented at the First National Conference on Cultural Conservation, May, Folklife Center, Library of Congress, Washington, D.C.

Mears, Helen. 1976. "The Way of the Gods." In *The Japan Reader,* edited by Jon Livingston, Joe Moore, and Felicia Oldfather. Vol. 2, *Imperial Japan: 1800–1945.* Harmondsworth, England: Penguin Books.

Merchant, Carolyn. 1980. *The Death of Nature: Women, Ecology, and the Scientific Revolution.* New York: Harper Collins.

———. 1989. *Ecological Revolutions: Nature, Gender, and Science in New England.* Chapel Hill: University of North Carolina Press.

————, ed. 1993. *The Racial Economy of Science.* Bloomington: University of Indiana Press.

Merrington, John, and Christian Marazzi. 1971. "Notes on Strategic Analysis of Class Struggle and Class Composition/Recomposition." Unpublished manuscript.

Merton, Robert K., and Robert Nisbet, eds. 1971. *Contemporary Social Problems.* New York: Harcourt, Brace, Jovanovich.

Metzner, Cliff. 1988. "Transboundary Sewage Problems: Tijuana/San Diego–New River/Imperial Valley." *Transboundary Research Report* no. 2 (spring).

Mexico City News. 1992 (15 November). "Mexico Getting Tough with Border Dumpers."

Meyer, Stephen. 1977. "Mass Production and Human Efficiency: The Ford Motor Company, 1908–1921." Ph.D. diss., Rutgers University.

Meza, Francisco Santacruz. 1992. "Las maquiladoras no ocasionan la anencefalia en México: Lugo." *Excélsior,* 25 October.

Microelectronics Group. Conference of Socialist Economists. 1980. *Capitalist Technology and the Working Class.* London: CSE Books.

Mies, Maria. 1987. *Patriarchy and Accumulation on a World Scale: Women in the International Division of Labour.* 2d ed. London: Zed Books.

Mies, Maria, Veronika Bennholdt-Thomsen, and Claudia von Werlhof. 1988. *Women: The Last Colony.* London: Zed Books.

Milbraith, Lester W. 1989. *Envisioning a Sustainable Society: Learning Our Way Out.* Albany: State University of New York Press.

Miller, Alan S. 1991. *Gaia Connections: An Introduction to Ecology, Ecoethics, and Economics.* Savage, Md.: Rowman & Littlefield.

Minh-ha, Trinh T. 1989. *Woman, Native, Other: Writing Postcoloniality and Feminism.* Bloomington: Indiana University Press.

Moberly, A. L. 1964. "Fences and Neighbors: El Chamizal and the Colorado River Salinity Disputes in United States–Mexico Relations." Ph.D. diss., University of California, Santa Barbara.

Moffett, Matt. 1984. "U.S. Companies with Factories in Mexico Are Having Difficulty Retaining Workers." *Wall Street Journal,* 17 July.

Moguel, J., and E. Velásquez. 1991. "Organización social y lucha ecológica en una región del norte de México." Paper presented at the Coloquio de Antropología e Historia Regional, Colegio de Michoacán. Morelia, Michoacán, Mexico.

Montgomery, David. 1976. "Workers' Control of Machine Production in the Nineteenth Century." *Labor History* 17 (fall).

————. 1979. *Workers' Control in America: Studies in the Control of Work, Technology, and Labor Struggles.* Cambridge: Cambridge University Press.

Monthly Review Press Staff, ed. 1976. *Technology, the Labor Process, and the Working Class: A Collection of Essays.* New York: Monthly Review Press.

Moro, Martín, Alfonso Bouzas, and Isaac Palacios S. 1978. *Control y luchas del movimiento obrero: Dos ensayos.* Mexico City: Editorial Nuestro Tiempo.

Mulcahy, Susan D., and Robert R. Faulkner. 1979. "Person and Machine in a New England Factory." In *Case Studies on the Labor Process,* edited by Andrew Zimbalist. New York: Monthly Review Press.

Mumme, Stephen P. 1988. "La Paz Agreement: Progress and Problems in Managing the Border Environment." *Transboundary Resources Report* no. 2 (spring).

———. 1992a. "New Directions in United States–Mexico Transboundary Environmental Management: A Critique of Current Proposals." *Natural Resources Journal* 32 (2): 539–562.

———. 1992b. "System Maintenance and Environmental Policy in Mexico." *Latin American Perspectives* 19 (winter): 123–143.

Mumme, Stephen P., and Joseph Nalven. 1988. "Managing the Border Environment: Advances, Issues, and Options." In *One Border, Two Nations: Policy Implications and Problem Resolutions,* edited by Óscar J. Martínez, Albert E. Utton, and Mario Miranda Pacheco. Mexico City: Asociación Nacional de Universidades e Institutos de Enseñanza Superior.

Mungaray Lagarda, Alejandro. 1983. "División internacional del trabajo y automatización de la producción: El futuro de las maquiladoras." *Investigación Económica* no. 164 (April–June).

Munro, David A., and Martin W. Holdgate, eds. 1992. *Caring for the Earth: A Strategy for Sustainable Living.* Project directed by David A. Munro. Gland, Switzerland: International Union for the Conservation of Nature and Natural Resources.

Muñoz Ríos, Patricia. 1992. "Amplio análisis de la Red de Acción Frente al Libre Comercio: El TLC fue diseñado para las élites financiera e industrial." *La Jornada,* 13 November.

Nadworny, Milton J. 1955. *Scientific Management and the Unions, 1900–1932: A Historical Analysis.* Cambridge: Harvard University Press.

Nandy, Ashis. 1992. "Oh What a Lovely Science." *Z Papers* 1 (4): 3–4.

Nash, June. 1983. "The Impact of the Changing International Division of Labor on Different Sectors of the Labor Force." In *Women, Men, and the International Division of Labor,* edited by June Nash and María Patricia Fernández-Kelly. Albany: State University of New York Press.

Nash, June, and María Patricia Fernández-Kelly, eds. 1983. *Women, Men, and the International Division of Labor.* Albany: State University of New York Press.

Nash, June, and Helen Icken Safa, eds. 1976. *Sex and Class in Latin America.* New York: Praeger.

Negri, Toni. 1980. *Del obrero-masa al obrero social.* Translated (from the Italian) by Joaquín Jorda. Barcelona: Editorial Anagrama.

———. 1984. *Marx beyond Marx: A Political Reading of the Grundrisse.* Translated by Harry Cleaver, Michael Ryan, and Maurizio Viano and edited by Jim Fleming. South Hadley, Mass.: Bergin & Garvey.

Nelson, Daniel. 1975. *Managers and Workers: Origins of the New Factory System in the U.S., 1880–1920.* Madison: University of Wisconsin Press.

————. 1980. *Frederick W. Taylor and the Rise of Scientific Management.* Madison: University of Wisconsin Press.

Nelson, Lin. 1990. "The Place of Women in Polluted Places." In *Reweaving the World: The Emergence of Ecofeminism,* edited by Irene Diamond and Gloria Feman Orenstein. San Francisco: Sierra Club Books.

Newsweek. 1989 (6 March). "The Electronic Goddess: Computerizing Bali's Ancient Irrigation Rites."

Noble, David F. 1979. "Social Choice in Machine Design." In *Case Studies on the Labor Process,* edited by Andrew Zimbalist. New York: Monthly Review Press.

————. 1984. *Forces of Production: A Social History of Industrial Automation.* New York: Knopf.

————. 1993. *Progress without People: In Defense of Luddism.* Harvey and Jessie Series, no. 1. Chicago: Charles H. Kerr.

Norberg-Hodge, Helena. 1991. *Ancient Futures: Learning from Ladakh.* San Francisco: Sierra Club Books.

North American Congress on Latin America (NACLA). 1975. "Hit and Run: U.S. Runaway Shops on the Mexican Border." *Latin America and Empire Report* 9 (5): 2–30.

Noss, Reed F. 1991. "From Endangered Species to Biodiversity." In *Balancing on the Brink of Extinction: The Endangered Species Act and Lessons for the Future,* edited by Kathryn A. Kohm. Washington, D.C.: Island Press.

Ocaranza, A., and V. Kerber. 1989. "La inversión japonesa en las maquiladoras." Paper presented at the Seminario sobre la Industria Maquiladora en México, June, Colegio de México, Mexico City.

O'Connor, James. 1991. *Is Sustainable Capitalism Possible?* CES/CNS Pamphlet Series, no. 1. Santa Cruz, Calif.: Center for Ecological Socialism.

Odum, Eugene P. 1971. *Fundamentals of Ecology.* 3d ed. Philadelphia: Saunders Publishing.

Old, Joe. 1992. "How Do You Clean up a 2,000-Mile Garbage Dump?" *Business Week,* 6 July.

Ong, Aihwa. 1987. *Spirits of Resistance and Capitalist Discipline: Factory Women in Malaysia.* Albany: State University of New York Press.

Orduña, Francisco. 1992. "Acelerará la cosmopolitización del mexicano: El TLC no implicará perder la identidad nacional." *La Jornada,* 30 October.

Orme, William A., Jr. 1991. "The Sunbelt Moves South." *NACLA Report on the Americas* 24 (6): 10–19.

Ortega, Gabriela R. 1992. "La iniciativa promueve desarrollo armónico del sector: Desaparece la excesiva reglamentación." *El Nacional,* 14 November.

Ortiz, Alfonso. 1976. *The Tewa World: Space, Time, Being, and Becoming in a Pueblo Society.* Chicago: University of Chicago Press.

Ortiz Monasterio, Fernando, Isabel Fernández Tijero, Alicia Castillo, José Ortiz Monasterio, and Alfonso Bulle. 1987. *Tierra profanada: Historia ambiental de México.* Mexico City: Instituto Nacional de Antropología e Historia and Secretaría de Desarrollo Urbano y Ecología.

Ortiz Monasterio, Fernando, Josefina Mena, and Ángel Parada. 1983. *Documentación y evaluación de experiencias tradicionales y alternativas para el manejo de residuos urbanos en zonas de bajos ingresos en el Valle de México.* Mexico City: Population Council and United States Agency for International Development.

Ortman, David E. 1992. "Environmental Effects of a NAFTA." In *Trading Freedom: How Free Trade Affects Our Lives, Work, and Environment,* edited by John Cavanagh, John Gershman, Karen Baker, and Gretchen Helmke. San Francisco: Institute for Food and Development Policy.

Otani, Kiyosho. 1987. "Japanese Firms Begin Moving Production from U.S. to Mexico." *Japan Economic Journal,* 9 May.

Ouchi, William G. 1982. *Theory Z: How American Business Can Meet the Japanese Challenge.* New York: Avon.

Oyarzabal-Tamargo, F. 1976. "Economic Impact of Saline Irrigation Water: Mexicali Valley, Mexico." Ph.D. diss., Colorado State University.

Paglabán, Enrique. 1978. "Philippines: Workers in the Export Industry." *Pacific Research* 9 (3, 4): 2–31.

Palliox, Christian. 1976. "The Labour Process: From Fordism to Neo-Fordism." In *The Labour Process and Class Strategies,* edited by the Conference of Socialist Economists. London: Stage One.

Park, Robert. 1928. "Human Migration and the Marginal Man." *American Journal of Sociology* 33 (6): 881–893.

Parker, Mike. 1985. *Inside the Circle: A Union Guide to QWL.* Boston: South End Press.

Pascale, Richard T., and Anthony G. Athos. 1981. *The Art of Japanese Management: Applications for American Executives.* New York: Simon & Schuster.

Pearson, Charles, ed. 1987. *Multinational Corporations, Environment, and the Third World: Business Matters.* Durham, N.C.: Duke University Press.

Peña, Devon G. 1979. "Trade Unionism, Strikes, Wildcats, and Mexican Women Workers in the Mexican Maquiladoras." Unpublished manuscript. Center for the Study of Human Resources, University of Texas at Austin.

———. 1980. "Las maquiladoras: Mexican Women and Class Struggle in the Border Industries." *Aztlán* 11 (2): 160–229.

———. 1981. *Maquiladoras: A Select Annotated Bibliography and Critical Commentary.* CSHR Bibliography Series, no. 7-81. Austin: Center for the Study of Human Resources, University of Texas at Austin.

———. 1983. "The Class Politics of Abstract Labor: Organizational Forms and Industrial Relations in the Mexican Maquiladoras." Ph.D. diss., University of Texas at Austin.

———. 1984. "Skilled Activities among Assembly Line Workers in Mexican-American Border Twin-Plants." *Campo Libre* 2 (1, 2): 189–207.

———. 1985. "Maquila Women Workers and the Refusal of Development: Gender, Class, and Community in the U.S.–Mexico Border." Prepared for the Silicon Valley Research Group workshop series Women, High Technology, and Society, June, University of California, Santa Cruz.

————. 1986. "Between the Lines: Toward a New Perspective on the Industrial Sociology of Women Workers in Transnational Labor Processes." In *Chicana Voices: Intersections of Race, Class, and Gender,* edited by Teresa Córdova, Norma Cantú, Gilberto Cárdenas, Juan García, and Christine M. Sierra. Austin: CMAS Publications. [Reprint, Albuquerque: University of New Mexico Press, 1993.]

————. 1987. "Tortuosidad: Shop Floor Struggles of Female Maquiladora Workers." In *Women on the U.S.–Mexico Border: Responses to Change,* edited by Vicki L. Ruiz and Susan Tiano. Boston: Allen & Unwin.

————. 1988. "When the Rivers Burn: Mexico's Environmental Movement." Unpublished manuscript. Department of Sociology, Colorado College.

————. 1989a. "The Andropositivist Vernacular and the Question of Method in Chicano Studies." Paper presented at the Seventeenth Annual Conference of the National Association for Chicano Studies, March, Albuquerque.

————. 1989b. "The 'Green' Marx: Capitalism and the Destruction of Nature." Unpublished manuscript. Rio Grande Bioregions Project, Hulbert Center for Southwestern Studies, Colorado College.

————. 1990a. "Diversity and Community: Maintaining Allegiances." *Liberal Education* 76 (5): 34–38.

————. 1990b. "Maquiladoras and Ethnocentrism: Conceptual Dilemmas in Theory and Practice." *Journal of Borderlands Studies* 5 (1): 15–19.

————. 1992a. "The 'Brown' and the 'Green': Chicanos and Environmental Politics in the Upper Rio Grande." *Capitalism, Nature, Socialism* 3 (1): 79–103.

————. 1992b. "'Forest Crimes' in the Subaltern Life of the Commons: A Site Ethnography of Power-in-Spacing." Paper presented at the Thirty-Third Annual Conference of the Western Social Science Association, April, Denver.

————. 1992c. "The U.S.–Mexico Border as a Disturbance Regime: Rapid Industrialization and Threats to Biodiversity in the Rio Grande Watershed— A Preliminary Assessment." Unpublished manuscript. Rio Grande Bioregions Project, Hulbert Center for Southwestern Studies, Colorado College.

————. 1993a. "Agroecology of a Chicano Family Farm." Paper presented at the Thirty-Fourth Annual Conference of the Western Social Science Association, April, Corpus Christi, Texas.

————. 1993b. "Letter from Mexico: Mexico's Struggle against NAFTA." *Capitalism, Nature, Socialism* 4 (4): 123–128.

————. 1993c. "Mexican Opposition to NAFTA and the Critique of the Neo-Liberal Project." Paper presented at the Thirty-Fourth Annual Conference of the Western Social Science Association, April, Corpus Christi, Texas.

————. 1998a. "Los Animalitos Son Inteligentes: Notes toward the Bioregional Study of Chicano Culture in the Upper Rio Grande." In *Chicano Culture, Ecology, Politics: Subversive Kin,* edited by Devon G. Peña. Tucson: University of Arizona Press. Forthcoming.

————, ed. 1998b. *Chicano Culture, Ecology, Politics: Subversive Kin.* Tucson: University of Arizona Press. Forthcoming.

————. Forthcoming. *Gaia in Aztlán: Culture, Ecology, and the Politics of Place in the Upper Rio Grande.*

Peña, Devon G., and Gilberto Cárdenas. 1988. "The Division of Labor in Microelectronics: A Comparative Analysis of France, Mexico, and the United States." *Studies in Comparative International Development* 23 (2): 89–112.

Peña, Devon G., and Joe Gallegos. 1993. "Nature and Chicanos in Southern Colorado." In *Confronting Environmental Racism: Voices from the Grassroots,* edited by Robert Bullard. Boston: South End Press.

Peña, Devon G., and Dawn Gettman. 1986. "Women, Mental Health, and the Workplace in a Transnational Setting." *Social Work* 31 (1): 5–11.

Peña, Devon G., and Louis McFarland. 1989. "The Rio Grande Bioregions: A Select Annotated Bibliography in the Study of Culture and Ecology in the Rio Grande Watershed." Unpublished manuscript. Rio Grande Bioregions Project, Hulbert Center for Southwestern Studies, Colorado College.

Peña, Devon G., Rubén Martínez, and Louis McFarland. 1993. "Rural Chicana/o Communities and the Environment: An Attitudinal Survey of Residents of Costilla County, Colorado." *Perspectives in Mexican American Studies* 4 (summer): 45–74.

Pérez U., Matilde. 1992a. "Deforestadas, 49.6 millones de hectáreas de bosques y selvas: Desmotes ilegales, la causa principal, SARH." *La Jornada,* 29 October.

————. 1992b. "El sistema de cuotas beneficia a los productores estadounidenses: Los porcicultores mexicanos enfrentarán serios problemas con el tratado comercial norteamericano." *La Jornada,* 8 November.

————. 1992c. "Tendencia privatizadora: Gonzalo Chapela." *La Jornada,* 16 November.

Pérez U., Matilde, and Óscar Camacho. 1992. "Cámara de Diputados: Listo el dictamen sobre la nueva ley forestal." *La Jornada,* 17 November.

Pérez U., Matilde, and Rosa Rojas. 1992. "Cenecistas y productores piden cambios: Imprecisa, la iniciativa de ley forestal que presentó el ejecutivo." *La Jornada,* 12 November.

Perfecto, Ignacio. 1990. "Pesticide Exposure of Farmworkers and the International Connection." In *The Proceedings of the Michigan Conference on Race and the Incidence of Environmental Hazards,* edited by Bunyan Bryant and Paul Mohai. Ann Arbor: School of Natural Resources, University of Michigan.

Perlman, Janice E. 1976. *The Myth of Marginality: Urban Poverty and Politics in Rio de Janeiro.* Berkeley: University of California Press.

Peterson, Jonathan, and Nancy Yoshihara. 1987. "Asian Firms Find Home in Mexico." *Los Angeles Times,* 19 March.

Petrikin, Jonathan S., ed. 1995. *Environmental Justice.* San Diego, Calif.: Greenhaven Press.

Piore, Michael J., and Charles F. Sabel. 1984. *The Second Industrial Divide: Possibilities for Prosperity.* New York: Basic Books.

Poore, Duncan. 1989. *No Timber without Trees: Sustainability in the Tropical Forests.* London: Earthscan.

Posey, Darrell Addison. 1983. "Indigenous Knowledge and Development: An Ideological Bridge to the Future." *Ciência e Cultura* 35 (7) (July).

———. 1987. *Alternatives to Destruction: Science of the Mebêngôkre.* 1987. Belém, Brazil: Museu Paraense Emilio Goeldi.

———. 1992. "Los derechos de propiedad intelectual de los pueblos indígenas." *La Jornada del Campo* no. 9 (10 November).

Potere Operaio. 1970. *Italy 1969–70: A Wave of Struggles.* Supplement to *Potere Operaio* no. 27 (June 27 – July 3).

Powell, John Wesley. 1892. "Institutions for the Arid Lands." *Century Magazine* no. 40 (May–October): 111–116.

President, Order. 1972. "Reglamento del párrafo tercero del artículo 321 del Código Aduanero de los Estados Unidos Mexicanos para el Fomento de la Industria Maquiladora." *Federal Government Executive Decrees.* Mexico City: Gobierno Federal de la República Mexicana.

Pulido, Laura. 1996. *Environmentalism and Economic Justice.* Tucson: University of Arizona Press.

Quadri, Gabriel. 1990. "Una breve crónica del ecologismo en México." *Revista Ciencias,* 4 July.

Quijano, Aníbal. 1970. "Redefinición de la dependencia y proceso de margina-lización en América Latina." Unpublished manuscript. Comisión Económica para América Latina (CEPAL), Santiago, Chile.

Ramos, Humberto. 1989. "A Transborder Pollution Case Study." Paper presented at the Thirty-First Annual Conference of the Western Social Science Association, April, Albuquerque.

Ranfla González, Arturo. 1989. "Growth Poles and Subregionalization of the Northern Border of Mexico." Paper presented at the Thirty-First Annual Conference of the Western Social Science Association, April, Albuquerque.

Ranger, Edward M., Jr. 1991. "Environmental Regulation and Enforcement in Mexico." *Maquiladora Industry Annual Review* no. 4.

Rascón, María Antonieta. 1979. "La mujer y la lucha social en la historia de México." *Cuadernos Agrarios* 4 (9): 105–118.

Red Notes/Conference of Socialist Economists (CSE). 1979. *Working Class Autonomy and the Crisis.* London: Red Notes/CSE Books.

Reisner, Marc. 1986. *Cadillac Desert: The American West and Its Disappearing Water.* New York: Viking.

Reno, Phillip. 1981. *Mother Earth, Father Sky, and Economic Development: Navajo Resources and Their Use.* Albuquerque: University of New Mexico Press.

Reuters. 1992. "Zona fronteriza: Empresa de EU admite que dejó basura tóxica." *La Jornada,* 7 November.

Robles, Isabel. 1984. "Para que no olvidemos." In *Folleto de solidaridad obrera,* edited by the Sociedad Cooperativa de Seleccionadores de Materiales (SOCOSEMA) and the Centro de Orientación de la Mujer Obrera (COMO). Ciudad Juárez: SOCOSEMA and COMO.

Rodd, R. Stephan. 1991. "Improved Assessment of Strategic Environmental Commodities." Paper presented at the Eleventh Annual Meeting of the International Association for Impact Assessment, June, Champaign-Urbana, Ill.

Rodríguez, Gregoria. 1993. "Anencephaly and the Maquiladoras: A Critique of Objectivist Semantics in Epidemiological Research." Paper presented at the Thirty-Fourth Annual Conference of the Western Social Science Association, April, Corpus Christi, Texas.

Rodríguez, Sylvia. 1990. "Ethnic Reconstruction in Contemporary Taos." *Journal of the Southwest* 32 (4): 541–555.

Roethlisberger, Fritz J., and William J. Dickson. 1939. *Management and the Worker: An Account of a Research Program Conducted by the Western Electric Company, Hawthorne Works, Chicago.* Cambridge: Harvard University Press.

Rohter, Larry. 1987. "Plants in Mexico Help Japan Sell to U.S." *New York Times*, 26 May.

Rojas, Rosa. 1992. "Clinton favorecerá al TLC, estima la CNC: Derechos de jornaleros, tema a tratar con la nueva administración de EU." *La Jornada*, November 6.

Rosaldo, Renato. 1989. *Culture and Truth: The Remaking of Social Analysis.* Boston: Beacon Press.

Rosenberg, Nathan. 1981. "Marx as a Student of Technology." In *Science, Technology, and the Labour Process*, edited by Les Levidow and Bob Young. Marxist Studies, vol. 1. London: CSE Books.

Roseneau, Pauline Marie. 1992. *Post-Modernism and the Social Sciences: Insights, Inroads, and Intrusions.* Princeton, N.J.: Princeton University Press.

Roy, Donald. 1952a. "Quota Restriction and Goldbricking in a Machine Shop." *American Journal of Sociology* 57 (5): 427–442.

———. 1952b. "Restriction of Output in a Piecework Machine Shop." Ph.D. diss., University of Chicago.

———. 1953. "Work Satisfaction and Social Reward in Quota Achievement." *American Sociological Review* 18: 507–514.

———. 1954. "Efficiency and the Fix: Informal Intergroup Relations in a Piecework Machine Shop." *American Journal of Sociology* 60: 255–266.

———. 1958. "'Banana Time': Job Satisfaction and Informal Interaction." *Human Organization* 18: 158–168.

Ruiz, Vicki L., and Susan Tiano, eds. 1987. *Women on the U.S.–Mexico Border: Responses to Change.* Boston: Allen & Unwin.

Russell, Dick. 1989. "Environmental Racism: Minority Communities and Their Battle against Toxics." *Amicus Journal* 11 (spring).

Rzedowski, Jerzy, and Miguel Equihua. 1987. *Atlas cultural de México: Flora.* Mexico City: Secretaría de Educación Pública and Grupo Editorial Planeta.

Sabel, Charles F. 1982. *Work and Politics: The Division of Labor in Industry.* Cambridge: Cambridge University Press.

Saldívar, Ramón. 1990. *Chicano Narrative: The Dialectics of Difference.* Madison: University of Wisconsin Press.

Sale, Kirkpatrick. 1985. *Dwellers in the Land: The Bioregional Vision.* San Francisco: Sierra Club Books.

Salinas de Gortari, Carlos. 1992. "Cuarto Informe de Gobierno." Published in *La Jornada* and *Uno Más Uno,* 2 November.

Salinas-León, Roberto. 1993. "'Green Herrings' Pose Environmental Distortion of Trade Pact." *Colorado Springs Gazette Telegraph,* 24 July.

Sánchez, Roberto. 1987. "El problema de los desechos industriales." *El Cotidiano* número especial 1.

———. 1989a. "Hazardous Wastes Generated by the Maquiladora: The Case of Mexicali." Paper presented at the Thirty-First Annual Conference of the Western Social Science Association, April, Albuquerque.

———. 1989b. "La negociación de conflictos ambientales entre México y Estados Unidos." *Frontera Norte* 1 (1): 77–96.

———. 1990a. "Health and Environmental Risks of the Maquiladora in Mexico." *Natural Resources Journal* 30 (1): 163–186.

———. 1990b. "Manejo transfronterizo de residuos tóxicos y peligrosos: Una amenaza para los países del tercer mundo." *Frontera Norte* 2 (3): 91–114.

Sanderson, Susan. 1987. "Automated Manufacturing and Offshore Assembly in Mexico." In *Face to Face with the New Technology,* edited by Cathryn Thorup. New Brunswick, N.J.: Transaction Books.

Sargent, Frederic O., Paul Lusk, José A. Rivera, and María Varela. 1991. *Rural Environmental Planning for Sustainable Communities.* Washington, D.C.: Island Press.

Satchell, Michael. 1991. "Poisoning the Border." *U.S. News and World Report,* 6 May.

Sayles, Leonard. 1977. *The Behavior of Industrial Work Groups.* New York: Wiley, 1958. Reprint, New York: Arno Press.

Schmink, Marianne. 1989. "Community Management of Waste Recycling in Mexico: The SIRDO." In *Seeds: Supporting Women's Work in the Third World,* edited by Ann Leonard. New York: Feminist Press.

Schueler, Donald. 1991. *Incident at Eagle Ranch: Predators as Prey in the American West.* Tucson: University of Arizona Press.

Scott, James C. 1985. *Weapons of the Weak: Everyday Forms of Peasant Resistance.* New Haven, Conn.: Yale University Press.

Seay, Janice, and Larry Trejo. 1979. "Is the Border Twin-Plant Concept for You?" *Texas Business* 4 (6).

Secretaría de Comercio y Fomento Industrial (SECOFI). 1992. *Tratado de libre comercio entre México, Canadá, y Estados Unidos: Resumen.* Mexico City: SECOFI.

Secretaría de Patrimonio y Fomento Industrial (SEPAFIN). 1979. *Indicadores socioeconómicos de la industria maquiladora en México.* Mexico City: SEPAFIN.

Selcraig, Bruce. 1992. "Poisonous Flows the Rio Grande." *Los Angeles Times Magazine,* 25 October.

Seligson, Michael, and Edward J. Williams. 1981. *Maquiladoras and Migration: Workers in the Mexico–United States Border Industrialization Program.* Office for Mexican Studies, Institute of Latin American Studies (ILAS), University of Texas at Austin. Austin: ILAS.

Shaffer, Mark. 1981. "Minimum Population Sizes for Species Conservation." *Bioscience* 31 (2): 131–134.

Shaiken, Harley. 1982. "El nuevo 'auto mundial.'" *Información Obrera* no. O (spring): 121–132.

———. 1984. *Work Transformed: Automation and Labor in the Computer Age.* New York: Holt, Rinehart & Winston.

Shapiro-Perl, Nina. 1979. "The Piece-Rate: Class Struggle on the Shop Floor." In *Case Studies on the Labor Process,* edited by Andrew Zimbalist. New York: Monthly Review Press.

Shefferman, Nathan. 1955. *The Shefferman Personnel Motivation Program.* Englewood Cliffs, N.J.: Prentice-Hall.

Shimizu, T. 1977. "Wirtschaftliche und humane Aspekte eines Systems zur Produktionssteuerung in der japanischen Automobilindustrie." *Humane Personal- und Organisationsentwicklung* 14 (2): 321–343.

Shiva, Vandana. 1988. *Staying Alive: Women, Ecology, and Development.* London: Zed Books.

Sierra Valencia, Griselda. 1992. "No garantiza la protección de los bosques la nueva ley forestal: Gonzalo Chapela." *Uno Más Uno,* 17 November.

Silver, Cheryl S., and Ruth S. DeFries. 1990. *One Earth, One Future: Our Changing Global Environment.* Washington, D.C.: National Academy of Sciences.

Sindicato de Empleados de Industria y Comercio–Zaragoza (SEICZ). 1979 (August 3). "A la opinión pública." Unpublished correspondence and manuscript. SEICZ-FROC-CROC, Tijuana.

Sklair, Leslie. 1988. *Maquiladoras: Annotated Bibliography and Research Guide to Mexico's In-Bond Industry, 1980–1988.* Monograph Series, no. 24. La Jolla: Center for U.S.–Mexican Studies, University of California, San Diego.

———. 1989. *Assembling for Development: The Maquila Industry in Mexico and the United States.* London: Unwin Hyman.

———. 1994. *Assembling for Development: The Maquila Industry in Mexico and the United States.* 2d ed. London: Unwin Hyman.

Snow, Robert T. 1983. "The New International Division of Labor and the U.S. Workforce: The Case of the Electronics Industry." In *Women, Men, and the International Division of Labor,* edited by June Nash and María Patricia Fernández-Kelly. Albany: State University of New York Press.

Sociedad Cooperativa de Seleccionadores de Materiales, S.A. (SOCOSEMA). 1975. *Desarrollo integral de una comunidad.* Ciudad Juárez: SOCOSEMA.

———. 1980. *Reporte anual.* Ciudad Juárez: SOCOSEMA.

———. 1988. *Reporte anual.* Ciudad Juárez: SOCOSEMA.

———. 1990. *Reporte anual.* Ciudad Juárez: SOCOSEMA.

Sohn-Rethel, Alfred. 1976. "The Dual Economics of Transition." In *The Labour Process and Class Strategies,* edited by the Conference of Socialist Economists (CSE). London: Stage 1.

Solís, Adriana. 1993. *An Analysis of EPA's Progress on the Integrated Border Environmental Plan's Hazardous Waste Commitments.* Austin: Texas Center for Policy Studies.

Solomonides, Tony, and Les Levidow, eds. 1985. *Compulsive Technology: Computers as Culture.* London: Free Association Books.

South, Robert B. 1990. "Transnational 'Maquiladora' Location." *Annals of the Association of American Geographers* 80 (4): 549–570.

Sprouse, Martin, ed. 1992. *Sabotage in the American Workplace: Anecdotes of Dissatisfaction, Mischief, and Revenge.* San Francisco: Pressure Drop Press.

Staudt, Kathy. 1986. "Economic Changes and Ideological Lag in Households of Maquila Workers in Ciudad Juárez." In *The Social Ecology and Economic Development of Ciudad Juárez,* edited by Gay Young. Boulder, Colo.: Westview Press.

———. 1987. "Programming Women's Empowerment: A Case from Northern Mexico." In *Women on the U.S.–Mexico Border: Responses to Change,* edited by Vicki L. Ruiz and Susan Tiano. Boston: Allen & Unwin.

Stavrianos, Leften Stavros. 1981. *Global Rift: The Third World Comes of Age.* New York: Morrow.

Steward, Julian. 1955. *Theory of Culture Change: The Methodology of Multilinear Evolution.* Urbana: University of Illinois Press.

Stewart, John Cary. 1990. *Drinking Water Hazards: How to Know If There Are Toxic Chemicals in Your Water and What to Do If There Are.* Hiram, Ohio: Envirographics.

Stoddard, Ellwyn R. 1978. "Functional Alternatives to Bi-National Border Development Models: The Case of the U.S.–Mexico Border." Paper presented at the annual meeting of the American Sociological Association, September, San Francisco.

———. 1979. "A 3-D Perspective of Water Gate Rip-offs along the Rio Grande: Water Allocations by Dam, District, and Ditchriders." In *Environmental Problems along the Border.* Occasional Paper no. 7. San Diego, Calif.: Border-State Consortium for Latin America.

———. 1987. *Maquila: Assembly Plants in Northern Mexico.* El Paso: Texas Western Press.

———. 1991. "Border Maquila Ownership and Mexican Economic Benefits: A Comparative Analysis of the 'Good,' the 'Bad,' and the 'Ugly.'" *Journal of Borderlands Studies* 6 (2): 23–50.

———. 1992a. "George Baker's 'Mexican Labor Is Not Cheap': A Rejoinder and Critical Commentary." *Río Bravo Journal* 2 (1): 107–125.

———. 1992b. "Maquiladora Ownership and Labor Turnover Rates: Transnational and National Processing Plants in Mexicali, B.C." Herberger Center Monographs (edited by D. F. G. Williams). Tempe: Arizona State University.

———, ed. 1990. *Border Maquiladoras and Research Interpretations: An International Symposium.* Special issue. *Journal of Borderlands Studies* 5 (1).

Sugimori, Y., et al. 1977. "Toyota Production System and Kanban System: Materialisation of Just-in-Time and Respect-for-Human System." *International Journal of Production Research* 6 (3): 553–564.

Suro, Roberto. 1993. "Pollution-Weary Minorities Try Civil Rights Tack." *New York Times,* 11 January.

Sward, Keith. 1948. *The Legend of Henry Ford.* New York: Rinehart.

Taddei Bringas, I. Christina. 1989. "La presencia japonesa en el norte de México." Paper presented at the international seminar Mexamérica: Empleo, Migración y Movimientos Sociales en los Ochenta, November, Hermosillo, Mexico.

Tagliazucchi, Pino. 1982. "La respuesta sindical a la introducción de los robots en la industria automotriz." *Información Obrera* no. O (spring): 133–137.

Talbot, Cindy, and Andrea Hricko. 1979. "Hazards of the Electronic Industry." *Labor Occupational Health Program Monitor* no. 8 (October).

Taylor, Frederick Winslow. 1903. *Shop Management.* New York: Harper & Brothers.

———. 1911. *The Principles of Scientific Management.* New York: Harper & Brothers.

Taylor, Kevin. 1990. "Why Supernatural Eels Matter." In *Lessons of the Rainforest,* edited by Suzanne Head and Robert Heinzman. San Francisco: Sierra Club Books.

Taylor, Peter. 1975. "'The Sons of Bitches Just Won't Work': Postal Workers against the State." *Zerowork: Political Materials* no. 1 (December): 85–113.

Tepperman, Jean. 1976. *Not Servants, Not Machines: Office Workers Speak Out!* Boston: Beacon Press.

Texas Center for Policy Studies. 1992. *A Response to the EPA/SEDUE Integrated Border Environmental Plan.* Austin: Texas Center for Policy Studies.

———. 1993. *Biodiversity Protection in the Texas-Mexico Border Region.* Austin: Texas Center for Policy Studies.

Thomis, Malcolm I. 1970. *The Luddites: Machine-Breaking in Regency England.* North Haven, Conn.: Shoe String Press.

Tiano, Susan. 1984. *Maquiladoras, Women's Work, and Unemployment in Northern Mexico.* WID Working Papers, no. 43. East Lansing: Michigan State University.

———. 1985. "Maquiladora Women: A New Category of Workers?" Paper presented at the annual meeting of the Association of Borderlands Scholars, April, Fort Worth, Texas.

———. 1987a. "Gender, Work, and World Capitalism: Third World Women's Roles in Development." In *Analyzing Gender: A Handbook of Social Science Research,* edited by Beth B. Hess and Myra Marx Ferree. Newbury Park, Calif.: Sage.

———. 1987b. "Women Workers in a Northern Mexican City: Constraints and Opportunities." *In Women on the U.S.–Mexico Border: Responses to Change,* edited by Vicki L. Ruiz and Susan Tiano. Boston: Allen & Unwin.

————. 1990. "Labor Composition and Gender Stereotypes in the Maquilas." *Journal of Borderlands Studies* 5 (1): 20–24.

Time. 1986 (5 May). "Deadly Gunk from El Norte: Illegal Disposal of California Toxic Waste in Mexico."

Tolan, Sandy. 1990. "The Border Boom: Hope and Heartbreak." *New York Times Magazine*, 1 July.

Tolan, Sandy, and Jerry Kammer. 1991. "Life in the Low-Wage Boomtowns of Mexico." *Utne Reader* (November–December).

Toledo, Alejandro, Julia Carabias, Cristina Mapes, and Carlos Toledo. 1985. *Ecología y autosuficiencia alimentaria: Hacia una opción basada en la diversidad biológica, ecológica y cultural de México.* Mexico City: Siglo Veintiuno.

Toledo, Víctor M. 1987. *La etnobotánica en Latinoamérica.* Bogotá, Colombia: ICFES.

————. 1988. "La diversidad biológica de México." *Ciencia y Desarrollo* 14 (81): 17–30.

————. 1991. "La crisis ecológica." In *México ante la crisis,* edited by Pablo González Casanova and Héctor Aguilar Camín. Mexico City: Siglo Veintiuno.

————. 1992. "Biodiversidad y campesinado: La modernización en conflicto." *La Jornada del Campo* no. 9 (10 November).

Tomaso, G., and A. Alm. 1990. "Economy vs. Ecology: Mexico's Drive for Growth Eclipses Concerns about Toxic Wastes from Border Plants." *Transboundary Resources Report* 4 (1).

Totsuka, Hideo. 1981. *Über die Gleichgültigkeit einiger Klischee-Vorstellungen zur Beschäftigungspolitik japanischer Unternehmen.* Berlin: Science Center, International Institute for Comparative Social Research/Labor Policy.

Truax, Hawley. 1990. "Beyond White Environmentalism: Minorities and the Environment." *Environmental Action* no. 21.

Trueba, José D. 1980. *Ecología para el pueblo.* Mexico City: Ediciones Edicol.

Trueba Urbina, Alberto, and Jorge Trueba Barrera. 1980. *Ley federal del trabajo de 1970: Reforma procesal de 1980.* 44th ed. Mexico City: Editorial Porrúa.

Tuan, Yi-Fu. 1974. *Topophilia: A Study of Environmental Perception, Attitudes, and Values.* Englewood Cliffs, N.J.: Prentice-Hall.

Tudiver, Neil. 1982. "Business Ideology and Management in Social Work: The Limits of Cost Control." *Catalyst* 4 (1): 25–48.

Turner, Victor. 1969. *The Ritual Process: Structure and Anti-Structure.* Chicago: Aldine.

"Unequal Protection: The Racial Divide in Environmental Law." 1992 (September 21). *National Law Journal* 15 (3): 2–12.

Unger, Kurt. 1989. "La inversión japonesa en México: Perspectivas industriales y de comercio." Paper presented at the Seminario sobre la Industria Maquiladora en México, June, Colegio de México.

United Nations Centre for Human Settlements. 1990. *Human Settlements and Sustainable Development: The Role of Human Settlements and of Human Settlement Policies in Meeting Development Goals and in Addressing the Issues of Sustainability at Global and Local Levels.* Paper prepared by Diana Mitlin and David Satterthwaite of the Human Resources Programme, International Institute for Environment and Development. Nairobi, Kenya: United Nations Centre for Human Settlements (Habitat).

United States General Accounting Office (GAO). 1983. *Siting of Hazardous Waste Landfills and Their Correlation with Racial and Economic Status of Surrounding Communities.* Washington, D.C.: GAO.

"United States, Mexico to Clean up Border." 1992. *EPA Journal* 18 (2): 4–5.

United States Office of the Trade Representative (USOTR). 1992a. *NAFTA Supplemental: Agreement on Environmental Cooperation.* Washington, D.C.: USOTR, Executive Office of the President.

———. 1992b. *NAFTA Supplemental: Agreement on Labor Cooperation.* Washington, D.C.: USOTR, Executive Office of the President.

United States Tariff Commission (USTC). 1969. *Economic Factors Affecting the Use of Items 807.00 and 806.30 of the Tariff Schedules of the United States.* Report to the President on Investigation 332-61 under Section 332 of the Tariff Act of 1930. Tariff Commission Publication 339. Washington, D.C.: USTC.

Uno Más Uno. 1992a (27 October). "El TLC convertirá a México en un punto importante para las manufacturas de Japón."

———. 1992b (15 November). "Cuarenta billones de pesos: Monto de la reprivatización."

Valdés de Villalva, Guillermina. 1981. "Empleo y transferencia de tecnología o mano de obra femenina desechable? El caso de Ciudad Juárez, Chihuahua." Paper presented at El Primer Encuentro sobre Impactos Regionales de la Integración México–Estados Unidos, July, Guanajuato, Mexico.

———. 1985. "New Policies and Strategies of the Multinational Corporations during the Crisis of 1982–3." In *The U.S. and Mexico: Borderland Development and the National Economies,* edited by Lay James Gibson and Alfonso Corona Rentería. Boulder, Colo.: Westview Press.

———. 1989. "Aprendizaje en la producción y transferencia de tecnología en la industria de maquila de exportación." In *Reestructuración industrial: Maquiladoras en la frontera México–Estados Unidos,* edited by Jorge Carrillo. Mexico City: Consejo Nacional para la Cultura y las Artes and Colegio de la Frontera Norte de México.

Valdés de Villalva, Guillermina, and Francisco Villarreal Torres. 1975. "Una injusticia que debe hacerse pública." *El Fronterizo,* 4 April.

Valette, Jim. 1987. *Waste Management Inc.: The Greenpeace Report.* Chicago: Greenpeace.

van Dijk, Teun A. 1993. *Elite Discourse and Racism.* Sage Series on Race and Ethnic Relations, no. 6. Newbury Park, Calif.: Sage.

The Vanishing Forest: The Human Consequences of Deforestation. 1986. Report prepared for the Independent Commission on International Humanitarian Issues. London: Zed Books.

Van Ness, John R. 1987. "Hispanic Land Grants: Ecology and Subsistence in the Uplands of Northern New Mexico and Southern Colorado." In *Land, Water, and Culture: New Perspectives on Hispanic Land Grants,* edited by Charles L. Briggs and John R. Van Ness. Albuquerque: University of New Mexico Press.

Van Waas, Michael. 1981. "The Multinationals' Strategy for Labor: Foreign Assembly Plants in Mexico's Border Industrialization Program." Ph.D. diss., Stanford University.

Vargas Márquez, Fernando. 1984. *Parques nacionales de México y reservas equivalentes: Pasado, presente y futuro.* Mexico City: Instituto de Investigaciones Económicas, Universidad Nacional Autónoma de México.

Vélez-Ibáñez, Carlos G. 1983. *Rituals of Marginality: Politics, Process, and Culture Change in Urban Central Mexico, 1969–1974.* Berkeley: University of California Press.

Venegas Aguilera, Lilia, and Dalia Barrera Bassols. 1985. "Condiciones de trabajo en la industria maquiladora de tipo electrónico: El caso de Ciudad Juárez." *Estudios Fronterizos* 2 (1).

Vera, Beatriz, and Gay Young. 1984. "Extensive Evaluation of Centro de Orientación de la Mujer Obrera in Ciudad Juárez." Unpublished manuscript. Prepared for the Inter-American Foundation, Washington, D.C.

Vogel, Ezra. 1980. *Japan as Number One: Lessons for America.* Cambridge: Harvard University Press.

Ward, Justin, and Glenn T. Pricket. 1992. "Prospects for a Green Trade Agreement." *Environment* 34 (4): 2–5.

Warner, David V. 1991. "Health Issues at the U.S.–Mexican Border." *Journal of the American Medical Association* 265 (2): 242–247.

Warner, W. Lloyd, and J. O. Low. 1947. *The Social System of the Modern Factory.* New Haven, Conn.: Yale University Press.

Watson, Bill. 1971. *Counter-Planning on the Shop Floor.* Somerville, Mass.: New England Free Press.

Weir, David. 1987. *The Bhopal Syndrome: Pesticides, Environment, and Health.* San Francisco: Sierra Club Books.

Weiss, Lawrence David. 1984. *The Development of Capitalism in the Navajo Nation: A Political-Economic History.* Minneapolis, Minn.: MEP Publications.

Wetherell, Margaret, and Jonathan Potter. 1992. *Mapping the Language of Racism: Discourse and the Legitimation of Exploitation.* New York: Columbia University Press.

Whitehead, T. N. 1938. *The Industrial Worker.* 2 vols. Cambridge: Harvard University Press.

Wibo, Gilbert Raúl. 1991. "Ecologistas y antinucleares en México, 1980–1989: Movimiento y contramovimiento social." Thesis, Facultad de Ciencias Políticas y Sociales, Universidad Nacional Autónoma de México.

Wiener, Norbert. 1948. *Cybernetics: or, Control and Communication in the Animal and the Machine.* New York: Wiley.

————. 1950. *The Human Uses of Human Beings.* London: Eyre & Spottis-woode.

Withorn, Ann. 1981. "Retreat from the Social Wage: Human Services in the 1980s." *Radical America* 15 (1, 2): 23–32.

Wolf, Eric. 1959. *Sons of the Shaking Earth.* Chicago: University of Chicago Press.

————. 1982. *Europe and the People without History.* Berkeley: University of California Press.

World Commission on Environment and Development. 1987. *Our Common Future.* Oxford: Oxford University Press.

World Environment Center. 1992. *Environmental, Health, and Housing Needs and Non-Profit Groups in the U.S.–Mexico Border Area.* Arlington, Va.: World Environment Center.

Worster, Donald, ed. 1988. *The Ends of the Earth: Perspectives on Modern Environmental History.* Cambridge: Cambridge University Press.

Wright, Angus. 1984. "Innocents Abroad: American Agricultural Research in Mexico." In *Meeting the Expectations of the Land: Essays in Sustainable Agriculture and Stewardship,* edited by Wes Jackson, Wendell Berry, and Bruce Colman. San Francisco: North Point Press.

————. 1990. *The Death of Ramón González: A Modern Agricultural Dilemma.* Austin: University of Texas Press.

Yakowitz, H. 1985. *Global Aspects of Hazardous Waste Management.* Report prepared for the World Commission on Environment and Development, U.S. Congress, Office of Technology Assessment. Washington, D.C.: GPO.

Young, Gay. 1987. "Gender Identification and Working-Class Solidarity among Maquila Workers in Ciudad Juárez: Stereotypes and Realities." In *Women on the U.S.–Mexico Border: Responses to Change,* edited by Vicki L. Ruiz and Susan Tiano. Boston: Allen & Unwin.

————, ed. 1986. *The Social Ecology and Economic Development of Ciudad Juárez.* Boulder, Colo.: Westview Press.

Yudelman, Sally W. 1987. *Hopeful Openings: A Study of Five Women's Development Organizations in Latin America and the Caribbean.* West Hartford, Conn.: Kumarian Press.

Zerowork. 1975. *Zerowork: Political Materials* no. 1 (December).

————. 1977. *Zerowork: Political Materials* no. 2 (fall).

Zimbalist, Andrew, ed. 1979. *Case Studies on the Labor Process.* New York: Monthly Review Press.

Zwerdling, Daniel. 1980. *Workplace Democracy: A Guide to Workplace Ownership, Participation, and Self-Management Experiments in the United States and Europe.* New York: Harper & Row.

Index

AAMSA (Autopartes y Arneses de México), 129
Absenteeism, 75, 82, 113
Absolute surplus labor time, 31
Acapulco Fashions, 122–123, 128, 129, 147, 148, 155, 352n19
Accidents. *See* Industrial accidents
ACI (automated component insertion), 55, 59, 60, 61, 68, 91, 246
Action Network on Free Trade. *See* Red de Acción Frente al Libre Comercio
AFL-CIO, 104
AFSC. *See* American Friends Service Committee
AFW. *See* Arizona Farmworkers' Union
Aglietta, Michel, 271
Agribusiness, 321–322
Agriculture, 315–317, 320–321
Allen Bradley, 364n65
Alvarado, Elena, 235, 279, 280
Álvarez Solórzano, Ticul, 287–289
AMAC. *See* Association of Maquiladoras
Amazonia, 341n21
American Friends Service Committee (AFSC), 303–304, 351n15
American Hospital Supply Company, 148
American Society of Mechanical Engineers, 342n34
AMF, 129
Anencephaly, 247, 280

Anthropogenic habitats, 284
Antonio J. Bermúdez Industrial Park, 370–371n21
Apprenticeship at COMO, 150–151, 206, 209–211
AQC. *See* Automated quality control
Araujo, Hugo Andrés, 315
Arbitration and conciliation system, 107, 352n19
Argyris, Chris, 345n65
Arizona Farmworkers' Union (AFW), 332, 351n4
Arkwright machine-smashers, 28, 340n13
Army, U.S., 306
Aronowitz, Stanley, 360n15
Artisan guilds, 29–30
Asistencialismo, 139
Assemblers, 65, 67
Assembly-line speedup
  and output restriction, 114–115
  in productivity drive, 81, 82, 87–90, 208
  and psychogenic illnesses, 299
  resistance to, 112–121
Assembly-line system
  Blauner on, 359n5
  decline of, in U.S., 45
  definition of, 35
  distribution of workers on assembly line, 82–84
  and Fordism, 3–6, 28, 34–39, 45–46, 49, 60, 68
  history of, 34

Hawthorne studies, 26–27, 97, 344–345n60
Health. *See* Occupational health hazards; Public health
Henn, 373n60
Hermosillo, 280
Hernández, Hortencia, 142
Herrera, Luis, 279
Herrera, Sylvia, 302–303
Homans, George, 26, 40, 345n60
Honda, 246, 267
Honeywell, 89
Hopi, 341n21
Hounshell, David A., 344n47
Hourly standards and quotas, 78–82, 349–350n29, 350nn31–32
Housing fund
   and SOCOSEMA, 232
Howard, Robert, 43, 57
Human Problems of an Industrial Civilization, The (Mayo), 344n57
Human relations, 26–27, 40–42, 94, 344n58
Human resource departments, 37, 39. *See also* Personnel departments; Personnel policies
Human Use of Human Beings, The (Wiener), 346n71
Humanistic-management model, 42–43, 345–346n66
Hyper-Toyotism, 272–275, 276
Hyperspecialization, 187–188, 191. *See also* Specialization

IAF. *See* Inter-American Foundation
IBM, 89
Identity narratives, 181–182
Ideology
   as category of social theory, 131–132
   of struggle in maquilas, 130–133
   and support of strikes, 132–133
IMISAC. *See* Instituto Mexicano de Investigación Social

Imported consciousness, 352n20, 360n14
IMSS (Mexican Social Security Institute), 381n106
Incentives. *See* Gimmes approach to worker rewards
Inductive apprenticeship, 150–151, 206, 209–211
Industrial accidents, 57, 129, 247, 294–298, 372n43, 380n95, 381n106
Industrial Ecology International, 380n83
Industrial engineering, 27
Industrial psychologists, 50, 51
Industrial Revolution, 29, 32
Industrial sociology, 25, 27, 40, 43
Industrial workers. *See* Workers
Industrial Workers of the World (IWW), 7, 28, 335n9
INFONAVIT (Instituto para el Fomento Nacional de la Vivienda de los Trabajadores), 169
Informal shop-floor networks
   and friendships, 71–72, 118–119
   group chiefs' participation in, 121
   lack of research on, 19
   managerial control and disruption of, 41–43, 51, 94–95, 121–122
   and managerial sociology, 41–43, 51, 345n60
   and militancy, 126–128
   and politics of production, 5
   and workers' rejection of promotions, 72
   and working knowledge, 196–197
Institute for Agriculture and Trade Policy, 369n11, 387n190
Institute for Policy Studies, 279, 369n11, 387n190
Inter-American Foundation (IAF), 144, 153–154, 156, 355n17
Intermediate Safeguard Zone, 348n13
Internal labor-market policies, 68–77

About the Author

A native of Laredo, Texas, Devon G. Peña received his doctorate in sociology from the University of Texas at Austin. Since 1984, he has been on the faculty of Colorado College, where he is an associate professor of sociology and the director of the Rio Grande Bioregions Project of the Hulbert Center for Southwestern Studies. He is a member of the executive council of the Western Social Science Association and of the board of directors of the Council for Responsible Genetics.

CMAS BOOKS

The Terror of the Machine: Technology, Work, Gender, and Ecology on the U.S.–Mexico Border was designed by Jace Graf and Víctor J. Guerra. The text was composed by CMAS Books, primarily in Minion, with Hiroshige used for the title page and chapter titles. The book was printed and bound by Edwards Brothers, of Ann Arbor, Michigan.